ORIGINS
OF
CATHOLIC
WORDS

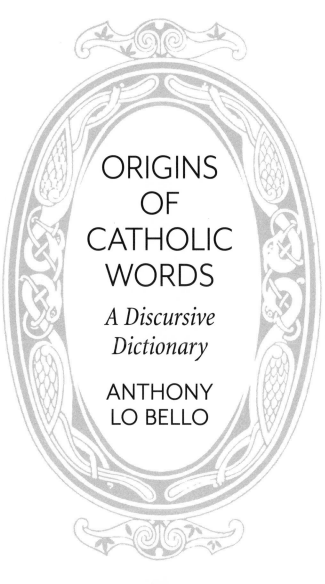

ORIGINS OF CATHOLIC WORDS

A Discursive Dictionary

ANTHONY LO BELLO

The Catholic University of America Press
Washington, D.C.

The paper used in this publication meets the requirements of American
National Standards for Information Science—Permanence of Paper for
Printed Library Materials, ANSI z39.48-1992.
∞

Cataloging-in-Publication Data available from the Library of Congress
ISBN 978-0-8132-3230-0

CONTENTS

PREFACE

In 1969, at the beginning of the second program of his television series *Civilisation*, Kenneth Clark declared, "It could be convincingly argued that Western civilization was basically the creation of the church."[1] In harmony with this proposition is the thesis that the study of the vocabulary of the Catholic religion may be taken as belonging to the liberal arts. And it is indeed from the perusal of the best literature, and of the arts and music that have adorned the liturgy, that the words defined in this dictionary have been chosen.

This book is a work of reference organized like a lexicon or encyclopedia. There is an entry for each word of importance having to do with the Catholic Church. I give the etymology of the word, describe what it means, and then add whatever further discussion I feel is needed. In some cases, this amounts to several pages. The book takes for its models Shipley's *The Origins of English Words: A Discursive Dictionary of Indo-European Roots* and my own *Origins of Mathematical Words: A Comprehensive Dictionary of Latin, Greek, and Arabic Roots*, both published by the Johns Hopkins University Press.

When writing on practically everything that concerns the Catholic Church during a period of two thousand years, an author cannot hope to present judgments or opinions (where he dares to do so) that will be accepted by everyone, but so long as such things are presented decently and are distinguished from fact, the learned world allows a man to have his say. The success of a book of this sort depends on such an allowance being made. Furthermore, a book of such length as this and on such a subject cannot avoid occasionally treating matters involved in controversy

1. Kenneth Clark, "The Great Thaw," episode 2 of *Civilisation*, first aired March 2, 1969, BBC video, 48:23.

on which, at least, there is more than one opinion that must be tolerated.

I have been ecumenical in my choice of authorities. I have quoted Newman when he was an Anglican and Döllinger when he was a Catholic. J. B. Bury, Lord Chesterfield, Mandell Creighton, S. R. Driver, Ferdinand Gregorovius, Dr. Johnson, Henry Charles Lea, Bishop Lightfoot, Thomas Babington Macaulay, John Stuart Mill, Dean Milman, Leopold von Ranke, and Bertrand Russell find their places alongside Alban Butler, Denzinger, the Abbé Duchesne, Adrian Fortescue, Bishop Hefele, Cardinal Gasparri, Msgr. Ronald Knox, Msgr. Horace K. Mann, Ludwig von Pastor, Wilfrid Ward, William George Ward, and Evelyn Waugh.

There have been many changes in the Catholic Church since 1962, and one of the goals of this book is to describe what will soon be missing from the memories of all living people. Alas, history, both ecclesiastical and secular, and the study of the ancient Greek and Latin languages, almost fall into that awful category. This book may, I hope, make its small contribution so that the situation not arise that would convict John Henry Newman of error when he wrote, "What the Catholic Church once has had, she never has lost."[2]

In giving the English translations of Classical Latin words, I have made constant use of the dictionary of Charlton T. Lewis and Charles Short and *Cassell's New Latin Dictionary*. Similarly, in translating Greek words I have always relied on the dictionary of Henry George Liddell and Robert Scott. I have therefore refrained from mentioning in every entry that the definition is taken from one of these authorities. Neither do I mention repeatedly that I have consulted and benefited from the *Oxford English Dictionary* or Ernest Weekley's *Etymological Dictionary*. I also depend heavily on the lexicons of Antonio Bacci and Karl Egger. For Hebrew I have relied on the lexicon of Francis Brown, S. R. Driver, and Charles A. Briggs, and for Arabic on the dictionaries of George Wilhelm Freytag, Edward William Lane, and Hans Wehr. For Aramaic I depend on the grammar of Gustaf Dalman.[3]

Passages are given in Greek or Latin when I consider it necessary or enjoyable to present the authoritative texts. It is a pleasant fallacy that one may study the Catholic religion without recourse to those languages. It is one of the great pleasures of life, and one of the valuable rewards of scholarship, to read all texts of importance exactly as they were first written.

2. John Henry Cardinal Newman, *Historical Sketches*, vol. 2, *The Mission of St. Benedict* (London: Longmans, Green, 1917), 368.

3. See the bibliography for complete publication information.

Translations for which no authority is given are my own.

The notes have been written and placed in such a manner as to avoid the inconvenience that caused David Hume to complain to Edward Gibbon that, in the first volume of his *History of the Decline and Fall of the Roman Empire*, an excessive and tedious amount of page-flipping was required of the reader.

Finally, I take this opportunity to acknowledge the assistance of Dr. Trevor Lipscombe, director of the Catholic University of America Press, whose idea this book was, as well as the cooperation of his colleagues, especially those who read the manuscript and made suggestions for its improvement. The criticisms of Anne Needham have been invaluable. Her work on a manuscript that presented many challenges to the copy editor was indispensable.

ORIGINS
OF
CATHOLIC
WORDS

Abbot The Hebrew noun אב means *father*. The vocative case of the same noun in Aramaic is אבא This was transliterated into Greek and then into Latin as we read in Mark 14:36:

> ἀββὰ ὁ πατήρ
> Abba, pater!

As a result, the Latin noun *abbas, abbatis, m.* became an address of respect to a male superior, and it has been taken over into English as *abbot*. It is now used as the title of the head of a monastery.

> Abbas qui praeesse dignus est monasterio ...[1]
> The abbot who is worthy to preside over a monastery ...

There is no difference between an *abbey* and a *monastery* other than the etymological one. The French title *Abbé* for a clergyman is vague. The French called Liszt an abbé, though he was not a priest and had progressed in orders no higher than acolyte.

Abdication The Latin verb *dĭco, dĭcare* means *to consecrate, dedicate, devote, deify*. What one devotes to the Deity one no longer possesses for oneself, and so the addition of the preposition *ab*, which introduces the element of separation, produces the compound verb *abdĭco, abdĭcare* meaning *to disown* or *renounce*, whether relatives or magistracies. From this latter verb, there arose the noun *abdicatio, abdicationis, f.,* with the

---

1. *Regula Sanctissimi Patris Nostri Benedicti*, Caput 2.

meaning *disowning, renouncing, abdication.* The most famous abdication in ancient history was that of the emperor Diocletian on the Kalends of May in 305, after which he retired to Spalato (Split) to grow vegetables. The most famous abdication in mediaeval history was that of Pope Celestine V on December 13, 1294, an act that got him placed in Hell by Dante.

> Poscia ch'io v'ebbi alcun riconosciuto,
> vidi e conobbi l'ombra di colui
> che fece per viltate il gran rifiuto.[2]

> When some of these I recognised, I saw
> And knew the shade of him, who to base fear
> Yielding, abjured his high estate.[3]

The most famous abdication in modern history was that of the emperor Charles V, who resigned his various thrones piecemeal over the two-year period from 1554 to 1556, after which he retired to the Monastery of San Yuste in Extremadura, where he remained until his death in 1558. This abdication is the subject of a famous poem, *Der Pilger vor Sankt Just*, by August, Graf von Platen (1796–1835). This poem was beautifully set to music by Carl Loewe (1796–1869).

> Nacht ist's, und Stürme sausen für und für.
> Hispanische Mönche, schließt mir auf die Thür!

> Laßt hier mich ruhn, bis Glockenton mich weckt,
> Der zum Gebet euch in die Kirche schreckt.

> Bereitet mir was euer Haus vermag,
> Ein Ordenskleid und einen Sarkophag.

> Gönnt mir die kleine Zelle, weiht mich ein,
> Mehr als die Hälfte dieser Welt war mein.

> Das Haupt, das nun der Scheere sich bequemt,
> Mit mancher Krone ward's bediademt.

> Die Schulter, die der Kutte nun sich bückt,
> Hat kaiserlicher Hermelin geschmückt.

> Nun bin ich vor dem Tod den Toten gleich,
> Und fall' in Trümmer, wie das alte Reich.

---

2. Dante, *Inferno*, 3.59–60.
3. Dante Alighieri, *Inferno*, trans. Henry Francis Cary (London: The Folio Society, 1998), 10.

'Tis night, the tempest howls, the torrents pour,
Hispania's monks, awake, and ope the door!

Here let me rest till waked by the bell's chime
That calls ye to the church at matins prime!

Prepare for me the bounties of your house,
A friar's cowl, and a sarcophagus!

Ordain me, and a little cell assign!
More than the half of this wide world was mine.

The head that to the shears now boweth down
Wore on its brow more than one jeweled crown.

The shoulders over which the cowl is laid
Oft in imperial ermine were arrayed.

I'm like the dead, ere death comes to o'erwhelm,
And fall to ruins like the ancient realm.[4]

The abdication of Pope Benedict XVI from the supreme pontificate on February 28, 2013, is an abdication within the memory of most people now living. To use the verb *resign* of a sovereign prince is incorrect since it reveals poverty of expression; *abdicate* is the precise technical term.

Ablution The Greek verb λύω and the associated Latin verb *luo, luere, lui, luiturus* mean *to loose*, and the compound Latin verb *abluo, abluere, ablui, ablutus* means *to loose from dirt, to wash*. From the fourth principal part of the latter verb comes the noun *ablutio*, a washing, whence proceeds the English *ablution*. The ablutions at the Mass are the washing of the hands, which is accompanied by the prayer *Lavabo*.

Abortion The Latin verb *orior, oriri, ortus sum* means *to rise*; the addition of the preposition *ab* introduces the notion of reversal of direction and produces the compound verb *aborior, aboriri, abortus sum* meaning *to set, to disappear*, and thus *to be born in an untimely manner*. The corresponding Latin nouns *abortio, abortionis, f.*, and *abortus, -ūs, m.*, both mean *miscarriage* in the general sense, whether induced or not. Abortion is forbidden by the Catholic Church as a violation of the Fourth Commandment. It is also forbidden in the original Hippocratic Oath, which doctors have since revised.

4. Alfred Baskerville, *The Poetry of Germany*, 6th ed. (New York: Leypoldt & Holt, 1867), 236–37.

ὁμοίως δὲ οὐδὲν γυναικὶ πεσσὸν φθόριον δώσω.

I will likewise not give any abortion-causing potion to a woman.

Abortion is explicitly condemned in the *Didache of the Twelve Apostles*, a document of the first or second century A.D.:

οὐ φονεύσεις τέκνον ἐν φθορᾷ, οὐ δὲ γεννηθὲν ἀποκτενεῖς.[5]

Thou shalt not murder a child by abortion, nor kill it once it has been born.

Absolution The Latin verb *solvo, solvere, solvi, solutus* means *to loosen, to release*, and the related compound verb *absolvo absolvere, absolvi, absolutus* means *to release from*, whence proceeds the English *absolve*. From the fourth principal part of *absolvo* comes the noun *absolutio*, from which is derived the English *absolution*. Absolution is the act whereby the priest absolves the penitent in the sacrament of confession with the formula:

Ego te absolvo a peccatis tuis in nomine Patris, et Filii, et Spiritus Sancti. Amen.

I absolve thee of thy sins in the name of the Father, and of the Son, and of the Holy Ghost. Amen.

Accession The Latin verb *cedo, cedere, cessi, cessus* means *to go, to yield*; and the addition of the preposition *ad* produces the compound verb *accedo, accedere, accessi, accessus*, with the meaning *to go to, to approach, to yield to, to be added to*. The associated fourth declension noun *accessus* means an *approach*, a *surrender*. The election of the pope *per accessum* or, in English, by accession, occurred in former times when, after an inconclusive scrutiny, cardinals transferred their votes from candidates who had little support to a candidate who was close to the required two-thirds majority. The idea was to save time. According to Sladen, the last time this method was available was in the Conclave of 1878. In 1903, he says, the cardinals unanimously agreed beforehand not to allow it, and it was formally abolished by Pius X shortly after he emerged from that assembly as supreme pontiff.[6] This transfer of votes in the accession was originally accomplished *viva voce*, but later was made by ballot. It is described by Sladen thus:

It is seldom that the first vote gives the necessary two-thirds majority. Unless it does, the second commences immediately. This is in order to transfer the votes

---

5. *Didache*, II 2.
6. Douglas Sladen, *The Secrets of the Vatican* (London: Hurst & Blackett, 1907), 69, footnote.

of those who have voted for someone who proves to have no chance to one of the Cardinals who have the largest number of votes at the first ballot. Each of the electors at the new ballot has to mark his vote with the same device and number as before; it is only the middle part of the voting paper which is altered to "*Accedo Reverendis[simo] D[omino] meo D[omino] Card....*" which signifies, "I transfer my vote to Cardinal So-and-So...." If any elector wishes to adhere to his first vote, he writes *Nemini* after this, signifying "I do not wish to transfer my vote to anyone." And this is what the electors do who have voted for a candidate who has received enough votes at the first ballot to give him a chance of being elected. If the *votes of accession*, combined with those of the first ballot, give any Cardinal his two-thirds majority, a minute verification commences. The scrutineers, who have preserved the ballots of the first vote, by breaking the seals of the lower parts and comparing the devices, establish the fact that the electors who by transferring their votes have conferred the election on one of their number, have not already voted for the same name on the first ballot. For a cardinal is not allowed to vote for the same name both in the first ballot and in the *vote of accession*, since the votes of accession are transferred in order to accumulate the requisite two-thirds majority. The secret of the ballot remains inviolate. The upper part of the voting paper which contains the name of the elector is unsealed in two cases only.

It may happen that the seals and devices adopted by several Cardinals are so alike that they can hardly be distinguished, and the doubts which then arise as to the correctness of the transfer of votes cannot be cleared up without opening the top part of the voting paper. In the second place, if the Cardinal who appears to be elected has received exactly two-thirds of the votes and not one more, he is asked to reveal his number and device, which has to be verified by opening the top part of his paper in order to prove that he has not voted for himself, which would invalidate his majority.[7]

This description of the *Accessus* is confirmed by the Papal Chamberlain Hartwell de la Garde Grissell.[8] The election by *Accessus* was used as early as in the Conclave of 1455, which produced the supreme pontiff Calixtus III. At the time, the accession was accomplished by voice without the bureaucracy of a paper ballot. The account of that conclave may be read in the *Commentaries* of Pius II.

When they came again to the scrutiny and tried the method which is called "accession", two thirds agreed upon the man who had been generally regarded as the least likely candidate. This was Alfonso, Cardinal of the Santi Quattro Coronati, a

7. Ibid., 69–70.
8. See Hartwell de la Garde Grissell, *Sede Vacante, Being a Diary Written during the Conclave of 1903, with Additional Notes on the Accession and Coronation of Pius X* (Oxford: James Parker, 1903), 81–83.

Spaniard from Valencia, of noble birth, an eminent jurist, a man of great and wide experience, but very old and almost decrepit, for he was over seventy.[9]

The method of election by accession after a scrutiny was abolished by Pius X in his apostolic constitution *Vacante Sede Apostolica* of December 25, 1904, probably because this method had previously resulted in unseemly or unedifying spectacles such as that recorded by Aeneas Silvius Piccolomini, Pope Pius II, in his account of his own election in the conclave of 1458.

On the third day after mass, when they came to the scrutiny, it was found that Filippo, Cardinal of Bologna, and Aeneas, Cardinal of Siena, had an equal number of votes, five apiece. No one else had more than three. On that ballot, whether from strategy or dislike, no one voted for Guillaume, Cardinal of Rouen.

The cardinals were accustomed, after the result of the scrutiny was announced, to sit and talk together in case any wished to change his mind and transfer the vote he had given to another (a method called "by accession"), for in this way they more easily reached an agreement. This procedure was omitted after the first scrutiny owing to the opposition of those who had received no votes and therefore could not now be candidates for accession....

The next day they went as usual to mass and then began the scrutiny.... When the result of the scrutiny was made known, it was found, as we have said before, that nine cardinals (Genoa, Orsini, Lerida, Bologna, San Marco, Santi Quattro Coronati, Zamora, Pavia, and Portugal) had voted for Aeneas; the Cardinal of Rouen had only six votes, and the rest were far behind. Rouen was petrified when he saw himself so far outstripped by Aeneas, and all the rest were amazed, for never within the memory of man had anyone polled as many as nine votes by scrutiny. Since no one had received enough votes for election, they decided to resume their seats and try the method that is called "by accession," to see if perhaps it might be possible to elect a pope that day. And here again Rouen indulged in empty hopes. All sat pale and silent in their places as if entranced. For some time no one spoke, no one opened his lips, no one moved any part of his body except the eyes, which kept glancing all about. It was a strange silence and a strange sight, men sitting there like their own statues; no sound to be heard, no movement to be seen. They remained thus for some moments, those inferior in rank waiting for their superiors to begin the accession. Then Rodrigo, the Vice-chancellor, rose and said, "I accede to the Cardinal of Siena," an utterance which was like a dagger in Rouen's heart, so pale did he turn. A silence followed and each man looking at his neighbor, began to indicate his sentiments by gestures. By this time it appeared that Aeneas would be pope, and some, fearing this result, left the con-

9. Pius II, *The Commentaries of Pius II*, trans. Florence Alden Gragg, with historical introduction and notes by Leona C. Gabel (Northampton, Mass.: Smith College Studies in History), vol. 22, nos. 1–2, October 1936–January 1937, 76.

clave, pretending physical needs, but really with the purpose of escaping the fate of that day. Those who thus withdrew were the Cardinals of Ruthen and San Sisto. However, as no one followed them, they soon returned. Then Jacopo, Cardinal of Sant'Anastasia said, "I accede to the Cardinal of Siena." At this all appeared even more stunned, like people in a house shaken by unprecedented earthquakes, and lost the power of speech. Aeneas now lacked but one vote, for twelve would elect a pope. Realizing this, Cardinal Prospero Colonna thought that he must get for himself the glory of announcing the pope. He rose and was about to pronounce his vote with the customary dignity, when he was seized by the Cardinals of Nicaea and Rouen and sharply rebuked for wishing to accede to Aeneas. When he persisted in his intention, they tried to get him out of the room by force, resorting even to such means to snatch the papacy from Aeneas. But Prospero, who, though he had voted for the Cardinal of Rouen on his ballot, was nevertheless bound to Aeneas by ties of old friendship, paid no attention to their abuse and empty threats. Turning to the other cardinals, he said, "I too accede to the Cardinal of Siena and I make him pope." When they heard this, the courage of the opposition failed and all their machinations were shattered.

All the cardinals immediately fell at Aeneas's feet and saluted him as Pope. Then they resumed their seats and ratified his election without a dissenting vote.[10]

Accident The Latin verb *cado, cadere, cecidi, casus* means *to fall,* and the addition of the preposition *ad* produces the compound verb *accido, accidere, accidi,* with the meaning *to fall down, to happen.* The Latin neuter plural participle of this last verb, *accidentia* or *accidents,* translates the Aristotelian technical term συμβεβηκότα (singular συμβεβηκός) applied to the nonessential properties of a thing; the Greek neuter perfect participle συμβεβηκός belongs to the verb συμβαίνω, compounded of the preposition σύν (*with*) and the verb βαίνω (*to go*) and meaning in the perfect tense *to be agreed on, to happen by chance.*

In Aristotelian metaphysics an accident is a property of a thing which is no part of the essence of the thing: something it could lose or have added without ceasing to be the same thing or the same substance. The accidents divide into categories: quantity, action (i.e., place in the causal order, or ability to affect things or be affected by them), quality, space, time, and relation.[11]

Nine of the ten categories of Aristotle were the categories of accidents. The first category, that of *being* (or *essence* or *substance*) was entirely different. See the entry **Categories**.

10. Ibid., 93–103.
11. Simon Blackburn, *The Oxford Dictionary of Philosophy* (Oxford: Oxford University Press, 1994), s.v. "Accident."

Acephaloi The Greek noun κεφαλή means *head*, and the addition of *alpha privativum* produces the adjective of two terminations ἀκέφαλος with the meaning *headless*. The *acephaloi* were a party of late-fifth-century Monophysites in the East who rejected the Council of Chalcedon and honored the memories of the Patriarch Dioscorus of Alexandria and the monk Eutyches, both of whom had been condemned by that Council. They were called *acephaloi* because they had no patriarch or head of their own.[12]

Acolyte The Greek verb ἀκολουθέω means *to follow*, and related to it is the noun ἀκόλουθος with the meaning, a *follower*. When the noun was transliterated into Latin in the Middle Ages, the *h* was lost because Latin has no theta. Similarly, the *h* is always dropped when Italian borrows a Greek word spelled with theta. In former times, the order of acolyte was directly below that of subdeacon and above that of exorcist. Today its functions are commonly performed by youngsters called altar boys and altar girls. Others call them altar servers to do away with the distinction of sex, a phrase that has the merit of including those adults who serve the Mass.

Adoptionism The Latin verb *opto, optare, optavi, optatus* means *to choose, to wish for*, and the associated compound verb *adopto, adoptare, adoptavi, adoptatus* means *to choose for oneself*. From this latter verb proceeded the noun *adoptio*, whence comes the English *adoption*. It became an *ism* in Spain in the seventh century, when a Nestorian type of heresy arose according to which God the Father had adopted Jesus of Nazereth to be his son. To rule out the possibility that the Christ is the *adopted* Son of the Father, the technical term μονογενής had already been employed in the fourth century.

But Scripture does not leave us here; in order to fix us in this view, lest we should be perplexed with another notion of the analogy, derived from that adopted sonship, which is ascribed therein to created beings, it attaches a characteristic epithet to His Name, as descriptive of the peculiar relation of Him who bears it to the Father. It designates Him as the *Only-begotten* or the *own*[13] Son of God, terms evidently referring, where they occur, to His heavenly nature, and thus becoming the inspired comment on the more general title.[14]

12. Henry Hart Milman, *History of Latin Christianity, Including That of the Popes, to the Pontificate of Nicholas V* (New York, Sheldon, 1860), 1:333.

13. John 1:1, 14, 18; 3:16; 5:18; Romans 8:32; Hebrews 1:1–14.

14. John Henry Cardinal Newman, *The Arians of the Fourth Century*, new ed. (London: Longmans, Green, 1897), 158.

— A —

Adoration The Latin noun *ōs, ōris, n.* means *mouth*, and from it was derived the verb *oro, orare* with the meaning *to speak, to beg, to pray, to entreat.* The compound verb *adoro* means *to speak to* someone, especially to the Deity, and therefore *to worship.* The associated noun *adoratio* means a *praying to, worship.* Thus we sing in the most beautiful of Christmas carols:

> Venite, adoremus.

The Greek word for this idea is λατρεία, originally the *service of the gods*; it is derived from the verb λατρεύω, which means *to work for hire, to serve,* especially the gods. (See, for example, the entry **Idolatry**.) Formerly a pope could be elected by a method called *adoration.* This happened when all the cardinals, without bothering to hold a scrutiny, prostrated themselves before one of their number and acclaimed him supreme pontiff. Sixtus V was so elevated to the papacy in 1585.[15]

Ad Orientem This Latin phrase means *toward the east* or *in the eastward position* and is an expression used to describe a liturgical celebration in which the priest faces the eastward direction. Facing east means facing the rising sun, and *ad orientem* is in fact an abbreviation for *ad orientem solem,* toward the rising sun. The expression *ad orientem* is found in the *Ritus Servandus* of the old Roman Missal (for example, at V 3), as is the related expression *versus populum.* If the priest indeed celebrated the Mass facing east, one would imagine that the congregation must have faced in the same direction so long as they did not have their backs toward him, which common sense would have prohibited. The orientation of the priest toward the east is said to have been usual in early times, as the rising sun was a metaphor for the risen Lord, and churches were constructed accordingly. The dead have even been interred with this consideration in mind.

Mr. Ward was buried with his face to the east.[16]

However, there are no video recordings of ancient liturgies whereby one might verify any hypothesis about the orientation of the celebrant, and, in due course, churches were constructed in whatever way was most convenient, irrespective of the points of the compass. The practice of having the priest and the people face in the same direction became standard at

---

15. Ludwig Freiherr von Pastor, *History of the Popes* (St. Louis, Mo.: Herder, 1932), 21:22.

16. Wilfrid Ward, *William George Ward and the Catholic Revival* (London: Macmillan, 1893), 418.

some point and must have been confirmed by the custom of reserving the Sacrament, to which it would have been discourteous to turn one's back.

The question that for some time has agitated pious souls is whether the priest should in modern times face the people or not. This question cannot be given an answer based on antiquarian considerations, for whether or not a practice was common two thousand years ago is not relevant to the question whether it is recommendable today. See the entry **Versus Populum**.

Adoro Te Devote This hymn of Thomas Aquinas (1225–1274) appears in the Missal in the preliminary matter "*Gratiarum actio post Missam.*"

> Adoro te devote, latens Deitas,
> Quae sub his figuris vere latitas:
> Tibi se cor meum totum subicit,
> Quia te contemplans, totum deficit.
>
> Visus, tactus, gustus in te fallitur,
> Sed auditu solo tuto creditur:
> Credo quidquid dixit Dei Filius:
> Nil hoc verbo Veritatis verius.
>
> In cruce latebat sola Deitas;
> At hic latet simul et humanitas:
> Ambo tamen credens atque confitens,
> Peto quod petivit latro paenitens.
>
> Plagas, sicut Thomas, non intueor,
> Deum tamen meum te confiteor:
> Fac me tibi semper magis credere,
> In te spem habere, te diligere.
>
> O memoriale mortis Domini,
> Panis vivus, vitam praestans homini:
> Praesta meae menti de te vivere,
> Et te illi semper dulce sapere.
>
> Pie pellicane, Jesu Domine,
> Me immundum munda tuo sanguine:
> Cuius una stilla salvum facere
> Totum mundum quit ab omni scelere.
>
> Jesu, quem velatum nunc aspicio,
> Oro, fiat illud, quod tam sitio:
> Ut, te revelata cernens facie,
> Visu sim beatus tuae gloriae. Amen.

The best translation is by John Mason Neale (1818–1866). Neale's translations are serviceable because they can be sung to the same tune as the Latin hymn.

> Humbly I adore Thee, hidden Deity,
> Which beneath these figures art concealed from me;
> Wholly in submission Thee my spirit hails,
> For in contemplating Thee it wholly fails.
>
> Taste and touch and vision in Thee are deceived:
> But the hearing only may be well believed:
> I believe whatever God's own Son declared;
> Nothing can be truer than Truth's very Word.
>
> On the Cross lay hidden but Thy deity:
> Here is also hidden Thy humanity:
> But in both believing and confessing, Lord,
> Ask I what the dying thief of Thee implored.
>
> Though Thy wounds, like Thomas, I behold not now,
> Thee my Lord confessing, and my God, I bow:
> Give me ever stronger faith in Thee above,
> Give me ever stronger hope and stronger love.
>
> O most sweet memorial of His death and woe,
> Living Bread, which givest life to man below,
> Let my spirit ever eat of Thee and live,
> And the blest fruition of Thy sweetness give!
>
> Pelican of mercy, Jesu, Lord and God,
> Cleanse me, wretched sinner, in Thy Precious Blood:
> Blood whereof one drop for humankind outpoured
> Might from all transgression have the world restored.
>
> Jesu, Thou, Whom thus veil'd, I must see below,
> When shall that be given which I long for so,
> That at last beholding Thy uncover'd Face,
> Thou wouldst satisfy me with Thy fullest grace?[17]

Adultery The Latin nouns *adultĕr, -ĕri, m.* and *adultĕra, -ae, f.* mean *adulterer* and *adulteress* respectively, and the noun *adulterium* means *adultery*. Adultery is the act of violating one's marriage vows by having sexual intercourse with someone other than one's husband or wife. In the

17. Rev. J. M. Neale, trans., *Mediaeval Hymns and Sequences*, 2nd ed. (London: Joseph Masters, 1863), 176–77.

first century or two of the Church, adulterers were urged to do penance, but they were "deprived of all hope of readmission to the congregation, even at their last hour."[18]

Advent The Latin verb *venio, venire, veni, venturus* means *to come*, and the compound verb *advenio, advenire, adveni, adventus* means *to come to*. From the fourth principal part of the latter verb proceeds the noun *adventus, adventūs, m.*, which means *the coming*, whence we have the English noun *advent*. The Advent season is the opening season of the liturgical year and begins with the fourth Sunday before Christmas. It is a penitential season that ends with the Midnight Mass on Christmas Eve, a vigil which was once a day of fast and abstinence. The Advent season was formerly the occasion for special sermons. A famous series of such *Adventspredigten* was delivered by Michael Cardinal Faulhaber in Munich in December, 1933, under the title *Judentum, Christentum, und Germanentum*.

Advocatus Diaboli The Latin verb *voco, vocare, vocavi, vocatus* means *to call*, and the compound verb *advoco* means *to call to one's aid*. Thus, the *advocatus* was *someone called in to help, legal counsel*. The phrase *Advocatus Diaboli* means the *Devil's Lawyer* and refers to a former official of the Sacred Congregation of Rites whose duty it was to mention those reasons why a candidate for sainthood should *not* be canonized and thereby to pull the plug on controversial causes. For example, had there been a Devil's Advocate when Pius IX came up for canonization, that authority would, I believe, have brought up the Mortara Case and the use of capital punishment in the Papal States and would have thrown them into the balance to try to prevent the proceedings from going any further. The abolition of this position is not uncorrelated with the multiplication of canonizations in recent decades, events that formerly were very rare. For the etymology of *diabolus*, see the entry **Devil**.

Aeterne Rex Altissime This hymn, of unknown authorship, is sung during the Corpus Christi procession and on the Feast of the Ascension *ad Officium Lectionis* (i.e., at the hour formerly called *Matins* and now denominated the *Office of Readings*). There are eight strophes, each consisting of four lines in iambic dimeter (two pairs of iambs), without rhyme.

---

18. Louis Duchesne, *Early History of the Christian Church from Its Foundation to the End of the Third Century* (London: John Murray, 1914), 298.

Aeterne Rex altissime,
Redemptor et fidelium,
Quo mors soluta deperit,
Datur triumphus gratiae.

Scandens tribunal dexterae
Patris, potestas omnium
Collata Jesu caelitus,
Quae non erat humanitus.

Ut trina rerum machina,
Caelestium, terrestrium,
Et infernorum condita,
Flectat genu iam subdita.

Tremunt videntes Angeli
Versam vicem mortalium:
Culpat caro, purgat caro
Regnat Deus Dei caro.

Tu Christe nostrum gaudium
Manens Olympo praemium,
Mundi regis qui fabricam,
Mundana vincens gaudia.

Hinc te precantes quaesumus,
Ignosce culpis omnibus,
Et corda sursum subleva
Ad te superna gratia.

Ut cum repente coeperis
Clarere nube Judicis,
Poenas repellas debitas,
Reddas coronas perditas.

Gloria tibi Domine,
Qui scandis super sidera,
Cum Patre, et Sancto Spiritu,
In sempiterna saecula. Amen.

The following translation is by Edward Caswall (1814–1878), whose translations, like those of John Mason Neale, have the merit of not requiring new music, since they can be sung to the same familiar tune as the original hymn:

O Thou eternal King most high!
Who didst the world redeem;
And conquering Death and Hell, receive
A dignity supreme.

Thou, through the starry orbs, this day,
Didst to thy throne ascend;
Thenceforth to reign in sovereign power
And glory without end.

There, seated in thy majesty,
To Thee submissive bow
The Heav'n of Heav'ns, the earth beneath,
The realms of Hell below.

With trembling there the angels see
The changed estate of men:
The flesh which sinn'd by Flesh redeem'd;
Man in the Godhead reign.

There, waiting for thy faithful souls,
Be Thou to us, O Lord!
Our joy of joys while here we stay,
In Heav'n our great reward.

Renew our strength; our sins forgive;
Our miseries efface;
And lift our souls aloft to Thee,
By thy celestial grace.

So, when Thou shinest on the clouds,
With thy angelic train,
May we be saved from deadly doom
And our lost crowns regain.

To Christ returning gloriously
With victory to Heaven,
Praise with the Father evermore
And Holy Ghost be given.[19]

Affusion The Latin verb *fundo, fundere, fudi, fusus* means *to pour*, and
the addition of the preposition *ad* produces the compound verb *affundo,
affundere, affudi, affusus* with the meaning *to pour upon*. From the fourth
principal part of this compound verb proceeds the noun *affusio, affusionis*

---

19. Edward Caswall, *Lyra Catholica: Containing All the Breviary and Missal Hymns, with Others
from Various Sources* (London: Burns & Oates, 1884), 197–99.

meaning *a pouring upon*. Baptism by affusion is the most common form of baptism in the Church; one merely pours water from a dish or shell onto the head of the child. See also the entry **Infusion**.

Agape This noun, which must be pronounced in three syllables, is the English transliteration of the Greek noun ἀγάπη, which means *brotherly love, charity*. It is related to the verb ἀγαπάω, *to welcome, to be fond of*, and ultimately to ἄγαμαι, *to wonder at, admire*. It was the name given to the communal meal important in the lives of the earliest Christians, a meal mentioned by Pliny in his ninety-sixth letter to the emperor Trajan, quoted below in full in the entry **Martyr**. The *Song of Agape* in 1 Corinthians 13 is a masterpiece worthy of being committed to memory. There is a close relationship between the *Song of Agape* and Agathon's *Hymn to Eros* in Plato's *Symposium*. *Eros* is a yearning love, whereas *agape* is a giving love; neither word had the erotic connotation of today's "love". *Eros* is a love of an experience of the past; *agape* is a love of the present, a state of mind that guides all actions. *Agape*, one of the three charisms (faith, hope, love), is a fruit of grace. One may ask whether grace is equal to love. No, abstractions cannot be set equal in such a manner, especially when the words used are translations from the original language. Ἔλεος, *mercy*, is the rock of *agape*; it is the basis of the world's meaning. There are two kinds of *agape*, there is the *agape* of Christ, and the *agape* of men inspired by that of Christ.

Agnostic The English word *agnostic* was introduced by Thomas Henry Huxley (1825–1895), who was of the opinion "that God was unknowable and Christianity a superstition."[20] It is formed from the Greek adjective ἄγνωστος, *unknown*, which appears in Acts 17:23 in the story of the unknown god. The adjective ἄγνωστος is formed from *alpha privativum* and the verb γιγνώσκω, *to know*. There is also in Greek the related verb ἀγνοέω, *to be ignorant, not to know*.

Agnus Dei This Latin phrase means the *Lamb of God*. It comes from the cry of John the Baptist:

Ecce agnus Dei, ecce qui tollit peccatum mundi.

Behold the Lamb of God. Behold him who taketh away the sin of the world.[21]

---

20. Wilfrid Ward, *William George Ward and the Catholic Revival* (London: Macmillan, 1893), 306.
21. John 1:29

It was taken into the Communion rite, albeit with the reading *peccata* instead of *peccatum*. *Agnus Dei* was also the name of a sacramental of former times, a wax wafer on which was impressed the figure of a lamb with the banner of the cross.

Agonistics The Greek noun ἀγών means an *assembly*, an *assembly for an athletic contest* (like the Olympic games, a *contest* or *struggle)*. From it is derived the verb ἀγωνίζομαι with the meaning *to contend*. The contestant himself is the ἀγωνιστής, and the related adjective ἀγωνιστικός means *fit for a contest*. The Greek name for the Circumcellion heretics was οἱ ἀγωνιστοί. See the entry **Circumcellions**.

Akkadian There was in Babylonia a city which the Jews called אַכַּד, which is mentioned once in the Bible at Genesis 10:10. Their language was called Akkadian.

Alb The Latin adjective *albus, -a, -um* means *white, dead white*, as opposed to *candidus, -a, -um*, which means *glittering white*. The alb is a white tunic worn by the clergy under all other vestments except the amice, which is now optional. The alb was also the garment worn by the newly baptized from the Easter Vigil until the first Sunday after Easter, which thus acquired the name *Dominica in albis*, the Sunday when you are dressed in white. This Sunday was also called *Quasi modo* Sunday, from the opening words of the Introit for the day. In English-speaking countries, the further name *Low Sunday* came into use; Weekley says that this was perhaps due to a reaction from the joys of Easter. *Dominica in albis, Quasi modo* Sunday, and Low Sunday are names that have all been displaced by the modern Divine Mercy Sunday devotion. The alb, like the surplice and rochet, should not be ironed like a sheet; it must be ironed so as to be pleated or crimped. Not to do so is a sign of laziness and lack of attention to detail. (See the comment of Msgr. Ronald Knox in this regard in the entry **Surplice**.) The alb is supposed to be so long as to trail on (or at least reach) the ground and require ministers to hold it up as the priest ascends a flight of steps. The purpose of this is to hide the pants and stockings, the sight of which was, in former times, considered a blameworthy distraction.

Albigenses The French city of Albi was in ancient times called *Albiga*, and its people *Albigenses*. The noun *Albigenses* is used to denominate certain numerous heretics of Provence who, in the twelfth and thirteenth centuries, were the object both of a crusade called by Innocent III and of the attention of the Dominican Inquisition. They were a species of Cathars or Manichees. Their solution to the problem of evil was to hold that all matter was the creation of the devil, with whom they identified the God of the Old Testament. Purgatory and hell were for them life on this earth. They had no use for the pope or for the Church. For them the resurrection of the body was both false and undesirable; salvation consisted of the escape of the soul from corporeal existence, which might be achieved after a series of reincarnations. Macaulay considered the rise of the Albigenses to be the first of the four great revolutions against the Roman Church (see his essay on von Ranke). Their doctrines and history are minutely investigated in the third and fourth chapters of the first volume of Lea's *History*.[22] The English adjective corresponding to the noun *Albigenses* is *Albigensian*.

Alexandrian School The English word *school* is the corruption of the Greek noun σχολή meaning *leisure, spare time*. The verb ἀλέξω means *to ward off*, hence, *to defend*, and the noun ἀνήρ, ἀνδρός means *man*; from these two words there arose the name Ἀλέξανδρος with the meaning *man-protector*, one who defends men. The most famous of Alexanders was Alexander the Great, who founded the city Ἀλεξάνδρεια in Egypt. The most famous confessor of the Christian Catechetical "School of Alexandria" was the Christian gnostic Titus Flavius Clemens (c. 150–c. 215), known as Clement of Alexandria. The method of pedagogy adopted by this School was the subject of comment by John Henry Newman:

What I have said about the method of teaching adopted by the Alexandrian, and more or less by the other primitive Churches, amounts to this; that they on principle refrained from telling unbelievers all they believed themselves, and further, that they endeavored to connect their own doctrine with theirs, whether Jewish or pagan, adopting their sentiments and even their language, as far as they lawfully could.[23]

The Abbé Duchesne describes the doctrines of Clement as follows (the Greek words are quotations from an evaluation by St. Photius the Martyr):

Clement taught the eternity of matter; he said the Son was only a creature; he believed in the transmigration of souls (metempsychosis), and in the existence

---

22. Henry Charles Lea, *A History of the Inquisition in the Middle Ages*, 3 vols. (New York: Harper & Brothers, 1887).

23. John Henry Cardinal Newman, *The Arians of the Fourth Century*, new ed. (London: Longmans, Green, 1897), 89.

of other worlds, prior to the creation of man. The history of Adam and Eve was treated in a shamelessly impious manner (αἰσχρῶς τε καὶ ἀθέως). According to Clement, the Word was made flesh only in appearance. Moreover, he acknowledged two or three Words, as the following phrase shows: "The Son is also called the Word, with the same name as the Word of the Father; but it was not He who was made flesh; neither was it the Word of the Father; but it was a Power of God, a sort of derivation from His Word, which in the form of reason (νοῦς γενόμενος) dwells in the heart of man."[24]

Another celebrity of the School was Origen (c. 185–c. 254), the father of textual criticism. Textual criticism is the science of determining the exact text of the sacred scriptures; if someone added or subtracted a verse, one wants to know who, what, and when. Origen attained this status by comparing the Hebrew text of the Old Testament with those of the Septuagint and of three other Greek translations, namely, the versions of Aquila, Symmachus, and Theodotion; the Hebrew text he gave both in the Hebrew alphabet and transliterated into Greek letters for the benefit of those unable to read Hebrew. For the purpose of comparison, he wrote these six versions next to one another in six columns, and as a result his book came to be called the *Hexapla*, from the Greek ἑξαπλάσιος, six-fold, from ἕξ, six, and ἁπλόος, simple, one-fold. In his fifth column, which contained his edition of the Septuagint, he used the obelus (—) to indicate passages in the Septuagint not found in the Hebrew Bible and the asterisk (※) to mark passages not found in the Septuagint but which he had added from Theodotion.[25] These symbols became standard and were later used by Jerome:

Notet sibi unusquisque vel iacentem lineam vel signa radiantia, id est vel obelos vel asteriscos, et ubicumque virgulam viderit praecedentem, ab ea usque ad duo puncta quae impressimus, sciat in Septuaginta translatoribus plus haberi; ubi autem stellae similitudinem perspexerit, de hebraeis voluminibus additum noverit, aeque usque ad duo puncta, iuxta Theodotionis dumtaxat editionem qui simplicitate sermonis a Septuaginta interpretibus non discordat.[26]

24. Louis Duchesne, *Early History of the Christian Church from Its Foundation to the End of the Third Century* (London: John Murray, 1914), 244–45.

25. The preeminent book on the textual criticism of the Bible is by Ernst Würthwein, *The Text of the Old Testament: An Introduction to Kittel-Kahle's Biblia Hebraica*, trans. Peter R. Ackroyd (Oxford: Basil Blackwell, 1957).

26. *Praefatio Eusebii Hieronymi in Libro Psalmorum*, in *Biblia Sacra Iuxta Vulgatam Versionem*. Adiuvantibus Bonifatio Fischer OSB, Ioanne Gribomont OSB, H. F. D. Sparks, W. Thiele, recensuit et brevi apparatu instruxit Robertus Weber OSB, editio tertia emendata quam paravit Bonifatius Fischer OSB cum sociis H. I. Frede, Ioanne Gribomont OSB, H. F. D. Sparks, W. Thiele, 2 vols (Stuttgart: Deutsche Bibelgesellschaft, 1985), 1:767.

The reader should pay attention to the horizontal line and the sunburst, that is, to the obelus and the asterisk, wherever he sees them. When you notice a passage with the slanted line in front and a colon at the end, then you know that that passage is an addition in the Septuagint. Where, however, you find a passage with the starlike mark at the beginning and a colon at the end, then you know that it is not original to the Septuagint but is precisely Theodotion's translation of a passage in the Hebrew text, for Theodotion's style is so straightforward that it is in harmony with that of the Septuagint.

Although Origen was at the frontier of knowledge in textual criticism, he went over the top in asceticism, for as a result of his literal interpretation of Matthew 19:12 he castrated himself. He is the best example of how a fellow can be outstanding in one discipline and insane in another.

Genius may in some matters raise a man above the level of his age; in others it is powerless, and every human intellect must remain subject to the current of the requirements, feelings, and conceptions of the time in which it dwells, and by which, as by the atmosphere, it is surrounded.[27]

Origen's theology was condemned in the sixth century, long after his death, when the Fifth Ecumenical Council inaugurated the practice of *post mortem* anathematizations. One of the peculiarities of his theology was that while the usual theory of metempsychosis had the soul travelling from body to body, Origen's system had the body being used by one soul after another. It is summarized by Duchesne as follows:

Now, this system had two aspects. According as the Word is viewed in relation to the finite transitory world, or to God, He appears distinct from God and partaking in some degree in the character of a created being; or else, as co-eternal with God, and deriving from the divine substance. The Modalists might be met by the first aspect; and the second was calculated to reassure those who were disturbed by the excessively clear cut lines of demarcation drawn between the different manifestations, or hypostases, and by their subordination. The transition from one aspect to another involved no contradiction; they were linked together in Origen's system; orthodoxy was safeguarded by the juxtaposition of complementary doctrines. But the whole system was academic; it formed no part of the teaching of the Church; it might even be said that the Church ignored it.[28]

---

27. Ferdinand Gregorovius, *History of the City of Rome in the Middle Ages*, 2nd ed., trans. Mrs. Gustavus W. Hamilton (London: G. Bell & Sons, 1902), 2:70.
28. Louis Duchesne, *Early History of the Christian Church from Its Foundation to the End of the Third Century* (London: John Murray, 1914), 354.

Allegory The Greek adjective ἄλλος means *other*, and the verb ἀγορεύω means *to speak in the assembly, to address an audience*. The combination of the two words produced the noun ἀλληγορία with the meaning *to say one thing but mean another*. The allegorical interpretation of scripture was once common; see the entry **Bible**. Writing of the Song of Songs, Sanday says:

> Its place in our Bibles is due to a method of interpretation which is now very generally abandoned....
>
> I do not think that we need deprecate the allegorical use of the Song of Songs, so long as it is quite understood that this is not its original meaning.[29]

The function of an allegory is to translate the past into the present.

Alleluia This is the transliteration of the Hebrew phrase הללו יה, which means *Praise the Lord*.

Alogoi The Greek noun λόγος means *word, reason*, and by the addition of *alpha privativum* there was formed the adjective ἄλογος with the meaning *unspoken, irrational*. In the second century, this adjective was used in the plural ἄλογοι to refer to a group of Christian heretics who rejected the fourth gospel, the gospel of the Logos, because they found it to be incompatible with the synoptic gospels.

ἐν ἀρχῇ ἦν ὁ λόγος.

In the beginning was the Logos. (John I 1)

Sanday evaluated them as follows:

> They seem to have been just a few rationalizing Christians who cut away all that seemed to them mystical or extravagant.[30]

Altar The Latin adjective *altus* means *high*, and places of sacrifice were located on high ground. The word *altar* is just the transliteration of the Ecclesiastical Latin noun *altare, altaris, n.* The Classical Latin word for *altar* is *ara, -ae, f.* The altar was the location of the sacrifice of animals, a practice that was common to most primitive religions, including that of the children of Israel. The abandonment of the old high altars that occurred after the Second Vatican Council was, from the artistic point of view, a calamity.

29. William Sanday, *Inspiration, Eight Lectures on the Early History and Origin of the Doctrine of Biblical Inspiration, Being the Bampton Lectures for 1893* (London: Longmans, Green, 1896), 211, 212.
30. Ibid., 64.

Altar Rails The Latin verb *rego, regere, rexi, rectus* means *to guide, direct, make straight*. From it is derived the noun *regula* with the meaning a *ruler, a bar*. Our noun *rail* is the corruption of this Latin noun through the medium of the Old French *reille*. The altar rails were removed from many churches where the traditional Latin Mass has since been attempted; the results have not been convenient for the elderly.

Ambo The Greek verb βαίνω means *to go*, and the preposition ἀνά means *up to*. Their combination produced the verb ἀναβαίνω with the meaning *to climb up*, and from it is derived the noun ἄμβων, ἄμβωνος, *m.*, meaning *the crest of a hill, the rim of a goblet, the steps of a ladder*, and finally a *pulpit*. (The unrelated Latin adjective *ambo* means *both*.) The ambo is the preacher's station reached by a flight of stairs, often helical to save space. The word should not be used of a mere lectern on a level with the sanctuary. The two pulpits of greatest artistic value are those of Nicola Pisano—one in the baptistery of the Cathedral of Pisa and the other in the Duomo of Siena.

Americanism This is the name of a heresy that Cardinal Gibbons said no one in America believed. It was the object of a letter of condemnation *Testem Benevolentiae* of Leo XIII in 1899 addressed to the aforementioned prelate. It may be defined as the attitude that such doctrines as freedom of the press, freedom of religion, and separation of church and state should, in 1899, have been accepted by the Catholic Church. "The name *America* is derived from the proper name Ἀμαλάριχος or *Amaláricus*, meaning *tireless ruler*, which was common among the Ostrogoths; it came into Italian as *Amerígo* and was the first name of the explorer Vespucci, from whence it was adopted as the name of our continent. The accent on the antepenult is due to the Spanish pronunciation *Américo*."[31]

Amice This word is the corruption of the Latin noun *amictus, -ūs, m.*, the putting on of a garment or the garment itself, from the verb *amicio, amicire, amicui, amictus*, which means *to clothe, to wrap around*. The amice is a rectangular piece of white cloth worn under the alb and tied with laces around the neck so as to prevent one from seeing skin or street clothes that might otherwise be visible and distracting. The amice is not mentioned in the instructions that come with the current Roman Missal:

31. Anthony Lo Bello, *Origins of Mathematical Words: A Comprehensive Dictionary of Latin, Greek, and Arabic Roots* (Baltimore, Md.: The Johns Hopkins University Press, 2013), 15.

Sacerdotis celebrantis vestis propria, in Missa aliisque sacris actionibus quae cum Missa directo conectuntur, est planeta seu casula, nisi aliud caveatur, super albam et stolam induenda.[32]

The proper vestment of a celebrating priest, in the Mass and in other sacred ceremonies directly connected with it, is the *planeta* or chasuble (unless there is an exemption otherwise), to be worn over the alb and stole.

Anathema The Greek verb ἀνατίθημι means *to set* (τίθημι) *up* (ἀνά), and the noun ἀνάθημα derived from it means *that which is set up*, a *votive offering*. Since such offerings were sometimes destroyed, the related word ἀνάθεμα eventually acquired the meaning of something consigned to perdition, as in the curse ἀνάθεμα ἔστω, "Let him be anathema." In this sense, it was added to the end of canons in the acts of councils as a warning to gainsayers:

Si quis dixerit, licere Christianis plures simul habere uxores, & hoc nulla lege divina esse prohibitum; anathema sit.[33]

If anyone should say that Christians are allowed to have many wives simultaneously and that this is forbidden by no divine law, let him be anathema.

Anathematisms The addition of the suffix -ισμός to the noun ἀνάθεμα produced the word ἀναθεματισμός with the meaning a *decree that levels an anathema*, a censure ending with the words ἀνάθεμα ἔστω. The English word is the transliteration of the Greek noun, which had been taken over into Latin as *anathematismus*. The anathematisms *par excellence* were the twelve canons of Cyril, Patriarch of Alexandria, submitted to Nestorius, Patriarch of Constantinople, with the demand that he accept them. The Council of Ephesus (431 A.D.) took notice of them, and the "Robber" Council of Ephesus (449) approved them, although they had not previously been seen and approved by Pope Julius. Furthermore, in the year 448, they had been condemned as smacking of Apollinarianism by the Bishops of Syria.[34] The Council of Chalcedon (451) included them in its acts and declared the letters of Cyril canonical, and the Fifth Ecumenical Council, the second at Constantinople (553), defended them. The first of them is the most important:

32. *Institutio Generalis Missalis Romani*, in *Missale Romanum, editio typica altera* (Vatican City: Libreria Editrice Vaticana, 1975), §299.

33. Council of Trent, twenty-fourth session, *De Sacramento Matrimonii*, Canon II, November 11, 1563.

34. John Henry Cardinal Newman, "Trials of Theodoret," in *Historical Sketches*, vol. 2 (London: Longmans, Green, 1917), 351.

Εἴ τις οὐχ ὁμολογεῖ, Θεὸν εἶναι κατὰ ἀλήθειαν τὸν Εμμανουὴλ, καὶ διὰ τοῦτο θεοτόκον τὴν ἁγίαν παρθένον γεγέννηκε γὰρ σαρκικῶς σάρκα γεγονότα τὸν ἐκ Θεοῦ λόγον· ἀνάθεμα ἔστω.³⁵

If anyone should not agree that the Emmanuel is in truth God, and for this reason the Holy Virgin is Mother of God (for she gave birth in the flesh to the Logos from God which became flesh), let him be anathema.

Anchorite The Greek verb χωρέω means *to make room, to give way,* and the addition of the preposition ἀνά (back) produces the compound verb ἀναχωρέω with the meaning *to retire.* The related noun ἀναχωρήτης signifies *someone who has withdrawn from society,* and from it is derived the English noun *anchorite,* a hermit. There is no connection with the word *anchor,* which clumsily descends from another Greek noun, ἄγκυρα.

Angel The Greek verb ἀγγέλλω means *to bring a message, to bear tidings.* The fellow bringing the message was called the ἄγγελος or *messenger.* The beings who bring the messages of Deity are therefore called ἄγγελοι. The English transliteration *angel* is used only in the case of such a celestial messenger. The Hebrew word for such a being is מלאך. The verb from the root לאך is not found in biblical Hebrew, though it is available in the fourth conjugation of modern written Arabic with the meaning *to send as a messenger.*

Angelus Domini The prayer *Angelus Domini* is recited at the beginning of the day, at noon, and in the evening.

> V. Angelus Domini nuntiavit Mariae
> R. Et concepit de Spiritu Sancto. Ave Maria, etc.
> V. Ecce ancilla Domini
> R. Fiat mihi secundum verbum tuum. Ave Maria, etc.
> V. Et Verbum caro factum est
> R. Et habitavit in nobis. Ave Maria, etc.
> V. Ora pro nobis, Sancta Dei Genetrix
> R. Ut digni efficiamur promissionibus Christi.

Oremus. Gratiam tuam, quaesumus, Domine, mentibus nostris infunde ut, qui, angelo nuntiante, Christi Filii tui incarnationem cognovimus, per passionem eius et crucem ad resurrectionis gloriam perducamur. Per eundum Christum Dominum nostrum. Amen.

---

35. Denzinger, *Enchiridion Symbolorum et Definitionum,* 7th ed. (Würzburg, Germany: V. J. Stahel, 1895), XII 21.

V. The angel of the Lord declared unto Mary

R. And she conceived of the Holy Ghost. Hail Mary ...

V. Behold the handmaid of the Lord

R. Be it done unto me according to thy word. Hail Mary ...

V. And the Word was made flesh

R. And dwelt among us. Hail Mary ...

V. Pray for us, O Holy Mother of God

R. That we may be made worthy of the promises of Christ.

Let us pray. Pour forth, we beseech thee, O Lord, thy grace into our hearts, that we, to whom the Incarnation of Christ, thy son, was made known by the message of an angel, may, by His Passion and Cross, be brought to the glory of His Resurrection. Through the same Christ our Lord. Amen.

In Catholic countries the appropriate times would be announced by the ringing of the church bell.

Sweetly over the village the bell of the Angelus sounded.[36]

In modern times the prayer would be recited on the radio or even televised. In Muslim countries, the authorities still alert the public when it is time to pray, though by boom boxes. In the Easter season the Angelus is replaced by the *Regina Caeli* (see **Regina Caeli**).

Anglican The *Angli* were a tribe of German barbarians who invaded Britannia in the fifth century and gave their name to the southern half of the island, *Anglia*. *England* means *land of the Angli*. The associated Late Latin adjective *anglicanus* means *English* and was used by Thomas à Becket in a letter of 1169 to the supreme pontiff Alexander III and by the authors of the Magna Carta:

Quod ecclesia anglicana libera sit.[37]

That the English Church be free.

It became the common appellation of a member of the established Church of England in the seventeenth century, as one can deduce from the quotations cited in the *Oxford English Dictionary*. The Church of England produced the greatest biblical scholars of the English-speaking world, including Charles, Driver, Gray, Lightfoot, Plummer, Westcott, and Word-

---

36. Longfellow, "Evangeline," I, iv. 127.

37. Ernest Weekley, *An Etymological Dictionary of the English Language* (New York: Dover, 1967), s.v. "Anglican."

sworth. It received Charles Augustus Briggs into its communion after he was convicted of heresy by the Presbyterians. It demonstrated with its Book of Common Prayer and the Authorized Bible that it is possible to have a vernacular liturgy of the first rank.

Anglican Orders The nineteenth century was agitated by the question of whether the priests of the Church of England were priests in the same way that priests of the Roman Catholic and Eastern Orthodox Churches are priests. It was the decision of Pope Leo XIII in his bull *Apostolicae Curae* (1896) that they were not. The bull called forth a Latin reply of the archbishops and bishops of the Church of England, composed by the historian Mandell Creighton, Bishop of London (1843–1901).[38] The current practice of the Catholic Church is to accept an Anglican priest-convert as a layman.

Animal *Animal, animalis, n.*, is a Latin noun meaning *that which has an anima or soul*. See the entry **Hell**. Thus, it is an etymological heresy to say that animals have no souls. That an animal has a soul may mean no more than it is a creature that breathes, or it may indicate agreement with the Platonic doctrine in the *Timaeus*, that the soul of animals is no different from that of men and travels back and forth between them in the process of transmigration and reincarnation, a great heresy. Concern about the welfare of animals may, in the opinion of some authorities, be dismissed in view of 1 Corinthians 9:

μὴ τῶν βοῶν μέλει τῷ θεῷ;

God doesn't care about oxen, does he?

This, though, is Paul at his weakest. More elevated thoughts are to be found in the Jewish tradition.

Have compassion towards all, not towards men only, but also towards beasts.[39]

The killing of animals for meat was not so common in biblical times as it is today, when it is an industry. People in those times were too poor to own an animal, or, if they owned one, to slay it, except on a rare occasion,

---

38. *Anglican Orders (Latin), The Bull of His Holiness Leo XIII, September 13, 1896 and the Answer of the Archbishops of England, March 29, 1897*, published for the Church Historical Society, London, Society for Promoting Christian Knowledge, 1932.

39. *Testaments of the Twelve Patriarchs, Zebulon*, §5, in R. H. Charles, *The Apocrypha and Pseudepigrapha of the Old Testament in English* (Oxford: Clarendon Press, 1913), 2:330.

such as for a feast. It is a problem for some, though not all, that animal sacrifices were imagined to be required by the express command of the Deity, as one may read on almost any page of the Pentateuch. Those who cannot accept this and yet wish to remain believers rely on the device of ascribing the call for sacrifices to the human element in the scriptures. (See the entry **Inspiration**.) The prophets of Israel commented as follows with regard to animal sacrifices:

For what purpose is the multitude of your sacrifices unto me? saith the Lord: I am full of the burnt offerings of rams, and the fat of fed beasts; and I delight not in the blood of bullocks, or of lambs or of he goats. When ye come to appear before me, who hath required this of your hand, to tread my courts? Bring no more vain oblations; incense is an abomination unto me; the new moons and Sabbaths, the calling of assemblies, I cannot away with; it is iniquity, even the solemn meeting. Your new moons and your appointed feasts my soul hateth; they are trouble unto me; I am weary to bear them. And when ye spread forth your hands, I will hide mine eyes from you: yea, when ye make many prayers, I will not hear: your hands are full of blood. Wash you, make you clean; put away the evil of your doings from before mine eyes; cease to do evil; Learn to do well; seek judgment, relieve the oppressed, judge the fatherless, plead for the widow.[40]

Thus saith the Lord of hosts, the God of Israel. Put your burnt offerings into your sacrifices, and eat flesh. For I spake not unto your fathers, nor commanded them in the day that I brought them out of the land of Egypt, concerning burnt offerings or sacrifices. But this thing commanded I them saying, "Obey my voice, and I will be your God, and ye shall be my people, and walk ye in all the ways that I have commanded you, that it may be well with you."[41]

I hate, I despise your feast days, and I will not smell in your solemn assemblies. Though ye offer me burnt offerings and your meat offerings, I will not accept them, neither will I regard the peace offerings of your fat beasts.[42]

For I desired mercy and not sacrifice, and the knowledge of God rather than burnt offerings.[43]

Wherewith shall I come before the Lord, and bow myself before the high God? Shall I come before him with burnt offerings, with calves of a year old? Will the Lord be pleased with thousands of rams, or with ten thousands of rivers of oil? Shall I give my firstborn for my transgression, the first of my body for the sin of

---

40. Isaiah 1:11–17. This and the following translations are taken from the Authorized Version, the King James Bible.
41. Jeremiah 7:21–23.
42. Amos 5:21–22.
43. Hosea 6:6.

my soul? He hath shewed thee, O man, what is good. And what doth the Lord require of thee, but to do justly, and to love mercy, and to walk humbly with thy God?[44]

> I will take no bullock out of thy house, nor he goats out of thy folds.
> For every beast of the forest is mine, and the cattle upon a thousand hills.
> I know all the fowls of the mountains, and the wild beasts of the field
>   are mine.
> If I were hungry, I would not tell thee, for the world is mine, and the fullness
>   thereof.
> Will I eat the flesh of bulls, or drink the blood of goats?[45]

For thou desirest not sacrifice, else would I give it. Thou delightest not in burnt offering. The sacrifices of God are a broken spirit; a broken and contrite heart, O God, thou wilt not despise.[46]

One of the criteria whereby one evaluates religions is what they have to say about the treatment of animals.

Anno Domini This phrase, abbreviated A.D., is Latin for "in the year of the Lord." As the Romans counted the years from the founding of their city, so the Christians eventually counted them from the birth of Christ. This system of dating from the Nativity of the Lord was introduced by the monk Dionysius Exiguus, who lived in the first half of the sixth century.[47] According to Gregorovius, the Church of Rome adopted this system of dating in the year 968; before then it used the system of indictions.[48] The system of indictions used by the Holy See in the period 584–968 identified a year by its place in a fifteen-year cycle. Thus, *indictione decima* meant "in the tenth year of the cycle," not "in the tenth cycle." This method was defective because one did not know which cycle was meant unless one could determine it from other information. In the system of indictions, the first day of the year was September 23, the birthday of the emperor Augustus and a close approximation of the autumnal equinox.

The use of the secular concoctions C.E. (common era) and B.C.E. (before the common era) is distracting; the best authors have never used

---

44. Micah 6:6–8.

45. Psalm 1:9–13.

46. Psalm 51:6–17. The most advanced textual critics hold that verses 18–19 are a later interpolation by an apologist, a poor ending to a psalm of such profound spirituality.

47. *Brewer's Dictionary of Phrase and Fable*, 18th ed., ed. Camilla Rockwood (Edinburgh: Brewer's, 2009), 49.

48. Ferdinand Gregorovius, *History of the City of Rome in the Middle Ages*, trans. Mrs. Gustavus W. Hamilton (London: G. Bell & Sons, 1909), 1:360n1.

these phrases. They are a device to avoid the reference to Jesus Christ. The expression A.D. has in its favor that it is a universal expression, whereas C.E. can be used only in English-speaking countries.

Annulment *Nullus, -a, -um* is the Latin adjective meaning *no, none, not any*. From this adjective there arose the late verb *annullo, annullare* with the meaning *to bring to nothing*. Such an act was called an *annullatio*. The Romans added the suffix *-mentum* to verb stems to create nouns. The French continued this practice and formed *annullement*, whence we have our English word. In the Catholic Church, it has the meaning of a declaration that no marriage ever existed. The abrogation of a valid marriage is called a *divorce*, an option not available in the Catholic Church. Annulments may be granted by diocesan courts, whose verdicts may be appealed to the Supreme Tribunal of the Roman Rota.

Annunciation The Latin word *nuntius* as an adjective means *announcing, bringing news of*, and as a noun it means *messenger*. There was thence formed the verb *nuntio, nuntiare, nuntiavi, nuntiatus* with the meaning *to bring news of*. This verb, when compounded with the preposition *ad*, produced the verb *adnuntio, adnuntiare, adnuntiavi, adnuntiatus* with the meaning *announce, tell*. From this verb came the noun *annuntiatio, annuntiationis, f.*, meaning *announcement*. The Annunciation is the feast commemorating the event of Luke 1:26–56. It is celebrated on March 25, nine months before the birth of Christ.

Anoint The Latin verb *unguo, unguere, unxi, unctus* means *to anoint, besmear*, and the compound verb *inunguo* means to *smear* (unguo) *on* (in). From the latter verb is derived the English verb *to anoint*. Anointing with oil is a part of many sacraments, including baptism, confirmation, holy orders, and extreme unction.

Anomoeans The Anomoeans were the strict Arians who rejected both the term ὁμοιούσιος (*homoiousios*) proposed by the Semi-Arians and the term ὁμοῖος (*homoeos*) of the Homoeans who followed Bishop Acacius of Caesarea.

A new variety of the heresy arose in the East ..., advocated by Aetius and Eunomius; who, by professing boldly the pure Arian tenet, alarmed Constantius, and threw him back upon Basil, and the other Semi-Arians. This new doctrine, called Anomoean, because it maintained that the *usia* or *substance* of the Son was unlike (ἀνόμοιος) the Divine *usia*, was actually adopted by one portion of the Eusebians,

Valens and his rude Occidentals; whose language and temper, not admitting the refinements of Grecian genius, led them to rush from orthodoxy into the most hard and undisguised impiety.[49]

Referring to the time of the Declaration of Sirmium (357), Duchesne wrote:

At the period of which we are now speaking, attention was directed towards the idea of resemblance. In the time of Arius, they preferred rather to say that the Word was not eternal, that He was a creature; now stress was laid on the point that He did not resemble the Father; He was unlike Him (ἀνόμοιος) from whence was derived the name of Anomoeans applied to the new Arians.[50]

Antependium The Latin word *pendo, pendere, pependi, pensus* means *to hang,* and the preposition *ante* means *before,* and from them is composed the noun *antependium* with the meaning of an *altar frontal* (see the entry **Frontal**). As a neuter noun of the second declension, its plural is *antependia.* Those of the high altar of St. Peter's are the gift of Clement XIII.[51]

Anthem The Greek preposition ἀντί means *over against,* and the noun ὕμνος means *song.* The combination of the two produced the noun ἄνθυμνος, defined by Dr. Johnson in his dictionary as follows:

Anthem: G. ἄνθυμνος, a hymn sung in alternate parts and should therefore be written *anthymn.*

Anticamera Pontificia See the entry **Camera**. When the Italians compounded words with the Latin preposition *ante* (before), the prefix was frequently changed to *anti.* The *anticamera pontificia*—the pontifical antechamber—was originally an entrance or audience hall before the private rooms of the pope where he received his visitors. The expression then became the name of the class of functionaries—*camerieri* or chamberlains—who assisted him in the well ordering of these visits. The personnel of the anticamera were divided into two classes, those of the *anticamera segreta* and those of the *anticamera d'onore*; the former busied themselves with the reception of sovereigns and other most high authorities, whereas the latter arranged the visits of small groups of less exalted but still respectable visitors. Pope Paul abolished the title *chamberlain* in the *motu proprio*

49. John Henry Cardinal Newman, *The Arians of the Fourth Century,* new ed. (London: Longmans, Green, 1897), 336.

50. Louis Duchesne, *Early History of the Christian Church from Its Foundation to the End of the Fifth Century,* vol. 2 (London: John Murray, 1931), 228.

51. Hartwell de la Garde Grissell, *Sede Vacante, Being a Diary Written during the Conclave of 1903, with Additional Notes on the Accession and Coronation of Pius X* (Oxford: James Parker, 1903), 60.

Pontificalis Domus of March 28, 1968;[52] the two clerics who do the same job are now called *prelati dell'anticamera*—prelates of the antechamber.

Antichrist For the etymologies of the constituent parts of this word, see the entries **Antipope** and **Christ**. The word *antichrist* appears four times in the Bible, three in the First Epistle of John (2:18, 22; 4:3) and once in the Second Epistle of John (verse 7); its plural, *antichrists*, appears once in the First Epistle of John (2:18). *Antichrist* means *counter-Christ*.

Children, it is the last hour; and as you have heard that antichrist is coming, so now many antichrists have come; therefore we know that it is the last hour.[53]

Who is the liar but he who denies that Jesus is the Christ? This is the antichrist, he who denies the Father and the Son.[54]

… and every spirit which does not confess Jesus is not of God. This is the spirit of antichrist, of which you heard that it was coming, and now it is in the world already.[55]

For many deceivers have gone out into the world, men who will not acknowledge the coming of Jesus Christ in the flesh; such a one is the deceiver and the antichrist.[56]

The Catholic doctrine of the antichrist is stated by the Rhemes translators in their note to 1 John 2:18:

Vvhereby vve may learne, that al Heretikes, or rather Arch-heretikes be properly the precursors of that one and special Antichrist, vvhich is to come at the last end of the vvorld, & vvhich is called here immediatly before, ὁ Ἀντίχριστος, *that peculiar and singular Antichrist.*

Antiphon The Greek preposition ἀντί means *over against*, and the noun φωνή means *sound*. The combination of the two produced the noun ἀντιφωνή with the meaning a *sound in reply*, an *answer*. An antiphon was originally a prayer or song, often sung, in which the congregation or choir or chorus is divided into two parts, one part answering the other in alternation. It is nowadays a highfalutin name for hymn. Thus, what used to be called the *Introit* is currently denominated *Entrance Antiphon*.

---

52. *Pontificalis Domus* (motu proprio of Pope Paul VI, March 28, 1968), III 7 §5. The text is available at http://w2.vatican.va/content/paul-vi/la/motu_proprio/documents/hf_p-vi_motu-proprio_19680328_pontificalis-domus.html.

53. 1 John 2:18 (Revised Standard Version).

54. 1 John 2:22 (Revised Standard Version).

55. 1 John 4:3 (Revised Standard Version).

56. 2 John 7 (Revised Standard Version).

Antiphonal (Chant) The addition of the Latin adjectival suffix *-al* to *antiphon* produced the adjective *antiphonal*. John Henry Newman, in his *History of the Arians*, quotes the following passage from the *History* of Theodoret (2:24):

Whereas he (the Bishop Leontius) took part in the blasphemy of Arius, he made a point of concealing this disease, partly for fear of the multitude, partly for the menaces of Constantius; so those who followed the Apostolical dogmas gained from him neither patronage nor ordination, but those who held Arianism were allowed the fullest liberty of speech, and were placed in the ranks of the sacred ministry. But Flavian and Diodorus, who had embraced the ascetical life, and maintained the Apostolical dogmas, openly withstood Leontius's machinations against religious doctrine. They threatened that they would retire from the communion of his Church, and would go to the West, and reveal his intrigues. Though they were not as yet in the sacred ministry, but were in the ranks of the laity, night and day they used to excite all the people to zeal for religion. They were the first to divide the singers into two choirs, and to teach them to sing in alternate parts the strains of David.[57]

Antiphonale For the etymology and formation of this word, see the entries **Antiphon** and **Missal**. The *Antiphonale* (called the *Antiphonal* in English) is the music book containing the antiphons or chants in the Divine Office that are sung before and after the psalms.

Antipope The Greek preposition ἀντί means *against*, and in compositions it may mean *in opposition to*; for example, ἀντιστρατηγός is *our general's opponent*, the *enemy's general*. The Romans did not adopt the Greek preposition ἀντί when they coined words; nevertheless on the analogy of *antichrist*, the noun *antipapa, -ae, m.* came into ecclesiastical use in the thirteenth century with the meaning a *claimant to the papal throne who illegitimately opposes the rightful pope*. The Germans are more original than their Latin and English colleagues and call such a being a *Gegenpapst*. The first antipope was St. Hippolytus, who, in 218, challenged the authority of Pope Calixtus I and his successors, whom he accused of being heretics, too sympathetic with the Modalists. He and his opponent Pope Pontian reconciled after both had been condemned *ad metalla* in Sardinia. The last antipope was Felix V, head of the House of Savoy, the ancestor of the kings of Italy, who, in the year 1439, was set up by the Council of Basel in

---

57. John Henry Cardinal Newman, *The Arians of the Fourth Century*, new ed. (London: Longmans, Green, 1897), 455.

opposition to Eugenius IV. A strange coincidence is that whereas the first antipope became a saint, the last antipope was crowned by a cardinal who became a blessed, Louis Aleman.

Anti-Semitism Opposition to the Children of Israel for the very reason that they are children of Israel is denominated *anti-Semitism*; in the modern world it means hatred, or at least malevolent suspicion, of Jews because they are Jews. It is an absurd word, since there is no such thing as Semitism. Semites are those people who descend from the biblical שם, Shem, eldest son of Noah (Genesis 6:10); for this reason the correct spelling ought to be *Shemite*, not *Semite*. The adjective *Semitic* has a well-defined scientific meaning in the phrase *the Semitic languages*, which include Akkadian, Amharic, Arabic, Aramaic, Assyrian, Babylonian, Ethiopic, Hebrew, Syriac, Ugaritic, and all languages related to them by means of a grammar based on the triliteral root. The restriction of the word *Semite* to the meaning *Jew* is common but unetymological.

The story of the relationship between the Jews and the Catholic Church is a hornets' nest. The depiction of the Jews in the gospels, especially in the passion narratives, is not such as would uniformly promote positive views about them in the minds of uncritical people; for reasons like this, the Church has always reserved to herself the authority to interpret scripture. The passages most often cited as presenting difficulties are the following:

Matthew 27:25: καὶ ἀποκριθεὶς πᾶς ὁ λαὸς εἶπεν Τὸ αἷμα αὐτοῦ ἐφ᾽ ἡμᾶς καὶ ἐπὶ τὰ τέκνα ἡμῶν.

Et respondens universus populus dixit, "Sanguis eius super nos et super filios nostros."

John 8:44: ὑμεῖς ἐκ τοῦ πατρὸς τοῦ διαβόλου ἐστὲ καὶ τὰς ἐπιθυμίας τοῦ πατρὸς ὑμῶν θέλετε ποιεῖν.

Vos ex patre Diabolo estis, et desideria patris vestri vultis facere.

Acts 7:51–52: Σκληροτράχηλοι καὶ ἀπερίτμητοι καρδίαις καὶ τοῖς ὠσίν, ὑμεῖς ἀεὶ τῷ πνεύματι τῷ ἁγίῳ ἀντιπίπτετε, ὡς οἱ πατέρες ὑμῶν καὶ ὑμεῖς. τίνα τῶν προφητῶν οὐκ ἐδίωξαν οἱ πατέρες ὑμῶν; καὶ ἀπέκτειναν τοὺς προκαταγγείλαντας περὶ τῆς ἐλεύσεως τοῦ δικαίου οὗ νῦν ὑμεῖς προδόται καὶ φονεῖς ἐγένεσθε.

Duri cervice et incircumcisi cordibus et auribus, vos semper Spiritui Sancto resistitis, sicut patres vestri et vos. Quem prophetarum non sunt persecuti patres vestri? Et occiderunt eos, qui pronuntiabant de adventu Iusti, cuius vos nunc proditores et homicidae fuistis.

1 Thessalonians 2:14–16: τῶν Ἰουδαίων, τῶν καὶ τὸν κύριον ἀποκτεινάντων Ἰησοῦν καὶ τοὺς προφήτας καὶ ἡμᾶς ἐκδιωξάντων, καὶ θεῷ μὴ ἀρεσκόντων, καὶ πᾶσιν ἀνθρώποις ἐναντίων, κωλυόντων ἡμᾶς τοῖς ἔθνεσιν λαλῆσαι ἵνα σωθῶσιν, εἰς τὸ ἀναπληρῶσαι αὐτῶν τὰς ἁμαρτίας πάντοτε. ἔφθασεν δὲ ἐπ᾽ αὐτοὺς ἡ ὀργὴ εἰς τέλος.

a Judaeis, quia Dominum occiderunt Iesum, et prophetas et nos persecuti sunt, et Deo non placent et omnibus hominibus adversantur, prohibentes nos gentibus loqui, ut salvae fiant, ut impleant peccata sua semper. Pervenit autem ira Dei super illos usque in finem.

I have followed here the custom of former times of leaving such strong tobacco in Latin. Since the Church would go bankrupt if, in the manner of Thomas Jefferson, it removed such passages from the gospels, it is its custom, in predicaments such as this, to put other documents on the table, in this case, §4 of the Declaration *Nostra Aetate* of the Second Vatican Council (October 28, 1965), which includes the following essential paragraphs:

Etsi auctoritates Iudaeorum cum suis asseclis mortem Christi urserunt, tamen ea quae in passione Eius perpetrata sunt nec omnibus indistincte Iudaeis tunc viventibus, nec Iudaeis hodiernis imputari possunt. Licet autem Ecclesia sit novus populus Dei, Iudaei tamen neque ut a Deo reprobati neque ut maledicti exhibeantur, quasi hoc ex Sacris Litteris sequatur. Ideo curent omnes ne in catechesi et in verbi Dei praedicatione habenda quidquam doceant, quod cum veritate evangelica et spiritu Christi non congruat.

Praeterea, Ecclesia, quae omnes persecutiones in quosvis homines reprobat, memor communis cum Iudaeis patrimonii, nec rationibus politicis sed religiosa caritate evangelica impulsa, odia, persecutiones, antisemitismi manifestationes, quovis tempore et a quibusvis in Iudaeos habita, deplorat.

Although the Jewish authorities and their followers pushed for the death sentence, nevertheless, the horrible things done at the time of the passion of Christ cannot be blamed on all the Jews of that time as a group, nor on the Jews alive today. For although the Church is the new people of God, nonetheless the Jews should be presented neither as condemned by God nor as under the sentence of damnation. Therefore, let everyone take care that in religious instruction and in preaching God's word, he not say anything that is not in harmony with Gospel truth and with the spirit of Christ.

Furthermore, the Church, which condemns all persecutions of any human beings whomsoever, mindful of the inheritance which it shares with the Jews, motivated not by politics but rather by the religious love of the Gospels, deplores hatred, persecution, and antisemitism directed against Jews throughout all history and by whatsoever personality.

Since the majority of Jews rejected Jesus, relations between them and the early Christians were most difficult. The once commonly accepted strict interpretation of the doctrine *Extra ecclesiam nulla salus* condemned them to hell, together with all other "unbelievers." By the time of the first Crusade, these feelings of antipathy erupted into pogroms. The events of the Hitler period have resulted in steps designed to prevent any recurrence of those crimes, such as the above-mentioned decree. Strange was the abolition of the Feast of the Circumcision, which would have afforded an obvious opportunity to celebrate the fraternity of Jews and Christians.

Anulus Piscatoris This Latin phrase means the *Fisherman's Ring*; it is a reference to the signet ring of the pope, the successor of Peter, who was a fisherman. It is of gold with the image of St Peter upon the bezel and is presented to the pope upon his election. (Pope Francis, however, decided to have a Fisherman's Ring of silver.) Above the image is then engraved his name, e.g., *Pius XI. Pont. Max.* To prevent forgery, the Fisherman's Ring is ceremoniously destroyed after the death of the pope. The ceremony of the smashing of the *anulus piscatoris* is described by Noonan:[58]

The cardinals enter the pope's apartments, each vested in scarlet choir dress. Accompanying them are the Papal Household officials and the commandant of the Swiss Guard as witnesses. The ring is inspected, first by the other cardinals present, to verify if it is truly the Fisherman's Ring. This completed, a silver knife is taken in hand by the Camerlengo, who scratches the seal twice, once horizontally and once vertically, in the sign of a cross, although not with theological intent. These scratches serve as a simple means of defacing or destroying the symbolic power of the ring, [which] is then inspected by those present. The ring is then placed on a lead block, which stands before the Camerlengo on a marble table. A silver mallet is produced and taken in hand by the Camerlengo, who, swiftly and with as much force as he can muster, administers a blow to the ring. This blow sometimes produces a split, other times a deep crack—either way, the ring is finally destroyed. The Camerlengo must continue to issue blows to the ring if it is not immediately destroyed. All present must visually verify its destruction and affirm this witness to the protonotary present, whose function it is to document these historic moments of the *Sede Vacante*. The ring, along with its broken pieces, is placed in a velvet sack, tied tightly, and carried away by the Camerlengo, who will place it inside the second casket, the lead tomb, along with all the important documents of a papacy now ended.

58. James-Charles Noonan Jr., *The Church Visible* (New York: Viking, 1996), 32–33.

The Latin word *anus* means the *fundament* and then anything of the same shape. The diminutive *anulus* denoted a finger ring or signet ring. According to Lewis and Short, the spelling *annulus* is incorrect; it is not clear that *annus* and *anulus* are related. Among the ancient Romans, only citizens had the right to wear a ring, which was of iron, unless the fellow happened to belong to the equestrian order, in which case he might wear a gold ring. Formerly prelates, like other princes, wore multiple rings, as one can see, for example, in Raphael's portrait of Leo X. Clergy who have earned a doctoral degree may wear a doctoral ring, but they should not do so while in choir dress or while celebrating a liturgical function.

Aphthartodocetic The Greek verb φθείρω means *to corrupt*, and from it was formed the adjective φθαρτός with the meaning *corruptible*. The addition of *alpha privativum* produced the negation of this adjective, ἄφθαρτος, with the meaning *incorruptible*. See also the entry **Docetic**. From the union of ἄφθαρτος and δοκητικός was produced the adjective ἀφθαρδοκητικός with the meaning *appearing to be incorruptible*. The aphthardocetic heresy was a doctrine taught by the emperor Justinian at the end of his life:

… that the body of Christ was incorruptible, and that his manhood was never subject to any wants or infirmities, the inheritance of our mortal flesh.[59]

This teaching was rejected by the clergy, and Justinian died before he could do anything to force it on the faithful. Justinian learned this heresy from Julian of Halicarnassus:

Julian, identifying the substance and qualities of the divinity and humanity of Christ, deduced that his body was indestructible from the moment at which it was assumed by the Logos.[60]

Apocalypse The Greek verb καλύπτω means *to cover or hide*; The addition of the preposition ἀπό adds the sense of *ceasing from* and produces the compound verb ἀποκαλύπτω meaning *to uncover, reveal*. The related noun ἀποκάλυψις means *uncovering, a revealing*. The Latin translation is *revelatio*, a pulling back of the veil that covers something, from the prefix *re-*, back, and *velo, velare*, to cover with a veil. *Apocalypse of John* is the title of the last book of the New Testament, and, because of the contents of that

---

59. Edward Gibbon, *The History of the Decline and Fall of the Roman Empire*, ed. Betty Radice (London: The Folio Society, 1995), 6:58.

60. J. B. Bury, *History of the Later Roman Empire* (New York: Dover, 1958), 2:375.

volume, the word came to mean *the final disaster at the end of the world.*
Ascribed to St. John the Evangelist, its Greek prose style is noticeably different from that of the fourth gospel. Commenting on the biblical criticism of Dionysius, Patriarch of Alexandria (247–264), Duchesne wrote:

According to Dionysius, the Apocalypse could not be by the same author as the Fourth Gospel, but is the work of another John, not the great apostle.[61]

Apocrisiary The Greek verb κρίνω means *to separate, divide, choose, judge,* and the addition of the preposition ἀπό (*from*) produces the compound verb ἀποκρίνω with the meaning *to distinguish,* and in the middle voice, *to reply.* From this verb came the noun ἀπόκρισις meaning a *separating,* an *answer.* From this noun proceeded the Greek noun ἀποκρισιάριος meaning a *secretary,* which was transliterated into Latin as *apocrisiarius,* and understood as *an official authorized to give and receive answers,* an *ambassador.* From the Latin noun comes our English word *apocrisiary.* The *apocrisiary* was for many centuries the permanent papal representative at the imperial Byzantine court; he was a sort of papal nuncio in Constantinople. The position fell into desuetude in the eighth century after the extinction of the Byzantine power in Italy.

Apocrypha The Greek verb ἀποκρύπτω means *to hide* (κρύπτω) *away from* (ἀπό), and from it is derived the adjective ἀπόκρυφος meaning *hidden.*

The Greek ἀπόκρυφος is a translation of a late Hebrew or Aramaic word meaning "hidden," "withdrawn from publicity." It had at first a much milder signification than that which we attach to it. In a literal sense it was used of the rolls which were put away because they were worn out or because of faults in the writing. In a more metaphorical sense it meant that a book was not suitable for public reading. It implied in itself nothing more than this, no suspicion as to authorship, no doubt as to doctrine.[62]

The Catholic Old Testament contains some books (Tobias, Judith, Wisdom, Ecclesiasticus, Baruch, Maccabees 1 and 2) whose Hebrew originals, if there were any, have not survived; such books were removed from the Bible by the reformers, who called them *apocryphal.* The Council of Trent, in its fourth session (April 8, 1546), listed which books were to be held as

---

61. Louis Duchesne, *Early History of the Christian Church from Its Foundation to the End of the Third Century* (London: John Murray, 1914), 350.

62. William Sanday, *Inspiration, Eight Lectures on the Early History and Origin of the Doctrine of Biblical Inspiration, Being the Bampton Lectures for 1893* (London: Longmans, Green, 1896), 205.

belonging to the Bible. One of the major biblical discoveries of modern times was that of three manuscripts of the Hebrew original of the Book of Jesus ben Sirach (Ecclesiasticus) among the Dead Sea Scrolls; these were published and edited by G. R. Driver, the son of the S. R. Driver of the Hebrew lexicon. Previously considerable fragments of them had been found by Solomon Schechter in the Cairo Geniza. The English adjective *apocryphal* is a hybrid word, a syllable of the Latin adjectival suffix *-alis* having been added on to a Greek stem.

Apollinarianism The Latin name *Apollinaris* means *devoted to Apollo*, and Apollinarianism is the name of a heresy of which an Apollinaris was the originator. His battle cry was "One incarnate nature of Christ." Apollinaris (c. 310–c. 390) deduced from the Book of the Apocalypse that the Temple would be rebuilt and the Law restored. This opinion did not find favor with most believers, and, as a result, the entry of the Book of the Apocalypse into the biblical canon was for some time postponed.

At the time when Apollinaris appeared upon the scene, the Church had settled upon the terms in which thenceforth it was to explain the sense in which it understands the relationship between the unity of God and the Divinity of Jesus Christ. The Divine being manifested in Jesus is absolutely identical with the One and Only God recognized by Christianity; He is distinguished, however, by a differentia (*spécialité*), obviously mysterious and incomprehensible, which, in the language of the New Testament, by which that of the Church guides itself, is expressed by the relationship of Son to Father. Hence arises the distinction of "Persons," to use the terminology of the West—of "Hypostases," in that of the East. To these two Hypostases or Persons of the Father and the Son is added, by an analogous distinction, the third Hypostasis of the Holy Spirit. In this way is constituted the "Trinity" of theology; thus the Christian tradition is formulated, as clearly as such a mystery allows, in the philosophical language of the time.[63]

The problem arose that certain skeptical people rejected this formulation. For Apollinaris, Jesus Christ was not a true man in the sense that he did not have a human mind (νοῦς) but rather a Divine mind.

Apart from this collocation, [Apollinaris] saw no means of preserving the Unity of Christ. Those who represented Him to themselves as formed of the Divinity and of a complete humanity, seemed to him madmen, capable of believing in centaurs, the hippogriff, and other fabulous creatures.[64]

63. Louis Duchesne, *Early History of the Christian Church from Its Foundation to the End of the Fifth Century*, vol. 2 (London: John Murray, 1931), 470.
    64. Ibid., 472.

We have seen above that at Antioch ever since the time of the Emperor Valens there had been considerable discussion as to the relations of the Divine element in Christ with his human element (*forma Dei, forma servi*). Apollinaris and his party endeavored to establish between these two elements a unity of nature, in which one of the two—the human element—was partly sacrificed. According to this theory, the Person of the Divine Word had united to itself, not an individual man, nor even all the components of humanity, but simply an animate body which it directed by fulfilling in it the functions of the Intellect. There were not two Persons but one only—that of the Word: there were not two Natures but one only, the Divine Nature, conceived, however, as possessing human aptitudes corresponding to the functions of the body and of the living soul: "One is the Incarnate Nature of the Divine Word."[65]

Gibbon describes the system of Apollinaris as follows:

He taught that the Godhead was united or mingled with the body of a man; and that the *Logos*, the eternal wisdom, supplied in the flesh the place and office of a human soul. Yet, as the profound doctor had been terrified by his own rashness, Apollinaris was heard to mutter some faint accents of excuse and explanation. He acquiesced in the old distinction of the Greek philosophers between the rational and sensitive soul of man; that he might reserve the *Logos* for intellectual functions, and employ the subordinate human principle in the meaner actions of animal life. With the moderate Docetes he revered Mary as the spiritual, rather than as the carnal, mother of Christ, whose body either came from heaven, impassible and incorruptible, or was absorbed, and as it were transformed, into the essence of the Deity.[66]

Apology The Greek deponent verb ἀπολογέομαι means *to make a speech in court in defense of oneself*; it is compounded of the preposition ἀπό, which gives it the sense of *in reply*, and λέγω, *to speak*. From them was formed the noun ἀπολογία, a *speech in self-defense*. The most famous apology is that of Socrates; next comes the *Apologia pro Vita Sua* of John Henry Newman. The earliest Christian apologies, like the famous one of Justin Martyr, were addressed to the Roman emperors, who, if they could be convinced, had the ability to do the most good. The apologists believed in the truth of the adage *Aut Caesar aut nihil*.

65. Louis Duchesne, *Early History of the Christian Church from Its Foundation to the End of the Fifth Century*, vol. 3 (London: John Murray, 1924), 221–22. Duchesne's note here reads: "Μία φύσις τοῦ θεοῦ σεσαρκωμένη, *Una natura Dei Verbi incarnata*. This celebrated formula, common to the Apollinarians and the Monophysites, was adopted also by the Church, but not without difficulty and with explanations which modified its original meaning."

66. Edward Gibbon, *The History of the Decline and Fall of the Roman Empire*, ed. Betty Radice (London: The Folio Society, 1995), 6:29.

Apostasy The Greek preposition ἀπό means *away from*, and the verb ἵστημι means *to stand*. Their combination resulted in the compound verb ἀφίστημι, *to revolt*, whence arose the noun ἀπόστασις, *defection*. In the Catholic system, the word means *to desert the Church*. Thus, Julian "the Apostate" had been brought up a Christian in the family of his uncle the emperor Constantine, but he abandoned Christianity and attempted to restore the worship of the traditional gods.

Apostate This word is the transliteration of the Greek noun ἀποστάτης, *someone who stands apart*, from the verb ἀφίστημι, *to stand apart*. An *apostate* is someone who has left the Catholic Church. It is a pejorative, condemnatory term. Formerly one would have nothing to do with apostates.

Again, it is plain that the tenderness of dealing, which it is our duty to adopt towards a heathen unbeliever, is not to be used towards an apostate. No *economy* can be employed towards those who have been once enlightened, and have fallen away. I wish to speak explicitly on this subject, because there is a great deal of that spurious charity among us which would cultivate the friendship of those who, in a Christian country, speak against the Church and its creeds. Origen and others were not unwilling to be on a footing of intercourse with the heathen philosophers of their day, in order, if it were possible, to lead them into the truth; but deliberate heretics and apostates, those who had known the truth, and rejected it, were objects of their abhorrence, and were avoided from the truest charity towards them. For what can be said to those who already know all we have to say? And how can we show our fear for their souls, nay, and for our own steadfastness, except by a strong action? Thus Origen, when a youth, could not be induced to attend the prayers of a heretic of Antioch whom his patroness had adopted, from a loathing, as he says, of heresy. And St. Austin himself tells us, that while he was a Manichee, his own mother would not eat at the same table with him in her house, from her strong aversion to the blasphemies which were the characteristic of his sect. And Scripture fully sanctions this mode of acting, by the severity with which such unhappy men are spoken of, on the different occasions when mention is made of them.[67]

Apostle The Greek noun ἀπόστολος, *messenger, someone sent*, is derived from the verb ἀποστέλλω, *to send* (στέλλω) *away* (ἀπό) *on a mission*. It is the technical term applied to the twelve students of Jesus sent by him to preach the good news to the whole world. St. Paul applied the term to himself, so that the phrase "the Holy Apostles Peter and Paul" appears in

---

67. John Henry Cardinal Newman, *The Arians of the Fourth Century*, new ed. (London: Longmans, Green, 1897), 85–86. He cites Romans 16:17; 2 Thessalonians 3:14; and 2 John 10, 11, among others.

the Canon of the Mass. Peter and Paul are the two patron saints of the Church of Rome, where they died and were buried. The Apostles' Creed is the earliest form of the creed. Duchesne says that it may date from the first half of the second century.[68]

Credo in Deum Patrem omnipotentem; et in Jesum Christum filium eius unicum, Dominum nostrum, qui natus est de Spiritu Sancto et Maria Virgine, sub Pontio Pilato crucifixus et sepultus, tertia die resurrexit a mortuis, ascendit in coelum, sedet ad dexteram Patris, inde venturus judicare vivos et mortuos. Et in Spiritum Sanctum, Sanctam Ecclesiam, remissionem peccatorum, carnis resurrectionem.[69]

I believe in God, the Father Almighty, and in Jesus Christ His only Son, Our Lord, who was born of the Holy Ghost and the Virgin Mary, was crucified under Pontius Pilate and was buried. On the third day he arose from the dead, ascended into heaven, and sitteth at the right hand of the Father, from whence he is about to come to judge the living and the dead. And I believe in the Holy Ghost, the Holy Church, the forgiveness of sins, and the resurrection of the flesh.

Those who have memorized a later version of this Creed will recognize that the primitive form lacks many familiar phrases added later on. For example, the phrase *the Creator of heaven and earth* was added to follow *Father Almighty* after the Gnostics had denied that the Almighty Father would so humble himself so as to create matter and this imperfect world. The Latin form of the Apostles' Creed currently in use in the Catholic Church is the following:

Credo in Deum, Patrem omnipotentem, creatorem caeli et terrae. Et in Iesum Christum, Filium eius unicum, Dominum nostrum: qui conceptus est de Spiritu Sancto, natus ex Maria Virgine, passus sub Pontio Pilato, crucifixus, mortuus et sepultus; descendit ad inferos; tertia die resurrexit a mortuis; ascendit ad caelos, sedet ad dexteram Dei Patris omnipotentis; inde venturus est iudicare vivos et mortuos. Credo in Spiritum Sanctum, sanctam Ecclesiam catholicam, Sanctorum communionem, remissionem peccatorum, carnis resurrectionem, vitam aeternam. Amen.[70]

I believe in God, the Father almighty, the Creator of heaven and earth. And in Jesus Christ his only Son, Our Lord, who was conceived by the Holy Ghost, born of the Virgin Mary, suffered under Pontius Pilate, was crucified, died, and was

---

68. Louis Duchesne, *Early History of the Christian Church from Its Foundation to the End of the Third Century* (London: John Murray, 1914), 368.

69. Denzinger, *Enchiridion Symbolorum et Definitionum*, 7th ed. (Würzburg, Germany: V. J. Stahel, 1895), I 1.

70. *Catechismus catholicus*, cura et studio Petri Cardinalis Gasparri concinnatus, 15th ed. (Vatican City: Typis Polyglottis Vaticanis, 1933), 21–22.

buried. He descended into hell, on the third day he arose again from the dead, he ascended into heaven and sits at the right hand of God the Father almighty. From thence he will come to judge the living and the dead. I believe in the Holy Ghost, the holy Catholic Church, the communion of Saints, the forgiveness of sins, the resurrection of the body, and life everlasting. Amen.

The names of the twelve apostles are given in Matthew 10:2–4, Mark 3:14–19, Luke 6:13–16, and (with the omission of Judas, who had committed suicide) Acts 1:13. The first of the apostles was Σίμων Πέτρος—Simon Peter. His Aramaic name was שִׁמְעוֹן בַּר־יוֹנָה—Σίμων Βαριωνᾶ—Simon Bar Jonah, as we learn from Matthew 16:17. He had the nickname כֵּיפָא—Κηφᾶς—Cephas, which means "the Rock" in Aramaic. *Rock* in Greek is πέτρα, and this noun was made masculine, Πέτρος, to render it appropriate for a man's name. The meaning of the name שִׁמְעוֹן is uncertain, though the verb שָׁמַע means *to hear*. The etymology of the name *Jonah* is similarly uncertain, since the meaning of the root יוֹן is not clear. The common feminine noun יוֹנָה, however, means *dove*.

The brother of Simon Peter was Ἀνδρέας—Andrew, a Greek name; we do not know his Aramaic given name. When Franz Delitzsch translated the New Testament into Hebrew for the conversion of the Jews, he merely transliterated the name by אַנְדְּרִי.[71] Ἀνδρέας is related to the Greek noun ἀνήρ, ἀνδρός, which means *man*, from which is derived the adjective ἀνδρεῖος with the meaning *manly*. Egger says that Ἀνδρέας is a term of endearment or pet name for Ἀνδρογένης (Androgenes), Ἀνδρόμαχος (Andromachos), or Ἀνδρόκλης (Androcles), just as Ἀντίπας (Antipas) is an endearing abbreviation for Ἀντίπατρος—Antipatros, in English, Antipater.[72]

The name of the third apostle is given as Ἰάκωβος, the Greek transliteration of the Hebrew יַעֲקֹב—Jacob. The name יַעֲקֹב means *he takes by the heel* or *he supplants* (see Genesis 25:26); it is derived from the noun עָקֵב, which means *heel*. The names *James*, *Giacomo*, and *Jaime* are corruptions of *Iacobus*, the Latin transliteration of Ἰάκωβος, the *b* having become *m* in the course of time.

The brother of James was Ἰωάννης, which was transliterated into Latin as *Ioannes* and thence came into English as *John*; this name is derived from the Hebrew יוֹחָנָן, which means *God has been gracious*. James and his

71. ספרי הבדית החדשה נעתקים מלשון יון ללשון עברית על ידי החכם פראפעסאר פראנץ דעליטש (Franz Delitzsch's *Hebrew New Testament* [London: Lowe & Brydone, 1960], 16).

72. Karl Egger, *Lexicon Nominum Locorum* (Rome: Libreria Editrice Vaticana, 1977), 17b.

brother John were the sons of Ζεβεδαῖος—Zebedee. The Hebrew root זבד means *to bestow upon, to endow with*, and זבד is a Hebrew proper name meaning a *gift* or *he hath given*. The Hebrew proper name זבדי means *my gift* or a *gift to me*. Dalman notes the existence of the Aramaic proper name זבדיה, *the Lord hath given*.[73] The Gospel according to Mark says that Jesus gave these brothers the nickname Βοανηργές—Boanerges, which the evangelist translates as *sons of thunder*—υἱοὶ βροντῆς, but it is not certain what *Boanerges* means. Dalman argues that the evangelist's translation is faulty and notes that Βοανηργές could be בני־רגז—*sons of anger*, which he says is possible, but that בני־רגיש—*sons of uproar*—is better.[74]

Only a Greek name is given for the fifth apostle—Φίλιππος, literally *horse-lover*, from the Greek ἵππος (horse) and φίλος (loving). Delitzsch transliterates the name by פילפוס.[75]

The sixth apostle is called by a mere patronymic, Βαρθολομαῖος—Bartholemew, the transliteration of the Aramaic name בר־תלמי, which means *the son of Tolmay*.[76] Tolmay—תלמי—is a Hebrew proper name of uncertain etymology.

The name of the seventh apostle was Θωμᾶς—Thomas, the transliteration of the Aramaic name תוֹמָא. The Hebrew noun תּוֹאָם means *twin*, and related to it is the Aramaic proper name תאוֹמא or, with suppression of the first aleph, תוֹמא.[77]

The name of the eighth apostle was Ματθαῖος—Matthew, the transliteration of the Aramaic name מתי. The name is related to the Hebrew root נתן, *to give*. This may be a shortened form of the fuller מתניה or מתתיה, *the gift of the Lord*.[78] However, it is disputed by the highest authorities whether י is a remnant of יה.[79]

The ninth apostle was another James, but this James was Ἰάκωβος ὁ τοῦ Ἀλφαίου—James the son of Alphaeus, in Aramaic, יעקב בר־חלפי. The Hebrew verb חלף means *to pass on, to pass through*. The same root خلف in

73. Gustaf Dalman, *Grammatik der Jüdisch-Palästinischen Aramäisch, nach den Idiomen des Palästinischen Talmud, des Onkelostargum und Prophetentargum und der Jerusalemischen Targume*, zweite Auflage (Leipzig: J. C. Hinrichs'sche Buchhandlung, 1905), 178–79, 178n7.

74. Ibid., 144n2.

75. ספרי הבדית החדשה נעתקים מלשון יון ללשון עברית על ידי החכם פראפעסאר פראנץ דעליטש (Franz Delitzsch's *Hebrew New Testament* [London: Lowe & Brydone, 1960], 16).

76. Dalman, *Grammatik der Jüdisch-Palästinischen Aramäisch*, 176n2.

77. Ibid., 145n6.

78. Ibid., 178.

79. G. Buchanan Gray, *Studies in Hebrew Proper Names* (London: Adam & Charles Black, 1896), 149–52.

– A –

Arabic means *to come after in succession*, whence proceeds the noun خَليفة, meaning a *vicar*, a *deputy*, a *caliph*. Dalman mentions the Aramaic proper name חלפיה—*The Lord hath passed over*.[80]

The name of the tenth apostle was Θαδδαῖος—Thaddeus. According to Dalman, this is the Greek Θευδᾶς, a shortening of Θεόδοτος, Θεόδοσιος, or Θεόδωρος.[81] Matthew does not give his Aramaic name. Plummer says that this Thaddeus is the Ἰούδας Ἰακώβου—יהודה בר־יעקב—Jude, Son of James—in the list of Luke 6:16; such an identification "makes all run smoothly."[82] *Jude* or *Judas* is of course the same name as *Judah*, the son of Jacob. The learned are not agreed on the etymology of יהודה. Thaddeus is called Λεββαῖος—Lebbaeus in the Codex Bezae; this name has nothing to do with *Levi*, which would be Λευεί—לוי.[83] *Lebbaeus* is explained by Allen as follows:

> It is best to suppose that in both Gospels Θαδδαῖος is original, and that Λεββαῖος was substituted in Western texts for reasons that can only be conjectured. It is possible that someone who supposed Thaddeus to be connected with the Aramaic word for "breast" substituted Lebbaeus, which he had formed from the Hebrew word for "heart," as a more fitting name for an Apostle. The Thaddeus of Mk. and Mt. may be a corruption of Judas, which Lk. has rightly replaced. Cf. *Encycl. Bib.* "Thaddeus."[84]

The eleventh apostle was Σίμων ὁ Καναναῖος—Simon the Cananaean. The Hebrew root קנא conveys the idea of *being livid*. The derived Hebrew verb קנא (in the *pi'el* conjugation) means *to be jealous, to be zealous*. The noun קנאה derived from this root means *ardor, zeal, jealousy*. The Aramaic adjective קנאן, like the Hebrew קנאי, means *zealous*.[85] Σίμων ὁ Καναναῖος is therefore likely to be the Aramaic שמעון קנאנא, קנאנא being the emphatic state of the adjective קנאן. If, though, the meaning intended was that Simon was a *Zealot* in the technical sense of one of the party of Jewish revolutionaries (and this conjecture is supported by Luke 6:15, where Simon is called ὁ ζηλωτής, then Dalman says that since the Zealots were called

80. Dalman, *Grammatik der Jüdisch-Palästinischen Aramäisch*, 179.

81. Ibid., 179n9.

82. Alfred Plummer, *A Critical and Exegetical Commentary on the Gospel according to St. Luke*, 10th ed., the International Critical Commentary (New York: Charles Scribner's Sons, 1914), 174.

83. Dalman, *Grammatik der Jüdisch-Palästinischen Aramäisch*, 178n3.

84. Willoughby C. Allen, *A Critical and Exegetical Commentary on the Gospel according to S. Matthew*, 3rd ed., the International Critical Commentary (Edinburgh, T&T Clark, 1977), 100.

85. Dalman, *Grammatik der Jüdisch-Palästinischen Aramäisch*, 174n2.

in Hebrew קַנָּאִים (singular קַנַּאי), our text should read Καvvαῖος instead of Καvαvαῖος. Allen writes:

Dalman (*Gram.* p. 174) thinks that the Greek form of the last word should be Καvvαῖος, and this has been changed into Καvαvαῖος by assimilation to the geographical term *Canaanite*.[86]

Two proposals to be rejected are that the name should be *Simon the Canaanite* or *Simon from Cana*. The former is impossible because the Greek transliteration for *Canaan* begins with *chi* and not *kappa*, and the latter would require the Greek to have ὁ Καvαῖος.

The twelfth apostle was Ἰούδας ὁ Ἰσκαριώτης—Judas Iscariot. Delitzsch, Dalman, and Cheyne all agree that in Hebrew this fellow was called יְהוּדָה אִישׁ־קְרִיּוֹת—*Judah, the guy from Kerioth*, a place name.[87] No one accepts the suggestion that *Iscariot* is a corruption of the Latin *sicarius*—an assassin.

Apostolic This adjective is the transliteration of the Greek ἀποστολικός, *pertaining to an apostle*. It is a mark of the Church, as descending from the apostles. Since the Roman pontiff is the successor of the apostle Peter, the adjective *apostolic* is rightly used of everything that pertains to him. Thus, for example, his blessing is the apostolic benediction, and a place where he dwells, whether it be the Lateran, the Vatican, or the Quirinale, is an apostolic palace.

Apparition The Latin verb *pareo, parere* means *to appear*, and the associated compound verb *appareo, apparere, apparui, apparitus* means *to appear* (pareo) *to* (ad). From the fourth principal part of the latter verb comes the noun *apparitio*, whence proceeds our *apparition*. An apparition is an appearance; in the Catholic Church the word is used of the appearances of Jesus Christ or a saint to a favored believer.

Aramaic Brown, Driver, and Briggs define the the Hebrew noun ארם as follows:

The Aramaeans, a leading branch of the Shemitic stock inhabiting Mesopotamia and northern Syria, in many tribes and settlements.[88]

---

86. Plummer, *Commentary on the Gospel according to St. Luke*, 101.

87. Rev. T. K. Cheyne and J. Sutherland Black, eds., *Encyclopaedia Biblica, A Critical Dictionary of the Literary, Political, and Religious History, the Archaeology, Geography, and Natural History of the Bible* (London: Adam & Charles Black, 1901), s.v. "Kerioth."

88. Francis Brown, S. R. Driver, and Charles A. Briggs, *A Hebrew and English Lexicon of the Old Testament* (Oxford: Clarendon Press, 1968), 74a.

The English word *Aramaic* is simply the stem of the Greek ἀραμαϊκός and its Latin transliteration *aramaicus*, adjectives which mean *Aramaean*. The Aramaean language is called in Hebrew ארמית. This is the language spoken by Jesus Christ, the language of the people of Galilee and Judaea in the first century A.D. It survives to this day as a liturgical language among Jews and certain communities of Eastern Christians. It is spoken as the vernacular language by a few thousand Syrian Christians. It is the language in which portions of the Old Testament were written, namely, Daniel 2:4b–7:28, Ezra 4:8–6:18, 7:12–26, Jeremiah 10:11, and Genesis 31:47aβ.

Archbishop The Greek prefix ἀρχι-, whence our *arch*, is derived from the verb ἄρχω, which means *to rule*. An archbishop, consequently, is a *ruler of bishops*, a sort of super-bishop. The connecting final iota of the prefix is dropped in English. Weekley says that *archbishop* is "the oldest of the *arch*-words."[89]

Archdeacon For the etymology, see the previous entry and the entry **Deacon**. The archdeacon of a diocese was the deacon who supervised the other deacons.

Archimandrate The Greek verb ἄρχω means *to rule*, and the noun μάνδρα means an *enclosed space*, a *cow barn*, a *stable*; somehow this noun acquired the meaning *monastery*, and the compound noun ἀρχιμανδρίτης means the *ruler of a monastery*, an *abbot*. It is a term used in the Greek, but not in the Latin, Church.

Archivist The Greek verb ἄρχω means *to rule*, and the corresponding noun ἄρχων means *ruler*, in particular, one of the nine chief rulers of Athens. The residence of their chief was called the ἀρχεῖον, which was translated into Latin as *curia*. The aforementioned Greek noun was also transliterated into Latin as *archium*; the letter *v* was then inserted for ease of pronunciation, and eventually the Greek nominal suffix *-ista* was added to the stem to produce *archivista*, whence is derived our noun *archivist*. The position of archivist of the Holy Roman Church is united with that of cardinal librarian. The most famous of these were Angelo Mai (1782–1854), Giovanni Mercati (1866–1957), and Eugène Tisserant (1884–1972).

---

89. Ernest Weekley, *An Etymological Dictionary of the English Language*, 2 vols. (New York: Dover, 1967), s.v. "arch."

Arian The followers of the fourth century heresiarch Ἄρειος, Patriarch of Constantinople, were called Ἀρειανοί, which became in Latin *Ariani* and in English *Arians*. The name Ἄρειος means *devoted to* Ἄρης, *warlike*. According to Milman,

Arianism had arisen out of that pronounced sense of the malignancy of matter, which in its grosser influence had led to the Manichean Dualism. The pure, primal, parental Deity must stand entirely aloof from all connection with that in which evil was inherent, inveterate, inextinguishable. This was the absolute essence of Deity; this undisturbed, unattainted Spiritualism, which disdained, repelled, abhorred the contact, the approximation of the Corporeal, which once assimilating to, or condescending to assume any of the attributes of Matter, ceased to be the Godhead.[90]

That Jesus was man is explicitly stated by St. Peter in Acts 2:22:

Ἰησοῦν τὸν Ναζωραῖον, ἄνδρα ἀποδεδειγμένον ἀπὸ τοῦ θεοῦ εἰς ὑμᾶς δυνάμεσι καὶ τέρασι καὶ σημείοις, ...

Iesum Nazarenum, virum approbatum a Deo in vobis, virtutibus, et prodigiis, et signis, ...

Jesus of Nazareth, a man attested to you by God with mighty works and wonders and signs, ...[91]

That he was God is implied in the preface to the Gospel according to John:

καὶ θεὸς ἦν ὁ λόγος.... Καὶ ὁ λόγος σὰρξ ἐγένετο ...

et Deus erat verbum.... Et verbum caro factum est ...

and the Word was God.... And the Word became flesh ...

and in the acclamation of the apostle Thomas at John 20:28

Ὁ Κύριός μου καὶ ὁ Θεός μου.

Dominus meus, et Deus meus.

My Lord and my God!

Since most ancient peoples had a hierarchy of gods, some greater and some less, the question was raised, was Jesus the Christ God just as much as the Father was God? Arriving at an answer to the question was made

---

90. Henry Hart Milman, *History of Latin Christianity, Including That of the Popes, to the Pontificate of Nicholas V* (New York, Sheldon, 1860), 1:202–3.

91. Translations of Scripture used in this entry are taken from the Revised Standard Version of the Bible.

complicated by the statement of Jesus that "the Father is greater than I" (John 14:28):

ὁ πατὴρ μείζων μού ἐστιν.

Pater maior me est.

... for the Father is greater than I.

Since there is no passage in the New Testament that says outright, "Jesus Christ is God," there arose Christians who denied this doctrine, even though the Christ does not correct Thomas at John 20:28. For them,

the Father was the only true God; and the Son and the Holy Spirit were beings clearly inferior to Him.[92]

Such gainsayers had to present another theory as to who the Christ was. One of these people was Arius (d. 336), a priest of Alexandria, whose teaching is denominated *Arianism*. The origins of this heresy lay in Antioch. Of the priest Lucian, the head of a school in Antioch operated by the partisans of the deposed Bishop Paul of Samosata, Duchesne wrote:

The theological trend of this school is shown by the well-established fact that Lucian was the originator of the doctrine, which soon became so famous as Arianism. Around him were grouped, even as early as this time we now speak of, the future leaders of this heresy, amongst others Arius himself, Eusebius, the future Bishop of Nicomedia, Maris, and Theognis. It was, they found, necessary to abandon the theories of Paul [of Samosata], and to admit the personal pre-existence of Christ, or in other words, the Incarnation of the Word. But they granted as little as possible. The Word, according to the new doctrine, was a celestial being, anterior to all visible and invisible creatures; He had indeed created them. But He had not existed from all eternity; He was created by the Father, as an instrument for the subsequent creation. Before that He did not exist. He was called out of nothing.[93]

Paul of Samosata had taught "that Christ became God by gradual development and by adoption."[94] Duchesne has summarized Arianism as follows:

God is One, eternal, and unbegotten. Other beings are His creatures, the Logos first of all. Like the other creatures, the Logos was taken out of nothingness (ἐξ

---

92. Louis Duchesne, *Early History of the Christian Church from Its Foundation to the End of the Fifth Century*, vol. 2 (London: John Murray, 1931), 377.

93. Louis Duchesne, *Early History of the Christian Church from Its Foundation to the End of the Third Century* (London: John Murray, 1914), 362.

94. Ibid., 341.

οὐκ ὄντων) and not from the Divine Substance; there was a time when He was not (ἦν ὅτε οὐκ ἦν); He was created, not necessarily, but voluntarily. Himself a creature of God, He is the Creator of all other beings, and this relationship justifies the title of God, which is improperly given to Him. God adopted Him as Son in prevision of His merits, for He is free, susceptible of change (τρεπτός), and it is by His own will that He determined Himself on the side of good. From this sonship by adoption results no real participation in the Divinity, no true likeness to It. God can have no like. The Holy Spirit is the first of the creatures of the Logos; He is still less God than the Logos. The Logos was made flesh, in the sense that He fulfilled in Jesus Christ the functions of a soul.[95]

The best work on the Arians is by John Henry Newman, *The Arians of the Fourth Century*. This book was published in 1833, when he was still an Anglican. Newman wrote:[96]

The fundamental tenet of Arianism was, that the Son of God was a creature, not born of the Father, but, in the scientific language of the times, made "out of nothing."[97]

Sozomen expressly says, that Arius was the first to introduce into the Church the formulae of the "out of nothing," and the "once He was not," that is, the creation and the non-eternity of the Son of God.[98]

If the professions of the Arians are to be believed, they confessed our Lord to be God, God in all respects,[99] full and perfect, yet at the same time to be infinitely distant from the perfections of the One Eternal Cause. Here at once they are committed to a ditheism; but Athanasius drives them on to the extreme of polytheism. "If," he says, "the Son were an object of worship for His transcendent glory, then every subordinate being is bound to worship his superior." But so repulsive is the notion of a secondary God both to reason, and much more to Christianity, that the real tendency of Arianism lay towards the sole remaining alternative, the humanitarian doctrine.[100]

It has been already observed that they explain the word Only-begotten in the sense of only-created; and considered the oneness of the Father and the Son to

---

95. Louis Duchesne, *Early History of the Christian Church from Its Foundation to the End of the Fifth Century*, vol. 2 (London: John Murray, 1931), 100–101. [Note of Duchesne]: "In those days scarcely any difference was recognized between γενητός (having come to be) and γεννητός (begotten), any more than between their contraries ἀγένητος and ἀγέννητος."

96. John Henry Cardinal Newman, *The Arians of the Fourth Century*, new ed. (London: Longmans, Green, 1897), 202.

97. ἐξ οὐκ ὄντων; hence the Arians were called *Exucontii*.

98. Newman, *The Arians of the Fourth Century*, 201.

99. πλήρης Θεός

100. Newman, *The Arians of the Fourth Century*, 230.

consist in a unity of character and will, such as exists between God and His Saints, not in nature.[101]

The doctrine of the Arians showed the influence of the Platonic mythology. In the *Timaeus* of Plato, the god who creates the physical world is himself a creature, created by the supreme god who could not be conceived as humbling himself to such an extent as to get involved with matter. There was thus a widely accepted belief in a hierarchy of gods, the more a god condescended to deal with man and matter, the lower was his station in the hierarchy. Furthermore, the monotheism of the Jews, inherited by the Christians, made the doctrine that Jesus Christ was a divine person a difficulty. The Council of Nicaea, the first of those assemblies now recognized as ecumenical, condemned the Arian doctrine in the Nicene Creed of 325, defining the Son to be just as divine (ὁμοούσιος— *homoousios*) as the Father, but the Arian doctrine nevertheless maintained a large following. The imperial authorities, observing that the debates of the Christians were degenerating into controversies that threatened the public order, attempted to impose compromises and to proceed against "extremists" on both sides. Pope Liberius, under pressure from the emperor Constantius II, signed such a compromise formula that avoided the Nicene doctrine of the *homoousios*; at the emperor's behest he also condemned St. Athanasius. His behavior in this regard was commented upon at the First Vatican Council, where his case, along with those of Pope Vigilius and Pope Honorius I, was presented as reason for proceeding with caution in making any proclamation about papal infallibility. Ignaz von Döllinger, in conversation with Alfred Plummer about the views of Cardinal Newman with regard to the infallibility question, commented:

"It is very strange," he said, "that a man who has written a history of the Arians should believe in the Pope's infallibility. No one asked a Pope to give an infallible judgment on that great question."[102]

Another such compromise was that of the Council of Ariminum (Rimini) in 359, in which it was declared that non-biblical vocabulary such as the word *homoousios* in the Nicene Creed should be set aside. After the Council of Rimini, St. Jerome commented:

---

101. Ibid., 227.

102. Robrecht Boudens and Leo Kenis, eds., *Alfred Plummer: Conversations with Dr. Döllinger, 1870–1890* (Leuven: Leuven University Press, 1985), 66.

Ingemuit totus orbis et se esse Arianum miratus est.[103]

The whole world woke up surprised to find that it was Arian.

Cardinal Newman had to explain in later life some of the statements to be found in his *History of the Arians*, wherein he had written that the faithful, and not the bishops, had preserved the Catholic faith in the fourth century.

The episcopate, whose action was so prompt and concordant at Nicaea on the rise of Arianism, did not, as a class or order of men, play a good part in the troubles consequent upon the Council; and the laity did. The Catholic people, in the length and breadth of Christendom, were the obstinate champions of Catholic truth, and the bishops were not.[104]

On the one hand, then, I say, that there was a temporary suspense of the functions of the "Ecclesia docens." The body of Bishops failed in their confession of the faith. They spoke variously, one against another; there was nothing, after Nicaea, of firm, unvarying, consistent testimony, for nearly sixty years ... general councils, &c., said what they should not have said, or did what obscured and compromised revealed truth.[105]

The Arians of Spain at last united with the Catholic Church in 589 after the Third Council of Toledo.[106]

Finally, Newman observed that the pure Arians "were the first among Christians to employ force in the cause of religion."[107]

Ascension The Latin verb *scando, scandere, scandi, scansus* means *to climb*. The associated compound verb *ascendo, ascendere, ascendi, ascensus* means *to climb* (scando) *to* (ad), whence proceeds the noun *ascensio*, a rising, a going up, an ascent. In the Catholic Church, the word is used with reference to the ascension of Christ forty days after Easter. For the ascension of the Virgin Mary, the word *Assumptio* is used; in German, however, the same word, *Himmelfahrt*, is employed in both cases, the distinction being made in the prefix: *Christihimmelfahrt, Mariähimmelfahrt*. With regard to the ascension of another person, we read in Genesis 5:21–24:

---

103. Newman, *The Arians of the Fourth Century*, 450. (Newman cites *In Lucif.* 19.)
104. Newman, *The Arians of the Fourth Century*, 445.
105. Ibid., 466.
106. Henry Charles Lea, *History of Sacerdotal Celibacy in the Christian Church* (University Books, 1966), 93.
107. Newman, *The Arians of the Fourth Century*, 301.

וַיְחִי חֲנוֹךְ חָמֵשׁ וְשִׁשִּׁים שָׁנָה וַיּוֹלֶד אֶת־מְתוּשָׁלַח:

וַיִּתְהַלֵּךְ חֲנוֹךְ אֶת־הָאֱלֹהִים אַחֲרֵי הוֹלִידוֹ אֶת־מְתוּשֶׁלַח שְׁלֹשׁ
מֵאוֹת שָׁנָה וַיּוֹלֶד בָּנִים וּבָנוֹת:

וַיְהִי כָּל־יְמֵי חֲנוֹךְ חָמֵשׁ וְשִׁשִּׁים שָׁנָה וּשְׁלֹשׁ מֵאוֹת שָׁנָה:

וַיִּתְהַלֵּךְ חֲנוֹךְ אֶת־הָאֱלֹהִים וְאֵינֶנּוּ כִּי־לָקַח אֹתוֹ אֱלֹהִים:

And Enoch lived sixty and five years, and begat Methuselah: And Enoch walked
with God after he begat Methuselah three hundred years, and begat sons and
daughters: And all the days of Enoch were three hundred sixty and five years: And
Enoch walked with God: and he was not; for God took him. (King James Version)

From this verse it was concluded that Enoch ascended into heaven, as we
see from Hebrews 11:5–6:

Πίστει Ἐνὼχ μετετέθη τοῦ μὴ ἰδεῖν θάνατον, καὶ οὐχ ηὑρίσκετο διότι μετέθηκεν
αὐτὸν ὁ θεός· πρὸ γὰρ τῆς μεταθέσεως μεμαρτύρηται εὐαρεστηκέναι τῷ θεῷ,
χωρὶς δὲ πίστεως ἀδύνατον εὐαρεστῆσαι, πιστεῦσαι γὰρ δεῖ τὸν προσερχόμενον
τῷ θεῷ ὅτι ἔστιν καὶ τοῖς ἐκζητοῦσιν αὐτὸν μισθαποδότης γίνεται.

By faith Enoch was translated that he should not see death; and was not found,
because God had translated him: for before his translation he had his testimony,
that he pleased God. But without faith it is impossible to please him: for he that
cometh to God must believe that he is, and that he is a rewarder of them that
diligently seek him. (King James Version)

Ascetic The Greek verb ἀσκέω means to *work curiously, to fashion*, and
then *to exercise, to practise*. From it arose the noun ἄσκησις (*exercise,
training, trade, profession*) and adjective ἀσκητός (*curiously wrought,
acquired by practice*). An ἀσκητής was a *tradesman* or *artist*; the other
possibility in Greece was to be an ἰδιώτης or *fellow without professional
knowledge*, a *layman*, from which we get our word *idiot*. The meaning
of ἀσκητής was eventually restricted to *one who practiced rigorous self-
restraint*, whence it acquired the meaning *monk* or *hermit*. The life style of
an ascetic was called *asceticism*.

Asceticism This English word is formed on the Greek model by adding
the suffix *–ism* to the adjective ἀσκητικός, *industrious, belonging to an
ascetic*.

Ashes This word is descended from the Anglo-Saxon noun *asce*. It is in
Latin *cinis*.

Memento homo quia cinis es, et in cinerem reverteris.

Remember, man, that thou art ashes, and unto ashes shalt thou return.

The imposition of ashes is traditional at the beginning of Lent, on Ash Wednesday. On that day the pope receives ashes from the Cardinal Major Penitentiary at the Church of Santa Sabina on the Aventine, and he then imposes ashes on the members of his entourage.

Asperges This is the first word of Psalm 50, verse 8, in the Vulgata, which begins the ceremony of the sprinkling of the congregation with holy water before Mass; it is derived from the Latin verb *aspergo, aspergere* (*to sprinkle*) and means, "Thou shalt sprinkle." During the Easter Season, the sprinkling rite begins with the verse *Vidi Aquam.* (See that entry.) The beautiful ceremony, which preceded the main Mass on Sunday, is now rarely used.

Aspergillum The Greek verb σπείρω means *to sow, to scatter like seed*, and related to it is the Latin verb *spargo, spargere, sparsi, sparsus* meaning *to sprinkle*. The addition of the preposition *ad* (to) produces the compound verb *aspergo, aspergere, aspersi, aspersus* which means *to sprinkle upon*. The Latin noun *aspergillum*, a *little sprinkler*, is derived from this verb. The liturgical *aspergillum* is a fistful of small branches or a wand with a perforated ball at the end, which is dipped into a pail of holy water and then used to sprinkle people or things. The priest wields the aspergillum with his right hand; an acolyte, not the priest, must carry the pail.

Aspergillum is also the name of a genus consisting of hundreds of mold species; it was thus named by the biologist Pier Antonio Micheli (1679–1737), a priest, since the spores reminded him of the aspergillum used for sprinkling before mass. I owe this observation to a learned friend.

Assessor The Greek verb ἕζομαι means *to sit*, and related to it is the Latin verb *sedeo, sedere, sedi, sessus* with the same meaning. The addition of the preposition *ad* (near) produces the compound verb *adsideo, adsidere, adsedi, adsessus* meaning *to sit beside*. From the fourth principal part there arose the noun *assessor* with the meaning *an attendant who sits beside one*, an *assistant*. The assessor of the Holy Office was the third-in-command of that congregation; the pope was the prefect, and after him came the secretary. In the reorganization of the Congregation undertaken by Pope Paul VI, the pope relinquished the title of prefect, the secretary assumed the duties and title of the prefect, the assessor assumed the duties and title of the secretary, and the position of assessor was abolished.

Assistant The Greek verb ἵστημι (second aorist ἔστην) means *to stand*, and related to it is the Latin verb *sto, stare, steti, status* with the same meaning. From *sto* there developed by reduplication the verb *sisto, sistere, steti, status* also meaning *to stand*, and the addition of the prefix *ad* produced the compound verb *adsisto, adsistere, adstiti, adstatus* with the meaning *to stand nearby*. The participle *assistens* denotes a fellow who is present and stands by some higher ranking personality. Thus, in the Roman court the Prince Colonna and the Prince Orsini were the prince assistants at the papal throne, *i principi assistenti al soglio pontificio*. They were those members of the Roman nobility who had the privilege of standing to the left and right of the pope, actually to the left and right of the two chief cardinal deacons, during solemn papal functions. The positions were hereditary. The position to the right of the supreme pontiff was the more exalted, and as neither the Prince Colonna nor the Prince Orsini would yield precedence to the other, the two did not appear at the same function in order to avoid a scene, notwithstanding the decree of Sixtus V, who had determined that the precedence should alternate, that is, he took precedence who had for the longer time been head of his family. This problem ceased when Pius XII replaced the Prince Orsini with the Prince Torlonia. Since the Prince Torlonia acknowledged the precedence of his colleague Colonna, the two did occasionally appear together, as, for example, at the opening of the second session of the Second Vatican Council. The prince assistant had the privilege of giving the pope the *lavabo*. The position of prince assistant was abolished by Pope Paul VI. The last prince assistant at the papal throne was Prince Aspreno II Colonna (1916–1987), whose memorabilia are displayed in the apartment of his mother, Princess Isabelle, in the Palazzo Colonna, Rome. The Roman nobles no longer assist the pope in liturgical functions but continue to serve as escorts to the members of the delegations accompanying foreign heads of state on official visits to the Holy See.

Assumption The Latin verb *emo, emere, emi, emptus* means *to buy*. The addition of the preposition *sub* produces the compound verb *sumo, sumere, sumpsi, sumptus* meaning *to take up*. The further addition of a second preposition *ad* results in the compound verb *adsumo, adsumere, adsumpsi, adsumptus* meaning *to take up* (sumo) *to oneself* (ad), and from it is derived the noun *assumptio*, a taking up, in this case, to God in heaven. The proclamation by Pius XII in 1950 of the dogma of the Assumption was the only exercise of papal infalliblity in a matter of doctrine since the definition made at the First Ecumenical Council of the Vatican in 1870.

The Italian language has the female personal name *Assunta* for women named to honor the assumption of the Holy Virgin.

Asterisk The Greek noun ὁ ἀστήρ, τοῦ ἀστέρος means *the star*, and the associated diminutive noun ἀστερίσκος means a *small star*. It is the name of the symbol ✳ used by Origen to set off certain passages, added to his edition of the Septuagint, contained in the fifth column of his *Hexapla*, namely, passages that were Theodotion's Greek translations of words in the Hebrew Bible that had nothing corresponding to them in the Septuagint:

As employed by Origen in the fifth column of the Hexapla, ... the asterisk called attention to words or lines wanting in the LXX, but present in the Hebrew.[108]

The asterisk is also a liturgical item.

The Asterisk is a gold star of twelve rays, on each of which is inscribed the name of an apostle. It is placed over the Host to preserve it from accidents.[109]

The asterisk was used in papal Masses when the Host needed to be transported the long distance from the Altar of the Confession to the papal throne set up before the Altar of the Chair, so that the supreme pontiff might communicate.

Atheism The Greek noun θεός means *god*, and when *alpha privativum* is prefixed to it, there is produced the adjective ἄθεος with the meaning *godless, not believing in the gods*. *Atheism* is the denial of the existence of God. It is not a Greek word; the Greek word for *atheism* is ἡ ἀθεότης. The most famous argument for atheism was given by Bertrand Russell in the book *Why I Am Not a Christian*.[110]

The English suffix *–ism* is the transliteration of the stem of the Greek

---

108. Henry Barclay Swete, *An Introduction to the Old Testament in Greek* (Cambridge: Cambridge University Press, 1900), 70.

109. Hartwell de la Garde Grissell, *Sede Vacante, Being a Diary Written during the Conclave of 1903, with Additional Notes on the Accession and Coronation of Pius X* (Oxford: James Parker, 1903), 70 note a.

110. Bertrand Russell, *Why I Am Not a Christian, and Other Essays on Religion and Related Subjects*, ed. Paul Edwards (New York: Simon & Schuster, n.d.).

suffix -ισμός, which forms nouns of action from verbs ending in -ίζω or -ίζομαι. Thus from χάρις (favor) came χαρίζομαι (to show favor) and thence χάρισμα (a gift). The Western Europeans began already in the sixteenth century to multiply *isms* by adding the suffix indiscriminately to various stems, and it was thus that the noun *atheism* was produced.

Audience The Latin noun *audientia* means a *hearing*, and is derived from the verb *audio, audire, audivi, auditus*, meaning *to hear*. It is the name of a private meeting with a preeminent personage who has granted one a hearing. In modern times, it is used only with reference to a sovereign such as the Roman pontiff; it may retain its original meaning or mean any admission into the presence of that figure, for example, to the rock star–like events in St. Peter's Square.

Auditor An *auditor* is *someone who hears*; it is a Latin noun of agent formed from the verb *audio, audire, audivi, auditus*, meaning *to hear*. In the Roman Curia, the judges of the Roman Rota are called *auditores*, since they hear the cases brought before that court.

Augustinian The Greek verbs αὔξω and αὐξάνω and the related Latin verb *augeo, augere, auxi, auctus* all mean *to increase*, and from the last verb was formed the adjective *augustus* with the meaning *majestic*. Beginning with Gaius Julius Caesar Octavianus (63 B.C.–14 A.D., this adjective became a title of the Roman emperors. The addition of the diminutive suffix produced the name Augustinus, little Augustus, the name of the bishop of Hippo and Doctor of the Church (354–430). The addition of the second suffix -*ianus* produced the adjective *augustinianus* with the meaning *pertaining to Augustine*. The Augustinians are the members of the Order of Saint Augustine (OSA), once called in England the *Austin Friars*. The *Confessions* of St. Augustine and his *City of God* are masterpieces of Western literature. In the *Confessions* are to be found many weighty utterances such as:

Inquietum est cor nostrum, donec requiescat in te.[111]

Our hearts are restless, until they rest in Thee.

Da quod iubes, et iube quod vis![112]

Grant what you command, and command what you will!

111. *Confessiones*, book 1, chapter 1.
112. Ibid., book 10, chapter 29.

Episodes from the saint's life were painted by Benozzo Gozzoli (c. 1420–1497) in a beautiful fresco cycle in the cathedral of San Gimignano.

Augustinianism The addition of the Greek suffix *-ism* to the root of the adjective *Augustinian* produced the noun *Augustinianism*, the name for the doctrine of St. Augustine of Hippo.

According to him, Free Will had no initiative in the work of Salvation; even the first movement of resort to God, the initial aspiration for faith, must be referred to Divine action. It was in vain that any one opposed to him the objection that if the Bible tells of startling conversions like that of St. Paul, we find in it also stories like that of Zacchaeus where grace follows as the sequel of a good motion, even though it be one of simple and pious curiosity. This first good motion Augustine claimed for grace exactly in the same way as that which might follow. In this he was following out the logic of his system. The human race is justly devoted to eternal condemnation. In this mass of persons under eternal condemnation, God chooses whom it pleases Him, and that without regard to merits acquired or possible. These elect persons are predestined to salvation; whatever they do or do not do, they will be saved by the power of grace, a grace admitting neither of failure nor resistance. "Help yourself and Heaven will help you," says the wisdom of the nations. "Whether you help yourself or do not help yourself," says Augustine, "Heaven will help you if you are predestined; if you are not, anything that you can do is useless." It is hardly necessary to say that in such a system God could not be considered as willing the salvation of all men. This conception to which Augustine had not been opposed in his youth was subsequently got rid of by him and with a decision that is remarkable. The text, 1 Timothy 2:4[113], in which it is distinctly inculcated, is submitted by him to exegesis so subtle and so strained, that if we were not dealing with St. Augustine one would be tempted to utter the word "juggling".

That a system so pitiless should have been able to be patronized by such a man is a thing which, at first sight, seems inexplicable. But in that day people were familiar with the ideas of Damnation, of Election, of free Predestination. They are the ground of Biblical history: Israel had always lived, was still living, under the feeling of its Predestination as a nation. The Christians, to some extent, had inherited this mental attitude. Though exaggerated and carried to extremity among the Gnostics and the Manicheans, it had in no way seemed detrimental to

---

113. ... ἐνώπιον τοῦ σωτῆρος ἡμῶν θεοῦ, ὃς πάντας ἀνθρώπους θέλει σωθῆναι καὶ εἰς ἐπίγνωσιν ἀληθείας ἐλθεῖν.

... coram Salvatore nostro Deo, qui omnes homines vult salvos fieri, et ad agnitionem veritatis venire.

... in the sight of God our Savior, who desires all men to be saved and to come to the knowledge of the truth. (Revised Standard Version)

their success. Rare in the spirits of people of that time were those humanitarian conceptions which among ourselves revolt at such rigour.[114]

According to him [Augustine], a man is virtuous, he does that which is good, because God gives us the will and the power thereto, in other words succours us by His grace; from ourselves we can extract only sin. And why are we so made? By the fault of Adam, from which proceeded all our frailties, all our weaknesses physical and moral, sicknesses, death, and that interior dislocation which sets at perpetual strife within us the consciousness of the Law and the promptings of concupiscence. Adam sinned: his whole posterity sinned in him, for what is here involved is not merely some sort of falling away, but a falling away which is culpable,[115] which entitles God to avenge on each of us the fault committed by our first father. In the sight of God, the human race is a sinful mass, *massa peccati, massa perditionis*, from which the Author of all Justice could not extract any other good save what he puts into it Himself.[116]

Autocephalous The Greek adjective αὐτός means *self*, the noun κεφαλή means *head*, and so the adjective αὐτοκέφαλος means *having one's own head*. It is used of Orthodox Churches in the East that are self-ruling and independent of any prelate appointed by a foreign authority.

Auxiliary The Latin noun *auxilium* means *help*, and the associated adjective *auxiliaris* means *helpful*.

Da robur, fer auxilium.

Thine aid supply; Thy strength bestow.

An auxiliary bishop is an assistant bishop assigned as a helper to a diocesan bishop; the Germans call such functionaries *Weihbischöfe*, consecrating bishops, because their principal duty is to save the diocesan bishop the trouble of travelling around the diocese administering the sacrament of confirmation, a time-consuming activity.

Ave Maria This Latin phrase means *Hail Mary* and is the name of the prayer based on Luke 1:28, 42.

---

114. Louis Duchesne, *Early History of the Christian Church from Its Foundation to the End of the Fifth Century*, vol. 3 (London: John Murray, 1924), 192–93.

115. [Note of Duchesne]: "St. Augustine is here emphasizing the famous passage of St. Paul (Romans V 12ff): it is right to note that the words ἐφ᾽ ᾧ πάντες ἥμαρτον on which he lays great stress are badly rendered in the Latin Vulgate by *in quo omnes peccaverunt*, and mean not '*in whom* all have sinned' but '*because* all have sinned.'"

116. Ibid., 143.

χαῖρε, κεχαριτωμένη, ὁ κύριος μετὰ σοῦ. εὐλογημένη σὺ ἐν γυναιξίν, καὶ εὐλογημένος ὁ καρπὸς τῆς κοιλίας σου.

Ave Maria, gratia plena. Benedicta tu in mulieribus, et benedictus fructus ventris tui.

The remaining portion of the prayer, viz., *Sancta Maria, mater Dei, ora pro nobis peccatoribus, nunc et in hora mortis nostrae* is of much later composition.

Ave Maris Stella This ancient Marian hymn dates at least from the ninth century.

Its very frequent occurrence in the Divine Office made it most popular in the Middle Ages, many other hymns being founded upon it.[117]

Each line consists of three trochees, and the meter is trochaic dimeter brachycatalectic, that is, each line fails by one foot to have the requisite two pairs of trochees.[118] It is without rhyme.

> Ave maris stella,
> Dei mater alma,
> Atque semper virgo,
> Felix caeli porta.
>
> Sumens illud "Ave,"
> Gabrielis ore,
> Funda nos in pace,
> Mutans Hevae nomen.
>
> Solve vincla reis,
> Profer lumen caecis,
> Mala nostra pelle,
> Bona cuncta posce.
>
> Monstra te esse matrem,
> Sumat per te preces,
> Qui pro nobis natus,
> Tulit esse tuus.
>
> Virgo singularis,
> Inter omnes mitis,
> Nos culpis solutos,
> Mites fac et castos.

117. *The Catholic Encyclopedia* (New York: The Encyclopedia Press, 1913), s.v. "Ave Maris Stella."
118. The verb καταλήγω means *to end*, and the adjective βραχύς means *short*. The line ends short.

Vitam praesta puram,
Iter para tutum,
Ut videntes Iesum,
Semper collaetemur.

Sit laus Deo Patri,
Summo Christo decus,
Spiritui Sancto,
Tribus honor unus. Amen.

The following anonymous translation is found in more than one work published in the old days when some liturgical books were printed with facing English translations.

Hail! Bright star of ocean,
God's own mother blest,
Ever sinless virgin,
Gate of heavenly rest.

Taking that sweet Ave,
Which from Gabriel came,
Peace confirm within us,
Changing Eva's name.

Break the captives' fetters,
Light on blindness pour;
All our ills expelling,
Every bliss implore.

Show thyself a Mother;
May the Word Divine,
Born for us thy Infant,
Hear our prayers through thine.

Virgin all excelling,
Mildest of the mild,
Freed from guilt preserve us,
Pure and undefiled.

Keep our life all spotless,
Make our way secure,
Till we find in Jesus,
Joy forevermore.

Through the highest heaven,
To the Almighty Three,
Father, Son, and Spirit,
One same glory be.[119]

Avignon This is the French city on the Rhône whose name is the corruption of the Latin *Avennio, Avennionis, m.*, an important town of the Gauls in the time of Caesar. In 1348, the Holy Father Clement VI purchased the city, where he and his predecessors had been living since 1309, from Joanna I, queen of Naples and countess of Provence. The period from 1309 to 1367 and from 1370 to 1378, during which the supreme pontiffs resided at Avignon, was called, by those who disapproved of this sojourn, the *Babylonian Captivity of the Papacy*, perhaps because the poet Petrarch had referred to Avignon as *Babylon*. The city of Avignon remained under the sovereignty of the popes until 1791, when it was annexed to France by brute force. At the fall of Napoleon, the victorious powers allowed the French to remain in possession despite the attempt of Cardinal Consalvi to have the place restored to the pontifical government.

---

119. *Hymns for the Year: A Complete Collection for Schools, Missions, and General Use*, new ed. (London: Burns, Lambert, & Oates, 1866), 114.

B

Baldacchino The Italians corrupted the Arabic, بغداد, Baghdad, into *Baldacco*, whence proceeded the diminutive *baldacchino* with the meaning, *a luxurious type of cloth imported from Baghdad*. This is the Italian word for the canopy, formerly of cloth, over the high altar or over the bishop's throne found in many churches. That over the high altar of St. Peter's Basilica in Rome, by Bernini, is the most famous. As regards the canopy or cloth of state over the bishop's cathedra:

The continuation of this practice in new construction has been forbidden; however, the Church has been careful to reaffirm the historic significance of those already existing.[1]

The baldacchino carried above the pope when he was seated upon the sedia gestatoria had eight poles, which were held by prelates of the Apostolic Segnatura.

Ban The Anglo-Saxon verb *bannen* means *to proclaim*, and from it was derived the noun *ban* (plural *bans* or *banns*) with the meaning *proclamation*. The *bans* or *banns* of marriage are the proclamation to the community of the intention of an engaged couple to marry. However, in former times, a proclamation was occasionally made to the effect that someone was an outlaw, and when such a proclamation was made by the Holy Roman Emperor, then such a criminal was said to be under the *ban of the Empire*. When such a proclamation was made by the pope, the fellow in question was under the *ban of the Church*, that is, excommunicated.

1. James-Charles Noonan Jr., *The Church Visible* (New York: Viking, 1996), 397.

Baptism The Greek verb βαπτίζω means *to dip*. From this the Greeks made the noun βάπτισμα, a sort of dunking. In the New Testament it refers to a ritual bathing, such as that of John the Baptist, or by the Christians in their solemn initiation ceremony. Infant baptism arose when the faithful began to have children. See the entry **Paedobaptism**. A great controversy arose in the third century about the baptism of heretics.

Christian initiation had two parts—baptism, and what we call confirmation. By the first came purification from sin; by the second, the gift of the Spirit. In the ritual of this second part, special importance was attached to the laying on of hands, accompanied by an invocation of the Sevenfold Spirit. The Roman usage was to accept baptism conferred by heretics; but it was thought that only the Church, the True Church, could invoke the Holy Spirit with any efficacy; and therefore the converted heretic had to submit to the imposition of hands, as if by way of penance, but really that he might receive the Holy Spirit. In Carthage, the absolute repudiation of the validity of the heretical rites had the authority of long established tradition.[2]

Thus St. Cyprian, Bishop of Carthage (c. 200–258), required the rebaptism of heretics, a practice forbidden today.

The Latin language transliterates the Greek verb and has the word *baptizo, baptizare*. The noun has three forms in Latin, *baptisma, baptismatis*; *baptismus, -i*; and *baptismum, -i*.

Basilica The Greek noun βασιλεύς means *king*, and from it is derived the adjective βασιλικός, *royal*. The second of the nine archons in Athens was called the ἄρχων βασιλεύς, and because he was in charge of criminal processes, his seat was referred to as ἡ βασίλειος στοά or *the royal pillared hall*. From this usage the name *basilica* was extended to all law courts, which were traditionally of rectangular shape with colonnades and without transepts. The four main churches of Rome were built in this manner and were denominated the *four major basilicas*. The term *basilica* was later extended to denote any church singled out for distinction by the pope. These *minor basilicas* number in the hundreds and may be found in every city of size. They receive a special multicolored processional umbrella as a symbol of their rank, and these have their place in all solemn parades (see the entry **Conopaeum**).

---

2. Louis Duchesne, *Early History of the Christian Church from Its Foundation to the End of the Third Century* (London: John Murray, 1914), 306.

Beatification The Latin verb *beo, beare, beavi, beatus* means *to bless, to make happy*, and the verb *facio, facere, feci, factus* means *to make*. From these is formed the first-conjugation ecclesiastical technical verb *beatifico* with the meaning *to declare blessed*. Someone so declared is called a *beatus*, a *blessed*. It is an intermediate step before canonization, introduced when the process of making saints became bureaucratic. A *beatus* is someone approved by the pope for veneration; a *beatus* differs from a *saint* in that beatification involves permitting the local cult of the *beatus*, whereas canonization requires the universal cult of the saint.

Bell This is a Low German word, the Anglo-Saxon *belle*. The small bells called in Latin *campanulae* are correctly sounded at those most sacred moments of the Mass to secure the attention of the people.

Paulo ante consecrationem, minister, pro opportunitate, campanulae signo fideles monet. Item pulsat campanulam ad unamquamque ostensionem, iuxta cuiusque loci consuetudinem.[3]

A little before the consecration, an attendant, if it is considered recommendable, alerts the faithful by the sound of a small bell. He similarly rings the small bell at each elevation, if it is the custom to do so in that place.

Their sound is numinous, and because of this connection the great bells in church towers are blessed when installed.

Benedictine The Latin verb b*enedico, benedicere, benedixi, benedictus* means *to speak* (dico) *well of* (bene); the past participle *benedictus* became a proper name in Christian times. The most famous of Benedicts was the monk Benedict of Nursia (c. 480–c. 547), and the monks who follow his rule are called *Benedictini* or *Benedictines*. The Benedictines were the saviours of classical literature after the disaster of the sixth century war in which the generals Belisarius and Narses of the emperor Justinian attempted to wrest Italy from the Goths.

And as in Rome, so throughout Italy, the war of annihilation between Goths and Byzantines swallowed up the priceless treasures of ancient literature, with the exception of such remnants as had happily been collected and saved in the rising monasteries of the Benedictines.[4]

---

3. *Institutio Generalis Missalis Romani*, in *Missale Romanum, editio typica altera* (Vatican City: Libreria Editrice Vaticana, 1975), §109.

4. Ferdinand Gregorovius, *History of the City of Rome in the Middle Ages*, trans. Mrs. Gustavus W. Hamilton (London: G. Bell & Sons, 1909), 1:489.

Benediction The Ecclesiastical Latin verb *benedico, benedicere, benedixi, benedictus* means *to bless*, and from it is derived the noun *benedictio, benedictionis* with the meaning *a blessing*. Benediction is the name of the ceremony of blessing the people with the sacred species inserted into a monstrance. It includes the hymns *O Salutaris Hostia* and *Tantum Ergo Sacramentum*, each being the last two stanzas of the poems *Verbum Supernum Prodiens* and *Pange Lingua Gloriosi Corporis Mysterium*, which were composed and set to music by Thomas Aquinas. I once heard the late Msgr. Robert J. Schuler, pastor of St. Agnes Church in St. Paul, Minnesota, say that when he celebrated Benediction of the Most Holy in Latin and chanted

"Panem de caelo praestitisti eis."

The people responded

"Omne delectamentum in se habentem."

But when a colleague celebrated in English and sang, "You have given them bread from heaven," no one knew what to answer.

Benedictus Dominus Deus Israel This is the prayer of Zacharias on the occasion of the circumcision of his son John the Baptist (Luke 1:68–79). It is sung at Lauds (*ad Laudes matutinas*).

> Benedictus Dominus Deus Israel,
> Quia visitavit, et fecit redemptionem plebis suae:
>
> Et erexit cornu salutis nobis:
> In domo David pueri sui.
>
> Sicut locutus est per os sanctorum, qui a saeculo sunt, prophetarum eius:
> Salutem ex inimicis nostris, et de manu omnium, qui oderunt nos:
>
> Ad faciendam misericordiam cum patribus nostris:
> Et memorari testamenti sui sancti.
>
> Iusiurandum, quod iuravit ad Abraham patrem nostrum,
> Daturum se nobis: Ut sine timore, de manu inimicorum nostrorum liberati,
>
> Serviamus illi in sanctitate, et iustitia
> Coram ipso, omnibus diebus nostris.
>
> Et tu, puer, propheta Altissimi vocaberis:
> Praeibis enim ante faciem Domini parare vias eius:

Ad dandam scientiam salutis plebi eius:
In remissionem peccatorum eorum:

Per viscera misericordiae Dei nostri:
In quibus visitavit nos, oriens ex alto:

Illuminare his, qui in tenebris, et in umbra mortis sedent:
Ad dirigendos pedes nostros in viam pacis.

Gloria …

The best translation is that to be found in the Book of Common Prayer:

Blessed be the Lord God of Israel:
for he hath visited, and redeemed his people;

And hath raised up a mighty salvation for us:
in the house of his servant David;

As he spake by the mouth of his holy Prophets:
which have been since the world began;

That we should be saved from our enemies:
and from the hands of all that hate us;

To perform the mercy promised to our forefathers:
and to remember his holy Covenant;

To perform the oath which he sware to our forefather Abraham:
that he would give us;

That we being delivered out of the hand of our enemies:
might serve him without fear;

In holiness and righteousness before him:
all the days of our life.

And thou, Child, shalt be called the Prophet of the Highest:
for thou shalt go before the face of the Lord to prepare his ways;

To give knowledge of salvation unto his people:
for the remission of their sins,

Through the tender mercy of our God:
whereby the day-spring from on high hath visited us;

To give light to them that sit in darkness, and in the shadow of death:
and to guide our feet into the way of peace.

Glory be …

Benefice The Latin verb *benefacio, benefacere, benefeci, benefactus* means *to do good to*, and from it is derived the noun *beneficium* with the meaning a *favor*. A benefice is an ecclesiastical appointment that generates income for the incumbent.

Bible The Greek noun βιβλίον means *a small book*. It is the diminutive of ἡ βίβλος, *the inner bark of the papyrus*, and then *the paper made from this bark*, and finally *the book or scroll itself*. It is applied to the Bible as the book *par excellence*, or, as the Greeks said, κατ' ἐξοχήν. The Bible is divided into Old Testament and New Testament; the former is a politically incorrect name for the Hebrew Bible. The authoritative enumeration of the books of the Bible was accomplished by the Council of Trent (Fourth Session, April 8, 1546) after the reformers had questioned the traditionally received list.

Sacrorum vero librorum Indicem huic Decreto adscribendum censuit, ne cui dubitatio suboriri possit, quinam sint, qui ab ipsa Synodo suscipiuntur, sunt vero infrascripti. Testamenti veteris, quinque Moysis, id est, Genesis, Exodus, Leviticus, Numeri, Deuteronomium; Iosue, Iudicum, Ruth, quattuor Regum, duo Paralipomenon, Esdrae primus, & secundus, qui dicitur Neemias, Thobias, Iudith, Hester, Iob, Psalterium Davidicum centum quinquaginta psalmorum, Parabole, Ecclesiastes, Canticum canticorum, Sapientia, Ecclesiasticus, Isaias, Hieremias cum Baruch, Ezechiel, Daniel, duodecim Prophetae minores, id est, Osea, Ioel, Amos, Abdias, Micheas, Naum, Abacuch, Sophonias, Aggaeus, Zacharias, Malachias, duo Machabaeorum, primus, & secundus. Testamenti novi, quattuor Evangelia, secundum Matthaeum, Marcum, Lucam, & Ioannem. Actus Apostolorum a Luca Evangelista conscripti, quattuordecim Epistolae Pauli Apostoli, ad Romanos, duae ad Corinthios, ad Galatas, ad Ephesios, ad Philippenses, ad Colossenses, duae ad Thessalonicenses, duae ad Timotheum, ad Titum, ad Philemonem, ad Hebraeos. Petri Apostoli duae, Ioannis Apostoli tres, Iacobi apostoli una, Iudae Apostoli una, & Apocalypsis Ioannis Apostoli. Si quis autem libros ipsos integros cum omnibus suis partibus, prout in Ecclesia Catholica legi consueverunt, & in veteri vulgata latina editione habentur, pro sacris, & canonicis non susceperit; & traditiones praedictas sciens, & prudens contempserit; anathema sit.[5]

[This Ecumenical Council] has determined that a list of the canonical books should be added to this decree, and lest any doubt insinuate itself into anyone's mind as to what those books actually are, which the Council accepts, those books are: Of the Old Testament, the Five Books of Moses (namely, Genesis, Exodus, Leviticus, Numbers, and Deuteronomy), Joshua, Judges, Ruth, the Four Books of Kings, the Two Books of Paralipomenon, I and II Esdras, (the latter of which is called Nehemias), Tobias, Judith, Esther, Job, the Psalter of David containing one hundred and fifty psalms, Proverbs, Ecclesiastes, the Canticle of Canticles, Wis-

---

5. The Latin quotation I have made from the first edition in my possession.

dom, Ecclesiasticus [Sirach], Isaias, Jeremias including Baruch, Ezechiel, Daniel, the Twelve Minor Prophets (namely, Osee, Joel, Amos, Abdias, Micheas, Nahum, Habacuc, Sophonias, Aggeus, Zacharias, and Malachias), and I and II Machabees. Of the New Testament: the Four Gospels (that is, those according to Matthew, Mark, Luke, and John), the Acts of the Apostles written by the Apostle Luke, the fourteen Letters of Paul the Apostle (namely, to the Romans, the two to the Corinthians, to the Galatians, to the Ephesians, to the Philippians, to the Colossians, the two to the Thessalonians, the two to Timothy, to Titus, to Philemon, and to the Hebrews), I and II Peter, I, II, and III John, the Letter of the Apostle James, the Letter of the Apostle Jude, and the Apocalypse of the Apostle John. If, however, anyone should not accept the whole of these books, with all their parts, as they are accustomed to be read in the Catholic Church, and which are contained in the venerable Latin Vulgate edition, and, though knowing the aforementioned traditions, should knowingly hold them in contempt, let him be anathema.

The following famous mediaeval epic verses present the four ways of interpreting passages in the Bible:

> Littera gesta docet, quid credas allegoria,
> Moralis quid agas, quo tendas anagogia.

These lines may be rendered by the doggerel verses:

> Of things long past the teacher is the letter.
> The moral tells us what conduct is better.
> Allegory makes doctrines to defend.
> Anagogy's about our latter end.

The first clause refers to the literal interpretation of scripture, which formerly was universal. Thus, the literal interpretation of Matthew 16:18–19 is that Christ actually spoke those words to Peter. The second clause refers to the allegorical interpretation, according to which it is believed that Christ did not actually hand physical keys to Peter, but rather meant thereby to appoint him his vicar on earth. Similarly, Thomas Aquinas saw the *Panem de caelo* of Exodus 16:4 as a figure of the Eucharist. The third clause refers to the moral interpretation of scripture, according to which the stories of Jonah and Ruth teach appreciation for what is now called diversity. The fourth clause refers to the mystical interpretation, according to which a passage may refer to the life to come; for example, to interpret the progress of the Israelites through the Red Sea or of Jonah coming forth from the belly of the "whale" as teaching the resurrection of the dead. Of these four classical methods of interpretation, the first is the one that has suffered the most with the passage of time. Higher critics will say that Noah was no more an actual person than Anna Karenina, but that the story of the ark was intended to teach a lesson. Similarly, they say that the superfluity of wine at the wedding feast in Cana, and the multiplication of the loaves and fishes in John 6 are fairytale motifs theologized by the evangelist. The difficulty for the Catholic system with this kind of approach is that, for example, if Adam and Eve were not real people, then what happens to the Pauline doctrine of original sin? On the other hand, there are certain benefits to being able to say that certain episodes that offend modern ears did not really happen but are fiction, a human element in the scripture. Thus Bertrand Russell was bothered by the story of the herd of swine being propelled over the cliff for no fault of their own,[6] and by the demands of the Deity for animal sacrifices recorded in the Book of Leviticus.[7]

This exegetical attitude [*viz.*, that the Old and New Testaments are incompatible] is, in fact, easy to understand. The religious thinkers of the 2nd century felt, as we do, a perpetual temptation to criticize Nature and Law. Man may well complain of the brutality of the forces of Nature, not only on his own account, but for the sake of all creatures; in other words, man from his very circumscribed point of view, is naturally inclined to maintain that the world is ill-arranged. So likewise, the Law being laid down for the general run of cases, ignores, and cannot but ignore, a thousand particular instances, and in consequence it often appears to be absurd and unjust. But the heart of man dimly discerns that, above this world with its miseries, there is an Infinite Goodness, manifesting itself in love, and not in simple justice. Suppose that a highly cultivated Greek, in this mood, had the Bible put into his hands. The Old Testament confronts him with an awful God, who creates man, it is true, but almost immediately punishes the whole human race for the sin committed by the original human pair He created; who then repents Him of having permitted the propagation of the human race, and destroys all but one family, with most of the animals, who assuredly were quite innocent of the misdeeds of which man is accused; who then befriends a company of adventurers, protects them against all other nations, sends them on conquering, pillaging raids, shares their spoils, and takes a leading part in the massacre of the vanquished; who endows them with a Law, containing by the side of many equitable provisions many others which are strange and most impracticable. Enlightened Jews and Christians explained these difficulties by ingeneous allegories. We cannot do this; but we have got out of the difficulty nevertheless, by denying the objectivity of

---

6. Bertrand Russell, *Why I Am Not a Christian, and Other Essays on Religion and Related Subjects*, ed. Paul Edwards (New York: Simon & Schuster, no date), 18–19.

7. The best discussion of these matters is by Cardinal Newman in his article "On the Inspiration of Scripture," in *The Nineteenth Century* 15, no. 84 (February, 1884): 184–89.

these tares in the Lord's field, and regarding them as an expression, in the sacred text, of a progressive purification of the conception of God, in the minds of the men of old. But no such explanation was within the reach of the early thinkers. The Gnostic philosophers did not make use of allegory which the orthodox did. And as they had to make someone responsible for Nature and the Law, they fell back on the God of Israel. The Gospel, on the contrary, where they though a different note was struck, seemed to them a revelation of supreme Goodness and of absolute Perfection.[8]

Bination The Latin adjective *bini* means *twofold*. *Bination* is the celebration of two Masses on the same day by the same priest. Bination, as well as *trination*, is now common, because of the scarcity of priests, but in former times it was a rarity allowed without dispensation only on Christmas and All Souls Day.

Biretta The Greek adjective πυρρός means *flame-colored*, and to it is related the Latin *birrus*, which means *red*. From this there was produced the barbarous word (the description is Bacci's) *biretum*, whence comes our noun *biretta*. Evidently, the biretta was originally a small red hat.

The biretta (beretta, biretum, birettum) is an ecclesiastical cap, square in shape, having three "horns" or projections on top, with a tuft ("pompon") of silk (not a tassel) attached where the three horns meet in the middle. In wearing the biretta, the part which has no horn should be to the left.[9]

Bacci says that the correct Latin expression for the clerical biretta is *quadratum pileum clericorum*.[10] The *pileum*, according to Cassell's Latin dictionary, was "a felt cap, a πῖλος fitting close to the head, worn at feasts, especially the Saturnalia, and by slaves after manumission." The cardinal's biretta is red and has no tuft; that of other bishops is purple. All other clergy wear a black biretta. The biretta is worn over the zucchetto. Scholars who have received the doctoral degree from a university authorized to grant such degrees by the Holy See have the privilege, of which they are bound to make use, of wearing a four-cornered biretta with a tuft on academic occasions, though not in choir if they happen to be priests. The color of the doctoral biretta should be black; the colors of the lining and

8. Louis Duchesne, *Early History of the Christian Church from Its Foundation to the End of the Third Century* (London: John Murray, 1914), 129–30.

9. John A. Nainfa, *Costume of Prelates of the Catholic Church according to Roman Etiquette* (Baltimore, Md.: John Murphy, 1909), 86.

10. Antonio Bacci, *Vocabolario Italiano-Latino delle Parole Moderne e Difficili a Tradurre* (Rome: Editrice Studium, 1963), 116.

of the tuft depend on the tradition of the institution that has granted the degree.

Bishop This word is the corruption of the Latin *episcopus*, the transliteration of the Greek noun ἐπίσκοπος, an *overseer*, from the noun ἐπισκοπέω, *to look* (σκοπέω) *upon* or *after* (ἐπί). Bishops chased out of their sees by the advance of Islam were called bishops *in partibus infidelium*. Because the Church operates on the principle that there can be no bishop without a diocese, the same description was applied to bishops appointed to those abandoned sees as a legal fiction, when their real purpose was merely to lighten the load of episcopal duties for a busy confrère; such prelates, called auxiliary bishops in America, are more aptly described in the German language as *Weihbischöfe*, i.e., confirmation-performing bishops. The dispute arose in the sixteenth century whether or not bishops were *iure divino*, that is, whether they were a divine or human invention.

The word ἐπίσκοπος occurs in five places in the New Testament: Acts 20:28, Philippians 1:1, 1 Timothy 3:2, Titus 1:7–9, and 1 Peter 2:25. In the Revised Standard Version, ἐπίσκοπος is sometimes translated *guardian* and sometimes *bishop*, and πρεσβύτερος is rendered by *elder*; this is because those translators considered it an anachronism uniformly to use *bishop* and *priest* for the titles of Christian clergy in the New Testament texts:

Acts 20:17–18, 28—(St. Paul's Farewell to the Ephesian πρεσβύτεροι): Ἀπὸ δὲ τῆς Μιλήτου πέμψας εἰς Ἔφεσον μετεκαλέσατο τοὺς πρεσβυτέρους τῆς ἐκκλησίας. ὡς δὲ παρεγένοντο πρὸς αὐτὸν εἶπεν αὐτοῖς ... προσέχετε ἑαυτοῖς καὶ παντὶ τῷ ποιμνίῳ, ἐν ᾧ ὑμᾶς τὸ πνεῦμα τὸ ἅγιον ἔθετο ἐπισκόπους ...

And from Miletus he sent to Ephesus and called to him the elders of the church. And when they came to him, he said to them, ... "Take heed to yourselves and to all the flock, in which the Holy Spirit has made you guardians ..."

Philippians 1:1: Παῦλος καὶ Τιμόθεος δοῦλοι Χριστοῦ Ἰησοῦ πᾶσιν τοῖς ἁγίοις ἐν Χριστῷ Ἰησοῦ τοῖς οὖσιν ἐν Φιλίπποις σὺν ἐπισκόποις καὶ διακόνοις· ...

Paul and Timothy, servants of Christ Jesus, to all the saints in Christ Jesus who are at Philippi, with the bishops and deacons ...

1 Timothy 3:2: δεῖ οὖν τὸν ἐπίσκοπον ἀνεπίλημπτον εἶναι, μιᾶς γυναικὸς ἄνδρα ...

Now a bishop must be above reproach, married only once ...

Titus 1:7: δεῖ γὰρ τὸν ἐπίσκοπον ἀνέγκλητον εἶναι ὡς θεοῦ οἰκονόμον ...

For a bishop, as God's steward, must be blameless ...

1 Peter 2:25: ἦτε γὰρ ὡς πρόβατα πλανώμενοι, ἀλλὰ ἐπεστράφητε νῦν ἐπὶ τὸν ποιμένα καὶ ἐπίσκοπον τῶν ψυχῶν ὑμῶν.

For you were straying like sheep, but have now returned to the Shepherd and Guardian of your souls.

In the *Acts of the Apostles* and in the letters of St. Paul, the terms ἐπίσκοπος and πρεσβύτερος (by transliteration *bishop* and *priest*, or, by etymology, *overseer* and *elder*) seem to be used interchangeably. The Presbyterians deduced therefrom that there was no difference in meaning between the two words ἐπίσκοποι and πρεσβύτεροι, that the two words were synonyms and should be translated by *overseers* and *elders* respectively, that the translations *bishops* and *priests* was an anachronism, and that the episcopal government of the Church was a human invention; furthermore, they etymologically and controversially referred to priests as *elders*. There is a note on this issue in the Rhemes New Testament at Philippians 1:1,[11] where the authors presented the traditional Catholic teaching with regard to this issue.

Vvicleffe and other Heretikes vvould proue by this that Priests are not here named, and for that there could not be many Bishops of this one tovvne, that there is no difference betvvixt a Bishop and a Priest, vvhich vvas the old heresie of Aërius, of vvhich matter,[12] in other places: for this present it is ynough to knovv that in the Apostles time there vvere not obserued alvvaies proper distinct names of either function, as they vvere quickly aftervvard, though they vvere alvvaies diuers degrees & distinctions.

With reference to Acts 20:28 and Philippians 1:1,[13] the Abbé Duchesne writes:

Here already appears an absence of clear distinction between priests and bishops and the collegiate government of the Church.[14]

---

11. "Paul and Timotheus the servants of Jesus Christ, to all the saints in Christ Jesus which are at Philippi, with the bishops and deacons" (Authorized Version).

12. See Annot. Tit, I, v. 5.

13. Acts 20:28: "Take heed therefore unto yourselves, and to all the flock, over the which the Holy Ghost hath made you overseers [ἐπισκόπους] to feed the Church of God, which he hath purchased with his own blood." This is the translation in the Authorized Version. The Rhemes New Testament has *bishops* instead of *overseers*, with the note, "Bishops or priests (for then these names were sometime vsed indifferĕtly) gouvernours of the Church of God, & placed in that roome & high functiõ by the Holy Ghost."

14. Louis Duchesne, *Early History of the Christian Church from Its Foundation to the End of the Third Century* (London: John Murray, 1914), 65.

In some places, as in Jerusalem, there appears to have been just one bishop in charge ("monarchical episcopacy"), whereas in others, it seems that there were several bishops ("collegiate episcopacy"). The reason for the transition from collegiate to monarchical episcopacy in those places where the former arrangement at first obtained is no doubt to be found in the *Iliad*, in a passage that was the favorite of the emperor Caligula:[15]

Οὐκ ἀγαθὸν πολυκοιρανίη· εἷς κοίρανος ἔστω,
Εἷς βασιλεύς, ᾧ δῶκε Κρόνου παῖς ἀγκυλομήτεω
Σκῆπτρόν τ᾽ ἠδὲ θέμιστας, ἵνα σφίσιν ἐμβασιλεύῃ. (2:204–6)

To one sole monarch Jove commits the sway;
His are the laws, and him let all obey.[16]

The Jews have no bishops, yet during the reign of the emperor Charles V, Rabbi Joseph (Joselmann) Ben Gershon of Rosheim (c. 1478–1554), who had earned the confidence of the emperor and whose opinions, therefore, had the most influence with that authority in any matter relating to the Children of Israel, was referred to as the *Episcopus Iudaeorum*, the bishop of the Jews. This was not the only occurrence of such an appointment.

Blaise, St. According to Abbot Karl Egger, this name was borrowed by the Romans from a non-Latin Italian language, which in turn had taken it over from the Greek βλαισός, which means *arthritic*. The associated adjective *blaesus* is used by Martial (10.65.10):

Os blaesum tibi debilisque lingua.

Your mouth stammers, and your tongue is weak.

In times past, on February 3, the feast of St. Blaise, Catholics would go to their parish church to receive the blessing of the throat. The suitability of this fourth-century bishop of Sebastea to help in such cases is due to his having cured a choking child who had been brought to him with a fishbone stuck in his throat.

In many places a blessing is given on the day of his feast or to individual sufferers at other times. Two candles (said to be in memory of the tapers brought to the saint in his dungeon) are blessed and held like a St. Andrew's cross either against

---

15. The third line is a later interpolation.
16. Homer, *The Iliad of Homer*, trans. Alexander Pope, 6 vols. (London, 1715), 1:101, lines 243–44.

the throat or over the head of the applicant, with the words *Per intercessionem Sancti Blasii liberet te Deus a malo gutturis et a quovis alio malo.*[17]

The tapers in question were brought to the saint in his unlit prison cell by a woman whose pig he had rescued from a wolf; the wolf had carried off the pig, but, upon being rebuked by the saint, restored the pig to its owner. Also edifying is the story of how animals fled to him for help in eluding the round-up of wild beasts being conducted by hunters for the purpose of supplying wild animals for the arena. For these persuasive reasons, the martyr Blaise became the patron saint of animals.

Breviary The Latin adjective *brevis* means *short, brief,* whence arose the noun *breviarium,* meaning a *summary.* It is the old name of the book containing the prayers said at special times of the day, that is, matins, lauds, prime, terce, sext, nones, vespers, and compline. It was usually published in four volumes, one for each of the seasons of the year. The recitation of the prayers was called the *Divinum Officium* or *Divine Office,* that is, one's duty vis-à-vis the Deity. Abbot Ferdinand Cabrol describes how the book acquired the name *Breviary*:

St. Gregory VII having, indeed, abridged the order of prayers, and having simplified the Liturgy as performed at the Roman Court, this abridgment received the name of *Breviary.*[18]

The new official name for the Divine Office is *Liturgia Horarum* or *Liturgy of the Hours.* It is an example of a modern name replacing a name that arose naturally over the centuries.

Brief The English word *brief* is a corruption of the Latin adjective *brevis,* which means *short.* The brief was a communication from the pope that was less formal and therefore shorter than such documents as a bull. Thus a brief began, for example, *Pius Pp. II* rather than *Pius Episcopus Servus Servorum Dei ad perpetuam rei memoriam.* A brief would be sealed with the Fisherman's Ring on wax rather than on melted lead. It might even suffer the indignity of being folded into an envelope. It was appropriate for personal letters, as when, for example, Pius II wrote a letter of condolence to Piero de' Medici on the occasion of the death of his father Cosimo.

---

17. *Butler's Lives of the Saints, Complete Edition,* ed. Herbert J. Thurston and Donald Attwater (Norwalk, Conn.: Easton Press, 1995), 1:238 (February 3). "By the intercession of St. Blaise may God free you from every ailment of the throat and from every other ailment."

18. *The Catholic Encyclopedia* (New York: The Encyclopedia Press, 1913), 2:769s, s.v. "Breviary."

Bull The Latin noun *bulla, -ae, f.* means *anything that swells and thereby becomes round*, a *bubble*, a *boss* or *knob*, whence there was derived the verb *bullio, bullire*, with the meaning *to bubble up, to boil*. In Late Latin it was the name of the seal, usually of lead, that was affixed to important documents, the lead having first been softened (by boiling it in water) in order to receive the impression. The word was then transferred from the seal to the document itself. The word is nowadays reserved for papal documents sealed in such a way. They are defined by Bacci as *litterae apostolicae sub plombo datae*, that is, *apostolic letters given under the lead* [*seal*].[19] The traditional opening formula for a papal bull is *N. Episcopus Servus Servorum Dei ad perpetuam rei memoriam*. The leaden seal was made optional in the reign of Leo XIII, so there are few real papal bulls any more. The letter of the nobility of England to Pope Clement VII requesting the dissolution of the marriage of Henry VIII with Catherine of Aragon was a true bull, though not of the pope; its many leaden seals have survived. This precious document, lost for centuries, was found by Cardinal Mercati (1866–1957) in the Vatican Library during his time there. The noun *bulla* is related to the Greek φαλλός, whence our adjective *phallic*.

Buskins Weekley says that the word results from metathesis in the phrase *buck-skin*, a combination used as an adjective with the noun *shoes* understood. *Buck* and *skin* are the metamorphoses of the Anglo-Saxon word *bucc*, meaning a *male deer*, and the Old Norse word *skinn* meaning *hide*. The buskins are the high, embroidered stockings formerly worn by bishops in the celebration of the pontifical high Mass. In Ecclesiastical Latin they are called *caligae*. The emperor Gaius, as a youth, wore baby-sized *caligae*, whence he acquired the nickname *Caligula*.

---

19. Antonio Bacci, *Vocabolario Italiano-Latino delle Parole Moderne e Difficili a Tradurre* (Rome: Editrice Studium, 1963), s. v. "Bolla."

C

Caesaropapism *Caesaropapism* is the system wherein the sovereign is pope. It was the system adopted by Henry VIII in England in 1533 and that which prevailed in the early Church from the conversion of Constantine until the debasement of the imperial dignity, which happened at different times in the Eastern and Western Empires. The word is the concatenation of *Caesar*, a family name (*cognomen*) of the clan (*gens*) Julia, *pope*, and the suffix *-ism*. Lewis and Short relate Caesar to *caesius* and *caeruleus*, both of which adjectives mean *dark blue*.

There was not then a guiding power, an effective expression of Christian unity. The Papacy, such as the West knew it later on, was still to be born. In the place which it did not yet occupy, the State installed itself without hesitation. The Christian religion became the religion of the emperor, not only in the sense of being professed by him, but in the sense of being directed by him. Such is not the law, such is not the theory; but such is the fact.

    The emperor, it is true, did not himself determine the formularies of faith; that was the business of the bishops. If he feels the necessity of fixing exactly, on some particular point, the theological language, it is to them that he addresses himself. Whether they are assembled in councils, more or less oecumenical, in one or in two divisions; or whether they meet in smaller gatherings on individual summonses despatched at will, it is always to the emperor that the meeting owes its formation, it is to him that it looks for its programme, for its general direction, and above all for the sanction of its decisions. If, like Theodosius, the emperor distrusts formulas, and has recourse more readily to persons, it is he who decides with whom it is right to hold communion. And upon what ground does his decision rest? Upon his own personal estimate of the situation. Theodosius was a

Nicene, like all the Westerns; when he was called to govern the East, he indicated to it as standards of orthodoxy the Bishops of Rome and of Alexandria. Later on, when he knew his episcopal world better, he perceived that these authorities were not so decisive as necessary, and he indicated others.

The emperor again does not assume, in theory, the right of deposing a bishop. That is the business of the Church which alone is in a position to know whether such an one of its representatives has or has not violated its internal statutes. In proceedings taken against bishops and other clergy, the State does not interfere, providing such proceedings relate only to statutory obligations, and do not affect the common law of the State. Thus, if a bishop teaches heresy, or a clerk breaks the law of celibacy (provided it was not a case of adultery), it is for the Church, and not the State, to recall him to his duty, and to apply to him its own penalties, dismissal (deposition) and exclusion (excommunication). Where the State intervenes, and at the request of the Church, is in relation to the consequences which may be produced in regard to public order by the execution of the ecclesiastical sentence. Then the State, by ordinary police measures, would eject, banish, or imprison such and such a bishop, or such and such a claimant as should be pointed out to it, either by its own officials or simply by episcopal authority, after a trial in due form.

Such is the theory. In practice it is evident that the government would have no difficulty in finding in the divisions amongst the episcopate, and the weaknesses of individual members, a basis of operations against any persons who presumed to displease it. Moreover, the common law, with its crimes of *lèse-majesté* and rebellion, provided it in certain cases with other means of action. In fact, a bishop, especially a bishop of important position, who wished to live a quiet life, had to be careful not to oppose the official dogmas and, generally speaking, the manifestations, even when they affected religion, of the will of the government.[1]

Rowan Williams, archbishop of Canterbury, had the following to say about the rise of caesaropapism in the fourth century, remarks of particular interest in view of the history of the Church of England in the sixteenth century.

And then everything appeared to change. Violence against Christians stopped quite abruptly in 311; and the emergence of an imperial figure sympathetic to Christianity, one who believed that the Christian God had in some way assisted his decisive military victory over a rival, led to a new policy of legal recognition for the Church—and, perhaps less predictably, of official interest in the internal business of the Church. Constantine, who finally became the sole ruler of the Empire in 324, not only allowed various civic and public privileges to the leaders

1. Louis Duchesne, *Early History of the Christian Church from Its Foundation to the End of the Fifth Century*, vol. 2 (London: John Murray, 1931), 522–23.

of the Church but believed himself authorized to sort out its controversies. The challenges of the fourth-century Church were not those of harassment or persecution, but of internal division, much complicated by the active involvement of successive emperors.[2]

The doctrine of the Church historian Eusebius with regard to caesaropapism was, in the words of Archbishop Williams, the following:

He was able to present himself again in the years ahead as one of the most loyal and eloquent spokesmen for an extravagant but coherent philosophy based on a kind of cosmic delegation of authority—from God to God's heavenly 'Logos', his image and deputy (like the subordinate co-emperors who sometimes appeared in Roman politics), and from the Logos to the emperor on earth. As the Logos guaranteed stability and rationality in the whole cosmos, so the emperor guaranteed the same in the (civilised) world. This scheme is already to be seen in the last pages of the *History* (with what was later to be an embarrassing reference to Constantine's son and co-emperor Crispus who was executed by his father in 326), and it was expressed most fulsomely in Eusebius' oration in 335 to mark the thirtieth anniversary of Constantine's accession.[3]

Bury quotes a statement that sums up the doctrine of caesaropapism made by the Patriarch Menas of Constantinople with regard to the Emperor Justinian in a synod of 536:

Προσήκει μηδὲν τῶν ἐν τῇ ἁγιοτάτῃ ἐκκλησίᾳ κινουμένων παρὰ γνώμην αὐτοῦ καὶ κέλευσιν γενέσθαι.[4]

It is fitting that none of those things being moved in the most holy church come to pass without his knowledge and command.

With regard to the theory and practice of caesaropapism by the emperor Justinian, Bury writes:

Justinian took his responsibilities as head of the Church more seriously than any Emperor had hitherto done, and asserted his authority in its internal affairs more constantly and systematically. It was his object to identify the Church and State more intimately, to blend them, as it were, into a single organism, of which he was himself the controlling brain. We must view in this light his important enactment that the Canons of the four great Ecumenical Councils should have the same validity as Imperial laws. And we can see in his legislation against heretics and pa-

---

2. Rowan Williams, preface to Eusebius, *The History of the Church from Christ to Constantine*, trans. G. A. Williamson (London: The Folio Society, 2011), xi.

3. Ibid., xiii.

4. J. B. Bury, *History of the Later Roman Empire* (New York: Dover Publications, 1958), 2:392n2.

gans that he set before himself the ideal of an Empire which should be populated only by orthodox Christians. He determined "to close all the roads which lead to error and so place religion on the firm foundations of a single faith,"[5] and for this purpose he made orthodoxy a requisite condition of citizenship. He declared that he considered himself responsible for the welfare of his subjects, and therefore, above all, for securing the salvation of their souls; from this he deduced the necessity of intolerance towards heterodox opinions.[6]

One can see here many similarities with the later theory of the Catholic state.

Calendar The Greek verb καλέω means *to call*. The root survives in the Latin *Kalendae*, the Kalends, the name for the first day of each of the twelve months, the days on which the beginning of the new month was announced—as is still done in Muslim countries, at least in the case of Ramadan—by the firing of a cannon. When I was a child, the Sicilians of the town announced the beginning of the feast of their three saints Alfio, Filadelfo, and Cirino by firing a cannon. From *Kalendae*, the Latin noun *calendarium* and our *calendar* are derived. The ecclesiastical calendar is published at the beginning of the Roman Missal to indicate which saints are to be commemorated on which days. In former times a day would be identified by its saint; so, for example, June 13 would be called St. Anthony's Day. The Germans used to call September 8 *Mariä Geburt:*

> Mariä Geburt,
> Fliegen die Schwalben fort!
> Bleiben sie da,
> Ist der Winter nicht nah.
>
> On Mary's birthday
> The swallows fly away,
> But if those birds stay,
> The winter will come late, they say.

Camauro The camauro is the velvet winter cap of the pope, lined with ermine, traditionally worn together with the mozzetta of corresponding material. It was not used by Pius XII, Paul VI, or John Paul II. The earliest depiction of the camauro that I have seen is in Melozzo da Forli's painting of Sixtus IV appointing Platina librarian of the Vatican. Bacci says that the correct Latin for this item is *galericulum* or *little galero*. According to Nainfa:

5. [Note of Bury]: Procopius, *Aed.*, i, 1.
6. Bury, *History of the Later Roman Empire*, 2:360–61.

This cap has probably retained the primitive shape of the biretta. This would explain why the Pope does not make use of a biretta like other members of the
Prelacy and clergy.[7]

The etymology of this Italian word is difficult. Bacci offers none. The
authorities of Wikipedia are more daring and propose that it is derived
from the Greek καμηλαύχιον (not in Liddell and Scott) which is supposed
to mean a *camel-skin cap*, but I find this most precarious.

Camera (Apostolic) The Greek noun καμάρα is an *important room with
a vaulted or arched ceiling*; it came into Latin as *camara* and then *camera*.
The important room could be the bedroom or the treasury. The *Apostolic
Camera* was the treasury of the Church; after the collapse of the Papal
States, Pius X redefined its responsibility to be that of administering the
finances of the Holy See during the vacancy of the papacy. The *Maestro
di Camera* was the name of the dignitary in charge of the pope's private
household.

Cameriere The Italian noun *cameriere* is the corruption of the Latin *camerarius*, which means *someone attached to the camera*. He was an intimate
attendant in the private apartment of the pope. There have been many categories of such attendants, both lay and clerical, and these are discussed in
the following entries. The lay chamberlains were called *camerieri di spada
e cappa*—chamberlains of sword and cape—from the sixteenth-century
Spanish court dress that they wore. These were divided into five categories: *Camerieri Segreti di Spada e Cappa Partecipanti, Camerieri Segreti di
Spada e Cappa di Numero, Camerieri Segreti di Spada e Cappa Soprannumerari, Camerieri d'Onore di Spada e Cappa di Numero*, and *Camerieri
d'Onore di Spada e Cappa Soprannumerari*. Those called *segreti* belonged
to the *anticamera segreta*, whereas the ones denominated *d'onore* were
part of the *anticamera d'onore*. All these titles were abolished by Pope
Paul VI in his motu proprio *Pontificalis Domus* of March 28, 1968 (III 7
§7);[8] instead, he designated the title *Honorati Viri Summo Pontifici Astan-
tes—Gentiluomini di Sua Santità*—Gentlemen of His Holiness—for laymen serving in the pontifical household and specified that the positions

---

7. John A. Nainfa, *Costume of Prelates of the Catholic Church according to Roman Etiquette*
(Baltimore, Md.: John Murphy, 1909), 93.

8. *Pontificalis Domus* (motu proprio of Pope Paul VI, March 28, 1968). The text is available at
http://w2.vatican.va/content/paul-vi/la/motu_proprio/documents/hf_p-vi_motu-proprio_19680328
_pontificalis-domus.html.

were henceforth not hereditary (I 3 §4). Until 1968, the clerical chamberlains had been divided into four categories, *Camerieri Segreti Partecipanti*, *Camerieri Segreti Soprannumerari*, *Camerieri d'Onore di Abito Violetto*, and *Camerieri d'Onore extra Urbem*, of which classes only the prelates in the first actually performed services at the papal court. By the same document referred to above, Pope Paul abolished these titles, eliminating the last two ranks altogether (III 7 §3); the first two categories he preserved, but he assigned different titles to the incumbents. He specified the new titles whereby the various former Participating Privy Chamberlains were henceforth to be designated, and he changed the name of the *Camerieri Segreti Soprannumerari* to *Cappellani Sanctitatis Suae*—Chaplains of His Holiness. In modern Italian, *cameriere* has become the name of a restaurant waiter.

Camerieri d'Onore di Abito Violetto The Latin noun *honos* or *honor, honoris, m.*, became in Italian *onore*. The Latin verb *habeo, habere, habui, habitus* means *to have, to hold*, and from its fourth principal part came the noun *habitus, -us, m.*, meaning *condition, deportment, bearing, style of dress*. Horace spoke of the Roman way of dressing (*Romanus habitus*) in the *Satires* (2.7.54):

> Tu, cum proiectis insignibus, annulo equestri
> Romanoque habitu, prodis ex iudice Dama
> Turpis, odoratum caput obscurante lacerna:
> Non es quod similas?

> When you intriguing go, to cheat the fight,
> You drop the robe and ring, and doff the Knight,—
> With the coarse cowl your perfumed tresses hide,
> And lay the terrors of the judge aside,
> You feign the slave; and in good sooth 'tis plain,
> You are the very character you feign.[9]

The Latin noun *viola* is the name of the flower; from it were derived the Italian adjective *violetto* and English adjective *violet*. The title *Camerieri d'Onore di Abito Violetto* means *Honorary Chamberlains Who Wear a Purple Habit*. Like doctors *honoris causa*, they had no duties to perform; the title was in this case truly honorary. There were hundreds of them, and they lost their title when the pope who promoted them died.

9. *The Epodes, Satires, and Epistles of Horace*, trans. Rev. Francis Howes (London: William Pickering, 1845), 132.

Camerieri d'Onore di Spada e Cappa di Numero The Greek noun σπάθη means a *broad blade*, and related to it is the Anglo-Saxon noun *spadu*, whence are derived the Italian noun *spada* and the English noun *spade*. The Latin word for this object is the unrelated *ensis, ensis, m*. For the etymology of "*cappa*," see the entry **Cap**. The Greek verb νέμω means *to distribute*, and related to it is the Latin noun *numerus* meaning *number*. There were four to six noblemen at the papal court who were called by the title *Camerieri d'Onore di Spada e Cappa di Numero*; they were the full time (for so I translate *di numero*) chamberlains of honor, formally attired in sixteenth-century court dress with sword and cap. They were naturally of higher rank than the "extras," who were denominated *soprannumerari*. The honorary lay privy chamberlains were so called not because their position was merely honorific, which it was not, but because they were not involved in escorting people to *private* audiences, which was the responsibility of the *camerieri segreti*. Instead they served at the audiences to honored *groups* that the popes held in the *Sala del Trono* of the Sistine Palace of the Vatican in times long ago, before Paul VI built the great audience hall and before the modern practice arose of holding mass audiences in St. Peter's Square. The lay officials who facilitated such audiences to honored groups formed what was called the *anticamera d'onore*. The Englishman Hartwell de la Garde Grissell (1839–1907), the founder of the "Newman Clubs," belonged to this category of chamberlain and described in his memoirs the duties he had to perform.[10] As noted above, additional *camerieri d'onore di spada e cappa*, as many as 144, were appointed to assist the permanent four to six, often without the expectation that they would ever perform duties, unless perchance they happened to visit Rome for an extended stay and were willing to serve for a week; these chamberlains were called *supernumerary*.

Camerieri d'Onore di Spada e Cappa Soprannumerari From the Latin phrase *supra numerum*—above the official number—there was produced the Italian adjective *soprannumerario* (plural *soprannumerari*) of the same meaning. These extra chamberlains assisted the chamberlains *di numero* when their services were required and they were available; there were over a hundred of them.

Camerieri d'Onore extra Urbem The Latin noun *urbs, urbis, f.*, means *walled town or city*; it may also refer to Rome as the city *par excellence*.

10. Hartwell de la Garde Grissell, *Sede Vacante, Being a Diary Written during the Conclave of 1903, with Additional Notes on the Accession and Coronation of Pius X* (Oxford: James Parker, 1903).

The title *Camerieri d'Onore extra Urbem* means *Honorary Chamberlains outside of Rome*. These fellows originally attended the pope's semiprivate audiences when he travelled outside the Eternal City to their vicinity. There were dozens of them, and they lost their title when the pope who promoted them died. In modern times they formed the lowest grade of clerical chamberlains, below that of the *camerieri d'onore di abito violetto*, and, like them, they actually performed no services.

Camerieri Segreti di Spada e Cappa di Numero The Latin verb *secerno, secernere, secrevi, sectretus* means *to separate, part, sunder*, and its fourth principal part is the origin of the Italian adjective *segreto* and the English adjective *secret*. Those chamberlains were called privy—*segreti*—who served at the private audiences granted to heads of state and similarly august personages and at no others. There were four full-time (*di Numero*) lay officials of the papal court with this title. The American Francis Augustus MacNutt (1863–1927) held this rank; his memoirs are a reliable source of information on the subject.[11] There were hundreds more supernumerary *camerieri segreti di spada e cappa* who assisted the aforementioned four, but most of these were often not resident in Rome and not expected to perform any duties. The *camerieri segreti di spada e cappa di numero* would pair off with the members of the delegations of foreign heads of state who were making a state visit to the pope and accompany them through the event.

Camerieri Segreti di Spada e Cappa Partecipanti The Latin noun *pars, partis, f.* means a *part*, and the verb *capio, capere, cepi, captus* means *to take*. From their combination was formed the adjective *particeps* with the meaning *sharing*. From *particeps* proceeded the verb *participo, participare* with the meaning *to share with someone*; from the participle of this verb came the Italian participle *partecipante* (plural, *partecipanti*) and the English participle *participating*. Those dignitaries were called *participating* who long ago enjoyed the privilege of dining at the pope's table. There were five chief noble officials of the papal court called *camerieri segreti di spada e cappa partecipanti*. They were the *Maestro del Sacro Ospizio*, hereditary in the family of the Prince Ruspoli; the *Foriere Maggiore dei Sacri Palazzi Apostolici*, hereditary in the family of the Marquis Sacchetti; the *Cavallerizzo Maggiore di Sua Santità*, hereditary in the family of the

---

11. *A Papal Chamberlain: The Personal Chronicle of Francis Augustus MacNutt* (London: Longmans, Green, 1936).

Marquis Serlupi Crescenzi; the *Soprintendente Generale delle Poste*, hereditary in the family of the Prince Massimo; and the *Latore della Rosa d'Oro*, which position in modern times was held by the counts of the Soderini family, then by the Princes Luigi Barberini and Enrico Massimo Lancellotti, and finally by Count Giuseppe Dalla Torre del Tempio di Sanguinetto, editor of *L'Osservatore Romano*. See the entry for each title. There were good reasons why these positions were made hereditary. For example, in 1455 the first printing press in Rome was set up in properties owned by and adjacent to the palace of Prince Massimo, who became its patron.[12] The Palazzo Massimo alle Colonne is open to the public once a year, on March 16, the anniversary of the day in 1584 when the Principino Paolo Massimo was raised from the dead at the intercession of the spiritual director of the family, St. Filippo Neri. On March 16 in 2014, the author of these pages stood in line and was fortunate to be admitted.

Camerieri Segreti di Spada e Cappa Soprannumerari There were hundreds of these "extra" lay privy chamberlains, who were eligible to assist their full time colleagues the chamberlains *de numero* when needed. See the entry Camerieri Segreti di Spada e Cappa di Numero.

Camerieri Segreti Partecipanti These were the clerical privy chamberlains who formerly enjoyed the privilege of participating at the pope's table at meal time. The *camerieri segreti partecipanti* were appointed by the pope at the time of his elevation to the papacy. These were the pope's closest collaborators and attendants, who functioned under the supervision of the majordomo and *maestro di camera*. They included the privy almoner (now known as the almoner of His Holiness), the prefect of the apostolic palace (now the pope's vicar general for Vatican City), the secretary for briefs to princes, and the secretary for Latin letters. There were numbered among them, in addition, a handful of intimate assistants with archaic titles revelatory of their original function, such as *pincernae* (cup bearers), *nuntii* (messengers), and *vestiarii* (men in charge of the wardrobe); these last three classes were abolished by Pope Paul VI in 1968 (*Pontificalis Domus*, III 7 §5 and §11)[13] and replaced by a total of two prelates called

---

12. Augustus J. C. Hare, *Walks in Rome*, 17th ed. (New York: George Routledge & Sons, n.d.), 526–28.

13. *Pontificalis Domus* (motu proprio of Pope Paul VI, March 28, 1968). The text is available at http://w2.vatican.va/content/paul-vi/la/motu_proprio/documents/hf_p-vi_motu-proprio_19680328 _pontificalis-domus.html.

*prelati pontificali aulae addicti—prelati dell'anticamera pontificia—*prelates of the pontifical antechamber. One of the last of the old *camerieri segreti participanti*, Mario Nasalli Rocca di Corneliano, wrote his memoirs, which I translated into English and published privately by agreement with the Libreria Editrice Vaticana.[14]

Camerieri Segreti Soprannumerari The *camerieri segreti soprannumerari*, who were all clergymen, had the title but no duties, so the dignity was for them merely titular. These extra clerical privy chamberlains numbered in the thousands and, like the other clerical chamberlains who were not bishops, were denominated prelates *di mantellone* from their distinctive habit.

Camerlengo The Late Latin noun *camerarius* indicated the fellow in charge of a *camera*. *Camera* became in German *Kammer*, and a member of the Kammer was called a *Kämmerling*. This latter word then came back into Italian as *camerlengo*. The cardinal camerlengo was originally the treasurer of the papal government. Since the man in charge of money is the key fellow in any enterprise, the cardinal camerlengo became the main authority in the Church during the vacancy of the Holy See.

It may also be mentioned here that no such ceremony as striking the dead Pope's forehead with a silver hammer takes place, and that the exact method of calling aloud his name is not tied down to any determinate form, but is left to the discretion of the Cardinal Camerlengo.[15]

Cancelleria The Greek word καρκίνος means *crab*, and its relative *cancer* in Latin means the same thing. The diminutive *cancelli* means *little crabs*, whence it developed the meaning, *lattice work, grating*. Those officials in charge of maintaining public records worked behind such gratings and were hence denominated *cancellarii* or *chancellors*, that is, grating-people. The office where they worked was the *cancellaria* or chancery. *Cancelleria* is the Italian metamorphosis of *cancellaria*. In times before the explosion of big government, an official in charge of issuing official documents and maintaining records was an important personality who amassed other responsibilities, especially judicial and financial ones; in Germany

---

14. Mario Cardinal Nasalli Rocca di Corneliano, *Accanto ai Papi* (Vatican City: Libreria Editrice Vaticana, 1976).

15. Hartwell de la Garde Grissell, *Sede Vacante, Being a Diary Written during the Conclave of 1903, with Additional Notes on the Accession and Coronation of Pius X* (Oxford: James Parker, 1903), 2.

and Austria even today the head of government is called the chancellor (Kanzler). In England, before the time of Walpole, the chancellor was the King's chief adviser; Cardinal Wolsey, for example, was Lord High Chancellor. In the Roman Curia, the office of chancellor (and even that of vice chancellor) was of great importance; this importance grew less in the twentieth century, until the office was abolished by Pope Paul VI; the last incumbent was Luigi Cardinal Traglia. For many centuries, the head of the papal chancery was the vice chancellor, since the position of chancellor was theoretically held permanently by the archbishop of Cologne. The palace of the chancellor in Rome is the now extraterritorial Palazzo della Cancelleria on the Corso Vittorio Emanuele; it is the home of various offices of the Roman Curia. It is a Renaissance masterpiece, constructed during the pontificate of Sixtus IV by his nephew Cardinal Riario. It was built around the Church of San Lorenzo in Damaso, of which the chancellor of the Holy Roman Church was always cardinal priest.

Candle The Latin verb *candeo, candere, candui* means *to be shining white*, and from it is derived the noun *candela* with the meaning *candle, taper*. The original purpose of the candle was, naturally, to produce light; this is the reason why candles were put upon the altar and why, formerly, an attendant held a candle next to a bishop as he read. The use of short, fat candles instead of tall, slim ones has become common in liturgical ceremonies. The bizarre location of candles upon or around the altar is to be blamed on the need that is felt not to block the face of the priest celebrating toward the people. The requirement that altar candles be of beeswax is considered to be satisfied if the candle is 65 percent of that substance. Candles should be of bleached wax, except at Requiem Masses, the Tenebrae, and the Mass of the Pre-Sanctified, when they should be of unbleached wax.

Candlemas Day On February 2 is celebrated the commemoration of three events that took place on the same day, the Presentation of Christ in the Temple, the Purification of the Blessed Virgin Mary, and the meeting (ὑπάντησις) of the Child Jesus with Simeon and Anna. According to Fr. Thurston,[16] this day came to be called Candlemas Day because the third of these events was celebrated in Palestine forty days after the Epiphany with a procession of candles, and this ceremony was imported to the West in order to counteract the pagan Lupercalia, celebrated around the same

---

16. *Butler's Lives of the Saints, Complete Edition*, ed. Herbert J. Thurston, SJ, and Donald Attwater (Norwalk, Conn.: Easton Press, 1995), 1:232–36 (February 2).

time. The feast and its procession were then moved forward to forty days after Christmas in order to join the Feast of the Purification.

Canon The Greek noun κανών means a *straight rod*, and, metaphorically, a *rule* or *standard*. In the plural, κανόνες, it referred to those ancient authors who were the model of excellence for aspiring authors, and thus those books acknowledged by the Church as determining the Catholic religion were denominated the *canonical scriptures*. The canon of scripture promulgated by the Council of Laodicea in Phrygia (c. 363) does not include Tobias, Judith, Wisdom, Ecclesiasticus (Ben Sirach), and I and II Maccabees in the Old Testament; its list of the contents of the New Testament is the same as that of the Council of Trent twelve hundred years later, except that it leaves out the Apocalypse of St. John. The canon of the Council of Carthage of 397 is the same as that made by the Council of Trent in 1546.[17]

The clergy of certain cathedral and collegiate churches are denominated *canons*. The reason for this is that in former times, what we call *regular* clergy were called *canonical* clergy or simply canons. The cathedral canons indeed had a Rule:

The organization of the Church, moreover, received at the same time an efficient impulse by the institution of the order of canons, founded virtually in 762, the year in which St. Chrodegang, Bishop of Metz, promulgated the Rule for their government. This Rule of course entirely forbids all intercourse with women, and endeavors to suppress it by deposition. The lofty rank of St. Chrodegang, who was a cousin of Pepin-le-Bref, and the eminent piety which merited canonization, gave him wide influence, which doubtless assisted in extending the new institution, but it also had recommendations of its own which were sufficient to ensure success. By converting the cathedral clergy into monks, bound by implicit obedience towards their superiors, it brought no little increase of power to the bishops, and enabled them to exert new authority and influence. It is no wonder, therefore, that the order spread rapidly, and was adopted in most of the dioceses.[18]

In the singular, the word *canon* may also refer to that portion of the Mass containing the consecration, which, in the traditional Roman Can-

17. William Sanday, *Inspiration, Eight Lectures on the Early History and Origin of the Doctrine of Biblical Inspiration, Being the Bampton Lectures for 1893* (London: Longmans, Green, 1896), 60. Sanday says that the list is not original, but that whatever its origin it is mentioned in the Acta of the Quinisextine Council ("in Trullo") of 692.

18. Henry Charles Lea, *History of Sacerdotal Celibacy in the Christian Church* (n.p.: University Books, 1966), 106.

on, is that part from the prayer *Te igitur* through the prayer *Per ipsum et cum ipso et in ipso*. The current word for *Canon* is *Eucharistic Prayer*, an example of the modern tendency to do away with all Latin or Greek words that, it is imagined, cannot be appreciated by the common people. Additional Canons were added to the Missal as part of its revision after the Second Vatican Council, each with its own raison d'être, such as brevity, in the case of the second Canon. The English adjective *canonical* is macaronic, the Latin adjectival suffix *-al* having been superimposed upon the stem of the Greek adjective κανονικός, *belonging to a rule*.

Canonization The Ecclesiastical Latin verb *canonizo, canonizare, canonizavi, canonizatus* means *to enroll in the calendar of the saints*. This calendar came to be called a *canon*, since it was an infallible indicator of whether someone was a saint. Canonization is the formal recognition that a dead fellow is a saint. When this declaration is made, the name of the saint is enrolled in the list of those who have achieved that standard, or canon, of sanctity, and the saint is given a place in the calendar.

Canopy This word is the corruption of the Greek κωνωπεῖον, which is the same as κωνωπέων. See the entry **Conopaeum**.

Cantor The Latin verb *cano, canere, cecini, cantus* means *to sing*, and from its fourth principal part is derived the noun of agent *cantor, cantoris, m.*, with the meaning *one who sings*. The word is reserved for a singer who sings solo. If such a fellow is musically challenged, the result is destructive of the *mysterium tremendum et fascinans*. It is now a common practice for cantors to stand up before the congregation and, with theatrical gestures, to indicate when the assembled multitudes are supposed to respond.

Cap This word is derived, according to Weekley, from the Late Latin *cappa*, which he says is of obscure origin. He mentions that *cappa* may be a shortened form of *capitulare*, head dress. In its preamble to the entry *cap*, the *Oxford English Dictionary* has the following remark:

Isidore, a. 636, has (xix.xxi. 3, De ornamentis capitis feminarum) 'cappa ... quia capitis ornamentum est'; Diez cites *cappa* from a document of 660 and an ancient gloss '*cappa* mitra'. Med. L. used indiscriminately cappa and capa (the latter, however, much more frequently), and commonly in the sense of 'cloak, cope'; *Chron. Treverti* anno 1146, has 'caracalla (i.e., a long cloak with a hood) quam nunc capam vocamus'. The presumption is that the name was transferred from a woman's cap, hood, or head-covering, as Isidore used it, to the 'hood' of a cloak, and then to a cloak or 'cape' having such a hood, and thus to a priest's 'cope'. The sense 'head-covering, esp. hat' was at an early period in Romanic appropriated by the dim. *cappellum, -ellus*, in It. *cappello*, Sp. *capelo*, Pr. *capel*, OF. *capel, chapel*, F. *chapeau*, 'hat'. (The sense 'little or short cloak' was retained by the fem. dim. *cappella, capella*, It. *cappello*, Pr., Pg. *capella*, Sp. *capilla*, ONF. *capelle*, F. *chapelle*, until this received the curiously transferred sense CHAPEL, q.v.)

Nainfa derives *cappa* from the Latin *capio, capere, cepi, captus*, meaning *to take, to take in*, "quia *capit* totum hominem—because it covers the whole person,"[19] but this is wrong.

Capi d'Ordine This Italian phrase means *Heads of the Orders*. It refers to the troika of the senior cardinal bishop, the senior cardinal priest, and the senior cardinal deacon, who sometimes acted as representatives of the whole Sacred College. For example, in the conclave they approached the newly elected pontiff together with the camerlengo when the latter asked him:

Acceptasne electionem de te canonice factam in Summum Pontificem?[20]

Do you accept your election to the supreme pontificate?

Capitoline The Greek noun κεφαλή means *head*, and related to it is the Latin noun *caput* with the same meaning. From it was derived the name *Capitolium* for the chief temple of Rome, dedicated to Jupiter. The hill on which it stood came to be called the *Mons Capitolinus* or Capitoline Hill. Our noun *capitol* is derived from the name of this temple and hill. Even today, the Capitoline Hill is the headquarters of the Roman city government. The buildings of the Capitol have, since the beginning of the last century, been dwarfed by the Monument to Victor Emmanuel II; to see how the hill looked before the construction of that edifice, consult the collection of photographs published by the Thorvaldsen Museum.[21] The Capitoline collection of antiquities became a public museum under Clement XII (1730–1740). The main building of Catholic interest on the Capitoline Hill is the Basilica of Santa Maria in Araceli (see the entry **Santo Bambino**).

19. John A. Nainfa, *Costume of Prelates of the Catholic Church according to Roman Etiquette* (Baltimore, Md.: John Murphy, 1909), 74.

20. Hartwell de la Garde Grissell, *Sede Vacante, Being a Diary Written during the Conclave of 1903, with Additional Notes on the Accession and Coronation of Pius X* (Oxford, James Parker, 1903), 49.

21. *Rome in Early Photographs, The Age of Pius IX, Photographs 1846–1878 from Roman and Danish Collections*, trans. Ann Thornton (Copenhagen: The Thorvaldsen Museum, 1977), 169, 172.

Cappa Magna This great cape (for that is what the phrase means in Latin) was worn by bishops, archbishops, and cardinals on occasions of particular solemnity (see the entry **Cap**). According to McCloud, the *cappa magna* developed from the cope and achieved its separate existence as an item of clothing in the fifteenth century.[22] The *cappa magna* of the cardinals and nuntios alone was of watered silk, with the lining of the hood being ermine in winter (from Vigil of All Saints to Holy Saturday) and silk in summer. Often the ermine would be decorated with the tails of the animals, a practice that would nowadays cause an outcry. The train of the *cappa magna* was fifteen meters long, until the motu proprio *Valde Solliciti* of Pius XII (1952), when it was reduced to seven meters. The hood was functional, and, when in use, could be covered by the *galero* or red hat. The use of the *cappa magna* was forbidden in Rome and became optional elsewhere as a result of the instruction of the Secretariat of State *Ut Sive Sollicite* dated March 31, 1969:

> Magna cappa sine pelle mustelina, scilicet sine hermellino, non amplius praescribitur, eademque tantum extra Urbem, in sollemnissimis quidem festivitatibus, adhiberi poterit.[23]

The cappa magna, without weasel fur, that is, without ermine, is no longer required and may only be worn outside of Rome, and then only on the most solemn feasts.

As a practical result, the garment has almost entirely disappeared, and when used, invites the charge of ostentation from critics who do not appreciate the beauty of it. The winter *cappa magna*, which has an ermine cape at the top, was expressly abolished by Pope Paul VI, but his decree has not prevented the Latin patriarch of Jerusalem from using it.

Capuchin The Italian noun *cappuccio* means a *big hood* (*cappa*), and the reformed Franciscans of the sixteenth century were called *cappuccini* from this distinctive article of their clothing. The Capuchins used to maintain untrimmed bushy beards, but this is now optional.

Carabinieri The *carabinieri* are the Italian police, and also the police of the Vatican City State. Originally, they were mounted troops who carried

---

22. Henry J. McCloud, *Clerical Dress and Insignia of the Roman Catholic Church* (Milwaukee, Wis.: Bruce Publishing, 1948), 104.

23. *Ut Sive Sollicite* (instruction of the Secretariat of State, March 31, 1969), *Acta Apostolicae Sedis* 61, no. 5 (1969), 334–40, A 12. The text is also available at www.shetlersites.com/clericaldress/utsivesollicite.html.

a *carbine*, a short-barreled rifle. Weekley declares the etymology of *carbine* to be unknown.

Cardinal The Greek verb κραδαίνω means *to swing*, and the associated Latin noun *cardo, -inis, m.*, means a *hinge*. From this noun is formed the adjective *cardinalis, -e*, which means *important* and was originally applied to the chief priest (*presbyter cardinalis*) of each of the major parish churches of Rome, at the time when the increase of the number of clergy caused these churches to have more than one priest each to serve them. Similarly, the main thoroughfare of Jerusalem in the time of the Roman occupation was called the *cardo*. From the color of the cardinal's robes is derived the name of the red bird.

In the last sixty years, the number of cardinals has been multiplied into the hundreds; such an increase is an effective way of debasing the honor. The inflation began with John XXIII, who made appointments that exceeded the number seventy set by Sixtus V, beginning on December 15, 1958, when he increased the number of cardinals to seventy-five. As I write these lines, there are two hundred and twenty-three cardinals, an unprecedented inflation. In 1461, when Pius II created seven cardinals and raised the number of the Church's senate to thirty-three, Cardinal Tebaldo protested against the intolerable cheapening of that honor, that the day would come when the dignity would go to destruction and three hundred cardinals be appointed.[24] I confidently predict that many readers of this book will live to the day when this prophecy will be fulfilled. Paul VI deprived those over eighty of the vote in the conclave, so for them the dignity is mere show. Perhaps there had been some instances in the 1958 and 1963 conclaves of senile cardinals complicating the proceedings. Inconsistent with the rule *octogenarii de ponte* is the fact that the popes themselves do not retire at eighty years of age. Benedict XVI, the first pope to abdicate since Celestine V, did so two months short of his eighty-sixth birthday.

Cardinale Nipote This is an Italian phrase meaning *Cardinal Nephew*, *nipote* being the corruption of the Latin noun *nepos, nepōtis, m.*, meaning *grandson, nephew*. As the popes required trustworthy assistants intimately associated with their person, there arose the precaution of a pope's ap-

---

24. *The Commentaries of Pius II*, trans. Florence Alden Gragg, with historical introduction and notes by Leona C. Gabel (Northampton, Mass.: Smith College Studies in History, 1951), vol. 35 (Books VI–IX), book 7, p. 503.

pointing one or two relatives to the cardinalate shortly after his accession to the papal throne. A competent nephew was selected to run the papal government, and his position was similar to what we now call the secretary of state. This custom became fixed by the fifteenth century and died out at the end of the eighteenth century.

Carmelite The Hebrew noun כרם means *vineyard*, and the related noun כרמל means *garden-land*. (Hebrew grammarians call the added letter ל an *afformative*.) The latter word became the name of the promontory and mountain in the Holy Land, Mt. Carmel. The word *carmine* in the Italian title of the Virgin, *la Madonna del Carmine*, and the Spanish name *Carmen* are simply corruptions of *Carmelo*; they are not related to the Latin noun *carmen*, song.

Cartesian The French name *Des Cartes* or Descartes became in Latin *Cartesius*, and that is the way the great philosopher was known to the learned world in his lifetime and thereafter. The corresponding adjective is *cartesianus*, which means *pertaining to Descartes*. In order to avoid error, Descartes adopted an attitude of skepticism in all investigations. His proof of the existence of God is unusual in that it makes no use of the argument from design in nature, because he thought that he had first to prove that the evidence of the senses was not a hallucination, and this he could accomplish only by proving a theorem that God existed, and then a corollary, that he would not deceive us. The Cartesian *a priori* approach to the proof of the existence of God is close to the intuitive method proposed by William George Ward (1812–1882), which depends on purely mental reasoning rather than on experimental reasoning.

Mental phenomena, if studied carefully and with prolonged attention, show the genuineness of this alleged intuition (*viz.*, the existence of a Superior Being).[25]

"Mind", he would say, "the two arguments to urge, for fifty years to come, are the arguments from conscience and from the persistence, in this weak and wayward world, of conscience's chief exponent and fullest realization, the Catholic Church."[26]

The cognizance of God

25. Wilfrid Ward, *William George Ward and the Oxford Movement* (London: Macmillan, 1889), 348.
26. Ibid., 368–69.

arises in the mind spontaneously, universally, irresistibly. This seems to me among the most important of theistic facts.[27]

For myself, I have always held strongly that the perception of right and wrong is the *strongest of all grounds* for our belief in God's existence.[28]

The surname Descartes was originally Des Quartes or Des Quartis.[29]

Carthusian *Cartusia* is the Latin name of a place in Gaul originally called *Catorissium*, an appellation perhaps related to the name of the local mountains, *Catursiani montes*.[30] The French now call this place *Chartreuse*. It is the site of the great establishment of St. Bruno in 1084. The hermits are called *Cartusiani* or *Carthusians*. Their establishments are called in English *charter houses*. Their green liqueur, the best in the world, is called *Chartreuse*.

Cassock Weekley, with some hesitation, derives this word from *Cossack*, as, for example, *cravat* comes from *Croatian* and *dalmatic* from *Dalmatian*. It is the clerical coat, of which there are two styles: the Roman, with buttons down the front, and the Jesuit, with hooks and sash. Prelates have two cassocks, a black one for ordinary use and a purple (bishops) or scarlet (cardinals) one for use in choir; the latter formerly had a train. The cassock is called in Latin the *vestis talaris*, or *dress reaching to the heels*, since *talus, -i, m.*, is the Latin noun meaning *ankle, heel*, or *die*; dies were originally made from the ankle bones of the hind feet of certain animals. An easy experiment will verify that the number of buttons is not universally fixed at thirty-three or any other number.

Catacombs The Latin verb *cubo, cubare* means *to lie down, to recline*. Under the influence of the Latin verb, the Greek expression κατὰ κύμβας came to mean *in the neighborhood of the underground cemeteries where the Christian dead were buried*. Gregorovius prefers this etymology,[31] and second best in his opinion is a derivation from the Greek noun κύμβος meaning *depth* or *excavation*, in which case κατὰ κύμβους would mean *in the vicinity of the excavations*. Also to be noted is the fact that the Greek noun κύμβη means a *hollow vessel*, whether a cup, bowl, or boat. On the

---

27. Ibid., 413.
28. Ibid., 453.
29. Elizabeth S. Haldane, *Descartes: His Life and Times* (London: John Murray, 1905), 2.
30. *Oxford English Dictionary*, compact ed., s.v. "Carthusian."
31. Ferdinand Gregorovius, *History of the City of Rome in the Middle Ages*, trans. Mrs. Gustavus W. Hamilton (London: G. Bell & Sons, 1909), 1:31n1.

other hand, Weekley says that *catacomb* is probably the corruption of a proper name associated with the area where the Christian burials took place, namely, in the vicinity of the present Basilica of St. Sebastian on the Via Appia Antica.

Catechism The Greek noun ἠχή means *sound*, and the related transitive verb ἠχέω means *to sound*. Related to it is the noun ἡ ἠχώ, *the reverberated sound, the echo*. The compound verb κατηχέω means *to echo down, to resound, to sound a thing in one's ears, to teach by word of mouth*, and became used especially of the elements of religion. The related adjective κατηχής means *resounding*, and from it was derived the noun κατήχησις, *oral instruction*. From this noun evolved the verb κατηχίζω, *to instruct orally*, a verb so late that it is not to be found in Liddell and Scott. Similarly late is the noun κατηχισμός with the meaning *a book containing such instruction*, which was transliterated into the Latin *catechismus*. The form of the old catechisms, wherein the obvious questions were listed and followed by the official answers, has not been superseded in cogency by the methods adopted in modern times. Lord Chesterfield wrote to his son that he should always refer to the latest edition of any book, since that volume would contain all the corrections and improvements of the author over the first edition. It is not so with catechisms. In the case of catechisms, it is best to refer to the 1933 catechism of Cardinal Gasparri for the traditional interpretation of doctrine.[32]

Catechumen This word is the transliteration of the stem of the Greek passive participle κατηχούμενος of the verb κατηχίζω mentioned in the previous entry; it means *someone being instructed*.

For, indeed, adult converts were not admitted without being proved in the Catechumenate, an institution which, towards the end of the 2nd century, we hear of almost everywhere. Converts who embraced Christianity, after attaining years of discretion, were not allowed to join the general body of the faithful at once. Initiation was only granted at the end of a prescribed time, during which they learnt what was the real meaning of Christianity and its doctrines, and of the many obligations they proposed to take upon themselves. And not only did they learn, but they also began to live the Christian life. Thus they tried their strength, and the Church kept her eye upon them, and was able to judge if their perseverance might reasonably be reckoned on. The catechumens were already considered as

---

32. *Catechismus catholicus, cura et studio Petri Cardinalis Gasparri concinnatus*, 15th ed. (Vatican City: Typis Polyglottis Vaticanis, 1933).

Christians; they shared the name, and in time of persecution, they shared also the risks of the faithful. In the Christian assemblies they might take part in the singing, the reading of the Scriptures, and in certain of the prayers; but not in the celebration of the Mystery of the Eucharist and several other rites, such as initiation and ordination.[33]

Categories The Greek verb ἀγείρω means *to collect, to gather*, and from it was derived the noun ἀγορά with the meaning *assembly*. From this noun there proceeded the verb ἀγορεύω meaning *to address an assembly*. The addition of the preposition κατά produced the compound verb καταγορεύω, *to accuse before the assembly*; the accuser was the κατηγορός, and the accusation was the κατηγορία. In due course this latter noun acquired the additional grammatical meaning of *predication*. By means of his ten κατηγορίαι (*categories*), Aristotle attempted to explain in how many senses the copula is used when we say, "X is [a] Y." The ten categories are listed below; categories 2 through 10 are called *accidents*:

GREEK	(meaning)	LATIN	ENGLISH
1. οὐσία	(being)	*substantia*	substance
2. πόσον	(how much?)	*quantum*	quantity
3. ποῖον	(how?)	*quale*	quality
4. πρὸς τί	(in what way?)	*relatio*	relation
5. ποῦ	(where?)	*locus*	place
6. πότε	(when?)	*tempus*	time
7. κεῖσθαι	(to lie)	*situs*	position
8. ἔχειν	(to have)	*habitus*	possession
9. ποιεῖν	(to do)	*actus*	activity
10. πάσχειν	(to have done to one)	*passio*	passivity

The Mediaeval Latin authors translated the Greek noun κατηγορία by *praedicamentum*, whence we get our noun *predicate*.

Cathars The Greek adjective καθαρός (plural καθαροί) means *clean*. It was a term of congratulation applied to themselves by certain Manichees to distinguish themselves from the mass of people soiled by ignorance. See the entry **Albigenses**.

Cathedral The Greek verb ἕζομαι means *to sit*, and the addition of the preposition κατά (*down*) produces the compound verb καθέζομαι meaning *to sit down*. The derived nouns ἕδρα and καθέδρα both mean *seat*, the

---

33. Louis Duchesne, *Early History of the Christian Church from Its Foundation to the End of the Third Century* (London: John Murray, 1914), 366.

object upon which one sits or sits down. The latter noun was taken over into Latin as *cathedra* and was used of the bishop's throne in the cathedral. From *cathedra* there developed the adjective *cathedralis* with the meaning *pertaining to the cathedra*, and thence the English noun *cathedral*, the main church of the diocese wherein is the bishop's throne.

Cathedra Petri   This Latin phrase means the *seat of Peter*. The wooden chair encased by Bernini in his *Cathedra Petri* in the apse of St. Peter's Basilica was made for Charles the Bald and donated by him to Pope John VIII in 875 on the occasion of his coronation as Holy Roman Emperor.[34] Gregorovius, who saw the chair in June of 1867, had the following to say about this relic:

Bishop Damasus placed in the Baptistery the chair which tradition, from the second century onwards, had alleged to be the actual chair and seat of Peter. This remarkable seat, the most ancient throne in the world, first occupied by simple unpretending bishops, then by ambitious Popes ruling nations and peoples, still survives. In the seventeenth century, Alexander VII had it inclosed within a bronze chair which, bearing the metal images of the Four Doctors of the Church, stands in the tribunal of the cathedral. On the feast of the Apostle in 1867 the chair was uncovered for the first time for two hundred years, and exposed to public view in a chapel. It is in reality an ancient sedan chair (*sella gestatoria*), to the now worm-eaten oak of which additions have from time to time been made in acacia wood. The front is decorated with ivory bands, on which fighting animals, centaurs and men are represented in diminutive arabesque figures; it also contains a row of ivory panels engraved with the labors of Hercules, an appropriate symbol for the Herculean work of the early Papacy in the history of the world. These panels did not originally belong to the chair, but were evidently affixed as ornaments in later times, occasionally with such carelessness that some are even fastened on upside down. Beyond doubt, this celebrated chair, if not belonging to apostolic times, is of very great antiquity, though the suggestion that it may be the *sella curulis* of the Senator Pudens is altogether untrustworthy.[35]

The Abbé Duchesne pointed out that this chair, enshrined by Bernini in the apse of St. Peter's Basilica, is not mentioned as one of the basilica's relics until the thirteenth century. During the reign of Pope Paul VI, it was taken out of the shrine and examined by experts, who reported that

34. Michele Maccarrone, "The Wooden Cathedra," in *The Vatican, Spirit and Art of Christian Rome*, by the Metropolitan Museum of Art, New York (New York: Henry N. Abrams, 1982), 88–89. This two-page contribution has a full-page color photograph of the wooden chair.

35. Ferdinand Gregorovius, *History of the City of Rome in the Middle Ages*, trans. Mrs. Gustavus W. Hamilton (London: G. Bell & Sons, 1909), 1:98.

in their opinion it was no older than the sixth century. The window of the Holy Ghost above the chair is meant to be viewed in the evening, when the sun shines through it (about 5 P.M. in March).

Catholic The Greek phrase κατὰ ὅλην τὴν οἰκουμένην γῆν means *throughout the whole inhabited earth*. From the first two words of this phrase developed the adjective καθολικός, which was applied to the Church and meant *universal*. Aristotle had previously used the word in the expression καθολικὸς λόγος with the meaning a *universal statement*.[36] The Latin adjective *catholicus* is merely the transliteration of the Greek word. The word appears in the Nicene Creed, and therefore many non-Catholic Christians who accept that statement call themselves *catholic* (e.g., Orthodox, Anglicans, Lutherans, and even some Pentecostals), but in common usage the word is applied only to those who accept the authority of the Roman pontiff. In England, however, it was for a long time offensive to refer to such people otherwise than *Roman* Catholics. It is one of the four defining marks of the Church: unity (*unam*), sanctity (*sanctam*), universality (*catholicam*), and apostolicity (*apostolicam*). The name *Catholic Church* was first used by St. Ignatius of Antioch in his *Letter to the Smyrnaeans* §8 (written about the year 107).

ὅπου ἂν φανῇ ὁ ἐπίσκοπος, ἐκεῖ τὸ πλῆθος ἤτω, ὥσπερ ὅπου ἂν ᾖ Ἰησοῦς Χριστός, ἐκεῖ ἡ καθολικὴ ἐκκλησία

Wherever the Bishop is, there let the people be, just as wherever Jesus Christ is, there is the Catholic Church.

The name *Old Catholics* was given to those people who, in the years after 1870, rejected the doctrine of papal infallibility. The most famous Old Catholic was Dr. Döllinger (1799–1890), who said:

The time is coming when Latin will cease to be the language of Catholicism, and with the cessation of Latin much of the power of Rome will go.[37]

Catholic Epistles For the etymologies of these words, see the individual entries. The Epistles of St. Paul are addressed to specific communities of believers—the Romans, Corinthians, Galatians, Ephesians, Philippians, Colossians and Thessalonians—or to specific individuals—Timothy,

---

36. *De Plantis* 2.6, cited by Bishop Lightfoot in *The Apostolic Fathers: Clement, Ignatius, Polycarp* 2nd ed. (London: Macmillan, 1889), part 2, vol. 2, 310n2.

37. Ignaz von Döllinger, in *Alfred Plummer, Conversations with Dr. Döllinger, 1870–1890*, ed. Robrecht Boudens (Leuven: Leuven University Press, 1985), 15.

Titus, and Philemon. The Letters of James, Peter, 1 John, and Jude, however, are addressed, it appears, to larger groups of believers, and for this reason are called the *Catholic* Epistles. (The Second Letter of John is addressed to an unnamed *elect lady*, and 3 John to *Dearest Gaius*; nevertheless these two are included among the Catholic Epistles.)

Catholicos This was the title that the Greeks used when speaking of the supreme pontiff of the Armenians, the first of whom was Gregory the Illuminator (third century).[38]

Caudatarius This word is the Ecclesiastical Latin noun for *train-bearer*, derived from *cauda, -ae, f.*, tail. Their services are required by prelates who wear the *cappa magna*, one train-bearer per prelate. According to Nainfa, the train-bearers of the cardinals at Rome formerly formed a fraternity, founded by Paul III in 1538, whose prefect was the train-bearer of the pope. They could be seen seated on long benches in front of the seats of the cardinals on occasions when those prelates were summoned to appear in the *cappa magna*. They would spread the *cappa* and pick it up as the occasion required. He says that they had charge of the Church of San Salvatore in Campo, near the Ghetto.[39] Naturally, this office is now extinct.

Cavallerizzo Maggiore di Sua Santità The Greek noun καβάλλης means *nag*, a small pack horse, and related to it is the Latin word *caballus* with the same meaning. The Latin noun came into Italian as *cavallo* and became the common name for *horse*, even one of the highest dignity.

The Italian phrase *Cavallerizzo Maggiore di Sua Santità* means *Equerry-in-Chief of His Holiness*. It *was* a position (for it was abolished by Pope Paul VI in the *motu proprio Pontificalis Domus* of 1968, III 7 §3)[40] hereditary in the noble family of the Marquesses Serlupi Crescenzi; the Marchese was in charge of the upkeep of the papal carriages and stables. Thus Bacci's translation of this phrase was *Praefectus Stabuli Pontificis Maximi*. Whoever is now in charge of the pope's fleet of automobiles (or at least of the papal Ford Focus) would be the corresponding contemporary official.

---

38. Louis Duchesne, *Early History of the Christian Church from Its Foundation to the End of the Fifth Century*, vol. 3 (London: John Murray, 1924), 370–71.

39. John A. Nainfa, *Costume of Prelates of the Catholic Church according to Roman Etiquette* (Baltimore, Md.: John Murphy, 1909), 77.

40. *Pontificalis Domus* (motu proprio of Pope Paul VI, March 28, 1968). The text is available at http://w2.vatican.va/content/paul-vi/la/motu_proprio/documents/hf_p-vi_motu-proprio_19680328_pontificalis-domus.html.

The cavallerizzo maggiore was one of the five great nobles denominated *camerieri segreti di spada e cappa partecipanti*. He always marched in front of the sedia gestatoria on the left in all solemn processions.

Celibate The Latin adjective *caelebs, caelibis* means *unmarried*. It is likely that the priests and Levites of the Children of Israel abstained from sexual contact with their wives during their time of service in the Temple, since such contact would have made them ritually unclean and therefore unsuitable for activities in the sanctuary.[41] Furthermore, celibacy was enjoined upon certain priests and women of the nations, like the Vestal Virgins of Rome. There seems to have developed a widespread opinion that there is something dirty about sexual activity, which appears to be at odds with the spiritual element in man. It is recorded in Luke 14:26 that Jesus said:

Εἴ τις ἔρχεται πρός με καὶ οὐ μισεῖ τὸν πατέρα ἑαυτοῦ καὶ τὴν μητέρα καὶ τὴν γυναῖκα καὶ τὰ τέκνα καὶ τοὺς ἀδελφοὺς καὶ τὰς ἀδελφάς, ἔτι τε καὶ τὴν ψυχὴν ἑαυτοῦ, οὐ δύναται εἶναί μου μαθητής.

Si quis venit ad me, et non odit patrem suum, et matrem, et uxorem, et filios, et fratres, et sorores, adhuc autem et animam suam, non potest meus esse discipulus.

If any man come to me, and hate not his father, and mother, and wife, and children, and brethren, and sisters, yea, and his own life also, he cannot be my disciple. (Authorized Version)

St. Paul considered celibacy preferable to the married state, as is clear from 1 Corinthians 7:8–9:

Λέγω δὲ τοῖς ἀγάμοις καὶ ταῖς χήραις, καλὸν αὐτοῖς ἐὰν μείνωσιν ὡς κἀγώ· εἰ δὲ οὐκ ἐγκρατεύονται, γαμησάτωσαν, κρεῖττον γάρ ἐστιν γαμεῖν ἢ πυροῦσθαι.

Dico autem non nuptis, et viduis: bonum est illis si sic permaneant, sicut et ego. Quod si non se continent, nubant. Melius est enim nubere, quam uri.

I say therefore to the unmarried and widows, It is good for them if they abide even as I. But if they cannot contain, let them marry: for it is better to marry than to burn. (Authorized Version)

His enthusiasm for this state was no doubt enforced by the common opinion that the end of the world was nigh (1 Corinthians 7:29).

41. Leviticus 15:18.

Τοῦτο δέ φημι, ἀδελφοί, ὁ καιρὸς συνεσταλμένος ἐστίν· τὸ λοιπὸν ἵνα καὶ οἱ ἔχοντες γυναῖκας ὡς μὴ ἔχοντες ὦσιν.

Hoc itaque dico, fratres, tempus breviatum est; reliquum est, ut et qui habent uxores, tamquam non habentes sint.

But this I say, brethren, the time is short; it remaineth, that both they that have wives be as though they had none ... (Authorized Version)

It is clear that married men became bishops, priests, and deacons in Apostolic times (1 Timothy 3:2). Whether in those times unmarried bishops, priests, or deacons could take a wife is unclear.

The chief authority on the history of clerical celibacy in the Catholic Church was the Quaker Henry Charles Lea (1825–1909) of Philadelphia, whose exhaustive *History of Sacerdotal Celibacy in the Christian Church* is not the less useful because its author disapproved of the obligation (for he considered clerical celibacy to be the chief cause of the evils which beset the Catholic clergy); his private library of manuscripts and books on this and related subjects is to be found on the sixth floor of the Van Pelt Library of the University of Pennsylvania. His antagonistic attitude requires, however, that his volume be used with caution.

In the early part of the third century Hippolytus, Bishop of Portus, in his enumeration of the evil ways of Pope Calixtus, taxes the pontiff with admitting to the priesthood men who had been married twice, and even thrice, and with permitting priests to marry while in orders.[42]

We thus reach the state of ecclesiastical discipline at the close of the third century, as authoritatively set forth in the Apostolic Constitutions and Canons— bishops and priests allowed to retain the wives whom they may have had before ordination, but not to marry in orders; the lower grades, deacons, subdeacons, etc., allowed to marry after entering the Church; but all were to be husbands of but one wife, who must be neither a widow, a divorced woman, nor a concubine.[43]

By the canons of Ancyra [314] we learn that marriage in orders was still permitted, as far as the diaconate, provided the postulate at the time of ordination declared his desire to enjoy the privilege and asserted his inability to remain single.[44]

By the Council of Neo-Caesarea [circa 315] it was provided that a priest marrying in orders should be deposed ...[45]

---

42. Henry Charles Lea, *History of Sacerdotal Celibacy in the Christian Church* (n.p.: University Books, 1966), 18–19.

43. Ibid., 20.

44. Ibid., 30.

45. Ibid., 31.

During the reigns of Pope Damasus (366–384) and his successor Pope Siricius (384–399), the Church of Rome demanded continence from those in the orders of deacon, priest, or bishop in the Western Church; married clergy of those ranks were to have no relations with their wives. A letter of Pope Siricius to the Archbishop of Tarragona to this effect "was the first definitive canon, prescribing and enforcing sacerdotal celibacy, exhibited by the records of the Church".[46] Church Councils held in Carthage in 390 and 401 required married priests to separate from their wives.[47] An edict of the emperor Honorius in the year 420 decreed that such a separation was not necessary for those married before their ordination to the diaconate.[48] Speaking of Gregory VII (1073–1085), Lea wrote:

Early in Lent of the next year (March 1074) he held his first synod, which adopted a canon prohibiting sacerdotal marriage, ordering that no one in future should be admitted to orders without a vow of celibacy, and renewing the legislation of Nicholas II, which commanded the people not to attend the ministrations of those whose lives were a violation of the rule. There was nothing in the terms of this more severe than what had been decreed in innumerable previous councils—indeed, it was by no means as threatening as many decretals of recent date; but Gregory was resolved that it should not remain, like them, a mere protest, and he took immediate measures to have it enforced wherever the authority of Rome extended.[49]

Two worldly motives suggested by Lea to account for the requirement of clerical celibacy in the Church after the legalization of Christianity by Constantine were (1) to discourage candidates for the priesthood who were motivated by ambition to acquire prestige, power, and wealth, and (2) to prevent ecclesiastical property from being turned over to the children of priests and bishops.[50] The ninth and tenth canons of the twenty-fourth session of the Council of Trent (November 11, 1563) had the following to say about the subject:

Canon 9. Si quis dixerit, Clericos in sacris ordinibus constitutos, vel regulares, castitatem solemniter professos, posse Matrimonium contrahare, contractumque validum esse, non obstante lege Ecclesiastica vel voto, et oppositum nil aliud esse, quam damnare Matrimonium, posseque omnes contrahere matrimonium, qui non sentiunt se castitatis, etiamsi eam voverint, habere donum, Anathema Sit:

46. Ibid., 45.
47. Ibid., 52.
48. Ibid., 55.
49. Ibid., 185.
50. Ibid., 42–43.

cum Deus id recte petentibus non deneget, nec patiatur nos supra id, quod possumus, tentari.

Canon 10. Si quis dixerit, statum conjugalem anteponendum esse statui virginitatis vel coelibatus, et non esse melius ac beatius manere in virginitate aut coelibatu, quam jungi matrimonio; Anathema Sit.[51]

Canon 9. If anyone should say that clerics in holy orders, or friars who have solemnly taken a vow of chastity, can contract a marriage, or, if they have already married, that the marriage is valid regardless of canon law or their vow, and that to deny this is equivalent to condemning marriage, and that anyone can get married who does not feel that he has the gift of chastity (even if he has taken such a vow), let him be anathema. For God does not turn away those who properly ask for this gift, nor does He allow us to be tempted beyond what we can bear.

Canon 10. If anyone should say that the married state is superior to that of virginity or celibacy, and that it is not better and more blessed to remain a virgin or celibate than to get married, let him be anathema.

About these canons, Lea says:

The dissolution of such marriages, as we have seen, was not suggested until the middle of the twelfth century, and the decision of the council thus condemned as heretics the whole body of the Church during three-quarters of its previous existence.[52]

It is currently debated by learned authorities whether married permanent deacons of the Latin Rite should be celibate.

We have seen that by the early fourth century the tradition in the Western Church was that no unmarried bishop, priest, or deacon could take a wife, and any candidate for the episcopacy, priesthood, or diaconate had to be unmarried, or, if married, had to live with his wife henceforth as brother and sister or even separate from her entirely. In the Eastern Church, however, married men were regularly raised to the rank of priest or deacon without having to commit to future celibacy; married men might also become bishops without surrendering conjugal relations, but this possibility died out by the early fifth century. In the East it was also possible early on for unmarried candidates for the diaconate (though not for the priesthood or episcopacy) to reserve the right to marry after ordination if their bishop approved, but this option was certainly no more after the Council in Trullo (692).[53]

51. Denzinger, *Enchiridion Symbolorum et Definitionum*, 7th ed. (Würzburg, V. J. Stahel, 1895), §855, §856.

52. Lea, *History of Sacerdotal Celibacy*, 465.

53. Carl Joseph von Hefele, *Conciliengeschichte, Nach den Quellen bearbeitet*, 2nd ed. (Freiburg im Breisgau: Herder, 1873), 1:431–35.

It is sometimes claimed that the third canon of the First Council of Nicaea prohibited bishops, priests, and deacons from having a wife, but Hefele denies this interpretation as contrary both to the meaning of the key word συνείσακτον and to the whole tradition of Greek Christianity.[54]

Ἀπηγόρευσεν καθόλου ἡ μεγάλη σύνοδος, μήτε ἐπισκόπῳ μήτε πρεσβυτέρῳ μήτε διακόνῳ μήτε ὅλως τινὶ τῶν ἐν κλήρῳ ἐξεῖναι συνείσακτον ἔχειν, πλὴν εἰ μὴ ἄρα μητέρα, ἢ ἀδελφὴν, ἢ θείαν, ἢ ἃ μόνα πρόσωπα πᾶσαν ὑποψίαν διαπέθευγε.

The General Council absolutely prohibits any bishop, priest, or deacon, or any other clergyman whomsoever, from having an additional woman [συνείσακτον] living with him other than his mother, sister, aunt, or other such person who is beyond suspicion.

The current discipline with regard to permanent deacons in the Western Church is that an unmarried man so ordained must henceforth be celibate, but a married man may continue to live with his wife in the usual way, though he must be celibate if he becomes a widower. This discipline is thus a break with the tradition of the Western Church, but in conformity with that of the Eastern Church.

Cenobite See **Coenobite**.

Censor Deputatus The Latin verb *censeo, censere, censui, census* means *to appraise, to estimate*, and the derived noun *censor, censoris, m.*, means a *magistrate*, particularly a severe one, like those who had anything to do with the revenue, who were proverbially harsh. The verb *puto, putare, putavi, putatus* means *to clear up, settle, consider*, and the addition of the preposition *de* (from) produced the compound verb *depŭto, depŭtare, depŭtatvi, depŭtatus* meaning *to clean up by cutting off, to prune, to detach for special service*. The *censor deputatus* is a person appointed by a diocesan bishop to read a manuscript and determine if it contains any heresy. If he finds none, the censor issues the decree *nihil obstat*—there is nothing to prevent [*sc.* publication]. The bishop may then proceed to issue an *imprimatur*.

Cerecloth The Latin noun *cera* means *wax*, and the Anglo-Saxon noun *clāth* means *garment*, like the German *Kleid*. A *cerecloth* is a waxed cloth that was used to cover the consecrated stone altar, which contained holy relics, before the three required linen cloths were applied. It protected the altar from desecration. The cerecloth is called in Latin *chrismale*.

54. Ibid., 379–81.

– C –

Ceremony The Latin noun *caerimonia, -ae, f.,* means *sacred work, divine rite.* The complicated rituals that developed over the centuries in the Catholic Church were swept away after the Second Vatican Council; precision in such matters came to be considered mere fuss inappropriate to the essence of religion. However, those rituals had intellectual content as the representation of history, whereas modern rites are the self-conscious compositions of modern scholars in an age of linguistic decline.

Cerinthus The Greek noun κήρινθος means *bee-bread.* It was transliterated into Latin as *cerinthus* and somehow became a personal name. The notorious Cerinthus was an early heresiarch whom St. John the Divine met by accident in the public baths of Ephesus; the apostle immediately fled out of the building, lest it come crashing down as a result of the presence of such a specimen.

Let us get out of here, for fear the place falls in, now that Cerinthus, the enemy of truth, is inside![55]

Cerinthus's system is described by Gibbon as follows:

A more substantial, though less simple hypothesis, was contrived by Cerinthus of Asia, who dared to oppose the last of the apostles. Placed on the confines of the Jewish and Gentile world, he labored to reconcile the Gnostic with the Ebionite, by confessing in the same Messiah the supernatural union of a man and a God; and this mystic doctrine was adopted with many fanciful improvements by Carpocrates, Basilides, and Valentine, the heretics of the Egyptian school. In their eyes, Jesus of Nazareth was a mere mortal, the legitimate son of Joseph and Mary: but he was the best and wisest of the human race, selected as the worthy instrument to restore upon earth the worship of the true and supreme Deity. When he was baptized in the Jordan, the Christ, the first of the aeons, the Son of God himself, descended on Jesus in the form of a dove, to inhabit his mind and direct his actions during the allotted period of his ministry. When the Messiah was delivered into the hands of the Jews, the Christ, an immortal and impassible being, forsook his earthly tabernacle, flew back to the *pleroma* or world of spirits, and left the solitary Jesus to suffer, to complain, and to expire. But the justice and generosity of such a desertion are strongly questionable, and the fate of an innocent martyr, at first impelled, and at length abandoned, by his divine companion, might provoke the pity and indignation of the profane. Their murmurs were variously silenced by the sectaries who espoused and modified the double system of Cerinthus. It was alleged that, when Jesus was nailed to the cross, he was endowed

---

55. Irenaeus, quoted by Eusebius in *The History of the Church from Christ to Constantine*, trans. G. A. Williamson (London: The Folio Society, 2011), IV 14, p. 105.

with a miraculous apathy of mind and body, which rendered him insensible of his apparent sufferings. It was affirmed that these momentary, though real pangs, would be abundantly repaid by the temporal reign of a thousand years reserved for the Messiah in his kingdom of the new Jerusalem. It was insinuated that if he suffered, he deserved to suffer; that human nature is never absolutely perfect; and that the cross and passion might serve to expiate the venial transgressions of the son of Joseph, before his mysterious union with the Son of God.[56]

The Cerinthian heresy was one of the two basic types from which the heresies of the next three hundred years descended, the other being the Apollinarian heresy. The Cerinthian heresy emphasized a difference between God and man in the Second Person of the Trinity, a difference that led Nestorius to reject the appellation Theotokos for Mary, the mother of Jesus. Apollinaris, on the other hand, emphasized the union of God and man with his expression Μία φύσις τοῦ θεοῦ Λόγου σεσαρκωμένη—One incarnate nature of God the Logos—an expression condemned by the Council of Chalcedon.

Chalcedonian Χαλκηδών was the name of a city in Bithynia, that is, in what is now the northwest portion of Asia Minor. Qualified authorities say that the more correct form of the name is *Calchedon*;[57] I have seen this latter name explained as if it meant "New Town" and was a corruption of a Semitic phrase קריה הדשׁח, but this is precarious, because what the Semites were doing in Bithynia I do not know. Conveniently situated across the Bosphorus from Constantinople, Chalcedon was the location of the Fourth Ecumenical Council in 451. At the time of the Latrocinium of Ephesus in 449, the government of the Eastern Roman Empire was in the hands of the eunuch Chrysaphius, whose godfather was the monk Eutyches of Constantinople. Eutyches taught the monophysite doctrine, "Two Natures before the union, only one afterwards." For this he had been condemned by Flavian, patriarch of Constantinople. With the approval of Chrysaphius, the Latrocinium reversed this decision. The fall of Chrysaphius and the rise of the orthodox emperor Marcian led to the summoning of an ecumenical council at Chalcedon to undo the decisions made at the Latrocinium. The doctrine taught by the Ecumenical Council of Chalcedon is the following:

---

56. Edward Gibbon, *The History of the Decline and Fall of the Roman Empire*, ed. Betty Radice (London: The Folio Society, 1995), 6:27–28

57. *Encyclopaedia Britannica*, 11th ed., s.v. "Chalcedon."

ἐπ᾽ ἐσχάτων δὲ τῶν ἡμερῶν τὸν αὐτὸν δι᾽ ἡμᾶς καὶ διὰ τὴν ἡμετέραν σωτηρίαν ἐκ Μαρίας τῆς παρθένου τῆς θεοτόκου κατὰ τὴν ἀνθρωπότητα, ἕνα καὶ τὸν αὐτὸν Χριστὸν Ἰησοῦν, υἱὸν μονογενῆ ἐν δύο φύσεσιν ἀσυγχύτως, ἀτρέπτως, ἀδιαιρέτως, ἀχωρίστως γνωριζόμενον, οὐδαμοῦ τῆς τῶν φύσεων διαφορᾶς ἀνηρημένης διὰ τὴν ἕνωσιν, σωζομένης δὲ μᾶλλον τῆς ἰδιότητος ἑκατέρας φύσεως, καὶ εἰς ἓν πρόσωπον καὶ μίαν ὑπόστασιν συντρεχούσης.

in novissimis diebus eundem propter nos et propter salutem nostram ex Maria virgine Dei genitrice secundum humanitatem: unum eundemque Christum Filium Dominum unigenitum, in duabus naturis inconfuse, immutabiliter, indivise, inseparabiliter agnoscendum, nusquam sublata naturarum differentia propter unitionem magisque salva proprietate utriusque naturae, et in unam personam atque subsistentiam concurrente.[58]

We believe ... in Jesus Christ ... who for us and for our salvation came forth from the Virgin Mary, Mother of God in relation to the humanity, as one single and the same Christ, Son, Lord, Only-begotten, in two natures, without confusion or change, without division or separation, the difference of the natures being in no wise suppressed by their union, each nature preserving on the contrary its particularity, both concurring to form a single person and a single hypostasis.[59]

The critical phrase was considered to be ἐν δύο φύσεσιν (*in two natures*), since to say ἀπὸ δυοῖν φύσεων (*from two natures*) would have raised and left unanswered the question of when the two natures were combined.

The twenty-eighth canon of the Council of Chalcedon was rejected by Pope Leo the Great, since it implied that the primacy of the Church of Rome was merely one of honor and a matter of politics.

Καὶ τῷ αὐτῷ σκοπῷ κινούμενοι οἱ ἑκατὸν πεντήκοντα θεοφιλέστατοι ἐπίσκοποι τὰ ἴσα πρεσβεῖα ἀπένειμαν τῷ τῆς νέας Ῥώμης ἁγιωτάτῳ θρόνῳ, εὐλόγως κρίναντες τὴν βασιλείᾳ καὶ συγκλήτῳ τιμηθεῖσαν πόλιν, καὶ τῶν ἴσων ἀπολαύουσαν πρεσβείων τῇ πρεσβυτέρα βασιλίδι Ῥώμῃ καὶ ἐν τοῖς ἐκκλησιαστικοῖς ὡς ἐκείνην μεγαλύνεσθαι πράγμασι, δευτέραν μετ᾽ ἐκείνην ὑπάρχουσαν.[60]

Motivated by the same point of view, the one hundred fifty God-loving bishops have assigned equal privileges to the Most Holy See of New Rome, having sensibly judged that the city which has been honored as the seat of the Empire and of the

---

58. Denzinger, *Enchiridion Symbolorum et Definitionum*, 7th ed. (Würzburg: V. J. Stahel, 1895), XVII 34–35.

59. Louis Duchesne, *Early History of the Christian Church from Its Foundation to the End of the Fifth Century*, vol. 3 (London: John Murray, 1924), 207.

60. Canon 28 of the Council of Chalcedon. Text is available at http://earlychurchtexts.com/main/chalcedon/canons_of_chalcedon_03.shtml.

Senate, and which enjoys equal privileges with the royal Old Rome, is worthy to be exalted likewise in ecclesiastical matters, coming next after her.

But the See of Constantinople had been of little account up to this time, the principal see of the East having always been Alexandria, on account of the preeminence of its Catholic bishops. Indeed, for fifty years before this Council, the cathedra of Constantinople had been occupied by heretics.

The circumstances which brought Gregory to Constantinople were the following:—It was now about forty years since the Church of Constantinople had lost the blessing of orthodox teaching and worship. Paul, who had been elected bishop at the beginning of this period, had been visited with four successive banishments from the Arian party, and at length with martyrdom. He had been superseded in his see, first by Eusebius, the leader of the Arians, who denied our Lord's divinity; then by Macedonius, the head of those who denied the divinity of the Holy Spirit; and then by Eudoxius, the Arianizer of the Gothic tribes. On the death of the last mentioned, A.D. 370, the remnant of the Catholics elected for their bishop Evagrius, who was immediately banished by the Emperor Valens; and, when they petitioned him to reverse his decision, eighty of their ecclesiastics, who were the bearers of their complaints, were subjected to an atrocious punishment for their Christian zeal, being burned at sea in the ship in which they had embarked.[61]

Chalice The Latin noun *calix* is the transliteration of the Greek noun κάλυξ, κάλυκος, *f.*, which means *the cup of a flower*. In the process of transliteration it changed grammatical gender. It acquired the meaning of a *goblet*. *Calix* is used in the words of consecration in the Latin Vulgata. The Greek uses the noun ποτήριον.

Matthew 26:17–28: Et accipiens calicem gratias egit: et dedit illis, dicens: Bibite ex hoc omnes. Hic est enim sanguis meus novi testamenti, qui pro multis effundetur in remissionem peccatorum.

Mark 14:23–25: Et accepto calice, gratias agens dedit eis: et biberunt ex illo omnes. Et ait illis: Hic est sanguis meus novi testamenti, qui pro multis effundetur. Amen dico vobis, quia iam non bibam de hoc genimine vitis usque in diem illum, cum illud bibam novum in regno Dei.

Luke 20:17–20: Et accepto calice gratias egit, et dixit: Accipite et dividite inter vos. Dico enim vobis quod non bibam de generatione vitis, donec regnum Dei veniat. Et accepto pane gratias egit, et fregit, et dedit eis dicens: Hoc est corpus meum, quod pro vobis datur: hoc facite in meam commemorationem. Similiter et cali-

---

61. John Henry Cardinal Newman, "Rise and Fall of Gregory," in *Historical Sketches*, vol. 2 (London: Longmans, Green, 1917), 78.

cem, postquam coenavit, dicens: Hic est calix novum testamentum in sanguine meo, qui pro vobis fundetur.

1 Corinthians 11:25–26: Similiter et calicem, postquam coenavit, dicens: Hic calix novum testamentum est in meo sanguine. Hoc facite quotiescumque bibetis, in meam commemorationem. Quotiescumque enim manducabitis panem hunc, et calicem bibetis: mortem Domini annuntiabitis donec veniat.

Chamberlain This English word is the corruption of the Italian *camer-lengo*. It is nowadays the equivalent of the Italian *cameriere*. See the entries **Camerlengo** and **Cameriere**.

Chapel From the Late Latin noun *cappa*, a coat, there was derived the diminutive *cappella*, a small cape, a cloak. The half cloak that St. Martin gave to the beggar became a great relic, and the places where pieces of it were enshrined were called in French *chapelles*, whence the English *chapels*. Those authorities in charge of maintaining the chapels were called *cappellani* or *chaplains*. The word *chapel* is most commonly used to designate independent sections of great churches or places of worship in private dwellings.

Chapter The Latin noun *caput, capitis, n.*, means *head*, and the addition of the suffix *–ulum* produces the diminutive noun *capitulum* with the meaning a *little head*. This latter word came to be applied to that portion of a book that had a special heading, that is, a chapter; the English word is merely the corruption of the Latin noun by the mediation of the French *chapitre*. The chapter of a church consisted of those clergy who gathered there and heard the reading of a *capitulum* from the breviary. It was therefore the assembly of the canons of that church.

Charism The Greek verb χαίρω means *to rejoice*, and related to it is the noun χάρις with the meaning *favor, grace*. From this noun there was derived the verb χαρίζομαι meaning *to show favor*, from whence proceeded the noun χάρισμα, χαρίσματος, *grace, favor, gift*, whence we derive our noun *charism*. The charisms are prophecies, visions, ecstasies, and gifts of healing.[62] According to Paul (1 Corinthians 12:4):

Διαιρέσεις δὲ χαρισμάτων εἰσίν, τὸ δὲ αὐτὸ πνεῦμα·

There are differences of gifts, but the spirit is the same.

---

62. Louis Duchesne, *Early History of the Christian Church from Its Foundation to the End of the Third Century* (London: John Murray, 1914), 144.

The *charismatics* are those who benefit from the charism of speaking in tongues.

Chastity The Greek adjective καθαρός means *clear, pure, spotless,* and related to it is the Latin adjective *castus* with the additional meaning *chaste. Castitas,* whence proceeds our *chastity,* is the state of being *chaste.* Of the Council of Bourges (1031), Lea writes:

> A vow of chastity was commanded as a necessary pre-requisite to assuming the subdiaconate, and no bishop was to ordain a candidate without exacting from him a promise to take neither wife nor concubine.... As this is apparently the earliest instance of a vow of chastity being imposed in conferring orders, it is as well to remark that this precaution has never been adopted by the Church, but such a duty is considered as implied, and became what was known in the schools as a votum adnexum.[63]

Chasuble The usual explanation of this word, that it is ultimately derived from the Latin *casula,* little house, is called dubious by Weekley. Dr. Johnson takes no notice of the word in the first edition of his dictionary (1755); the *Oxford English Dictionary* mentions many mediaeval forms such as cassibula, casubula, cassubula, and casubla, each fellow spelling the word as he pronounced it. It refers to a mediaeval sleeveless hooded garment. The preferred Latin word for *chasuble* is *planeta, -ae, f.* The chasuble is the required outer garment of the celebrant of the Mass. The once common Roman or fiddleback style of chasuble is currently in eclipse as a result of the revival of the Gothic style. In this context, it is useful to remember that *Gothic* was originally a pejorative word, used to denominate what was considered by people of taste to be in the style of barbarians.

Chi-Rho The Chi-Rho is the symbol consisting of a Greek capital *rho* P superimposed upon a Greek capital *chi* X. Since *chi* and *rho* are the first two letters of the name of Christ, ΧΡΙΣΤΟΣ, the symbol is an abbreviation for the name of the Savior.

The victory of Constantine over Maxentius was universally considered as an extraordinary event, in which the intervention of the Divinity could scarcely fail to be recognized. The senate expressed this idea by causing to be engraved upon the arch raised in commemoration of the event the two famous words: INSTINCTV DIVINITATIS.... While marching against [Maxentius], the soldiers of Constan-

---

63. Henry Charles Lea, *History of Sacerdotal Celibacy in the Christian Church* (n.p.: University Books, 1966), 144.

tine had displayed upon their shields the sign ☧, formed from the first two letters of the name of Christ.[64]

Constantine told Eusebius that while reflecting on how best to ensure that the divine favor would bless his enterprise,

to assist him in coming to a decision, he asked God to enlighten him by some marvelous sign. Shortly afterwards, he saw in the sky, and his whole army saw it with him, a Cross of light, with these words: "In this sign, conquer."[65]

Choir The chorus of a Greek tragedy or comedy was a band of singers who danced as they sang their lines. The Greek noun χορός means *a dance in a ring* and, eventually, the band of singers who performed such dances. This word was transliterated into Latin as *chorus*, which eventually degenerated into the French *choir*. Each church should have a trained choir competent to sing the propers of the Mass from the *Graduale Romanum*. This is nowadays never the case, even in cathedrals and basilicas.

Chorbishop The Greek noun χώρα means *place*, in particular a *rural place*, as opposed to an urban location. Χωρεπίσκοπος was therefore a title given to an ecclesiastical authority, not a bishop, in those places; it corresponds to *rural dean* in the Latin Church.

Elsewhere, in lands where there were few towns, and the branch churches were in large villages and other country places, their superintendents were called *Chorepiscopi*.[66]

Chrism The Greek verb χρίω means *to rub over, to anoint*, and from it was formed the noun χρῖσμα (chrism) with the meaning *anything smeared on*.

Chrismale For the etymology, see the entry **Chrism** above. The chrismale was a cloth formerly placed on the lap of a prelate for him to place his hands upon while seated. The purpose was to prevent him from soiling his sacred vestments with his greasy hands. Evidently the chrismale came into use quite early on, before the habit of wearing pontifical gloves became established. The cerecloth on an altar stone is also called in Latin a *chrismale*.

---

64. Louis Duchesne, *Early History of the Christian Church from Its Foundation to the End of the Fifth Century*, vol. 2 (London: John Murray, 1931), 45–47.

65. Ibid. Duchesne gives the Greek in a note: τούτῳ νίκα.

66. Louis Duchesne, *Early History of the Christian Church from Its Foundation to the End of the Third Century* (London: John Murray, 1914), 382.

Christ The Greek adjective χριστός means the *anointed one*. It is derived from the verb χρίω, *to rub on, to smear, to anoint*. It is the translation of the Hebrew noun and Aramaic adjective מְשִׁיחָ, Messiah, applied to Jesus by his followers. The Hebrew verb מָשַׁח means *to smear or anoint* with holy oil.

Christening For the etymology, see the entries **Chrism** and **Christ** above. Because the faithful are anointed at baptism, the word *christening* became a synonym for *baptism*.

Christian Disciples of a leader are usually called after the name of their master; thus arose the names Benedictines, Calvinists, Dominicans, Franciscans, Lutherans, Mohammedans (no longer allowed), a list that can be extended without limit. In many cases, this sort of name was intended as a pejorative. The members of the Community of Saints were first called *Christians* in Antioch, as we read in Acts 11:26.

χρηματίσαι τε πρώτως ἐν Ἀντιοχείᾳ τοὺς μαθητὰς Χριστιανούς.

The disciples were called *Christians* for the first time in Antioch.

It was probably not intended as a compliment. In his life of Nero, Suetonius refers to the Christians in an unflattering way.

Adflicti suppliciis Christiani, genus hominum superstitionis novae et maleficae.[67]

Punishments were imposed upon the Christians, a body of men belonging to a new and wicked cult.

Christmas This noun is the concatenation of *Christ* and *Mass*. The Feast of Christmas (the "Mass of Christ") has been celebrated on December 25 since time immemorial.

How December 25 came to be pitched on for the commemoration is not known, and has been the subject of lively discussions. The notion of an origin in the Roman *Saturnalia* of December can be safely disregarded; but there is some likelihood that the solar feast of *natalis Invicti* (the Birthday of the Unconquered [Sun]), itself observed at the winter solstice about December 25, helped to determine the date.[68]

The Eastern Churches also celebrate it on that day, but according to the Julian Calendar, which, since 1900, is thirteen days behind the Gregorian

67. Suetonius, "Nero," §16.
68. *Butler's Lives of the Saints, Complete Edition*, ed. Herbert J. Thurston, SJ, and Donald Attwater (Norwalk, Conn.: Easton Press, 1995), 1:610 (December 25).

Calendar; the difference will increase to fourteen days in 2100, to fifteen days in 2200, and to sixteen days in 2300. What the Eastern Churches call December 25 we call January 7.

This feast is not among the most primitive in the Church, and liturgically considered, ranks not only below Easter, but also below Pentecost and the Epiphany. The commemoration of the birth of Our Lord by a separate feast began only in the fourth century (before 336), and at Rome, from whence it soon spread to the East where hitherto the birth had been commemorated as a lesser aspect of the feast of the Epiphany.[69]

Christus Vincit These are the first words of a chant, the tune of which is used as the signal of the Vatican Radio. They form the first verse of the *Laudes Regiae*.

Christus vincit, Christus regnat, Christus imperat.

Christ conquers, Christ reigns, Christ commands.

Church This word is the corruption, through Anglo-Saxon, of the Greek κυριακόν [δῶμα], the Lord's [house], from κύριος, lord. The Latin language uses *ecclesia*, the transliteration of the Greek ἐκκλησία composed of the preposition ἐκ (*from*) and the verb καλέω (*to call*); it is the assembly of those singled out. It was the opinion of the historian Gregorovius that the Church is in her essence the guardian of the theory of the unity of the human race, or the Christian republic.[70]

Circumcellions The Latin preposition *circum* means *around, about*, and the noun *cella* means a *room, garret, mean apartment*. The *Circumcelliones* were North African Donatist heretics of the mid fourth century who loitered about the meaner neighborhoods to prey upon passers-by. If this behavior led to their death, they became, in their own estimation, martyrs. Speaking of the Donatists, Duchesne writes:

It was about this time that there was formed under their auspices the strange body called Agonistics, or Circumcellions. This name was given to bands of fanatics, who travelled all over the country, especially in Numidia, to lend a hand to the good cause and wage war against the *traditores*. They claimed to observe strict chastity, and this was why the Donatists, later on, compared them with the Catholic monks. Armed with stout cudgels, they appeared everywhere, on the public

---

69. Ibid., 4:609.
70. Ferdinand Gregorovius, *History of the City of Rome in the Middle Ages*, trans. Mrs. Gustavus W. Hamilton (London: G. Bell & Sons, 1909), 1:13.

roads and in the markets, prowled about cottages, whence came their name of Circumcellions, and kept a strict watch over farms and country houses. It was not only in the quarrel of Donatus and Caecilian that they interested themselves. Sturdy redressors of wrongs, the enemies of all social inequalities, they eagerly took the part of small holders against proprietors, of slaves against their masters, and of debtors against their creditors. At the first call of the oppressed, or those who pretended to be so, and especially of the Donatist clergy when they found themselves hemmed in at close quarters by the police, the Circumcellions appeared on the scene in fierce gangs, uttering their war-cry: *Deo laudes!* and brandishing their famous clubs. One of their chief amusements, when they met a carriage preceded by running slaves, was to put the slaves inside the carriage, and make the masters run in front. Even to those who did not belong to any of the classes regarded with dislike by these extraordinary people, it was not at all pleasant to meet the Circumcellions upon lonely roads. The sons of martyrs often had the intention of being martyrs themselves; and as, to their uneducated minds, the meaning of martyrdom was simply and solely a violent death, they sought for it with the greatest eagerness. When the madness seized them, they appeared to passers-by, and endeavored to compel them to kill them. If such an one refused, they killed *him*, and then hastened on to find someone who would be more obliging. If necessary, they procured martyrdom for themselves, burnt themselves alive, threw themselves into rivers or, very commonly, from precipices. Once dead, they were buried by their companions with the greatest respect; the plains of Numidia were studded with their tombs, to which the same honours were paid as to those of the real martyrs.[71]

Circumcision The Latin verb *circumcido, circumcidere, circumcidi, circumcisus* means *to cut* (caedo) *around* (circum); it is a literal translation of the Greek περιτέμνω used in the Septuagint to translate the Hebrew מול‎, *to cut off*. From *circumcido* is derived the noun *circumcisio*; the corresponding Greek noun is περιτομή. Circumcision was the sign of the covenant between the Almighty and the House of Abraham, as is explained in Genesis 17. The fifth-century mosaic in the apse of the Church of Santa Sabina in Rome portrays two virgins, who represent the two parts of the Church; they are marked *ecclesia ex circumcisione* and *ecclesia ex gentibus*, the Church from the Circumcision and the Church from the Gentiles. The same church has the oldest depiction of the crucifixion, an engraving into the wood of the main door. The Roman court traditionally celebrated the beginning of Lent at this church.

---

71. Louis Duchesne, *Early History of the Christian Church from Its Foundation to the End of the Fifth Century*, vol. 2 (London: John Murray, 1931), 189–90.

Cistercian *Cistertium* is the Latin name of a place in Gaul that became in French Cîteaux. The Benedictine monks of the monastery founded there in 1098 were called *Cistercienses* or *Cistercians*. From their attire, they were known in England as the *White Friars*.

Clappers The word *clap* is onomatopoetic and of Germanic origin. *Clappers* is the English name for the *crotalus*, which is supposed to be used instead of bells during the Easter Triduum after the *Gloria* of the *Missa in Cena Domini* until the *Gloria* of the Mass of the Easter Vigil.

Classics The Greek noun κλῆσις means a *calling*, a *summons*, a *name*, and is derived from the verb καλέω, *to call*. The related Latin noun, *classis*, means *one of the divisions into which Servius Tullius, the sixth legendary King of Rome, divided the people*, and later, the *fleet*, in the sense of the whole body of citizens assembled in the naval forces. The adjective corresponding to the noun *classis* is *classicus*, with the meaning *belonging to a class*, and then, by specialization, *belonging to the first class*. A book is a *classic* if it has deserved that preeminence among other books that the Greek and Latin languages and literatures were at one time held to enjoy among other languages and literatures; those products of the human mind are *classical* that enjoy the authority and respect due to that which is sublime. According to Gibbon, there are three reasons to study the classics:

But the Moslems deprived themselves of … the principal benefits of a familiar intercourse with Greece and Rome, the knowledge of antiquity, the purity of taste, and the freedom of thought.[72]

Since the gospels and creeds of the Catholic religion are written in the Greek language, and since the affairs of the Church of Rome were conducted in Latin until 1965, the neglect of the Greek and Latin languages is inseparable from a decline in the understanding of the Catholic religion.[73]

There was, in the nineteenth century, a disagreement between Cardinal Newman and William George Ward about whether the classics should form the foundation of a liberal education. Ward held that there was an essential distinction between ecclesiastical and secular education.

---

72. Edward Gibbon, *History of the Decline and Fall of the Roman Empire* (London: Strahan & Cahill, 1776–88), 5:430.

73. Much of this paragraph is adapted from the entries on pages 71–72 of my *Origins of Mathematical Words* (Baltimore, Md.: Johns Hopkins University Press, 2013).

If you could secure half an hour's careful meditation on some doctrinal book every morning, this would be an immense deal, for it would, in fact, be an intellectual training.

But nowadays you can't do this; and classical education without it is (to my mind) simply the road to the devil.[74]

Ward thought that the Fathers of the Church might be profitably substituted for Homer and Vergil. In this he was following a tradition that went back to the earliest centuries of the Church.

Tertullian and St. Jerome, though they reviled poets, orators, and philosophers, continued to read and quote them. But Cyprian, once a Christian, abjured all literature except the Bible.[75]

Monsignor Ronald Knox, when an Oxford don, lectured on logic, Homer, and Vergil.[76] This prepared him for the masterpiece of his life, his translation of the Vulgata into English. Cardinal Newman, in his youth, discussed the importance of the study of the ancient Latin classics for Catholics.

Would that Christianity had a Virgil to describe the old monks at their rural labours, as it has had a Sacchi or a Domenichino to paint them![77]

I observe that, whatever the monks had not, a familiar knowledge and a real love they had of the great Latin writers, and I assert, moreover, that that knowledge and love were but in keeping with the genius and character of their institute. For they instinctively recognized in the graceful simplicity of Virgil or of Horace, in his dislike of the great world, of political contests and of ostentatious splendor, in his unambitious temper and his love of the country, an analogous gift to that religious repose, that distaste for controversy, and that innocent cheerfulness which were the special legacy of St. Benedict to his children.... As far as they allowed themselves in any recreation, which was not of a sacred nature, they found it in these beautiful authors, who might be considered as the prophets of the human race in its natural condition.[78]

74. Wilfrid Ward, *William George Ward and the Catholic Revival* (London: Macmillan, 1893), 454–55.

75. Louis Duchesne, *Early History of the Christian Church from Its Foundation to the End of the Third Century* (London: John Murray, 1914), 289.

76. Evelyn Waugh, *Monsignor Ronald Knox, Fellow of Trinity College, Oxford and Protonotary Apostolic to His Holiness Pope Pius XII* (Boston: Little, Brown, 1959), 120.

77. John Henry Cardinal Newman, "The Mission of St. Benedict," in *Historical Sketches*, vol. 2 (London: Longmans, Green, 1917), 407.

78. John Henry Cardinal Newman, "The Benedictine Schools," in *Historical Sketches*, vol. 2 (London: Longmans, Green, 1917), 467.

The classical studies and tastes which I have been illustrating, even though foreign to the monastic masses, as they may be called,—even though historically traceable to the mission of St. Theodore from the Holy See to England,—must still be regarded a true offspring of the Benedictine discipline, and in no sense the result of seasons or places, of relaxation and degeneracy.... When, then, I am asked whether these studies are but the accidents and the signs of a time of religious declension, I reply that they are found in those very persons, on the contrary, who were preëminent in devotional and ascetic habits, and who were so intimately partakers in the spirit of mortification, whether of St. Benedict or St. Romuald, that they have come down to us with the reputation of saints,—nay, have actually received canonization or beatification.[79]

This analogy between the monastic institute and Virgil is recognized by Cassiodorus, who, after impressing on his monks, in the first place, the study of Holy Scriptures and the Fathers, continues, "However, the most holy Fathers have passed no decree, binding us to repudiate secular literature; for in fact such reading prepares the mind in no slight measure for understanding the sacred writings."[80]

The collapse of the classics has resulted in a free fall of the humanities, a consequence that one can see every day. John Stuart Mill, speaking of grammar, wrote:

It is the most elementary part of logic.... The structure of every sentence is a lesson in logic.... The languages which teach it [grammar] best are those which have the most definite rules and which provide distinct forms for the greatest number of distinctions of thought.... In these qualities, the classical languages have an incomparable superiority over every other language.

It is of no use saying that we may know them [ancient authors like Plato, Aristotle, or the evangelists] through modern writings.... Modern books do not teach us ancient thoughts; they teach us some modern writer's notion of ancient thought.... Translations are scarcely better. When we really want to know what a person thinks or says, we seek it at first hand from himself. We do not trust to another person's impression of his meaning, given in another person's words; we refer to his own.[81]

Those who want to study Greek and Latin the tried and true way learn Latin first, then Greek. The reading of Caesar is the most recommendable

79. Ibid., 472–73.
80. Ibid., 453.
81. John Stuart Mill, "Inaugural Address Delivered to the University of St. Andrew's," February 1, 1867. This address is available online at https://jotamac.typepad.com/jotamacs_weblog/files/Inaugural Address.pdf, pages 228 (first paragraph) and 227 (second paragraph).

choice for the first Latin prose author to be attempted. One will often have occasion to refer to the passages about the construction of the bridge over the Rhine and about the wild bull in the Hyrcanian forest. There is great value in choosing Xenophon's *Anabasis* to be the first Greek prose text to be studied. There is educational value even in the constant repetition of the words ἐντεῦθεν ἐξελαύνει. Methods of instruction that require the student to read more advanced authors than he has sufficient command of the language to be able to do are disastrous.

Clausura The verb *claudo, claudere, clausi, clausus* means *to close*, and the associated noun *clausura* means a *shutting up*. It is used of the immuring of the Sacred College of Cardinals in the conclave. The related English noun is *closure*.

Clementine The Latin adjective *Clementinus* is related to the proper name *Clemens* (mild, merciful) as *Paulinus* to *Paulus* and *Sistinus* to *Sixtus*. The Clementine Chapel of St. Peter's Basilica is that built by Clement VIII; it is on the left side, directly opposite the Gregorian Chapel, and contains the monument of Pius VII by Thorwaldsen. The Sala Clementina of the Vatican Palace is the hall in the palace of Sixtus V built by Clement VIII between the pope's private library and the Hall of Consistories; it is used for medium-sized audiences and was the room where the corpse of John Paul II was laid out before being ceremoniously transferred to St. Peter's Basilica.

Clergy The Greek noun κλῆρος means a *lot*, an *inheritance*, and the Latin noun *clerus* is merely its transliteration. The clergy are those who have a part in the Church's ministry, as we read in Acts 1:17:

καὶ ἔλαχεν τὸν κλῆρον τῆς διακονίας ταύτης.

And he drew the lot of this ministry.

The Latin noun and adjective *clericus* is, similarly, the transliteration of the Greek adjective κληρικός, which means, as an adjective, *concerning inheritances*, and as a noun, *an official so concerned, a clerk*. It became corrupted into *clergé* in French, whence we have the English *clergy*. The adjective *clerical* was formed by adding the Latin adjectival suffix *–alis* to the stem of the Greek adjective κληρικός. Our noun *clerk* is merely the stem of the Latin noun *clericus*. The clergy are those men admitted to the order of deacon or to a higher order. Formerly it was used of anyone who had received tonsure, a practice abolished (along with the orders of subdeacon, porter, lector, exorcist, and acolyte) by the motu proprio *Ministeria Quaedam* of Paul VI of August 15, 1972.

Clericalism This modern noun was formed by taking the root of the Greek adjective κληρικός (see the previous entry), adding the Latin adjectival suffix -*al* (which was unnecessary), and then superimposing the Greek nominal suffix -*ism*. *Clericalism* is a pejorative term used to refer disapprovingly to that attitude according to which priests should have the final say in all matters, especially political. Anti-clericalism is the attitude that priests should be prevented from any activity except the performance of religious functions. Typical of the anti-clerical attitude are the views expressed by Gregorovius, speaking about the Gothic Wars in sixth-century Italy:

The decay of all political virtue and manliness, and the decline of learning were the chief causes that contributed to raise the priesthood to power; and we may observe, that only in periods of exhaustion of thought and demoralization of literature such as this, does the priesthood ever attain supremacy.[82]

Coadjutor The Latin verb *adiuvo, adiuvare, adiuvi, adiutus* means *to help*; from it were derived the nouns *adiutor* (helper) and *adiutorium* (help).

Dominus adiutor mihi.[83]

Adiutorium nostrum in nomine Domini.[84]

The noun *coadjutor*, the combination of *cum* (with) and *adiutor*, is the name of a bishop appointed to help a diocesan bishop, usually with the understanding that he, and not the diocesan bishop, is to wield the actual power. The coadjutor bishop usually has the right of succession to the diocese.

Codex The Latin noun *codex, codicis, m.*, means the *trunk of a tree,* a *wooden tablet,* and then a *book formed by stacking pages one on top of the other,* the appearance of which recalled the appearance of a slab of wood. Speaking of the famous library founded in the third century by Alexander, Bishop of Jerusalem, Sanday writes:

---

82. Ferdinand Gregorovius, *History of the City of Rome in the Middle Ages*, trans. Mrs. Gustavus W. Hamilton (London: G. Bell & Sons, 1909), 1:490.
83. These words, the motto of Cardinal Wolsey, can be seen everywhere at Hampton Court Palace. They are translated "The Lord is my helper."
84. "Our help is in the name of the Lord" is one of the verses of the Pontifical Blessing, to which the response is, "who made heaven and earth" (Qui fecit caelum et terram).

The founding of this library fell just at that critical moment when the sacred books were being transferred from the smaller rolls of papyrus, which seldem held more than a single work, to the larger *codices* of vellum shaped like our present books, in which it was usual to combine a number of cognate texts and where they soon acquired a definite order.[85]

Coenobite The Greek adjective κοινός means *common*, and the noun βίος means *life*, and their combination produces the noun κοινόβιον, whose meaning is explained in the following passage:

Μοναστήριον means properly a place where one lives alone; this is exactly the contrary of the usually received meaning; Κοινόβιον, of which we have no literal equivalent in French, means a place where men live in common; this is the correct term, but it is Greek.[86]

A coenobite is thus the opposite of an anchorite.

Coinherence The Latin verb *haereo, haerere, haesi, haesus* means *to stick*, and the addition of the preposition *in* produces the compound verb *in-haereo* with the meaning *to stick in* or *cleave to*. There is no Latin verb *coinhaereo* attested, but in the nineteenth century some excellent authors (Coleridge, J. S. Mill, Newman) invented the English word *coinherence*; the doctrine of coinherence is defined by Newman as follows:

It is the clear declaration of Scripture, which we must receive without questioning, that the Son and Spirit are in the one God, and He in Them. There is that remark-able text in the first chapter of St. John which says that the Son is "in the bosom of the Father." In another place it is said that "the Son is in the Father and the Father in the Son" (John XIV 11). And elsewhere the Spirit of God is compared to "the spirit of a man which is in him" (I Corinthians II 11). This is, in the language of theology, the doctrine of the coinherence (περιχώρησις or *circumincessio*); which was used from the earliest times on the authority of Scripture, as a safeguard and witness of the Divine Unity.[87]

Collect The Latin verb *conligo, conligere, conlegi, conlectus* means *to gath-er* (lego) *together* (cum), and the noun *collect* was very early used to de-nominate the prayer, which is said in the Mass before the Old and New

85. William Sanday, *Inspiration, Eight Lectures on the Early History and Origin of the Doctrine of Biblical Inspiration, Being the Bampton Lectures for 1893* (London: Longmans, Green, 1896), 9.

86. Louis Duchesne, *Early History of the Christian Church from Its Foundation to the End of the Fifth Century*, vol. 2 (London: John Murray, 1931), 395n2.

87. John Henry Cardinal Newman, *The Arians of the Fourth Century*, new ed. (London: Long-mans, Green, 1897), 172–73.

Testament readings, that sums up the purpose of the day's rite. This prayer is simply called *oratio* in the Roman Missal.

Communicatio Idiomatum The Greek phrase ἀντίδοσις ἰδιομάτων, translated into Latin by *communicatio idiomatum*, is defined by Gibbon to be

a mutual loan or transfer of the idioms or properties of each nature to the other.[88]

It is the device whereby one admits such terms as "Mother of God." The Greek verb ἀντιδίδωμι means *to give* (δίδωμι) *in return* (ἀντί) and the noun ἰδίωμα means *that which is personal to one*, a *peculiarity*, derived from the adjective ἴδιος which means *private*. The noun ἰδίωμα was merely transliterated into Latin. For the etymology of *communicatio* see the following entry.

Communion The Latin verb *munio, munire, munivi, munitus* means *to build*, especially a wall, and the noun *moenia, moenium, n.*, derived from it means *walls, bulwarks*. The related noun *munus, muneris, n.*, means an *office* or *function*, for the public offices were seen as bulwarks for the state. The addition of the prefix *com-* with the noun *munus* produces the adjective *communis* with the meaning *that which is shared with all*. It was a principle of Roman law that

In casu extremae necessitatis, omnia sunt communia.

In case of absolute necessity, there is no private property.

From this adjective proceeds the noun *communio* meaning a *sharing* or *mutual participation*. From the adjective *communis* there also proceeded the verb *communico*, of the first conjugation, with the meaning *to share*, and from it was derived the noun *communicatio* meaning a *sharing*, a *fellowship*. The English noun *communion* is used both for the body of the faithful and for the sacrament of the Eucharist. The current habit of frequent communion, though encouraged by the Church, was condemned by William George Ward, the first of the converts from the Oxford Movement to the Catholic Church.

Yet he had a horror of anything like taking liberties with God or the Sacraments, especially if people's lives were not altogether consistent with it. He did not like

---

88. Edward Gibbon, *The History of the Decline and Fall of the Roman Empire*, ed. Betty Radice (London: The Folio Society, 1995), 6:35, note §.

too frequent communion, except in those who were leading very holy mortified lives, and was very particular not to go himself if not well enough to prepare properly.[89]

Compline The Latin verb *compleo, complere, complevi, completus* means *to fill up, to complete*, and, as the prayers before going to bed completed the worship of the day, their time was called the *hora completa*, whence we get the corruption *compline*.

Concelebration The Latin adjective *celeber* means *filled, crowded*, and the associated first-conjugation verb *celebro* means *to visit frequently or in large numbers*. From its fourth principal part comes the noun *celebratio* with the meaning a *numerous assembly*. The Latin verb *concelebro, concelebrare, concelebravi, concelebratus* means *to celebrate* (celebro) *together* (cum). Formerly, if there were several priests at a Mass, one would celebrate and the others would assist in choir. Concelebration is the practice of several priests reciting the words of consecration at the same time.

Conception The Latin verb *capio, capere, cepi, captus* means *to take*, and the addition of the prefix *con-* produces the compound verb *concipio, concipere, concepi, conceptus* with the meaning *to take* or *hold together, take in, absorb, conceive*. From the fourth principal part of this verb proceeds the noun *conceptio, conceptionis, f.*, meaning *comprehending, becoming pregnant, conception*. For the *Immaculate Conception*, see the entry **Immaculate**.

Conclave The Greek noun κλείς, κλειδός, *f.*, means a *bolt, bar*, or *key* used to close a door with. The Greek verb κλείω and the related Latin verb *claudo* both mean *to close*. To the latter verb is related the noun *clavis, clavis, f.*, with the meaning *key*. The Latin phrase *cum clave* thus means *with a key*. This developed into a neuter noun *conclave, -is* of the third declension with the meaning of a *room that can be locked with a key*. Since the cardinals met under such conditions for the election of a new pope, the word became the name of their assembly. The conclave was instituted by Gregory X in his bull *Ubi periculum* of July 7, 1274. He decreed that no cardinal could be barred from the conclave for any reason whatsoever, even excommunication, so it was quite daring (in the opinion of Cardinal Tisserant) for Pope Paul VI to bar those over eighty years old from participating. However, what one pope decrees another may revoke. In order to avoid a long

---

89. Wilfrid Ward, *William George Ward and the Catholic Revival* (London: Macmillan, 1893), 70.

interregnum, the conclave in modern times used to open on the eleventh day following the death of the pope. Thus, Pius IX died on February 7, 1878, and the conclave to elect his successor opened on February 18; Leo XIII was elected on February 20. This did not allow Cardinal McCloskey of New York sufficient time to get to Rome in order to participate. Leo XIII died on July 20, 1903, and the conclave began on July 31. Cardinal Gibbons was already in Rome when Pope Leo died, so he was able to take part in the election of Pius X, which occurred on August 4. This was the first time that an American participated in a conclave. Pius X died on August 20, 1914, and the conclave began on August 31. Cardinal Farley was in Rome at the time and so was able to participate in the election of Benedict XV on September 3; Cardinals Gibbons and O'Connell arrived after Benedict had been elected. Benedict XV died on January 22, 1922, and the conclave to elect his successor opened on February 2. Cardinals O'Connell and Dougherty arrived after the election of Pius XI on February 6. Cardinal O'Connell complained to the new pontiff that the rules did not allow enough time for American cardinals to take part in the conclave. Pius XI thereupon issued the *motu proprio Cum Proxime* of March 1, 1922, in which he increased the number of full days between the death of a pope and the opening of the conclave to a minimum of fifteen and a maximum of eighteen, the exact length being left to the congregation of cardinals in Rome during the *sede vacante* to decide. When Pius XI died on February 10, 1939, the cardinals decided to allow the maximum interval of eighteen full days to pass, so the conclave to elect his successor was not opened until the nineteenth day after the death, on March 1. This allowed Cardinal O'Connell sufficient time to arrive, and he participated in the election of Pius XII on March 2. The most astonishing eye-witness account of any conclave is that given by Aeneas Silvius Piccolomini, Pope Pius II, of the conclave of 1458, contained in his Commentaries.[90] See the entry **Accession**.

Concordat The Latin adjective *concors, concordis* means *of one mind, agreeing*, and is compounded of *cum* (with) and *cors* (heart). From it was produced the verb *concordo, concordare*, to agree, whose past participle *concordatum* means *something agreed to*. This became *concordato* in Italian and thence *concordat* in English. Bacci says that the correct Latin

---

90. *The Commentaries of Pius II*, trans. Florence Alden Gragg, with historical introduction and notes by Leona C. Gabel (Northampton, Mass.: Smith College Studies in History), vol. 22, nos. 1–2, October 1936–January 1937, pp. 93–105.

name for a *concordat* is *pactum conventum*. A concordat is a treaty made between the Holy See and a foreign state, to regulate the affairs of the Catholic Church in that country. The most famous concordats were those with Italy (1929) and Germany (1933). For a discussion of these, see the entry **Lateran Pacts**.

Conference The Latin verb *fero, ferre, tuli, latus* means *to bring* or *carry*. The addition of the prefix *con-*, from *cum*, together, produces the compound verb *confero, conferre, contuli, collatus* with the meaning *to bring together*. The Late Latin noun *conferentia* and the derived French noun *conference* mean a *gathering for the exchange of ideas*. It may be little more than a lecture with a question and answer period following.

Confession This noun is formed from the third principal part of the Latin verb *confiteor*. For its etymology, see **Confiteor**.

Confessional The addition of the Latin adjectival suffix *-alis* to the stem of the Latin noun *confessio, confessionis* produced the ecclesiastical adjective *confessionalis* with the meaning *pertaining to confession*. In English, the stem of *confessionalis* was used as a noun to refer to the place where the priest heard the confession of the penitent. Henry Charles Lea gives the following summary of the history of the confessional, although the motive he assigns for its introduction seems contrary to reason. Referring to the Council of Trent, he writes:

About that time, however, a preventive effort was commenced by the invention of the confessional. Hitherto the priest had heard confessions in the open, with the penitent at his knees or seated by his side, which gave ample opportunity for temptation and solicitation. To remedy this the confessional was gradually evolved—a box in which the confessor sits, while the penitent outside pours the tale of his sin through a grille, neither being visible to the other. The earliest allusion to such a contrivance that I have met occurs in a memorial to Charles V by Siliceo, Archbishop of Toledo, in 1547. In 1565 a Council of Valencia ordered its use, especially for the confession of women, and between 1565 and 1575 S. Carlo Borromeo introduced it in his province of Milan, while the Roman Ritual of 1614 prescribes its employment in all churches. The command was obeyed but slackly, for the innovation had to win its way against the pronounced opposition of the priesthood, who objected to this seclusion from their penitents. In Spain we find the Inquisition, between 1710 and 1720, busy in endeavoring to enforce the use of the confessional, and as late as 1781 it issued a decree to be printed and sent to all parish priests and superiors of convents, who were to post it in their sacristies.

In this it alludes to its previous repeated orders and its sorrow at the evils arising from their non-observance or from the devices used to elude them, of which it gives a curious enumeration.[91]

Confessor For the etymology, see the entry **Confiteor**. A *confessor* is someone who suffers for the faith without, however, losing his life. Such were those Christians condemned to the mines or to the galleys. The word is the Latin translation of the Greek noun ὁμολογητής, from the verb ὁμολογέω, which means *to speak one language, to agree*. Bishop Lightfoot has the following to say on the distinction between *martyr* and *confessor*.

The distinction between μάρτυς and ὁμολογητής (more rarely ὁμόλογος), which the humility of these sufferers suggested, became afterwards the settled usage of the Church; but that it was not so at the close of the second century appears from the Alexandrian Clement's comments on Heracleon's account of ὁμολογία in *Strom.* Iv. 9, p. 596; comp. also Tertull. *Prax.* I "*de jactatione martyrii inflatus ob solum et simplex et breve carceris taedium.*" Even half a century later the two titles are not kept apart in Cyprian's language. The Decian persecution however would seem to have been instrumental in fixing the distinction ...[92]

The noun *confessor* has also the additional meaning of a priest who is chosen to hear the confession of a distinguished personality on a regular basis. Thus, the confessor of Pius XII was Augustine Bea.

Confirmation The Latin verb *confirmo, confirmare* means *to make strong*, and is compounded of *cum* (with) and *firmus* (strong); such a strengthening is called a *confirmatio*, whence comes the English noun. The proof texts for the sacrament of confirmation are Acts 8:14–17 and 19:1–6. The Greek name for this sacrament is ἡ βεβαίωσις, *the strengthening*. Duchesne writes:

From the time of the apostles, the rite of initiation included two principle parts; the bath, or baptism with water, and the laying on of hands. The first rite conveyed the special gift of remission of sin; it was the symbol of the purification of the soul, by conversion, and grafting into Jesus; the second rite carried with it sanctification by the descent of the Holy Ghost upon the soul of the neophyte. As time went on, other ceremonies were introduced. Tertullian speaks not only of baptism and the

---

91. Henry Charles Lea, *History of Sacerdotal Celibacy in the Christian Church* (n.p.: University Books, 1966), 499.

92. Joseph Barber Lightfoot, *The Apostolic Fathers: Clement, Ignatius, Polycarp*, 2nd ed. (London: Macmillan, 1889), part 1, vol. 2, 27n2. The Latin quotation from Tertullian means, "Boasting that he [Praxeas] was a martyr just because he had been in jail for a short period of time."

laying on of hands, but also mentions unction, the consignation or imposition of the sign of the cross, and lastly, a mixture of milk and honey given the newly initiated to drink.[93] And as he adds that all these ceremonies were practiced by the Marcionites, they must date back at least to the first half of the 2nd century.[94]

Confiteor The Latin verb *fateor, fateri, fassus sum* means *to admit, to allow*, and the compound verb produced by the addition of the intensifying prefix *con-* produces the verb *confiteor, confiteri, confessus sum* with the meaning *to acknowledge, to confess*. The *Confiteor* is one of the opening prayers of the Mass whose text was abbreviated by the authors of the liturgical reform. The traditional *Confiteor* is as follows:

Confiteor Deo omnipotenti, beatae Mariae semper Virgini, beato Michaeli archangelo, beato Ioanni Baptistae, sanctis apostolis Petro et Paulo, omnibus sanctis, et vobis, fratres: quia peccavi nimis cogitatione, verbo, et opera: mea culpa, mea culpa, mea maxima culpa.

Ideo precor beatam Mariam semper Virginem, beatum Michaelum archangelum, beatum Ioannem Baptistam, sanctos apostolos Petrum et Paulum, omnes sanctos, et vos, fratres, orare pro me ad Dominum Deum nostrum.

From this prayer the words *mea culpa, mea culpa, mea maxima culpa*, entered the vocabulary of all Christian peoples. In 1969, the *Confiteor* became:

Confiteor Deo omnipotenti, et vobis, fratres, quia peccavi nimis cogitatione, verbo, opere, et omissione: mea culpa, mea culpa, mea maxima culpa. Ideo precor beatam Mariam semper Virginem, omnes Angelos et Sanctos, et vos, fratres, orare pro me ad Dominum Deum nostrum.

It is the difference between poetry and prose.

Conopaeum The Greek noun κώνωψ means a *gnat*, and the name κωνωπεών, κωνωπεῶνος, *m.*, was given to an Egyptian bed or litter with mosquito curtains. There is an alternative form, τὸ κωνωπεῖον. It was transliterated into Latin by *conopĕum* or *conopium*. The *conopaeum* is the canopy granted to basilicas, which is displayed inside and carried about in solemn processions. It is also called an *umbraculum* in Latin, an *ombrellone* in Italian, and a *pavilion* in English. Some basilicas have more

---

93. Duchesne adds in a footnote: "This last ceremony is no longer in use; the anointing with oil, and the sign of the cross, form with the imposition of hands the special ritual of Confirmation."

94. Louis Duchesne, *Early History of the Christian Church from Its Foundation to the End of the Third Century* (London: John Murray, 1914), 366–67.

than one; at St. Peter's in Rome one formerly saw four of them in the procession of Corpus Domini. Such canopies are the relics of another age, when they were kept ready in certain great buildings to be ceremoniously carried above the heads of the highest authorities, such as the Roman pontiffs, during their visits. It is also the name of the veil or curtain before the tabernacle, which, in a time before screen windows, served the purpose of keeping insects out.

Consecration The verb *consecro, consecrare, consecravi, consecratus* means *to make especially* (con) *sacred* (sacer), and, indeed, episcopal consecration adds to what has already been received, namely, priestly ordination. The modern replacement of *consecration* by *ordination* in the making of a bishop was not an improvement. Ordination confers a sacrament, whereas consecration does not. The verb *ordino, ordinare, ordinavi, ordinatus* means *to put in order*, and, in the ecclesiastic sense, *raise to the priestly order*. Since one also raises a fellow to the episcopal order, the use of *ordination* is not wrong but is nonetheless undesirable, because it is better to use different words in service of precision rather than to use one word, which cancels all differences. The noun *consecration* is also used of that most solemn part of the Canon, the words of institution of the Holy Eucharist.

Hoc est enim corpus meum.

Hic est enim calix sanguis mei, novi et aeterni testamenti, mysterium fidei, qui pro vobis et pro multis effundetur in remissionem peccatorum.

The words *mysterium fidei*, not in the gospels, were removed in 1969.

Consistory The Greek verb ἵστημι means *to stand*, and related to it is the Latin verb *sto, stare, steti, status* with the same meaning; connected with this latter word is the verb *sisto, sistere, steti, status* with the meaning *to set, to place, to present oneself, to stand*. The addition of the intensifying prefix *con* (from *cum, with*) produces the compound verb *consisto, consistere, constiti, constitus* meaning *to take one's place, to stand with*. From this last verb was derived the noun *consistorium* with the meaning, a *place of assembly*, namely, of the emperor's cabinet.

Augustus had instituted a council or cabinet of fifteen, comprising the consuls and chief functionaries, with whom he prepared his measures, and to whom he partly opened the secrets of his policy. Under the Claudii this intimacy had been doubtless obstructed by the personal interest of Sejanus and Macro, of Pallas and

Narcissus. But [under] Domitian, who amidst all his vices retained at least no favourite and kept his freedmen in check, the council recovered some portion of its authority: even the burlesque debate of the turbot shows that functions which could be so caricatured were not wholly in abeyance. This council or Consistorium, as it came to be designated, continued to gain in dignity; while other advisers, taken also from the highest nobility, formed, under the name of the Auditorium, a bench of assessors in the emperor's court of justice.[95]

With the passage of time, the intimate council of advisers of the supreme pontiff came similarly to be called the Consistory, and when Sixtus V built his addition to the Vatican Palace intended for his personal residence, he included a hall at a corner of the top floor for the sittings of the Consistory, called in Italian the *Sala del Concistoro*. This hall was decorated at the direction of Clement VIII. It was there that on February 11, 2013, Benedict XVI announced to the assembled cardinals his imminent abdication. Its use nowadays allows for some small audiences to be held there. A consistory used to be called private, semiprivate, or public depending on the quality of the people admitted to it. For example, only cardinals were admitted to the secret consistory, whereas bishops resident in Rome could attend the semiprivate consistory, and even laymen might be allowed in the public consistory. For the arrangements of consistories Sixtus V established a special dicastery of the Roman Curia which eventually came to be called the Sacred Consistorial Congregation, which was abolished at the time of the general reorganization of the central offices of the Church by Paul VI.

Consubstantial The Latin adjective *consubstantialis* was invented to translate the Greek technical term ὁμοούσιος, *homoousios*. Commenting on the situation at the time of the Council of Sardica (343), Duchesne observes:

For people who translated ὁμοούσιος by *consubstantialis*, the terms οὐσία and ὑπόστασις were equivalent. We must note carefully that the word *essentia*, by which we translate οὐσία, was not at that time in use; that, for the two Greek words οὐσία and ὑπόστασις, there was but one Latin term, *substantia*. We can therefore understand the Council of Sardica being tempted to pass from the "consubstantial" to the unity of hypostasis.[96]

95. Charles Merivale, *A History of the Romans under the Empire* (London: Longman, Green, Longman, & Roberts, 1862), 7:550–51.

96. Louis Duchesne, *Early History of the Christian Church from Its Foundation to the End of the Fifth Century*, vol. 2 (London: John Murray, 1931), 176n1. For more on the relation between hypostasis and *ousia*, see the entries **Hypostasis** and **Hypostatic Union**.

Thus, *con-* gives the strength of the Greek ὁμός, and *substantia* is the literal rendering of ὑπόστασις.

Consulta The Latin verb *consulo, consulere, consului, consultus* means *to reflect, consult, consider*. From its fourth principal part was formed the Italian noun *consulta*, which was a name given to any body that consisted of advisers. In the Catholic Church it was the name given to the Supreme Court of the Pontifical State. Ferdinando Fuga built the Palace of the Consulta in Rome across the street from the Piazza of the Quirinale in the reign of Clement XII. It borders the Palazzo Pallavicini-Rospigliosi. It was seized by the Italians in 1870 and used first for the home of the Crown Prince Umberto (1871–1874), then for the Ministry of Foreign Affairs (1874–1922), then for the Ministry for Colonies (1924–1953), and now, since 1955, for the home of the Italian Constitutional Court. During the time when the palace served as the headquarters of the Italian Foreign Ministry, one spoke of the Consulta in the same way one now speaks of the Vatican, the White House, the Pentagon, or the Quai d'Orsay.

Contraception This is an odd word, formed by appending the preposition and adverb *contra* to the last two syllables of the noun *conception*. It is a comical word, but it is commonly not recognized as such, because people have gotten used to it. The verb *concipio* means *to take* (capio) *together* (cum), *to conceive*, and *contra* means *against*. When the Foundation *Latinitas* had to come up with a Latin noun for contraception, they decided on *atocium, -i, n.*, the transliteration of the Greek ἀτόκιον [φάρμακον], a drug mentioned by Pliny (*Historia Naturalis*, 29, 85) as impeding conception; it is the union of *alpha privativum* and a derivative of the noun τόκος (a bringing forth), which comes from the verb τίκτω, τέξω, ἔτεκον (to bring into the world). The word ἀτόκιος is another form of the Greek adjective ἀτοκεῖος meaning *causing barrenness*.

Contrition The Greek verb τείρω means *to rub*, or *wear away*, and related to it is the Latin verb *tero, terere, trivi, tritus* with the same meaning. The meaning is intensified by the addition of the prefix *con-*, which produces the compound verb *contero, conterere, contrivi, contritus*, from the fourth principal part of which come our adjective *contrite* and the Latin noun *contritio, contritionis*, whence proceeds our *contrition*.

The *Ordo Paenitentiae*, published by the Holy See in 1974, is 119 pages long, although the only necessity for the sacrament is the Act of Contrition, the recitation of sins, and the priest's recitation of the formula: *Et ego te absolvo a peccatis tuis in nomine Patris, et Filii, et Spiritus Sancti.*

Convent The Latin verb *convenio, convenire, conveni, conventus* means *to come* (venio) *together* (cum), and from its fourth principal part was formed the noun *conventus* of the fourth declension with the meaning a *home where monks* (or, more commonly, nuns) *live together.*

Conventual The combination of the suffix *–alis* and the noun *conventus* produces the adjective *conventualis*, from which is derived our adjective *conventual*, used to describe that *which pertains to a convent* or to *living together in common*. The Conventual Mass is the Mass at which a community of priests, monks, or nuns gathers to celebrate the Divine Liturgy in common. The Conventual Franciscans are those who are allowed to hold property in common; they are entrusted with the basilicas of Assisi and Padua and have their headquarters in the Basilica of the Twelve Apostles in Rome, where is found Bernini's monument to Clement XIV, the last pope of their order. Bacci calls the Conventual Franciscans *Franciscani atrati* (attired in black) and condemns the adjective *conventualis* as low Latin.

Convert The Latin noun *converto, convertere, converti, conversus* means *to turn*; the prefix *con-* has an intensifying force. From the first principal part was formed the English verb *to convert*, and from this verb came the noun *convert*. A convert is someone who joins the Church as an adult, usually after having left another religion or from a state of irreligion.

Cope Weekley derives this Middle English noun from the Late Latin *capa* with the meaning a *mantle*. See the entry **Cap**. The Latin word for this article of clothing is *pluviale* or *rain coat*, from *pluvia, -ae, f.*, rain. The cope was originally worn out-of-doors for the indicated reason. It eventually was promoted to the vestment worn indoors at the *asperges*, vespers, and other familiar ceremonies. It was held together at the breast by a clasp, which in the case of a great prelate developed into the morse.

Copt The inhabitants of ancient Egypt called themselves *Copts*. The Greeks imitated this sound for the name of the country and produced the word Αἴγυπτος. In Latin, this became *Aegyptus*, whence we get *Egypt*. In Hebrew the name for that country is entirely different, מצרים, and the modern Egyptians call their country by the related Arabic word, مصر. The word *Copt* is now used solely as a name for an Egyptian Christian subject to the patriarch of Alexandria, who is acknowledged to be the successor of St. Mark. These people were formerly called Monophysites, which was not a compliment.

Corona Aurea super Caput Eius These are the opening words of a hymn that used to be sung by the choir immediately before the senior cardinal deacon crowned the pope. They are adapted from Ecclesiasticus 45:14 (where the text has *mitram* instead of *caput*) and mean "The golden crown upon his head." The musical setting used in 1958 was composed by Domenico Bartolucci, at that time director of the Sistine Chapel Choir.

Coronation The Greek adjective κορωνίς, κορωνίδος means *curved* and as a feminine noun means *anything curved*, as, for example, a *garland*. The Latin noun *corona* was derived from it and has been corrupted into the English *crown*. The associated verb *corono, coronare, coronavi, coronatus* means *to put a wreath on someone's head*, and this, indeed, was done to champion athletes who nowadays would be given a gold medal. Thurston, an infallible authority, in his article "Coronation" in the *Catholic Encyclopedia* of 1911, says that the Roman emperors began to wear a diadem at the time of Constantine and submitted to a formal coronation ceremony beginning in the fifth century. Contrary to the ICEL explanatory statement to its translation of Psalm 72 ("perhaps composed for the coronation of a new king in Jerusalem,")[97] Hebrew kings were anointed, not crowned. Yet, in 2 Kings 11:11–12, we are told that when the priest Jehoiada anointed Jehoash King of Judah, he placed a diadem (נזר) of some sort upon his head as a sign of his consecration. During the Middle Ages, popes began to be viewed as sovereigns and were accordingly crowned. The use of the triple crown originated in the fourteenth century. In 1978, John Paul I refused to be crowned with the tiara, and since then popes have "inaugurated their pontificate" (for so it is officially described—*inauguratio pontificatus*) by being vested with a pallium. The coronation ritual for the coronation of an English sovereign is the subject of a great book, *The Coronation Ceremonial*, by Herbert Thurston, SJ; the ritual was composed on the occasion of the coronation of George V.

Formerly the pope received the pallium from the senior cardinal deacon at his Coronation Mass after the prayers at the foot of the altar and the

---

97. *Psalms for All Seasons: From the ICEL Liturgical Psalter Project* (Silver Spring, Md.: National Association of Pastoral Musicians, 1987), 66.

Confiteor. The cardinal deacon recited the following verse before placing the pallium on the shoulders of the Pontiff:

Accipe Pallium Sanctum, plenitudinem Pontificalis officii ad honorem Omni-potentis Dei, gloriosissimae Virginis Mariae Eius Matris, beatorum Apostolorum Petri, et Pauli, et Sanctae Romanae Ecclesiae.

Receive the Holy Pallium, the fullness of the Pontifical dignity, to the honor of Almighty God, of the most glorious Virgin Mary His Mother, of the Holy Apostles Peter and Paul, and of the Holy Roman Church.

The first time that the clergy took part in the political ceremony of the coronation of the new emperor was at the coronation of the Emperor Leo at Constantinople on February 7, 457.

As there was no longer any member of the Theodosian family to give him the investiture, it occurred to them to have recourse to the Patriarch Anatolius, and the latter presided at the coronation of the new Emperor.[98]

Corpus Christi This Latin phrase means the *Body of Christ*, and is the name of a great feast instituted by Urban IV in 1264 and celebrated on the Thursday following Ascension Day. In Italy, the feast is called *Corpus Domini*, and in America the long English expression *Solemnity of the Most Holy Body and Blood of Christ* is becoming standard. As a result of secularization, Corpus Christi has been transferred in most countries to the following Sunday. There is an associated traditional procession once celebrated with great pomp and dignity but nowadays all too often spoiled by people inappropriately dressed.

Corso The Latin verb *curro, currere, cucurri, cursus* means *to run*, and from it was derived the noun *cursus, -ūs, m.*, a race-track. The Italian noun *corso* is derived from the aforementioned Latin noun. The Corso is the main street of Rome, leading from the Capitoline Hill to the Flaminian Gate (the *Porta del Popolo*). It acquired its name from the pontiff Paul II (1464–1471), who inaugurated the custom of holding the Carnival races on that thoroughfare.[99] A description of these festivities in the years 1869 and 1870 may be found in the memoirs of a Pontifical Zouave who witnessed them.[100]

98. Louis Duchesne, *Early History of the Christian Church from Its Foundation to the End of the Fifth Century*, vol. 3 (London: John Murray, 1924), 331.

99. Ferdinand Gregorovius, *The Tombs of the Popes, Landmarks in the History of the Papacy*, trans. Mrs. L. W. Terry (Rome: Victoria Home, 1895), 120.

100. Joseph Powell, *Two Years in the Pontifical Zouaves, A Narrative of Travel, Residence, and Experience in the Roman States* (London: R. Washbourne, 1871), 84–85, 152–53.

– C –

Cotta This noun is a mediaeval corruption of the Anglo-Saxon word *coat*. It is the name of a short-sleeved white vestment, not so long as the surplice, whose use was described by Nainfa:

If Canons have the privilege of the canonical *cappa magna*, their summer costume in choir consists in wearing the *cotta* over the rochet; unless they have obtained also the privilege of a summer *cappa* (a *cappa* without fur). In both cases, they put on the cotta over the rochet when they have to administer a sacrament.

The cotta is worn over the rochet by the Prelates *di mantelletta* for ecclesiastical functions and the administration of sacraments. This rule applies to the Prelates *di mantellone* who have obtained the privilege of wearing the rochet. Bishops wear the cotta over the rochet when performing ecclesiastical functions in presence of the Pope and especially when they receive holy communion at the Pope's hands on Holy Thursday.[101]

This use of the cotta over the rochet was abolished by Pope Paul VI. Elderly readers of this book may remember seeing the Papal Master of Ceremonies Enrico Dante so attired at the time of the Second Vatican Council.

In usum remanet rochetum e lino similive e textili. Eidem vero numquam super-pelliceum imponetur.

The rochet of linen or of similar material remains in use, though a cotta will never be worn over it.[102]

The Latin name of the cotta, *superpelliceum*, was condemned by the Latinist Giacomo Pontano since it is not worn over the skin (*pellis*), nor is it made of leather.[103] The cotta is nowadays commonly worn over the cassock by altar boys.

Council The Greek verb καλέω means *to call*, and related to it is the Latin *calo, calare, calavi, calatus*, which also means *to call* or *summon*, but was a technical term used exclusively of religious assemblies. The Latin noun *concilium* is the combination of the prefix *cum-*, together, and the verb *calo*. It means an *assembly* of any sort, but in the Catholic Church it is reserved to an assembly of clergy, especially of bishops, and the highest

---

101. John A. Nainfa, *Costume of Prelates of the Catholic Church according to Roman Etiquette* (Baltimore, Md.: John Murphy, 1909), p. 62, §6.

102. *Ut Sive Sollicite* (instruction of the Secretariat of State, March 31, 1969), *Acta Apostolicae Sedis* 61, no. 5 (1969), 334–340, A 11. The text is also available at www.shetlersites.com/clericaldress/utsivesollicite.html.

103. Antonio Bacci, *Vocabolario Italiano-Latino delle Parole Difficili a Tradurre* (Rome: Editrice Studium, 1963), 229.

form of council is the ecumenical or general council of the bishops of the whole world, of which there have been twenty-one. The infallible source for the history of the councils is the *Conciliengeschichte* (nine volumes) of Carl Josef von Hefele, bishop of Rothenburg (1809–1893). As Plato's *Crito* ends in the middle of a sentence, so does this great work end in the middle of the reign of Paul III.

Counter Reformation See the entry **Reformation**. The English word *counter* is derived from the Latin preposition *contra*, which means *against*. *Counter Reformation* is a term coined by von Ranke in his *History of the Popes*. The title of book 5 is *Gegenreformationen* (Counter Reformations), and he uses the term to denote the Catholic response to the Protestant Reformation in the period 1563–1629.

Court The Greek noun χόρτος means a *feeding-place*, a *poultry yard*, and the related Latin noun *hortus* has the meaning *garden*. Another related Latin noun, *cohors, cohortis, f.*, means an *enclosure*, a *yard*. (The *coh-* is an expansion of the Greek χ.) The English word *court* is the descendant of this latter noun. The court of a sovereign prince is the set of officials who assist him in the performance of his duties and accompany him when he appears in state. The court of the Roman pontiff consists of both spiritual and temporal personalities and once presented a magnificent spectacle, but the slate has been wiped clean in the past half century of *aggiornamento*.

Credence The Latin verb *credo, credere, credidi, creditus* means *to trust, to believe*. Formerly the food of dignitaries would be tested for poison at a side table before being presented for consumption. From this practice, the Italian word *credenza* acquired the meaning of any such side table. The *credence table* of the sanctuary is the side table where the cruets of wine and water are kept.

Credo This Latin verb means *I believe* and is the usual beginning of a profession of faith. The word was eventually corrupted into the English *creed*. It is commonly used in reference to the profession of faith found in the Mass after the gospel. The *Credo* was officially inserted into the Mass by Benedict VIII (1012–1024) at the request of Emperor St. Henry II. Since I cannot believe for you, the former translation *We believe* was daring as well as grammatically wrong. (The translators translated instead the Greek text that begins πιστεύομεν, for the plural was more in harmony

– C –

with their program.) Speaking of the Christian neophytes of the earliest times, Duchesne wrote:

> At baptism, they were required to renounce publicly, before the whole Christian assembly, Satan, his pomps, and his works, which meant, in fact, paganism,[104] its worship, and its lax morality. Then they declared their faith in Jesus Christ, and in token thereof they recited a profession of faith.[105]

See the entry **Apostles** for the earliest form of a creed, and the entry **Nicene Creed** for the form promulgated in the fourth century.

Criticism The Greek verb κρίνω means *to judge*, and the associated adjective κριτικός means *pertaining to a judge*. The activity of a judge became an *ism* in English. The word *criticism* was in use in English at least as early as the seventeenth century. The connection with the Catholic religion is through the terms *higher* and *lower criticism* of biblical studies. *Lower criticism* is the study of determining the correct text of the biblical books; *higher criticism* is the enterprise of discovering the authors, the dates, and the constituent parts of those books.

> Indeed criticism is only the process by which theological knowledge is brought into line with other knowledge; and as such it is inevitable.[106]

> In speaking of critical theories of the Old Testament the layman may wish to be reminded what the critical points in these are. Two may be described as general and two as particular. The *general* points are (i) the untrustworthy character of Jewish traditions as to authorship unless confirmed by internal evidence; they are not in fact traditions in the strict sense at all, but only inferences and conjectures without historical basis: (ii) the composite character of very many of the books—the Historical Books consisting for the most part of materials more or less ancient set in a frame-work of later editing; some of the Prophetical Books containing as we now have them the work of several distinct authors bound up in a single volume; and books like the Psalms and Proverbs also not being all of a piece but made up of a number of minor collections only brought together by slow degrees. Two *particular* conclusions are of special importance: (i) the presence in the Pentateuch of a considerable element which in its present shape is held by

---

104. [Note of Duchesne]: "This renunciation was only intended for neophytes who had been pagans. It is certain that converts from Judaism were not called upon to renounce Satan. This formula was not for them."

105. Louis Duchesne, *Early History of the Christian Church from Its Foundation to the End of the Third Century* (London: John Murray, 1914), 367.

106. William Sanday, *Inspiration, Eight Lectures on the Early History and Origin of the Doctrine of Biblical Inspiration, Being the Bampton Lectures for 1893* (London: Longmans, Green, 1896), 116.

many to be not earlier than the Captivity; and (ii) the composition of the Book of Deuteronomy not long, or at least not very long, before its promulgation by King Josiah in the year 621, which thus becomes a pivot-date in the history of Hebrew literature.[107]

Sanday has the following to say on how the ancients wrote books.

In the first place, it must be remembered that Hebrew history was as a rule, and especially for the earlier periods, anonymous. The writers had not a literary object in the sense of seeking any fame or reputation for themselves. Their object was either simply to record the facts, or else more often to draw a religious lesson from the facts. They might at times wish to advance the interests of a particular class or order; but all personal interests, and in particular interests connected with literary composition, were not only in the background, but were absolutely non-existent. No Hebrew historian thought either of himself or of his predecessors as possessing a right of property in their work. He was just as ready to have the products of his pen used by others as he was to use himself the stores which had come down to him....

Lastly, we have to remember that their writings did not take the form of printed books. They were not produced in wholesale editions, but by single copies at a time. And the writer of each new copy would not consider himself slavishly bound to the text of his predecessor. He would be something between a scribe and an author or editor. He was bound by no rules; and he would either simply transcribe or add and subtract as he felt moved to do at the moment. Both his additions and subtractions would be due to different motives—sometimes to the use of other authorities, and sometimes to the particular religious interest which was dominant with him in writing.[108]

Lower criticism, as has been noted, is the study that determines the correct text; examples of lower criticism may be found at the end of the entry **Neo-Vulgata**. Higher criticism, which is the more controversial variety, was defined by S. R. Driver of the Hebrew Lexicon as follows:

The proper function of the "Higher Criticism" is to determine the origin, date, and literary structure of an ancient writing.[109]

Higher Criticism came most forcibly to the notice of the American public as a result of the 1891 heresy trial of Charles Augustus Briggs, whom the Presbyterians excommunicated for the teaching contained in

107. Ibid., 120–21.
108. Ibid., 156–58.
109. S. R. Driver and A. F. Kirkpatrick, *The Higher Criticism* (New York: Hodder & Stoughton, 1912), vii.

his inaugural address as professor of biblical theology at the Union Theological Seminary:

It may be regarded as the certain result of the science of the Higher Criticism that Moses did not write the Pentateuch or Job; Ezra did not write the Chronicles, Ezra, or Nehemiah; Jeremiah did not write the Kings or Lamentations; David did not write the Psalter, but only a few of the Psalms; Solomon did not write the Song of Songs or Ecclesiastes, and only a portion of the Proverbs; Isaiah did not write half of the book that bears his name. The great mass of the Old Testament was written by authors whose names or connection with their writings are lost in oblivion.[110]

William R. Harper, in a Yale College lecture, weighed in on this issue:

"I for one," he admitted candidly, "reached the position long ago that there were discrepancies, inconsistencies, and contradictions and mistakes in the Bible."

Nevertheless, Harper, like many other American higher critics of the evangelical school, devoutly upheld his belief in the Bible. "I see these errors," he remarked, "yet I accept the Bible and admit the existence in it of errors."[111]

Sanday, in commenting on the interpretation of the Book of Daniel, observed:

The human mind will in the end accept that theory which covers the greatest number of particular facts and harmonizes best with the sum total of knowledge.[112]

The same author, discussing the question of the infallibility of the historical books of the Old Testament, wrote:

[According to the critical view], inspiration is not inherent in the Bible as such, but is present in different books and parts of books in different degrees. More particularly on this view—and here is the point of greatest divergence—it belongs to the Historical Books rather as conveying a religious lesson than as histories, rather as interpreting than as narrating plain matter of fact. The crucial issue is that in this last respect they do not seem to be exempted from possibilities of error.[113]

Because higher criticism emphasized a certain dependence of the Israelite culture and religion on Babylonian civilization, thereby depriving it (so

110. Carl E. Hatch, *The Charles A. Briggs Heresy Trial* (New York: Exposition Press, 1969), 34–35. The quoted words are those of Briggs.

111. Ibid., 106.

112. William Sanday, *Inspiration, Eight Lectures on the Early History and Origin of the Doctrine of Biblical Inspiration, Being the Bampton Lectures for 1893* (London:Longmans, Green, 1896), 215.

113. Ibid., 400.

some believed) of absolute originality, Solomon Schechter said that higher criticism was higher anti-Semitism.[114]

The net result of these discoveries is that the ancient Hebrews are taken out of the isolation in which, as a nation, they formerly seemed to stand; and it is seen now that many of their institutions and beliefs were not peculiar to themselves; they existed in more or less similar form among their neighbors; they were only in Israel developed in special directions, subordinated to special needs, and made the vehicle of special ideas.[115]

the tablets brought from the library of Ashurbanipal have disclosed to us the source of the material elements upon which the Biblical narratives of the Creation and the Deluge have been constructed.[116]

The conclusions of the higher critics, all proposed before the First World War, included the following: The Pentateuch was not written by Moses, as the book you are now reading was written by Anthony Lo Bello, but is rather a compilation of various documents denominated J, E, P, and D. So, for example, there are two creation stories Genesis 1:1–2:3 (P) and Genesis 2:4–2:25 (J). The prophecy of Isaiah consists of three different books combined by an editor (1–39, 40–55, 56–66), the last of whom lived in the period after the return from the Babylonian Exile. The Psalms were not all written by David, but by various authors, some perhaps, like Psalm 2, as late as the second century B.C. The Gospel according to John is a late work written by someone who had no personal contact with Jesus. The Letter to the Hebrews, and probably some of the other epistles as well, was not written by Paul.

The historical books are now seen to be not, as was once supposed, the works (for instance) of Moses, or Joshua, or Samuel. They are seen to present a multiplicity of phenomena which cannot be accounted for, or reasonably explained, except upon the supposition that they came into existence gradually; that they are compiled out of the writings of distinct and independent authors, characterized by different styles and representing different points of view, which were combined together and otherwise adjusted, till they finally assumed their present form. The various documents thus brought to light reveal, further, such mutual differences that in many cases they can no longer be held to be the work of contemporary writers, or to spring, as used to be thought, from a single generation: in the Pentateuch, espe-

114. *Seminary Address and Other Papers* (Cincinnati, Ohio: Ark Publishing, 1915), 35–39.

115. S. R. Driver and A. F. Kirkpatrick, *The Higher Criticism* (New York: Hodder & Stoughton, 1912), 42.

116. Ibid., 43–44.

cially, the groups of laws contained in the different strata of narrative differ in such a way that they can only be supposed to have been codified at widely different periods of the national life, to the history and literature of which they correspond, and the principles dominant in which they accurately reflect.[117]

These alarming conclusions were condemned by the Pontifical Biblical Commission founded by Leo XIII, to whom investigations such as these seemed subversive of Christianity. Questions were posed to the Commission, to which it replied *Yes* or *No*, for example:

Utrum varia systemata exegetica, quae ad excludendum sensum litteralem historicum trium priorum capitum libri Geneseos excogitata et scientiae fuco propugnata sunt, solido fundamento fulciantur? *Resp*. Negative.[118]

Are the diverse ways of interpreting the Bible, which have been devised in order to rule out the literal, historical sense of the first three chapters of the Book of Genesis, and which have been promoted under the guise of science, supported by a sound foundation? *Reply*: No.

Utrum solida prostent argumenta, etiam cumulative sumpta, ad evincendum Isaiae librum non ipsi soli Isaiae, sed duobus, immo pluribus auctoribus esse tribuendum? *Resp*. Negative.[119]

Are those arguments convincing, even if taken all together, that purport to establish that the Book of Isaiah must be assigned not to Isaiah himself alone, but to two, yea, even more authors? *Reply*: No.

The question of interest is whether these responses have any authority today. Certainly their authority is that to which the learning of their authors and constant tradition entitle them. Since, in the Christian system, the Christ is acknowledged to have come around 4 B.C. and not before, it is necessary to accept that the Deity revealed himself gradually; thus, it is not obvious that it can be ruled out that He also revealed the truth about the scriptures gradually. That the human beings themselves would not have thought to do it this way is, in view of Isaiah, not a convincing argument.

My thoughts are not your thoughts and your thoughts are not my thoughts, sayeth the Lord. (Isaiah 55:8)

---

117. Ibid., 40.
118. *Acta Apostolicae Sedis* 1 (1909), 567.
119. *Acta Sanctae Sedis* 41 (1908), 613s.

The *Catechism of the Catholic Church* has the following to say on the subject:

Libri inspirati veritatem docent. "Cum ergo omne id, quod auctores inspirati seu hagiographi asserunt, retineri debeat assertum a Spiritu Sancto, inde Scripturae libri veritatem, quam Deus nostrae salutis causa Litteris sacris consignari voluit, firmiter, fideliter, et sine errore docere profitendi sunt."

The inspired books teach the truth. "Since therefore all that the inspired authors or sacred writers affirm should be regarded as affirmed by the Holy Spirit, we must acknowledge that the books of Scripture firmly, faithfully, and without error teach that truth which God, for the sake of our salvation, wished to see confided in the Sacred Scriptures."[120]

Croccia The Italian word *croccia* denotes a *crook* or *hook*. The word is now used of various species of great mantles, some open in the front, formerly worn by the train bearers of the cardinals at papal ceremonies and by the cardinals themselves when in conclave. Hartwell de la Garde Grissell, cameriere segreto di numero, speaking of the Conclave of 1903, wrote:

The 'Croccia' was not worn by the Cardinals either at this or at the last Conclave. It is in the form of a mantle, made of silk or stuff according to the season, and worn over the 'Mozzetta'. The colour is purple for those who are not regulars, and for those who are it should be the colour of their Mozzetta.[121]

The name comes from the fact that the mantle is fastened at the neck by a hook.

Crosier A crook or a hook was called in mediaeval times a *croccia* in Italian and in Old French *croce*; thus, *crochet* is a kind of knitting done with a hooked needle. The words *croccia* and *croce* came to be applied to a staff with such a hook at the top. The French called the fellow who carried the bishop's staff *le crosier*. In Latin, this servant was the *crociarius*. Eventually *crosier* came to mean the bishop's staff itself. The word has no connection with *crux*, cross; the carrier of the cross was called the *cruciarius*. The

---

120. The Latin is quoted from *Catechismus Catholicae Ecclesiae*, Typica Editio (Vatican City: Libreria Editrice Vaticana, 1993), Article 3, II, §107, available online on the website of the Holy See: http://www.vatican.va/archive/catechism_lt/index_lt.htm. The English is quoted from *The Catechism of the Catholic Church*, 2nd ed. (Vatican City: Libreria Editrice Vaticana, 2003), §107, available online at http://www.vatican.va/archive/ENG0015/_INDEX.HTM. The quotation within the passage is from the Dogmatic Constitution on Divine Revelation of the Second Vatican Council, *Dei Verbum*, §11.

121. Hartwell de la Garde Grissell, *Sede Vacante, Being a Diary Written during the Conclave of 1903, with Additional Notes on the Accession and Coronation of Pius X* (Oxford: James Parker, 1903), 33, note a.

Latin word for the bishop's pastoral staff is *baculus pastoralis*. In former times, high-ranking dignitaries who were not bishops were occasionally granted the privilege of carrying a crosier. This practice was frowned upon after the Second Vatican Council. The only non-episcopal functionaries whom I have seen doing so in the past half century are three high officials of the cathedral chapter of Cologne, who still carry their pastoral staffs in the Corpus Christi procession each year. When carried by a prelate, the crosier always faces out.

Cross This word is the corruption of the Latin noun *crux*. On the Palatine Hill in Rome there was found during excavations in 1856 a graffito with the inscription Ἀλεξάμενος σέβετε θεόν. The middle word would be marked wrong in Greek 101; one expects σέβεται. The meaning is *Alexamenos worships his god*. It is accompanied by a picture of a man worshipping a crucified donkey. It is the first appearance of a crucifix in an illustration. Its date is within two centuries of the crucifixion. The earliest non-blasphemous representation of the crucifixion that I know of is on the fifth-century wooden door of the Church of Santa Sabina in Rome.

Crotalum The Greek noun κρόταλον means a *rattle*, and the Latin *crotalum* is its transliteration. It is the device used at Mass in place of bells during the Easter Triduum, after the Gloria of the Maundy Thursday Mass until the Gloria of the Easter Vigil Mass. A Jewish teacher of mine, who, as a child, used to attend Mass with the rest of his for the most part Catholic village in the Rhenish Palatinate, always remembered the *crotalum* and spoke of it as having the aura of the numinous about it. The crotalum is not something that you will commonly find in a Catholic Church any more. In biology, *Crotalus* is the genus of the *crotalidae*, the rattlesnakes.

Crucifix The Latin noun *crux, crucis, f.*, means *cross*, and the verb *figo, figere, fixi, fixus* means to *attach*. They were concatenated to form the compound verb *crucifigo* with the meaning *to attach to a cross*. Crucifixion was among the Romans a slave's punishment—*supplicium servile*; Roman citizens could not be crucified.

The custom of representing Christ naked on the cross was unknown in the early centuries of Christianity. Even the celebrated Graffito, a Pagan caricature of the Crucifixion, found on the Palatine in 1856, represents the Crucified as clothed. F. X. Kraus, *Das Spottcrucifix vom Palatin*, Freiburg, 1872. There is no instance of a crucifix being discovered in any of the oldest churchyards of Rome. The ancient crucifix of Lucca represents the Saviour as clad in a decent tunic, and diademed. The Byzantine oil-vases in Monza, moreover, presented to Queen Theodolinda, which depict the Saviour's passion, represent the two thieves hanging on their crosses, while Christ is raised in glory above His cross. The use of the crucifix was still very rare in the time of Gregory I.[122]

Cruet This noun, the Anglo-French diminutive of the Old French *cruit*, or *pot*, is related to the German noun *Krug* and the English noun *crock*. It is the name for the vessels used to hold the wine and water in the Mass before they are poured into the chalice for consecration.

Crusades The Latin noun *crux, crucis, f.* means *cross*. The pious soul or adventurer who set out on the Holy Crusades wore a cross on his garment, wherefore he was called in French (for French most of them were) *un croisé*. The sacred enterprise upon which he was embarked therefore acquired the name *croiserie*, from which our noun *crusade* descends. The Crusades were the campaigns of the eleventh, twelfth, and thirteenth centuries in which the Catholics of the West invaded the Muslim conquests in the east and established control over certain areas; they established the Kingdom of Jerusalem, the Principality of Antioch, the County of Tripoli, and the County of Edessa, which entities were denominated the *Crusader states*. The standard history of the Crusades is that in three volumes by Steven Runciman. The main positive result of the Crusades was the establishment of intellectual intercourse between the Latin Christians and the Muslims, as the former made Latin translations of the Arabic translations of the Greek authors. The bad behavior of some crusaders made the enterprise an embarrassment in modern times, though Muslim rule was scarcely uniformly benign.

Crux Fidelis These are the first two words of an antiphon sung at the Creeping to the Cross on Good Friday. The English translation is by Edward Caswall (1814–1878).

> Crux fidelis, inter omnes
> Arbor una nobilis;
> Nulla silva talem profert,
> Fronde, flore, germine.
> Dulce lignum, dulces clavos,
> Dulce pondus sustinet.

122. Ferdinand Gregorovius, *History of the City of Rome in the Middle Ages*, 2nd ed., trans. Mrs. Gustavus W. Hamilton (London: George Bell & Sons, 1902), 2:222n3.

— C —

Faithful Cross, O Tree all beauteous!
Tree all peerless and divine!
Not a grove on earth can show us
Such a leaf and flower as thine.
Sweet the nails, and sweet the wood,
Laden with so sweet a load!

Cubicularii ab Ense et Lucerna The Latin verb *cubo, cubare, cubui, cubitus* means *to lie down*, and from it is derived the noun *cubile* with the meaning a *bed*. From this noun is derived the word *cubicularius* with the meaning *bedroom servant, valet*. The Latin noun *ensis* means *sword*, and the noun *lucerna*—from *luceo, lucere, luxi*, (to be bright), and *lux*, (light)—means *lamp*. The *cubicularii ab ense et lucerna* (in Italian: *camerieri de spada e cappa*) were pontifical attendants who protected the pope in his progress, clearing and lighting the way before him. Equivalent characters may be seen today at the Church of the Holy Sepulcher in Jerusalem clearing the tourists out of the way before the daily processions.

Cuius Regio Eius Religio This Latin phrase means *Whose state, his religion*. It was the compromise formula adopted at the Peace of Augsburg (1555) in an attempt to settle the religious wars in the Holy Roman Empire; the religion of the prince was to be the religion of his people. Those subjects unwilling to follow the religion of their prince were to emigrate to some other territory.

Cult The Latin verb *colo, colere, colui, cultus* means *to till, take care of, worship*. The noun *cultus, cultūs, m.*, means *worship*; its stem has come into English as *cult*. In the Catholic Church, one speaks, for example, of the *cult of the saints*, meaning thereby the honors paid to those beings. In everyday language, the word has a negative connotation and is an appellation given to religious communities which are considered to be founded upon ignorance and irrational behavior.

Curia The *curia* was a division of the nobility of ancient Rome; the dividing was fabulously attributed to Romulus himself. There were thirty such *curiae*. The meeting place of a curia also became known as a curia. The Roman Senate met in one such curia, called the *Curia Hostilia* because it was built by Tullius Hostilius, third king of Rome. The word *curia* thus came to designate the senate house. The advisers of a bishop form a curia, and those of the bishop of Rome form the Roman Curia.

Cushion The Latin verb *cubo, cubare, cubui, cubitus* means *to lie down*, and from it is derived the nouns *cubitum*, with the meaning the *elbow*, and *coxa*, meaning the *thigh*. The *x* in *coxa* became *ss* in French (*coussin*) and *sc* in Italian (*cuscino*), and from the latter noun we get the English *cushion*. The ecclesiastical cushion is the device used to enable a prelate to kneel without pain to his knees.

D

Dalmatic The dalmatic is the outer garment of the deacon at Mass, originally a white sacerdotal vestment with purple stripes. Its origin is in Dalmatia, whence its name. In a similar way, *cravat*, tie, is the corruption of *Croatian*, since Croatia was the place of origin of that scarf. Fra Angelico painted the deacons Stephen and Lawrence wearing dalmatics in the frescoes of their lives in the Chapel of Pope Nicholas V in the Vatican. This chapel is no longer open to visitors who purchase the general admission ticket to the Vatican Museums. One has to go on a special tour to see it.

Da Pacem This ancient hymn is based on 2 Kings 20:19, 2 Chronicles 12:15, and Psalm 72:6–7.

Da pacem, Domine, in diebus nostris, quia non est alius qui pugnet pro nobis, nisi tu Deus noster.

Grant peace, O Lord, in our time, for there is none other to fight for us but you, our God.

Datary The Latin verb *do, dare, dedi, datus* means *to give*, and from the use of the past participle in expressions such as *datum Romae Kalendis Ianuariis MMXVI* ("given at Rome on January 1, 2016") at the end of documents, that past participle *datum* acquired the meaning *date*. Thence there arose the late verb *dato, datare* with the meaning *to date* (sc. a document). The fellow who dated the document, who most likely also prepared it in its final form, was called the *datarius*, and his office was denominated the *dataria*. English, by a poverty of expression, expresses both *datarius* and *dataria* by the single word *datary*. The Datary was the office of the Roman Curia that prepared official documents.

La Dataria Apostolica è quel Dicastero della Santa Sede, per mezzo del quale il Sommo Pontefice accorda Benefizi Ecclesiastici, Dispense Matrimoniali dagli impedimenti pubblici e dirimenti, ed altre grazie, a seconda delle Costituzioni Apostoliche all'uopo promulgate.[1]

The Apostolic Datary is that congregation of the Holy See by means of which the Supreme Pontiff grants ecclesiastical benefices, matrimonial dispensations from public impediments and diriments, and other graces in accordance with the Apostolic Constitutions promulgated for that purpose.

The Palace of the Datary is attached to the Apostolic Palace of the Quirinale, where the popes lived for most of the seventeenth, eighteenth, and nineteenth centuries. It was one of the many edifices in Rome given extraterritorial status in 1929. The Holy See exchanged it in the 1970s in return for getting extraterritorial status for the Palazzio Pio in the Borgo. It is now occupied by the Italian News Agency ANSA. As a result of a reorganization of the Roman Curia by Paul VI, the Apostolic Datary had meanwhile ceased to exist as of January 1, 1968.

Deacon The Greek verb διακονέω means *to serve*, and the corresponding noun διάκονος means *servant, minister*; Latin just transliterates the noun into *diaconus*, of which *deacon* is the stem. The story of the institution of the office of deacon is to be found in Acts 6:1–6. Thereupon follows the story of the martyrdom of the deacon Stephen. Gregorovius observed:

The deacon played a conspicuous part in Rome, and administering, as they did, the ecclesiastical property, mixed largely with the world. On this account the archdeacon, next to the bishop, was the most important person in the church.[2]

Deaconesses A female deacon might be called in Greek a διακονίσσα, just as a queen was a βασιλίσσα. The English noun *deaconess* is just the offspring of the Greek διακονίσσα. St. Paul calls the Lady Phoebe a deacon (not a deaconess) in Romans 16:1–2:

---

1. From the *Regolamento della Dataria Apostolica*, published February 6, 1901, to be found in *La Storia e il Diritto della Dataria Apostolica dalle Origini ai Nostri Giorni* by Nicola Storti (Naples: Athena Mediterranea Editrice, 1969), 385.

2. Ferdinand Gregorovius, *History of the City of Rome in the Middle Ages*, trans. Mrs. Gustavus W. Hamilton (London: George Bell & Sons, 1909), 1:148n1.

Συνίστημι δὲ ὑμῖν Φοίβην τὴν ἀδελφὴν ἡμῶν, οὖσαν καὶ διάκονον τῆς ἐκκλησίας τῆς ἐν Κεγχρεαῖς, ἵνα αὐτὴν προσδέξησθε ἐν κυρίῳ ἀξίως τῶν ἁγίων, καὶ παραστῆτε αὐτῇ ἐν ᾧ ἂν ὑμῶν χρῄζῃ πράγματι, καὶ γὰρ αὐτὴ προστάτις πολλῶν ἐγενήθη καὶ ἐμοῦ αὐτοῦ.

I commend our sister Phoebe to you, who is a deacon of the Church in Cenchrea, so that you receive her in the Lord in a manner worthy of the saints, and that you stand by her in whatever matter in which she needs your assistance, for she has been a great help to many, even to me.

Female assistants were useful, even indispensable, as intermediaries between the clergy and females; there is no evidence that deaconesses had a liturgical function. In fact, as if to rule this possibility out, Jerome translates οὖσαν καὶ διάκονον τῆς ἐκκλησίας in the passage cited above by *quae est in ministerio ecclesiae*, that is, "who is in the service of the Church." Yet Lea speculated as follows:

it would have been strange if women, to whom the propagation of the Gospel was so greatly owing, had not been sometimes admitted to the function of conducting the simple services of the primitive Church. We learn from St. Paul that Phoebe was a deacon (διάκονος) of the Church of Cenchrea; the Apostolic Constitutions contain a regular formula for their ordination; and the canon of Laodicea shows that until the middle of the fourth century they still occasionally occupied recognized positions in the active ministry of the Church.[3]

In our own times, Pope Francis has appointed a committee to examine what information is available about women and the deaconate.

Dean The Greek numeral δέκα means *ten*, and a δεκανός was the supervisor of a set of ten monks. This noun was transliterated into Latin as *decanus*. The English word *dean* is the corruption, through the medium of the French *doyen*, of this Latin noun, the *c* having fallen out. Nowadays the dean is the highest in rank of the canons of a cathedral or collegiate chapter.

Death The English word *death* is derived from the Anglo-Saxon noun *dēath*; it is related to the German *Tod*. Plato gave a definition of death in the dialogue *Gorgias*:

3. Henry Charles Lea, *History of Sacerdotal Celibacy in the Christian Church* (n.p.: University Books, 1966), 40.

ὁ θάνατος τυγχάνει ὤν, ὡς ἐμοὶ δοκεῖ, οὐδὲν ἄλλο ἢ δυοῖν πραγμάτοιν διάλυσις, τῆς ψυχῆς καὶ τοῦ σώματος, ἀπ᾽ ἀλλήλοιν.[4]

Death, it seems to me, is nothing other than the separation of two things, the soul and the body, from one another.

Decretals The Greek verb κρίνω means *to judge*. The related Latin verb *cerno, cernere, crevi, cretus* means *to separate, distinguish, resolve, determine*. The addition of the preposition *de* results in the compound verb *decerno* with the meaning *to decide, to decree after making a determination*. From the fourth principal part *decretus* comes the noun *decretum* with the meaning a *resolve* or *decree*, which is the equivalent of the Greek δόγμα. The addition of the suffix *-alis* produced the adjective *decretalis* with the meaning *pertaining to a decree*. From this developed the mediaeval noun *decretal, decretalis, n.*, meaning a *papal decree*. The False Decretals are pretended papal decrees, which Lea says are probably of the ninth century.[5]

Deism The Latin word *deus* means *god*, and the suffix *-ism* is the transliteration of the stem of the Greek suffix -ισμός, which forms nouns of action from verbs ending in -ίζειν. The noun *deism* is therefore a macaronic construction, a concoction of the seventeenth century. Deism is the point of view that there is a god, but that he takes no interest in human affairs and that all teaching to the contrary is a fraud. It became popular during the Enlightenment of the eighteenth century, and its professors were of the opinion that organized religion is the promotion of superstition. The Catholic Church was the particular object of their disapproval. Thomas Jefferson was a deist; the Jefferson Bible is an edition of the gospels that he produced by striking out all texts involving miracles.

When a matter-of-fact mind, averse to allegory, takes up biblical criticism, the outcome is often the mutilation and alteration of the sacred text.[6]

Deo Gratias This Latin phrase means *Thanks be to God*. The giving or adoption of bizarre names is not an idiosyncrasy solely of the modern era. Names such as Deogratias, Dominusvobiscum, Habetdeum, and Quodvultdeus were common enough among bishops, particularly North African bishops, until the extinction of Catholicism there in the fifth century.

4. Plato, *Gorgias*, 524b

5. Henry Charles Lea, *History of Sacerdotal Celibacy in the Christian Church* (n.p.: University Books, 1966), 107.

6. Louis Duchesne, *Early History of the Christian Church from Its Foundation to the End of the Third Century* (London: John Murray, 1914), 219.

– D –

Some of these names, such as Adeodatus, have maintained their place to the present day. Milman observes:

The successor of Cyprian, "Quod vult Deus," ("What God wills,"—the African prelates had anticipated our Puritans in their Scriptural names), and many of his clergy were embarked in crazy vessels, and cast on shore on the coast of Naples.[7]

Deo Laudes! This exclamation, which means *Praises to God!*, was the battle cry of the Circumcellions.

Deputy The Latin verb *pŭto* of the first conjugation means *to cleanse, clear, lop, prune, settle, reckon, think*, and the preposition *de* means *off* or *from*. From their combination was produced the verb *depŭto* with the meaning *to prune* or *cut off*. A fellow sent off on special assignment was therefore said to be *deputatus*, and from the French form of this word, *député*, we get our noun *deputy*, meaning *agent*. It was once used of the pope as the deputy or Vicar of Christ. This particular usage of the word *deputy* became notorious in the 1960s as the result of the play of Hochhuth, *Der Stellvertreter*, translated into English as *The Deputy*.

Deus Passus This is a Latin phrase meaning the *God who suffered*. It was a controversial expression at the time of the early controversies about the Holy Trinity.

Peter [the Fuller] was a great liturgist. He knew to what an extent customs in worship can exert influence upon religious thought. It is to him that the practice goes back of reciting in the Mass the Credo of Nicaea. In his view it was a protest against the Council of Chalcedon. The Monophysites took every opportunity of repeating that they desired only the Creed of Nicaea and repudiated all others. He attempted also to complete the Trisagion. To the hallowed words, "Holy God, Holy and Mighty, Holy and Immortal," he added, "Crucified for us, ὁ σταυρωθεὶς δι' ἡμῶν." This was equivalent to the formula *Deus passus*, which had been used without specific implication before all these controversies. Now it was plainly a profession of the unity of nature.[8] Calendion, with a view to settling matters, had conceived the idea of inserting between the primitive text and the heretical addition the words, "Christ our God"—which saved the situation and orthodoxy. But this correction, like many other wise things, met with little success. The "Cru-

---

7. Henry Hart Milman, *History of Latin Christianity, Including That of the Popes, to the Pontificate of Nicholas V* (New York: Sheldon, 1860), 1:269.

8. [Note of Duchesne]: "The *Theotokos* is in itself quite as open to criticism as the *Crucifixus pro nobis*. We may note the analogy between Calendion's combination and that which Nestorius had proposed with his *Christotokos*."

cified for us" without any softening became the battle cry of the Monophysites, just as the Deo Laudes had been that of the Donatists.[9]

Deuterocanonical This is a word coined in the sixteenth century to describe those books of the Catholic Old Testament that are not to be found in the *Biblia Hebraica*,[10] and about whose canonicity there had therefore been more than the usual discussion; the Protestants removed them from the Bible, calling them *apocryphal* and their sum total the *Apocrypha*, a denomination that had the consequence of imparting a negative connotation to those words. The word *Deuterocanonical* is a combination of the Greek adjectives δεύτερος (second) and κανωνικός (pertaining to the Canon) and the Latin adjectival suffix *-al*. The analogous word *protocanonical* was contemporaneously invented to denominate those books that had been admitted to the Canon first.

Devil The Greek verb βάλλω means *to throw*, and the compound verb διαβάλλω means *to throw across, to slander*; from this latter word arose the associated noun διάβολος with the meaning a *slanderer*. The word διάβολος was used in the Septuagint to translate the Hebrew שׂטן, *Satan*. It was transliterated into Latin as *diabolus*, which was itself later corrupted into the English *devil*. The devil is mentioned in the Lord's Prayer, where he is denominated the *Evil One*: *Sed libera nos a Malo*.

Dialogue Mass The Greek verb λέγω means *to speak*, and with the addition of the distributive preposition διά there is produced the compound verb διαλέγω, with the meaning *to converse*. From this verb there was derived the noun διάλογος with the meaning *conversation*. The dialogue was the genre of literature perfected by Plato. The modern *Dialogue Mass* was an invention of the twentieth century; the idea was to get the congregation talking during the Mass by encouraging them to give all the responses of the servers, and even to sing along with the choir in chanting the parts of the prayers reserved for those singers. Except in those rare cases where the people joining in are expert musicians and Latinists, the practice can be a distraction.

9. Louis Duchesne, *Early History of the Christian Church from Its Foundation to the End of the Fifth Century*, vol. 3 (London: John Murray, 1924), 352.
10. William Sanday, *Inspiration, Eight Lectures on the Early History and Origin of the Doctrine of Biblical Inspiration, Being the Bampton Lectures for 1893* (London: Longmans, Green, 1896), 273.

Diatessaron The Greek prepositional phrase διὰ τῶν τεσσάρων εὐαγγελίων means *through the four gospels,* and from its first and third words was derived the name *Diatessaron.* The *Diatessaron* was the first harmony of the four gospels; it was composed either in Syriac or Greek by Tatian, a second-century Syrian pupil of Justin Martyr.[11] It is mentioned by Eusebius,[12] who says that Tatian was an Encratite heretic.

Dicastery The Greek noun δίκη means *right, justice.* From it were derived the verb δικάζω (to judge) and the nouns δικαστής (judge) and δικαστήριον (court of justice). The meaning was later extended to encompass any bureau or department of government. It is a relatively new word in the terminology of the Holy See, introduced during the time of Pope John Paul II as a generic all-encompassing name for any department of the Roman Curia.

Didache The old Greek root δάω means *to learn,* and the reduplicated causal form διδάσκω means *to teach.* The noun διδαχή formed from this latter verb means *teaching,* in Latin, *doctrina.* The *Didache,* or *The Teaching of the Twelve Apostles* is the name of a book of the first century A.D. It is known to have existed since ancient times, for it is mentioned by Eusebius:

Among spurious books must be placed the 'Acts' of Paul, the 'Shepherd', and the 'Revelation of Peter'; also the alleged 'Epistle of Barnabas', and the 'Teachings of the Apostles', together with the Revelation of John, if this seems the right place for it: as I said before, some reject it, others include it among the Recognised Books.[13]

However, no manuscript of the *Didache* had been discovered until the nineteenth century, when one dated 1056 was found by the Metropolitan Bryennios in the library of the patriarch of Jerusalem, in Constantinople; this discovery was announced in 1875. Bishop Lightfoot prepared an edition of the Greek text with an introduction and translation, which was published after his death.[14] The modern reader notices those portions that support the early date assigned to the document; for example, it con-

11. William Sanday, *Inspiration, Eight Lectures on the Early History and Origin of the Doctrine of Biblical Inspiration, Being the Bampton Lectures for 1893* (London: Longmans, Green, 1896), 301–2.
12. Eusebius, *The History of the Church from Christ to Constantine,* trans. G. A. Williamson (London: The Folio Society, 2011), IV 29, p. 124.
13. Eusebius, *The History of the Church from Christ to Constantine,* trans. G. A. Williamson (London: The Folio Society, 2011), III 25, p. 81.
14. J. B. Lightfoot, *The Apostolic Fathers,* ed. J. R. Harmer (London: Macmillan, 1891), 213–35.

tains instruction on the offices of apostle, prophet, bishop (not distinguished from *priest*), and deacon and recommends that catechumens be baptized in a stream, although the modern method by affusion is permitted. Astrologers, called mathematicians (μαθηματικοί), are condemned. The confession of sins in the church is prescribed. Fasting is ordered on Wednesdays and Fridays. The Lord's Prayer is given with the Doxology. There is a formula for the words of consecration, and the end of the world is considered imminent. See the entry **Abortion**.

Dies Irae These are the opening words of the sequence in the old requiem Mass; they mean the *Day of Wrath*. The *Dies Irae* is the most famous poem of the Middle Ages and the chief work of art in the Catholic liturgy. To be present when it is chanted at a funeral is to participate in sublimity. The "Dies Irae" of the Verdi *Requiem* is the supreme masterpiece of all music. To understand this poem is the definition of education. This poem, like so many other of the old prayers, is remarkable for its intellectual content.

> Dies irae, dies illa,
> Solvet saeclum in favilla:
> Teste David cum Sibylla.
>
> Quantus tremor est futurus,
> Quando iudex est venturus,
> Cuncta stricte discussurus!
>
> Tuba mirum spargens sonum
> Per sepulchra regionum,
> Coget omnes ante thronum.
>
> Mors stupebit, et natura,
> Cum resurget creatura,
> Iudicanti responsura.
>
> Liber scriptus proferetur,
> In quo totum continetur,
> Unde mundus iudicetur.
>
> Iudex ergo cum sedebit,
> Quidquid latet, apparebit:
> Nil inultum remanebit.
>
> Quid sum miser tunc dicturus?
> Quem patronum rogaturus,
> Cum vix iustus sit securus?

Rex tremendae maiestatis,
Qui salvandos salvas gratis,
Salva me, fons pietatis.

Recordare, Iesu pie,
Quod sum causa tuae viae:
Ne me perdas illa die.

Quaerens me, sedisti lassus:
Redemisti crucem passus:
Tantus labor non sit cassus.

Iuste iudex ultionis,
Donum fac remissionis
Ante diem rationis.

Ingemisco, tamquam reus:
Culpa rubet vultus meus:
Supplicanti parce, Deus.

Qui Mariam absolvisti,
Et latronem exaudisti,
Mihi quoque spem dedisti.

Preces meae non sunt dignae:
Sed tu bonus fac benigne,
Ne perenni cremer igne.

Inter oves locum praesta,
Et ab haedis me sequestra,
Statuens in parte dextra.

Confutatis maledictis,
Flammis acribus addictis:
Voca me cum benedictis.

Oro supplex et acclinis,
Cor contritum quasi cinis:
Gere curam mei finis.

Lacrimosa dies illa,
Qua resurget ex favilla
Iudicandus homo reus:
Huic ergo parce, Deus.

Pie Iesu Domine,
Dona eis requiem. Amen.

Here follows the English translation by Thomas Babington Macaulay (1800–1859).

On that great, that awful day,
This vain world will pass away.
Thus the Sibyl sang of old
Thus hath Holy David told.

There shall be a deadly fear
When the Avenger shall appear,
And unveiled before his eye
All the works of man shall lie.

Hark! to the great trumpet's tones
Pealing o'er the place of bones;
Hark! it waketh from its bed
All the nations of the dead,—
In a countless throng to meet,
At the eternal judgment seat.

Nature sickens with dismay
Death may not retain his prey;
And before the Maker stand
All the creatures of his hand.

The great book shall be unfurled,
Whereby God shall judge the world:
What was distant shall be near,
What was hidden shall be clear.

To what shelter shall I fly?
To what guardian shall I cry?
Oh, in that destroying hour,
Source of goodness, Source of power,
Show thou, of thine own free grace,
Help unto a helpless race.

Though I plead not at thy throne
Aught that I for thee have done,
Do not thou unmindful be,
Of what thou hast borne for me:

Of the wandering, of the scorn,
Of the scourge, and of the thorn.
Jesus, hast thou borne the pain,
And hath all been borne in vain?
Shall thy vengeance smite the head
For whose ransom thou hast bled?

Thou, whose dying blessing gave
Glory to a guilty slave:
Thou, who from the crew unclean
Didst release the Magdalene:
Shall not mercy vast and free,
Evermore be found in thee?

Father, turn on me thine eyes,
See my blushes, hear my cries;
Faint though be the cries I make,
Save me for thy mercy's sake,
From the worm and from the fire,
From the torments of thine ire.

Fold me with the sheep that stand
Pure and safe at thy right hand.
Hear thy guilty child implore thee,
Rolling in the dust before thee.

Oh the horrors of that day!
When this frame of sinful clay,
Starting from its burial place,
Must behold thee face to face.

Hear and pity, hear and aid,
Spare the creatures thou hast made.
Mercy, mercy, save, forgive,
Oh, who shall look on thee and live? [15]

The latest news on the *Dies Irae* was reported by Lentini:

Testo attribuito a vari autori, più lungamente al francescano Tommaso da Celano
(† c. 1260); ma sembra certo che sia almeno del sec. XII e forse anche anteriore,
di autore ignoto.

Ritmico. Dimetro trocaico; strofe di 3 versi, con rima bisillabica perfetta a a a.

È la celebre sequenza, "sacrae poeseos"—dice il Daniel (Thes. l. c.[16])—"summum decus et Ecclesiae Latinae κειμήλιον pretiosissimum", tanto a lungo cantata,
e con molta partecipazione dei fedeli, nella Messa per i defunti. Espunta, purtrop-
po, dal Messale, è stata introdotta nella LH, perché non andasse perduto questo
gioiello di arte e di pietà, tanto più che si adatta bene alla settimana ultima che
precede la 1ª Domenica di Avvento, nella quale—sembra—si soleva cantare in
consonanza col Vangelo. La composizione infatti si svolge in referimento al finale

---

15. Thomas Babington Macaulay, *The Miscellaneous Writings* (London: Longman, Green, Longman, Roberts, 1860), 2:394–95.

16. H. A. Daniel, *Thesaurus Hymnologicus* (Halle and Leipzig, 1855–1862).

giudizio universale. Benché stesa in prima persona singolare, è degna del suo posto nella liturgia per il magnifico contenuto.[17]

Text attributed to various authors, for the longest time to the Franciscan Thomas of Celano (died c. 1260), but it seems certain that it is at least as early as the twelfth century and perhaps even earlier, of unknown authorship.

Rhythm: trochaic dimeter, each strophe of three verses, with a perfect two-syllable rhyme a a a.

It is the famous sequence, "the supreme glory of sacred poetry"—so, Daniel in his dictionary—"and the most precious treasure of the Latin Church," so long sung, and with the full participation of the faithful, in the Requiem Mass. Expunged, unfortunately, from the Missal, it has been introduced into the Liturgy of the Hours in order that this jewel of art and of piety not be lost, and even more because it is well adapted to the last week before the First Sunday of Advent in which—it seems—one should sing compatibly with the Gospel of the day. The composition in fact deals with the Last Judgment. Although written in the first person singular, it is worthy of its place in the liturgy because of its wonderful contents.

A casualty of the modern liturgical changes, the *Dies Irae* survives in the Liturgy of the Hours, in the thirty-fourth week, Monday through Saturday, where it has been divided into three parts; the first part is an optional hymn for the *Office of Readings* (formerly Matins), the second part is an optional hymn for Lauds (*ad Laudes matutinas*), and the third part is an optional hymn for Vespers (*ad Vesperas*). To each third there has been added, to serve as a doxology, a final stanza not part of the original poem, but composed for other purposes in the fifteenth century:

> O tu, Deus maiestatis,
> Alme candor Trinitatis,
> Nos coniunge cum beatis. Amen.
>
> Do Thou, O God of majesty,
> All caring, glorious Trinity,
> Grant us a bless'd eternity. Amen.

In its new home, the verse *Qui Mariam absolvisti* has been changed to *Peccatricem qui solvisti* to accommodate those who accept the discovery of the textual critics, that the woman caught in sin (Luke 7:37) was not the same as Mary Magdalene.

---

17. Anselmo Lentini, *Te Decet Hymnus, L'Innario della "Liturgia Horarum"* (Vatican City: Typis Polyglottis Vaticanis, 1984), 70.

Diet The Mediaeval Latin noun *dieta* stood for two ideas, that of the Greek δίαιτα (*life, way of living, mode of life*) and that of the Latin *dies* (*a day, a day's work*). In the second sense, it was the word used to describe the meetings of the legislative body of the Holy Roman Empire, which gatherings were not restricted to a particular city. The Diets of Worms (1521) and of Speyer (1529) were of particular importance for the relationship between the Catholic Church and the reformers; the former congress was distinguished by the appearance of Luther, whereas at the latter Diet there was coined the word *Protestant*.

Digamy The Greek adverb δίς means *twice*, and the noun γάμος means *marriage*, whence proceeds the adjective δίγαμος with the meaning *twice-married*. The English noun *digamy* is formed from the Greek adjective; it is the state of having married again after the death of one's first wife. To remarry is an impediment to receiving the sacrament of Holy Orders. That digamy is a disqualification from the episcopacy, or even from the priesthood, is announced in 1 Timothy 3:2:

δεῖ οὖν τὸν ἐπίσκοπον ἀνεπίλημπτον εἶναι, μιᾶς γυναικὸς ἄνδρα …

Oportet ergo episcopum irreprehensibilem esse, unius uxoris virum …

The bishop must be beyond criticism, married only once …

The Pauline rule that prohibits a twice-married man from being ordained is still enforced in the Orthodox Church.

Dignitatis Humanae This is the name of the declaration made by the Second Vatican Council on religious liberty; it begins, "In our time, men have become more and more conscious of the dignity of the human person." It had long been the complaint of critical people that while the Catholic Church demanded freedom for herself, she denied it, when she could, to those of other religions under the pretext that error has no rights. The Catholic Church was not unique in denying religious liberty to dissidents in past ages; all nations and all churches did so at one time or another. The foremost proponents of religious liberty in America would hesitate, no doubt, to permit the bloody Ashura processions of the Shiite Muslims down Broadway or Park Avenue. In an age when the law *Cuius regio eius religio* was in force, religious liberty was another name for treason. *Dignitatis Humanae* teaches that it is a human right to be free to practice one's religion publicly, provided one does not thereby disturb public order.

Haec Vaticana Synodus declarat personam humanam ius habere ad libertatem religiosam. Huiusmodi libertas in eo consistit, quod omnes homines debent immunes esse a coërcitatione ex parte sive singulorum sive coetuum socialium et cuiusvis potestatis humanae, et ita quidem ut in re religiosa neque aliquis cogatur ad agendum contra suam conscientiam neque impediatur, quominus iuxta suam conscientiam agat privatim et publice, vel solus vel aliis consociatus, intra debitos limites. Insuper declarat ius ad libertatem religiosam esse revera fundatum in ipsa dignitate personae humanae qualis et verbo Dei revelato et ipsa ratione cognoscitur. Hoc ius personae humanae ad libertatem religiosam in iuridica societatis ordinatione ita est agnoscendum, ut ius civile evadat.[18]

This Vatican Council declares that the human being has the right to freedom of religion. This type of freedom consists in all men being free from pressure either from individuals or from groups or from any human authority, so that in the matter of religion no one is forced to act against his conscience, nor is anyone prevented from acting privately or publicly as his conscience directs, either alone or in association with others, within due boundaries. What is more, it declares that the right to freedom of religion is truly based on the very dignity of the human being as understood from the revealed word of God and by means of reason itself. This right of the human being to freedom of religion must be so recognized in the legal ordering of society that it becomes a civil right.

This declaration was different from that which had previously emanated from such authorities as Gregory XVI and Pius IX.

Ex qua omnino falsa socialis regiminis idea haud timent erroneam illam fovere opinionem catholicae Ecclesiae, animarumque saluti maxime exitialem, a rec. mem. Gregorio XVI. Praedecessore Nostro *deliramentum* appellatam, nimirum "libertatem conscientiae et cultuum esse proprium cuiuscumque hominis ius, quod lege proclamari et asseri debet in omni recte constituta societate, et ius civibus inesse ad omnimodam libertatem nulla vel ecclesiastica, vel civili auctoritate coarctandam, quo suos conceptus quoscumque sive voce, sive typis, sive alia ratione palam publiceque manifestare, ac declarare valeant."[19]

From this altogether wrong notion of the ordering of society, they hardly hesitate to embrace that false hypothesis, altogether catastrophic to the Catholic Church and the salvation of souls, and called by our recently deceased predecessor Gregory XVI *pure madness*, namely, "that freedom of conscience and of religions is a prerogative of every man which ought to be declared and asserted by law in every

18. Sacrosanctum Oecumenicum Concilium Vaticanum II, *Constitutiones, Decreta, Declarationes*, Cura et Studio Secretariae Generalis Concilii Oecumenici Vaticani II (Vatican City: Typis Polyglottis Vaticanis, 1974), §2, pp. 513–14.

19. *Quanta Cura*, in Denzinger, *Enchiridion Symbolorum et Definitionum*, 7th ed. (Würzburg: V. J. Stahel, 1895), §1540, p. 372.

properly constituted society, and that citizens have the innate right, not alienable by any ecclesiastical or civil power, to every sort of freedom, a right that permits them openly and publicly to announce and declare whatever opinions they have by voice, in print, or in any other manner."

The traditional teaching of the Catholic Church was that in ideal circumstances, such as were most closely approximated in the Middle Ages, the Catholic religion should be the religion of the state, and dissenters should be allowed to practice their religion privately but certainly not in public. The teaching of the Second Vatican Council was defended on the basis that its truth had been discovered from the book of human experience.

Etsi in vita Populi Dei, per vicissitudines historiae humanae peregrinantis, interdum exstitit modus agendi spiritui evangelico minus conformis, immo contrarius, semper tamen mansit Ecclesiae doctrina neminem esse ad fidem cogendum.

Evangelicum fermentum in mentibus hominum sic diu est operatum atque multum contulit, ut homines temporum decursu latius agnoscerent dignitatem personae suae et maturesceret persuasio in re religiosa ipsam immunem servandam esse in civitate a quacumque humana coercitione.[20]

Although from time to time there have been evident in the progress of the People of God, during their pilgrimage through history, examples of behavior scarcely in conformity with, and even opposite to, the spirit of the Gospel, all have nevertheless accepted the teaching that no one may be forced to join the Church.

The evangelical leaven has for so long done its work in the hearts of men that as the centuries passed, people more and more recognized the dignity of their person, and the point of view matured that that dignity should be kept immune in the state from any human coercion.

Diocese The Greek verb οἰκέω means *to inhabit*, or, of states, *to be settled, situated, governed*. From the addition of the preposition διά (*throughout*) to this word there arose the compound διοικέω with the meaning *to manage, direct, conduct*. From διοικέω was produced the noun διοίκησις with the meaning *housekeeping, management*, whose Latin transliteration is *dioecēsis*, a district. The emperor Diocletian (284–305) reorganized the government of the Roman Empire, dividing it into thirteen dioceses: Africa, Asia, Britain, Dacia, the East, Egypt, Gaul, Italy, Macedonia, Pontus, Rome, Spain, and Thrace, each governed by a *vicarius*. Similarly, the Church organized itself into dioceses, each governed by an *episcopus*.

20. Sacrosanctum Oecumenicum Concilium Vaticanum II, *Constitutiones, Decreta, Declarationes*, Cura et Studio Secretariae Generalis Concilii Oecumenici Vaticani II (Vatican City: Typis Polyglottis Vaticanis, 1974), §12, p. 527.

Diphysite The Greek verb φύω means *to bring forth*, and from it was derived the noun φύσις, which means *nature*. The adverb δίς means *twice* (from δύο, two), and from the combination of the two words was formed in the fifth century the technical term διφυσίτης (plural διφυσῖται), a believer in the doctrine that Christ had two natures. Thus, a diphysite formula is any formula teaching that there are two natures in Jesus Christ. Such a formula was imposed as a condition of orthodoxy at the Fourth Ecumenical Council at Chalcedon in 451.

Diptych The Greek verb πτύσσω means *to fold*, and from it was derived the feminine noun πτύξ, πτυχός, *a fold*. The adverb δίς means *twice* (from δύο, *two*), so the adjective δίπτυχος means *folded over so as to be made double*. The diptychs were folded tablets on which were inscribed the names of the chief prelates of Christendom to be commemorated in the Mass. To erase someone's name from the diptychs was to declare him a heretic. In modern times in the Latin Church, only the names of the pope and the local bishop are commemorated in this manner. The noun *diptych* is also the name for an icon painted on two hinged tablets.

Disciples The Greek verb διδάσκω means *to teach*, and the related Latin verb *disco, discere, didici* means *to learn*. A *disciplina* is *that which is learned*, or the act of learning itself. One who learns, invariably someone young, is a *discipulus*, a learner, and it is from this word that we have the English *disciple*. The Disciples were the twelve students of Jesus. They are called in the Greek of the gospels μαθηταί, *pupils*.

It has been pointed out by Weizsäcker [*Apost. Zeitalt.* p. 36] that the regular word for disciples, μαθηταί, though constantly used in the Gospels and Acts, disappears entirely from the rest of the New Testament, where the substitutes are ἀδελφοί and ἅγιοι.[21]

Dispensation The Latin verb *pendo, pendere, pependi, pensum* means *to cause to hang down, to weigh*, and from it was formed the compound verb *dispendo, dispendere*, with the meaning *to weigh out*. From the latter verb was formed the frequentative verb *dispenso, dispensare* with the meaning *to be constantly weighing or paying out*, and he who paid out the money was called a *dispensator*, and his paying out, a *dispensatio*. According to Weekley, the meaning of the giving out of exemptions instead of money is

---

21. William Sanday, *Inspiration, Eight Lectures on the Early History and Origin of the Doctrine of Biblical Inspiration, Being the Bampton Lectures for 1893* (London: Longmans, Green, 1896), 288–89.

a late, mediaeval development. For the dispensations requested by Henry VIII from Clement VII, see the entry **Divorce**.

Dissident The Latin verb *sedeo, sedere, sedi, sessus* means *to sit*. The addition of the prefix *dis-*, which imparts the force of *apart, asunder*, produces the compound verb *dissideo, dissidere* with the meaning *to sit apart from, to be distant, to disagree*. Those who do so are called *dissidentes*, whence comes our English word *dissidents*. The word *dissidents* was many years ago a common appellation given to the Orthodox; indeed, Donald Attwater once wrote a good book entitled *The Dissident Eastern Churches*.[22]

Divorce The Latin verb *verto, vertere, verti, versus* means *to turn*, and the addition of the prefix *dis-* produces the compound verb *diverto, divertere, diverti, diversus* with the meaning *to turn different ways, to differ*. From this last verb is derived the noun *divortium*, divorce, which word, together with the more common *repudium*, was used to indicate the transaction whereby a valid marriage was dissolved. This possibility does not exist in the Catholic religion, since it was condemned *expressis verbis* by Jesus Christ, in Mark 10:2–9. The exception mentioned in Matthew 5:32 and 19:9 allows a loophole. The most famous and instructive case in the history of the Church was that of Henry VIII, King of England (1509–1547), whose divorce was the proximate cause of the Reformation in that country.[23]

Henry VIII always maintained that he had never been divorced. He did not believe in divorce. What we call his divorces, he called his *annulments*, declarations that no marriage had existed in the first place, that the marriage had been null and void from the beginning. According to him, the famous jingle should have been:

Annulled, beheaded, died,
annulled, beheaded, survived.

We begin with two passages from the Old Testament, the happy hunting grounds of so many reformers. These verses are relevant to Henry's initial divorse, because his first wife was his older brother's widow.

22. Donald Attwater, *The Dissident Eastern Churches* (Milwaukee, Wis.: Bruce Publishing, 1937).
23. The best sources upon which to rely for the story of the divorce are the introductions of John Sherren Brewer to his editions of the *Letters and Papers, Foreign and Domestic, of Henry VIII*, which he issued during his tenure as Keeper or Master of the Rolls and Records of the Chancery of England, afterwards collected and published separately in two volumes in 1884 as *The Reign of Henry VIII*, and the four papers by James Gairdner in the *English Historical Review* listed in the bibliography. Also important is the paper by Fr. Herbert Thurston, SJ, "The Canon Law of the Divorce," *English Historical Review* 19, no. 76 (October 1904): 632–45.

Leviticus 20:21: And if a man should take his brother's wife, it is an unclean thing; he hath uncovered his brother's nakedness. They shall be childless.

Deuteronomy 25:5–6: If brethren dwell together, and one of them die and have no child, the wife of the dead shall not marry without unto a stranger; her husband's brother shall go in unto her and take her to him to wife, and perform the duty of an husband's brother unto her. And it shall be that the firstborn which she beareth shall succeed in the name of his brother which is dead, that his name not be put out of Israel. (Authorized Version)

Upon first glance, it seems that these two verses state contradictory laws with regard to whether or not one of the children of Israel was allowed to marry his brother's widow. Those most successful in harmonizing the verses say that one may marry one's brother's widow if the brother was childless, in which case the firstborn of the new marriage would be the heir of the deceased. This is called the Levirate Marriage, and was the law among the Jews. If, however, the brother was still alive, or died with surviving children, then the marriage of the brother and sister-in-law was strictly forbidden. It was such an attempt on the part of Herod Antipas to marry his brother Philip's divorced wife during his brother's lifetime that got him into trouble with John the Baptist.

When the Christian Church was established, certain Old Testament practices were continued, and others were discontinued. Among those discontinued was the Levirate Marriage. Continued was the prohibition against marrying one's brother's widow, extended now to both cases, whether or not she had provided heirs to her first husband.

All societies have laws forbidding people from marrying their closest relatives. In the United States, a man may not marry his mother, his sister, or his daughter. In the Commonwealth of Pennsylvania, no man may marry his first cousin. In Germany, it is allowed by the state to marry one's first cousin, and both Lutherans and Jews avail themselves of this permission. In England Queen Victoria, and, in Germany, four of her grandchildren, all married their first cousins. The Catholic Church, however, does not allow the marriage of first cousins without a papal dispensation; such a dispensation allowed the marriage of the future King Umberto I of Italy with his first cousin (their fathers were brothers), the future queen consort Margherita di Savoia.

Marriage in former times was regulated not by the state but by the Church, and in 1509, when Henry VIII married Catherine of Aragon, that meant the Catholic Church. Even into modern times, in Catholic countries like Italy, Spain, Belgium, and Ireland, the laws of the Church with regard to marriage (called *canon law*) were simply taken over *en masse* by the state.

The following famous verse from the Gospel according to St. Matthew must now be considered.

Matthew 16:18–19: And I say unto thee, that thou art Peter, and upon this rock I will build my church, and the gates of hell shall not prevail against it. And I will give thee the keys of the kingdom of heaven, and whatsoever thou shalt bind on earth shall be bound in heaven, and whatsoever thou shalt loose on earth shall be loosed in heaven. (Authorized Version)

At the time of King Henry's first marriage, it was believed in all of Europe that Jesus Christ, during the time of his physical presence upon earth, had authorized St. Peter and his successors, the popes of Rome, to dispense with good cause from laws in cases of extreme necessity. There was some debate about how far the pope could go, but there was no debate that he could go far. The most common sort of dispensation sought from the pope was to be allowed to marry someone so closely related to one that the laws of the Church prohibited the marriage.

In the sixteenth century, the people whom one was forbidden to marry were much more numerous than they are today. This is because some restrictions were abolished in a revision of the Code of Canon Law made in 1917. At the time of Henry VIII, a man was forbidden by canon law to marry the following people:

1. His second cousin or anyone related by blood more closely to him than the second cousin.

2. Any of the widows of the aforementioned second cousins or closer relatives, including his brother's widow. (It was this prohibition that required Henry to get a dispensation to marry Catherine of Aragon, his brother's widow.)

3. The sister, mother, or daughter of anyone with whom he had had sexual intercourse, even if out of wedlock. (It was this prohibition that required Henry to get a dispensation to marry Ann Boleyn, the younger sister of his former mistress, Mary Boleyn.)

4. His godmother.

Two people related in any of these four ways were said to be prohibited from contracting marriage by the *impediment of affinity*. The last two of these restrictions apply to our story because, if a fellow like Henry VIII wanted to marry within the forbidden limits, he applied to the Holy See of Rome for a dispensation, which was to be granted only for serious reasons, such as to allow marriages between royal houses to cement an alliance for the establishment of peace.

It was quite common for people to apply to the pope for dispensations from the rules, especially for sovereigns to do so. For example, in 1527 Emperor Charles V, Henry VIII's nephew by marriage, applied for a dispensation from Pope Clement VII to marry his first cousin, the Infanta Isabella of Portugal. The serious reason behind the request for the dispensation was a reason of state, that it promoted peace between Spain and Portugal. The dispensation was granted, and one of the children of this marriage was the future King Philip II.

In 1501, King Henry VII of England and Ferdinand and Isabella, the Catholic Kings of Spain, made a treaty that was sealed by the marriage of Henry's heir, Arthur, Prince of Wales, to the Infanta Catherine, daughter of Ferdinand and Isabella. The prince was fifteen years old, the princess sixteen years old. They lived together for six months until the sickly prince died of tuberculosis. The sovereigns then decided that the princess should now marry Henry, the new Prince of Wales, younger brother of Prince Arthur. But first they waited several months to see if Catherine was pregnant by her late husband. When it was clear that she was not, they proceeded with the arrangements. Since such a marriage between a man and his sister-in-law was prohibited by the Church, they applied to Pope Julius II for a dispensation in 1503. His Holiness granted the request. The marriage, however, did not take place immediately, for Henry was but twelve years old. Furthermore, King Ferdinand had not yet paid his daughter's dowry in full, and King Henry waited until he should do so. To encourage the Spaniard to hurry up, he applied pressure by pretending to look around for other young ladies for his son to marry. In 1505, he had Prince Henry make a solemn, notarized declaration before lawyers that he did not want to marry the princess. Time passed. Queen Isabella died in 1504. King Henry VII died in 1509. On his deathbed, he advised his son Henry to marry Catherine. So, the first act of Henry VIII was to use the papal dispensation of 1503 to marry Catherine in 1509, shortly after his accession to the throne.

Queen Catherine bore six children to King Henry, but all died at birth or in infancy except the fifth, the future Queen Mary, born in 1516. Queen

Catherine's last pregnancy was in 1518. The king was not faithful to her. In 1520, his affair with Elizabeth Blount produced an illegitimate son, Henry Fitzroy. Henry also had an affair with Mary Boleyn, elder sister of the soon-to-be-notorious Ann Boleyn. By 1527, Queen Catherine was forty-two years old and had had no pregnancy for nine years, so all hope of a male heir from her was abandoned.

At this time, a change took place in English foreign policy that further weakened the position of Queen Catherine. Queen Catherine was the aunt of the emperor Charles, who had amassed a universal empire through the marriages of his father and grandfather.

Bella gerant alii; tu, felix Austria, nube.

Let other princes go to war. Thou, happy Austria, marry!

Henry began to tilt toward an alliance with King Francis I of France. Catherine was not happy about this, and this tension aggravated the situation.

The switch from alliance with the House of Austria to alliance with France was not popular in England, since the English economy depended on trade with the Netherlands, which was part of the empire of the Habsburgs. Furthermore, Catherine of Aragon was a popular queen.

Although it was accepted that the crown could be inherited through the female line, and the crown had indeed been so passed on, no woman had ever been sovereign in England.[24] It was thought possible that, should Henry die, several men would try their luck and challenge a queen regnant under whatever pretexts they cared to put forward and attempt to prevail by force. Henry therefore conceived the desire to rid himself of Catherine and marry a younger woman capable of producing a male heir. The matter was complicated by the fact that he had become infatuated with Ann Boleyn, the younger sister of his recent concubine Mary Boleyn, and this Ann was the candidate that he had in mind to succeed Queen Catherine. Ann Boleyn was unpopular and denominated by the people "the great whore."

The king therefore decided that he should find a pretext to seek from Pope Clement VII an annulment of his marriage with Catherine. He then intended to marry Ann Boleyn. Henry's first step was to bring his plan to the attention of his chief minister, Cardinal Wolsey. Wolsey was the most

24. Matilda, daughter of Henry I, ought to have succeeded to the throne upon the death of her father in 1135, but her succession was contested by her cousin Stephen, another claimant in the female line, and civil war broke out. She eventually retired to France.

powerful minister in the history of England. In addition to being what today would be called Prime Minister, he was also the head of the Catholic Church in England in his capacity as the legate of the pope. He was archbishop of York, bishop of Winchester, bishop of Durham, and abbot of St. Albans. His income was enormous, and his power absolute. He was the object of professional jealousy. There was some good in him, because during his fifteen years of power, no one was burned at the stake, whereas many of his successors for one hundred years reduced their enemies to ashes for heresy, or decapitated them for treason. His motto was *Dominus mihi adiutor*, as one can see at his palace of Hampton Court.

Henry told Wolsey that he wanted the marriage with Catherine annulled, and he wanted Wolsey to use his power as papal legate, or his influence with the pope, to arrange this, but he did not tell him that he intended to replace Catherine with Ann Boleyn. Wolsey was thinking that the queen might be replaced with a French princess to cement that alliance. Wolsey knew that Ann was Henry's concubine, but he did not imagine that Henry intended to make the strumpet his wife. Wolsey had a low opinion of Ann and called her "the night crow."

Wolsey and the king decided to seek an annulment of the marriage with Catherine on the grounds that Pope Julius had been tricked by Henry VII, Ferdinand, and Isabella into granting the dispensation, which would therefore have been invalid; in other words, they decided to argue that the dispensation was, in the technical term of canon law, *obreptitious*, obtained by falsehood. The falsehood that Wolsey and the king claimed to have been perpetrated had been the representation to the pope that the marriage between Henry and Catherine was necessary for peace between England and Spain, whereas those countries were in no danger of going to war at the time. Since Wolsey was the papal legate in England, they decided that he would secretly summon the king to appear before his legatine court and there declare the marriage annulled. Catherine was not to be informed as yet of what was going on.

Wolsey held his clandestine hearing in May 1527, but before long it was decided that this was not really the best way to go. Wolsey did not have the power as papal legate to prohibit Catherine from appealing his verdict to Pope Clement in Rome, which, they thought, she would certainly do. His Holiness would have to be brought into the loop sooner or later, and they decided that it would be preferable to bring him in sooner.

At this point, the situation of the pope was most unsatisfactory. His freedom of action was nonexistent. Rome was occupied by the Imperial Army of Charles V, Queen Catherine's nephew. The officers had lost control, since they had not the money to pay the troops. The soldiers had therefore sacked the city and chased the pope into the Castel Sant'Angelo, a fortress near the Vatican where he was a virtual prisoner.

Henry and Wolsey devised the following plan. Wolsey would travel to France and get the cooperation of King Francis and of the French cardinals in requesting that Pope Clement appoint Wolsey substitute pope for the time that he was not free to act because of his imprisonment in the Castel Sant'Angelo. During the time that he was acting pope, Wolsey would annul the marriage of Henry and Catherine. At this point, Henry finally told Catherine that he would have their marriage declared null and void, and Catherine made clear that she would oppose his scheme to discard her.

Wolsey set off for France. Henry, however, behind Wolsey's back, sent his secretary Dr. Knight to Rome with orders somehow to break into the Castel Sant'Angelo and present a unique request to the pope. Henry requested from Pope Clement a dispensation for bigamy; he asked for permission to take a second wife. No pope had ever granted such a dispensation; in fact the only Christian authority ever to grant a license for bigamy was Martin Luther, who issued one in 1540 for the benefit of Philip, Landgraf of Hesse, whose wife was an alcoholic and therefore disgusting to him. Although it was argued that polygamy could not be contrary to divine law, since God had allowed it at the time of the Hebrew patriarchs, the popes were not sure that they had the power to allow bigamy, and therefore none of them had ever permitted it.

Pope Clement was generous in handing out dispensations, because he had himself received one to become a priest. Since he was illegitimate, he could not have been ordained a priest without a dispensation from his cousin, Pope Leo X. Clement, though quite willing to grant dispensations of all sorts, would never grant a request for bigamy, despite the opinion of Henry that it was within his apostolic authority. Note that at this point of the affair, Henry magnified the authority of the pope to grant dispensations, because he wanted that authority to be exercised for his own benefit.

Before Knight got to Rome, Wolsey's spies reported to him what Henry was doing behind his back. Wolsey knew quite well that Rome would never grant a license for bigamy. At the same time, his attempt to get the French to support his plan to be declared acting pope failed, and he rushed back to England to deal with the marriage issue. He then persuaded the king that the application for bigamy would cause him to lose all credibility at the papal court and that it was therefore a bad idea. Instead, he asked the king to allow him to write up a proper petition for annulment to His Holiness. Henry agreed, but once again did something behind Wolsey's back. He sent a secret petition of his own to the pope through his secretary Knight. In this petition, he asked the pope to issue a dispensation to allow him, after his marriage to Catherine was declared null and void, to marry a woman with whose sister he had previously engaged in illicit sexual intercourse. Recall that according to canon law, to marry a woman with whose sister one had had sexual intercourse was forbidden. Henry's secret petition alerted the court of Rome to his infatuation with Ann Boleyn and ruined his credibility with the pope. Henry had hitherto enjoyed much prestige at the Holy See because of his book against Luther published in 1521. In reward for that publication, Clement's cousin and predecessor Leo X had awarded Henry the title "Defender of the Faith," a title still used by the monarchs of England to this day.

Wolsey again found out what Henry was doing behind his back. He realized that he no longer had the complete confidence of his master, and that Henry intended to replace Catherine with Ann Boleyn. A modern minister with any shame would resign in such a position, but that was not the way of the sixteenth century. In those times, it was expected that a minister carry on and implement the policy of the sovereign, even if he personally disagreed with it. He wrote up a petition of his own to the pope, less clumsy that Henry's, whose terms would allow Henry to marry Ann.

Pope Clement was one of those people who hate to say no, and who put off unpleasant decisions for as long as possible. He could not really afford to annoy Catherine's nephew the emperor, nor did he want to insult Henry, who had hitherto been a useful son of the Holy Church. He therefore granted Henry's request. He issued a dispensation for Knight to bring back to England allowing Henry to marry a woman with whose sister he had previously had illicit sexual intercourse, *provided that the marriage with Queen Catherine should first be declared null and void.*

Wolsey realized that, because of this *proviso*—that the marriage with Catherine had to be declared null before Henry could marry Ann—the dispensation had no practical effect; it was putting the cart before the horse. He therefore decided to send ambassadors to Clement to request from the pope the establishment of a *Decretal Commission*, consisting of himself, or, if necessary, at most one other additional prelate, to settle the matter.

The purpose of the Decretal Commission would be to decide whether Pope Julius had been tricked into granting the dispensation of 1503. According to Wolsey, the Commission would investigate whether five assertions were true and, if they found them to be so, declare Pope Julius to have been deceived, and the bull of dispensation consequently null and void. The annulment of the marriage of Henry and Catherine, which depended on the bull of dispensation, would be an immediate consequence. The five assertions were:

First, it was alleged in the bull that Henry desired the marriage, which was not true, for he never asked for it, or knew of the obtaining of the dispensation.

Second, it was stated that the marriage was contracted for the sake of preserving peace and alliance—an insufficient reason, especially as there had been no war, and there was no danger of one at the time.

Third, because Henry was only twelve years old when the dispensation was obtained, and therefore not of lawful age.

Fourth, because some of the persons named in the bull, namely, Queen Isabella and King Henry VII, were dead before it was put into force.

Fifth, that Henry, on reaching the age of fourteen, had made a protestation that he would not marry Catherine, by which the previous dispensation was rendered null, and a subsequent marriage was not valid without a new one.

Furthermore, Wolsey requested through his ambassadors that the pope also issue a *pollicitation*, that is, a promise not to accept any appeal from the decision of the Decretal Commission. He warned Pope Clement that the king would have his way, and if he, the pope, should not do as he was asked, it would lead to his, Wolsey's, fall and to the collapse of the Catholic Church in England.

Pope Clement was intimidated to establish the Decretal Commission and issue the pollicitation. However, he proceeded with great cunning. He associated with Wolsey as a second judge in the case Cardinal Campeggio, one of the most respected members of the Sacred College and a man well acquainted with England (he was absentee bishop of Salisbury). Wolsey and Campeggio were to try the case in England. However, he told Campeggio to delay as much as he could as often as he could. He told him to show the decree establishing the Decretal Commission to Henry and Wolsey only, and then to burn it.

Campeggio set out for London from Rome; it was convenient that he was suffering from gout, since it gave him an excuse to take several months for the trip. He arrived in London in October 1528. The first thing he did was to try to solve the problem by convincing Queen Catherine to enter a nunnery. When Wolsey and Campeggio tried to get Catherine of Aragon to enter a nunnery, perhaps they were thinking like Alexander III (1159–1181):

Alexander adopted the principle that a simple vow of chastity did not prevent marriage or render it null, but that *a formal vow, or the reception of orders, created a dissolution of marriage*,[25] or a total inability to enter into it; but Celestin III carried the principle still farther, and decreed that a simple vow, while it did not dissolve an existing connection, was sufficient to prevent a future one.[26]

Naturally, the supposed teaching of Alexander III was not serviceable to the two cardinals. Entrance into a nunnery would probably have been equivalent to what is nowadays called a plea of *nolo contendere*. Catherine refused; she said that her vocation in life was that of a wife and mother, not that of a nun. Then something unexpected happened that allowed the legates to postpone the trial for seven months. Queen Catherine suddenly exhibited a copy of a *Brief*, a letter from Pope Julius II to her mother Queen Isabella in 1503, in which the pope wrote that he granted a dispensation for Henry and Catherine to marry, not only for the establishment of peace between England and Spain, *but also because of many other serious reasons*. This was a catastrophe for Henry and Wolsey. If this brief existed, then even if Wolsey and Campeggio were to rule the bull of dispensation null and void because obtained by deception, the marriage would still be legitimate because of the brief. Henry spent half a year trying to prove the brief a forgery. He insisted on seeing the original, which the Spaniards would not give him, since they were sure he would destroy it. Henry, Wolsey, and Campeggio then decided to start the trial in May 1529 before things deteriorated any further, for Catherine was threatening to appeal to the pope to transfer the case to Rome. The speech of Queen Catherine on the opening day of the trial is very famous and recorded in

25. Italics mine.
26. Henry Charles Lea, *History of Sacerdotal Celibacy in the Christian Church* (n.p.: University Books, 1966), 270–71.

Cavendish's contemporary *Life of Wolsey*.[27] She walked out of the court after her speech and never again returned.

The trial continued for three months. Some bishops, led by John Fisher of Rochester, defended the marriage. At the end of July, Campeggio announced that even though they were sitting in England, he must follow the calendar of the Roman Curia and adjourn the proceedings for the late summer recess. He then made preparations to return to Rome. This inconclusive result enraged the king, who violated the prelate's diplomatic immunity by having his baggage ransacked at the port of Dover. The agents did not, however, find the love letters of Henry to Ann Boleyn, which the cardinal is believed to have brought to show the pope, and which now are one of the treasures of the Vatican Archives.

The adjournment of the trial without any result caused the fall of Wolsey. Henry saw that his minister did not have the clout with the pope to arrange the divorce, so he dumped him. Wolsey survived one more year, during which time his enemies brought many charges against the fallen tyrant. He died in 1530 on his way to London to be tried on trumped-up charges of treason. He died regretting the part he had played in the divorce. The famous last words of Shakespeare's Wolsey are the last verses of *Henry VIII*, Act III:

> Had I but serv'd my God, with halfe the Zeale
> I serv'd my King: he would not in mine Age
> Have left me naked to mine Enemies.

These lines are based on actual words spoken by Wolsey and recorded by his gentleman usher George Cavendish in his biography of his master:

I see the matter against me, how it is framed. But if I had served God as diligently as I have done the King, He would not have given me over in my grey hairs.[28]

Henry now changed his policy. Instead of asking for the dispensation of Pope Julius to be set aside on the pretext that it was obtained by fraud, he decided to argue that the pope had no power to overrule Leviticus 20:21. That Deuteronomy 25:5–6 required him to marry Catherine did not bother him, since the Catholic Church had always considered that regulation of the Jewish Law to have been abrogated by the coming of

---

27. George Cavendish, *Thomas Wolsey, late Cardinal, his Life and Death*, ed. Roger Lockyer (London: The Folio Society, 1962), 113–15.

28. Ibid., 224.

Christ. On the advice of Thomas Cranmer, chaplain of the Boleyn family, Henry addressed a circular question to the university faculties of Europe, "Does the pope have the authority to abrogate Leviticus 20:21?" His agents bribed the professors and got the reply "No!" from many schools; other professors, bribed by the emperor, replied "Yes!" It is useful to remember that Henry VIII was fluent in Latin, but knew neither Hebrew nor Greek.

Catherine, meanwhile, exercised the right of every Catholic and appealed her case to the pope, so that the trial in England could never be resumed. The pope was in no hurry to make a decision because, politically, he lost no matter what he did. If he decided for Catherine, he lost England; if he decided for Henry, he insulted the emperor, nephew of Catherine. The case dragged on at Rome year after year. With each year, the dependency of the pope on the emperor increased.

Henry refused to appear in Rome, either personally or by proxy. It was beneath his dignity to do so. On the contrary, he took for himself the title of *majesty*, one previously reserved for the Holy Roman Emperor. Mere kings of England had hitherto been traditionally addressed as "Your Highness" or "Your Grace." He decided to enforce the law against making appeals to the pope, called the *Statute of Praemunire*, which had rarely been enforced and was mainly a bargaining chip of the kings of England in disputes with the Holy See. He struck at the pope's sources of income by abolishing *Annates*, a tax consisting of one-year's income of a diocese, traditionally sent to the pope by bishops who had just been appointed to a see. He asked the bishops' conference, or Convocation, to give him the title Supreme Head, under God, of the Church in England. Archbishop Warham of Canterbury added the saving proviso, "insofar as the law of God permits"; he then asked his colleagues what they thought. They all remained silent, and he said, quoting a principle of Roman law, *Qui tacet consentire videtur*, "He who is silent is assumed to agree." One bishop then added, "Then we are all silent." Warham died shortly thereafter, in 1532. Henry decided to appoint Thomas Cranmer his successor. He asked Pope Clement for the bulls of appointment in the usual manner, and, to expedite matters, paid the usual fees. Even at this late point he was still beginning his letters to the pope with the traditional formula, "I kiss the blessed feet of Your Holiness." Pope Clement made the appointment, since he would do anything to please Henry other than grant the annulment. Cranmer was now in place to perform the function that Henry intended for him.

In 1533, Ann Boleyn got pregnant. King Henry expected a son, and decided to cut the Gordian knot. He had Cranmer declare the marriage with Catherine null and void. Cranmer then married Henry and Ann. This forced the pope's hand, and he issued a decree of excommunication against Henry (July 13, 1533), to take effect if he did not set aside Ann and return to Catherine. Henry's response was to have the parliament pass the Act of Supremacy (voted by parliament on November 11 and accepted by the king on December 18, 1534), which made him pope in England and declared that the bishop of Rome had no more authority in England than any other foreign bishop.

Two years later, Henry had Ann Boleyn beheaded for witchcraft and incest. Before the execution, he had Archbishop Cranmer declare that marriage too to have been null and void; the reason given was that Henry had previously had sexual intercourse with her sister Mary.

The verdict of Macaulay on the English Reformation is to be found in the famous "Essay on Hallam's *Constitutional History of England*":

a King, whose character may be best described by saying, that he was despotism itself personified, unprincipled ministers, a rapacious aristocracy, a servile Parliament, such were the instruments by which England was delivered from the yoke of Rome. The work which had been begun by Henry, the murderer of his wives, was continued by Somerset, the murderer of his brother, and completed by Elizabeth, the murderer of her guest.[29]

Dixit Dominus These are the opening words of Psalm 109 (110 in the Hebrew Bible), "Jahweh said unto my Lord ...," the most famous of the Vespers psalms of the Catholic liturgy. As such, it has been put to music by all of the great composers. For a discussion of its text, see the entry **Neo-Vulgata**. The traditional numbering of the psalms in Catholic Bibles usually differs from that in the Hebrew Bible, because the Vulgate follows the Septuagint, in which what are called Psalms 9 and 10 in the Hebrew Bible are correctly recognized to be one alphabetical psalm and called Psalm 9; it is a mistake to begin a new psalm after verse 21. Psalm 9 contains the verses corresponding to the Hebrew letters א through כ, whereas Psalm 10 contains those corresponding to the letters ל through ת. As a result of this confusion, the Catholics and the Protestants assigned different numbers to most of the psalms, the Protestants following the Hebrew

---

29. Thomas Babington Macaulay, *Critical and Historical Essays Contributed to the Edinburgh Review*, 6th ed. (London, Longman, Brown, Green, & Longmans, 1849), 1:126.

numbering, and the Catholics following the numbering in the Septuagint and the Vulgate. As a compromise, *Dixit Dominus*, for example, used to be called Psalm 109 (110) in old Catholic Bibles. In the Neo-Vulgata edition published by the Vatican in 1979, it is noteworthy that *Dixit Dominus* is denoted Psalm 110 (109), the traditional numbering of the Vulgata having been relegated to second place.[30]

Docetic The Greek verb δοκέω means *to think, to seem, to appear*, as especially in the phrase ὡς ἐμοῖ δοκεῖ, *as it appears to me, as I believe*. The *docetic* heretics of the primitive Church denied that the Deity would condescend to assume a body and therefore held that the Christ only appeared to have flesh. Such people were called in Greek δοκηταί (plural of δοκητής) and their belief δοκητισμός. The adjective describing such a belief was δοκητικός, whence proceeds our *docetic*.

Doctor The Greek verb δοκέω means *to think, to appear*. Related to it is the Latin verb *doceo, docere, docui, doctus*, which means *to teach*, for thinkers are the most appropriate teachers. From the fourth principal part of this verb comes the noun *doctor*, which means *a teacher*. The four original Doctors of the Church, whose statues were sculpted by Bernini above the Altar of the Chair in St. Peter's Basilica, were Athanasius, John Chrysostom, Ambrose, and Augustine. The number has now been multiplied to thirty-six.

Doctrine The Latin verb *doceo, docere, docui, doctus* means *to teach*, and the associated noun *doctrina* means *that which is taught*. *Doctrine* is the teaching of the Catholic Church. The corresponding Greek noun is διδαχή.

Dogma The Greek verb δοκέω means *to think, suppose*, and from it was derived the noun δόγμα with the meaning *that which one thinks true, an opinion*, and then a *decree*. In the Catholic Church it acquired the meaning of a belief that the Church declares to be true and that must be accepted as such by all believers.

Josephus says that the Jews from their very birth regard their Scriptures as the "decrees of God" (Θεοῦ δόγματα).[31]

---

30. For the confusion in the numbering of the psalms, see Charles Augustus Briggs, *A Critical and Exegetical Commentary on the Book of Psalms*, vol. 1 (Edinburgh: T&T Clark, 1906), xlviii–xlix, §13.

31. William Sanday, *Inspiration, Eight Lectures on the Early History and Origin of the Doctrine of Biblical Inspiration, Being the Bampton Lectures for 1893* (London: Longmans, Green, 1896), 79.

– D –

Evelyn Waugh tells the story of the reaction of Msgr. Ronald Knox to a symposium in which various celebrities in all walks of life discussed the major issues of religion.

Conan Doyle had succinctly stated: "The less dogma, the more Christ." Dogma, Ronald patiently explains, is not derived from the Latin word meaning to teach, but from the Greek meaning to be acceptable; dogmas are the tenets on which a school or party are agreed; he wished to discover the dogmas of the symposiasts, and his quest led him through a miasma of undefined premises and irrational conclusions, of huge omissions and assumptions, of an almost meaningless vocabulary and fatuous self-complacency.[32]

D.O.M. This abbreviation for *Deo Optimo Maximo* is frequently found in inscriptions. It means *to the best and supreme god*. The words *Optimus Maximus* were a standing epithet of Jupiter. The Christians applied the phrase to the one God, *to God, the best, the supreme*.

The following inscription is on the façade of the Church of La Madeleine in Paris:

D·O·M·SVB·INVOC·S·M·MAGDALENAE

[Dedicated] to God, the best, the supreme, [and] under the protection of St. Mary Magdalene.

Domestic Prelate The Greek verb δέμω means *to build*, and related to it is the Latin noun *domus* meaning *home*. From this noun was formed the adjective *domesticus* with the meaning *belonging to one's home*. Domestic prelates are clergy admitted to the pope's family and therefore raised to the papal nobility; in the old way of thinking, bishops are *ipso facto* nobles, so the title *domestic prelate* is usually reserved for a clergyman who is not a bishop.

Domine, Salvum Fac Regem Nostrum N. This prayer for the monarch or the state was formerly sung at the conclusion of the Sunday high Mass. It is now rarely heard. The word *regem* is changed as the occasion demands to *reginam, imperatorem,* or *rem publicam*.

> Domine, salvum fac imperatorem nostrum Napoleonem
> Et exaudi nos in die qua invocaverimus te.

---

32. Evelyn Waugh, *Monsignor Ronald Knox, Fellow of Trinity College, Oxford and Protonotary Apostolic to His Holiness Pope Pius XII* (Boston: Little, Brown, 1959), 234.

Domine, salvum fac regem nostrum Ludovicum
Et exaudi nos in die qua invocaverimus te.

Domine, salvam fac reginam nostram Elisabeth
Et exaudi nos in die qua invocaverimus te.

Domine, salvam fac rem publicam
Et exaudi nos in die qua invocaverimus te.

Save the state, O Lord,
And hearken unto us on the day on which we cry out unto thee.

Among the many famous musical settings are those of Paisiello for the coronation of Napoleon I and of Gounod in honor of Napoleon III.

Dominical The Latin noun *domus* means *house*, and from it was derived the related noun *dominus*, meaning *master of the house* or *lord*; it was the Latin equivalent of the Greek κύριος and the Hebrew רבּי. From *dominus* was derived the adjective *dominicus* with the meaning *pertaining to the master*. Hence the Latin-speaking Christians called Sunday *dies dominica* or simply *dominica*, the Lord's Day. In this regard they followed their Greek-speaking brethren, who called it ἡ ἡμέρα ἡ κυριακή. The English adjective *dominical* is a super-adjective, having one adjectival ending (*-al*) heaped upon another (*-ic*). Sunday is the Dominical Day. The Dominical Use was the habit of ending the Lenten fast on the Sunday following Nisan 14. The Dominical or Sunday Letter of a given year is the letter obtained by assigning the letters A through G to the days January 1 through 7 and then picking the letter corresponding to the day that is a Sunday. It was formerly used in a table at the beginning of the Missal to help priests in inaccessible places determine the date of Easter in a given year.

Dominican The Latin noun *dominus* means *lord, master*, and the associated adjective *dominicus, -a, -um* means *pertaining to the master*. From this adjective arose the Italian name *Domenico* or *Dominic*. Saint Dominic was called *Dominicus* in Latin, and his followers were denominated *dominicani* or *Dominicans*. The official name of this group is *Ordo Praedicatorum*, the Order of Preachers, for learned preaching was their calling (see the entry **Preachers**). Because of the similarity of *Dominicani* to *Domini canes* (the dogs of the Lord), the Dominican friars are often to be identified in mediaeval paintings by the Dalmatian dogs that accompany them.

– D –

Dominus Vobiscum *The Lord be with you* was a common greeting among Latin-speaking early Christians, and for this reason made its way into the Mass. The courteous reply was *Et cum spiritu tuo*. Similarly, in the old days, people in Italy, upon meeting priests on the street, would greet them by saying "Sia lodato Gesù Cristo." The phrase means "May Jesus Christ be praised," and is a translation of the Latin *Laudetur Jesus Christus*. The tradition made somewhat of a comeback under Pope John Paul II.

Donation The Latin verb *dono, donare, donavi, donatus* means *to give*, and from its fourth principal part is formed the noun *donatio, donationis, f.*, with the meaning a *gift*. Gregorovius gives the following account of the Donation of Constantine, a fable of the eighth century that was believed for many centuries thereafter.[33]

> It represented that Constantine, cured by Bishop Sylvester of leprosy by baptism, out of reverence to the Prince of the Apostles, had humbly quitted Rome and retired to a corner of the Bosphorus, resigning the capital of the world and Italy to the successors of S. Peter.

The Donation seems to be alluded to by Pope Adrian I in a letter to Charlemagne of the year 777:

> ... through whom [Constantine] God had deigned to bestow everything on the Holy Church of the Apostolic Prince.[34]

Doway Douai, which the English pronounced and spelled *Doway*, is the French corruption of the Latin name of the town, *Duacum*, probably taken from a Celtic name. A college for English seminarians was established in Douai in 1565, since those students could not prepare for the priesthood in their native land. At that time, Douai was under the authority of the Catholic King Philip II in his capacity as Duke of Burgundy. The head of the college, William Allen (1532–1594), later cardinal, established a committee of scholars to translate the Vulgate into English for the benefit of English Catholics and to supply whatever notes they considered necessary. Preeminent among these scholars were Gregory Martin (c. 1540–1582)

---

33. Ferdinand Gregorovius, *History of the City of Rome in the Middle Ages*, 2nd ed., trans. Mrs. Gustavus W. Hamilton (London: George Bell & Sons, 1902) 2:362–363. See also Ignaz von Döllinger, *Fables respecting the Popes of the Middle Ages, A Contribution to Ecclesiastical History*, trans. Alfred Plummer (London: Rivingtons, 1871), 107–78.

34. Gregorovius, *History of the City of Rome in the Middle Ages*, 2:362.

and Richard Bristow (1538–1581). The translation was complete by 1582, but only the New Testament was published in that year because of the lack of funds; by that time, the revolution in the Spanish Netherlands had caused the college to move to Rheims in France. See the entry **Rhemes**. Sufficient funds for the publication of the Old Testament in two volumes became available by 1609, and by that time, the situation in Douai was sufficiently pacified that the college had returned thither. The first volume of the Old Testament was published in 1609 and the second volume in 1610. The two volumes were therefore called the *Doway Old Testament*. The Rhemes-Doway Bible thus consists of three volumes; it was published on the continent because, at that time, the public practice of the Roman Catholic religion in England was prohibited by law. The English eventually abandoned their phonetic spellings of French names, and this edition of the scriptures is commonly known today as the Douai-Rheims Bible, the order assigned to the cities having been reversed.

The Old Testament was written in Hebrew in the first millennium before Jesus Christ. It was translated into Greek for the benefit of Greek speaking Jews outside of Palestine. This translation, called the Septuagint because it was made, according to legend, by seventy scholars, was actually done by various people at various times and varies in quality from poor to excellent. The New Testament was written in Greek within a century of the death of Christ. So, except for certain portions of the books of Daniel and Ezra, which are in Aramaic—the language related to Hebrew and spoken by Jesus Christ and now nearly extinct—the original languages of the Bible are Hebrew and Greek. Some books were lost in the original Hebrew and survived only in the Greek translation. For this reason, the reformers excluded them from their scripture and collectively called them the Apocrypha. However, a manuscript containing the Hebrew text of one of these books, *Ecclesiasticus* or *Ben Sirach*, was discovered in the nineteenth century, but I am not aware that the Reformed churches thereupon restored the Book of *Ecclesiasticus* to their Old Testament.

As the early Christians failed to win over the Children of Israel, they shook what they considered the dust of the synagogue from their feet and sought converts among the nations. Thus Christianity quickly became a gentile religion. The Western gentiles spoke Latin, and so translations of the Bible were made into Latin. The quality of these early Latin translations was so poor that the pope of Rome, Damasus (366–384), asked St. Jerome to make a good translation, which he did. Jerome was the best biblical scholar of his time and of the next thousand years, so his translation was competent and came into common use; for this reason, it was called the *Common Bible*, or, in Latin, the *Biblia Vulgata*. There was no knowledge of Hebrew in the world at that time except among Jews, and after the barbarians, that is, the Germans, conquered Rome in 476, knowledge of Greek pretty much disappeared, whence arose the expression "It's all Greek to me." Therefore, Jerome's Latin Vulgate Bible became the Bible of Western Christianity for the next millennium. During this period, the translation of the Bible into everyday languages was discouraged; the reason was that the vernacular languages were considered inappropriate for such a holy thing as God's word, for those languages had no literature. There may also have been a desire to prevent commotions. This does not square with modern notions of freedom of speech, but those were times when people were lucky to have an enlightened, benign dictator, a Charlemagne or an Akbar, when they were so fortunate as to find one, as John Stuart Mill (1806–1873) admitted in his essay *On Liberty*.[35]

This all changed with the Protestant Reformation in the sixteenth century. The situation in England with respect to Bibles in the 1560s and 1570s was this: The most popular Bible in the country was the Geneva or "Breeches" Bible, which had been made by English Protestant exiles in Geneva and first appeared in 1560. It is called the Breeches Bible because of the translation of Genesis 3:7:

They [Adam and Eve] sewed fig tree leaves together and made themselves breeches.

The translators made their translation from the Hebrew and the Greek, as best they could, given the state of Hebrew and Greek studies at the time, with the help of Luther's German translation, Beza's Latin translation of the New Testament, and other such works. The translators were Presbyterians and were therefore considered heretics by both the Roman Catholics and the Anglicans. In the margins and at the end of each chapter, they added notes in which they defended Calvin's interpretation of the passage in question and contradicted the Catholic view. Some of the doctrines attacked were also held by the Church of England. For example, Revelation 9:3 reads:

And there came out of the smoke Locustes upon the earth, and unto them was given power, as the Scorpions of the earth have power.

35. John Stuart Mill, *On Liberty & Considerations of Representative Government* (London: The Folio Society, 2008), section 1, "Introductory," p. 14.

The marginal note on this verse was:

Locustes are false teachers, heretikes, and worldlie suttil Prelates, with Monkes, Freres, Cardinals, Patriarkes, Archebishops, Bishops, Doctors, Baschelers, & masters which forsake Christ to mainteine false doctrine.

As a result of the many comments such as these, the Anglican Bishops tried to put the Geneva Bible out of business and issued their own, official, version of the Bible for use in churches, which was called the *Bishops' Bible*, without "bitter notes"; it came out in 1568. It was a revision of the previous official English version, the Great Bible from the reign of Henry VIII, which in turn depended on the work of the pioneer Tyndale (c. 1492–1536) for the New Testament and the pioneer Coverdale (c. 1488–1569) for the Old Testament.

After the accession of Queen Elizabeth in 1558, the promotion of the Catholic religion in England became dangerous. The leading figures therefore migrated to Douai, which was then under the authority of Philip II, king of Spain, the champion of the Catholics. The chief of the exiles was Fr. William Allen of Oriel College, Oxford, who established a seminary at Douai and appointed one of his fellow scholars, Fr. Gregory Martin of St. John's College, Oxford, to prepare an English translation of the Bible for the use of their Catholic fellow countrymen, who had nothing English in their hands to oppose the Protestant Geneva and Bishops' Bibles. Martin finished his translation in 1582. By then the exiles had moved to Rheims in France on account of the civil war in the Netherlands, which was raging around Douai. They did not have enough money to print the whole Bible, so they put out the New Testament only. This is the Rhemes New Testament.[36] The English government immediately prohibited the importation of the books into the country, and most copies were impounded at the Channel ports and destroyed. The reason for this was that Allen and his second-in-command, Fr. Richard Bristow, had added what the government considered an inflammatory commentary to Martin's translation, published in tiny print sixty-three lines to a page after each chapter. (The Bible itself is printed at forty-one lines to a page; the page

36. *The New Testament of Iesus Christ, translated faithfvlly into English, out of the authentical Latin, according to the best corrected copies of the same, diligently conferred vvith the Greeke and other editions in diuers languages: vvith arguments of books and chapters, annotations, and other necessarie helps, for the better vnderstanding of the text, and specially for the discouerie of the corrvptions of diuers late translations, and for cleering the controversies in religion of these daies*: In the English College of Rhemes, Printed at Rhemes, by John Fogny, 1582.

size is approximately six inches by eight-and-a-half inches, depending on how closely to the text block the page was cropped.) It was furthermore decreed that any oath sworn on this Rhemes Bible was null and void and without any legal force whatsoever.

Here is an example of the commentary to which the English government objected. It concerns Hebrews 13:17, which reads "Obey your prelates." This phrase is their translation of St. Jerome's *Obedite praepositis vestris*, which is itself the translation of the original πείθεσθε τοῖς ἡγουμένοις ὑμῶν. It means, "Obey your rulers," but since the rulers mentioned are, from the context, clearly *religious* rulers, the translation *prelates* is not false. The commentary that is provided for this verse is an attack on the Act of Parliament of 1559, whereby Queen Elizabeth was declared to be the Supreme Governor, after God, of the Church in England, and the authority of the Pope of Rome rejected.

There is nothing more inculcated in the holy Scriptures, then obedience of the lay people to the Priests and Prelates of Gods Church, in matters of soule, conscience, and religion. Vvereof the Apostle giueth this reason, because they haue the charge of soules, and must ansvver for them; vvhich is an infinite preeminence and superiority, ioyned vvith burden, and requireth maruelous submission and most obedient subiection of al that be vnder them and their gouernement. From this obedience there is no exception nor exemption of kings and Princes, be they neuer so great. If they haue soules, and be Christian men, they must be subiect to some Bishop, Priest, or other Prelate. And vvhatsoever he be (though Emperour of all the world) if he take vpon him to prescribe and giue laws of religion to the Bishops and Priests, vvhom he ought to obey and be subiect vvnto in religion, he shall be damned vndoubtedly, except he repent, because he doth against the expresse vvord of God and law of nature. And by this you may see the difference of an heretical and disordered time, from other catholike Christian daies. For heresie and the like damnable reuoltes from the Church of God, is no more than a rebellion and disobedience to the Priests of Gods Church, vvhen men refuse to be vnder their discipline, to heare their doctrine and interpretation of Scriptures, to obey their laws and counsels. This disobedience and rebellion from the Spiritual Gouernour, vnder pretence of obedience to the Temporal, is the bane of our daies, and specially of our Countrie, vvhere these new sects are properly maintained by this false principle, That the Prince in matters of soule and religion may command the Prelate: vvhich is directly and euidently against this Scripture and all other, that command the sheepe of Christs fold to obey their spiritual Officers.[37]

37. Ibid., 639.

The Rhemes New Testament is a small quarto. There is an engraved title page, then the sixteenth-century equivalent of the *imprimatur*, and then a famous and controversial *Preface* introducing the work to the reader.

The Preface to the Rhemes Bible deals with three important issues:

1. Why the Catholic Church had discouraged vernacular translations of the Bible.

2. Why the translators had decided to translate from Jerome's Latin Vulgate edition and not from the Hebrew and Greek.

3. Why their translation was so literal.

Here follows a summary of what they had to say on each of these matters.

The Catholic Church, they said, had never opposed the circulation of the Bible, provided that the circulation was of the original Hebrew and Greek Bible, or of the Latin translation by St. Jerome; this way, only people qualified by learning could take a look. Up until now, they said, she had discouraged vernacular editions for the multitude because translators generally translate according to what they think God must have meant, rather than according to what is actually written. Such translations would then have fallen into the hands of people who were incompetent to evaluate what they were reading.

As to why they were translating the Latin translation of Jerome instead of the original Hebrew and Greek texts, they answered that they would have translated the original Hebrew and Greek texts if those texts were available, but that the Hebrew and Greek manuscripts that were then in circulation were so corrupt that they were unsuitable for use as the basis of a translation. On the other hand, they said, there *were* excellent and reliable manuscripts around of Jerome's version, and Jerome was well known to have been an outstanding Hebrew and Greek scholar. Therefore, it was better for the time being to follow him rather than the adulterated Hebrew and Greek manuscripts that were available. In writing this, Allen and company had a point. Now although Fr. Martin translated from the Latin, he always compared the Latin text with what the available Hebrew and Greek manuscripts read in those cases where the Latin was incapable of precision, for example, whether a noun should have the definite or indefinite article. (Latin has neither, but both Hebrew and Greek have the definite article.) As a result, his translation excelled in the correct use of *the* and *a*. So, for example, he alone in that time correctly translated Matthew 4:5:

Then the Deuil tooke him vp into the holy citie, and set him vpon *the* pinnacle of the Tẽple ...

Everyone else, including King James twenty nine years later, has *a* pinnacle.

There are other cases in which the Rhemes New Testament is better than all competition. One is Matthew 2:1–2:

When Iesus therefore vvas borne in Bethlehem of Iuda in the days of Herod the King, behold, there came Sages from the East to Hierusalem, saying, vvhere is he that is borne King of the Ievves? For vve haue seene his starre in the East, and are come to adore him.

Another nice rendering is of Matthew 18:28:

And vvhen that seruant vvas gone forth, he found one of his felovv seruants that did ovve him an hundred pence: and laying hands vpon him thratled him, saying, Repay that thou ovvest.

Martin's translation is extremely literal, so much so that one often has to understand Latin to make sense of it, and in many cases it is incomprehensible. This was all according to plan. Martin wanted his readers to refer to the original at difficult passages, not to be fooled into thinking that there was no difficulty. He helped his readers out by including at the end of the volume a famous short dictionary of new words that he had coined, which were really nothing but transliterations of Hebrew, Greek, or (mostly) Latin words. When we read this dictionary now, we are astonished to see that words that are quite common today were evidently meaningless to a literate fellow of 1582. This is because these words entered into common use in our language only after the King James translators later (1611) borrowed them from Martin's work. They include such surprises as *acquisition, advent, adulterate, allegory, assumption, calumniate, catechize, character, holocaust, paraclete, resuscitate,* and *tetrarch.* This infusion of mostly Latin words into our vocabulary was the main contribution of the Rhemes-Doway Bible to the English language. What Martin wanted to avoid by his literal method was the fault of theologizing, which translators of religious texts often do. This theologizing method of translating scripture and liturgy was censured by Ernest Colwell, President of the University of Chicago:

It [sc. the modernizing method] plainly means that the Bible cannot say anything which the interpreter regards as unworthy of God. But this can be a sound rule for interpretation only if the interpreter's ideas as to what is worthy of God coincide with all the Biblical author's ideas—or with God's own thoughts. Unless the student is willing to make these assumptions, he should avoid interpretations based on this dogma. In practice, the appeal to this dogma gives the interpreter license to edit scripture into conformity with his own ideas.[38]

This sort of thing happens all the time, but Martin did not do it.

A typical example of a passage where the Rhemes New Testament is not comprehensible to the modern reader is Hebrews 13:16, which reads:

And beneficence and communication do not forget, for vvith such hostes God is promerited.

This is St. Jerome's Latin:

Beneficentiae autem et communionis nolite oblivisci; talibus enim hostibus promeretur Deus.

Jerome in turn is translating the Greek:

τῆς δὲ εὐποιίας καὶ κοινωνίας μὴ ἐπιλανθάνεσθε, τοιαύταις γὰρ θυσίαις εὐαρεστεῖται ὁ θεός.

In plain English, this means "Do not forget to do good to one another and to maintain fellowship with one another, for these are the sort of sacrifices that please God." It is the attitude of the prophets of Israel toward sacrifices. Martin, however, saw it as a verse that contradicted the Lutheran doctrine *sola fides*, that by faith alone does one achieve salvation. This is his note justifying his translation:

This latin vvord promeretur cannot be expressed effectually in any one English vvord. It signifieth, Gods fauour to be procured by the foresaid vvorkes of almes and charitie, as by the deserts and merites of the doers. Which doctrine and vvord of merites the Aduersaries like so il, that they flee both here and els vvhere from the vvord, translating here for, promeretur Deus, *God is pleased*, more neare to the Greeke, as they pretend. Which in deede maketh no more for them then the latin, vvhich is agreeable to most auncient copies, as vve see by Primasius, S. Augustines scholer. For if God be pleased vvith good vvorkes and shew fauour for them, then are they meritorious and then only faith is not the cause of Gods fauour to men.

38. Ernest Cadman Colwell, *The Study of the Bible* (Chicago: Phoenix Books / The University of Chicago Press, 1964), 103–4.

It was not until 1609, long after Martin and Allen had died, that the money was at hand to publish Martin's translation of the Old Testament. By that time, the seminary had moved back to Douai. The first volume of the Old Testament was published there in 1609, and the second volume in 1610. The two volumes together are called the Doway Old Testament, and are in the same format as the Rhemes New Testament. Later editions of the Rhemes-Doway Bible were published at Rouen. The later editions of the New Testament were printed with larger, easier to read type, and were illustrated with fine full-page engravings. Furthermore, some of the more inflammatory notes were removed.

The Rhemes New Testament and Doway Old Testament became known simply as the "Doway Bible" in England. It was revised by Bishop Richard Challoner (1691–1781), who changed many antiquated spellings and Latinisms, so that his edition is really an entirely new work. Evelyn Waugh wrote in 1959:

For a hundred years or more the Douay version of the Bible, as amended by Challoner, the official text of the Catholic Church in England, had been generally recognized as unsatisfactory. The second Synod of Oscott in 1855 had recommended that Newman should edit a new English version. The editorship as then conceived was more than the composition of the philosophic *Prolegomena* which he had in mind, and the choice of the translators; Newman's literary taste was to inform the whole work. As W. G. Ward wrote: 'It will be most pleasing to your friends in making your *name* immortal; for every Catholic reading his vernacular Bible will have your name on his lips. Your name will be imbedded as it were in the English Bible.'

A number of causes—the commercial interests of a bookseller, the apathy of Cardinal Wiseman, Newman's diffidence—contributed to frustrate this great project, but the primary impediment was the protest of the American Bishops on the ground that Archbishop Kendrick of Baltimore was already engaged on the same task and that it was undesirable that there should be two competing English versions (of which Newman's would without doubt have been the superior). To Newman's chagrin the matter was dropped with few expressions of regret. The Baltimore Bible was not adopted in England; the Douay stayed in use; but the sense of the resolution of 1855 was never entirely forgotten. All that was required was human energy to put it into effect. In 1938 the matter was recognized as being urgent, for the American Bishops were again busy preparing their own version.[39]

---

39. Evelyn Waugh, *Monsignor Ronald Knox, Fellow of Trinity College, Oxford and Protonotary Apostolic to His Holiness Pope Pius XII* (Boston: Little, Brown, 1959), 268–69.

On September 19, 1938, the Archbishop of Birmingham (England) wrote to Msgr. Ronald Knox:

Shrewsbury has sent me the letter you received from the U.S.A. about revising S. John's Gospel or the whole Bible 'in the idiom of our time'. I can well imagine what that will be. Can you wait until after the bishops' meeting on October 25th and 26th for an answer? I am proposing to put it to them that they appoint you our representative with power to coopt any other workers you desire. But I should also like to put it to them, if you do not strongly object, that they appoint *you* to do a new version of the New Testament first of all, and then the O.T. if the work goes on as I trust it will.[40]

Cardinal Hinsley wrote to Knox on November 8 of the affirmative vote of the bishops on the above-mentioned proposal.

With all the other Bishops I welcomed the proposal to commission you to translate the New Testament. We have confidence in you as the one man who can give us an English text readable and understood of the people.[41]

In the event, Knox decided to disregard the Doway-Challoner version totally and produced his own independent translation of the Vulgate, which the Bishops of England approved for private use.

Doxology The Greek verb δοκέω means *to think*, and the noun δόξα means *opinion, good report, glory*. The verb λέγω means *to lay, to lay in order, to relate, to speak*. Related to this verb is the noun λόγος, which means *word* or *reason*, and from this noun proceeded the adjective δοξολόγος, -ον meaning *speaking praise*. The resulting substantive δοξολογία thus means the *speaking of praise*, a doxology. The *Great Doxology* is the hymn *Gloria in Excelsis Deo*. The most common doxology is the *Gloria Patri*.

Dualism The Greek numeral δύο means *two*; it is the same word in Latin, *duo*. The associated adjective *dualis* means *double*, and from this adjective was formed in modern times the noun *dualism*, a theory involving two of something. Thus, the belief that there are two gods, one good and one bad, who wage perpetual warfare with one another is religious dualism, as would be the heresy that there are two gods, one the father of the other.

Dubium The Greek numeral δύο means *two*, and related to it is the Latin adjective *dubius* with the meaning *doubtful*. From the neuter singular of

40. Ibid.
41. Ibid.

this adjective comes the noun *dubium*, the Latin word for *doubt*. A dubium is a question formally proposed for an answer to a Roman Congregation or even to the pope himself. Thus, in former times various dubia were submitted to the Pontifical Biblical Commission, such as

Utrum solida prostent argumenta, etiam cumulative sumpta, ad evincendum Isaiae librum non ipsi soli Isaiae, sed duobus, immo pluribus auctoribus esse tribuendum? *Resp*. Negative.[42]

Are those arguments convincing, even if taken all together, that purport to establish that the Book of Isaiah must be assigned not to Isaiah himself alone, but to two, yea, even more authors? *Reply*: No.

The dubia most recently in the news are the five submitted publicly to Pope Francis in September 2016 by four cardinals (Brandmüller, Burke, Caffarra, Meisner) who did not see how the pope's apostolic exhortation *Amoris Laetitia* could be reconciled with traditional teaching and discipline:

It is asked whether, following the affirmations of *Amoris Laetitia* (300–305), it has now become possible to grant absolution in the sacrament of penance and thus to admit to holy Communion a person who, while bound by a valid marital bond, lives together with a different person *more uxorio* without fulfilling the conditions provided for by *Familiaris Consortio*, 84, and subsequently reaffirmed by *Reconciliatio et Paenitentia*, 34, and *Sacramentum Caritatis*, 29. Can the expression "in certain cases" found in Note 351 (305) of the exhortation *Amoris Laetitia* be applied to divorced persons who are in a new union and who continue to live *more uxorio*?

After the publication of the post-synodal exhortation *Amoris Laetitia* (304), does one still need to regard as valid the teaching of St. John Paul II's encyclical *Veritatis Splendor*, 79, based on sacred Scripture and on the Tradition of the Church, on the existence of absolute moral norms that prohibit intrinsically evil acts and that are binding without exceptions?

After *Amoris Laetitia* (301) is it still possible to affirm that a person who habitually lives in contradiction to a commandment of God's law, as for instance the one that prohibits adultery (Matthew 19:3–9), finds him or herself in an objective situation of grave habitual sin (Pontifical Council for Legislative Texts, "Declaration," June 24, 2000)?

After the affirmations of *Amoris Laetitia* (302) on "circumstances which mitigate moral responsibility," does one still need to regard as valid the teaching of St. John Paul II's encyclical *Veritatis Splendor*, 81, based on sacred Scripture and on the Tradition of the Church, according to which "circumstances or intentions

---

42. *Acta Sanctae Sedis* 41 (1908), p. 613 s.

can never transform an act intrinsically evil by virtue of its object into an act 'subjectively' good or defensible as a choice"?

After *Amoris Laetitia* (303) does one still need to regard as valid the teaching of St. John Paul II's encyclical *Veritatis Splendor*, 56, based on sacred Scripture and on the Tradition of the Church, that excludes a creative interpretation of the role of conscience and that emphasizes that conscience can never be authorized to legitimate exceptions to absolute moral norms that prohibit intrinsically evil acts by virtue of their object?[43]

Duplication The Greek numeral δύο means *two*; it is the same word in Latin, *duo*. The Latin verb *plico, plicare, plicavi, plicatus* means *to fold*. From the combination of the two proceeds the adjective *duplex, duplicis* with the meaning *double*. From this adjective is formed the noun *duplicatio, duplicationis* meaning a *doing twice*. *Duplication* is a synonym for *bination*, that is, the celebration of two masses in one day.

43. The *National Catholic Register*, which published this translation, identified it as the "translation provided by the Cardinal signatories." See http://www.ncregister.com/blog/edward-pentin/full-text-and-explanatory-notes-of-cardinals-questions-on-amoris-laetitia.

E

Easter Weekley derives the word *Easter* from the Anglo-Saxon noun *Eastre*, plural *Eastron*, which was the name of a pagan German festival at the vernal equinox, celebrated in honor of the Teutonic goddess of the dawn. (The German noun *der Ost* means the *East*.) When the Germans converted to Christianity, the name was adopted for the Christian paschal feast, since the two celebrations happened around the same time.

Ebionite The Hebrew adjective אביון means *poor*, and the masculine plural אביונים was transliterated into the Greek Ἐβιωναῖοι, whence we have our noun *Ebionite*.

This term, which later was derived from the name of an imaginary founder Ebion, really signified poor.[1]

The Ebionites were a Christian heretical sect of the first century A.D. From their name it is clear that these sectaries were from the humbler element of the population.

In St. Irenaeus' description the Ebionites are characterized by their fidelity to the Mosaic ordinances, circumcision, and the rest; they hold Jerusalem in great veneration, and turn towards it to pray; and their belief that the world was created by God Himself distinguishes them from all the gnostic sects.[2]

The Ebionites believed that Jesus was the physical son of Joseph and Mary.

1. Louis Duchesne, *Early History of the Christian Church from Its Foundation to the End of the Third Century* (London: John Murray, 1914), 91.
2. Ibid.

Ecce Sacerdos Magnus This antiphon is traditionally sung upon the entrance of a bishop into a church. It was set to music by Perosi with especial success. The verses are modelled after passages in Ecclesiasticus 44.

> Ecce sacerdos magnus, qui in diebus suis placuit Deo, et inventus est iustus. Alleluia.
> Non est inventus similis illi, qui conservaret legem Excelsi. Alleluia.
> Ideo iureiurando fecit illum Dominus crescere in plebem suam. Alleluia.
> Benedictionem omnium gentium dedit illi, et testamentum suum confirmavit super caput eius. Alleluia.
> Ideo iureiurando fecit illum Dominus crescere in plebem suam. Alleluia.
> Gloria Patri, et Filio, et Spiritui Sancto ...
> Ideo iureiurando fecit illum Dominus crescere in plebem suam. Alleluia.
>
> Behold the great priest, who in his days hath pleased God, and he was found just. Alleluia.
> There was found no one like unto him, who would keep the law of the Most High. Alleluia.
> Therefore hath the Lord sworn, that he should increase among his people. Alleluia.
> He hath given unto him the blessing of all nations, and hath confirmed his covenant upon his head. Alleluia.
> Therefore hath the Lord sworn, that he should increase among his people. Alleluia.
> Glory be to the Father, and to the Son, and to the Holy Ghost ...
> Therefore hath the Lord sworn, that he should increase among his people. Alleluia.

In days gone by, Catholics would hear this sung when the local bishop entered the church for the purpose of administering the sacrament of confirmation.

Eclecticism The Greek verb λέγω means *to gather, to pick up*, and when compounded with the preposition ἐκ produces the verb ἐκλέγω with the meaning *to select*. From this latter verb were produced the adjectives ἐκλεκτός with the meaning *chosen, select* and ἐκλεκτικός with the meaning *selective*. From this latter adjective there was in the nineteenth century produced the English noun *eclecticism*. This was Newman's name for the Neoplatonic school of Ammonius, whose "first promulgator and chief luminary"[3] was Plotinus. It is also called *Neologism*; see the entry for that word.

---

3. John Henry Cardinal Newman, *The Arians of the Fourth Century*, new ed. (London: Longmans, Green, 1897), 107.

Economical Method The Greek noun οἶκος means *house*, and the verb νέμω means *to deal out, distribute, control*. From their combination is produced the adjective οἰκονόμος, -ον, with the meaning *managing a household*; in 1 Corinthians 4:1 St. Paul calls the saints οἰκονόμοι of the mysteries of God. From οἰκονόμος there was further produced the adjective οἰκονομικός meaning *practiced in management, thrifty*. The addition of the stem of the Latin adjectival ending -*alis* produced the English word *economical*. The *economical method* is a method of reasoning called in Greek κατ᾽ οἰκονομίαν, whereby one conceals the full, difficult truth in disputation with an adversary who has not yet been prepared to accept it. It is the policy of public reserve with regard to the mysteries of the faith. The Latin name for this method of instruction is *Disciplina Arcani*.[4]

Ecthesis The Greek verb τίθημι means *to place*, and from it is derived the noun θέσις with the meaning a *putting* or *placing*. The addition of the preposition ἐκ produces the noun ἔκθεσις, which means a *putting out*. This noun is translated into Latin by *expositio*, an *exposition*. The *Ecthesis* of the emperor Heraclius (610–641) was a decree of 638 whereby that autocrat, in an attempt to impose an end to divisive domestic theological quarrels between Orthodox and Monophysites in the face of the Muslim advance, sought, by means of an imposed compromise, to put an end to the debate about the details of the unity of divinity and humanity in the Second Person of the Trinity. The Muslims had just captured Jerusalem, and in the decisive battle beforehand many Syrian Christians in the imperial army had deserted to the Muslims, for they were Monophysites and had, for almost two centuries, suffered discrimination at the hands of the Orthodox. As a concession to the Orthodox, the Emperor decreed that all were to hold that in Christ there was one hypostasis and two natures, but in compensation for the benefit of the Monophysites, he declared that there was one will and one source of activity ("one theandric energy"—μία θεανδρικὰ ἐνέργεια). This attempt at producing peace through compromise failed; though favored by Pope Honorius and the patriarchs of Constantinople, Antioch, and Alexandria, it was opposed as heretical by the patriarch of Jerusalem, St. Sophronius, and it was eventually withdrawn. Within three years the Muslims had conquered Egypt, where

---

4. The Greek verb ἀρκέω means *to ward off*. Related to it is the Latin verb *arceo* meaning *to shut in*. From *arceo* came the noun *arca*, a chest or coffer, and from *arca* came the adjective *arcanus* meaning *shut, closed, secret*.

the monophysite population preferred the rule of Islam to that of the Orthodox.[5]

Ecumenism The Greek verb οἰκέω means *to inhabit*, and the present passive particple οἰκούμενος means *inhabited*. The expression [ἡ γῆ] ἡ οἰκουμένη means *the inhabited* [*world*]. The addition of the adjectival suffix -ικός produces the super-adjective οἰκουμενικός with the meaning *pertaining to the inhabited world*. In modern times there was formed the noun *ecumenism* with the meaning a *friendly attitude toward people of other religions*, and individuals with such an outlook were called *ecumenical*. Not all religious people are ecumenical in this sense, for Eusebius tells the story of how Origen, orphaned at the age of sixteen, his father having been martyred, was admitted into the house of a pious lady who provided for him, yet he would not pray together with the lady's stepson, because the stepson was a heretic.[6] There is, however, another attitude, called the *Divinity of Traditionary Religion* or the *Dispensation of Paganism*, explained by John Henry Newman as follows.

It would seem, then, that there is something true and divinely revealed, in every religion all over the earth, overloaded, as it may be, and at times even stifled by the impieties which the corrupt will and understanding of man have incorporated with it. Such are the doctrines of the power and presence of an invisible God, of His moral law and governance, of the obligation of duty, and the certainty of a just judgment, and of reward and punishment, as eventually dispensed to individuals; so that Revelation, properly speaking, is an universal, not a local gift; and the distinction between the state of Israelites formerly and Christians now, and that of the heathen is, not that we can, and they cannot attain to future blessedness, but that the Church of God ever has had, and the rest of mankind never has had, authoritative documents of truth, and approved channels of communication with Him.[7]

Similar to the opinion of Newman is that of his contemporary Sanday:

It must not be thought that God is present only in a single creed and that all others alike are destitute of Him. It is rather His method to lead men gradually, and sometimes by circuitous routes, to the better understanding of Himself.[8]

5. See Steven Runciman, *A History of the Crusades* (London: The Folio Society, 1994), 1:1–16.

6. Eusebius, *The History of the Church from Christ to Constantine*, trans. G. A. Williamson (London: The Folio Society, 2011), VI 2, p. 164.

7. John Henry Cardinal Newman, *The Arians of the Fourth Century*, new ed. (London: Longmans, Green, 1897), 84.

8. William Sanday, *Inspiration, Eight Lectures on the Early History and Origin of the Doctrine of Biblical Inspiration, Being the Bampton Lectures for 1893* (London: Longmans, Green, 1896), 395.

Education The Latin verb *duco, ducere, duxi, ductus* means *to lead*, and related to it is the verb *educo, educare, educavi, educatus* meaning *to bring up, to rear*, from whose fourth principal part is derived the noun *educatio, educationis, f.*, with the meaning *bringing up, training, education*. James Anthony Froude said, "I have long though that, to educate successfully, you should first ascertain clearly, with sharp and distinct outline, what you mean by an educated man."[9] When William James was asked what he thought was the point of a liberal education, he replied that such an education "should enable us to know a good man when we see him."[10] Catholic theology is very difficult and requires education on the part of those who interest themselves in it. The quality of the education depends on the quality of the books. Dr. Jowett once wrote to Margot Tenant:

It is a great principle in all serious reading to stick to the works of great writers.[11]

Ego N. Catholicae Ecclesiae Episcopus This phrase means, "I, N., Bishop of the Catholic Church." Such a manner of signing one's name, now reserved for the pope on special occasions, was once used by bishops who wished to distinguish themselves from heretical colleagues who claimed the same title. For example, the Roman pontiff Pope Hilary used this manner to distinguish himself from the Arian pretender to the Papal See.[12] St. Augustine used it so as not to be confused with the Donatist bishop of Hippo.

Elector The Greek verb λέγω means *to lay, to lay in order*, and related to it is the Latin verb *lego, legere, legi, lectus* meaning *to collect, gather*. The addition of the preposition *e (out)* results in the compound verb *eligo, eligere, elegi, electus*, meaning *to choose out of some group, to select*. From the fourth principal part is formed the noun *elector* with the meaning *one who chooses*. The electors of the Holy Roman Empire were seven princes who elected the emperor during an interregnum, three spiritual (the archbishops of Cologne, Mainz, and Trier) and four temporal (the king of Bohemia, the duke of Saxony, the count of the Palatinate, and the margrave

---

9. Inaugural address at the University of St. Andrew's, March 19, 1868.

10. William James, "The Social Value of the College-Bred," an address delivered at a meeting of the Association of American Alumnae at Radcliffe College, Cambridge, Mass., November 7, 1907.

11. Geoffrey Faber, *Jowett, a Portrait with Background* (Cambridge, Mass.: Harvard University Press, 1958), 366.

12. Louis Duchesne, *Early History of the Christian Church from Its Foundation to the End of the Fifth Century*, vol. 3 (London: John Murray, 1924), 458–59.

of Brandenburg). The emperor was the one temporal prince mentioned in the Good Friday Liturgy:

Oremus et pro Christianissimo Imperatore nostro N., ut Deus et Dominus noster subditas illi faciat omnes barbaras nationes, ad nostram perpetuam pacem. Oremus,

> Flectamus genua.
>
> Levate.

Omnipotens sempiterne Deus, in cuius manu sunt omnium potestates, et omnium iura regnorum, respice ad Romanum benignus Imperium, ut gentes, quae in sua feritate confidunt, potentiae tuae dextera comprimantur. Per Dominum nostrum Iesum Christum ...

Let us also pray for our most Christian Emperor N., that the Lord our God may subject all the barbarian peoples to him, for our lasting peace.

> Let us kneel.
>
> Arise!

Almighty everlasting God, in whose hand are the powers of all peoples and the governments of all kingdoms, regard kindly the Roman Empire, so that the nations that trust in their savagery may be subdued by your mighty right hand. Through our Lord Jesus Christ ...

Those cardinals who are not superannuated by having celebrated their eightieth birthday are nowadays called *cardinal electors*, since they are the only ones allowed into the conclave. Their number was capped at 120, but this limit has not always been observed.

Elevation The Latin verb *levo, levare, levavi, levatus* means *to lift, to raise*, and when compounded with the preposition *e* there is produced the verb *elevo, elevare, elevavi, elevatus* with the meaning *to raise up, to elevate*. From the fourth principal part of this latter verb is derived the noun *elevatio, elevationis, f.*, with the meaning a *raising up*. The raising of the Host in the Mass after the consecration is called the *elevation*. The *Elevation Candle* was a candle that was lit on the Epistle side of the altar during the Canon of the Mass.

Emancipation The Latin verb *emancipo, emancipare* means *to release the son from the authority of his father, to transfer or make over property*, including people. From this verb proceeded the noun *emancipatio*, a transfer of property, a setting free. The Catholic Emancipation was the name for a series of laws passed by the British Parliament in the eighteenth and nineteenth centuries that removed the civil disabilities of Roman Catholics.

— E —

Ember Days The Ember Days were (for they have disappeared from the Missal) three special days of fast and abstinence at the beginning of each season. They were fixed by Gregory VII to be the Wednesday, Friday, and Saturday after December 13, St. Lucy's Day (*feria quarta, sexta, sabbato quatuor temporum Adventūs*), after the First Sunday of Lent (*feria quarta, sexta, sabbato quatuor temporum Quadragesimae*), after Pentecost Sunday (*feria quarta, sexta, sabbato quatuor temporum Pentecostis*), and after September 15, the Exaltation of the Holy Cross (*feria quarta, sexta, sabbato quatuor temporum Septembris*). The noun *Ember* is an Anglo-Saxon corruption of the Latin *Tempora*, which means *seasons*; the *quatuor tempora* are the four seasons.

Eminence The Latin deponent verb *minor, minari* means *to jut out, project*, and related to it is the verb *mineo, minere* meaning *to overhang*. The addition of the preposition *e* (out) to the latter verb produced the compound verb *emineo, eminere, eminui* meaning *to project, stand out*, and from this compound verb was derived the noun *eminentia* meaning *prominence*. By the decree of Urban VIII of June 10, 1630, the title *Eminence* is reserved for cardinals. Before his time, cardinals would be called Your Highness, Your Brilliance, Your Grace, Your Magnificence, Your Magnitude, Your Eminence, or whatever compliment came to mind. The title of *Eminence* had previously been reserved for the three spiritual prince electors of the Holy Roman Empire, the archbishops of Cologne, Mainz, and Trier.

Enchiridion The Greek preposition ἐν means *in*, and the noun χείρ means *hand*. From the concatenation of these two words there proceeded the adjective ἐγχειρίδιος, -ον, with the meaning *in the hand*. The neuter singular of this adjective, τὸ ἐγχειρίδιον, was used as a noun with the meaning *something held in the hand*, such as a *dagger*, or a *manual*. The *Enchiridion Indulgentiarum* is the handbook that lists all the means whereby one may gain an indulgence. The Italian name for this volume is *Raccolta*, that is, *Collection*. See the entry **Indulgence**.

Encratite The Greek noun τὸ κράτος, τοῦ κράτεος means *strength*, and the addition of the preposition ἐν produces the adjective ἐγκρατής with the meaning *having a firm hold on*. The related noun ἐγκράτεια means *self-control*, and the deponent verb ἐγκρατεύομαι means *to exercise self-control*. The Encratites were an early Christian heresy first mentioned by Irenaeus, who is quoted by Eusebius:

Borrowing from Saturninus and Marcion, the so-called Encratites preached celibacy, setting aside the original creation of God and tacitly condemning Him who made male and female for the generation of human beings. They also introduced abstention from "animate things", as they call them, showing ingratitude to God who made all things. Again, they deny the salvation of the first created man. This notion they adopted quite recently; one Tatian was the first to introduce this blasphemy. He had been a pupil of Justin …[13]

Thus, not only did they disapprove of sex as something wicked and consequently reject marriage, but they also seem to have been vegetarians, a lifestyle that did not find favor in the eyes of the learned author. They had a significant influence on the Priscillian heretics of fourth century Spain. See the entry **Priscillianists**.

Encyclical The Greek noun κύκλος means *circle*, and from it is derived, upon the addition of the preposition ἐν, the adjective ἐγκύκλιος with the meaning *circular*. In late Latin this was transliterated by *encyclius* and then corrupted to *encyclicus*. The additional suffix *-al* is a mistake added on when the word became English. The encyclicals are official letters of the popes (*litterae enciclicae*) addressed to the episcopate and sometimes even to a wider audience. The term became common in the nineteenth century as a name for such pronouncements.

Energumen The Greek adjective ἐνεργός, *active, working*, is derived from the obsolete root ἔργω, which meant *to do work*. From it was produced the verb ἐνεργέω with the meaning *to be in action, to work*:

ὁ γὰρ ἐνεργήσας Πέτρῳ εἰς ἀποστολὴν τῆς περιτομῆς ἐνέργησεν καὶ ἐμοὶ εἰς τὰ ἔθνη.

For he that vvrought in Peter to the Apostleship of the circumcision, vvrought in me also among the Gentils (Galatians 2:8, Rhemes translation).

In the passive voice this verb means *to be the object of action*, especially by a supernatural agent. Thus an ἐνεργούμενος is a fellow subjected to supernatural activity. The derivative English word *energumen* denotes someone suspected of being possessed by a devil.

Eparchy The Greek verb ἄρχω means *to rule*, and the compound verb ἐπάρχω means *to rule over a province of the Roman Empire as* ἔπαρχος,

---

13. Eusebius, *The History of the Church from Christ to Constantine*, trans. G. A. Williamson (London: The Folio Society, 2011), IV 29, p. 123.

that is, *as governor*. The Latin term to which ἔπαρχος corresponded was *praefectus*, prefect, commander. The noun ἐπαρχία was used to translate the Latin *provincia*. In the Eastern Churches, *eparchy* is used instead of *diocese* for the unit of government, but the use of the corresponding *eparch* for *bishop* is uncommon.

Epiphany The Greek verb φαίνω means *to appear*. The addition of the preposition ἐπί produces the compound verb ἐπιφαίνω with the meaning *to show forth*, and in the middle and passive voices *to show oneself*. The phrase τὰ ἐπιφάνια, whence we get our word *epiphany*, is the name for the feast of the manifestation of Christ to the gentiles.

Episcopalian The Latin noun *episcopus* is the transliteration of the Greek noun ἐπίσκοπος. See the entry **Bishop**. From it was derived the English noun and adjective *Episcopalian* with the meaning *an adherent of the Church of England or its associated churches*, as distinguished from those Protestants, such as the Presbyterians, whose system of government dispensed with bishops.

Epistle The Greek verb στέλλω means *to set in order, to dispatch on an expedition, to send*. The addition of the preposition ἐπί produces the compound verb ἐπιστέλλω with the meaning *to send to, impose orders on*. From this verb is derived the noun ἐπιστολή, which means *message* or *letter*, from which, through the medium of the Latin transliteration *epistola*, we get our noun *epistle*. The letters of the apostles contained in the New Testament are called *epistles*, and it is because of this fact that the word *epistle* acquired a higher dignity than the humbler word *letter*.

Epitaph The Greek verb θάπτω, θάψω, ἔθαψα, τέταφα, τέθαμμαι, ἐθάφθην (second aorist ἐτάφην) means *to perform the funeral rites, to bury*. From this word is derived the noun τάφος with the meaning, *a burial*. The addition of the preposition ἐπί, *on*, produced the compound adjective of two terminations ἐπιτάφιος, ἐπιτάφιον with the meaning *on* or *over a tomb*. From the root of this adjective comes the English noun *epitaph* meaning an *inscription on a tombstone*. The most famous papal epitaph is that on the worthy monument to Adrian VI (1522–1523) in the Church of Santa Maria dell'Anima, Rome:

Proh dolor! Quantum refert in quae tempora vel optimi cuiusque virtus incidat.

Alas! How much depends on the times in which even the most capable of men is cast!

This was one of that pontiff's favorite sayings, whereby he lamented the limits that the bankrupt condition of the Church set to his enterprises. Another phrase of his was the customary reply he gave when pressed to make a decision before he was ready to do so—"Exspectabimus, et videbimus"—that is, "Let's wait and see."[14]

Eschatology The Greek adjective ἔσχατος means *last, farthest*. The original sense of the word *eschatology* is geographical, as may be illustrated by quoting from the first book of the *Odyssey*, verse 23:

> Αἰθίοπας τοὶ διχθὰ δεδαίαται, ἔσχατοι ἀνδρῶν.
>
> The Ethiopians, a race divided, the remotest of men.

Its meaning is now temporal; it is the study of what happens at the end of the world. When one reads 1 Corinthians 7, one should keep in mind that it was a problem for Christianity to adjust to the idea that the world might go on. The book of R. H. Charles may be consulted on the subject.[15]

Essence This English word is derived from the Late Latin noun *essentia* (from *esse*, to be), which, according to Seneca, Cicero invented to translate the Greek noun οὐσία, being.[16] In the liturgy it appears in the Preface of the Most Holy Trinity:

Ut in confessione verae sempiternaeque Deitatis, et in personis proprietas, et in essentia unitas, et in maiestate adoretur aequalitas.

So that in the praise of the true and everlasting Godhead, there may be adored distinction in persons, oneness in being, and equality in majesty.

It was not the only Latin word used to render οὐσία; see the entry **Substance**. Blackburn defines *essence* as it is understood by modern philosophers:

---

14. Leopold von Ranke, *The History of the Popes during the Last Four Centuries*, trans. Mrs. Foster and G. R. Dennis (London: G. Bell and Sons, 1912), 1:77.

15. R. H. Charles, *A Critical History of the Doctrine of a Future Life* (London: Adam & Charles Black, 1913). The book was republished in 1963 under the title *Eschatology: The Doctrine of a Future Life in Israel, Judaism, and Christianity, A Critical History* (New York: Schocken Books).

16. "Ciceronem auctorem huius verbi habeo" (I take it that Cicero concocted this word). Seneca, *Epistles* 58.6.

The basic or primary element in the being of a thing; the thing's nature, or that without which it could not be what it is. A thing cannot lose its essence without ceasing to exist, and the essential nature of a natural kind, such as water or gold, is that property without which there is no instance of the kind. Locke contrasted real essences, in something like this sense, with the nominal definition provided by a description of the common properties of a thing. Throughout Greek, scholastic, and some modern philosophy, there have been many proposals of ways for finding the essences of things, and views about what science would be like if we did not know them. The distinction between essential and accidental properties is rejected by holistic approaches to science, such as that advocated by Quine.[17]

Essenes The etymology of this name is uncertain; these people were called by the Greeks Ἐσσηνοί or Ἐσσαῖοι. They were a Jewish party of the time of Christ who produced the writings called the *Dead Sea Scrolls*, which were discovered in caves at Qumran in the mid-twentieth century. They had moved to the wilderness to get away from the Jewish establishment in Jerusalem, of which they disapproved.

Et cum Spiritu Tuo This is the standard reply to the greeting *Dominus Vobiscum*. The translation "And also with you," which was used for forty years in the English speaking world, was replaced by "And with your Spirit" in the most recent revision of the Missal. The expression is a Hebraism. It was not originally a theological statement. In Hebrew, *my soul, your soul, his soul* are euphemisms for *I, you,* and *he.* "My soul is tired" just means "I am tired." The Hebrew point of view was that you *are* a soul, not that you *have* a soul.

Etiquette (Church) The German verb *stecken* means *to stick,* and related to it was the Old French noun *estiquette* and its modern equivalent *étiquette,* which, according to Weekley, was originally the name of a notice stuck on a post. Our English noun *ticket* is related to it. The progress of the meaning from *ticket* to *proper behavior* is unclear. The first occurrence of this word in English has a Catholic connection; it is in the letter of March 19, 1750, from Lord Chesterfield to his natural son, who was visiting Rome at that time at the age of 17 years. The episode is very instructive. Speaking of the supreme pontiff of the time, Benedict XIV, the father wrote:

I do not think that the present Pope was a sort of man, to build seven modern little chapels at the expense of so respectable a piece of antiquity as the *Colliseum.*

17. Simon Blackburn, *The Oxford Dictionary of Philosophy* (Oxford: Oxford University Press, 1994), 125, s.v. "essence."

However, let His Holiness's taste of *Virtù* be ever so bad, pray get somebody to present you to him, before you leave Rome; and without hesitation kiss his slipper, or whatever else the *étiquette* of that Court requires. I would have you see all those ceremonies; and I presume that you are, by this time, ready enough at Italian to understand and answer *il Santo Padre* in that language. I hope, too, that you have acquired address, and usage enough of the world to be presented to any body, without embarrassment or disapprobation. If that is not yet quite perfect, as I cannot suppose that it is entirely, custom will improve it daily, and habit at last complete it.[18]

The Earl had previously instructed his son:

A propos of the Pope; remember to be presented to him before you leave Rome, and go through the necessary ceremonies for it, whether of kissing his slipper or his b—h, for I would never deprive myself of any thing that I wanted to do or see, by refusing to comply with an established custom. When I was in Catholic countries, I never declined kneeling in their churches at the elevation, nor elsewhere, when the Host went by. It is a complaisance due to the custom of the place, and by no means, as some silly people have imagined, an implied approbation of their doctrine. Bodily attitudes and situations are things so very indifferent in themselves, that I would quarrel with nobody about them. It may, indeed, be improper for Mr. Harte to pay that tribute of complaisance, upon account of his character.[19]

Eucharist The Greek verb εὐχαριστέω means *to return thanks*, and the noun εὐχαριστία derived from it means *thankfulness, gratitude*. It is compounded of the adverb εὖ, *well*, and the noun χάρις, *favor, grace*.

Eusebians The Greek verb σέβω means *to worship, to be religious*, and the adverb εὖ means *well*. From their combination was formed the adjective εὐσεβής with the meaning *pious*. The adjective became a proper name, like the Latin *Pius*. The Eusebians were a party of Arians named after Eusebius, Bishop of Nicomedia (died 341), whose leadership they followed. They were the court party, who supported the policies of Emperor Constantius II (337–361). Their enemies in later times called them Semi-Arians. They were the champions of the word ὁμοιούσιος; see the entry **Homoiousios**.

---

18. *Letters Written by the Late Right Honourable Philip Dormer Stanhope, Earl of Chesterfield, to his Son, Philip Stanhope, Esq., Late Envoy Extraordinary at the Court of Dresden, together with Several other Pieces on various Subjects*, ed. Eugenia Stanhope (London: J. Dodsley, 1774), 1:566.

19. The Mr. Harte mentioned is Mr. Raphael Harte, his son's tutor and travelling companion, probably in Church of England orders. Chesterfield, *Letters*, Letter of September 22, 1749.

Eutychian The Greek adverb εὖ means *well*, and the noun τύχη means *fortune*, and their concatenation produced the adjective εὐτυχής with the meaning *successful, lucky, prosperous*. The adjective became a proper name, and its most notorious bearer was the the holy man Eutyches, the head of a monastery of hundreds of monks in Constantinople, who in the fourth century, after the Council of Ephesus, taught that the Christ, though consubstantial with the Father with respect to divinity, was not consubstantial with us with respect to humanity. Another teaching of Eutyches, "Two Natures before the union, only one afterwards," was approved at the Robber Council of Ephesus, presided over by Dioscorus, patriarch of Alexandria. This teaching is the exact opposite of the Catholic doctrine.

He [Eutyches] challenged entirely the view that the humanity of Christ was a humanity like ours or, in technical language, that Christ was "consubstantial" with other men.[20]

The doctrine of Eutyches was condemned by the Council of Chalcedon in 451.

Evil This word is of Germanic origin. It descends from the Anglo-Saxon *yfel* and the Middle English *evel*. The German cognate is *Übel*. Weekley says that it is "probably related to *up, over*, as exceeding bounds." But the corresponding words in the Biblical languages are what concern us here. *Evil* in Hebrew is רע from the root רעע, whose original meaning Brown, Driver, and Briggs declare to be dubious. In Greek it is κακόν; in Latin *malum*. The problem of evil is one of the major issues in philosophy and religion and has always attracted the attention of thinking people. Eusebius mentions that, during the reign of Septimius Severus, the churchman Maximus composed a book with the title *The Origin of Evil*, and that this was a "question so much discussed among the heretics."[21] In his three essays on religion, John Stuart Mill followed Voltaire and argued that if God is omnipotent, then he cannot be all good because he tolerates evil, and if he is good, then he cannot be omnipotent or he would do away with evil. On this matter, one may quote Isaiah 45:7, which is the expression of absolute monotheism:

20. Louis Duchesne, *Early History of the Christian Church from Its Foundation to the End of the Fifth Century*, vol. 3 (London: John Murray, 1924), 277.

21. Eusebius, *The History of the Church from Christ to Constantine*, trans. G. A. Williamson (London, the Folio Society, 2011), V 27, p. 159.

עֹשֶׂה שָׁלוֹם וּבוֹרֵא עָר

אֲנִי יהוה עֹשֶׂה כָל אֵלֶּה

The maker of peace and the creator of evil, I the Lord do all these things.

Similarly do the Arabs say, when a disaster has happened,

كذالك شاء الله

"it was God's will that it should happen." This problem of evil was, in the opinion of William George Ward, the major issue in religion.

The unanswerable objection to an infinite Creator is, of course, the existence of evil.[22]

Exarch The Greek verb ἄρχω means *to begin* as well as *to rule*, and the compound verb ἐξάρχω means *to lead off, to be the first to do something*. Thus, the corresponding noun ἔξαρχος is in the Latin *princeps*, a leader, a chief. After the Byzantine conquest of the Gothic Kingdom of Italy in the sixth century, the governor appointed by the emperor was called the *exarch*, and his headquarters were at Ravenna. The same title was given in the Eastern Churches to the head of a church who did not have patriarchal rank, a sort of primate. Thus, the Bulgarian Orthodox, in their struggle to rid themselves of Greek bishops, had in the period 1872–1915, over the objections of the patriarch of Constantinople, an exarch.

Ex cathedra This Latin phrase means *from the Chair [of Peter]* and is employed to refer to any official pronouncement of the Roman pontiff, acting in his capacity as the successor of St. Peter, that defines a matter of faith or morals to be held by all believers. For the etymology, see the entry **Cathedral**. The official description of this authority is that in the fourth chapter of the constitution *Pater Aeternus* of the First Vatican Council (Fourth Session, July 18, 1870):

Itaque Nos traditioni a fidei Christianae exordio perceptae fideliter inhaerendo, ad Dei Salvatoris nostri gloriam, religionis Catholicae exaltationem et Christianorum populorum salutem, sacro approbante Concilio, docemus et divinitus revelatum dogma esse definimus: Romanum Pontificem, cum ex Cathedra loquitur, id est, cum omnium Christianorum Pastoris et Doctoris munere fungens pro suprema sua Apostolica auctoritate doctrinam de fide vel moribus ab universa Ecclesia tenendam definit, per assistentiam divinam, ipsi in beato Petro promissam, ea

---

22. Wilfrid Ward, *William George Ward and the Catholic Revival* (London: Macmillan, 1893), 456.

infallibilitate pollere, qua divinus Redemptor Ecclesiam suam in definienda doc-trina de fide vel moribus instructam esse voluit; ideoque eiusmodi Romani Pon-tificis definitiones ex sese, non autem ex consensu Ecclesiae, irreformabiles esse.

Si quis autem huic Nostrae definitioni contradicere, quod Deus avertat, prae-sumpserit; anathema sit.[23]

The following translation is that of Henry Edward Manning, Archbishop of Westminster and later cardinal:

Therefore, faithfully adhering to the tradition received from the beginning of the Christian faith, for the glory of God Our Savior, the exaltation of the Catholic Religion, and the salvation of Christian people, the Sacred Council approving, We teach and define that it is a divinely-revealed dogma: that the Roman Pontiff, when he speaks *ex Cathedra*, that is, when in discharge of the office of Pastor and Teacher of all Christians, by virtue of his supreme Apostolic authority, he defines a doctrine regarding faith or morals to be held by the Universal Church, by the divine assistance promised to him in blessed Peter, is possessed of that infallibility with which the divine Redeemer willed that His Church should be endowed for defining doctrine regarding faith or morals: and that therefore such definitions of the Roman Pontiff are irreformable of themselves, and not from the consent of the Church.[24]

Excellency The Latin adjective *celsus* means *upraised*, *high*, *lofty*, and the addition of the preposition *ex* (out) results in the compound verb *excello*, *excellere*, *excelsi*, *excelsus* meaning *to stand out*, *to be distinguished*. From this last verb comes the noun *excellentia* with the meaning *distinction*, *eminence*. In America, the way to address a bishop used to be "Your Excel-lency." Today, one instead hears merely the abrupt "Bishop" from the part of people uncomfortable with formality. Comical is the now common juxtaposition of a title with a nickname, for instance, Bishop Jim or Car-dinal Billy. Such methods of address are permitted only by persons with a low sense of the dignity of their office. The use of such forms of address as *Your Majesty*, *Your Excellency*, *Your Grace*, and the like was unknown in Europe until, according to Voltaire, the reign of Constantine. Von Ranke wrote, with regard to the sixteenth century:

It is worthy of note that titles came into use at this time. As early as the year 1520, it was remarked with disgust, that all desired to be called "Sir": this was attributed to the influence of the Spaniards. About the year 1550, the old forms of address,

23. Denzinger, *Enchiridion Symbolorum et Definitionum*, 7th ed. (Würzburg: V. J. Stahel, 1895), CXXXIX, §§1682–83, p. 400.

24. Available at http://catholicplanet.org/councils/20-Pastor-Aeternus.htm.

so noble in their simplicity, were encumbered, whether in speech or writing, by ponderous epithets of honour; at the end of the century duke and marquis were titles prevailing everywhere; all wished to possess them, every man would fain be "Excellency".[25]

Excommunication The Latin verb *munio, munire, munivi, munitus* means *to build*, especially a wall, whence the associated noun *moenia, moenium* means *the walls* or *fortifications* of a city. Related to *moenia* is *munus, muneris, n.*, which means *office, function, duty*; etymologically, the office is a bulwark for the state. The addition of the preposition *cum* (with) produces the adjective *communis* meaning *that which is shared* rather than private. Thence came the verb *communico, communicare* meaning *to share, to take a share in*, whence proceeded the noun *communicatio, communicationis* meaning *a sharing, a participation*. The noun *excommunicatio, excommunicationis, f.*, the ban of the Church, and the verb *excommunico, excommunicare*, to put under the ban, seem to have arisen in the fourth century and are to be found in the writings of Saints Jerome and Augustine. The Greek word for an excommunicated person is ἀποσυνάγωγος, that is, *someone expelled from the synagogue*. Speaking of excommunication in the fourth century, Milman wrote:

> For in the awful meaning which the act of excommunication conveyed to the Christian mind of that age, it meant total exclusion, unless after humiliating penance, and hard-wrung absolution, from the mercy of the Most High,—inevitable, everlasting damnation.[26]

Exequial Mass The Latin deponent verb *sequor, sequi, secutus sum* means *to follow*. The addition of the preposition *ex* emphasizes the finality of the act, producing the compound verb *exsequor, exsequi, exsecutus sum* with the meaning *to follow to the grave*. The related noun *exsequiae* means the *funeral procession*, and the adjective *exsequialis* has the meaning *having to do with the funeral procession*. The Exequial Mass is the Requiem Mass celebrated in the presence of the body of the deceased before the burial. It is to be distinguished from a Requiem Mass, which may be celebrated for any dead person at any time and at any place.

---

25. Leopold von Ranke, *The History of the Popes during the Last Four Centuries*, trans. Mrs. Foster and G. R. Dennis (London: G. Bell and Sons, 1912), 1:388.

26. Henry Hart Milman, *History of Latin Christianity, Including That of the Popes, to the Pontificate of Nicholas V* (New York: Sheldon, 1860), 1:224.

Exorcist The Greek noun ὅρκος means *oath*, and the addition of the preposition ἐξ (out) produces the compound verb ἐξορκίζω meaning first *to administer the oath of office to a person*, and secondly, *to banish an evil spirit by abjuration*, that is, by imposing solemnly an obligation on the spirit to leave the possessed person. The related noun ἐξορκιστής means the *person who does the banishing*. An exorcist ranked lower than an acolyte but higher than a lector. That he had much to do is a certain corollary of the belief of Pope Leo XIII:

… satanam aliosque spiritus malignos, qui ad perditionem animarum pervagantur in mundo.

… Satan and the other evil spirits, who prowl about the world seeking the ruin of souls.

Exposition The Latin verb *pono, ponere, posui, positus* means *to put* or *place*, and the compound verb *expono, exponere, exposui, expositus* means *to put* (pono) *out* (ex) *for display*. From the fourth principal part of the second verb is derived the noun *expositio*, a showing, from whence is derived our noun *exposition*. Exposition of the Blessed Sacrament is the public showing of the sacred species preserved in a monstrance.

Extra Ecclesiam Nulla Salus This Latin phrase means "Outside the Church there is no salvation." It is a dogma of the Catholic religion and rests upon Mark 16:15–16 and John 3:5.

καὶ εἶπεν αὐτοῖς: Πορευθέντες εἰς τὸν κόσμον ἅπαντα κηρύξατε τὸ εὐαγγέλιον πάσῃ τῇ κτίσει. ὁ πιστεύσας καὶ βαπτισθεὶς σωθήσεται, ὁ δὲ ἀπιστήσας κατακριθήσεται.

And he said unto them, Go ye into all the world, and preach the gospel to every creature. He that believeth and is baptized shall be saved; but he that believeth not shall be damned.[27]

ἀπεκρίθη ὁ Ἰησοῦς: Ἀμὴν ἀμὴν λέγω σοι, ἐὰν μή τις γεννηθῇ ἐξ ὕδατος καὶ πνεύματος, οὐ δύναται εἰσελθεῖν εἰς τὴν βασιλείαν τοῦ θεοῦ.

Jesus answered, Verily, verily, I say unto thee, Except a man be born of water and of Spirit, he cannot enter into the kingdom of God.[28]

It is customary to trace the dogma back to St. Cyprian of Carthage (letter 72, section 21). St. Augustine also taught it:

27. Mk 16:15–16
28. Jn 3:5 (Authorized Version)

Salus extra ecclesiam non est.

There is no salvation outside the Church.[29]

That the doctrine was understood literally for centuries is clear, for example, from the decree of the Fourth Lateran Council against the Albigensian and other heretics (1215):

Una vero est fidelium universalis Ecclesia, extra quam nullus omnino salvatur.[30]

For there is one worldwide Church of believers, outside of which no one at all is saved.

Leaving little to the imagination is the Bull *Cantate Domino* of Eugenius IV, published as the Decree of the Council of Florence (1441) regarding union with the Jacobites:

Firmiter credit, profitetur et praedicat, nullos intra catholicam Ecclesiam non existentes, non solum paganos, sed nec Iudaeos aut haereticos atque schismaticos, aeternae vitae fieri posse participes; sed in ignem aeternum ituros, qui paratus est diabolo et angelis eius, nisi ante finem vitae eidem fuerint aggregati: tantumque valere ecclesiastici corporis unitatem, ut solum in ea manentibus ad salutem ecclesiastica sacramenta proficiant, et ieiunia, eleëmosynae ac caetera pietatis officia et exercitia militiae christianae praemia aeterna parturiant. Neminemque, quantascumque eleëmosynas fecerit, etsi pro Christi nomine sanguinem effuderit, posse salvari, nisi in catholicae Ecclesiae gremio et unitate permanserit.[31]

[The Holy Roman Church] firmly believes, professes, and teaches, that no one not found within the Catholic Church, neither pagans, nor Jews, nor heretics, nor schismatics, have any share in eternal life, but instead will go down into eternal fire, which was prepared for the Devil and his angels, unless before their last breath they should be joined unto her. Furthermore, the unity of the ecclesiastical body is so important, that the Church's sacraments avail for salvation only for those who remain in her, and for those only do fasts, almsgiving, and all other acts and exercises of charity bear the fruit of eternal rewards. What is more, no one, however so many alms he should give, even if he should shed blood for Christ's name's sake, can be saved unless he remain in the bosom and unity of the Catholic Church.

Modern man takes a doctrine of this sort to be an example of offensive obscurantism. Since it is not possible within the system of an infallible

---

29. Augustine, *De Baptismo contra Donatistas*, 4.17.24.

30. Denzinger, *Enchiridion Symbolorum et Definitionum*, 7th ed. (Würzburg, V. J. Stahel, 1895), §357, p. 120.

31. Ibid., §605, p. 170.

Church to declare the pronouncements of ecumenical councils to be false, the severity of the doctrine *Extra ecclesiam nulla salus* is now attenuated by the device of regarding all men as somehow members of the Church in a miraculous manner.

Once when I [Dean Goulburn is speaking] had expressed surprise to him [William George Ward] that seriously-minded Roman Catholics could, in view of the dogma *Extra Ecclesiam nulla salus*, have any comfort or happiness in thinking of their Protestant relations and friends, he expounded to me the theory of "invincible ignorance", as excusing a large amount of heresy, and placing heretics who have erred under its influence within the pale of salvation. "And I am quite sure, my dear Goulburn," he added, with the greatest earnestness and emphasis, *"that your ignorance is MOST invincible."*[32]

William George Ward quoted from an allocution of Pius IX in support of the doctrine of invincible ignorance:

Notum nobis vobisque est eos qui invincibili ignorantia laborant, qui naturalem legem ... sedulo servantes ac Deo obedire parati posse aeternam consequi vitam.[33]

We and you both know, that those who struggle in the state of invincible ignorance, who dutifully adhere to the natural law and are prepared to obey God, can obtain life eternal.

Extraordinary The Latin adjective *extraordinarius* means *outside* (extra) *the usual order* (ordo). Thus, when Urban VI was elected pope in 1378 without having been a cardinal first, it was extraordinary. The bureaucratic way of referring to the Mass as celebrated in the traditional manner is to call it the *Extraordinary Form of the Mass*. On the contrary, it is the Mass celebrated in the common vernacular languages that is really extraordinary, there having been no such thing in the Catholic Church for fifteen hundred years.

Extreme Unction The Latin adjective *extremus* is the superlative degree of *exter*, which means *outward, foreign, strange*. *Extremus* therefore means *outermost, last, at the end*. The verb *unguo, unguere, unxi, unctus* means *to anoint*, whence arose the noun *unctio, unctionis* with the meaning *anointing*. The phrase *Extrema Unctio*, of which *Extreme Unction* is obviously the literal translation, literally means the *Last Anointing*; it used to be

---

32. Wilfrid Ward, *William George Ward and the Catholic Revival* (London: Macmillan, 1893), 77. Edward Meyrick Goulburn (1818–1897) was Dean of Norwich.
    33. Ibid., 458.

commonly called in English the *Last Rites*, but the approved name nowadays is the *Anointing of the Sick*. The Council of Trent and the *Catechismus Catholicus* of Cardinal Gasparri referred to the sacrament in question as *Extrema Unctio*.

Q. 469. *Quid est sacramentum Extremae Unctionis?*

R. Sacramentum Extremae Unctionis est sacramentum a Iesu Christo institutum, quo omnibus, post usum rationis vita periclitantibus, spiritualia auxilia, in mortis periculo maxime proficua, conferuntur, et aliquando etiam solamen ab infirmitatibus corporis.

Q. 469. What is the sacrament of Extreme Unction?

R. The sacrament of Extreme Unction is the sacrament instituted by Jesus Christ whereby spiritual assistance, most efficacious when there is danger of death, is granted to all who have attained the age of reason and whose life is despaired of; occasionally it may also provide comfort from bodily illnesses.[34]

The biblical proof-text for this sacrament is the Epistle of St. James 5:13–15.

Κακοπαθεῖ τις ἐν ὑμῖν; προσευχέσθω· εὐθυμεῖ τις; ψαλλέτω. ἀσθενεῖ τις ἐν ὑμῖν; προσκαλεσάσθω τοὺς πρεσβυτέρους τῆς ἐκκλησίας, καὶ προσευξάσθωσαν ἐπ᾿ αὐτὸν ἀλείψαντες ἐλαίῳ ἐν τῷ ὀνόματι τοῦ κυρίου καὶ ἡ εὐχὴ τῆς πίστεως σώσει τὸν κάμνοντα, καὶ ἐγερεῖ αὐτὸν ὁ κύριος· κἂν ἁμαρτίας ᾖ πεποιηκώς, ἀφεθήσεται αὐτῷ.

Is any among you afflicted? Let him pray. Is any merry? Let him sing psalms. Is any sick among you? Let him call for the elders of the church; and let them pray over him, anointing him with oil in the name of the Lord. And the prayer of faith shall save the sick, and the Lord shall raise him up; and if he have committed sins, they shall be forgiven him. (Authorized Version)

---

34. *Catechismus Catholicus*, cura et studio Petri Cardinalis Gasparri concinnatus, 15th ed. (Vatican City: Typis Polyglottis Vaticanis, 1933), 228.

F

Fabbrica di San Pietro The Mediaeval Latin noun *fabrĭca* means *building*. The Liberian Catalogue says of Pope Fabian:

Hic regiones divisit diaconibus et multas fabricas per cymiteria fieri iussit.

He assigned the various districts to the deacons and ordered many buildings to be constructed all over the catacombs.[1]

The Fabric of St. Peter's (*Fabbrica di San Pietro*) is the entity in charge of the upkeep of the Basilica. At its head is the cardinal archpriest.

Faith The semi-deponent Latin verb *fido, fidere, fisus sum* means *to trust, to believe*. To it is related the noun *fides, fidĕi, f.*, with the meaning *trust, confidence*, from which descends our word *faith*. It is the translation of the Greek noun πίστις, which plays such an important role in the theology of St. Paul. The genitive singular *fidĕi* of *fides* is accentuated on the antepenultimate syllable (in this case, the first syllable); the accentuation on the penultimate syllable is the most common mistake of inexpert celebrants of Latin Masses.

Falda This word is the Latin corruption of the Anglo-Saxon verb *faldan*, to fold, in German *falten*. It is a skirt of the popes, formerly worn over the cassock; it has not been employed by them, however, for several decades. Its extraordinary length produced the many folds that gave it its name.

---

1. Louis Duchesne, *Early History of the Christian Church from Its Foundation to the End of the Third Century* (London: John Murray, 1914), 235. The Latin text is available at www.tertullian.org/fathers/chronography_of_354_13_bishops_of_rome.htm.

Pius XI called this vestment the *calda* (hot), because he used to sweat profusely when covered by it.[2] This vestment is excessively long and thereby cripples the wearer, who must have two lackeys holding up the trains of the skirt so that he can walk without tripping.

Faldstool This word is the compound of the Anglo-Saxon verb *faldan*, which means *to fold*, and the noun *stōl*, which means *seat* or *throne*. The folding stool is a chair used by a prelate pontificating outside his diocese. It also conveniently serves as a prie-dieu for such a fellow.

Fanaticism The Latin noun *fanum, -i, m.* means a *place solemnly consecrated to a god*, a *temple*. The associated adjective *fanaticus* meant *inspired by a deity*, or *enthusiastic*. Dr. Johnson defined *fanaticism* as *enthusiasm, religious frenzy*; it often appears as *violence in the name of religion*, and is the offspring of arrogance and folly. Bertrand Russell used to say that it was the most dangerous thing in the world.

Fanaticism is *the* danger of the world. It always has been and has done untold harm. No, I think fanaticism is the greatest danger there is. I might almost say that I was fanatically against fanaticism.[3]

Fanon The Greek noun πῆνος means *cloth*. Related to it is the Latin *pannus* with the same meaning, which became *fano* in Late Latin and *fanone* in Italian, and then *fanon* in English. The article by Joseph Braun in the *Catholic Encyclopedia* remains the authority on this vestment. The fanon, though in use as early as the eighth century, fell into disuse, like many things, after the first few years of the reign of Paul VI.

[The fanon is] a shoulder cape worn by the pope alone, consisting of two pieces of white silk ornamented with narrow woven stripes of red and gold; the pieces are nearly circular in shape but somewhat unequal in size and the smaller is laid on and fastened to the larger one. To allow the head to pass through there is made in the middle a round opening with a vertical slit running down farther. The front part of the fanon is ornamented with a small cross embroidered in gold.

The fanon is like an amice; it is, however, put on not under but above the alb. The pope wears it only when celebrating a solemn pontifical Mass, that is, only when all the pontifical vestments are used. The manner of putting on the fanon recalls the method of assuming the amice universal in the Middle Ages and still

---

2. So reported Mother Pasqualina in her biography of his successor Pius XII, *His Humble Servant: Sister M. Pascalina Lehnert's Memoirs of Her Years of Service to Eugenio Pacelli, Pope Pius XII*, trans. Susan Johnson (South Bend, Ind.: St. Augustine's Press, 2014), 52.

3. Bertrand Russell, interview by John Freeman, *Face to Face*, BBC, March 4, 1959.

observed in some of the older orders. After the deacon has vested the Pope with the usual amice, alb, the cingulum and sub-cinctorium, and the pectoral cross, he draws on, by means of the opening, the fanon and then turns the half of the upper piece towards the back over the pope's head. He now vests the pope with the stole, tunicle, dalmatic, and chasuble, and finally arranges the whole upper piece of the fanon so that it covers the shoulders of the pope like a collar.[4]

Fascia The Latin noun *fascia, -ae, f.*, means *bandage* or *band*. It is the Latin name for the ecclesiastical sash called in Greek ζώνη. See the entry **Zona**.

Feast The Latin adjective *festus, -a, -um*, which is related to the noun *feriae* (holidays), means *of a holiday*. Formerly, a *feast* was the highest rank awarded in the ecclesiastical calendar, but nowadays that supremacy is assigned to the new word *solemnity*.

Feria The Latin noun *feriae, feriarum, f.*, means *holidays*; it is related to the adjective *festus, -a, -um*, which means *pertaining to a holiday*. However, in Ecclesiastical Latin, the singular *feria, -ae, f.*, came to mean an *ordinary day of the week*, a day not a holiday. Thus the word has the meaning opposite to that which it originally had.

Ferraiolo This noun is probably the corruption of the Latin *pilleolum*, a cloak. A less likely hypothesis is the derivation from the noun *feriae*, meaning *holidays*. The doubling of the *r* is against this latter derivation, but such a gemination is not unprecedented; for example, the first element of the Italian *Ferragosto* is also *feriae*. The *ferraiolo* and *ferraiolone* (big *ferraiolo*) are holiday cloaks, the former more like a cape, reaching only to the elbows, but the latter more ample, reaching to the feet. In practice, however, the former word is used for the longer cape, the word *ferraiolone* having fallen out of use. It is this longer cape, incorrectly called *ferraiolo*, that is the ecclesiastical item of dress. The elbow-length ferraiolo has no place in ecclesiastical costume. The ferraiolo used to be required attire for clergy admitted to the presence of the pope; in 1969, however, this requirement was dropped,[5] and now no one wears the ferraiolo to papal audiences, which have consequently lost much of their dignity. The cloak

---

4. *The Catholic Encyclopedia* (New York: The Encyclopedia Press, 1913), volume 5, page 785, s.v. "Fanon."

5. *Ut Sive Sollicite* (instruction of the Secretariat of State, March 31, 1969), *Acta Apostolicae Sedis* 61, no. 5 (1969): 334–40. The text is also available at www.shetlersites.com/clericaldress/utsivesollicite.html.

is still occasionally to be found at non-liturgical events such as graduations. That prelates no longer wear the ferraiolo over the simar is a simplification that will receive no high mark from experts on fashion.

Ferula The Latin verb *ferio, ferire, ferivi, feritus* means *to strike*. Related to it is the noun *ferula*, the *giant fennel*, a *stick, cane,* or *switch* used to punish slaves, or a *scepter* of authority. It is the name for the pastoral staff used by the modern popes since Pope Paul VI. Benedict XVI, the most cultivated of recent popes, dispensed with the unusual ferula of Pope Paul and used ones of more traditional style.

Fibulae The Latin verb *figo, figere, fixi, fixus* means *to fix* or *fasten*, and from it arose the noun *fibula, -ae, f.,* with the meaning, a *clasp, buckle,* or *broach*. Pope Paul VI prohibited prelates from wearing buckles on their shoes, as we see from section A 10 of the decree *Ut Sive Sollicite* of March 31, 1969:

Usus rubrorum calceorum atque fibularum, earum etiam quae argenteae super nigros calceos imponuntur, tollitur.

The use of red shoes and buckles, and even of silver buckles which are worn over black shoes, is abolished.

Figure The Latin verb *fingo, fingere, finxi, fictus* means *to shape, fashion, mold*. Related to this verb is the noun *figura* with the meaning *form, shape*. A *figure* is thus an allegorical representation of some reality.

> Panis angelicus fit panis hominum;
> Dat panis coelicus figuris terminum.
>
> Now is the bread of angels bread of men;
> Of types and figures this bread made an end.

Filioque With regard to the Holy Ghost, the original Creed of the First Council of Constantinople read, in its Latin form, *qui ex patre procedit*, that is, "Who proceeds from the Father." The word *filioque* was inserted into the Creed after *ex patre* in Spain in the fifth, sixth, and seventh centuries to combat the Adoptionist heresy.[6] The addition produced the read-

---

6. On the addition of the *filioque*, see Denzinger, *Enchiridion Symbolorum et Definitionum*, 7th ed. (Würzburg: V. J. Stahel, 1895), §48, p. 14, who cites the Councils of Galicia (447), Toledo III (589), Toledo IV (633), Toledo VIII (653), Toledo XII (681), Toledo XIII (683), and Toledo XV (688). On the Adoptionist heresy, see John Henry Cardinal Newman, "The Benedictine Schools," in *Historical Sketches*, vol. 2 (London: Longmans, Green, 1917), 485.

ing *qui ex patre filioque procedit,* "Who proceeds from the Father and the Son." The Greeks considered this to be impermissible unilateral tinkering with the Creed, and they reject the addition to this day. When Pope Benedict XVI and Patriarch Bartholomew recited the Nicene Creed in Greek in St. Peter's Basilica on June 28, 2008, they did not make the addition of the *Filioque,* probably the first time in a millennium that any pope omitted the phrase, in any language.

Fistola   The Latin noun *fistŭla* means a *tube* or *pipe*; it became in Italian *fistola.*

The Fistola is the tube through which the Pope receives the Sacred Blood. It is composed of three pipes which pass through a small bowl in the upper part; the centre pipe is longer than the others. The bowl is to protect the Sacred Blood from any accident through effusion.[7]

Flabellum   The Latin verb *flo, flare, flavi, flatus* means *to blow,* and from it was formed the noun *flabra, -orum, n.,* blasts of wind, breezes. The singular *flabrum* (not used) had the diminutive *flabellum* with the meaning a *small fan.* The flabellum was a fan used to cool an exalted dignitary in the heat of the day and to keep flies away; it is a neuter Latin noun of the second declension, so the plural is *flabella.* In solemn processions, one flabellum was carried on each side of the pope when he was seated on the sedia gestatoria. It was last used by Pope Paul VI and was one of the earliest items to be abolished by that pontiff. It used to be exhibited in a museum in the Lateran Palace, but that museum has also been abolished, and the flabella have been relocated to the museum at Castel Gandolfo. The following useful paragraph of Francis Mershman indicates the connection between the flabellum and the United States:

Through the influence of Count Ditalmo di Brozza, the fans formerly used at the Vatican were, in 1902, presented to Mrs. Joseph Drexel of Philadelphia, U. S. A., by Leo XIII, and in return she gave a new pair to the Vatican. The old ones are exhibited in the museum of the University of Philadelphia. They are splendid creations. The spread is formed of great ostrich plumes tipped with peacock feathers; on the sticks are the papal arms, worked in a crimson field in heavy gold, the crown studded with rubies and emeralds.[8]

---

7. Hartwell de la Garde Grissell, *Sede Vacante, Being a Diary Written during the Conclave of 1903, with Additional Notes on the Accession and Coronation of Pius X* (Oxford: James Parker, 1903), 69, note a.

8. *The Catholic Encyclopedia* (New York: The Encyclopedia Press, 1913), s.v. "Flabellum."

Those who cannot travel to Philadelphia for this purpose can see the old flabella in the painting of *Pius VIII in St. Peter's on the Sedia Gestatoria*, by Horace Vernet, at the Château de Versailles. Although the flabella are fans, they were held erect and never waved to make a breeze for the pope, who was assumed to be beyond such considerations. The flabella were carried by two *camerieri segreti soprannumerari*—supernumerary privy chamberlains—who were colleagues of the master of pontifical ceremonies.

Flectamus Genua These Latin words mean "Let us kneel," and are derived from *flecto, flectere, flexi, flectum*, to bend, and *genua*, the plural of *genu*, knee. They are followed after a decent interval by the command "*Levate*," get up, derived from *levo, levare*, to lift. These commands were made optional, that is, effectively abolished, in the reform of the Missal after the Second Vatican Council.

Folded Chasuble For the etymology of *folded* see the entry **Faldstool**. Prior to 1960, the folded chasuble was used instead of the dalmatic by the deacon and subdeacon in penitential seasons. The Italian name for this vestment is *planeta picata*; the Latin name is *casula plicata*. The front half of the chasuble was simply folded up halfway underneath and stitched, so as not to drop.

Foriere Maggiore dei Sacri Palazzi Apostolici The Greek noun θύρα means *door*, and related to it is the Latin adverb *foras* meaning *out-of-doors*. In times past, the *foriere* was originally someone who went out ahead of a travelling pope in order to prepare the lodgings that would be needed for the night; the Italian word is probably derived from the Latin *foras*. The position of *foriere maggiore perpetuo*, one of the five *camerieri segreti di spada e cappa partecipanti*, was hereditary in the Florentine family of the Marquesses Sacchetti, who have a great palace at 66 Via Giulia in Rome. Francis D'Arcy Godolphin Osborne, British minister at the Vatican during the period 1936–1947, and twelfth and last Duke of Leeds (1884–1964), took rooms at the Sacchetti Palace after his retirement from diplomacy; his memoirs are a major source of information about life in the Vatican City State during the Second World War.[9] The foriere maggiore was a sort of quartermaster who had the supervision of the furnishings of the apostolic palaces, including the sedia gestatoria, in front of

---

9. They are the principal resource for the excellent book by Owen Chadwick, *Britain and the Vatican during the Second World War* (Cambridge: Cambridge University Press, 1986).

which on the right he always marched in solemn processions. When Pope Paul VI abolished the position in 1968, the incumbent, Marchese Giulio Sacchetti (died 2010), was retained at the Governatorato for three decades with a range of duties such as presiding over the transformation of the Santa Marta Residence, the issuing of coins and stamps, contracts for the restoration of the Sistine Chapel, and the supervision of the Gensdarmes.

Fraticelli The Greek noun φράτρα means *clan*, and each Athenian φυλή or *tribe* was divided into three φράτραι; the members of the clan were denominated φράτερες or *clansmen*, singular φράτηρ. Related to this word is the Latin noun *frater*, meaning *brother*, and derived from it is the Italian noun *frate* with the meaning *brother, friar*. Those Franciscans who observed the vow of absolute poverty were called in Italy, out of humility, *fraticelli*, that is, *little friars*. They began as a moderate party of the *Zelanti* or Spiritual Franciscans, but since some of them went so far as to criticize the clergy who owned property, they were eventually viewed as a threat and declared to be heretics.

The test of heresy, as I have said, was the assertion that Christ and the Apostles held no property. This appears from the abjuration of Frà Francesco d'Ascoli in 1344, who recants that belief and declares that in accordance with the bulls of John XXII, he holds it to be heretical. That such continued to be the customary formula appears from Eymerich, who instructs his inquisitor to make the penitent declare under oath, "I swear that I believe in my heart and profess that Our Lord Jesus Christ and his apostles while in this mortal life held in common the things which Scripture declares them to have had, and that they had the right of giving, selling, and alienating them."[10]

Yet, trivial as was apparently the point at issue, it was impossible that men could remain contentedly under the ban of the Church without being forced to adopt principles destructive of the whole ecclesiastical organization. They could only justify themselves by holding that they were the true Church, that the papacy was heretical and had forfeited the claim of obedience, and could no longer guide the faithful to salvation.[11]

Those who might be tempted by the life of the *Fraticelli* were accommodated by the institution of the Franciscans of the Strict Observance, founded in 1368 by Paoluccio da Trinci (died 1390) and whose foremost champion was St. Bernardino of Siena (1380–1444).

10. Henry Charles Lea, *A History of the Inquisition in the Middle Ages* (New York: Harper & Brothers, 1887), 3:160.
11. Ibid., 161.

Friar The Latin noun *frater* means *brother*. *Friar* is a corruption of *frater*, probably through the mediation of the French *frère*. A friar is a member of a begging or mendicant order, the four major ones being the Order of St. Augustine (the Austin Friars), the Order of Friars of the Blessed Virgin Mary of Mount Carmel (the Carmelites), the Order of Preachers (the Dominicans or Black Friars), and the Order of Friars Minor (the Franciscans or Grey Friars).

Frontal The Latin noun *frons, frontis, f.,* means the *forehead*, the *brow*. The derived plural noun *frontalia* means the *frontlet* of a horse. The *frontal* is a decorative cloth sometimes used to cover the front of an altar.

Galero The *galerum* (also *galerus* and *galera*) was a Roman leather hat with fur. It is mentioned in the Aeneid:

> Pars maxima glandes
> Liventis plumbi spargit, pars spicula gestat
> Bina manu, fulvosque lupi de pelle galeros
> Tegmen habet capiti.[1]

> Some whirl from leathern slings huge balls of lead,
> While others hurl twin darts that all men dread,
> Galeros of blond wolf's hide on their head.

It is the iconic symbol of the cardinalate, the *red hat*. To see how it was worn in times past, one need only consult the fresco of Raphael *Leo I repulsing Attila* in the Stanza di Eliodoro. Upon the death of a cardinal who was also a diocesan bishop, the galero was suspended from the ceiling of the cathedral church and allowed to fall to pieces with time. The galero was abolished in 1969.

Ruber galerus et petasus e rubro item gausapo abolentur.[2]

The red galero and the woolen red wide brimmed hat are abolished.

---

1. Virgil, *Aeneid*, 7.686–89. The translation that follows is a mixture of Ogilby, Dryden, and Lo Bello.

2. *Ut Sive Sollicite* (instruction of the Secretariat of State, March 31, 1969), *Acta Apostolicae Sedis* 61, no. 5 (1969): 334–40, A 9. The text is also available at www.shetlersites.com/clericaldress/utsivesollicite.html.

In the modern consistory, the Pope places a biretta on the head of the new cardinal.

Genealogy The Greek verb γίγνομαι means *to be born*, and from it is derived the noun γενεά with the meaning *descent*. The appending of the suffix -λογία from λόγος, *account*, produced the noun γενεαλογία, which was transliterated into the English *genealogy*, an account of one's descent. The disagreement between the Gospels of Matthew and Luke with regard to the genealogy of the Christ has for two thousand years been a *crux interpretum*. Matthew 1:15–16 says that Matthan (Ματθάν) begat Jacob and Jacob begat Joseph, whereas Luke 3:23–24 says that Joseph was the son of Heli and Heli was the son of Matthat (Ματθάτ). The earliest known attempted solution to this discrepancy is that reported circa 325 by Eusebius in his *Ecclesiastical History* (I, 7.1), that, Heli having died without children, his brother Jacob married the widow in accordance with Jewish law and raised up the heir Joseph to his late brother. Joseph would then have been the begotten son of Jacob but the legal son of Heli. This so-called Levirate marriage was required by Deuteronomy 25:5–6. This is the resolution adopted by the authors of the Rhemes New Testament in their note on this issue. On the other hand, the higher critic Plummer, in his commentary on Luke, wrote:

The various attempts which have been made at reconciling the divergences, although in no case convincingly successful, are yet sufficient to show that reconciliation is not impossible. If we were in possession of all the facts, we might find that both pedigrees are in accordance with them. Neither of them presents difficulties which no addition to our knowledge could solve.[3]

Genitum Non Factum This is the Latin phrase for "begotten, not made" from the Nicene Creed. It translates the Greek γεννηθέντα, οὐ ποιηθέντα.

The word ἀγέννητος, *ingenitus*, (*unborn, ingenerate*), was the philosophical term to denote that which had existed from eternity. It had accordingly been applied by Aristotle to the world or to matter, which was according to his system without beginning; and by Plato to his ideas. Now since the Divine Word was according to Scripture *generate*, He could not be called *ingenerate* (or *eternal*), without a verbal contradiction. In process of time a distinction was made between ἀγένητος and ἀγέννητος (*increate* and *ingenerate*) according as the letter n was or was not doubled, so that the Son might be said to be ἀγενήτως γεννητός (increately generate).[4]

---

3. Alfred Plummer, *A Critical and Exegetical Commentary on the Gospel according to St. Luke*, 10th ed., The International Critical Commentary (New York: Charles Scribner's Sons, 1914), 103.

4. John Henry Cardinal Newman, *The Arians of the Fourth Century*, new ed. (London: Longmans, Green, 1897), 181.

Gensdarmes The English word *gensdarmes* is the French phrase *gens d'armes*, men at arms, written without spaces or apostrophe. The interior *s* is usually omitted, so most people will only see the spelling *gendarmes*. The Gensdarmes are the police force of the Vatican City State.

For the maintenance of order and other police duties there are the Papal *Carabinieri*, called the *Gendarmeria Pontificia*, consisting of a Captain-Commandant (Count Paolo Ceccopieri), and one-hundred and twenty gensdarmes. They have to guard the staircases, the Cortile di S. Damaso, the corridors and the gardens. A stranger walking about the Vatican is constantly being challenged by them; he meets them at every corner. The Gendarmeria are the police of the Vatican.[5]

Gentiluomini di Sua Santità The Greek adverb χαμαί means *on the earth*, and related to it is the Latin noun *humus, humi, f.*, meaning the *ground*. Derived from *humus* is the noun *homo, hominis, m.*, meaning *human being, man*, and to it are related the Italian noun *uomo* and the English noun *man*. The Latin noun *gens, gentis, f.*, means *clan*; the associated adjective *gentilis* means *pertaining to the clan*. A clan was a group of families fabulously descended from a common ancestor. The name of the clan was the second of the three names of an ancient Roman. Marcus Tullius Cicero had the personal name Marcus and belonged to the family Cicero of the clan supposedly descended from some Tullus. In the Romance languages, but not in Latin, the adjective corrupted from *gentilis* came to mean *courteous*; thus, *gentiluomo* or *gentleman* was a man with good manners. As the lower classes were assumed not to know how to behave, the expression came to denote an individual of some rank in society. The *gentiluomini di sua santità* are the modern equivalent of the old *camerieri segreti di spada e cappa partecipanti*. They line up in the courtyard of San Damaso to await the arrival of a visiting head of state, and, when he arrives, they are introduced to that dignitary by the prefect of the pontifical household. They then escort the members of his delegation to the audience. They do not wear fifteenth century Spanish court dress anymore; instead they wear white tie and tails. They still, however, are distinguished by the great gold chain that was part of the uniform of their predecessors.

Genuflexorium The Latin noun *genu* means *knee*. The Latin verb *flecto, flectere, flexi, flexus* means *to bend*. The *genuflexorium* is a *prie-Dieu*, a device that allows a distinguished personality to kneel and be able to rise without pain or display of clumsiness.

5. Douglas Sladen, *The Secrets of the Vatican* (London: Hurst & Blackett, 1907), 155.

Ghost This noun descends from the Anglo-Saxon *gāst* and is related to the German *Geist*; it translates the Greek πνεῦμα and the Latin *spiritus*. Because of the influence of the American Halloween, the name *Holy Ghost* for the Third Person of the Blessed Trinity was changed during the sixties to *Holy Spirit*. Not unrelated was the change at the same time in Germany of the phrase *unter den Weibern* of the *Ave Maria* to *unter den Frauen*.

Gloria in Excelsis Deo The hymn, which is very ancient, is known as the Great or Angelic Doxology. It begins with the song of the angels in Luke 2:14:

Δόξα ἐν ὑψίστοις θεῷ καὶ ἐπὶ γῆς εἰρήνη ἐν ἀνθρώποις εὐδοκίας.

The Latin text is known to all lovers of music, or at least of Vivaldi:

Gloria in excelsis Deo, et in terra pax hominibus bonae voluntatis. Laudamus te, benedicimus te, adoramus te, glorificamus te. Gratias agimus tibi propter magnam gloriam tuam. Domine Deus, Rex caelestis, Deus Pater omnipotens. Domine Fili unigenite, Iesu Christe. Domine Deus, Agnus Dei, Filius Patris. Qui tollis peccata mundi, miserere nobis. Qui tollis peccata mundi, suscipe deprecationem nostram. Qui sedes ad dexteram Patris, miserere nobis. Quoniam tu solus Sanctus. Tu solus Dominus. Tu solus Altissimus, Iesu Christe. Cum Sancto Spiritu in gloria Dei Patris. Amen.

The following translation is by Archbishop Cranmer (1489–1556) and is found in the Communion Service of the Book of Common Prayer:

Glory be to God on high, and in earth peace, good will towards men. We praise thee, we bless thee, we worship thee, we glorify thee, we give thanks to thee for thy great glory, O Lord God, heavenly King, God the Father Almighty.

O Lord, the only-begotten Son Jesu Christ; O Lord God, Lamb of God, Son of the Father, that takest away the sins of the world, have mercy upon us. Thou that takest away the sins of the world, have mercy upon us. Thou that takest away the sins of the world, receive our prayer. Thou that sittest at the right hand of God the Father, have mercy upon us.

For thou only art holy; thou only art the Lord; thou only, O Christ, with the Holy Ghost, art most high in the glory of God the Father. Amen.

Almost all high musical settings of the Mass begin by repeating the opening words sung by the celebrant; this practice was condemned most forcefully by Fortescue:

Every Gloria in a figured Mass must begin: "Et in terra pax". The custom—once very common—of ignoring the celebrant and beginning again "Gloria in excelsis" is an unpardonable abomination that should be put down without mercy, if it still exists anywhere.[6]

Gloria, Laus, et Honor George Mason Neale (1818–1866) tells the traditional story of this hymn; the translation given below after the Latin text is his.

This processional Hymn for Palm Sunday is said to have been composed by S. Theodolph at Metz, or as others will have it, at Angers, while imprisoned on a false accusation: and to have been sung by him from his dungeon window, or by choristers instructed by him, as the Emperor Louis and his Court were on their way to the Cathedral. The good Bishop was immediately liberated.[7]

St. Theodulph died in 821. As for the story, as the Italians say, *Se non è vero, è ben trovato.*

> Gloria, laus, et honor, tibi sit, Rex Christe Redemptor:
> Cui puerile decus prompsit Hosanna pium.
>
> Gloria, laus, et honor, tibi sit, Rex Christe Redemptor:
> Cui puerile decus prompsit Hosanna pium.
>
> Israël es tu Rex, Davidis et inclyta proles:
> Nomine qui in Domini, Rex benedicte, venis.
>
> Gloria, laus, et honor, tibi sit, Rex Christe Redemptor:
> Cui puerile decus prompsit Hosanna pium.
>
> Coetus in excelsis te laudat caelicus omnis,
> Et mortalis homo, et cuncta creata simul.
>
> Gloria, laus, et honor, tibi sit, Rex Christe Redemptor:
> Cui puerile decus prompsit Hosanna pium.
>
> Plebs Hebraea tibi cum palmis obvia venit:
> Cum prece, voto, hymnis, adsumus ecce tibi.
>
> Gloria, laus, et honor, tibi sit, Rex Christe Redemptor:
> Cui puerile decus prompsit Hosanna pium.
>
> Hi tibi passuro solvebant munia laudis:
> Nos tibi regnanti pangimus ecce melos.

6. *The Catholic Encyclopedia* (New York: The Encyclopedia Press, 1913), s.v. "Gloria in Excelsis Deo."

7. Rev. J. M. Neale, trans., *Mediaeval Hymns and Sequences*, 2nd ed. (London: Joseph Masters, 1863), 23.

Gloria, laus, et honor, tibi sit, Rex Christe Redemptor:
Cui puerile decus prompsit Hosanna pium.

Hi placuere tibi, placeat devotio nostra:
Rex bone, Rex clemens, cui bona cuncta placent.

Gloria, laus, et honor, tibi sit, Rex Christe Redemptor:
Cui puerile decus prompsit Hosanna pium.

All glory, laud, and honor
To Thee, Redeemer, King.
To whom the lips of children
Made sweet hosannas ring.

Thou art the King of Israel,
Thou David's royal Son,
Who in the Lord's name comest,
The King and Blessed One.

All glory, laud, and honor
To Thee, Redeemer, King.
To whom the lips of children
Made sweet hosannas ring.

The company of angels
Are praising Thee on high,
And mortal men and all things
Created make reply.

All glory, laud, and honor
To Thee, Redeemer, King.
To whom the lips of children
Made sweet hosannas ring.

The people of the Hebrews
With psalms before Thee went;
Our praise and prayer and anthems
Before Thee we present.

All glory, laud, and honor
To Thee, Redeemer, King.
To whom the lips of children
Made sweet hosannas ring.

In hast'ning to Thy Passion,
They rais'd their hymns of praise;
In reigning 'midst Thy glory,
Our melody we raise.

All glory, laud, and honor
To Thee, Redeemer, King.
To whom the lips of children
Made sweet hosannas ring.

Thou didst accept their praises;
Accept the prayers we bring,
Who in all good delightest,
Thou good and gracious King.[8]

Fr. George William Rutler had a nice program, aired on EWTN, about this hymn.

Gloria Patri These are the first two words of an ancient doxology.

Gloria Patri, et Filio, et Spiritui Sancto, sicut erat in principio, et nunc, et semper, et in saecula saeculorum. Amen.

Glory be to the Father, and to the Son, and to the Holy Ghost, as it was in the beginning, is now, and ever shall be, world without end. Amen.

The subject of the verb *erat*, the "it," must be *glory*. However, Fortescue thought that there may have been no "it" in the beginning.[9] He referred to the version in the Greek liturgy:

Δόξα πατρὶ καὶ υἱῷ καὶ ἁγίῳ πνεύματι, καὶ νῦν καὶ ἀεὶ καὶ εἰς τοὺς αἰῶνας τῶν αἰώνων. ἀμήν.

Glory be to the Father, and to the Son, and to the Holy Ghost, now and forever. Amen.

Thus the phrase "as it was in the beginning" appears to be an addition in the Latin, probably added in the fourth century to contradict the Arian notion that there was no Son in the beginning.

Glossolalia The Greek noun γλῶσσα means *tongue*, and the Greek verb λαλέω means *to chatter, to make an inarticulate sound*. From the latter word was derived the noun λαλία with the meaning *talking, chatter*. The combination of γλῶσσα and λαλία produced the English noun *glossolalia* with the meaning *speaking in tongues*. The reference is to the phenomena reported in the New Testament.

---

8. Ibid., 25n1.
9. *The Catholic Encyclopedia* (New York, The Encyclopedia Press, 1913), s.v. "Doxology."

καὶ ἐπλήσθησαν πάντες πνεύματος ἁγίου, καὶ ἤρξαντο λαλεῖν ἑτέραις γλώσσαις καθὼς τὸ πνεῦμα ἐδίδου ἀποφθέγγεσθαι αὐτοῖς.

And they were all filled with the Holy Spirit, and began to speak in other tongues, as the Spirit gave them utterance.[10]

εὐχαριστῶ τῷ θεῷ, πάντων ὑμῶν μᾶλλον γλώσσαις λαλῶ· ἀλλὰ ἐν ἐκκλησίᾳ θέλω πέντε λόγους τῷ νοῒ μου λαλῆσαι, ἵνα καὶ ἄλλους κατηχήσω, ἢ μυρίους λόγους ἐν γλώσσῃ.

I thank God that I speak in tongues more than you all; nevertheless, in church I would rather speak five words with my mind, in order to instruct others, than ten thousand words in a tongue.[11]

In the former case, the believers speak in foreign languages on the first Pentecost Sunday; in the latter case, St. Paul tries to moderate the enthusiasm of those speaking incomprehensibly at the regular services.

Gloves This word is the corruption of the Anglo-Saxon noun *glōf*, which has the same meaning. Weekley notes the possible connection with the Old Norse word *lōfe*, which means *hand*. Episcopal gloves were worn by a bishop when he celebrated pontifical Mass; he took them off, however, at the beginning of the Offertory. The color of the gloves was the liturgical color of the day, although white was always permissible. The 1984 edition of the *Caeremoniale Episcoporum* makes no mention of liturgical gloves, so their use in the modern Mass would be an error. The Greek word for *glove* is χειροθήκη; its transliteration *chirotheca* is used in ecclesiastical Latin.

Gnostic The Greek word for *knowledge* is γνῶσις, derived from the second aorist infinitive γνῶναι of the verb γιγνώσκω, *to know*. From this noun was derived the adjective γνωστικός, with the meaning *pertaining to knowing, cognitive, theoretical*; the English noun *gnostic* is merely the transliteration of the stem. The Gnostics were people whose attitude toward the world may be described by the following paragraphs of the Abbé Duchesne.

Heresy, as we have seen, is as old as the Gospel itself. The field of the householder was hardly sown before tares showed themselves among the wheat. And so the early Christian leaders were tormented with anxiety, perpetually betrayed in the

---

10. Acts 2:4 (Revised Standard Version).
11. 1 Corinthians 14:18–19 (Revised Standard Version).

Epistles of St. Paul, the Pastoral Epistles, the Apocalypse, the Epistles of St. Peter, of St. Jude, and of St. Ignatius. The teaching that they had to guard against, so far as these documents disclose it, may be summed up as follows:—

1st. Neither Nature nor Law, whether Mosaic or natural, emanates from God the Father, the Supreme and True God, but they are the work of inferior spirits.

2nd. This Supreme God manifests Himself in Jesus Christ.

3rd. The true Christian can and must free himself from the influence of the creative and ruling powers, if he would draw near to God the Father.

These doctrines must not be regarded as simple perversions of apostolic teaching. They contain indeed Christian elements. But exclude from them the position assigned to Jesus Christ and His work, and the rest is complete in itself, and is easily accounted for by the evolution of Jewish thought, stimulated by Greek philosophic speculation. This is clear if we recall the characteristics of Philo's doctrine. God, Infinite Being, is not only far above all imperfection, but also above all perfection, and even beyond definition. Matter stands apart from the Supreme Being and does not emanate from Him, and He acts upon it by manifold Powers; the chief of these is the Word. These Powers, and the Word Himself, are represented now as being immanent in God, now as distinct hypostases; they correspond to the "ideas" of Plato, or the "efficient causes" of the Stoic, or again to the angels of the Bible and the demons (δαίμονες) of the Greeks. They shaped the world out of already existing material elements. Some of these powers are imprisoned in human forms, and it is from the incompatibility of their divine nature with the tangible body with which they are enveloped, that the moral conflict between duty and desire arises. The aim of moral life is to defeat the influence of body on mind. Asceticism is the best means to this end, but knowledge and well-regulated activity avail also, with the help of God. Thus the soul draws nearer God; in the next life, it will attain to Him, and even here it may, in ecstasy, attain to momentary union with Him.

Thus God stands apart from the world, and has no connection with it except through intermediaries emanating from Himself; in humanity, divine elements subsist, imprisoned, as it were in matter, from which they struggle to get free.

This is the basis of Gnosticism. If now we add to it the personality of Jesus and His redemptive work, ever drawing back to God the Divine elements which have strayed here below, we shall have the very doctrines controverted by the earliest Christian writers. Another step, however, must be taken before true Gnosticism is reached: the antagonism postulated between God and matter must be transferred to the Divine entity; the creator must be represented as being the more or less avowed enemy of the Supreme God, and—in the scheme of salvation—as the enemy of redemption.

This involves a complete break with the religious traditions of Israel. Neither Philo with his great respect for his own religion, nor the teachers of the Law, whose "Jewish fables" the apostles opposed, could have entertained the thought of including the God of Abraham, Isaac, and Jacob amongst the spirits of evil.[12]

The name *Gnostics* was first given to these sectaries by St. Irenaeus, bishop of Lyons. Their founder was Simon Magus.

God It is a reasonable hypothesis that this noun is etymologically connected with the Greek verb χέω, *to pour* (for example, a libation to a deity). It has nothing to do with the English adjective *good*. In the Hebrew language, the word *God* is sometimes used to convey a superlative; the *Spirit of God* in Genesis 1:2 could possibly mean *a mighty wind*. The learned world at the time of the rise of Christianity was much influenced by Plato, whose teaching about God was a contributing factor to some heresies. According to Plato, there is a universal spirit and an individual spirit. The universal spirit is comparable to the Spirit of God. The Platonic conception of God ascribed to the Deity the status of *beingly being*, ὄντως ὤν. One thing Plato was sure of was that God does not exist; by this he did not mean that he was an atheist, but that existence was the wrong technical term to ascribe to the Deity; God was beyond existence. This sort of speculation was not serviceable to Christianity, which discovered too many heresies in the Platonic dialogues. Aristotle, however, stayed away from such speculations, a difference in temperament that Raphael captured so well in the *School of Athens*.

The doctrine of Design in Nature is the point of view that the universe did not come about by chance but shows evidence of a creator. According to John Stuart Mill (1806–1873), it is the strongest argument for the existence of God and affords "a large balance of probability in favour of creation by intelligence".[13] William George Ward (1812–1882), on the other hand, believed that conscience was the strongest argument for the existence of God. The two carried on a famous correspondence on this topic.[14]

Gonfaloniere di Santa Romana Chiesa Weekley derives the Italian noun *gonfalone* from the Old High German *guntfano*, a compound of *gunt* (battle) and *Fahne* (flag). The fellow who carried the standard was

---

12. Louis Duchesne, *Early History of the Christian Church from Its Foundation to the End of the Third Century* (London: John Murray, 1914), 112–14.

13. John Stuart Mill, "On Theism," in *Three Essays on Religion* (New York: Henry Holt, n.d.), 174 (in the chapter "Marks of Design in Nature").

14. See Wilfrid Ward, *William George Ward and the Catholic Revival* (London: Macmillan, 1893), 275–95.

the *gonfaloniere*. The title was already current in the eighth century, when Pope Adrian sent the banner of the Church to Charlemagne, who became the first *Confalonerius Ecclesiae*—Gonfaloniere, that is, Standard-Bearer (or General) of the Church.[15] This position of standard-bearer of the Holy Roman Church became in later times hereditary in the family of the Marquesses Patrizi Naro Montoro. The gonfaloniere was a lieutenant general in the Papal Noble Guard. The position was abolished by Pope Paul in 1968. Referring to the Corpus Christi procession in Rome in 1861, Gregorovius, an eyewitness, wrote:

General Goyon headed the French troops in the procession, Kanzler the papal, and the Marchese Patrizi, as hereditary standard-bearer, carried the banner of the Church.[16]

Good Friday The word *good* originally had the connotation of *holy*. On the other hand, *good* here may simply be a corruption of *God*, as in the expression *good-bye*, which originally was *God be with you*, the English equivalent of *Dominus vobiscum*.

Gospel This is the Anglo-Saxon *gōd spel*, good tidings, a translation of the Greek εὐαγγέλιον. The Greek word was transliterated into Latin and became *evangelium*.

Once set side by side, the Gospels could not but invite comparison. Written with only relative attention to correctness of detail and precision of chronology, and coloured by pre-conceptions which were not always identical, they presented many variations which could not fail to arrest attention. Consequently, many attempts were made to complete or correct them, by each other, or even to blend their narratives into a kind of harmony. Fragments of these combinations are embedded in manuscripts still extant, and in quotations of ancient authors: some of them date back to very remote antiquity. Others impress us by their genuine appearance, though they lack the same authentication. Here, however, we dare not be too precise. It is wisest not to peer too far into the darkness, where we strain our eyes without any appreciable result.[17]

15. Ferdinand Gregorovius, *History of the City of Rome in the Middle Ages*, 2nd ed., trans. Mrs. Gustavus W. Hamilton (London: G. Bell & Sons, 1902), 2:469.

16. Ferdinand Gregorovius, *The Roman Journals of Ferdinand Gregorovius 1852–1874*, ed. Friedrich Althaus, trans. Mrs. Gustavus W. Hamilton (London: G. Bell & Sons, 1911), 135.

17. Louis Duchesne, *Early History of the Christian Church from Its Foundation to the End of the Third Century* (London: John Murray, 1914), 107–8.

Gothic The Goths were a Germanic people who called themselves Gut-thiuda, whence the Greeks denominated them Γόθοι. Because of their incomprehensible speech, the Greeks called them βάρβαροι and the Romans *barbari*, that is, *barbarians, babblers*. Their destructive behavior in the fifth century caused anything ugly, deformed, or vulgar to be called *Gothic*. Chasubles and architecture were so called by people who preferred classical clothing and buildings. The Gothic Art of the Middle Ages, however, was a supreme performance of the human being and recognized to be so by E. W. Pugin (1834–1875).

Governatorato The Greek verb κυβερνάω means *to steer*, and related to it is the noun κυβερνήτης meaning *helmsman*. The Latin language has the same verb and noun with the same meanings, viz., *guberno, gubernare, gubernavi, gubernatus* and *gubernator, gubernatoris, m.* From this last noun is derived our word *governor* and the Italian noun *governatore*. When the State of the Vatican City was established in 1929, Pius XI appointed Marchese Camillo Serafini *Governor of Vatican City*, and built a palace, the Governatorato, behind St. Peter's Basilica to house his administration, which lasted until Serafini's death in 1952. The position was not filled thereafter.

Grace The Latin noun *gratia* means *favor* and is the translation of the Greek χάρις. The Greek in turn is translating the Hebrew חן. The Hebrew verb חנן means *to show favor, to be gracious*. Grace is therefore divine favor. Who gets this favor is explained in Exodus 33:19:

וחנתי את־אשר אחן ורחמתי את־אשר ארחם

I will show favor to whom I will show favor, and I will be merciful to whom I will be merciful.

Graduale, Graduale Romanum The Latin verb *grador, gradi, gressus sum* means *to walk*, and the related noun *gradus, gradūs, m.*, means *step*. The adjective *gradualis* therefore means *having to do with steps, done in steps* or *on steps*. Why the Gradual Prayer of the Mass is so called is not clear. The *Graduale Romanum* is the book that contains the music for the changeable parts of the Mass. A *Graduale Simplex* or *Easy Gradual* was published by the Holy See in 1988 to make it easy for clergy and musicians of limited ability to use some of the ancient texts in their performances, but it has failed to detrude from their places the pitiful hymnals commonly found in churches.

Greek The Γραικοί were a tribe of western Greece. The Latin transliteration of Γραικός is *Graecus*, whence our *Greek*. The Romans applied this word to all those people who called themselves Ἕλληνες, Hellenes. Since the New Testament is written in Greek, that language is the foundation for the study of Christianity, just as the Hebrew language is the foundation for the study of Judaism.

The chief masterpieces of the Greek language are the epic poems of Homer, the *Iliad* and the *Odyssey*.

> Μῆνιν ἄειδε θεὰ Πηληϊάδεω Ἀχιλῆος
> οὐλομένην, ἣ μυρί᾽ Ἀχαιοῖς ἄλγε᾽ ἔθηκε,
> πολλὰς δ᾽ ἰφθίμους ψυχὰς Ἄϊδι προῖαψεν
> ἡρώων, αὐτοὺς δὲ ἑλώρια τεῦχε κύνεσσιν
> οἰωνοῖσί τε πᾶσι, Διὸς δ᾽ ἐτελείετο βουλή,
> ἐξ οὗ δὴ τὰ πρῶτα διαστήτην ἐρίσαντε
> Ἀτρεΐδης τε ἄναξ ἀνδρῶν καὶ δῖος Ἀχιλλεύς.

The most beautiful translation of them into English is by Alexander Pope (1688–1744), a Catholic.

> The Wrath of Peleus's Son, the direful Spring
> Of all the Grecian Woes, o Goddess, sing;
> That Wrath which hurl'd to Pluto's gloomy Reign
> The Souls of mighty Chiefs untimely slain;
> Whose Limbs unbury'd on the naked Shore
> Devouring Dogs and hungry Vultures tore.
> Since great Achilles and Atrides strove,
> Such was the sov'reign Doom, and such the Will of Jove.

These are the opening verses of Pope's translation of the *Iliad*, of which Dr. Johnson wrote:

It is certainly the noblest version of poetry which the world has ever seen; and its publication must therefore be considered as one of the great events in the annals of learning.[18]

That the study of the classical authors, whether Greek or Latin, is a noble and necessary foundation for ecclesiastical studies is clear from the life of Antonio Cardinal Bacci (1885–1971)[19] and, even more tellingly, of Pope

---

18. Samuel Johnson, *Lives of the Most Eminent English Poets; with Critical Observations on Their Works,* (London, 1781), 4:47.

19. See Antonio Bacci, *Con il Latino a Servizio di Quattro Papi* (Rome: Editrice Studium, 1964),

Leo XIII, who composed a famous Latin ode in the style of Horace for the inauguration of the twentieth century.[20]

Gregorian The Greek verb ἐγείρω means *to awaken*, and its fourth (perfect) principal part is ἐγρήγορα, *to be awake*. From this verb was formed the late verb γρηγορέω with the meaning *to be awake*. From this verb was formed the proper name Γρηγόριος meaning *vigilant, having a lively spirit*. The Latin transliteration of this Greek name is *Gregorius*, our *Gregory*. The adjective *Gregorianus, -a, -um* means *having to do with Gregory*. In the Catholic Church, the Gregory in question is usually either Gregory the Great (590–604) or Gregory XIII (1572–1585). The beautiful Gregorian Chant is fabulously attributed to Gregory the Great, and the Gregorian Calendar is correctly ascribed to Gregory XIII. The Gregorian Chapel in St. Peter's Basilica was built by that pontiff to receive the body of his namesake Gregory Nazianzen.

Gremiale The Latin noun *gremium* means *lap* or *bosom*. The *gremiale* is an apron placed on the lap of a celebrating prelate when he is seated; its function is to prevent the transfer of dirt from his hands to his vestments. For this reason it may also be worn during such activities as washing of the feet or imposition of ashes. A bishop will also wear a gremiale during the ceremony of the consecration of a church while he anoints the walls with chrism, to prevent an accident to his person.

---

which I translated into English with the permission of the cardinal's nephew, Professor Marsilio Bacci.

20. See *Carme Secolare del Sommo Pontefice Leone XIII Tradotto in Varie Lingue* (Rome: Federico Pustet, 1901).

H

Habemus Papam This is the ceremonial phrase "We have a pope," with which the senior cardinal deacon announces the election of a pope from the central balcony (loggia) of St. Peter's Basilica. The complete announcement is:

Annuntio vobis gaudium magnum. Habemus Papam, Eminentissimum ac reverendissimum Dominum, Dominum N., Sanctae Romanae Ecclesiae Cardinalem N., qui nomen sibi imposuit N.

I announce to you a great joy. We have a pope, the most eminent and most reverend lord, N. Cardinal N., who has taken the name N.

This ceremony was ruined by Cardinal Medina Estévez in 2005, who began, not with *Annuntio vobis*, but with "Dear Brothers and Sisters" in Italian, Spanish, French, German, and English. This was not the first time that the senior cardinal deacon did not prove up to the task.

On the last occasion, in 1878, Cardinal Caterini, whose duty it was to proclaim Leo XIII, being an old man of eighty-three years, entirely broke down, having said "Annuntio vobis," and the proclamation was made by a young Conclavist who was standing near, Don Bartolomeo Grassi Landi, now a Minor Canon of St. Peter's, who called aloud to the people, "Il Cardinale Pecci col nome di Leone XIII."[1]

The chosen name of the new pope should appear in the accusative case after the verb *imposuit*. However, the genitive case is allowed, as happened

---

1. Hartwell de la Garde Grissell, *Sede Vacante, Being a Diary Written during the Conclave of 1903, with Additional Notes on the Accession and Coronation of Pius X* (Oxford: James Parker, 1903), p. 45, note a. Don Bartolomeo's Italian means, "Cardinal Pecci, with the name Leo XIII."

twice in 1978. One competent author, who must have relied on authority, wrote:

Grammatically, nominative, genitive, dative, or accusative are all possible.[2]

The senior cardinal deacon, or cardinal protodeacon, formerly served at the pope's right hand on solemn occasions; the second cardinal deacon served at the pope's left hand. This is no longer the case, their places having been taken by masters of ceremonies, who are even allowed to sit at the side of the pontiff; in former times, though ceremonies were longer, they had to stand. I never saw Enrico Dante sit, even when he was a very old man. The position of senior cardinal deacon was a great prize that people usually held on to for the rest of their lives; for example, Nicola Cardinal Canali (1874–1961) held the position for fifteen years. Nowadays, it amounts to nothing unless a pope dies on the incumbent's watch; people just move up into the order of cardinal priests after a few years.

Hagiographa The Greek adjective ἅγιος means *sacred*, and the verb γράφω means *to write*. The compounding of the two produced the adjective ἁγιόγραφος with the meaning *written by inspiration*. The neuter plural of this adjective, ἁγιόγραφα, means *holy writings*. It is the Greek name for what the Jews called the כתובים or *Writings*, that is, those books of the Old Testament that did not make it into the Law or the Prophets. The *Hebrew Bible* consists of three parts: the Law, the Prophets, and the Writings. The Books of the Law come first, then the Books of the Prophets, then the Books called Writings. Thus, the Jews understood the Law to consist of the Books of Genesis, Exodus, Leviticus, Numbers, and Deuteronomy. The Prophets they defined as consisting of the Books of Joshua, Judges, Samuel 1 and 2, Kings 1 and 2, Isaiah, Jeremiah, Ezekiel, Hosea, Joel, Amos, Obadiah, Jonah, Micah, Nahum, Habakkuk, Zephaniah, Haggai, Zechariah, and Malachi. The rest belonged to the Writings. The order of the books in the *Hebrew Bible* is not preserved in the Septuagint and Vulgate, where the Prophets, Writings, and Apocrypha are intermingled.

Hebdomadarian The Greek word ἑπτά means *seven*, and from it were derived the adjective ἕβδομος with the meaning *seventh* and the Greek feminine noun ἑβδομάς, ἑβδομάδος meaning a *set of seven*. From the latter came the Latin noun *hebdomada, -ae, f.*, meaning *week*. The *hebdo-*

---

2. Ibid., 46.

madarian was the priest appointed by the abbot of a monastery or the dean of a collegiate church to sing the conventual Mass each day of a given week.

Hebrew The Hebrew verb עבר means *to pass over*, and a Child of Israel was called an עברי, that is, a Hebrew, in the sense of being someone who had come from beyond the Euphrates or the Jordan. His language was called עברית, Hebrew. The learned study of the Old Testament cannot be accomplished without the knowledge of this language.

Nothing can supersede an acquaintance, as intimate as it can be made, with the original languages of the Bible; it is that knowledge which brings us as nearly face to face as is possible with the original writers, and enables us to perceive many links of connection and shades of meaning, which can with difficulty, if at all, be brought home to us by a translation.[3]

Hebrew is best learnt from Weingreen's *A Practical Grammar for Classical Hebrew*. The student may then acquire "Gesenius-Kautzsch-Cowley," that is, Cowley's English edition of *Gesenius' Hebrew Grammar* edited by Kautzsch. Equally indispensable is "Brown-Driver-Briggs," that is, *A Hebrew and English Lexicon of the Old Testament* compiled by those three authorities. Finally, Kittel's *Biblia Hebraica* is the most beautiful critical edition of the Hebrew Bible; those who cannot find it will be satisfied with its successor, the *Biblia Hebraica Stuttgartensia*. It is bizarre that the Württembergische Bibelanstalt did not use the correct adjective *Stutgardiensis*, there being no such adjective Stuttgartensius, -a, -um.[4]

It has been said of the Hebrew language, that its every word is a poem.[5]

Yet not all were of this opinion.

He [Jerome] also devoted himself to Hebrew, a hard penance for a disciple of Cicero.[6]

The promotion of the academic study of the Hebrew and Greek languages was the life work of Johannes Reuchlin (1455–1522), who in 1506

---

3. S. R. Driver and A. F. Kirkpatrick, *The Higher Criticism* (New York: Hodder & Stoughton, 1912), 58.

4. Karl Egger, *Lexicon Nominum Locorum* (Vatican City: Libreria Editrice Vaticana, 1977), 298.

5. Edmund Clarence Stedman, *The Nature and Elements of Poetry* (Boston: Houghton Mifflin, 1892), 87.

6. Louis Duchesne, *Early History of the Christian Church from Its Foundation to the End of the Fifth Century*, vol. 2 (London: John Murray, 1931), 379.

wrote the first Hebrew grammar for Christian scholars, *De Rudimentis Hebraicis*. Desiderius Erasmus (1466–1536) published the Greek New Testament in 1516, which he provided with his own Latin translation.

The fame of Erasmus and Reuchlin is familiar to all; if we inquire what constitutes the principal merit of the latter, we find it to be his having written the first Hebrew grammar,—a monument of which he hoped, as did the Italian poets of their works, that "it would be more durable than brass;" as by him the study of the Old Testament was first facilitated, so was that of the New Testament indebted to Erasmus. To this it was that his attention was devoted; it was he who first caused it to be printed in Greek, and his paraphrases and Commentaries on it have produced an effect far surpassing the end he had proposed to himself.[7]

Hell This word is an Anglo-Saxon noun meaning the *abode of the dead* and is cognate with the verb *helan*, which means *to hide*. At death, the Greeks supposed that the soul went to a place called ᾅδης, which was ruled over by a god of the same name, Hades. This word was therefore used in the Septuagint to translate the Hebrew name for the abode of the dead, שאול, a word whose etymology is uncertain. When Zeus needed to get rid of the Titans, he sent them to a world even more remote than Hades, namely, to τάρταρος (Tartarus), a word, perhaps, of onomatopoetic origin, from the quivering and gnashing of the teeth at the tortures that were supposed to be inflicted there. In Christian times, both names interchangeably indicated the place of abode of the damned. In the Apostles' Creed, there is the phrase *descendit ad inferos*, and one may ask, What does it mean? The Latin adjective *inferus* means *below, low*; its comparative is *inferior* (lower), and its superlative *infimus* (lowest). *Inferi*, the plural of *inferus*, means, as a substantive, the *dead*, the inhabitants of the world below. Thus, *descendit ad inferos* is translated, "He descended into Hell." Inquiring minds were agitated by the question, Why did the Christ descend into Hell? Probably, it was a poetic way of saying that Jesus was dead. This was not satisfactory to some, who determined that he had gone to the nether world to collect the souls of the just and bring them to the newly opened gates of paradise. The adjective *infernus* is a synonym of *inferus* and means *that which comes from below*. Its neuter singular *infernum*, as a noun, means the *nether world*, that is, *hell*; in Italian this became *inferno*, whence we get our word for a place where people are tortured by fire.

---

7. Leopold von Ranke, *The History of the Popes during the Last Four Centuries*, trans. Mrs. Foster and G. R. Dennis (London: G. Bell & Sons, 1912), 1:60.

~ H ~

Henotikon The Greek numeral εἷς means *one*, and from it was derived the verb ἑνόω meaning *to unite*. From this verb was produced the adjective ἑνωτικός with the meaning *unity-producing*. The neuter singular Ἑνωτικόν of this adjective was used as the equivalent of *Decree of Union*. The Henotikon was a compromise formula issued by Emperor Zeno in 482, which attempted to reconcile the Catholic and Monophysite faiths. It pleased neither, the Catholics for reasons given in the third paragraph below, the Monophysites because it did not *expressly* condemn the Tome of Leo and the Council of Chalcedon.

The decree of union or Henotikon, obviously drawn up by the Patriarch of Constantinople, takes the form of a letter addressed by the Emperor Zeno "to the bishops, clergy, monks, and faithful of Alexandria, Egypt, Libya, and Pentapolis." In it the sovereign sets forth his faith, represented by the Creed of Nicaea and that of Constantinople (381). Saddened by existing discords, and in deference to the prayers which have been addressed to him with a view to the restoration of unity, he declares his attachment to these documents while adhering none the less to what was done at Ephesus against Nestorius and against "those who subsequently have thought as he did,"[8] as well as to the condemnation of Eutyches; he accepts also the twelve Anathemas of the Blessed Cyril. He protests that Mary is the Mother of God; that the Son of God made man is one and not two; that He is consubstantial with us by His humanity; that in the manner of conceiving of Him, there must be excluded all idea of division, of confusion, of appearances without reality; that there are not two Sons; further that One of the Trinity became incarnate. Whosoever thinks or has thought otherwise, whether at Chalcedon or in any other synod of any kind, he is anathematized, but especially Nestorius and Eutyches.

Of one nature, of two natures, there is no mention. At bottom the document was in agreement with the feelings of which the Greek Episcopate had given evidence at Chalcedon: it left outside the Creed certain controversial formulas, the sense of which had not yet been sufficiently elucidated. It bluntly, openly, gave authority to the doctrine of Cyril and to the formulation of it in the twelve Anathemas. In its substantial content, if we leave out of account the circumstances in which it was put forward, it could not raise any objection from the side of orthodoxy.

The worst of it was that implicitly it allowed to fall both the Tome of Leo and the Dogmatic Decree of Chalcedon, two formulas which for the past thirty years the government and its officials, the Patriarch of Constantinople, and the Greek

---

8. [Note of Duchesne]: "An allusion to the second Council of Ephesus, that of 449, and particularly to the condemnation of Ibas and Theodoret. On the other hand the reprobation of Eutyches agrees implicitly with Flavian's Synod and the Council of Chalcedon."

Episcopate as a whole, in agreement with the Holy See of Rome, had been putting forward and defending as the two-fold symbol of orthodoxy. It was a retreat.[9]

Heresiarch The Greek noun αἵρεσις means *choice* and then *heresy*, and the noun ἀρχή means *rule*; the compound noun αἱρεσιάρχης, *heresiarch*, therefore means *ruler of heretics* or *heretic-in-chief*. In less ecumenical times, it was a term of opprobrium reserved for the likes of Arius, Nestorius, Luther, and Calvin.

Heresy The Greek verb αἱρέω means *to choose*, and from it is derived the noun αἵρεσις, which means *a choice*. A heresy is, etymologically, a bad choice made as to doctrine in contradiction to the express definition of the Church.

Heretic The Greek adjective αἱρετικός means *able to choose*, but in Ecclesiastical Greek it came to denote *one who has made a choice of doctrine different from that of the Church*. It was translated into Latin as *hereticus*, whence we get the English word *heretic*. The word originally meant *sect* or *party*, as in Acts 15:5: τινες τῶν ἀπὸ τῆς αἱρέσεως τῶν Φαρισαίων. Among Christians it soon acquired a most wicked connotation, which endured into modern times.

Many a man would be deterred from outstepping the truth, could he see the end of his course from the beginning. The Arians felt this, and therefore resisted a detection, which would at once expose them to the condemnation of all serious men. In this lies the difference between the treatment due to an individual in heresy, and to one who is confident enough to publish the innovations which he has originated. The former claims from us the most affectionate sympathy, and the most considerate attention. The latter should meet with no mercy; he assumes the office of the Tempter, and so far forth as his error goes, must be dealt with by the competent authority, as if he were embodied Evil. To spare him is a false and dangerous pity. It is to endanger the souls of thousands, and it is uncharitable towards himself.[10]

Hermit The Greek adjective ἔρημος means of places *lonely*, *desert*, and of persons *lone*, *solitary*, and from it are derived the nouns ἐρημία, a solitary place, and ἐρημίτης, a fellow who lives alone in a desolate place. The word ἐρημίτης became in Latin *eremita*, and in the Middle Ages an unoriginal *h* was sometimes added to produce *heremita*, whence we get

9. Louis Duchesne, *Early History of the Christian Church from Its Foundation to the End of the Fifth Century*, vol. 3 (London: John Murray, 1924), 348–49.

10. John Henry Cardinal Newman, *The Arians of the Fourth Century*, new ed. (London: Longmans, Green, 1897), 234–35.

our *hermit*. The first hermit was St. Antony of the Desert (fourth century). The Church has for two thousand years sanctioned the eremitic life; it therefore may come as an unexpected shock to some readers to read the comments of the Abbé Duchesne on the enterprise of St. Antony:

Yet, when we look closely into the matter, the hermit was a living criticism of ecclesiastical society. The mere fact of his retirement proved that in his estimation the Church had become an impossible dwelling-place for anyone who wished to lead a really Christian life, and this judgment was founded upon an ideal of religious life which differed markedly from that of the Church. For him the very essential of Christianity was asceticism. Fraternal union, meetings for public worship, the liturgy, and instruction from the bishop, all these things were of secondary importance in comparison with that cultivation of the soul which consists above all in personal mortification and continual prayer. We cannot see how Antony, during his twenty years of seclusion, can ever have been enabled to receive the Eucharist.[11]

Hexateuch The Greek word ἕξ means *six*, and the noun τεῦχος means *implement* or, later on, a *book*. The adjective ἑξάτευχος, therefore, means *consisting of six books*. It is a name for the six books of Genesis, Exodus, Leviticus, Numbers, Deuteronomy, and Joshua. It was coined after the wide acceptance of the hypothesis of the higher critics, that the Book of Joshua was compiled by the same authors who compiled the Pentateuch.

Hierarchy The Greek adjective ἱερός means *pertaining to the gods*, and as a noun it means a *consecrated person*, what we would call a *priest*. The Greek verb ἄρχω means *to rule*, the noun ἀρχή means *rule*, and so the noun ἡ ἱεραρχία means *clerical leadership*, the *hierarchy*. The noun ἱεράρχης denominates a *clerical leader*, a *hierarch*.

High Mass The English adjective *high* is the descendant of the Anglo-Saxon *hēah*. The *High Mass* was that form of the traditional Latin Mass celebrated with a choir that sang the Propers and Ordinary. The adjective indicated the level of solemnity. If there is a procession to the altar, it should be accompanied by the Introit (unless the *Asperges* is to take place) or by an organ prelude, not by a hymn. English hymns are especially inappropriate. A *solemn high Mass* is a high Mass celebrated with priest, deacon, and subdeacon. Sung Latin Masses require a trained choir or become the occasion for a comedy of errors.

---

11. Louis Duchesne, *Early History of the Christian Church from Its Foundation to the End of the Fifth Century*, vol. 2 (London, John Murray, 1931), 390.

His Vel Similibus Verbis This is one of the most common phrases in the rubrics of the revised liturgical books. They mean "With these or the like words." They allow the celebrant to add personal touches—*proh dolor!*—to the rite in question, an activity which in most cases does away with all solemnity. There was at one time a high opinion of the ability of the average priest to compose liturgical texts.

Holy Ghost This was the name of the Third Person of the Blessed Trinity until the phrase *Holy Spirit* came into vogue. Our word *Holy* comes from the Anglo-Saxon adjective *hālig*, which means *whole*. The word once indicated physical rather than spiritual wholeness and health, like the Latin *incolumis* of the Mass. *Ghost* is the Anglo-Saxon *gāst*, an incorporeal entity. The *Holy Ghost* in Hebrew is רוח הקדש. In Greek it is τὸ πνεῦμα τὸ ἅγιον. In Latin it is *Spiritus Sanctus*. In each of these three holy languages, there is a connection with *wind*, something missing in the word *Ghost*. *Holy Ghost* was changed to *Holy Spirit* in the sixties because of the fear that the former made a Halloweenish impression on simple people, but the change from an Anglo-Saxon to a Latin-based noun is often a mistake. It had been used occasionally before then.

Whether or not the Macedonians explicitly denied the divinity of the Holy Spirit, is uncertain; but they viewed Him as essentially separate from, and external to, the One Indivisible Godhead. Accordingly, the Creed (which is that since incorporated into the public services of the Church), without declaring more than the occasion required, closes all speculations concerning the incomprehensible subject, by simply confessing his *unity with* the Father and Son. It declares, moreover, that He is the *Lord* (κύριος) or Sovereign Spirit, because the heretics considered Him to be but a minister of God; and the supreme *Giver* of life, because they considered Him a mere instrument, by whom we received the gift. The last clause of the second paragraph in the Creed, is directed against the heresy of Marcellus of Ancyra.[12]

"The last clause" referred to by Newman is "cuius regni non erat finis." The heresy of Marcellus is described by Arendzen as follows:

Marcellus wrote a book against Asterius, a prominent Arian. In this work he maintained that the trinity of persons in the Godhead was but a transitory dispensation. God was originally only One Personality, but at the creation of the universe the Word or Logos went out from the Father and was God's activity in the world. This Logos became incarnate in Christ and was thus constituted Son

12. John Henry Cardinal Newman, *The Arians of the Fourth Century*, new ed. (London: Longmans, Green, 1897), 392n5.

of God. The Holy Ghost likewise went forth as Third Divine personality from the father and from Christ according to St. John XX 22. At the consummation of all things, however (I Corinthians XV 28), Christ and the Holy Ghost will return to the Father and the Godhead be again an absolute Unity.[13]

The Holy Ghost is mentioned in the Old Testament at Psalm 51:13:

אל־תשליכני מלפניך

ורוח קדשך אל־תקח ממני

Cast me not away from thy presence; and take not thy holy spirit from me.

Holy Office On July 21, 1542, by the apostolic constitution *Licet ab Initio*, Pope Paul III founded the Sacred Congregation of the Roman and Universal Inquisition (*Sacra Congregatio Romanae et Universalis Inquisitionis*). The name *inquisition* having become untenable in modern times, Pope Pius X, by the apostolic constitution *Sapienti Consilio* of June 29, 1908, changed the name of this entity to the Sacred Congregation of the Holy Office (*Sacra Congregatio Sancti Officii*). Finally, even that name having become odious, Pope Paul VI, by the Motu Proprio *Integrae Servandae* of December 7, 1965, changed the name again to the Congregation for the Doctrine of the Faith (*Congregatio pro Doctrina Fidei*). The headquarters of this dicastery, a beautiful Renaissance palace, is still called the Palazzo del Sant'Uffizio, but the name of the street leading up to it has been changed to Via Paolo VI. It is an extraterritorial property of the Holy See on the very border of the Vatican City. It was assigned by Pius V to be the home of the Inquisition, but during the period 1870–1929 it served as an Italian army barracks.

Homoeans The Homoeans were a group of fourth-century Christians who tried to arrange a compromise between the Catholics, who accepted the adjective ὁμοούσιος as a technical term for the Christ, and the Semi-Arians, who used the term ὁμοιούσιος. The Homoeans, whose preeminent figure was Acacius, the successor of the historian Eusebius as bishop of Caesarea in Palestine, rejected both ὁμοούσιος and ὁμοιούσιος because they were not found in scripture, and instead proposed the term ὁμοῖος, *like*, saying that the Son was like the Father, some of them going even further and adding the phrase κατὰ πάντα, *in all ways*. Because the Homoeans refused to use non-scriptural theological vocabulary, they were denominated *scripturalists*.

13. J. P. Arendzen, "Marcellus of Ancyra," in *The Catholic Encyclopedia* (New York: The Encyclopedia Press, 1913), 9:642a.

Homoiousios The Greek adjective ὁμοιούσιος is compounded of the adjective ὅμοῖος (*like*) and the noun οὐσία (*being*) and means *of a similar being*; it was concocted by the Semi-Arian party in an attempt to approximate as closely as possible the Catholic doctrine of the ὁμοούσιος, *of the same being*, from which it differed by one vowel. The Semi-Arian Party had for its leaders Eusebius, bishop of Nicomedia, and Eusebius, bishop of Caesarea, and for this reason was called the Eusebian faction.

From the time that the Eusebians consented to subscribe the Homoüsion in accordance with the wishes of a heathen prince, they became nothing better than a political party. They soon learned, indeed, to call themselves Homoeüsians, or believers in the "like" substance (*homoeüsion*), as if they still held the peculiarities of a religious creed; but in truth it is an abuse of language to say that they had any definite belief at all.[14]

Homoousios The Greek adjective ὁμοούσιος is compounded of two parts, the adjective ὁμός (*same*) and the noun οὐσία (*being*) and means *of the same being*. It is the technical term agreed upon at the Council of Nicaea as expressing with accuracy the relationship between the divinity of the Father and the divinity of the Son.

The plain question was, whether Our Lord was God in as full a sense as the Father, though not to be viewed as separable from Him; or whether, as the sole alternative, He was a creature; that is, whether He was literally of, and in, the one Invisible Essence which we adore as God, "consubstantial with God" or of a substance which had a beginning. The Arians said that He was a creature, the Catholics that he was very God; and all the subtleties of the most fertile ingenuity could not alter, and could but hide, this fundamental difference.[15]

Some bishops, like Eusebius of Nicomedia, would not admit that ὁμοούσιος was an attribute of Jesus Christ with respect to his relation to God the Father. The term is not found in the Bible, and this fact strengthened their reluctance to adopt it.

Homosexuality The Greek adjective ὁμός means *same*, and the Latin verb *seco, secare, secavi, secatus* means *to cut, divide*. Related to the verb are the adverb *secus* with the meaning *otherwise than* (ac) or *differently from* (ac) and the noun *sexus, -ūs, m.*, which means *sex*. An adjective *sex-*

---

14. John Henry Cardinal Newman, *The Arians of the Fourth Century*, new ed. (London: Longmans, Green, 1897), 257.

15. Ibid., 253–54.

ualis is unknown to Lewis and Short; neither is a noun *sexualitas* to be found there. The Latin suffix *-itas* becomes *-ité* in French and therefore *-ity* in English. *Homosexuality* is thus a modern macaronic word like *automobile*, *neuroscience*, *sociology*, and *television*, half Greek and half Latin.

The first instance cited by the *O.E.D.* is from Havelock Ellis in 1897. Ellis thought it a "barbarously hybrid word" and disclaimed all responsibility for it.[16]

Honorius *Honorius* is a proper name formed by adding the suffix *-ius* to the noun *honor*. Pope Honorius I (625–638) is one of the three popes whose history was reviewed at the First Vatican Council to determine if it had any implications for the proposed doctrine of papal infallibility. His case, however, was more serious than those of Liberius and Vigilius. Alfred Plummer wrote:

On the vexed question of Honorius a few words will be found in an Appendix. It must ever remain the great, though by no means the only historical obstacle in the way of infallibilists.[17]

The reason for the difficulty is that, almost a half century after his death, Honorius was anathematized by the Sixth Ecumenical Council, the third held at Constantinople (680–681), the only pope ever to have been damned in this manner. These facts are admitted by the main modern preeminent Catholic authors who have discussed this matter, for example, Hefele and Mann. Therefore, any theory of papal infallibility must be interpreted in a manner that is consistent with this event. The facts may be summarized as follows.[18] In the fourth decade of the seventh century, the advance of Islam threatened the Syrian and Egyptian provinces of the Roman Empire. Most of the Syrian and Egyptian Christians had rejected the decrees of the Council of Chalcedon and denominated by the pejorative appellation "Melkites" or "Royalists" those Christians who followed the official line. The Orthodox party, on the other hand, condemned as "Monophysites"

---

16. Geoffrey Faber, *Jowett, a Portrait with Background* (Cambridge, Mass.: Harvard University Press, 1958), 92. The author is referring to the book *Sexual Inversion* by Henry Havelock Ellis and John Addington Symonds.

17. Alfred Plummer, introduction to *Fables respecting the Popes of the Middle Ages, A Contribution to Ecclesiastical History*, by Ignaz von Döllinger (London, Rivingtons, 1871), xxviii.

18. There is an excellent and full discussion in Horace K. Mann, *The Lives of the Popes in the Early Middle Ages* and *The Lives of the Popes in the Middle Ages*, vol. 1, pt. 1 (St. Louis, Mo.: B. Herder 1914), 330–45; and in Carl Joseph von Hefele, *Conciliengeschichte, Nach den Quellen bearbeitet*, vol. 3 (Freiburg im Breisgau: Herder, 1877), §324. Hefele's account had to be rewritten after the First Vatican Council.

or "one-nature-heretics" the majority of Armenians, Egyptians, and Syrians who rejected the Council. This internal division in the Christian ranks threatened to make impossible any successful resistance to the Muslim foe. There was therefore reason to come up with some sort of arrangement to unify the Christian population. In the year 634, Sergius, patriarch of Constantinople, wrote to Pope Honorius that Cyrus, patriarch of Alexandria, had reconciled large numbers of Egyptian heretics to the Orthodox Catholic Church by telling them that although there were two natures in Christ, there was only one will in him and only one operative force. Sergius, Cyrus, and the patriarch of Antioch were happy with this arrangement, but the monk Sophronius (soon to be patriarch of Jerusalem) had condemned it as heresy. Sergius asked the pope to make a call. Honorius replied in a letter that became notorious. The story is told by Plummer:

Of the four oriental patriarchs three had declared for the famous *Nine Articles*, which were an attempt to make peace by means of a doubtful expression.[19] The new patriarch of Jerusalem, Sophronius, disregarding the promise which he had made as a private theologian, had called a synod and solemnly condemned the *Nine Articles*. Now came the time when Honorius, hitherto quite passive, could keep silence no longer. He was formally asked for his decision. It would seem as if he never clearly understood the question. He gave *four* different answers. (1.) We must confess that Christ had only one will. (Which was heretical.) (2) We must not say that Christ had two conflicting wills, of which the divine will compelled the human will to act in harmony with it. (Which no one had ever dreamed of saying.) (3) It would be better not to talk either of one will or of two wills, but to leave such a mere question of language to grammarians. (Which was no answer at all.) (4) We *must* not talk either of one will or of two wills. The question cannot lawfully be discussed. (Which was a return to the absurd and disastrous policy of Zeno's *Henoticon*; attempting to settle a vexed question by forbidding its discussion.)

In the *Ecthesis* the emperor gave this fourth dictum of Honorius the authority of an imperial decree. The *Ecthesis* was received with great favour in the East; and Honorius would no doubt have accepted it. He died, however, before it reached Rome, October, A.D. 638.[20]

Forty-three years later, in its thirteenth session, the Sixth Ecumenical Council, the third to be held in Constantinople, rejected the *Ecthesis* and

---

19. [Note of Plummer]: "Θεανδρικὰ ἐνέργεια—words capable of an orthodox, but also of a monothelite interpretation. They occur in the seventh and crucial article. The first six are introductory; the last two are anathemas."

20. Alfred Plummer, appendix F to *Fables respecting the Popes of the Middle Ages, A Contribution to Ecclesiastical History*, by Ignaz von Döllinger (London: Rivingtons, 1871), 300–302.

condemned Honorius. After anathematizing Sergius, patriarch of Constantinople, Cyrus, patriarch of Alexandria, and other such authorities, the Council proceeded to decree:

Cum his vero simul proiici a sancta Dei catholica ecclesia simulque anathematizari praevidimus et Honorium ... eo quod invenimus per scripta, quae ab eo facta sunt ad Sergium, quia in omnibus eius mentem secutus est, impia dogmata confirmavit.[21]

Furthermore we have provided that Honorius not only be expelled from the Holy Catholic Church of God together with these, but that he also be anathema, because we have found that he confirmed impious doctrines in the letters which he sent to Sergius, for he followed that fellow in all things.

In confirming the decrees of the Council, the Emperor Constantine wrote:

[Ἀναθεματίζομεν] ἔτι δὲ καὶ τὸν Ὀνώριον τὸν πρεσβυτέρας Ῥώμης πάπαν γενόμενον τὸν κατὰ πάντα τούτοις συναιρέτην καὶ σύνδρομον καὶ βεβαιωτὴν τῆς αἱρέσεως.[22]

[We] furthermore [anathematize] Honorius, Pope of Elder Rome, who was in every way a fellow heretic and collaborator and strengthener of the heresy.

Even more importantly, the anathema was confirmed in several letters by Pope Leo II in 682, four of which are extant. including one to the emperor Constantine Pogonatus, one to Ervigius, king of the Visigoths, and one to the Spanish bishops. In the latter, the pope indicated that the anathema was imposed because of the culpable negligence of Honorius.

Qui vero adversum apostolicae traditionis puritatem perduelliones exstiterunt ... aeterna condemnatione mulctati sunt, i. e. Theodorus Pharanitanus, Cyrus Alexandrinus, Sergius, Paulus, Petrus Constantinopolitani, cum Honorio qui flammam haeretici dogmatis non, ut decuit apostolicam auctoritatem, incipientem extinxit, sed negligendo confovit.[23]

Those who proved themselves enemies of the purity of the apostolic tradition were punished by eternal damnation, namely, Theodore of Pharan, Cyrus of Alexandria, and Sergius, Paul, and Peter of Constantinople, together with Honorius, who did not put out the first flames of heretical teaching, as he ought to have, but by his negligence assisted in their spread.

21. Horace K. Mann, *The Lives of the Popes in the Early Middle Ages* and *The Lives of the Popes in the Middle Ages*, vol. 1, pt. 2 (St. Louis, Mo., B. Herder, 1925), 42n4.

22. Carl Joseph von Hefele, *Conciliengeschichte, Nach den Quellen bearbeitet*, 2nd ed., vol. 3 (Freiburg im Breisgau: Herder, 1877), 293.

23. Ibid., 294.

Thus it is clear that Pope Honorius, in a letter in reply to a request from Patriarch Sergius of Constantinople to weigh in on the doctrine of the One Will, wrote what was condemned as heresy by an ecumenical council held forty-two years after his death, and that the decree of this ecumenical council was confirmed by one of his papal successors, who said that the anathema was imposed for blameworthy incompetence.

Hood *Hood* is the development of the Anglo-Saxon *hōd*, as is the German *Hut*, hat. The Latin is *cucullus*. The fragmentary hood on the mozzetta was considered worthy of express condemnation in §1 of the instruction *Ut Sive Sollicite* of March 31, 1969.[24] The only such hoods to be seen any more are those on the mozzettas of some cathedral canons, evidently not covered by the aforementioned document.

Huguenot The German noun *Eidgenossen* means *confederates by oath*, and this word, according to Weekley, corrupted by the French into *Huguenots* under the influence of the proper name *Hughes*, was applied by them to the Protestants in their kingdom who followed the teachings of John Calvin. The *Oxford English Dictionary* declares the origin of the word to be uncertain, but presents this etymology and no other.

Hymn The Greek noun ὕμνος means a *song*. It was transliterated into Latin as *hymnus*, and the stem of this latter word became the English *hymn*. Hymns are not supposed to be sung at Mass, or one would find them in the *Missale Romanum* and the *Graduale*. If there is "down time," that is what silence or the organ are for.

Hypostasis The Greek verb ὑφίστημι means *to stand* (ἵστημι) *upon* (ὑπό), and from it was derived the noun ὑπόστασις, with the meaning *foundation*. This is the Greek name for what in English is called a Person of the Blessed Trinity.

The words *usia* and *hypostasis* were, naturally and intelligibly, for three or four centuries, practically synonymous, and were used indiscriminately for two ideas, which were afterwards respectively denoted by the one and the other.[25]

---

24. *Ut Sive Sollicite* (instruction of the Secretariat of State, March 31, 1969), *Acta Apostolicae Sedis* 61, no. 5, (1969), 334–40, A 1. The text is also available at www.shetlersites.com/clericaldress/utsivesollicite.html.

25. John Henry Cardinal Newman, *The Arians of the Fourth Century*, new ed. (London: Longmans, Green, 1897), 444.

Duchesne says that the Western Church started making a distinction be-tween *ousia* and *hypostasis* about 375;[26] hitherto both had been translated by *substantia*. The opinion of Duchesne was confirmed by Karl Rahner; the entry for the word "Hypostasis" in his theological dictionary begins as follows:

A philosophical expression for "concrete reality" (Gr. ὑπόστασις). This term orig-inally had the same meaning as οὐσία (nature); so that the Latin substantia (sub-stance) was used to render both. But when theological reflection on the Trinity began this usage proved unfortunate, given the relations that then obtained be-tween Greek and Latin theologians. Origen described the three divine Persons as ὑποστάσεις united by a single οὐσία; Tertullian spoke of three Persons in one sunbstance. Nevertheless the First Council of Nicaea still treated ὑπόστασις and οὐσία as synonyms. The classic theology of the Trinity was only formulated in 380: in the one divine nature (essence) there are three ὑποστάσεις, that is, three sub-sistences, or three Persons.[27]

Hypostatic Union For the etymologies, see the entry above and the entry **Union**. Rahner defines the hypostatic union as follows:

[It is] a technical term in theology which means that in Jesus Christ a human being became the created self-expression of the Word of God through the perma-nent union of a human nature (ὑπόστασις) with the divine Person of the Logos.[28]

---

26. Louis Duchesne, *Early History of the Christian Church from Its Foundation to the End of the Fifth Century*, vol. 2 (London: John Murray, 1931), 325.

27. Karl Rahner and Herbert Vorgrimler, *Theological Dictionary*, ed. Cornelius Ernst, OP, trans. Richard Strachan (New York: Herder & Herder, 1965), 218, s.v. "Hypostasis."

28. Ibid., 218, s.v. "Hypostatic Union".

Icon The Greek verb εἴκω means *to be like*. From it arose the noun εἰκών with the meaning *likeness*. *Icon* is the English transliteration of εἰκών. In religious art *icon* denotes a picture or painting. A statue may be a likeness, but it would not be called an icon. Some very few icons were held to be ἀχειροποίηται—made without human hands. Thus the icon of Christ in the Holy of Holies at the top of the Scala Sancta in Rome was held to have been begun by St. Luke but finished by an angel; it was placed there by Pope Stephen III in 752.

Iconoclasm The Greek noun εἰκών, εἰκόνος, *f.*, means a *likeness*. The Greek verb κλάω means *to break into pieces*. *Iconoclasm* is the stem of the Greek noun εἰκονόκλασμα, which means the *smashing* (κλάσμα) of *pictures* (εἰκόνες). It was the declared policy of some of the Byzantine emperors of the eighth century, beginning with Leo III the Isaurian, who, by his decree of the year 726, directed that all images were to be removed from the churches. The Imperial Majesty, perhaps under the influence of the spread of Islam, imagined that this order would make Christianity more palatable to non-believers and heretics.

Idol The Greek verb εἶδον (the aorist of the obsolete present εἴδω or, more properly, ϝίδω) and the related Latin verb *video* mean to see. There thence arose the noun εἴδωλον with the meaning *something that can be seen*. Our noun *idol* is merely the transliteration of the stem of the Greek noun. In religious art *idol* denotes something three-dimensional. A painting or mosaic is something that is seen, but it would not be called an idol.

Furthermore, the word *idol* nowadays has the connotation of something illegitimately worshipped, something that is not the case with *icon*.

Idolatry   This is the Greek word εἰδωλάτρεια, which means the *worship* (λάτρεια) *of graven images* (εἴδωλα).

Image   The Latin noun *imago, imaginis, f.*, means a *copy*, a *likeness*, and from it is derived the English noun *image*, which is the name of any likeness, whether graven or painted. The former were called in Greek εἴδωλα (*idols*), the latter εἰκόνες (*icons*).

Immaculate   The Latin noun *macula, maculae, f.*, means *stain*, and from it was derived the verb *maculo, maculare, maculavi, maculatus* with the meaning *to stain*. From the past participle *maculatus*, stained, there proceeded, upon the addition of the negating prefix *in-*, the adjective *immaculatus* with the meaning *without stain*. Pius IX defined the dogma of the *Immaculate Conception* in 1854.

On December 8, 1854, after many and long deliberations, the Dogma of the Immaculate Conception was promulgated in St. Peter's in the presence of fifty-four cardinals, forty-two archbishops, twenty-three bishops, and several patriarchs. By Pius IX's order, the names of those who assisted were engraved on two tablets inserted beside the Confessional altar in St. Peter's.

The festival on that day, sacred to the Virgin, was magnificent. After chanting the Gospel, first in Latin, then in Greek, Cardinal Macchi, deacon of the Sacred College, together with the senior archbishops and bishops present, all approached the Papal throne, pronouncing these words in Latin: "Deign, most Holy Father, to lift your Apostolic voice and pronounce the dogmatic Decree of the Immaculate Conception, on account of which there will be praise in heaven and rejoicings on earth." The Pope replying, stated that he welcomed the wish of the Sacred College, the episcopate, and the clergy, and declared it was essential first of all to invoke the help of the Holy Spirit. So saying he intoned the *Veni Creator*, chanted in chorus by all present. The chant concluded, amid a solemn silence, Pius IX's finely modulated voice read the following Decree:

"It shall be Dogma, that the most Blessed Virgin Mary, in the first instant of the Conception, by singular privilege and grace of God, in virtue of the merits of Jesus Christ, the Saviour of mankind, was preserved from all stain of original sin." The senior cardinal then prayed the Pope to make this Decree public, and, amid the roar of cannon from Fort St. Angelo and the festive ringing of church bells, the solemn act was accomplished. Pius IX then proceeded to the Sistine Chapel and crowned the Virgin's image.[1]

---

1. Raffaele de Cesare, *The Last Days of Papal Rome, 1850–1870*, ed. and trans., Helen Zimmern (London: Archibald Constable, 1909), 129–30.

Imprimatur The Latin verb *premo, premere, pressi, pressus* means *to press*, and the addition of the preposition *in* produces the compound verb *imprĭmo, imprĭmere, impressi, impressus* meaning *to press upon, to print*. *Imprimatur* means *Let it be printed*. The *imprimatur* is a license issued by a competent authority that a book is authorized to be published under the aegis of the corresponding entity. In 1687, Pepys gave the *imprimatur* of the Royal Society for the publication of the Newton's *Principia Mathematica*. In the Catholic Church, it is a declaration by a diocesan bishop that a book dealing with religion contains no heresy. Such a declaration is not the last word. There are examples of books that received the *imprimatur* that were afterwards placed on the Index of Forbidden Books; one such work was the three-volume *Early History of the Church* by the Abbé Duchesne. An imprimatur had been granted for this work by Giuseppe Ceppetelli, Patriarch of Constantinople and Vice Regent of the Diocese of Rome, a man who had ordained such people as the future Pope John XXIII and Cardinal Spellman, but the volumes were nonetheless later placed on the Index, an act which was a cause of embarrassment in later generations. His rehabilitation was made clear in the *New Catholic Encyclopedia*.

Duchesne frequently provoked violent reaction by his intolerance of pious fraud in history.... [His *Early History of the Christian Church* served] as a standard introduction to the complex problems of the first 5 centuries of the Church's development.... Though many of Duchesne's opinions have to be modified in the light of new documents and research, his fundamental judgments, based on deep and solid investigation, have proved invaluable.... A conscientious historian and a sincere churchman, he suffered unflinchingly under the suspicions of the anti-Modernists, but continued his invaluable contributions to the study of the Church's origins and early development in all its phases.[2]

Imprimi Potest This Latin phrase means *it can be printed*. It is a decree issued by the superior of a member of a religious order, permitting a manuscript submitted by that member to be forwarded to a diocesan bishop for examination prior to publication. It is a declaration that the superior has no objection to the publication of the book. The bishop will then delegate a censor to read the book and make a recommendation; a positive recommendation by the censor is called a *nihil obstat—there is nothing to prevent publication*. The bishop may then grant his approval, the *imprimatur*.

2. F. X. Murphy, "Duchesne, Louis," in *New Catholic Encyclopedia* (Washington, DC: Catholic University of America, 1967), 4:1088.

Improperia The Greek verb προφέρω means *to bring* (φέρω) *forward* (πρό), especially words of reproach. This is the same word as the Latin *profĕro*, from which was formed the noun *probrum*, a reproach. From this noun was formed the verb *impropĕro*, *impropĕrare* with the meaning *to cast reproaches on*. From this verb there was formed the noun *improperium*, a reproach. The *Improperia* are the reproaches sung during the adoration of the cross of the Good Friday service; they begin with the verses Micah 6:3, Jeremiah 2:21, and Isaiah 5:2, 4, after each of which is chanted the Trisagion in Greek and Latin. There then follow nine other reproaches, with Micah 6:3 chanted as a refrain after each verse. See the entry **Trisagion**.

Incardination The Late Latin first declension verb *incardino* means *to swing on* (in) *a hinge* (cardo); it came to be used of the installation of one of the chief priests, or cardinals, of Rome in his parish church, and then of the enrolling of any priest anywhere among the clergy of a diocese.

Incarnation The Latin noun *caro, carnis, m.*, means *flesh*, and from it and the preposition *in* was formed the first declension verb *incarno* with the meaning *to enter into the flesh*. It was used to translate the Greek verb σαρκόω, *to make fleshy*, *to make into flesh*, and from its fourth principal part proceeded the noun *incarnatio*, a making into flesh.

Newman said of St, Cyril of Alexandria:

He was not content with anathematizing Nestorius; he laid down a positive view of the Incarnation, which the Universal Church accepted and holds to this day as the very truth of Revelation. It is this insight into, and grasp of the Adorable Mystery, which constitutes his claim to take his seat among the Doctors of Holy Church.[3]

Incense The Latin verb *candeo, candere, candui*, means *to be shining white, to glow with heat*, and the addition of the preposition *in* produces the compound verb *incendo, incendere, incendi, incensus* with the meaning *to set on fire*. From the fourth principal part of this verb is derived the noun *incensum, -i, n.*, meaning a *setting fire to*, and then *incense*. The corresponding Greek word is θυμίαμα. See the entry **Thurible**. The use of incense has been traditional in the Christian liturgy since antiquity, and it is edifying to see priests who have been taught properly how to wield the chain censer.

3. John Henry Cardinal Newman, "Trials of Theodoret," in *Historical Sketches*, vol. 2 (London: Longmans, Green, 1917), 345.

Index Librorum Prohibitorum The Latin verb *indĭco, indĭcare* means *to point out*, and from it was formed the noun *index, indĭcis, m.*, meaning an *informer* or *something that informs, such as a catalogue*, a *table*, or a *list*. The Latin phrase *Index Librorum Prohibitorum* means the *List of Forbidden Books*. It was maintained by the Sacred Congregation of the Index, formerly a dicastery of the Roman Curia, established by Pius V in 1571. In 1916, this congregation was merged with the Supreme Congregation of the Holy Office. The Index was abolished by Pope Paul VI in 1966 as no longer suited to modern times. The censorship of books was originally the responsibility of the Roman Inquisition founded by Pope Paul III.

The whole body of men of letters was subjected to the most rigorous supervision. In the year 1543, Caraffa decreed that no book, whether new or old, and whatever its contents, should for the future be printed without permission of the Inquisitors. Booksellers were enjoined to send in a catalogue of their stock, and to sell nothing without their assent. The officers of customs also received orders to deliver no package, whether of printed books or MS to its address, without first laying them before the Inquisition. This gradually gave rise to an Index of prohibited books; the first examples were set in Louvain and Paris.[4]

Indulgence The Latin verb *indulgeo, indulgere, indulsi, indultus* means *to be forbearing, patient*. It is of uncertain etymology. From this verb proceeds the noun *indulgentia* with the meaning *tenderness, kindness*. In Ecclesiastical Latin, this noun acquired the meaning of *concession*, whereby by the performance of a certain act one would be exempted from doing penance for a certain period, yet still reap the rewards thereof. Thus, in my copy of the *New Catholic Edition of the Holy Bible* (1957), one reads on the half title:

Indulgence

Pope Leo XIII granted to the faithful who spend at least a quarter of an hour in reading the Holy Scriptures with the veneration due to the Divine Word and as spiritual reading, an indulgence of 3 years.—*Enchiridion Indulgentiarum*, 694.

The technical meaning of this was that the person in question reaped the benefits of three years of penance for himself or his beneficiary. It did not mean, as was commonly supposed, that if the beneficiary was dead, then he would spend three fewer years in Purgatory.

---

4. Leopold von Ranke, *The History of the Popes during the Last Four Centuries*, trans. Mrs. Foster and G. R. Dennis (London: G. Bell & Sons, 1912), 1:166–67.

Indult From the fourth principal part of the verb *indulgeo*, noted in the preceding entry, there was formed the noun *indultum, -i, n.*, with the meaning an *act of favor*, in particular, a delay in or exception from the enforcement of a law. The most famous case of an indult in modern times was the one granted by Pope Paul VI to the Catholics of England for the continued celebration of the traditional Latin Mass. The introduction of the revised *Missale Romanum* after the Second Vatican Council caused the old Latin Mass to be replaced by a new rite which was celebrated almost exclusively in English and in a method disagreeable to traditionally minded people. The following *Appeal* appeared in the July 6, 1971, edition of the *Times* of London. It was signed by fifty-seven distinguished people, including Vladimir Ashkenazy, Maurice Bowra, Agatha Christie, Kenneth Clark, Robert Graves, Graham Greene, Yehudi Mehunin, Nancy Mitford, Malcolm Muggeridge, Ralph Richardson, and Joan Sutherland. The result was the Indult of October 30, 1971 for the celebration of the Tridentine Mass in England.

One of the axioms of contemporary publicity, religious as well as secular, is that modern man in general, and intellectuals in particular, have become intolerant of all forms of tradition and are anxious to suppress them and put something else in their place.

But, like many other affirmations of our publicity machines, this axiom is false. Today, as in times gone by, educated people are in the vanguard where recognition of the value of tradition is concerned, and are the first to raise the alarm when it is threatened.

If some senseless decree were to order the total or partial destruction of basilicas or cathedrals, then obviously it would be the educated—whatever their personal beliefs—who would rise up in horror to oppose such a possibility.

Now the fact is that basilicas and cathedrals were built so as to celebrate a rite which, until a few months ago, constituted a living tradition. We are referring to the Roman Catholic Mass. Yet according to the latest information available in Rome, there is a plan to obliterate that Mass by the end of the current year.

We are not at the moment considering the religious or spiritual experience of millions of individuals. The rite in question, in its magnificent Latin text, has also inspired a host of priceless achievements in the arts—not only mystical works but works by poets, philosophers, musicians, architects, painters and sculptors in all countries and epochs. Thus, it belongs to universal culture as well as to churchmen and formal Christians.

In the materialistic and technocratic civilization that is increasingly threatening the life of mind and spirit in its original creative expression—the word—it seems particularly inhuman to deprive man of word-forms in one of their most grandiose manifestations.

The signatories of this appeal, which is entirely ecumenical and non-political, have been drawn from every branch of modern culture in Europe and elsewhere. They wish to call to the attention of the Holy See the appalling responsibility it would incur in the history of the human spirit were it to refuse to allow the traditional Mass to survive, even though this survival took place side by side with other liturgical forms.

Inerrancy The Latin verb *erro, errare* means *to wander, to err,* and its participle *errans* means *erring, being in the wrong.* The addition of the negative prefix *in-* produced the adjective *inerrans,* unerring, and from there the noun *inerrantia* and then the English *inerrancy.* The *inerrancy of scripture* is the teaching that there is no mistake of any sort in the Bible. The main objections to this view have always been based on the verses Matthew 27:9, Mark 2:26, and Acts 7:4, 16. In the first, Christ ascribes to Jeremiah a statement to be found in the Book of Zechariah. In the second case, Christ ascribes to the High Priest Abiathar a story in 1 Samuel 21:2–7 about the priest Ahimelech. In the third case, St. Stephen says that Abraham left Haran after his father died there, but from Genesis 11:26, 32, and 12:4 it may be deduced that Abraham left Haran when his father was one hundred and forty-five years old and still had sixty more years to live before he died in Haran. Apparent internal contradictions of this sort are always the most serious. A different sort of example occurs at Matthew 12:40, where Christ, commenting on the episode of Jonah and the great fish, says that the Son of Man will remain in the heart of the earth for three days and three nights, yet in the gospel accounts he lay dead for just two nights.

It must however be frankly admitted that even when deductions have been made, on critical grounds, there still remains evidence enough that Our Lord while upon earth *did* use the common language of His contemporaries in regard to the Old Testament; that He did speak—if not of Daniel as the author of the book which bears his name, yet of Moses as the author of the Pentateuch and of David as the author of one of the later Psalms; and that He did apply to His own day some part at least of the story of Jonah and the story of Noah as literal narrative.[5]

Sanday proposes the following solution to the problems noted above:

And although it cannot be said that there is complete agreement among them, many of the most reverent and most careful of our theologians, men of the most scrupulous and tender loyalty to the historical decisions both of the Universal

---

5. William Sanday, *Inspiration, Eight Lectures on the Early History and Origin of the Doctrine of Biblical Inspiration, Being the Bampton Lectures for 1893* (London: Longmans, Green, 1896), 413–14.

Church and of our own, have pronounced that there is no inconsistency, that limitations of knowledge might be and were assumed along with other limitations by Him Who was in all things made like unto His brethren, though without sin.[6]

Infallibility The Greek verb σφάλλω means *to trip, to baffle,* and related to it is the Latin verb *fallo, fallere, fefelli, falsus* meaning *to deceive.* From the stem of this verb, upon addition of the suffix *-abilis,* indicating capability, was formed the Late Latin adjective *fallibilis* meaning *capable of error.* The addition of the prefix *in-* then negated the meaning, producing the adjective *infallibilis,* incapable of error. Bacci says that the word *infallibilis,* of which the English *infallible* is a mere transliteration, is low Latin, and that the proper expression of the idea is *errorum immunitas,* and that the person so immune is *errorum omnium expers.*

The doctrine of infallibility has as a consequence that it is very daring for the Church to change long-standing traditions, teachings, and practices, lest it appear that it admits to having made a mistake. For example, the popes John Paul II and Francis have taken a stand on capital punishment quite different from that held by their predecessors for many centuries. From a conversation of Dr. Johnson of the year 1773, we discover an earlier attitude with regard to the popes and the death penalty:

It is told of Sixtus Quintus that on his death-bed, in the intervals of his last pangs, he signed death warrants.... Sixtus Quintus was a sovereign as well as a priest; and, if the criminals deserved death, he was doing his duty to the last.[7]

The guillotine was in standard use in Rome under the papal administration until the end of the secular power.[8]

Infusion The Latin verb *fundo, fundere, fudi, fusus* means *to pour,* and the addition of the preposition *in* produces the compound verb *infundo, infundere, infudi, infusus* with the meaning *to pour on.* From the fourth principal part of this compound verb proceeds the noun *infusio, infusionis, f.,* meaning a *pouring into* or *on.* As the name of a way of administering baptism, *infusion* is a synonym of *affusion;* one merely pours water from a shell onto the head of the person being baptized.

6. Ibid., 415.

7. James Boswell, *The Journal of a Tour to the Hebrides with Samuel Johnson, LL. D.,* Wednesday, 22d September.

8. For photographs of executions from 1865 and 1868, see numbers 165 and 172 in *Rome in Early Photographs, The Age of Pius IX, Photographs 1846-1878 from Roman and Danish Collections,* trans. Ann Thornton (Copenhagen: The Thorvaldsen Museum, 1977).

Initiation *Initium* is the Latin word for *beginning*; it is related to the verb *ineo, inire, inivi, initus*, which means *to go in*. Among Catholics, this is a cant word for *baptism*. Its use is deplorable, because it conjures up ideas of fraternity and sorority initiations. In its favor is the fact that the corresponding French word is used by Duchesne, a great authority.

In Partibus Infidelium This Latin phrase means *in the territory of the unbelievers*, that is, of the Moslems. It refers to those dioceses in the East that came under the government of the Caliphs in the seventh century and thereafter, and whose Christian populations were reduced to zero or became negligible. Such dioceses are given to auxiliary bishops or functionaries of the Roman Curia to maintain the legal fiction that each bishop must have a diocese.

Inquisition The Latin verb *quaero, quaerere, quaesivi, quaesitus* means *to ask*, and the compound verb *inquiro, inquirere, inquisivi, inquisitus* means *to ask about, to look into*. The resulting investigation is called an *inquisitio*, and the person who makes it is called the *inquisitor*. Inquisitors were appointed by the emperor Theodosius *ad conquirendos et eruendos hereticos* (to investigate and get rid of heretics). The Inquisition of the Middle Ages developed gradually from the existing usual methods of investigation available to the ecclesiastical and secular authorities. The foremost expert on the Inquisition commented as follows on this process.

A similar legendary halo exaggerates the exclusive glory, claimed by the Order, of organizing and perfecting the Inquisition. The bulls of Gregory IX alleged in support of the assertion are simply special orders to individual Dominican provincials to depute brethren fitted for the purpose to the duty of preaching against heresy and examining heretics, and prosecuting their defenders. Sometimes Dominicans are sent to special districts to proceed against heretics, with an apology to the bishops and an explanation that the friars are skillful in convincing heretics, and that the other episcopal duties are too engrossing to enable the prelates to give proper attention to this. The fact simply is that there was no formal confiding of the Inquisition to the Dominicans any more than there was any formal founding of the Inquisition itself. As the institution gradually assumed shape and organization in the effort to find some effectual means to ferret out concealed heretics, the Dominicans were the readiest instrument at hand, especially as they professed the function of preaching and converting as their primary business.

This is a fair illustration of the gradual development of the Inquisition. It was not an institution definitely projected and founded, but was moulded step by step out of the materials which lay nearest to hand fitted for the object to be attained.

In fact, when Gregory, recognizing the futility of further dependence on episcopal zeal, sought to take advantage of the favorable secular legislation against heresy, the preaching friars were the readiest instrument within reach for the accomplishment of his object. We shall see hereafter how, as in Florence, the experiment was tried in Aragon and Languedoc and Germany, and the success which on the whole attended it and led to an extended and permanent organization.

... Gregory soon adopted a more practical expedient. Shortly after the issue of the above bulls, we find him ordering the Provincial Prior of Toulouse to select some learned friars who should be commissioned to preach the cross in the diocese, and to proceed against heretics in accordance with the recent statutes. Though here there is still some incongruous mingling of duties, yet Gregory had finally hit upon the device which remained the permanent basis of the Inquisition—the selection by the provincial of certain fitting brethren, who exercised within their province the delegated authority of the Holy See in searching out and examining heretics with a view to the ascertainment of their guilt.[9]

By contrast, the Supreme Sacred Congregation of the Roman and Universal Inquisition, different from the mediaeval inquisition, was established on July 21, 1542 by Pope Paul III in the bull *Licet ab initio*.

In Saecula Saeculorum The phrase *in saecula saeculorum*, well known to all Catholics of a certain age, means *for centuries of centuries*, that is, *for all time*. It translates the Hebrew לְעוֹלָם, and the Greek εἰς τοὺς αἰῶνας τῶν αἰώνων used by St. Paul at *Philippians* 4:20. In baroque and classical music, it was frequently the occasion of a good fugue. Also found is the less common *in saeculum saeculi*, which a rationalist would translate *for ten thousand years*.

Inspiration The Latin verb *spiro, spirare, spiravi, spiratus* means *to breathe*, and the addition of the preposition *in* produces the compound verb *inspiro* with the meaning *to breathe upon*. The noun *inspiratio* therefore means *breathing upon*. George Barker Stevens of the Yale Divinity School wrote:

Inspiration is a name for that guiding and enlightening influence of the Divine Spirit upon the Biblical writers which enabled them in different degrees of fullness and in varying forms to present in their writings, accounts, examples an interpretation of the divine self-revelation, such as, when taken together and rightly interpreted, constitute an adequate and authoritative guide to religious faith and conduct.[10]

9. Henry Charles Lea, *A History of the Inquisition in the Middle Ages* (New York: Harper & Brothers, 1887), 1:300–301, 328, 329–30.

10. Carl E. Hatch, *The Charles A. Briggs Heresy Trial* (New York: Exposition Press, 1969), 108.

Sanday had the following to say on the two theories of biblical inspiration, the traditional theory and the critical theory:

So far it may well seem that the object of these lectures has been only to state and advocate the inductive or critical theory in opposition to the traditional. And it is true that where the two come into direct collision, as in other matters of human thought, the more scientific statement is to be accepted.[11]

The traditional theory needs little description.... But speaking broadly, the current view may be said to have been that the Bible as a whole and in all its parts was the Word of God, and as such that it was endowed with all the perfections of that Word. Not only did it disclose truths about the Divine nature and operation which were otherwise unobtainable, but all parts of it were equally authoritative, and in history as well as in doctrine it was exempt from error....

This was the view commonly held fifty years ago. And when it comes to be examined, it is found to be substantially not very different from that which was held two centuries after the Birth of Christ.[12]

The term *inspiration* is derived, or course, from the well-known passage in which St. Paul speaks of scripture as θεόπνευστος (2 Timothy 3:16–17), a word that is translated into the Latin of the *Vulgata* by *divinitus inspirata*. Thus, πᾶσα γραφὴ θεόπνευστος is rendered *Omnis Scriptura divinitus inspirata est*. S. R. Driver defined *inspiration* as follows:

By inspiration I suppose we may understand a Divine afflatus which, without superseding or suppressing the human faculties, but rather using them as its instruments, and so conferring upon Scripture its remarkable manifoldness and variety, enabled holy men of old to apprehend, and declare in different degrees, and in accordance with the needs and circumstances of particular ages or occasions, the mind and purpose of God.[13]

The advance of knowledge led Driver to propose the following theory of inspiration:

Elsewhere, again, literary considerations show that sayings and discourses are strongly coloured by the individuality of the narrator; the writers themselves also afford indications that they are subject to the limitations of culture and knowledge imposed by the age in which they lived. *A priori*, no doubt, we might have

11. William Sanday, *Inspiration, Eight Lectures on the Early History and Origin of the Doctrine of Biblical Inspiration, Being the Bampton Lectures for 1893* (London: Longmans, Green, 1896), 391.

12. Ibid., 394–95.

13. S. R. Driver and A. F. Kirkpatrick, *The Higher Criticism* (New York: Hodder & Stoughton, 1912), 50–51.

expected these things to be otherwise; but our *a priori* conceptions of the works and ways of God are apt to be exceedingly at fault.[14]

... as inspiration does not suppress the individuality of the biblical writers, so it does not altogether neutralize human infirmities, or confer upon those who have been its instruments immunity from error.[15]

Inspiration did not always, in precisely the same degree, lift those who were its agents above the reach of human weakness and human ignorance.[16]

In the words of the prophet, or other inspired writer, there is a human element not less than a Divine element; it is a mistake, and a serious mistake, to ignore either.[17]

Wilfrid Ward noticed that Leo XIII was the first supreme pontiff to allow some small place for the theory of inspiration promoted by Driver.

In 1894 he published an Encyclical on Biblical Studies—the Encyclical *Providentissimus Deus*—which seemed to reflect this duality of attitude. The bulk of it was conservative. But some passages not obviously reconcilable with the rest pointed to the recognition that inaccuracies in scientific and historical statements were not incompatible with inspiration.[18]

The Muslims, as is well known, apply a much different theory of inspiration to the production of their Quran; according to them, it is the very word of God recited by the Deity and taken down word for word by the Prophet Mohammed. As a result, there is little room for "modernism" in Islam.

Interdict The Greek verb δείκνυμι means *to show*, and related to it is the Latin verb *dīco, dīcere, dixi, dictus* meaning *to indicate, to say*. The addition of the preposition *inter* (*between, among*) to the latter verb produced the compound verb *interdīco, interdicere, interdixi, interdictus* meaning *to speak between, to interpose by speaking, to forbid*. From it was derived the noun *interdictum* meaning *prohibition*. The interdict was an ecclesiastical censure requiring the cessation of the public celebration of the liturgy. The last occasion on which a whole state was placed under this ban occurred in 1606, when Paul V proceeded against Venice. Most famous was the in-

---

14. Ibid., 49–50.
15. Ibid., 50.
16. Ibid., 54.
17. Ibid., 55.
18. Maisie Ward, *The Wilfrid Wards and the Transition*, vol. 1, *The Nineteenth Century* (New York: Sheed & Ward, 1934), 309–10.

terdict placed on England by Innocent III in 1208, a penalty that humbled King John.

Interim *Interim* is the Latin word for *meanwhile*. The *Interim* was a compromise regulation of the emperor Charles V, announced at the Diet of Augsburg in 1548, according to which married priests could keep their wives until an ecumenical council settled the issue of clerical celibacy.

Internuncio The Latin noun *internuntius* means a *messenger sent to act as mediator*, and the denominative verb *internuntio, internuntiare* means *to act as a mediator between two sides*. In the diplomatic language of the Holy See, *internuncio* retained its meaning of envoy but lost the connotation of mediator between two sides. As the *interrex* held the supreme power in the Roman state in the interregnum between the death of one king and the election of his successor, so the *internuncio* in the pontifical diplomatic service used to be the head of the embassy in the period after the departure or death of one nuncio and the arrival of his successor. However, in 1815 the Congress of Vienna recognized three ranks of diplomatic authorities: the ambassador, the envoy extraordinary and minister plenipotentiary, and the minister resident. In the papal diplomatic service, the nuncio henceforth corresponded to the ambassador, and the internuncio to the envoy extraordinary and minister plenipotentiary. (There was no title in the papal service corresponding to minister resident.) Thus, the internuncio became the papal diplomatic envoy of the second class. An internuncio would usually be appointed to second-class powers like Argentina, Bolivia, Brazil, Chile, Luxembourg, the Netherlands, Peru, and Venezuela. In modern times, it was perceived to be an unseemly act of discrimination to denominate certain states second rate in this way, so the title is now abolished.

Introibo ad Altare Dei These words were the beginning of the Mass (after the sign of the cross) for well over a thousand years. They are taken from Psalm 42:4 (43:4). They mean, "I will go in unto the altar of God."

Introit The Latin adverb *intro* means *inward, within*, and the verb *eo, ire, ivi, itus* means *to go*. Their concatenation produces the compound verb *introeo, introire* meaning *to enter, to go in*, and the word *introit* means *he enters*. It is the name of the chant sung at the beginning of Mass. In English, now it is called the *entrance antiphon*.

Islam This word is the Arabic noun meaning *submission*; it is the infinitive of the fourth conjugation verb اسلم *to submit*, derived from the first conjugation verb سلم, *to be whole*. Arabic is the language of the Quran, believed by the Muslims to be composed of the very words of God. The knowledge of the Arabic language was always important for the study of the related language Hebrew, but nowadays it is also necessary in view of the immigration into Europe and into the Americas of Moslems from Asia and Africa. The study of Arabic has indeed been introduced into American colleges that formerly taught Latin and Greek; students, however, are less likely to learn how to read the Quran than they are to learn modern conversational Arabic.

J

Jacobite The Christians who rejected the Council of Chalcedon were called Monophysites. They predominated among the Egyptians, Syrians, and Armenians. The most famous Syrian Monophysite was the sixth-century bishop James, or Jacobus, of Edessa, and on this account the Syrian Monophysites came to be denominated *Jacobites*.

It is possible that under the stress of persecution the Monophysitic faith might have expired, had it not been for the indefatigable labours of one devoted zealot, who not only kept the heresy alive, but founded a permanent Monophysitic Church. This was Jacob Baradaeus, who was ordained bishop of Edessa (about 541) by the Monophysitic bishops who were hiding at Constantinople under the protection of Theodora. Endowed with an exceptionally strong physical constitution, he spent the rest of his life in wandering through the provinces of the East, Syria, Mesopotamia, and Asia Minor, disguised as a beggar, and he derived the name Baradaeus from his dress, which was made of the saddle-cloths of asses attached together. His disguise was so effective, and his fellow-heretics were so faithful, that all the efforts of the Imperial authorities to arrest him were vain, and he lived till A.D. 578. His work was not only to confirm the Monophysites in their faith and maintain their drooping spirit, but also to ordain bishops and clergy and provide them with a secret organization. His name has been perpetuated in that of the Jacobite Church which he founded.[1]

For the etymology of the name *James*, see the entry **Apostle**.

Jehovah This word was composed by adding the vowels ְ of the Hebrew word for *Lord* (אדני—*Adonai*) to the consonants of the Tetragrammaton

---

1. J. B. Bury, *History of the Later Roman Empire* (New York: Dover, 1958), 2:391.

(יהוה—*Yahweh*). The result is *Yahowah*, which was corrupted into the English *Jehovah*. The purpose of this concoction was to prevent the careless uttering of the ineffable name of God, which crime was blasphemy. It was a signal that when one saw יהוה, one should say אדני. No one ever said *Jehovah*.

This is a reminder that at one time, words were considered to have power. Even into the memory of people now living, it was considered dangerous to utter the word *death*; if an Italian did so, he would immediately ward off the danger by adding the phrase *salute a noi—Health to us!*

Jesuit The Company or Society of Jesus, founded by Ignatius of Loyola, was approved by Paul III in 1540. The Latin name for a member of the Society is *Iesuita, -ae, m.* as if from Ἰησουίτης, produced by the addition of the Greek suffix -ίτης to the stem of the proper name Ἰησοῦς. Bacci prefers *sodalis societatis Iesu* or *Ignatianus sodalis societatis Iesu.*

They pleased themselves with the thought of making war as soldiers against satan, and in accordance with the old military propensities of Loyola, they assumed the name of the Company of Jesus, exactly as a company of soldiers takes the name of the captain.[2]

Jesu Nostra Redemptio This is now the hymn for First and Second Vespers of the Feast of the Ascension. It is also one of the hymns traditionally sung during the procession on Corpus Christi. It is a composition of the seventh or eighth century, of unknown authorship.

> Jesu nostra redemptio,
> Amor et desiderium,
> Deus Creator omnium,
> Homo in fine temporum.
>
> Quae te vicit clementia,
> Ut ferres nostra crimina,
> Crudelem mortem patiens,
> Ut nos a morte tolleres!
>
> Inferni claustra penetrans,
> Tuos captivos redimens:
> Victor triumpho nobili
> Ad dextram Patris residens.

---

2. Leopold von Ranke, *The History of the Popes during the Last Four Centuries*, trans. Mrs. Foster and G. R. Dennis (London: G. Bell & Sons, 1912), 1:152.

Ipsa te cogat pietas,
Ut mala nostra superes
Parcendo, et voti compotes
Nos tuo vultu saties.

Tu esto nostrum gaudium,
Qui es futurus praemium:
Sit nostra in te gloria
Per cuncta semper saecula. Amen.

The best translation is that by Edward Caswall (1814–1878).

O Jesu! our Redemption!
Loved and desired with tears!
God, of all worlds Creator!
Man, in the close of years!

What wondrous pity moved Thee
To make our cause thine own
And suffer death and torments,
For sinners to atone!

O thou, who piercing Hades,
Thy captives didst unchain!
Who gloriously ascendedst
Thy Father's Throne again.

Subdue our many evils
By mercy all divine;
And comfort with thy presence
The hearts that for Thee pine.

Be thou our joy, O Jesu!
In whom our prize we see;
Always through all the ages,
In Thee our glory be.

Jesus The Hebrew verb ישׁע means *to save*, and from it was derived the personal name of the Christ יהושׁע, literally, *Yahweh saves*. Since the Greeks had no letters that sounded like the Hebrew consonants ע, שׁ, ה, or י, their transliteration of the name יהושׁע, Ἰησοῦς, was most inaccurate. When transcribed into the Latin alphabet, it became *Iesus*, whence proceeds our *Jesus*. The Latin *Iosue*, the name in the *Vulgata* for the successor of Moses, is an alternative transliteration of the Hebrew name; it became *Joshua* in English.

Johannine This is an English adjective formed from the Latin *Ioannes*, John; an extra *h* has been added in the manner of the Germans and some Mediaeval Latin writers. The Johannine Literature are those books of the New Testament ascribed to the apostle John, namely, the gospel, the three letters, and the Apocalypse. For John, Jesus is the incarnation of the preexistent Torah. The fourth gospel plays with the literal (*proprie*) and figurative (*translate*) meanings of words, and the two are interwoven in a κόσμος συμβολικός that points to theological surrealism. In the prologue, for example, there is a continuous play on the literal and figurative meanings of λαβεῖν, παραλαβεῖν, and καταλαβεῖν. John's σκηνή is a double one, connected by a perpetual shuttle train, which makes the neutral observer dizzy. There is a bifurcation in the fourth gospel; Christ speaks the allegorical language, such as, for example, when he says that he will rebuild the temple in three days, but the Jews think in the proper, earthly meaning of the words.

Less commonly, *Johannine* may refer to the activity of anyone called John, for example, Pope John XXIII.

Jubilee This word is the corruption of the Hebrew noun יובל, which means a *ram's horn*, which was used as a musical instrument. Leviticus 25 prescribed the sounding of the ram's horn to announce the opening of the Holy Year of Jubilee (every fiftieth year) among the Hebrews. The jubilees of the Roman Catholic Church were inaugurated by Boniface VIII in 1300. After some confusion as to the proper interval of time between them, the period of twenty-five years was settled upon in the fifteenth century, and so it remained until 1933, when Pius XI held an extraordinary Holy Year on the anniversary of the redemption. Extraordinary Holy Years are becoming common; they were celebrated in 1983 and 2016. The best book on the Holy Year celebrated by the Roman Church is the work of Herbert Thurston, SJ, *The Holy Year of Jubilee*, written for the celebration of 1900. It has never been superseded.

Justice The Latin neuter noun *ius, iuris, n.*, means *right, law*, and from it was derived the adjective *iustus* with the meaning *fair, lawful*. The combination of *ius* and the verb *sisto, sistere, stiti, status—to set up, to stand—* produced the noun *iustitia*, our *justice*.

Justification The Greek noun δίκη means *justice*, and the related adjective δίκαιος means *just*. The noun δικαιοσύνη means *innocence* or *declara-*

tion of innocence. In Latin, such a verdict of innocence is called *iustificatio,* whence our noun *justification. To be justified* is the Greek way of saying *to be declared innocent.* The Catholic Church rejected the doctrine of the reformers that faith alone suffices (*sola fides sufficit*) for justification before the Deity; the Catholic doctrine of justification was set forth in the decree of the sixth session of the Council of Trent (January 13, 1547), Canon 9:

Si quis dixerit, sola fide impium iustificari, ita ut intelligat, nihil aliud requiri, quod ad iustificationis gratiam consequendam cooperetur, et nulla ex parte necesse esse, eum suae voluntatis motu praeparari atque disponi, anathema sit.

If anyone should say that the sinner is justified by faith alone, and by that mean that nothing else is required that helps to gain the grace of justification, and that it is not at all necessary that he be prepared and disposed by the activity of his own will, let him be anathema.

Kerygma The Greek verb κηρύσσω means *to proclaim*, and the associated nouns κῆρυξ and κήρυγμα mean *herald* and *proclamation* respectively. Karl Rahner defined *kerygma* as follows:

[It is] a NT term which in modern use means the word that is preached (Gr. κήρυγμα, preaching) to the Christian community or individual ("unto destruction" or "unto edification") in the name of God, by lawful commission of God and the Church, as the very word of God and Christ, and which efficaciously makes present its utterance in the situation of the hearer whom it summons.[1]

Kiss The English word *kiss* is descended from the Anglo-Saxon verb *cyssan* and the related noun *coss*. The *Kiss of Peace* in the Mass is the embrace that takes place after the words *Pax Domini sit semper vobiscum*.

Knight The Anglo-Saxon noun *cniht* means *youth, servant*, like the German *Knecht*. In the Middle Ages, many youths and servants became soldiers, and the word was translated into Latin by *miles*. The elevation of the military dignity led to the word acquiring in English the force of semi-nobility. See Weekley on this word. In ancient Rome, the *equites*, originally men who could provide themselves with horses (*equi*) in time of war, developed into an intermediate class between the senatorial order and the common, plebeian, folk. The English word *knights* now translates *equites*; the Germans use *Ritter* for this dignity, for they preserve the original meaning of *Knecht*. The popes, as sovereigns, in former times

---

1. Karl Rahner and Herbert Vorgrimler, *Theological Dictionary*, ed. Cornelius Ernst, O. P., trans. Richard Strachan (New York: Herder & Herder, 1965), 249–50, s.v. "Kerygma."

raised worthy individuals to the rank of knight, the five orders being the Supreme Order of Christ, the Order of the Golden Spur, the Order of Pius IX, the Order of St. Gregory the Great, and the Order of St. Sylvester. The Sovereign Military Order of Malta and the Order of the Holy Sepulcher are independent orders of Catholic knights founded in the period of the Crusades. The books by Archbishop Cardinale and Peter Bander van Duren treat this subject most thoroughly.[2] The recent intervention of the Holy See in the affairs of the Sovereign Military Order of Malta led to the abdication of the prince and grand master, a great embarrassment. These knights have been very sensitive about their sovereignty, even to the point of issuing postage stamps, whose validity is recognized by dozens of states. The book by Sire is a good study of the Order, with interesting information about the difficult relations between the Grand Master Prince Ludovico Chigi Albani della Rovere and Nicola Cardinal Canali.[3]

Kyriale *Kyriale* is an Ecclesiastical Latin word formed by the addition of the Latin adjectival suffix *-ale* to the stem of the Greek noun κύριος, *lord*; the name *Kyriale* is in reference to the chant *Kyrie eleison*. See the entry **Missal**. The Kyriale is a liturgical book that contains the musical notation for the chants of the unchangeable parts of the Mass (viz., the Kyrie, Gloria, Credo, Sanctus-Benedictus, and Agnus Dei). Although in naming the various liturgical books we may write *Antiphonal*, *Gradual*, *Pontifical*, and *Ritual* in English, we may not refer to the *Kyriale* as the *Kyrial*.

Kyrie Eleison These words are the transliteration of the Greek phrase κύριε ἐλέησον, which means *Lord, have mercy*. The prayer *Kyrie eleison* (three times), *Christe eleison* (three times), *Kyrie eleison* (three times) is recited antiphonally at the beginning of the Mass; it is the remnant of a litany that was, in the old days, chanted in procession before the celebration of the Eucharist. Nowadays it has been shortened from the traditional nine-fold form to a six-fold form, because it was considered too complicated for the common people to keep track of whether they should reply *Kyrie eleison* or *Christe eleison*.

2. Hyginus Eugene Cardinale, *Orders of Knighthood, Awards and the Holy See*, ed. Peter Bander van Duren (Buckinghamshire, England: Van Duren Publishers, 1984); and Peter Bander van Duren, *The Cross on the Sword, A Supplement to Orders of Knighthood, Awards and the Holy See* (Buckinghamshire, England: Van Duren Publishers, 1987), respectively.

3. H. J. A. Sire, *The Knights of Malta* (New Haven, Conn.: Yale University Press, 1994).

Labarum The etymology of this word is unknown.

The monogram of Christ, painted upon the shields of his soldiers, displayed at the top of the military standards (*labarum*), soon stamped upon the coins, and reproduced in a thousand different ways, gave an unmistakable expression of the opinions of the emperor.[1]

Lapsed The Latin deponent verb *labor, labi, lapsus sum* means *to slip, to fall down*. The *lapsi* are people who have fallen away from the practice of the Catholic religion. People who are not lapsed were formerly called *stantes*, that is, those who stood firm.

Lateran The Latin noun *later, latĕris, m.*, means a *brick*, and from it was formed the name *Lateranus*, the god of the hearth, for hearths are made of bricks. *Lateranus* was also a Roman cognomen or family name, like Caesar, Cicero, Maro, and Flaccus. The Lateran family had a home on the Caelian Hill, which was given by Emperor Constantine to Pope Sylvester. The cathedral of Rome was then built on this spot and was consequently described as being *in Laterano*. A palace was built next to the cathedral and was for centuries the seat of the papacy. The palace burnt down during the absence of the popes in Avignon but was rebuilt by Sixtus V (1585–1590), under the supervision of Domenico Fontana. For many years, visitors could make a tour of the palace and visit the Sala della Conciliazione, where the Lateran Pacts of 1929 were signed, but this is no longer the

---

1. Louis Duchesne, *Early History of the Christian Church from Its Foundation to the End of the Fifth Century*, vol. 2 (London: John Murray, 1931), 48.

case, and the historical museum that was once lodged in the palace has been dissolved and its treasures moved elsewhere. The story of how the Lateran Basilica became the St. John Lateran Basilica is told by Gregorovius. After relating how the Lombard barbarians destroyed Monte Cassino around 577, he reports:

The unfortunate monks, however, found time to escape, and fled to Rome, bearing with them the book of the institution of their order, written by the hand of the saint. Pelagius gave them shelter near the Lateran basilica, and here they founded the first Benedictine monastery within the city. This they dedicated to the Evangelist and the Baptist, and, as they later undertook the liturgical services in the basilica, the church of Constantine received from the adjoining monastery the title of St. John Baptist.[2]

Lateran Pacts The Greek verb πήγνυμι means *to stick* or *fix in*. Related to it is the Latin verb *pango, pangere, panxi* with the same meaning. However, with third and fourth principal parts *pepigi, pactus* the verb means *to fix, settle, agree upon*. The related verb *paciscor, pacisci, pactus sum* means *to make a bargain* or *agreement*. From *pactus* comes the noun *pactum, -i, n.*, an *agreement, covenant*, or *treaty*.

The most famous concordats were those of 1929 with fascist Italy and 1933 with National Socialist Germany. The concordat with Italy was signed the same day as the treaty restoring the temporal power of the pope, which treaty, together with the accompanying financial agreement and the concordat, constituted the *Lateran Pacts*. By the Concordat with the German Reich, the Holy See obtained much that it had been unable to secure from the Imperial and Weimar governments, and Hitler acquired the prestige that naturally devolved upon a government that concluded an agreement with the Holy See. The willingness of the Holy See to conclude these agreements with now discredited totalitarian states has been a cause of complaint. Competent historians have weighed in on the matter. It is therefore recommendable to give the issue some attention.[3]

---

2. Ferdinand Gregorovius, *History of the City of Rome in the Middle Ages*, 2nd ed., trans. Mrs. Gustavus W. Hamilton (London, G. Bell & Sons, 1902), 2:20.

3. The following books have been consulted: David I. Kertzer, *Prisoner of the Vatican* (Boston: Houghton Mifflin, 2004); David I. Kertzer, *The Pope and Mussolini* (Oxford: Oxford University Press, 2014); Susan Zuccotti, *The Italians and the Holocaust: Persecution, Rescue, Survival* (New York: Basic Books, 1987); Susan Zuccotti, *Under His Very Windows: The Vatican and the Holocaust in Italy* (New Haven, Conn.: Yale University Press, 2000); Robert Katz, *Death in Rome* (New York: Macmillan, 1967); Robert Katz, *Black Sabbath* (London: Arthur Barker, 1969); Robert Katz, *The Battle for Rome* (New York: Simon & Schuster, 2003); Denis Mack Smith, *Garibaldi*, The Stratford Library (London:

1. The Lateran Pacts with Italy

The Lateran Pacts were the conventions of February 11, 1929, between the Holy See and the Kingdom of Italy whereby the Vatican City became an independent and sovereign state and the temporal power of the popes was restored after an interval of fifty-nine years. They were signed in the Lateran Palace, which accounts for their name. They were the accomplishment of Pius XI and Benito Mussolini. The association with Mussolini became an embarrassment because of his crimes, and it is a useful investigation to inquire how this arrangement came about.

What we today call *Italy* consisted in 1850 of six independent states and some northern territories, Milan and Venice, which were occupied by Austria-Hungary and had been incorporated into the Habsburg dominions. Italy was then, and had been since the creation, a mere geographical term, like Scandinavia. If you asked an Italian what he was, he would probably have replied, "Catholic," or, if pressed, "Neapolitan" or "Sicilian"; no one would have said "Italian." In the middle of the peninsula was the oldest country in Europe, the *Pontifical State* or *States of the Church*, of which the pope was king. It consisted of Lazio, Umbria, the Marches of Ancona, and the Romagna. The Pontifical State had its origins in the chaos of sixth-century Italy, where the forceful personality of Gregory the Great filled a vacuum in a manner that laid the foundation for eventual territorial sovereignty. Further steps towards territorial sovereignty occurred in the eighth century, when the iconoclastic policies of the Byzantine emperors further discredited the Greek regime in the eyes of the Italians. It is incorrect, I believe, to imagine that the temporal power of the popes is an anachronism in modern times and counterproductive to the mission of the Church. The fact that the temporal power of the popes was something desirable became clear in the First World War. After Italy entered the conflict on the side of the entente powers, the Prussian, Bavarian, and Austro-Hungarian envoys to the Holy See were compelled to leave Rome and settle in Switzerland, from which distant location they could hardly function. Thus, the sovereignty of the pope was violated, for

Hutchinson, 1957); Denis Mack Smith, *Mussolini: A Biography* (New York: Alfred A. Knopf, 1982); Denis Mack Smith, *Cavour: A Biography* (New York: Alfred A. Knopf, 1985); Denis Mack Smith, *Italy and Its Monarchy* (New Haven, Conn.: Yale University Press, 1989); Denis Mack Smith, *Mazzini* (New Haven, Conn.: Yale University Press, 1994); Christopher Hibbert, *Il Duce: The Life of Benito Mussolini* (Boston: Little, Brown, 1962); C. S. Forester, *Victor Emmanuel II and the Union of Italy* (London: Methuen, 1927).

the Holy See was not at war with Germany and Austria. By the time of the Second World War, the State of the Vatican City had been established, but events proved that, if anything, it was too small. When Italy entered the war on the side of Germany, the diplomats accredited to the Holy See from the Allied powers were compelled by the Italians to move into the Vatican City, where they operated from rooms in a building on the location of what is now called the Santa Marta Residence. This was certainly an improvement over the situation in World War I, but the crowded circumstances within the walls of the Vatican were most inconveniencing, and there were those who argued that that the temporal domain of the pope was too small, that he should have a corridor to the sea.

But it would seem that the following reforms are necessary. Firstly, the Lateran treaty will have to be replaced by a new one in which the Vatican State will receive an *international*, as distinct from an Italian, guarantee of its independence and inviolability. Under such a statute, the Papal territory would be enlarged to enable the Vatican City to possess its own electricity plant, telephone system, water supply, bakery, etc., as well as quarters for the Cardinals resident in Rome and the diplomatic corps accredited to the Vatican. The Papal State should also include an airport and a seaport at or near Ostia, with a corridor—or at least a private road or railway accessible to the outside world—connecting it with the Vatican. This too would be guaranteed internationally.[4]

Once again history demonstrated that the temporal power had much to recommend itself in times when Italy went to war.

To the south of the Papal States was the Kingdom of the Two Sicilies, that is, the united kingdoms of Naples and Sicily. This had been an independent state for a thousand years and was ruled by kings of the House of Bourbon. Northwest of the Papal States were the three duchies, the Duchy of Parma, the Duchy of Modena, and the Grand Duchy of Tuscany. The first of these was ruled by a prince of the House of Bourbon, the second by a prince of the House of Austria-Este, and the third by a prince of the House of Habsburg-Lorraine. Princes of Bourbon and Habsburg had acquired those territories by right of inheritance, as a result of marriages with the heirs of the native dynasties. To the northwest of the three duchies was the Kingdom of Sardinia, with its capital at Turin, ruled by the House of Savoy, the oldest royal house in Europe. Although called the Kingdom of *Sardinia*, the island of Sardinia was actually the least important part of

---

4. Anthony Rhodes, *The Vatican in the Age of the Dictators (1922–1945)* (New York: Holt, Rinehart, & Winston, 1973), 356.

its territory, which in addition consisted of French-speaking Savoy, the Riviera, and the Italian-speaking provinces of Piedmont and Liguria. Finally, Lombardy, with its capital Milan, and Venetia, with its capital Venice, were together called the Kingdom of Lombardy and Venetia under the direct government of the emperor Francis Joseph of Austria-Hungary. Milan and Venice had been independent states for centuries (in the case of Venice, formerly one of the great powers of Europe, for over a millennium), but Milan came under the Habsburgs in the sixteenth century, and Napoleon overthrew the Venetian Republic in 1797. When Napoleon was in turn overthrown in 1814, the Congress of Vienna did not want any more republics in Europe, so they did not restore its independence but instead assigned Venice as a spoil of victory to her neighbor Austria. It is essential to realize that as a result of the experiences of the French revolution, the early nineteenth century European governments had a fear of republics and would tolerate only one, Switzerland. Finally, South Tyrol (Bozen—Bolzano, Brixen—Bressanone, Meran—Merano, Trient—Trento) and the port of Trieste were considered part of Austria, although many Italians lived there.

These six states and Austrian provinces did not become Italy in the German way. In 1870, twenty-five sovereign German states, that is, four kingdoms, six grand duchies, five duchies, seven principalities, and three free cities, peacefully agreed to form a federation to be called the *German Empire*, with the king of Prussia as *German Emperor*. Austria was left out because the overwhelming majority of its population was non-German and its emperor was the direct successor of the Holy Roman Emperor, the temporal head of Catholic Christianity, and could not accept second place to the Protestant king of Prussia. Germany was thus united by mutual consent of the states involved, and each of the uniting states theoretically remained sovereign; the Kingdom of Bavaria, for example, continued to maintain separate diplomatic relations with Austria, Spain, Portugal, Belgium, and the Holy See. This was not the case with Italy.

Change had been set in motion by Napoleon, who dared to sweep the slate clean of the accumulated heritage of a thousand years and to start over; he abolished all the Italian states except Naples, where he merely replaced the Bourbon king with his own general, Marshal Murat. He made his son king of Rome in place of the pope, and united northern Italy first into a republic, the Cisalpine Republic, and then into a kingdom, the Kingdom of Italy, with himself as king. Many modifications were made in the Quirinale Palace in anticipation of his taking up residence there, but he never came. When he was finally overthrown at Waterloo and the *status quo ante*, with some exceptions (Austria annexed the Republic of Venice, and Sardinia took the Republic of Genoa) restored, the precedent had nevertheless been set to think big and start over.

The founding fathers of Italy were Giuseppe Mazzini (1805–1872), Giuseppe Garibaldi (1807–1882), Victor Emmanuel II, king of Sardinia (1820–1878), and Camillo Benso, Count Cavour (1810–1861). The first two were republicans; how then did united Italy end up being a kingdom?

Mazzini was born in Genoa, the son of a professor of medicine at the local university. He thought that Napoleon was correct to unite northern Italy, but he saw no reason why he should have stopped there; the whole peninsula should be united. He would have preferred a republic, but he was willing to accept a kingdom if that was the only way unification could be accomplished. Of the Italian kings, he thought that the pope was the obvious choice to be king of Italy, but since the pope was not interested, Mazzini was willing to accept, reluctantly, his own monarch, Charles Albert, the king of Sardinia, and after him, his son Victor Emmanuel II. However, those fellows did not trust republicans, and Mazzini was exiled and spent his life mostly in England, agitating for revolution in the various Italian states and living off money sent to him by his widowed mother.

Whereas Mazzini was a conspirator, Garibaldi was an adventurer. Garibaldi was born in Nice, at that time part of the Kingdom of Sardinia, which had developed over time from the French Duchy of Savoy. His father earned his living on the sea as a fisherman and a sailor. Garibaldi wanted to unite Italy by getting rid of the princes, including his own king, so he was condemned for treason and fled to South America, where he became a professional soldier meddling in wars that were none of his business, like Uruguay's war of independence from Argentina and the revolt of the southernmost Brazilian state of Rio Grande do Sul, which tried to secede from Brazil. Garibaldi imagined himself a freedom fighter. He was a republican, but he believed that the best form of government for Italy would be benign dictatorship.

Victor Emmanuel II, king of Sardinia, became the first king of united Italy. He managed it in conjunction with his Prime Minister Cavour, almost reluctantly, and mainly in order to get in control of the Italian unification movement before it became republican and the two of them became its victims.

The first movement towards Italian unification was precipitated by, of all people, the pope of the time, Pius IX, commonly called Pio Nono. Pio Nono is one of the five or ten most important popes of all time. People were fascinated by him. One could not be neutral when he was concerned; one had to take a stand either for or against him. He so entered the popular imagination that, like Bismarck and Napoleon, a pastry was named after him, the *pio nono*; it is a sort of jelly roll. He is also the only pope whose cologne, made from a private formula, is still for sale; we know precisely how he smelled. He was elected pope in 1846 and was the hero of the liberals. He granted a general amnesty for all political prisoners, such as the *carbonari* or revolutionary republicans, started negotiations toward a customs union of all the Italian states, and called for the Austrians to withdraw from those fortresses in the Pontifical State that they had occupied the better to keep down revolutionaries in those areas. Things, however, got out of hand when the Milanese rose in revolt against the Austrians, and Pio Nono refused to declare war against Austria; after all, he could not realistically be expected to wage war against the Catholic Austrians. The revolutionaries in Rome were disgusted, rose in revolt, and assassinated the pope's prime minister, Count Rossi, in the Palazzo della Cancelleria. Pio Nono then fled to Naples, and the revolutionaries proclaimed the end of the Pontifical State and the establishment of the Roman Republic. Mazzini and Garibaldi arrived to run it. It lasted for about a year, until Napoleon's nephew, Louis Napoleon, sent in troops to put it down, which they did after a famous siege. The reason Louis Napoleon did this was that he wanted to make himself emperor like his uncle (he was at the moment merely president), and to do this he needed the help of the Church, and what better way to deserve this than by restoring the States of the Church to the pope? Mazzini and Garibaldi escaped, and Pio Nono returned, never to be a liberal again. A famous souvenir of the French siege may be seen to this day in the Palazzo Colonna, a cannonball that landed on the staircase leading to the grand gallery, which has been left in place as a κτῆμα εἰς ἀεί.

One of the results of the commotions of 1848 was the emancipation of the Jews in the Kingdom of Sardinia. As the House of Savoy went from strength to strength in the next quarter century, the emancipation was extended to the territories they acquired. By comparison, it could still happen in the Pontifical State that if a Catholic housemaid should secretly baptize a sick Jewish child, the child would be removed from his parents' care by the Inquisition and brought up as a Catholic. This happened to the boy Edgardo Mortara in Bologna in 1858.[5]

Upon the revolt of the Milanese in 1848 against the Austrian occupation, northern Italian public opinion drove Carl Albert, king of Sardinia, to declare war against the Austrians. He was defeated in two major battles (Custozza and Novara) by the octogenarian Austrian general field marshal Johann Josef, Graf Radetzky, in honor of whose two victories over the Italians Josef Strauss the elder then wrote a famous march, now heard universally on New Year's Eve. Carl Albert was forced to abdicate in favor of his son, because his people were convinced that he had not waged the war competently. Thus, by the end of 1849, the Italian revolutionaries had suffered two disasters, at Rome and in Milan, but the process of Italian unification had been started. As a result of the disasters, a new prime minister came to power in Sardinia, Camillo Benso, Count Cavour.

Cavour decided that the republican revolutionaries like Mazzini and Garibaldi were dangerous, and he was in time persuaded that if there had to be any unification, it should only be by annexation of the other Italian states to the Kingdom of Sardinia. He realized that this would eventually lead to war with Austria, so in order to win international support, he adopted a policy of ingratiating himself with England and the France of Louis Napoleon, who had now succeeded in establishing himself as Emperor Napoleon III. Cavour did this by joining England and France in the Crimean War against Russia, although the Italians had no business there at all. As a result of involving his people in a war that did not concern them, Cavour won the support of Napoleon III, who agreed to join him, were he attacked, in a campaign to clip the wings of Austria and drive her forces out of Milan. As war broke out in late April, 1859, between the combined forces of France and Sardinia on one side and Austria on the other, the Grand Duke Leopold II abandoned Tuscany. After the Austrian defeat at Magenta (June 4), revolutions broke out in Parma and Modena, and the dukes fled. The Austrian garrison was withdrawn from the Pontifical territories of Emilia and Romagna, and as a result the papal government was overthrown in those places. Cavour sent in troops to occupy those areas in order to prevent the republicans from taking over. The Austrians then suffered a second defeat at Solferino (June 24). The emperor Napoleon had now accomplished his goal of putting an end to the supremacy of Austria in northern Italy; he did not intend to destroy the temporal

---

5. See David Kertzer, *The Kidnapping of Edgardo Mortara* (New York: Knopf, 1997).

power of the pope, an eventuality that would have enraged his Catholic subjects. He therefore concluded the Armistice of Villafranca with Francis Joseph (July 11). As a result of this peace, he received Lombardy (except for Mantua) from the Austrians, a territory that he immediately handed over to Victor Emmanuel. The other provisions of the treaty were never implemented (for Victor Emmanuel disclaimed all power to impose them), namely, the pope was to have been acknowledged as the head of an Italian confederation, the three dukes were to have been allowed to return to their states, and the government of the Pontifical State was to be reformed so as, for example, to prevent further incidents like the Mortara case. Instead, plebiscites were held in the three duchies, in Emilia, and in the Romagna; these resulted in 99% majorities in favor of annexation to Sardinia, and those territories were accordingly absorbed into the Sardinian state. The papal government was able to retain control over the Marches, Umbria, and the Patrimony of St. Peter. In return for the help of the French, Cavour ceded Savoy and Nice to France; this infuriated Garibaldi, who had been born in Nice.

At this point, it became clear that the unification of Italy was going to be accomplished at the expense of the temporal power of the popes. The Church thus became an opponent and a victim of the unification of Italy. A secondary victim of Italian unification was the pope's main ally in Europe, Francis Joseph, the grandson of the last Holy Roman Emperor, who ruled, as the national hymn said, *durch des Glaubens Stütze*.

In the spring of 1860, Garibaldi invaded Sicily with a revolutionary force of a thousand republicans to overthrow the Bourbon government there. After succeeding in this enterprise, he crossed over to the mainland in late summer and entered Naples on September 7. At this point Victor Emmanuel, who could not control Garibaldi, fearing that the revolutionary would proceed to overthrow the Pontifical government in Rome and complicate his relations with the emperor Napoleon, decided to intervene. For such an intervention he required a land route, and for this reason his army crossed the frontier into Umbria and the Marches, deposed by force the papal government in those provinces, and proceeded into Neapolitan territory to take control of the situation there. The papal army resisted at Castelfidardo in an attempt to prevent the fall of Ancona, but the Pontifical troops were defeated in the famous battle there on September 11.

Garibaldi, to avoid civil war, handed over his Neapolitan conquest to the king. A plebiscite was held, 99% of the southerners voted to join the

Kingdom of Sardinia, and Italy was now complete except for Rome, still under the pope, and Venice and South Tyrol, still under Austria. At this point it was considered recommendable to change the name of the country, and on March 17, 1861, the Kingdom of Italy was proclaimed, with Victor Emmanuel as first king. Cavour then died, and Victor Emmanuel was on his own. Garibaldi determined to complete the unification by adding the Patrimony of St. Peter and the Austrian province of Venetia to the new state, and landed in Calabria with an irregular force in the summer of 1862. Victor Emmanuel, in order not to lose control of the unification process, sent troops to head him off and defeated his revolutionaries at Aspromonte (August 29). By a convention of September 15, 1863, Napoleon III agreed to withdraw the French troops who were supporting the papal government in Rome in return for the Italians moving their capital from Turin to Florence, the implication being that Rome would be left to the pope. This arrangement fell apart in the fall of 1866, when Garibaldi made an unsuccessful invasion of the Patrimony that caused the emperor to send his troops back.

Just as Italy owed the acquisition of Milan to a foreigner, Napoleon III, so did it owe the acquisition of Venice to another foreigner, Bismarck. Prussia and Austria were in competition to be the leader of the Germans. Bismarck decided to go to war, and he planned a two front war against the Austrians. He would move in from the north, and the Italians would move in from the south. The Italians would receive Venice as their reward. Victor Emmanuel agreed. The war began, and the Italians were promptly defeated both on land and on sea. In the north, however, the Prussians prevailed and routed the Austrians at Königgrätz (July 3, 1866). The Austrians had to surrender, but they refused to hand over Venice to the Italians, whom they had defeated. Instead, they gave it to the French, who in turn handed it over to the Italians. A plebiscite was held, and the Venetians voted by a 99% majority to join Italy. Rome with the Patrimony of St. Peter was now the last holdout.

In the fall of 1867, Garibaldi made one final attempt to invade the remaining Pontifical territories and overthrow the papal government. He was, however, defeated at Mentana (November 3) by the pope's army, and the campaign ended in a fiasco.

In the late summer of 1870, war broke out between Prussia and France, and Napoleon had to withdraw his army from Rome in order to send it against the Germans. As soon as the French forces departed, Victor Emmanuel moved in under the pretext of protecting the pope from the revolutionaries. Rome fell on September 20, 1870, and the temporal power of the popes came to an end. A plebiscite was held, and 99% of the Romans voted to join Italy.

Italy was thus united by force; the Kingdom of Sardinia simply annihilated the other existing states. Sham plebiscites were held as window dressing. All officials in the new Italy, even the local authorities, were appointed by the central government. There was a parliament, but only 5% of the people had the suffrage; to vote one had to be male, literate, and the owner of a certain amount of property. One of the despoiled sovereigns was the pope, from whom the new capital city of Rome and the whole Pontifical State had been wrested by brute force. Pio Nono refused to recognize the new state. He excommunicated the king and issued a decree forbidding Catholics to vote in the elections or to serve in governmental positions. Since 99% of Italians were Catholics, at least nominally, only liberals, socialists, anticlericals, and similar types took part in running the country. No Catholic political party could be established in Italy to play the part that the Center Party played in Germany. Church and state were separated. The Church viewed the unification as a sacrilegious takeover by unbelievers. Wilfrid Ward, who was a seminarian in Rome in 1877–1878, wrote:

> We looked upon the king as simply a victorious brigand.... We regarded Victor Emmanuel as outside the pale of civilization, as a pretender and without any mitigating hereditary claim.[6]

Many people, however, were happy to see education and marriage taken out of the hands of the Church. Monasteries and convents, considered absurdities in modern times, were confiscated.

The politicians who ran the new Italy decided to seek validation by amassing colonies like the other European powers. There was not much left to be taken. The Italians moved in on Eritrea and Somalia. They then set their criminal eyes on the adjacent empire of Ethiopia. Unexpectedly, they were routed and their army almost wiped out by the Ethiopians in the battle of Adowa in 1896, a great national calamity. With lesson unlearned, they next set their eyes on the Ottoman province of Libya, a great desert. They invaded and were defeated, but fortunately for them, war

6. Maisie Ward, *The Wilfrid Wards and the Transition*, vol. 1, *The Nineteenth Century* (New York: Sheed & Ward, 1934), 56.

broke out in the Balkans, and the Turks had to withdraw their forces from Libya to protect Constantinople, so Libya became Italian, though in name only, because there were constant insurrections.

The Italian colonies were nothing but trouble. They never paid for themselves and became bottomless pits into which the Italian state threw money. The Italian people preferred to emigrate to Boston and New York rather than to Benghazi and Mogadishu.

The repeated defeats that the Italian armed forces suffered were due to poor military leadership and poor equipment, the result of rampant corruption.

At this point, World War I broke out. The Italians determined to enter on the winning side. If they fought against Austria, they planned to take Trent and the eastern coast of the Adriatic from Trieste down to Greece. If they fought against France, they hoped to get Savoy and Nice back as well as take over Corsica, Tunisia, and Algeria. If the British came in on the side of the French, they intended to occupy Malta. The question was, which side to join? By May 24, 1915, they had decided that Austria was a loser, so on that day they came in on the side of the Entente and declared war on Austria.

The Italians suffered a massive defeat at Caporetto in the autumn of 1917, and the Austrians advanced almost to Venice. The British and French sent in troops to shore up the Italians, and the Austrian progress was stopped. In September, 1918, as Austria fell apart, the Italians attacked again, and this time they were victorious; Austria gave up on November 4.

The results of the war were a disaster for Italy. They thought that they would get the South Tyrol and a good deal of Slovenia, Croatia, Dalmatia, Bosnia, Montenegro, Albania, and many Greek islands and German colonies. Instead, they received only the South Tyrol and some additional territory in the northeast, including Trieste. The government was seen to have bungled everything, and then the veterans came back to find no jobs, and, to make it worse, most of them were unqualified to vote. Then appeared Mussolini.

Mussolini was the son of an anticlerical Socialist blacksmith father and a pious schoolteacher mother. He was born in the Romagna, part of the former Pontifical State. He learned as a boy that he could get his way by bullying the other children, and he was twice expelled from school for shanking other students. He became a school teacher and a left-wing journalist. He was not a dunce and taught himself to speak French, German, and English; later in life he never used a translator when dealing with diplomats from those countries. To use a translator he considered a humiliating indication of stupidity. This caused problems during World War II, when Hitler often talked faster than Mussolini could follow. He joined the Socialist Party and rose to be the editor of their newspaper *Avanti!* The Socialists had opposed foreign entanglements, and Mussolini fled to Switzerland to avoid the draft when the Libyan War started. By 1914 he had changed his mind, and he broke with the Socialists because he was in favor of joining in the world war, believing that if Italy stayed on the sidelines, it would become a cipher in the international arena. He served and was wounded, and when he returned to Italy, he founded the Fascist Party, named for the local chapters which were called *fasci* (bundles of rods, or groups of people) in Italian. He was the party's leader or *Duce*. This party wanted to restore order by beating up the Socialists, whom they condemned as unpatriotic for opposing the World War and for calling strikes in the factories and thereby upsetting the economy. The moneyed classes donated generously to the Fascists for taking a stand on this latter issue. One incompetent government succeeded another. Government incompetence is a proverb in Italy; I remember times when there would not be enough coins minted for change to be made. In 1922, in the general chaos, Mussolini, although he controlled only a few seats in the Parliament, announced that he would march on Rome, and he was appointed Prime Minister by the king before he could do so; the Liberals agreed because their many factions could not unite behind one of their own. The march took place anyway and served to announce that there was a new king in Israel.

Order was restored, and those who refused to obey were beaten up. A new law was passed stipulating that whatever party got the most votes in the next election would get 75% of the seats. The popular demand for law and order was so great that the Fascists got the most votes and so took over Parliament. The Socialist leader Matteotti was assassinated, and the opposition deputies seceded from Parliament and were then ignored. It was decreed that the Fascist Party hymn *Giovinezza* should be played immediately after the National Anthem at all events. Toscanini refused to do so at La Scala, so he was roughly handled and left the country.

Mussolini's style of government was to take over many ministries for himself; in addition to prime minister he was also at various times minister of war, minister for the army, minister for the navy, minister for the air force, and so on. Since he could not possibly know what was going on in so many departments, everything depended on his subordinates, who were usually scoundrels whom he could blackmail. They told him what he wanted to hear, and when Italy went to war, all branches of the armed forces were unprepared.

Having become dictator, Mussolini next patched up the feud with the Church. For fifty-nine years, the popes had condemned the Kingdom of Italy as a criminal country, but Pope Pius XI, who began his reign in 1922, saw that the restoration of the Pontifical State was a pipe-dream and so was open to a compromise. Mussolini grasped the opportunity to remove the thorn in the side of the state. He showed good will by putting a crucifix in every courtroom and classroom, and in 1929 he and the greatest of papal secretaries of state, Cardinal Gasparri, signed a peace treaty as part of the Lateran Pacts of February 11, 1929. Italy gave the pope a large sum of money in compensation for the loss of the Papal States. Italy had previously been a secular state, but now the Roman Catholic religion was declared to be the state religion. Religious education in the Catholic faith was introduced into the schools, and all questions regarding marriage were to be decided by Church tribunals. The pope was recognized as the sovereign head of a state called *Vatican City,* which consisted of the area enclosed by the ninth-century Vatican walls and the Bernini Colonnade. In return, the pope recognized Italy united under the Royal House of Savoy with Rome as its capital. This treaty was widely popular in Italy, and Mussolini started to build a great highway in Rome leading to St. Peter's Basilica; he called it *Reconciliation Street.* With the Lateran Pacts, the Church received more than it could ever have received from the secular Italian state in the period before 1922. Mussolini acquired the prestige of having solved the "Roman Question" in a manner satisfactory to both sides and was acclaimed as one of the greatest statesmen of all times.

Mussolini next determined to get revenge on Ethiopia for the defeat and humiliation of 1896. He invaded Ethiopia and made it a colony. Italy was declared an empire, and the king was declared emperor of Ethiopia. England and France condemned this act of aggression and got the League of Nations to impose sanctions on Italy, but Hitler, who admired Mussolini, applauded it, so Mussolini tilted towards Germany, which he had up to then opposed. When Hitler tried to take over Austria in 1934, Mussolini had mobilized and prevented it. Now, he did nothing to prevent the *Anschluss* of 1938.

When civil war broke out in Spain in 1936, Mussolini intervened on the side of Franco, who also received help from Hitler. The intervention was popular in Italy, because the republicans, against whom Franco was rebelling, were anticlericals and had communist support. During this period Germany surpassed Italy in power, and Mussolini began to take second place to Hitler. He started copying the Germans, although he disliked it if anyone pointed that out.

A direct result of the German alliance was Mussolini's introduction of anti-Semitic legislation in 1938. Fifty thousand Jews lived in Italy in 1938, something like one-half of one percent of the population. They were completely assimilated; unlike in Poland, one could not tell that someone was a Jew by the way he dressed or spoke. The Jews had been in Italy for two thousand years; Suetonius tells of how the emperor Claudius rebuked them when people who lived next to their synagogues complained that they were making too much noise arguing about some Chrestus.

Iudaeos impulsore Chresto assidue tumultuantis Roma expulit. (*Divus Claudius*, 25)

He expelled the Jews from Rome, for, at the instigation of Chrestus, they were upsetting public order.

Of all Italians they were the most enthusiastic supporters of the royal government, since they had benefitted the most from the secular state introduced at the unification. The Jews had become equal citizens for the first time and were the most grateful and loyal subjects of the House of Savoy. They joined the Fascist Party in the same proportion as other Italians. They remained loyal despite the Lateran Pacts and the accommodation with Hitler, but now Mussolini sacrificed them. Jews were no longer allowed to practice most professions except among their own kind. Jews were prohibited from marrying Catholics, and if Jews converted to the Catholic religion, they and their children were still considered Jews. This violated the Concordat with the Holy See, according to which the Catholic Church was in charge of marriage. For the Church, a converted Jew was just as much a Catholic as any other baptized person. This aspect of the racial laws Pius XI protested, but Mussolini replied that in the main his policy was no different from that of the popes in the times of the Papal States. Things were progressing poorly when the pope suddenly died when he was at the point of provoking a major confrontation. His successor, Pius XII, was scarcely elected when, in a matter of months, World War II broke out. It is important to note that despite all the discrimination, no

Italian Jew was physically harmed or put into a camp until the Germans occupied most of the country in September 1943. In fact, the parents of one of my teachers, German Jews, escaped to the United States through the port of Genoa in April 1940. The family of a friend of mine, Austrian Jews, escaped through the port of Trieste after the Anschluss of 1938. On the other hand, after September 1943 the Jews suffered unspeakable enormities under the German occupation and the Salò regime. The history of the Italian Jews in this period is the subject of books by Robert Katz, Daniel Kertzer, Primo Levi, and Susan Zuccotti.

Mussolini remained neutral until June 1940, when he decided to enter the war and attacked France. At the end of that year he attacked Greece without consulting Hitler, and the result was a disaster. The Greeks defeated the Italians, and Hitler postponed Operation Barbarossa and rescued the Italians before the British should enter the Balkans and push the Italians into the sea. At the same time, the Italians lost Somalia, Eritrea, and Ethiopia to the British. Hitler did not rescue him there, because the Germans had no interest in Somalia. Hitler had to intervene, however, when the British pushed into Libya and occupied half that colony. If they finished the job and drove the Italians out entirely, they would be able to invade Italy from the south and turn Hitler's flank. So, he sent Rommel with the Afrika Korps, and that delayed defeat for a year and a half.

Mussolini's entry into the War was a disaster for Hitler. It involved him in places where he had not planned to get involved and delayed his attack on the Soviet Union by a month, which might have made a difference.

By the summer of 1943, the allies had driven the Axis out of Africa, had occupied Sicily, and on July 18 they bombed Rome. This came as a shock to the Italians, who thought that the presence of the pope in Rome made the city inviolable. The presence of the pope meant nothing to the Americans and British, who flattened the San Lorenzo neighborhood, causing thousands of casualties and levelling the ancient Basilica of St. Lawrence, one of the seven most important churches of Rome. The king arrested Mussolini on July 25, 1943, and on September 8 the Italians surrendered unconditionally to the Allies. Hitler, who was in irrational awe of Mussolini, sent Otto Skorzeny to rescue him and then invaded and occupied most of the country. He set up Mussolini as the figurehead *Duce* of an Italian republic. Mussolini henceforth had no power at all. Fifteen percent of the Jews were shot or shipped to Auschwitz and gassed; the eighty-five percent who survived was the highest percentage in any occupied country. Most were hidden by fellow Italians. When the war ended, Mussolini was captured by partisans, shot, and hung upside down by the ankles from a hook at a gas station in downtown Milan.

Life in the Vatican City state during the Second World War may be studied in the pages of Owen Chadwick, who edited the diary of Francis D'Arcy Godolphin Osborne, British minister to the Holy See. The relationship between the Holy See and the Kingdom of Italy is the subject of recent books by Professor David Kertzer of Brown University, who became famous as the author of the definitive study of the Mortara case. The personality of Pius XI, the most important pope of the twentieth century, may be glimpsed in the memoirs of his secretary, Carlo Confalonieri,[7] and in the memoirs of his chamberlain, Mario Nasalli Rocca di Corneliano,[8] both of which have been translated into English.

The German Rolf Hochhuth wrote a play entitled *Der Stellvertreter—The Deputy*—that opened a hornets' nest in 1963; the author claimed that Pius XII was blameworthily silent when the Germans proceeded against the Jews during the Hitler times. The issue is the subject of several books, one of the most recent being *Under His Very Windows* by Susan Zuccotti. In defense of Pius it might by pointed out that one wrong word from him and he would have destroyed himself, everyone around him, and two-thirds of the art in the world. It is also not always remembered that the greatest enemy of the Catholic Church at that time was not Hitler, but Stalin, who was an ally of the United Kingdom and the United States.

2. The Concordat with Germany

The Concordat between the Holy See and the German Reich signed on July 20, 1933 in the Vatican Palace was actually the fourth concordat between the Holy See and a German government within ten years; concordats had previously been signed with the Länder of Bavaria (1924), Prussia (1929), and Baden (1932). The position of Catholics in Germany and of their Center Party was significantly better in the Weimar Republic than it had been during the Imperial regime.[9] When the German Reich

---

7. Carlo Confalonieri, *Pius XI: A Close-Up*, trans. Regis N. Barwig (Altadena, Calif.: Benziger Sisters, 1975).

8. Mario Nasalli Rocca di Corneliano, *Accanto ai Papi* (Vatican City: Libreria Editrice Vaticana, 1976).

9. The best source for the relations between the Holy See and Germany in the period 1918–1933

was proclaimed in 1871, each of the component states retained for itself the determination of all matters pertaining to religion. Upon the fall of the Imperial and Royal House of Hohenzollern, this arrangement persisted. This made possible the Vatican's signing of concordats with Bavaria, Prussia, and Baden at the same time that negotiations were underway for a *Reichskonkordat* for the whole Republic. The settlement after the World War had resulted in French and Belgian occupation of territories on the left bank of the Rhine (and eventually even of the Ruhr on the right bank); the German side wanted to ensure that only loyal Germans were appointed bishops and pastors in these places, not separatist or pro-French clergymen. They also wanted to prevent any portion of these territories from being detached from the German dioceses to which they belonged. Similar problems arose with the establishment of the new states of Czechoslovakia, Lithuania, Poland, and the Free City of Danzig in the east; portions of the diocese of Breslau, for example, were now in Czechoslovakia and Poland. The main objectives of the Holy See were to vindicate for itself the sole appointment of bishops and to ensure the teaching of the Catholic religion in the schools.

In the Bavarian Concordat of 1924, the teaching of the Catholic religion was made compulsory in the primary schools, and the privilege of the former kings of Bavaria to appoint bishops was declared not to devolve upon the new republican government; the Holy See would in the future make all such appointments. In return, the Bavarians, whose Diocese of Speyer in the Palatinate contained a portion of the Saarland that the French wanted to detach from the Reich, were assured that the boundaries of the Bavarian dioceses were not to be modified and that only loyal Germans would be appointed to head those sees. One of my late teachers, who grew up in the Rhenish Palatinate, went to this religious instruction as a child, though he was a Jew. When some of his father's friends asked him why he did not apply for an exemption to extricate his son from this situation, the father replied, "They won't hurt him." In his old age, my teacher enjoyed telling the stories of the saints that he had learned, that of Saint Agnes being his favorite. Though a rabbi, he kept pictures

is Stewart A. Stehlin, *Weimar and the Vatican 1919–1933* (Princeton, N.J.: Princeton University Press, 1983). Not to be ignored are the following important works: Gordon Zahn, *German Catholics and Hitler's Wars* (New York: Sheed & Ward, 1962); Saul Friedländer, *Pius XII and the Third Reich: A Documentation* (New York: Alfred A. Knopf, 1966); Guenter Lewy, *The Catholic Church and Nazi Germany* (New York: McGraw-Hill, 1964); John F. Morley, *Vatican Diplomacy and the Jews during the Holocaust 1939–1943* (New York: KTAV Publishing House, 1980).

of the village priest and the village nuns in his house until he died at 87.

In the Prussian Concordat of 1929, the whole issue of the Catholic Church and education was left out, because, had the agreement contained an article authorizing the involvement of the Catholic Church in education, it would not have passed the Prussian Landtag. The Holy See further conceded to the cathedral chapter the election of a diocesan bishop from a list previously approved by Rome; the Prussian government was allowed to veto any candidate whose political activities it considered unacceptable. The Prussians obtained the concession that the Holy See would safeguard the religious rights of German populations now under foreign rule; for example, Germans would not be required to go to confession in Polish, and portions of German dioceses now in Poland would not be incorporated into Polish dioceses.

The former Grand Duchy of Baden was co-extensive with the Archdiocese of Freiburg im Breisgau. Catholics amounted to 60 percent of the population. In the Concordat of 1932, the teaching of the Catholic religion was made compulsory in the primary and secondary schools. Only German citizens who had studied at German universities were to be appointed archbishop, auxiliary bishop, member of the cathedral chapter, or instructor in the seminary. Upon the vacancy of the archiepiscopal see, the Holy See was to present a *terna* of candidates to the chapter, which was to elect one of them. The Holy See was to compose its *terna* after taking note of lists of recommendable candidates submitted to it by the chapter and annually by the previous archbishop. The Holy See would confirm the chapter's choice after ascertaining from the government of the Free State that it had no objection of a political nature to the elected candidate.

The National Socialist Party had opposed the three above-mentioned concordats, and upon Hitler's assumption of power on January 30, 1933, it was uncertain whether he would continue the negotiations for a *Reichskonkordat* that had been conducted off and on during the previous fourteen years. However, Hitler wished to benefit from the prestige that would follow from his concluding a treaty with the Holy See, the main stumbling block to which in the past had been lack of agreement on the place of the Catholic Church in education. Protestants and Socialists in the Reichstag and the Prussian Landtag would never have approved the teaching of the Catholic religion in the public schools by instructors authorized by the Church; however, by the *Ermächtigungsgesetz* of March 24, 1933, Hitler did not need parliamentary sanction for his acts, and he determined to give the Church what it most wanted in return for the benefit that an agreement with such a respected personality as the Roman pontiff would bring to his regime. He also wanted to obtain from the Holy See the exclusion of priests from politics, for Catholic priests were most conspicuous in the ranks of the Center Party, which he wanted to eliminate without protests from Rome. The Holy See, on the other hand, was anxious to obtain the protection of an internationally recognized treaty while the opportunity was there, in view of the previous unfavorable attitude of the National Socialist movement to the Catholic religion. The Concordat was therefore signed on July 20, 1933, each side getting what it wanted most.

Hitler's government was still an unknown quantity; his methods and ideology were viewed at best with suspicion and at worst with condemnation by foreign governments and many people within Germany. He needed recognition for his regime as soon as possible, particularly from such a symbol of moral authority as the Holy See. Such recognition could remove the last bit of reluctance on the part of Catholics at home to endorse his regime and could bolster the diplomatic standing of his government by trading on the moral prestige of the Papacy, which by negotiating with Germany would recognize the new government and by implication show that it was worthy of trust. A treaty which could accomplish this quickly was worth large concessions.

For the Holy See, the concordat looked on paper like a great victory, for it granted Rome many of the concessions that had evaded the Church in other treaties. But Hitler was not interested in the details of what had been granted, and he dismissed any objection that the accord had been too generous. What he desired was to use the document for its political effect at home and abroad; the rest was unimportant and could be disregarded, reinterpreted, or changed later.[10]

Latin The region around Rome was in ancient times called *Latium*, and from this noun was formed the adjective *Latinus* with the meaning *belonging to Latium*, whence we have our word *Latin*. Lewis and Short connect *Latium* with *lătus, lăteris, n.*, which means *side, coast*. The Latin language was the language of the Roman Empire and, until recently, the language in which the liturgy and business of the Western Church was conducted. Latin replaced Greek as the language of the Roman Church by the middle of the third century. Because of the collapse of classical studies, the number of educated people who can function in Latin is infinitesimal, even in the Catholic Church. The top man in charge of Latin at the Holy

---

10. Stewart A. Stehlin, *Weimar and the Vatican 1919–1933* (Princeton, N.J.: Princeton University Press, 1983), 436, 440.

See used to be called the *Secretary of Briefs to Princes*. The preeminent such secretary in the Church of Rome during the twentieth century was Antonio Bacci, whose book *Vocabolario Italiano-Latino delle Parole Moderne e Difficili a Tradurre* is indispensable; examples of his compositions may be found in *Inscriptiones, Orationes, Epistulae.*[11]

I thus began to wonder whether it would be useful and timely to compose an Italian-Latin dictionary of modern words. The work was not easy; however, it appeared necessary, especially for me, for which it was an indispensable tool of work. It was first necessary for me to brush up by reading all the Latin classics, even those of the Christian period; then I went on to the humanists, the epigraphists, and finally that most rich mine of Latinity, the *Acta Leonis*.

Before beginning, I asked the advice of the Holy Father, Pius XII, who not only encouraged me to undertake the work, but also told me that right from that moment on, he would be blessing my undertaking.

The fourth edition of this *Italian-Latin Dictionary of Modern and Difficult-to-Translate Words* appeared in 1963; it was published by *Editrice Studium* of Rome and consisted of 846 pages, each with two columns, on which about 12,000 words were considered and translations proposed. It was also enriched with various modern terms which had been collected and examined by my gallant colleagues of *Latinitas, Palaestra Latina*, and other similar publications during the last ten years. A long time ago, the humanists worked worthily to enlarge the domain of Latin to help it adapt to modern requirements and new needs. Writers of inscriptions worked to the same end, and among them S. A. Morcelli is worthy of special mention, for he produced the famous *Morcelli Lexicon of Inscriptions*, which was published by Filippo Schiassi. In more recent times, other works, of lesser value, have been completed, all, however, worthy of praise for the noble and useful goal which motivated their authors.

I don't pretend that my *Dictionary* is without defects, gaps, or inevitable omissions; for this very reason I tried, as my friends and competent scholars advised, to perfect and enrich it more and more. One critic complained that there were occasionally exceptionally long circumlocutions. That's for sure, but one can't always translate new words and phrases by just one word, unless one wants to fall into the Latin style of Folengo, as Renzo has done. Circumlocutions can often be inserted into a sentence in such a clear, natural, and unobtrusive manner that all ponderousness and prolixity are removed. It's a question of knowing how to do it, and in any case, the *Dictionary* cannot teach or suggest everything. It would be quite something if one could write good Latin just by having a dictionary in one's hand.

---

11. See Antonio Bacci, *Vocabolario Italiano-Latino delle Parole Moderne e Difficili a Tradurre* (Rome: Editrice Studium, 1963); also idem, *Inscriptiones, Orationes, Epistulae*, 3rd ed. (Rome: Editrice Studium, 1954)

Horace, in his *Ars Poetica*, not only allows poets to introduce prudently, when necessary, new words, which derive, with a slight deviation (*parce detorta*) from a Grecian source, but also advises them to join words together in order to render new ideas.

> Dixeris, egregie, notum si callida verbum
> Reddiderit iunctura novum.[12]

> A skillful arrangement may be able
> To give a new air and cast to old words.

This is what I tried to do, and it is not for me to judge whether or not I succeeded. In any case, I can say that this book of mine, which required the most exhausting labor, has had a good press and has been read far and wide.[13]

In his memoirs Bacci tells the story of how his predecessor as secretary of briefs to princes, Nicola Sebastiani, helplessly suffered the indignity of having his name declined incorrectly by the celebrant of his funeral Mass.[14] After Bacci may be mentioned the abbot Karl Egger of the Vatican's *Latinitas* foundation, whose valuable works *Lexicon Nominum Virorum et Mulierum* and *Lexicon Nominum Locorum* are a source of joy to the scholar.[15] Pius X, in his letter of July 10, 1912, to Archbishop Dubois of Bourges, directed that the Roman pronunciation of Latin be used in the Catholic Church.[16] The amount of learning required to celebrate the Latin Mass is no longer available in the education offered by the American public school system.

Luther himself, in his *Formulae Missae* of 1523, prescribed a form of the Mass and Vespers in Latin for the churches of Wittenberg and Zwickau, a liturgy that persisted in some places until the eighteenth century. Of course, he produced in 1526 a vernacular German Mass for use in parish churches, but he later wrote:

Now there are three different kinds of Divine Service. [I] The first, in Latin; which we published lately, called the Formula Missae. This I do not want to have set aside or changed; but, as we have hitherto kept it, so should we be still free to use

---

12. Horace, *Ars Poetica*, 47.

13. Antonio Bacci, *Con il Latino a Servizio di Quattro Papi* (Rome: Editrice Studium, 1964). I have translated from section 3 of chapter 3.

14. Ibid., chapter 2, section 2.

15. See Karl Egger, *Lexicon Nominum Virorum et Mulierum*, 2nd ed. (Rome: Editrice Studium, 1963); and idem, *Lexicon Nominum Locorum* (Vatican City: Libreria Editrice Vaticana, 1977), with a supplement issued in 1985.

16. *Acta Apostolicae Sedis*, Annus IV, vol. 4, no. 17, pp. 577–78.

it where and when we please, or as occasion requires. I do not want in anywise to let the Latin tongue disappear out of Divine Service; for I am so deeply concerned for the young. If it lay in my power, and the Greek and Hebrew tongues were as familiar to us as the Latin, and possessed as great a store of fine music and song as the Latin does, Mass should be held and there should be singing and reading, on alternate Sundays in all four languages—German, Latin, Greek and Hebrew. I am by no means of one mind with those who set all their store by one language.[17]

The chief masterpiece of the Latin language is the *Aeneid* of Vergil. The most beautiful translation of this poem into English was by John Dryden (1631–1700), a Catholic.

> Arma, virumque cano, Troiae qui primus ab oris
> Italiam, fato profugus, Laviniaque venit
> Litora; multum ille et terris iactatus et alto,
> Vi superum, saevae memorem Junonis ob iram:
> Multa quoque et bello passus, dum conderet urbem,
> Inferretque Deos Latio: genus unde Latinum,
> Albanique patres, atque altae moenia Romae.[18]

> Arms and the Man I sing, who, forc'd by Fate,
> And haughty Juno's unrelenting Hate;
> Expell'd and exil'd, left the Trojan Shoar;
> Long Labours, both by Sea and Land he bore;
> And in the doubtful War, before he won
> The Latian Realm, and built the destin'd Town:
> His native Gods restor'd to Rites divine,
> And settl'd sure Succession in his Line:
> From whence the Race of Alban Fathers come,
> And the long Glories of Majestick Rome.

As for the value of Dryden's Vergil as a work of art, the opinion of Dr. Johnson, from his *Life of Dryden*, is to be accepted, when he wrote that the reason for its success was that it met the following criterion:

Works of imagination excel by their allurement and delight; by their power of attracting and detaining the attention. That book is good in vain, which the reader throws away. He only is the master, whose pages are perused with eagerness, and

---

17. B. J. Kidd, ed., *Documents Illustrative of the Continental Reformation* (Oxford: Clarendon Press, 1911), 195. Available online at https://www.questia.com/read/102387728/documents-illustrative-of-the-continental-reformation.

18. *Publii Virgilii Maronis Bucolica, Georgica, et Aeneis* (Birmingham: Baskerville, 1757), 104.

in hope of new pleasure are perused again; and whose conclusion is perceived with an eye of sorrow, such as the traveller casts upon departing day.[19]

Episodes from the *Aeneid* were painted by Pietro da Cortona in the gallery of the Palazzo Pamphili in Piazza Navona, the residence built by Girolamo Rainaldi for Olimpia Maidalchini, sister-in-law of Innocent X. During the reign of Leo XIII, this palace was leased by Francis Augustus MacNutt, the first American chamberlain at the papal court, whose accounts of the receptions held there for the black nobility of Rome may be studied in the pages of his memoirs.[20]

When Pius XI gave the inaugural broadcast at the Vatican Radio in 1931, he addressed the world in Latin. Today, such an event would be in Italian.

Latrocinium Ephesinum The Greek noun λάτρις, λάτριος, ὁ and ἡ, means a *hired servant*, and the related Latin noun *latro, latronis, m.*, had originally the same meaning, which was later expanded to include that of *freebooter* or *thief*. The related first declension deponent verb *latrocinor* meant *to serve as a mercenary, to be a robber*, and the noun *latrocinium* meant *mercenary service, highway robbery*, a *band of robbers*.

In the year 449, the emperor Theodosius II summoned a council, intended to be ecumenical, to review the condemnation of the speculations of the Archimandrite Eutyches by Flavian, patriarch of Constantinople. The council met at Ephesus under the presidency of Diodorus, patriarch of Constantinople, whose irregular management of affairs caused an uproar. The council's decisions were reversed at the Council of Chalcedon two years later. According to Duchesne, the name of *Robber Synod* was given to this Council by Pope Leo the Great.[21] A good summary account of the Robber Council of Ephesus was written by John Henry Newman.[22]

Lauda Sion Salvatorem Thomas Aquinas composed this sequence for the Feast of Corpus Christi. It is a great example of a hymn with intellectual content.

---

19. Samuel Johnson, *Lives of the Most Eminent English Poets; with Critical Observations on Their Works* (London, 1781), 2:173.

20. *A Papal Chamberlain: The Personal Chronicle of Francis Augustus MacNutt* (London: Longmans, Green, 1936).

21. Louis Duchesne, *Early History of the Christian Church from Its Foundation to the End of the Fifth Century*, vol. 3 (London: John Murray, 1924), 313n3.

22. John Henry Cardinal Newman, "Trials of Theodoret," in *Historical Sketches*, vol. 2 (London: Longmans, Green, 1917), 350–52.

Lauda, Sion, Salvatorem,
Lauda ducem et pastorem,
In hymnis et canticis.

Quantum potes, tantum aude,
Quia maior omni laude,
Nec laudare sufficis.

Laudis thema specialis,
Panis vivus et vitalis,
Hodie proponitur.

Quem in sacrae mensa cenae,
Turbae fratrum duodenae,
Datum non ambigitur.

Sit laus plena, sit sonora,
Sit iucunda, sit decora,
Mentis iubilatio.

Dies enim solemnis agitur,
In qua mensae prima recolitur
Huius institutio.

In hac mensa novi Regis
Novum Pascha novae legis,
Phase vetus terminat.

Vetustatem novitas,
Umbram fugat veritas,
Noctem lux eliminat.

Quod in cena Christus gessit,
Faciendum hoc expressit
In sui memoriam.

Docti sacris institutis,
Panem, vinum in salutis
Consecramus hostiam.

Dogma datur Christianis,
Quod in carnem transit panis,
Et vinum in sanguinem.

Quod non capis, quod non vides,
Animosa firmat fides,
Praeter rerum ordinem.

Sub diversis speciebus,
Signis tantum, et non rebus,
Latent res eximiae.

Caro cibus, sanguis potus,
Manet tamen Christus totus,
Sub utraque specie.

A sumente non concisus,
Non confractus, non divisus,
Integer accipitur.

Sumit unus, sumunt mille,
Quantum isti, tantum ille,
Nec sumptus consumitur.

Sumunt boni, sumunt mali,
Sorte tamen inaequali,
Vitae vel interitus.

Mors est malis, vita bonis,
Vide paris sumptionis
Quam sit dispar exitus.

Fracto demum sacramento,
Ne vacilles, sed memento,
Tantum esse sub fragmento,
Quantum toto tegitur.

Nulla rei fit scissura,
Signi tantum fit fractura,
Qua nec status, nec statura,
Signati minuitur.

Ecce panis Angelorum,
Factus cibus viatorum,
Vere panis filiorum,
Non mittendus canibus.

In figuris praesignatur,
Cum Isaac immolatur,
Agnus paschae deputatur,
Datur manna patribus.

Bone pastor, panis vere,
Jesu, nostri miserere;
Tu nos pasce, nos tuere,
Tu nos bona fac videre
In terra viventium.

Tu, qui cuncta scis et vales,
Qui nos pascis hic mortales,
Tuos ibi commensales,
Coheredes et sodales
Fac sanctorum civium.

The best English translation is by Edward Caswall (1814–1878):

Sion, lift thy voice and sing:
Praise thy Savior and thy King;
Praise with hymns thy Shepherd true:
Dare thy most to praise him well;
For he doth all praise excel;
None can ever reach his due.

Special theme of praise is thine,
That true living bread divine,
That life-giving flesh adored,
Which the brethren twelve received,
As most faithfully believed,
At the supper of the Lord.

Let the chant be loud and high;
Sweet and tranquil be the joy
Felt today in every breast;
On this festival divine
Which recounts the origin
Of the glorious Eucharist.

At this table of the King,
Our new paschal offering
Brings to end the olden rite;
Here, for empty shadows fled,
Is reality instead;
Here, instead of darkness, light.

His own act, at supper seated,
Christ ordained to be repeated,
In his memory divine;
Wherefore now, with adoration,
We the host of our salvation
Consecrate from bread and wine.

Hear what holy Church maintaineth,
That the bread its substance changeth
Into Flesh, the wine to Blood.
Doth it pass thy comprehending?
Faith, the law of sight transcending,
Leaps to things not understood.

Here in outward signs are hidden
Priceless things, to sense forbidden;
Signs, not things, are all we see:—
Flesh from bread, and Blood from wine;
Yet is Christ in either sign,
All entire confessed to be.

They too who of Him partake
Sever not, nor rend, nor break,
But entire their Lord receive.
Whether one or thousands eat,
All receive the selfsame meat,
Nor the less for others leave.

Both the wicked and the good
Eat of this celestial Food;
But with ends how opposite!
Here 'tis life; and there 'tis death;
The same, yet issuing to each
In a difference infinite.

Nor a single doubt retain,
When they break the Host in twain,
But that in each part remains
What was in the whole before;
Since the simple sign alone
Suffers change in state or form,
The Signified remaining One,
And the Same forevermore.

Lo! Upon the altar lies,
Hidden deep from human eyes,
Angels' bread from Paradise
Made the food of mortal man:
Children's meat to dogs denied;
In old types foresignified;
In the manna from the skies,
In Isaac, and the Paschal Lamb.

Jesu! Shepherd of the sheep!
Thy true flock in safety keep.
Living Bread! Thy life supply;
Strengthen us, or else we die;
Fill us with celestial grace:
Thou, who feedest us below!
Source of all we have or know!
Grant that with Thy Saints above,
Sitting at the Feast of Love,
We may see Thee face to face.

Lauds The Latin noun *laus, laudis, f.*, means *praise*, and from it was derived the verb *laudo, laudare, laudavi, laudatus* meaning *to praise*. Psalm 148 (*Laudate Dominum de Caelis*) and Psalm 150 (*Laudate Dominum in Sanctis Eius*), which used to be sung daily at the first of the canonical hours, are full of clauses beginning with the word *Laudate*, whence this hour acquired the name *Lauds*.

Legate The Latin noun *lex, legis, f.* means *the law*, and related to it is the verb *lēgo, lēgare, lēgavi, lēgatus*, which means *to appoint, to make second-in-command*, whence comes the noun *legatus* with the meaning *a deputy, one with delegated authority*. A legate is the highest rank of papal emissary, always a cardinal. Cardinals Campeggio and Wolsey were papal legates for the trial concerning the divorce of Henry VIII and Catherine of Aragon (see the entry **Divorce**). A *legatus a latere*, a legate from the very side of the pope, is a sort of super-legate, a legate in a situation where it is felt necessary to emphasize the connection between the pope and the prelate so designated. When the papal legate Cardinal Lauri arrived in Dublin in 1932, his ship was escorted into the harbor by a squadron of airplanes flying in the formation of a cross, he was met at the port by the whole government, and he was escorted into town by a troop of hussars through streets crowded with a tumultuous multitude who had waited for hours to salute him. A *legatus natus* is a prelate who holds the legatine dignity by virtue of his appointment to a prominent see, such as the archbishop of Esztergom, primate of Hungary.

Lent According to Weekley, our noun *lent* descends from the Anglo-Saxon word *lencten* meaning *spring*, which was created by combining the words for *long* and *day*. Lent is the penitential season before Easter.

Leonine The Greek noun λέων, λέοντος, *m.*, means *lion*, and related to it is the Latin word *leo, leonis, m.*, with the same meaning. It became a common proper name in the early centuries of Christianity, the most famous Leo being Pope Leo the Great. From the proper name proceeded the adjective *leoninus* meaning *pertaining to Leo*, whence we get our adjective *leonine*. The *Leonine City* is the neighborhood of Rome around the Vatican that had been fortified in the ninth century by Pope Leo IV. It had been the intention of the Italian government in 1870 to leave this area under the temporal administration of the pope, but Pius IX denied the offer. The Leonine Prayers are the prayers formerly recited after low Mass on Sunday by order of Leo XIII. They begin with three Ave Marias and the Salve Regina, followed by the verses:

> Ora pro nobis, sancta Dei Genetrix.
> Ut digni efficiamur promissionibus Christi.
>
> Pray for us, O Holy Mother of God,
> That we may be made worthy of the promises of Christ.

There follow the prayers:

Oremus. Deus, refugium nostrum et virtus, populum ad te clamantem propitius respice, et intercedente gloriosa et Immaculata Virgine Dei Genetrice Maria, cum beato Ioseph eius Sponso, ac beatis Apostolis tuis Petro et Paulo, et omnibus Sanctis, quas pro conversione peccatorum, pro libertate et exultatione Sanctae Matris Ecclesiae preces effundimus, misericors et benignus exaudi. Amen.

Sancte Michael Archangele, defende nos in proelio; contra nequitiam et insidias diaboli esto praesidium. Imperet illi Deus, supplices deprecamur; tuque, Princeps militiae caelestis, Satanam aliosque spiritus malignos, qui ad perditionem animarum pervagantur in mundo, divina virtute in infernum detrude. Amen.

Let us pray. O God, our refuge and our strength, look down graciously upon Thy people who cry out unto Thee, and by the intercession of the glorious and Ever-Virgin Mary, Mother of God, of Blessed Joseph her spouse, of Thy blessed Apostles Peter and Paul and of all Thy saints, mercifully and kindly hear the prayers which we pour forth unto Thee for the conversion of sinners and for the freedom and exultation of Holy Mother Church.

Saint Michael the Archangel, defend us in battle. Be our defense against the wickedness and snares of the Devil. May God rebuke him, we humbly pray, and may thou, Prince of the Heavenly Host, by the power of God, cast into hell Satan and all the evil spirits, who prowl about the world seeking the ruin of souls.

Liberal Education The Latin adjective *liber* means *free*, and the adjective *liberalis* formed from it means *pertaining to a free man*. The verb *educo*, *educare*, *educavi*, *educatus* means *to rear*, and the noun *educatio* formed from its fourth principal part means *upbringing*. Thus, liberal education is the bringing up of free-born children. The Greek word for education is παιδεία.

The Catholic theory of liberal education was the subject of the book *Idea of a University*, a masterpiece by John Henry Newman; it is a collection of lectures and essays. Newman pointed out the subject matter that ought to form the foundation of a liberal education in his lecture *Christianity and Letters*, delivered in November 1854, at the opening of his university's School of Philosophy and Letters. The basis of that inaugural address was the following famous thesis:

Looking, then, at the countries which surround the Mediterranean Sea as a whole, I see them to be, from time immemorial, the seat of an association of intellect and mind, such as to deserve to be called the intellect and mind of the human kind.... Considering, then, the characteristics of this great civilized society, which I have already insisted on, I think it has a claim to be considered as the representative society and civilization of the human race, as its perfect result and limit, in fact—those portions of the race which do not coalesce with it being left to stand by themselves as anomalies, unaccountable indeed, but for that very reason not interfering with what on the contrary has been turned to account and has grown into a whole. I call then this commonwealth pre-eminently and emphatically human society, and its intellect the human mind, and its decisions the sense of mankind, and its disciplined and cultivated state civilization in the abstract, and the territory on which it lies the *orbis terrarum*, or the world.[23]

Newman then went on to describe how almost coextensive with this natural association, which we may call Western Civilization, is the divine association of Christianity, and continued:

We know that Christianity is built upon definite ideas, principles, doctrines and writings, which were given at the time of its first introduction, and have never been superseded, and admit of no addition.... Civilization too has its common principles, and views, and teaching, and especially its books, which have more or less been given from the earliest times, and are, in fact, in equal esteem and respect, in equal use now, as they were when they were received in the beginning. In a word, the classics, and the subjects of thought and the studies to which they

23. John Henry Cardinal Newman, *Idea of a University* (Garden City, N.Y.: Image Books, 1959), 249–51.

give rise, or, to use the term most to our present purpose, the arts, have ever, on the whole, been the instruments of education which the civilized *orbis terrarum* has adopted; just as inspired works, and the lives of saints, and the articles of faith, and the catechism, have ever been the instruments of education in the case of Christianity.[24]

In a delightful section of his *Utopia*, Thomas More reported the zeal of the Utopians for classical studies:

When they heard us speak of the literature and learning of the Greeks, ... it was wonderful to see how eagerly they sought to be instructed in Greek.[25]

Today the preeminence of classical studies is no longer universally recognized. Even before Newman's time, loud voices had been raised against them. Thomas Paine looked upon them as part of a conspiracy to inhibit the development of mankind:

From what we know of the Greeks, it does not appear that they knew or studied any language but their own, and this was one cause of their becoming so learned: it afforded them more time to apply themselves to better studies.... As there is nothing new to be learned from the dead languages, all the useful books being already translated, the languages are become useless, and the time expended in teaching and learning them is wasted.... The best Greek linguist that now exists does not understand Greek so well as a Grecian ploughman did, or a Grecian milkmaid.... It would therefore be advantageous to the state of learning to abolish the study of the dead languages, and to make learning consist, as it originally did, in scientific knowledge.[26]

But Newman in no way denied the necessity of those scientific studies upon which Paine would have concentrated all the energies of the student to the exclusion of the classics; indeed, in his second discourse, he agrees whole-heartedly with the definition given by Dr. Johnson in his *Dictionary*, and holds that a university is a school "where all arts and faculties are taught." If, then, a certain science is excluded, the school that excludes it participates, as Plato would say, that much less in the idea of a university. Newman did, however, insist upon a preeminence for Greek and Latin letters and believed that if a university determined

24. Ibid., 252–53.

25. Thomas More, *Utopia*, trans. H. V. S. Ogden (Northbrook, Ill: AHM Publishing, 1949), 54.

26. Thomas Paine, *The Age of Reason* (New York: The World's Popular Classics Books, n.d.), 47–48.

how best to strengthen, refine, and enrich the intellectual powers (sc. of its students), the perusal of the poets, historians, and philosophers of Greece and Rome will accomplish this purpose, as long experience has shown, but that the study of the experimental sciences will do the like is proved to us as yet by no experience whatsoever. . . . The question is not what department of study contains the more wonderful facts, or promises the most brilliant discoveries, . . . simply which out of all provides the most robust and invigorating discipline for the unformed mind. . . . Whatever be the splendor of the modern philosophy, the marvelousness of its disclosures, the utility of its acquisitions, and the talent of its masters, still it will not avail in the event, to detrude classical literature and the studies connected with it from the place which they have held in all ages of education.[27]

The great Macaulay, who, though holding the Greeks to have produced "the most perfect of human compositions," and their tongue to be "the most powerful and flexible of human languages," was nevertheless able to write in his essay on *Lord Bacon*:

We are guilty, we hope, of no irreverence towards those great nations to which the human race owes art, science, taste, civil and intellectual freedom, when we say, that the stock bequeathed by them to us has been so carefully improved that the accumulated interest now exceeds the principal. We believe that the books which have been written in the languages of western Europe, during the last two hundred and fifty years,—translations from the ancient languages of course included,—are of greater value than all the books which at the beginning of that period were extant in the world.[28]

The book *Broadcast Minds* by Msgr. Ronald Knox "is a brilliant example of the old claim that a mind properly schooled in *Litterae Humaniores* can turn itself effectively on any subject connected with man."[29]

Liberian The Late Latin adjective *liberianus* means *pertaining to Liberius*. The adjective is therefore applied to anything connected with Pope Liberius, who reigned 352–366. In particular, the Church of Santa Maria Maggiore in Rome is called the *Liberian Basilica* because its construction was begun by that pontiff. It maintains the highest standard of liturgical excellence of the four Roman patriarchal basilicas.

27. Newman, *Idea of a University*, 258–59.

28. Thomas Babington Macaulay, *Criticial and Historical Essays, Contributed to the Edinburgh Review*, 6th ed. (London: Longman, Brown, Green, & Longmans, 1849), 2:295.

29. Evelyn Waugh, *Monsignor Ronald Knox, Fellow of Trinity College, Oxford and Protonotary Apostolic to His Holiness Pope Pius XII* (Boston: Little, Brown, 1959), 235.

Liberius *Liberius* is a proper name formed by adding the suffix *-ius* to the adjective *līber*, which means *free*. It was the name of a pope, one of the three whose biographies complicated the discussions about papal infallibility at the First Vatican Council. Arthur Plummer wrote:

> It was reserved for Liberius to commence his pontificate by excommunicating Athanasius, and to regain it by signing the semi-Arian creed of Sirmium, and once more renouncing communion with the great champion of the creed of Nicaea.[30]

Liber Usualis This is a Latin phrase meaning the *book to be used*. The *Liber Usualis* was the customary book used in the celebration of the divine office and Mass in choir, since it has all the texts and music needed for the proper celebration of those performances. It was never reissued after the changes brought on by the Second Vatican Council, a failure that created a problem for that handful of places that wanted to maintain the Latin liturgy in their celebration of the canonical hours.

Library The Latin word *līber*, *lǐbri*, *m.*, means the *inner bark of a tree*, upon which one could write. Hence it later came to mean a *book*. The associated noun *librarium*, *-i*, *n.*, means a *place to keep books*, a *bookcase*, and from it we get our word *library*. The Romans, however, were satisfied to transliterate the Greek noun βιβλιοθήκη to get their word for what we call a *library*, and so in Latin *library* is *bibliotheca*. At some point *libreria* came to mean *bookstore*, for that is its meaning in Italian. The Holy See possesses the greatest library in the world, that of the Vatican, whose prefect is always a cardinal. Among the masterpieces to be found there are the Codex Vaticanus, the most authoritative of biblical manuscripts, and the Peyrard Manuscript, the most important manuscript of Euclid's *Elements*. The Vatican Library was founded by Nicholas V (1447–1455), and his successor Sixtus V (1585–1590) built a hall for it across the Cortile della Pigna, cutting that open space in two and forever rendering impossible a resumption of the bull fights held there for the amusement of Julius III (1550–1555). Decades ago it used to be possible to visit display cases of rarities in the Sistine Hall of the Library, but this practice has unfortunately been discontinued, probably on account of the large and uncontrollable numbers of tourists who visit the Vatican Museums, for whom items like the Codex Vaticanus and MS Peyrard are of no interest.

---

30. Alfred Plummer, introduction to *Fables respecting the Popes of the Middle Ages, A Contribution to Ecclesiastical History*, by Ignaz von Döllinger (London: Rivingtons, 1871), xxvi.

Limbo The Latin noun *limbus* means *edge, border*. It is a pious hypothesis that the souls of those who die without baptism, with only original sin, dwell neither in heaven nor in hell, but at the *border* of one or the other, that is, *in limbo*.

According to Mark 16:15–16 and John 3:5, baptism is necessary for salvation.

Q. 359. Quid erit de anima illorum, qui sine Baptismo cum solo peccato originali moriuntur?

R. Anima illorum qui sine Baptismo cum solo peccato originali moriuntur, caret beatifica Dei visione propter originale peccatum, quod per naturam habet, absque dolore possidet, citra poenas, quibus personalia peccata puniuntur.[31]

Q. 359. What happens to the souls of those who die without baptism, with only original sin?

R. The souls of those who die without baptism with only original sin do without the beatific vision of God because of the original sin which they naturally have and possess without sorrow, without the punishments by which personal sins are penalized.

This sentence seemed unnecessarily harsh to many thinking people, who therefore posited on the outskirts of heaven or hell what they called a *limbus patrum* and a *limbus infantium*, in the former of which the souls of the like of Abraham, Isaac, Jacob, Moses, and Elijah waited, and in the latter of which the souls of unbaptized infants repose. Belief in the existence of such a limbo is neither a dogma nor a heresy. Since St. Joseph and St. John the Baptist were not baptized and yet have always been recognized by the Church as dwelling in paradise, some sort of device to allow for the alleviation of the general rule was required.

Q. 360. Potestne aliquid supplere vicem Baptismi?

R. Vicem Baptismi supplere potest actus fidei et perfectae caritatis, qui martyrio maxime comprobatur et necessario continet perfectam de peccatis contritionem et Baptismi votum; sed unus aquae Baptismus et characterem imprimit et capacitatem confert alia sacramenta recipiendi.[32]

Q. 360. Can anything supply the place of baptism?

R. An act of faith and perfect love, such as is best demonstrated by martyrdom, and which necessarily involves perfect sorrow for sins and the desire for

---

31. *Catechismus catholicus, cura et studio Petri Cardinalis Gasparri concinnatus*, 15th ed. (Vatican City: Typis Polyglottis Vaticanis, 1933), 197–98.

32. Ibid., 198.

baptism, can supply the place of baptism, but only baptism with water imparts a mark on the soul and confers the ability of receiving the other sacraments.

This is the famous baptism of desire and baptism of blood. It takes care of the Old Testament Fathers, St. Joseph, and St. John the Baptist, but does nothing for the infants and other unbaptized people of good will. It is this concern that in all times motivates the missionary spirit.

Litany The Greek λίττομαι means *to beg* or *pray*, and from it was derived the noun λιτή with the meaning *prayer*. Related to these words is the verb λιτανεύω and the noun λιτανεία, *entreaty*, whence came the Latin transliteration *litania*, reserved for a long repetitious prayer. Of the litanies of the Catholic Church, the most important is the Litany of the Saints.

Liturgy The Greek noun λαός means *people*, and from it was formed the adjective of two terminations λέϊτος, -ον (or λεῖτος, -ον), *of the people*. The adjective was compounded with the noun ἔργον, *work*, to form the adjective λειτουργός with the meaning *performing public duties*. The associated noun is λειτουργία, which has the meaning *public service*. The Latin noun *liturgia* is merely the transliteration of this Greek noun. Whereas the Greek noun is accented on the penult, the Latin noun must be accented on the antepenult, since the iota in question is short. (This is clear from the plural λειτουργίαι used by Demosthenes.) As an Italian word, however, *liturgia* is accented on the penult. Among the Athenians, burdensome public duties were discharged by citizen volunteers of means. Since divine service was one of these charges, λειτουργία acquired the meaning of *divine service*, as the public office *par excellence*. William George Ward had the following to say about the variety of liturgies available in the Christian world.[33]

And similarly, the Anglican communion service, beautiful as he found its prayers, *oppressed* him from the obligation it involved of his following at another's pace and in another's train of thought. He often went to the Catholic chapel in Spanish Place to mass instead—long before he joined the Puseyite party. The music and solemn ceremonial raised his feelings to God, and he could choose his own train of religious thought and prayer. He considered that for himself the greatest freedom in the form of his devotions was necessary to make them profitable. A public prayer, which did not appeal to him, led to irritation and distractions.

---

33. Wilfrid Ward, *William George Ward and the Oxford Movement* (London: Macmillan, 1889), 93–94.

A long sermon, or too long service not suited to his taste, would "bore" him so much, he said, that he came out in a state of rebellion against God, for inflicting on him something so intolerable, rather than nearer to God. He did not deny that in limits such things might be good as opportunities of enduring patiently what was irksome. But with his temperament the irksomeness was in some cases so intolerable that such occasions were purely and simply occasions of irreligion. The Anglican service made him often feel so "wicked", he said, that he abstained from taking the sacrament. "If only I might go to the play first," he maliciously said to an Evangelical friend, "I should feel pious enough; but the communion service makes me impious." He refers to this subject frequently in his writings of the period immediately succeeding that of which I am now speaking. "Religious ordinances," he says in the *British Critic*, "may be either a support or an oppression; either mold the spiritual life or repress it and stunt its growth; and so far as they belong to the latter category their very object is perverted, that object being, not to increase the difficulties of doing good, but to diminish them. Perhaps one of the most striking instances that can be named of this abuse is in the Kirk of Scotland, where the whole external duties and appliances of religion seem to consist of coming each Sunday twice to church, in order to hear a long extempore prayer, and a still longer sermon; of which regulation it is perhaps not too much to say that some persons of right religious principles and keen religious feelings might find life hardly endurable under so heavy a burden."

The so-called formalism of Catholicism was quite different, consisting either in the expression of natural feeling on the part of the congregation, as when the congregation kneel in silent prayer after Christ's death in the "passion" has been read on Good Friday, or in the illustrative representation in the liturgy of religious mysteries, which in no way interfered with freedom in the form of their devotions on the part of the faithful. "The real fact is," he says, speaking of Catholic churches, "that their alleged formalism, when contrasted with our practical system, mainly consists in this—that the people are not restrained by forms, that they are allowed and encouraged to vent their warm devotional feelings in such external acts and gestures as naturally express them, instead of being bound by harsh and cruel custom to an exterior of polite indifference, a cold, cramping, stifling uniformity."

Locum Tenens The Latin phrase *locum tenens* means *holding the place*. It is the name of a substitute who performs the duties associated with a vacant office until an incumbent is appointed. It is the French *lieutenant*, which has been carried over into English. The equivalent Italian noun is *luogotenente*; it was the title of Crown Prince Humbert during the period before his accession to the throne, when he exercised the royal powers surrendered by his father King Victor Emmanuel III.

Loggia The Italian word *loggia* means *porch*. It is most often used in reference to the main porch of St. Peter's Basilica, from which the pope imparts his solemn blessings. It is a word of barbarian origin related to the French *loge* and the English *lobby* and *lodge*. Weekley cites a presumed Old High German word *laubja* meaning *porch*.

Logos This word is the transliteration of the Greek noun λόγος, which means *word* or *reason*, for it was a sign of reason to be able to express oneself in words. Philo's doctrine of the Logos was adopted in the preface to the Gospel according to St. John.

The aim was to reach some understanding as to what exactly the Divinity incarnate in Jesus Christ really was. Starting from the Johannine axiom, "the Word was made flesh," many writers, and especially the Apologists, began to study Philo's theory of the Logos. They found in that theory a means of reconciling their own faith with their philosophical education, and also a point of contact with the educated hearers or readers, to whom they were defending Christianity. But what exactly was the Logos? At bottom, in whatever form their thought clothed itself, the Logos was for them God revealing Himself externally, acting outside Himself, allowing Himself to be known, or making Himself known. God is ineffable, abstract, and unknowable: between Him and the world an intermediary was necessary. This intermediary could only be Divine: the Word proceedeth from God. All external action on the part of God must be attributed to Him, first the Creation, then the divine manifestations (theophanies) in the Old Testament, and at last the Incarnation.[34]

Newman wrote the following about the prologue to the Gospel according to John:

Scripture is express in declaring both the divinity of Him who in due time became man for us, and also His personal distinction from God in His pre-existent state. This is sufficiently clear from the opening of St. John's Gospel, which states the mystery as distinctly as an ecclesiastical comment can propound it. On these two truths the whole doctrine turns, viz. that our Lord is one with, yet personally separate from God. Now there are two appellations given to Him in Scripture, enforcing respectively these two essentials of the true doctrine; appellations imperfect and open to misconception by themselves, but qualifying and completing each other. The title of the Son marks His derivation and distinction from the Father, that of the *Word* (i.e., Reason) denotes His inseparable inherence in the Divine Unity; and while the former taken by itself, might lead the mind to conceive of

34. Louis Duchesne, *Early History of the Christian Church from Its Foundation to the End of the Third Century* (London: John Murray, 1914), 221–22.

Him as a second being, and the latter as no real being at all, both together witness to the mystery, that he is at once *from*, and yet *in* the Immaterial, Incomprehensible God.[35]

Newman had the following to say about Christ as the Logos:

On the whole it would appear that Our Lord is called the Word or Wisdom of God in two respects; first, to denote His essential presence in the Father, in as full a sense as the attribute of wisdom is essential to Him, secondly, His mediatorship, as the Interpreter or Word, between God and His creatures. No appellation, surely, could have been more appositely bestowed, in order to counteract the notions of materiality or of distinct individuality, and of beginning of existence, which the title of the Son was likely to introduce into the Catholic doctrine.[36]

Low Mass The English adjective *low* is a descendant of the Anglo-Saxon *lāh*. A *low Mass* is a traditional Latin Mass celebrated without singing. It was the common form of the liturgy before the changes in the period 1963–1970. Such a Mass was called *low* in comparison with the sublimity of the sung mass, accordingly called *high*. A low Mass with a sermon should take no more than forty-five minutes to celebrate.

---

35. John Henry Cardinal Newman, *The Arians of the Fourth Century*, new ed. (London: Longmans, Green, 1897), 156–57.

36. Ibid., 169.

Macedonians Macedonia (Μακεδονία) was a territory to the north of Greece, between Thessaly and Thrace. In the history of Christian theology, the Macedonians were a heretical party that took its name from Macedonius, patriarch of Constantinople in the fourth century, who, they claimed, had denied the divinity of the Holy Ghost.

He now became avowed leader of the sect of Pneumatomachi, Macedonians, or Marathonians, whose distinctive tenet was that the Holy Spirit is but a being similar to the angels, subordinate to and in the service of the Father and the Son, the relation between whom did not admit of a third.[1]

St. Athanasius called the Macedonians πνευματομάκοι—adversaries of the Holy Ghost.

Maestro di Camera The Latin adverb *magis* means *more*, and derived from it is the noun *magister* with the meaning *chief, head, director*. It was corrupted into the Italian *maestro* and the English *master*. The *maestro di camera* was the member of the papal court who arranged all papal audiences. He ranked next in dignity after the *majordomo*. The two positions were united in 1968. See the entry **Majordomo**.

Maestro del Sacro Ospizio The Latin noun *hospes, hospitis, m.*, means *host* or *guest*, and related to it is the noun *hospitium* meaning *hospitality*. This latter noun came over to Italian as *ospizio*. The maestro del sacro

1. *Encyclopaedia Britannica,* 11th ed. (New York: The Encyclopaedia Britannica Company, 1911), s.v. "Macedonius."

ospizio, the master of the sacred hospice, was the highest ranking layman in the papal court, whose responsibilities at one time extended to political and economic affairs. After the return of the popes from Avignon, many of his duties were transferred to a cleric whose position was denominated *Prefect of the Apostolic Palace* and then *Majordomo*. He remained, however, in charge of the reception of exalted guests. The position was hereditary in the House of Ruspoli. The Prince Alessandro Ruspoli is easily identified in old newsreels and pictures because he wears a patch over one eye. It was his honor to escort the Queen of Italy on his arm when she and her husband, Victor Emanuel III, visited Pope Pius XI after the conclusion of the Concordat. The king was paired with the maestro di camera Monsignor Camillo Caccia Dominioni, who had been performing the duties of the majordomo since the retirement of Monsignor Ricardo Sanz De Samper the preceding year.

Magi The Greek noun μάγος means a *magus*, a member of a certain tribe of Medes. Probably due to the preeminence of that tribe in occult knowledge, the word came to mean one of the wise men or seers of Persia, who interpreted dreams and excelled in astronomy. Some of their activities were called *magic*, and so, in a negative sense, the word *magi* came to mean *wizards, magicians*. The magi of the Gospel according to St. Matthew saw the star in the eastern sky and came to worship Jesus.

Vidimus stellam eius in oriente, et venimus adorare eum.

The idea that they were three in number is first expressed by Pope Leo the Great. The relics of these three wise men are held in a golden cask at the high altar of the Cathedral of Cologne. The tradition that the magi were kings is due to a messianic interpretation of Psalm 72:10–11.

> The kings of Tarshish, and those of the isles, shall bring presents: and the
>   kings of Sheba and Seba shall offer gifts.
> Yea, all kings shall fall down before him: all nations shall serve him.

Magnificat The Latin adjective *magnus* means *great*, and the verb *facio, facere, feci, factus* means *to make*, and from their combination is produced the adjective *magnificus* meaning *grand, splendid*. From this adjective comes the verb *magnifico* of the first conjugation meaning *to prize highly, to esteem*. This most famous prayer is that of the Virgin Mary during the Visitation (Luke 1:46–55). It is sung daily at Vespers. The Gregorian melody was at one time familiar to all Catholics. The *Magnificat* was set to music by many composers, most notably by Bach.

Magnificat anima mea Dominum,
Et exsultavit spiritus meus in Deo salutari meo.
Quia respexit humilitatem ancillae suae:
Ecce enim ex hoc beatam me dicent omnes generationes.
Quia fecit mihi magna qui potens est, et sanctum nomen eius.
Et misericordia eius a progenie in progenies timentibus eum.
Fecit potentiam in brachio suo:
Dispersit superbos mente cordis sui.
Deposuit potentes de sede, et exaltavit humiles.
Esurientes implevit bonis, et divites dimisit inanes.
Suscepit Israel puerum suum, recordatus misericordiae suae.
Sicut locutus est ad patres nostros, Abraham et semini eius in saecula.

The best translation is that in the *Book of Common Prayer*:

My soul doth magnify the Lord,
And my spirit hath rejoiced in God my Saviour.
For he hath regarded the lowliness of his hand-maiden.
For behold, from henceforth all generations shall call me blessed.
For he that is mighty hath magnified me: and holy is his Name.
And his mercy is on them that fear him throughout all generations.
He hath shewed strength with his arm;
He hath scattered the proud in the imagination of their hearts.
He hath put down the mighty from their seat,
And hath exalted the humble and meek.
He hath filled the hungry with good things, and the rich he hath sent empty
    away.
He, remembering his mercy, hath holpen his servant Israel,
As he promised to our forefathers, Abraham and his seed, for ever.

Major Archbishop The Latin adjective *maior* is the comparative of *magnus*, great. *Greater archbishop* is a term invented by the Roman Curia in 1963 as a title for Joseph Slipyj, Ukrainian metropolitan of Lviv (Lwow, Lemberg, Leopoli), and his successors, who, for political reasons, could not, they imagined, be given the usual title for the head of a church with its own rite, *patriarch*. It has since been used, for similar political reasons, for the heads of some other Eastern Rite Churches.

Majordomo The Latin comparative adjective *maior* means *greater*, and the noun *domus* means *house*. The *maior domūs* or "mayor of the palace" was the preeminent official in the household of the Merovingian kings; in 751, the majordomo Pepin put his sovereign aside and assumed the throne himself. The name became *maggiordomo* in Italian and *majordomo* in English. The majordomo was the chief officer of the papal palace; he was in charge of all the ceremonies, both public and private, at which the pope appeared. He usually appeared at the pope's right hand in public and semipublic audiences, the maestro di camera standing at the left hand. After his term of office was complete, he became a cardinal. For good reason, the stipulated number of years could be abbreviated, as we learn from the following story about the maggiordomo Msgr. Ranuzzi de' Bianchi; Pope Benedict XV is speaking:

> Monsignore, according to the way things are done here, you should still have to wait two more years before becoming a Cardinal, but I hear that your mother isn't doing well, so I'll make you a Cardinal right away so that she can enjoy seeing her son in the purple.[2]

And that is exactly what happened. When the maggiordomo Ricardo Sanz di Samper retired in 1928, the *maestro di camera* at the time, Monsignor Caccia Dominioni, assumed the position. This union of the two positions became permanent in 1968, when, in the *motu proprio Pontificalis Domus*,[3] Pope Paul VI suppressed the individual titles, creating the position of Prefect of the Apostolic Palace for the combined position (see the entry **Maestro del Sacro Ospizio**), Monsignor Nasalli Rocca di Corneliano being the inaugural incumbent. Upon the promotion of the last-named prelate to the purple in 1969, the title was further changed to Prefect of the Pontifical Household.

Manichaeism Mani (مانی) was a third-century Persian who was the originator of the religion Manichaeism named after him. His name became in Greek Μανιχαῖος and from thence in Latin *Manichaeus*. Manichaeism (also Manicheism or Manichaeanism) was defined by Simon Blackburn as follows:

2. Mario Nasalli Rocca di Corrneliano, *Accanto ai Papi* (Vatican City: Libreria Editrice Vaticana, 1976), 11 (my translation).

3. *Pontificalis Domus* (motu proprio of Pope Paul VI, March 28, 1968). The text is available at http://w2.vatican.va/content/paul-vi/la/motu_proprio/documents/hf_p-vi_motu-proprio_19680328_pontificalis-domus.html.

The doctrine that the world is not governed by one perfect Being, but by a balance of the forces of good and evil. The doctrine elevates the devil, as the personification of evil, into a position of power comparable to that of God. It derives from Zoroastrianism and was held by the manichees, followers of the Persian teacher Manes or Manichaeus. It flourished between the 3rd and 5th centuries AD.[4]

Thus the main idea was that there were two worlds, the spiritual world of light and the material world of matter. A devil created man and put into some men bits of the light that he had stolen from the spiritual world. It was the duty of such men to free the light from the body so that it could return from whence it had been taken. The followers of Mani were denominated Manichees, and their religion was called Manichaeanism. St. Augustine had been a Manichee before his conversion to Christianity; thereafter he wrote against them as their declared enemy.

Maniple The Greek verb πλέω means *to fill*, but the corresponding Latin verb *pleo* is not found except in compounds like *compleo* and *expleo*. The noun *manus, manūs, f.*, means *hand*. From the combination of *manus* and *pleo* comes the noun *manipulus, -i, m.*, with the meaning a *handful*, a *troop of soldiers*. By mediaeval times it had acquired the meaning of a certain ecclesiastical vestment worn on the left arm between the elbow and the hand. The maniple is a sort of handkerchief worn on the left arm at Mass by the priest, deacon, and subdeacon. It was first imposed on the cleric when he attained the rank of subdeacon. It was made optional by the Congregation of Rites in the instruction *Tres Abhinc Annos*, May 4, 1967, §25: "*Manipulus semper omitti potest.*"[5] When the new order of Mass was introduced in the years 1969–1970, no mention of the maniple was made in the "General Instruction" of the revised Roman Missal; from this it may be deduced that its further use was not anticipated. It was not to be expected that a special prohibition against it would be included in the "Instruction." To wear the maniple in the celebration of the modern Mass would therefore be to sin by eccentricity. To single the maniple out for attention was a violation of the principle *De minimis non curat lex*. While this action has little effect when one wears a gothic chasuble, celebrants wearing the Roman fiddle-back chasubles look incompletely attired without a maniple.

4. Simon Blackburn, *The Oxford Dictionary of Philosophy* (Oxford: Oxford University Press, 1994), s.v. "Manichaeanism."

5. *Tres Abhinc Annos* (instruction of the Sacred Congregation of Rites, May 4, 1967), *Acta Apostolicae Sedis* 59 (1967), 442–48. The text is also available at http://www.vatican.va/archive/aas/documents/AAS-59-1967-ocr.pdf.

Mantelletta The Latin noun *mantēlum* or *mantellum* means a *cloth* or *napkin*, a *cloak* or *mantle*. The addition of the Italian diminutive suffix *-etta* produced the noun *mantelletta*, a sleeveless cape not quite reaching to the knees, with slits for the arms, open in the front, and fastened at the neck with a hook. It is now the outer choir dress of the seven apostolic protonotaries of the Roman Curia, who register the official acts of the Holy See, and a few other Roman authorities. Formerly it was ubiquitous, since it was prescribed for all prelates in the presence of higher prelates, but this usage was abolished by Pope Paul VI.

Pallium, seu manteletum, aboletur.[6]

The privilege of wearing it was formerly accorded as an honor to distinguished clergymen, who were therefore termed *prelates di mantelletta*, but this usage has been cut way back.

Mantellone The addition of the Italian suffix *-one* to the stem of the Latin noun *mantēlum* or *mantellum* produced the noun *mantellone*, a sleeveless cape reaching to the feet, with slits for the arms, open in the front and fastened at the neck with a hook. The word means a *big cape*.

The mantellone has two narrow bands, four inches wide, of the same material attached to the shoulders in back and reaching to the ankles.[7]

It was formerly the outer garment of the chamberlains and chaplains of the papal household, but it is not worn any more except by train bearers of bishops and cross bearers of metropolitan archbishops at "Tridentine" masses.

Mantum The Late Latin noun *mantum, -i, n.*, was the name of a Spanish cloak that reached down to the hands but not all the way down to the feet. It nevertheless became the name of an extremely long cope worn by the popes, though it has not been seen since the early years of the reign of Paul VI, who wore one embroidered with the arms of John XXIII.

Manuscript The Latin phrase *manu scriptum* means *written by hand*. A *manuscript* is a document or book written by hand rather than produced on a printing press. Ancient authors did not always write the manuscripts

---

6. *Ut Sive Sollicite* (instruction of the Secretariat of State, March 31, 1969), *Acta Apostolicae Sedis* 61, no. 5, (1969), 334–40, A 1. The text is also available at www.shetlersites.com/clericaldress/utsivesollicite.html.

7. Henry J. McCloud, *Clerical Dress and Insignia of the Roman Catholic Church* (Milwaukee, Wis.: Bruce Publishing, 1948), 98.

of their own works, as we learn from Eusebius, commenting on the method followed by the prolific Origen:

It was at this period that Origen started work on his *Commentaries on Holy Scripture*, at the urgent request of Ambrose, who not only exerted verbal pressure and every kind of persuasion, but supplied him in abundance with everything needful. Shorthand writers more than seven in number were available when he dictated, relieving each other regularly, and at least as many copyists, as well as girls trained in penmanship, all of them provided most generously with everything needful at Ambrose's expense.[8]

Marcionism The second century heretic Μαρκίων (Marcion) originated the eponymous heresy, which Duchesne describes in the next paragraph. The suffix -ίων creates a patronymic, so the name Marcion means *son of Mark.*

Marcion was a disciple of St. Paul. The antithesis between Faith and the Law, between Grace and Justice, between the Old Testament and the New Covenant, on which the apostle lays stress, was according to Marcion the foundation of all religion. Paul had with regret resigned himself to part from his brothers in Israel. But Marcion transformed this severance into deep-rooted antagonism. According to him, there was no agreement possible between the Revelation of Jesus Christ and the teaching of the Old Testament. A choice must be made between the infinite love and supreme goodness, of which Jesus was the ambassador, and the rigid justice of the God of Israel. "You must not," said he to the Roman presbytery, "pour new wine into old bottles, nor sew a new piece upon a worn-out garment." His real meaning was disclosed even more clearly, by one antithesis after another. The God of the Jews, of Creation, and of the Law, could not be identical with the Father of Mercy, and must therefore be regarded as inferior to Him....

Marcion's teaching laid claim to no secret tradition or prophetic inspiration. It did not seek to accommodate in any way its ideas to those of the Old Testament. Its method of exegesis has no touch of the allegorical, but is purely literal. This led to an entire repudiation of the Old Testament. Of the New Testament, or rather of all the apostolic writings, nothing was retained, except those of St. Paul and the third Gospel. And even so, the collection of St. Paul's letters did not include the Pastoral Epistles, and in the ten epistles retained, as well as in the text of St. Luke, there were omissions. The Galilean apostles were considered to have but imperfectly understood the Gospel: they had made the mistake of considering Jesus as the envoy of the Creator. This was why the Lord had raised up St. Paul to

---

8. Eusebius, *The History of the Church from Christ to Constantine*, trans. G. A. Williamson (London: The Folio Society, 2011), VI 23, p. 180.

rectify their teaching. Even in the letters of Paul, passages occur too laudatory of the Creator; these passages could only be interpolations.[9]

Maresciallo Perpetuo di Santa Romana Chiesa The Old High German noun *marahscalh* meant a *horse groom*; the word is related to the Anglo-Saxon *mearh* (*mare*) and *scealc* (*knave*, the German *Schalk*). Weekley observes that over the centuries the word underwent a rise in dignity. The Maresciallo Perpetuo di Santa Romana Chiesa was a high military officer of the papal armed forces whose duties were in time restricted to the security of the conclave. The position was hereditary and held by the head of the House of Chigi Albani. It was abolished by Pope Paul VI in 1968. The last holder of this office was the Prince Sigismondo Chigi Albani, a photograph of whom locking up the cardinals in the conclaves of 1958 and 1963 appeared in all the newspapers. His father, the Prince Ludovico Chigi Albani della Rovere, was, in the period 1931–1951, grand master of the Sovereign Military Order of Malta.

Maronite The monk Maron is believed to have been a Syrian hermit, a contemporary of St. John Chrysostom; he is the fabulous or actual originator of the Maronites, or Christians of Mount Lebanon. His name was transliterated into Greek as Μάρων, and his followers were therefore denominated Μαρωνῖται, or Maronites. The root of the name is the Aramaic noun מרא (*mārē'*) meaning *lord*. Their eponymous leader in the eighth century was St. John Maron, who conducted them to the Lebanese mountains and was styled *patriarch of Antioch*. The Maronites are the predominant Christian body in Lebanon, where they at one time predominated numerically, before the multiplication of the Shia Muslims, who more successfully obeyed the biblical injunction to be fruitful and multiply. The scientific view of the origin of the Maronites is found in Gibbon and is summarized in the entry by David George Hogarth that may be found in the eleventh edition of the *Encyclopaedia Britannica*:[10]

It seems most probable that the Lebanon offered refuge to Antiochene Monothelites flying from the ban of the Constantinopolitan Council of A.D. 680; that these converted part of the old mountain folk, who already held some kind of Incarna-

---

9. Louis Duchesne, *Early History of the Christian Church from Its Foundation to the End of the Third Century* (London: John Murray, 1914), 134, 136.

10. Edward Gibbon, chapter 47 of *The History of the Decline and Fall of the Roman Empire*, ed. Betty Radice (London: The Folio Society, 1995), 6:72–74.

tionist creed; and that their first patriarch and his successors, for about 500 years at any rate, were Monothelite, and perhaps also Monophysite.[11]

This theory is approved by Donald Attwater in his standard work *The Catholic Eastern Churches*.[12] The alternative view, that the Maronites were never Monothelites, has found a modern champion in E. El-Hayek.[13]

Martyr The Greek noun μάρτυρ, -υρος, *m.*, means a *witness*, and the word was simply transliterated into Ecclesiastical Latin, and thence into English, where the meaning was that of a Christian put to death for the faith; the standard Latin word for *witness* is *testis*. There are two surviving secular documents about the persecution of the Christians in the Roman Empire in the first century after the death of Christ. First comes Tacitus's account of their sufferings under the emperor Nero (*Annals* 15.44):

... iussum incendium crederetur. Ergo abolendo rumori Nero subdidit reos et quaesitissimis poenis adfecit quos per flagitia invisos vulgus Christianos appella-bat. Auctor nominis eius Christus Tiberio imperitante per procuratorem Pontium Pilatum supplicio adfectus erat; repressaque in praesens exitiabilis superstitio rursum erumpebat, non modo per Iudaeam, originem eius mali, sed per urbem etiam quo cuncta undique atrocia aut pudenda confluunt celebranturque. Igitur primum correpti qui fatebantur, deinde indicio eorum multitudo ingens haud proinde in crimine incendii quam odio humani generis convicti sunt. Et pere-untibus addita ludibria, ut ferarum tergis contecti laniatu canum interirent, aut crucibus adfixi aut flammandi, atque ubi defecisset dies in usum nocturni luminis urerentur. Hortos suos ei spectaculo Nero obtulerat et circense ludicrum edebat, habitu aurigae permixtus plebi vel curriculo insistens. Unde quamquam adversus sontis et novissima exempla meritos miseratio oriebatur, tamquam non utilitate publica sed in saevitiam unius adsumerentur.

... it was believed that the fire had been set. Therefore, to quash the rumor, Nero came up with suspects and afflicted them with the most exquisite tortures, people odious for their crimes, whom the common folk called Christians. The originator of this name, Christ, during the reign of Tiberius, had suffered capital punish-ment under the procurator Pontius Pilate. This damnable cult, kept down until now, was once again making headway, not only throughout Judea, the homeland of this evil, but all over the city [Rome] as well, whither everything horrible and disgusting flows in from everywhere, and flourishes. The first to be laid hold of

11. David George Hogarth, "Maronites," in *Encyclopaedia Britannica*, 11th ed. (New York: The Encyclopaedia Britannica Company, 1911), 17:747.

12. Donald Attwater, *The Catholic Eastern Churches* (Milwaukee, Wis.: Bruce Publishing, 1935), 180.

13. *The New Catholic Encyclopedia* (Washington, D.C.: The Catholic University of America, 1967), s.v. "Maronite Rite."

confessed, and by their evidence an enormous number were convicted, not really of the crime of setting the fire so much as of hatred of the human race. Their deaths were transformed into public spectacles, as when, sewed up in the hides of beasts, they perished as they were mangled by dogs; they were crucified or set on fire and burned in dark places for street lamps. Nero offered his private gardens for this show, and organized circus games, rubbing shoulders with the populace dressed as a charioteer, or setting foot on the racetrack. Wherefore, the people felt pity for the victims, however much they deserved the severest penalties, perceiving that they were being punished not for the public welfare, but on account of the rage of one madman.

Then there is Letter 96 of Pliny to Emperor Trajan, and the latter's reply:

C. Plinius Traiano Imperatori. Sollemne est mihi, domine, omnia de quibus dubito ad te referre. Quis enim potest melius vel cunctationem meam regere vel ignorantiam instruere? Cognitionibus de Christianis interfui numquam: ideo nescio quid et quatenus aut puniri soleat aut quaeri. Nec mediocriter haesitavi sitne aliquod discrimen aetatum an quamlibet teneri nihil a robustioribus differant, detur paenitentiae venia an ei qui omnino Christianus fuit desisse non prosit, nomen ipsum, si flagitiis careat, an flagitia cohaerentia nomini puniantur. Interim in eis qui ad me tamquam Christiani deferebantur hunc sum secutus modum. Interrogavi ipsos an essent Christiani. Confitentes iterum ac tertio interrogavi, supplicium minatus; perseverantes duci iussi. Neque enim dubitabam, qualecumque esset quod faterentur, pertinaciam certe et inflexibilem obstinationem debere puniri. Fuerunt alii similis amentiae quos, quia cives Romani erant, adnotavi in urbem remittendos. Mox ipso tractatu, ut fieri solet, diffundente se crimine, plures species inciderunt. Propositus est libellus sine auctore multorum nomina continens. Qui negabant esse se Christianos aut fuisse, cum praeeunte me deos appellarent et imagini tuae, quam propter hoc iusseram cum simulacris numinum adferri, ture ac vino supplicarent, praeterea male dicerent Christo, quorum nihil posse cogi dicuntur qui sunt re vera Christiani, dimittendos esse putavi. Alii ab indice nominati esse se Christianos dixerunt et mox negaverunt; fuisse quidem, sed desisse, quidam ante plures annos, non nemo etiam ante viginti. Hi quoque omnes et imaginem tuam deorumque simulacra venerati sunt et Christo male dixerunt. Adfirmabant autem hanc fuisse summam vel culpae suae vel erroris, quod essent soliti stato die ante lucem convenire carmenque Christo quasi deo dicere secum invicem, seque sacramento non in scelus aliquod obstringere, sed ne furta, ne latrocinia, ne adulteria committerent, ne fidem fallerent, ne depositum appellati abnegarent: quibus peractis morem sibi discedendi fuisse, rursusque coëundi ad capiendum cibum, promiscuum tamen et innoxium; quod ipsum facere desisse post edictum meum, quo secundum mandata tua hetaerias esse vetueram. Quo magis necessarium credidi ex duabus ancillis, quae ministrae dicebantur, quid esset veri et per tormenta quaerere. Nihil aliud inveni quam superstitionem pravam, immodicam. Ideo dilata cognitione ad consulendum te decucurri. Visa est enim mihi res digna consultatione, maxime propter periclitantium numerum. Multi enim omnis aetatis, omnis ordinis, utriusque sexus etiam, vocantur in periculum et vocabuntur. Neque civitates tantum sed vicos etiam atque agros superstitionis istius contagio pervagata est; quae videtur sisti et corrigi posse. Certe satis constat prope iam desolata templa coepisse celebrari et sacra sollemnia diu intermissa repeti pastumque venire victimarum, cuius adhuc rarissimus emptor inveniebatur. Ex quo facile est opinari quae turba hominum emendari possit, si sit paenitentiae locus.

Gaius Pliny to the Emperor Trajan. It has been my practice, sir, to refer to you all matters of which I am doubtful, for who can better moderate my hesitation, or instruct my ignorance? I have never been present at the trials of Christians; therefore, I am unaware what, and to what extent, one is accustomed to punish, or to investigate. I have hesitated not a little about whether there should be some allowance made for youth, or whether the youngsters should in no wise be treated differently from their elders; whether one should pardon those who repent, or whether to him who was once a Christian, ceasing to be one should be of no avail; whether the mere fact of being a Christian is punishable, no other crime having been committed, or whether the crimes commonly associated with that fact are what are to be punished. Up to now, this is the procedure I have been following in the trials of those who have been hauled before me as Christians: I ask them whether they are Christians. If they say *yes*, I ask them again, and a third time, with threats of punishment. If they are contumacious, I order them to be led away to execution, for I do not doubt that, whatever it was that they were confessing, their pertinacity and inflexible obstinacy ought surely to be punished. There were others of like foolishness, whom, insofar as they were Roman citizens, I sent to Rome for punishment. Soon word got out, and, as usually happens, accusations were multiplied, and a greater variety of cases arose. I received an anonymous list containing many names. Of these I thought that those who denied that they were or had been Christians should be set free if, at my invitation, they called upon the gods, reverencing with incense and libations your image (which I had ordered for this purpose to be included with the idols of the deities), all the while cursing Christ, for those who are really Christians, so they say, can in no wise be persuaded to do that. Others who had been pointed out as Christians admitted it, but soon reneged, saying that they had been such at one time, but had desisted, some, many years ago, a few, even more than twenty years back. All these too venerated your image and the statues of the gods, and cursed Christ. They furthermore asserted that this was the sum total of their crime and mistake: That they were accustomed to come together on a certain day of the week, before sunrise, to sing together a hymn to Christ, their god, and to bind themselves by oath against any evil, not to commit burglaries, muggings, or adultery, not to give false testimony, or to refuse to their rightful owners anything that had been entrusted to them for safe keeping. After this, it was their custom to study; then they assembled again to eat some ordinary and harmless food, but they stopped doing this after my decree, by which, at your command, I had prohibited all secret societies. What is more, I thought it necessary to see if this was the truth by interrogating two female slaves, called deaconesses, whom I put to the torture. I found out nothing more than that this was an extravagant and ridiculous cult. I then suspended the trial so I could have recourse to you, for this seems to me to be a matter worthy of your attention, especially on account of the number of cultists, for many people of every age, or every rank, and even of both sexes are falling into danger and will continue to do so. The infection of this cult has spread not only to the cities, but to the small towns as well, and to the rural regions. Yet it seems capable of being stopped and pushed back. It is certainly now admitted that the temples, recently empty, have begun to be crowded again, and the sacred ceremonies, for some time suspended, have recommenced. Furthermore, pasture land for sacrificial animals, which up to now could scarcely find a buyer, is once again being sold. Wherefore it is easy to suppose that the common folk can be corrected, if an opportunity be given them to recant.

Traianus Plinio S. Actum quem debuisti, mi Secunde, in excutiendis causis qui Christiani ad te delati fuerant secutus es. Neque enim in universum aliquid quod quasi certam formam habeat constitui potest. Conquirendi non sunt: si deferantur et arguantur, puniendi sunt, ita tamen ut qui negaverit se Christianum esse idque re ipsa manifestum fecerit, id est, supplicando deis nostris, quamvis suspectus in praeteritum, veniam ex paenitentia impetret. Sine auctore vero propositi libelli in nullo crimine locum habere debent. Nam et pessimi exempli nec nostri saeculi est.

Trajan to Pliny, Greetings! In dealing with the cases of those who have been denounced to you as Christians, you have followed that procedure which you ought, for there is no easy rule which can be laid down for all cases. Do not go looking for Christians, but if they are brought before you and are convicted, they must be punished, except that whosoever denies that he is a Christian and makes this manifest by worshipping our gods, should receive pardon on account of his repentance, however much his behavior in the past is suspect. Anonymous accusations are not to be admitted in any trial. They set the worst possible precedent and are not in accordance with the spirit of these advanced times.

It frequently happens that when a numerous class of people is abused, the number of victims is exaggerated by those in sympathy with them and attenuated by those motivated to be apologists for the criminals. Thus in our own times has arisen the class of holocaust deniers. Similarly the Turks reduce the number of Armenians murdered at their hand, and the defenders of the Confederacy minimize the sufferings of slaves. So in the eighteenth century there arose a great controversy over the number of the early Christian martyrs, a controversy brought forth by the publication in 1775 of the first volume of the *History of the Decline and Fall of the Roman Empire*, by Edward Gibbon.

The sixteenth chapter of Gibbon's volume is of sixty-eight quarto pages, and is entitled "The conduct of the Roman government towards the Christians, from the reign of Nero to that of Constantine." It was called a whitewash by the historian Milman, dean of St. Paul's, and Gibbon's chief nineteenth-century editor:

The sixteenth chapter I cannot help considering as a very ingenious and specious, but very disgraceful extenuation of the cruelties perpetrated by the Roman magistrates against the Christians. It is written in the most contemptibly factious spirit of prejudice against the sufferers; it is unworthy of a philosopher and of a man of humanity.

Gibbon himself stated the purpose of the sixteenth chapter at the end of the second paragraph:

To separate (if it be possible) a few authentic as well as interesting facts from the undigested mass of fiction and error, and to relate, in a clear and rational manner, the causes, the extent, the duration, and the most important circumstances of the persecutions to which the first Christians were exposed, is the design of the present Chapter.

Gibbon claimed that the Jews and Christians, alike in so many ways, received different treatment from the state because the former were a nation that followed the religion of their fathers, whereas the latter were viewed as a sect that had deserted the religion of their ancestors. Furthermore, the Christians never had a temple or sacrifices at a time when such things were commonly considered the essence of religion, and were therefore open to the charge of atheism, which was imagined to call down the indignation of heaven upon the Empire and its people. Nevertheless, Gibbon insisted that the attitude of the authorities toward the new religion was remarkably restrained. He made four claims: (1) During the first century A.D., the Christians were not even considered an object worthy of the attention of the government. The persecution of Nero was a local affair, restricted to the city of Rome itself, where the emperor required a scapegoat to deflect from his own person the accusation of incendiary. The persecution of Domitian thirty years later, Gibbon said, was no real persecution, but the mere execution of a few members of his own family whom the emperor suspected of plotting to overthrow him. (2) The authorities proceeded cautiously and

– M –

reluctantly in trying the cases of those Christians who were brought before them. As evidence of this, he alluded to the letter of the younger Pliny, governor of Bithynia and Pontus, to Emperor Trajan, asking for advice on how to proceed in such matters. The emperor replied that the authorities were not to seek out Christians, nor were they to accept the testimony of anonymous informers, but they were indeed to punish those Christians convicted on the testimony of a fair and open accuser. (3) The Romans were moderate in their punishments. There were three common ways of escaping the punishment for professing Christianity. First, upon notification by the government that he was under investigation, the accused could flee the province and wait until the persecution, which was usually of short duration, should end. Second, he could bribe a notary and purchase a certificate which falsely stated that he had sacrificed to the gods, and, third, if convicted, he would be set free if he threw a few grains of incense into the fire before the divine or imperial image. (4) The persecutions were brief, with long intervals of peace in between. To make his point, he discussed each of the persecutions, which tradition had enumerated as ten: those of Nero, Domitian, Trajan, Marcus Aurelius, Septimius Severus, Maximinus, Decius, Valerian, Aurelian, and Diocletian. He then proceeded to count the number of martyrs in the last persecution, that of Diocletian, which was the most bloody; he estimated the number at less than 2,000, arriving at this figure in the following way: He counted in the pages of Eusebius the names of no more than ninety-two victims in Palestine during the course of the persecution, and Palestine was, he pointed out, but one-sixteenth of the Eastern Roman Empire, where the persecution was bloodiest. He therefore supposed that there were no more than $16 \times 92 = 1{,}472$ victims in the Eastern half of the Empire. But in the West, the persecution was much less severe, since the Emperors Constantius, Maxentius, and Constantine protected the Christians. Gibbon therefore allowed no more than five hundred martyrs in the western half of the Empire, thereby arriving at a total of no more than two thousand for the whole world, and therefore far fewer than twenty thousand for all ten persecutions combined over the course of three hundred years. With regard to the number of the martyrs, which is the major issue of the sixteenth chapter, we are not in a position to settle the matter. Estimates range from a low of ten to twenty thousand to a high of hundreds of thousands, or even millions, but to assign an accurate approximation is impossible. With regard to whether Gibbon was fair or not, we may agree that Macaulay had a point:

I read a good deal of Gibbon. He is grossly partial to the pagan persecutors, quite offensively so.... He writes like a man who has received some personal injury from Christianity, and wished to be revenged on it and all its professors.[14]

Dr. Arnold of Rugby had the following to say on the subject after viewing the paintings of the sufferings of the martyrs in the Church of San Stefano Rotondo in Rome:

No doubt many of the particular stories thus painted will bear no critical examination; it is likely enough, too, that Gibbon has truly accused the general statements of exaggeration. But this is a thankless labour, such as Lingard and others have undertaken with regard to the St. Bartholomew massacre, and the Irish massacre of 1642. Divide the sum total of reported martyrs—by fifty if you will—but after all you have a number of persons of all ages and sexes suffering cruel torments and death for conscience sake and for Christ's, and by their sufferings manifestly, with God's blessing, ensuring the triumph of Christ's Gospel.[15]

A typical modern conclusion about the number of the early martyrs by an authoritative figure was attempted by the archbishop of Canterbury, Rowan Williams:

During the second decade of the fourth century, the Christian communities of the Roman world suddenly found themselves in a radically new situation. Until then they had generally been seen as rather suspect: their loyalty to the imperial administration was in doubt and they were secretive about their actual practices; not surprisingly, lurid rumours circulated. From time to time local Roman officials had rounded up a handful of them for trial—and execution if they failed to recant their beliefs. In the middle of the third century there had been for the first time an Empire-wide initiative against them, producing a good many martyrs and rather more apostates. And in the first decade of the fourth century another imperial pogrom had been in train; there had been a significant number of executions (some by very gruesome methods) and mutilations, with others condemned to forced labour in the terrible conditions of the state-owned mines. Once again, the pressure thus created led some to compromise with their persecutors, handing over church property and sacred books—an issue that was to generate long-lasting and savagely bitter controversy in later decades.[16]

14. George Otto Trevelyan, *The Life and Letters of Lord Macaulay* (London: Longmans, Green, 1876), 2:39–40.

15. Arthur Penrhyn Stanley, *The Life and Correspondence of Thomas Arnold, D. D.*, 5th ed. (London: B. Fellowes, 1845), 2:419.

16. Rowan Williams, preface to *The History of the Church from Christ to Constantine*, by Eusebius, trans. G. A. Williamson (London: The Folio Society, 2011), xi.

– M –

Masoretic It is a matter of debate among the authorities whether the origin of this word lies in the Hebrew root אסר to bind, or in the root מסר, *to deliver, hand down*. In the former case, the derived noun מסרת (*masoreth*) means *bond* or *link*; in the latter case, the derived noun מסרת (*massoreth*) means *tradition*. Other etymologies have also been proposed by those competent to have an opinion, and these may be found in the entry *Masorah* in the *Encyclopaedia Judaica*.[17] The Masorites were Jewish scholars of the first millennium who produced the standard, "Masoretic," text of the Hebrew Old Testament. The word *Masorite* comes from their Greek name, Μασωρῖται. The vowel marks and signs of their creation are learned by all students of biblical Hebrew, for whom the best resource is Jacob Weingreen's *A Practical Grammar for Classical Hebrew*.

Mass The Latin verb *mitto, mittere, misi, missus* means *to send*. From it was formed the noun *missa*, which first appeared, according to the *Oxford English Dictionary*, in the fourth quarter of the fourth century as a name for a religious service in general, and, with the passage of time, solely for the Holy Eucharist, as the religious ceremony *par excellence*. Why it should have become the name for a religious service is not clear. Furthermore, the *Oxford English Dictionary* says:

In secular application it occurs, though rarely, in the 5th and 6th centuries with the sense "dismissal".

If this is so, then the words *Ite, missa est* mean "Go, it is the time for dismissal." Bacci gives the Latin word *sacrum, -i, n.,* as the correct equivalent of the word *Mass*.

Since the doctrine of the Church teaches that the Mass is the unbloody sacrifice of Jesus Christ offered to God the Father, it came to be conducted with the solemnity due to its awesome significance. The accompanying ceremonial reached the highest achievable level of artistic beauty and intellectual content of any human performance. The modification of the Order of Mass that took place after the Second Vatican Council brought with it considerable change in the manner of Catholic worship. These changes were for some few Catholics part of a universal trend in the Western world, a trend that Bertrand Russell once commented upon.

---

17. *Encyclopaedia Judaica*, vol. 16, *Supplementary Entries* (Jerusalem: Keter Publishing House, n.d.), s.v. "Masorah," 1418b.

The world was much more beautiful to look at than it is now. Every time I go back to a place that I knew long ago, I think, "Oh how sad it is! This place used to be beautiful, and now it is hideous." And one thing after another, one piece of beauty after another, is destroyed, and that I do profoundly regret.[18]

Master of Ceremonies For the etymologies, see the entries **Ceremony** and **Maestro di Camera**. The common Latin name for *master of ceremonies* is *caerimoniarius*, although Bacci favors the title *caerimoniarum magister*. In the twentieth century, the preeminent masters of ceremonies at the papal court were Carlo Respighi (1918–1947) and Enrico Dante (1947–1965). The latter was quoted in the November 9, 1962, issue of *Time* magazine as complaining to the assembled fathers at the Second Vatican Council, "Everything has been ordained by tradition, and now you want to change it all." In truth, it was, and they did. He received a cardinal's hat from Pope Paul VI in 1965.

Matins The Latin indeclinable noun *mane* means *morning*, and from it proceeded the adjective *matutinus* with the meaning *belonging to the morning*. From *matutinus* came the French noun *matin* meaning *morning*, and from this noun came the name for the morning prayer, *Matins*.

Matrimony The Greek nouns πατήρ and μήτηρ mean *father* and *mother* respectively, and the related Latin nouns are *pater* and *mater*. The Latin suffix *-monium*, when added to roots or verb stems, forms a noun that names something associated with the idea in the root or verb stem. Thus from *pater* is formed *patrimonium*, and from *mater* is produced *matrimonium*, but whereas the former means *that which comes to us from the father*, the latter means *marriage*.

Maundy The Latin verb *mando, mandare, mandavi, mandatus* means *to command*, and from its fourth principal part was formed the noun *mandatum*, an order. The English *Maundy*, as in the phrases *Maundy Thursday* or *Maundy money*, is the corruption of *mandatum*. The adjective *Maundy* is applied to the day before the crucifixion because of the following words spoken by Jesus, which were believed to have been uttered on that day:

Mandatum novum do vobis ...

I give you a new commandment ...[19]

18. Bertrand Russell, interview by John Freeman, *Face to Face*, BBC, March 4, 1959.
19. John 13:34

– M –

Mediaeval The Greek noun αἰών means a *period of time*, particularly a long one, and related to it is the Latin noun *aevum* with the meaning *eternity*, or a *period of time* in general. The Greek adjective μέσος means *middle*, and related to it is the Latin adjective *medius* with the same meaning. The *Medium Aevum* was the Middle Ages, an expression that arose in the Renaissance period to denominate, usually with disparagement, the period hovering between antiquity and modernity. Ferdinand Gregorovius, however, defined the Middle Ages with admiration when he wrote:

> The Middle Ages are the development of the Western races, by the influence of the principles of the Christian religion operating on the foundations of ancient culture; they are the great factory and the treasure-house of all the ideas of our culture. The farther we are separated from them, the more mysterious and deserving of reverence do they appear. The sublimity of their ideals and the fervor of their religion, the grandeur of their world-embracing system, the visionary subordination of the earthly to the spiritual, the many-sided forms of their life, the profound antagonism between the supernatural and the actual world, and their destructive but at the same time fruitful struggle; all these things exhibit a cosmos of ideas and phenomena, whose essential nature seems veiled in mystery.[20]

From the phrase *Medium Aevum* was formed the Late Latin adjective *mediaevalis*, whence proceeded our *mediaeval*. The wonderful temporal reign of the saints was widely believed to have been realized in mediaeval times.[21]

Melkite The Hebrew מלך means *king*. The *Melkites*, or *royalists*, *partisans of the emperor*, were those Christians in the East who, in the fifth century, followed the lead of the Byzantine Emperor and accepted the decisions of the Council of Chalcedon. The name is the transliteration of the Greek word Μελκίτης coined for the occasion. Today the word is restricted in meaning and denotes only Catholics of the Eastern Rite subject to the patriarch of Antioch, currently Joseph I. His predecessor Maximos IV Saigh was conspicuous enough at the Second Vatican Council to incur the disapproval of the "traditionalists," who said that every disagreeable decision there had been adopted *Bea culpa, Bea culpa, Bea Maximos culpa*.

20. Ferdinand Gregorovius, *History of the City of Rome in the Middle Ages*, trans. Mrs. Gustavus W. Hamilton (London: G. Bell & Sons, 1902), vol. 8, pt. 2, pp. 703–4.

21. John Henry Cardinal Newman, "The Benedictine Schools," in *Historical Sketches*, vol. 2 (London: Longmans, Green, 1917), 437.

Mendicant The Latin verb *mendīco, mendīcare* means *to go begging*, and from its present participle *mendicans, mendīcantis* there proceeded the English adjective *mendicant*. In the thirteenth century, the friars of the newly founded Dominican and Franciscan orders were supposed to earn their living by begging, whence they were called the *mendicant orders*. In due course, the Augustinians and Carmelites were also recognized as mendicant orders.

Metempsychosis The Greek preposition μετά means *after* or *across*, and the noun ψυχή means *soul*. *Metempsychosis* is the doctrine of the transmigration of souls, or reincarnation, taught by Plato in the dialogue *Timaeus*. It is the reason why the Aristotelian and not the Platonic philosophy was more serviceable to the mediaeval scholastic philosophers, for that doctrine is a great heresy.

Minister The Latin comparative adjective *minus* means *less*, and related to it is the second declension noun *minister*, with the meaning a *subordinate, servant, attendant, assistant*. Weekley says that the ecclesiastical sense, after the French *ministre*, "is found in pre-Reformation times of an ecclesiastic charged with some spec. function." He says that the political meaning dates to the seventeenth century. In current ecclesiastical language, it is used only of Protestant clergymen of churches that deny the priesthood. Pliny, in his Letter 96 (to Trajan), uses the words "female ministers"—*ministrae*—to name what appear to be deaconesses. See the entry **Martyr**.

Miracle The Latin adjective *mirus* means *wonderful, astonishing, extraordinary*, and from it was derived the verb *miror, mirari, miratus sum* with the meaning *to marvel at*. From *miror* came the noun *miraculum*, the event causing the wonder. In the etymological sense, everyone accepts miracles. The Reformers and Deists tended to reject miracles, at least after the time of Christ, if miracles are defined as events contrary to the laws of physics; the rejection of miracles found its champion in David Hume (1711–1776), who expounded the thesis in the tenth section of his *Enquiry concerning Human Understanding*.

Miserere The Latin verb *misereor, misereri, miseratus sum* means *to have mercy*. The imperative singular is *miserere*, which translates the Greek ἐλέησον. It is the first word and therefore the name of the penitential Psalm 51. A beautiful musical setting of this psalm is by Gregorio Allegri (died 1652). In the eighteenth century, Allegri's *Miserere* was the most famous piece in the repertoire of the Sistine Chapel, and, for fear of its being stolen, the music was never published. Mozart is believed to have gone to hear it in 1769 with the intention of writing down the notes from memory thereafter.

Missal See the entry **Mass** for a more complete etymology. The addition of the adjectival suffix *-alis* to the stem of the Ecclesiatical Latin noun *missa* produced the adjective *missalis* with the meaning *pertaining to the Mass*; the neuter singular *missale* of this adjective then became a noun in its own right with the meaning the *Mass Book*. In similar fashion were formed the nouns *Antiphonale*, *Graduale*, *Pontificale*, and *Rituale*. After people became comfortable with this method of giving names to liturgical books, there was daringly produced the name *Kyriale* by adding the suffix to the stem of κύριε, the first word of the exclamation κύριε ἐλέησον. The *Missale Romanum* is the Latin name for the Mass book of the Western Church; its English translation is the *Roman Missal*.

Missalettes The silly noun *missalette* is formed by adding the French feminine diminutive ending *-ette* to the noun *missal*. Missalettes are the throw-away booklets, found in churches, that contain the prayers of the Mass. One would think that they are a sin against the environment. After the liturgical reforms in the wake of the Second Vatican Council, the *Missale Romanum* became an enormous book, and it is now published in four volumes instead of the former one volume. This is a result of all the options allowed by modern fancy. As a result, people can no longer be expected to own it, and are instead provided with missalettes. After their time is up, they are thrown away or recycled. The Jews put their unwanted prayer materials into a גניזה or *geniza*, or buried them in the ground. They could not be thrown into the garbage, because they were in the sacred language and contained the name of God. Such is the difference in attitude.

Missionary The Latin verb *mitto, mittere, misi, missus* means *to send*, and the related noun *missio* means *a sending*. From this noun is formed the ecclesiastical adjective and noun *missionarius*, from which we derive our adjective and noun *missionary*. Christianity, like Islam, is a missionary religion. Judaism is not. Missionary activity is ordered by Christ himself in Matthew 28:19–20:

πορευθέντες οὖν μαθητεύσατε πάντα τὰ ἔθνη, βαπτίζοντες αὐτοὺς εἰς τὸ ὄνομα τοῦ πατρὸς καὶ τοῦ υἱοῦ καὶ τοῦ ἁγίου πνεύματος, διδάσκοντες αὐτοὺς τηρεῖν πάντα ὅσα ἐνετειλάμην ὑμῖν·

Euntes ergo docete omnes gentes, baptizantes eos in nomine Patris et Filii et Spiritus Sancti, docentes eos servare omnia, quaecumque mandavi vobis.

Go ye therefore, and teach all nations, baptizing them in the name of the Father, and of the Son, and of the Holy Ghost, teaching them to observe all things whatsoever I have commanded you. (Authorized Version)

In the fifteenth chapter of his *History of the Decline and Fall of the Roman Empire*, Gibbon treats "The progress of the Christian religion, and the sentiments, manners, numbers, and condition of the primitive Christians." Since Gibbon's book is considered the greatest work of history in the English language and had a wide influence, it is worthwhile reviewing his explanation for the spread of Christianity in the three centuries after its institution. The fifteenth chapter is sixty-nine quarto pages long, with thirty-two lines to the page. Gibbon began by taking out an insurance policy: he would not deal with the divine causes for the spread of Christianity, but only the human causes. He said that there were five of these. The first was the inflexible zeal of the early Christians. Christianity, he said, proceeded out of Judaism, but, unlike the Jews, who did not care to propagate their religion, to which propagation, indeed, the physical pain of circumcision was a real impediment, the Christians were a missionary lot who held that outside the Church there was no salvation. The second cause was the doctrine of a future life. Although authorities like Cicero, following Plato, had taught the immortality of the soul, this was mixed up with the notion of reincarnation, where the soul, and not the body, was the principle of individuality; the Christians taught that both soul and body were specific to the individual. Furthermore, the commonality of mankind mostly followed Homer (book 11 of the *Odyssey*) and Vergil (book 6 of the *Aeneid*), who both represented the next life as a shadowy affair, certainly not something to be anticipated with enthusiasm. The third cause was the report of the many miracles wrought by the early saints. The fourth cause was the pure and austere way of life of the early Christians. The fifth and final cause was the union and discipline of the Christian commonwealth, which developed into an independent state in the midst of the Roman Empire. Since the believers took no part in politics, they devoted all their energies to the building up of the Church, which they organized into dioceses, archdioceses, and patriarchates, like the state itself, with its provinces, dioceses, and prefectures. Gibbon then recapitulates the five causes in the following passage:

It was by the aid of these causes, exclusive zeal, the immediate expectation of another world, the claim of miracles, the practice of rigid virtue, and the constitution of the primitive church, that Christianity spread itself with so much success in the Roman empire. To the first of these the Christians were indebted for their invincible valour, which disdained to capitulate to the enemy whom they were resolved to vanquish. The three succeeding causes supplied their valour with the most formidable arms. The last of these causes united their courage, directed their arms, and gave their efforts that irresistible weight, which even a small band of well-trained and intrepid volunteers has so often possessed over an undisciplined multitude, ignorant of the subject, and careless of the event of the war.[22]

He then proceeded to the estimation of the fraction of the population of the Empire before the time of Constantine who professed the Christian religion. Upon the scanty evidence available, for example, that later on, when Christianity was the official religion, it accounted for only twenty percent of the population of Antioch, the greatest city of the East, and that in Rome itself there were fewer than fifty priests, he concluded that this proportion was about five percent. With regard to the number of priests in Rome during the third century of our era, Gibbon relied upon a letter from Pope Cornelius to Fabius, bishop of Antioch, quoted by Eusebius in his *History*,[23] from which we learn that at that time (251–53) there were in the diocese of Rome forty-six priests, seven deacons, seven subdeacons, forty-two acolytes, and a total of fifty-two exorcists, lectors, and porters.

The issue treated in the fifteenth chapter was, how did Christianity happen to establish itself so completely in the centuries following the death of Christ? The theological reason, given by those who adhere to the Community of Saints, must always be that which is given in Galatians 4:4:

ὅτε δὲ ἦλθεν τὸ πλήρωμα τοῦ χρόνου ...

But when the fullness of time was come ...

The scientific reason was that the adjacent religions were declining, and had no influence any more on the population.

22. Edward Gibbon, *The History of the Decline and Fall of the Roman Empire*, ed. Betty Radice (London: The Folio Society, 1995), 2:134.
23. Eusebius, *The History of the Church from Christ to Constantine*, trans. G. A. Williamson (London: the Folio Society, 2011), VI 43, page 195.

We may end by asking whether, as Gibbon believed, the rise of Christianity was a contributing factor in the fall of the Roman Empire. The philosopher Celsus had early on written that the activities of the Christians could lead to the collapse of the state.

> He even winds up by an exhortation to the Christians to abandon their religious and political isolation, and to conform to the common religion, for the sake of the State and the Roman Empire, which these divisions weaken. That is his chief anxiety.[24]

At the most, one can say that Christianity gave it a gentle push. It was time for a change, and the influx of oriental religions, long before Christianity, had a foreboding impact on Roman religion. Christianity, indeed, had an impact only when it became the imperial religion; before that, it was like any other imported religion. The end came with Constantine. The Roman Empire fell like a ripe fruit that falls from the tree; the trees cannot hold them anymore, and one has only to use some rough handling. We may take a famous line of Horace for our conclusion:

> Suis et ipsa Roma viribus ruit.[25]
>
> Of its own weight did the Empire of Rome fall.

Miter The Greek noun μίτρα was the name of a Persian headband. The word was used by the Septuagint translators to render the turban מצנפת of the high priest (cf. Exodus 28:37), and from there it came to denote the bishop's hat. The current custom of a pontificating bishop putting on and removing his own miter is unseemly and is typical of the lack of attention to detail that is the main problem with modern liturgy; formerly, a minister did this, except when there were too many bishops in miters, in which case everyone took care of himself.

Mithraism The worship of the Persian god of light Mitrā, whom the Greeks called Μίθρας—Mithras—was introduced into the Roman Empire and became popular among men, particularly soldiers, in the third century of the Christian Era. A sanctuary of Mithras and the remains of a school of that cult, two floors *beneath* the Basilica of San Clemente in Rome, are not the least of the wonders to be appreciated at that site.

---

24. Louis Duchesne, *Early History of the Christian Church from Its Foundation to the End of the Third Century* (London: John Murray, 1914), 147.
25. Horace, Epode 16.2.

The Mithraic cult was practised by confraternities, and celebrated in subterranean caves, in the depths of which was a sculptured representation of Mithras killing the bull. The god, in Persian dress, stands out against the background of a cavern, hewn in the living rock, a symbol of the firmament whence shines forth the celestial light. He holds beneath him a bull, which he stabs in the shoulder, a symbolic sacrifice, representing, according to legend, the creation of the world. These mysteries, with many others, were revealed by degrees to the initiates. They were divided into seven classes, each having its own name.... The transit from one class to another involved many quaint ceremonies, not unlike those of our freemasons.[26]

... the religion of Mithras contained elements—in theology, morality, ritual, and in its doctrine of the end of all things—bearing a strange resemblance to Christianity. The Christians themselves perceived this. As mediator between the world and the Supreme Divinity, as creator, and, in a certain sense, as redeemer of mankind, the advocate of all moral good, and the adversary of all the powers of evil, Mithras certainly does present some analogy with the Logos, the creator and the friend of Man. The followers of Mithras, like the disciples of Christ, held the soul to be immortal, and that the body would rise again. Closely united with each other by a common religious bond, the Mithraites entered their confraternity by a baptismal rite; other ceremonies of theirs closely resembled confirmation and communion. Both religions observed the Sunday, the Day of the Sun. December 25, *natale Solis invicti*, was a feast-day to the followers of Mithras, as it became to the Christians. Mithraism had its ascetics, of both sexes, like the Christian Church.[27]

Mixed Marriages The Greek verb μίγνυμι means *to mix*, and related to it is the Latin verb *misceo, miscere, miscui, mixtus* with the same meaning. The Latin noun *mas, maris, m.*, means the *male*, and from it was derived the adjective *marītus, -a, -um* with the meaning *having to do with marriage*. From this adjective there proceeded the verb *marīto, marītare, marītavi, marītatus* meaning *to marry*, and thence came the Late Latin noun *maritaticum*, another word for *matrimony*. Our English noun *marriage* comes from *maritaticum*, via the French *mariage*. A mixed marriage is a marriage in which one party is a Catholic and the other party is not a Catholic. One of the complaints that St. Cyprian made about the Carthaginian Christians was that they were given to mixed marriages.[28]

---

26. Duchesne, *Early History of the Christian Church from Its Foundation to the End of the Third Century*, 394–95.

27. Ibid., 396.

28. Ibid., 290.

Modalism The Greek verb μέδομαι means *to measure, to weigh*, and related to it is the Latin noun *modus* with the meaning a *measure*, a *manner*. From this noun was formed the Mediaeval Latin adjective *modalis* with the meaning *pertaining to mode rather than to substance*, and the addition of the Greek suffix *-ism* produced the modern noun *modalism*. Modalism was a heresy that arose in the first half of the third century, when it was introduced in Rome by the confessor Praxeas, who had gone thither to oppose the Montanists, whose leader, Montanus, was called the *Paraclete*.

In Asia, in very early days, there were people who would not hear of any intermediary between God and the world, especially in the work of redemption, and they declared that they knew but one God, He who was incarnate in Jesus Christ. According to them the names of Father and Son corresponded only to different aspects of the same Person, playing transitory parts, and not to divine realities. This is what is called Modalism.[29]

If the Father and the Son were the same person, just as a single man may be both a father and a son, then it was correct to say that the Father suffered on the Cross—Pater passus est.

Praxeas was a Modalist. His doctrines spread so much that Tertullian said of him that in Rome he had done two diabolical works: "He had put to flight the Paraclete, and crucified the Father." This last shaft soon brought the new doctrine into ridicule. It exposed pretty clearly one outcome of the doctrine quite contrary to Scripture. The Modalists were called Patripassians.[30]

Modernism The Latin noun *modus, -i, m.* means a *unit of measurement*, and in the ablative singular, *modo*, it becomes an adverb with the meaning *just now*; in fact, the Romans still say *mo'* when they mean *now*. Just as the adjective *hodiernus* was formed from the adverb *hodie*, so was the adjective *modernus* formed from *modo* with the meaning *having to do with the present*. The Greek nominal suffix -ισμός was added in modern times to the stem of the Latin adjective *modernus* to form the noun *modernism*. *Modernism* is a term of abuse directed against Catholics who accept the higher criticism in the study of the Bible, with all the consequent results. It became a technical term when it appeared in the encyclical *Pascendi* of September 8, 1907.

29. Ibid., 223–24.
30. Ibid.

Thus we come to the key idea of Modernism—that dogmas are not the statements of truths revealed by God, but expressions of the religious mind at the stage to which religious experience has brought it; and the value of dogma is measured, not by the objective truth of what they tell us about God, but by the adequacy with which (provisionally and for the time being) they express our own religious consciousness.[31]

Modernist This is a word that appears in the title of the encyclical *Pascendi* in the phrase *De Modernistarum doctrinis*. A *modernista* or *modernist* is someone who is held to profess modernism. The term is pejorative and would not be used by anyone of himself.

Monachism The Greek adjective μόνος means *alone*, and from it was derived the noun μόναχος with the meaning *someone who lives alone*. This word was transliterated into Latin as *monacus* or *monachus*, and the addition of the Greek suffix *-ism* produced the modern noun *monachism*, the *life style of those who live alone*. The English noun *monasticism* is a synonym, transliterated from the Greek μοναστής, *someone who lives alone*. Lea suspects that the Christian monastic enterprise may have been promoted by the influence of the similar Buddhist institution,[32] but he admits that the instinct may be a natural response to a human need. The scriptural foundation for Christian monasticism he finds in the institution of widows discussed in 1 Timothy 5:9–16.[33] The Egyptian St. Antony of the Desert was the first solitary or hermit, and his countryman St. Pachomius the first monk. By 348, the first Council of Carthage was already legislating for hermits, and in 381 the Council of Saragossa published decrees on the subject of nuns.[34] The emperor Jovian had meanwhile, in 364, decreed the death penalty for any man who married a runaway nun;[35] such a crime was considered particularly heinous because of the opinion of Innocent I (401–417) and St. Augustine, that the nun was married to Christ.

In later times a variety of holy objects might present themselves for devotion to choose from, such as the care of the poor, or of the sick, or of the young, the re-

---

31. Maisie Ward, *The Wilfrid Wards and the Transition*, vol. 2, *Insurrection versus Resurrection* (New York: Sheed & Ward, 1937), 195. This book has an excellent discussion of the modernist controversy.

32. Henry Charles Lea, *History of Sacerdotal Celibacy in the Christian Church* (n.p.: University Books, 1966), 71, 72.

33. Ibid., 73.

34. Ibid., 76.

35. Ibid., 79.

demption of captives, or the conversion of the barbarians; but early monachism was flight from the world, and nothing else.[36]

The Reformers rejected monasticism and declared it a counterproductive enterprise. Their attitude is reflected in the following violent passage of Lea. He is speaking of a fifteenth-century account of the life of a Carthusian hermit.

He rarely slept on the couch provided for each brother, but passed his nights in prayer on the steps of the altar. In the hair shirt worn next his skin he cultivated lice and maggots so assiduously that they were often seen crawling over his face, and he scourged himself for every unhallowed wandering thought. He had preserved his virginity to old age, and his life had been passed in the Church, yet in his daily confessions he accused himself of every sin possible to man, and he rigorously performed whatever penance was assigned to him. With all this maceration, the flesh would still assert itself, and he was tormented with evil desires which the sharp cords of the discipline failed to subdue. His office of procurator of the abbey required him to make frequent visits on business to the neighboring town, and he never left the gates of his retreat without lamenting and expressing the fear that he should not return to it the same as he left it. If we consider what might have been effected by the energies of thousands of men such as this, had those energies not been absorbed in lifelong asceticism, we may conceive in some measure the retardation of human progress wrought by the influence of monachism.[37]

However, even a Protestant scholar like Gregorovius recognized that without the sixth-century monks, all culture would have disappeared from the face of the earth.

Monastery The Greek adjective μόνος means *alone*, and from it was derived the noun *monasterium* with the meaning the *home of those who live alone*. The inhabitants of a monastery live together, not alone, so the word has lost its original meaning. Speaking of St. Pachomius, Duchesne wrote:

He was the inventor of what we wrongly call the monasteries, and of the cenobitic life.[38]

36. John Henry Cardinal Newman, "The Mission of St. Benedict," in *Historical Sketches*, vol. 2 (London: Longmans, Green, 1917), 374–75.

37. Lea, *History of Sacerdotal Celibacy*, 306.

38. Louis Duchesne, *Early History of the Christian Church from Its Foundation to the End of the Fifth Century*, vol. 2 (London: John Murray, 1931), 395. See the entry **Coenobite** for Duchesne's comment on the words *monastery* and *coenobite*.

Monk The English noun *monk* is derived from the Latin noun *monacus* with the same meaning. For the etymology, see the entry **Monachism**.

Monophysite The Greek word μονοφυσίτης is a term of opprobrium for someone who rejected the decree of the Council of Chalcedon (451) concerning the two natures in Christ. It is compounded of μόνος, *single*, and φύσις, *nature*. Such people were also denominated (by their enemies) *Jacobites* in honor of one of their chief bishops, the sixth century James of Edessa. This form of Christianity is paramount in Armenia, Egypt, and Ethiopia, and is well represented in Syria and India. They were mistreated as heretics by the Byzantine authorities, wherefore they welcomed the advent of the Muslims in the seventh century.

Monotheism The Greek adjective μόνος means *alone*, and the noun θεός means *God*. From the latter word proceeded the adjective θεῖος with the meaning *pertaining to God*, and the concatenation of the words μόνος, θεῖος, and the suffix -ισμός produced the modern noun *monotheism* with the meaning *belief in one sole God*.

Monothelite The name μονοθελίτης is a term of opprobrium for someone who taught that there was but one will in the Christ, and who thus rejected the decree of the Third Council of Constantinople (681) that he had two wills; it is compounded of the words μόνος, *single*, and θέλημα, *will* (from ἐθέλω, *to want*). The main modern interest in the quarrel was the posthumous condemnation of Pope Honorius by the aforementioned Council, which matter came up for discussion at the time of the First Vatican Council. Passages such as Mark 14:36 were the subject of investigation to determine what they implied on the issue of one or two wills in the Christ:

οὐ τί ἐγὼ θέλω ἀλλὰ τί σύ.

Not what I will, but what Thou willest.

Monsignor The pope, as a sovereign prince, has, over the centuries, awarded titles of nobility to clergy and laity alike. An ennobled priest is called a *monsignor* in English, from the French *mon seigneur*, my lord. The Germans call such a celebrity *Prälat*. The creation of monsignors continues to this day, but the creation of lay papal nobility ended with Pius XII. Pope Pius named the American philanthropist Carrie Estelle Doheny a countess in 1939, and although such titles of nobility are not recognized in the United States, she was called Countess Doheny by her friends. She was a great book collector, but she willed her collection to a Catholic seminary, that of the Archdiocese of Los Angeles, which later sold them at auction at Christies during the period 1987–1989, the most valuable library ever dispersed in that manner.

Montanism The Latin noun *mons, montis, m.*, means a *mountain*, and from it was derived the adjective *montanus, -a, -um*, which means *pertaining to a mountain*, and which, as a noun, means *mountaineer*. *Montanus* was also a common Roman cognomen or surname. The noun *Montanism* described the system of the followers of the second century enthusiast Montanus, who emphasized prophecy, private inspiration, asceticism, and the imminent end of the world, occasionally over against the authority of the hierarchy. The supreme governors of the Montanists were not bishops and priests, which they had, but prophets and prophetesses. They admitted women to the priesthood and episcopate. They did away with mathematics by adopting a fixed date for Easter, April 6. Their most famous convert was Tertullian, and in Africa the Montanists were called *Tertulliani*. The Montanists denied that the Holy Spirit was a person, a doctrine which they thought contradicted the fact that there was but one God.

Monti The Latin noun *mons, montis, m.*, means *mountain*, and it came into Italian as *monte* with the plural *monti*. In Italian it was used as the name for a means of raising cash in the Papal States, adopted by the popes beginning with Clement VII (1523–1534). In this case, it evidently meant *piles* or *stacks of cash*. It was a sort of annuity. A subject who deposited cash with the state upon the announcement of a *monte* would receive a regular payment at a published interest rate for the remainder of his life. If the *monte* was termed *vacabile*, the deposit fell to the state when the depositor died; if the monte was *non vacabile*, then the interest payments would be continued after the death of the depositor for the life of his heir, and only upon the death of the heir would the principal fall to the state. It was an effective means of raising cash for an immediate need. Another, similar method was the sale of offices. A fellow would purchase his job in the papal administration and then make his living from the fees he collected in the performance of his duties.

Morse The Latin verb *mordeo, mordere, momordi, morsus* means *to bite*, and from it was formed the noun *morsus, morsūs, m.*, with the meaning a *bite*. This degenerated into the Italian *morso*, whence our *morse*, with the meaning a *clasp*, used to fasten a cloak at the top. It is the name of the prominent brooch used to close the copes of cardinals and bishops. Its use, along with that of buskins, sandals, and gloves, was made optional by Pope Paul VI in the instruction *Pontificales Ritus* of June 21, 1968, §15 c.[39] Nowadays it is a prohibited adornment, except when a pope should choose to wear one. In Latin, the morse is called *formale* or *pectorale*.

Mosaic The word *mosaic* is the corruption of the Greek adjective μουσεῖος, pertaining to the Muses; see the entry **Music**. The Greek μουσεῖος developed into the Late Latin *musaicus*, as if there had been an intermediate Greek adjective μουσαϊκός, but no such adjective is attested. *Musaicus* became *mosaicus*, which became the Italian *mosaico* and then the French *mosaïque*. The connection of the muses with patterns of little rocks or tiles is at least as old as the third century after Christ. The mosaics to be found in the churches of Rome and Ravenna are worthy of investigation either in person or through the book of Poeschke.[40]

Motet The French noun *mot* means *word*, and its diminutive *motette* means *little word*. *Motet* is merely the English spelling of *motette*. In the Catholic Church, *motet* is used of a musical polyphonic composition of the sixteenth century, usually of one or two movements, in which the text is a prayer; the word is not used if the composition is one of the proper or ordinary parts of the Mass.[41] How the word *motet* developed this meaning is unclear.

Mozzetta The Italian verb *mozzo, mozzare* means *to cut off*, and from it is derived the adjective *mozzo* meaning *cut short*. The Italian verb is a mutilation of the Latin *mutilo, mutilare* which means *to maim, to cut off*, whence comes the adjective *mutilis*, maimed. The mozzetta is a shortened cape that bishops wear over the rochet. It is etymologically related to *mozzarella*, the famous cheese, in the making of which the balls of cheese are cut off from the kneaded mass. Formerly bishops outside of

---

39. *Pontificales Ritus* (instruction of the Sacred Congregation of Rites, July 29, 1968), *Acta Apostolicae Sedis* 60, no. 7 (1968), 406–12. The text is also available at www.vatican.va/archive/aas/documents/AAS-60-1968-ocr.pdf.

40. Joachim Poeschke, *Italian Mosaics 300–1300*, trans. Russell Stockman (New York: Abbeville Press, 2010).

41. *Encyclopaedia Britannica*, 11th ed. (New York: The Encyclopaedia Britannica Company, 1911), s. v. "Motet."

their dioceses and auxiliary bishops wore not the mozzetta but rather the mantelletta, but this rule was abolished by Pope Paul VI. In winter, the pope's mozzetta is of crimson red bordered with violet; when wearing this mozzetta he usually also wears the hat called the *camauro*. In summer, the pope's mozzetta is of red silk without fur. John Paul II never used the winter mozzetta. Pope Paul VI abolished the small ornamental cap at the back of the mozzetta; one sees this cap nowadays only in the dress of certain canons, like those of Cologne cathedral, who, not being bishops, were not affected by his decree. From a purely sartorial point of view, this decree was a mistake, as the cap provided a sort of balance, and prelates wearing the new mozzettas now seem about to fall forward.

Mumpsimus A fifteenth-century copyist who knew no Latin wrote this word instead of *sumpsimus* while copying the text of the Mass when making a Missal. This Missal was then used by an English priest, who celebrated Mass by rote and said *Quod ore mumpsimus* for forty years. When he was given a new Missal with the corrected text, he refused to use it, saying, that he would not give up his old *mumpsimus* for the new-fangled *sumpsimus*. The story became a proverb to describe people who reject any change, even when it is required by knowledge.

Muratorian Canon The Latin noun *murus* means a *wall*, and derived from it are the adjective *muratus, -a, -um*, walled, and the noun *murator*, a builder of walls. In 1740, the historian Ludovico Antonio Muratori (1672–1750) published the text of a fragment of a seventh-century manuscript that he had found in the Ambrosian Library in Milan, which fragment contained a list of the canonical books of the Bible. The fragment is believed to be a copy of a much older document.

A complete canon, a list of all the books received by the Church as sacred and canonical, appeared for the first time in Rome towards the end of the 2nd century. This is called the Muratorian Canon. To tell the truth, this document is rather enigmatical, as only the end of it exists, and it is still a disputed point whether it was written in Greek or in Latin; it can, therefore, scarcely be considered an official document involving the responsibility of the Roman Church. But at least, it testifies to certainty reached on some points, and to other questions still undecided in Rome when it was written. It acknowledged as canonical the four gospels, the thirteen epistles of St. Paul, the Acts of the Apostles, the epistles of St. John and St. Jude, and two Apocalypses, that of John and that of Peter. Strong opposition existed, however, to the admission of the latter. The Shepherd was mentioned, but was set aside as too recent. Its author could neither be included amongst the prophets, nor amongst the apostles; he had written at a time, still recent (*nuperrime, temporibus nostris*), when his brother Pius occupied the episcopal throne at Rome. Other writings, such as the epistles of St. Paul to the Laodiceans and the Alexandrians, are classed as heretical, and resolutely set aside.[42]

In 1950, the Italian Republic issued a postage stamp in honor of Muratori; the work selected to be expressly commemorated on the stamp was not the Canon, but his twelve volume *Annali d'Italia*.

Music The Greek noun μοῦσα means *Muse*, one of the nine daughters of Zeus, the goddesses of the fine arts. A temple devoted to them was called a Μουσεῖον or *museum*, and from the noun μοῦσα was derived the adjective μουσικός with the meaning *pertaining to the Muses*, whence proceeds our word *music*. There were nine Muses: Calliope, Clio, Erato, Euterpe, Melpomene, Polymnia, Terpsichore, Thalia, and Urania. Since music was an essential component of the arts over which they presided, the word *music* naturally developed its current connotation. Life without music is death. The liturgy of the Church is supposed to be sung, and therefore music forms part of the education of the clergy. The education systems of the Western world have produced, at great expense, a generation uncomfortable with Perosi, and the music used for the Mass has been adjusted accordingly. Pugin was of the opinion that Gregorian Chant with organ accompaniment was the preferred type of music for the Mass.

It was of little use building Catholic churches, Pugin was wont to say, if they were to be used as fiddling rooms.

When the church at Derby was to be opened, he insisted on Gregorian with organ accompaniment; but "what was his disgust, the night before, when he saw a man with a fiddle-case making his way to the organ loft. He could hardly forbear," he said, "knocking him down with his own fiddle." He at once left the place and refused to attend the opening.[43]

The high quality of the Latin liturgical music of the Catholic Church in the era that began with Palestrina's *Missa Papae Marcelli* was the subject of comment by von Ranke.

42. Louis Duchesne, *Early History of the Christian Church from Its Foundation to the End of the Third Century* (London: John Murray, 1914), 369. [Note of Duchesne]: "The Epistle of St. James is not mentioned any more than those of St. Peter; but the text is doubtful, and possibly this omission, which is indefensible, especially as regards the First Epistle of Peter, did not occur in the original."

43. Wilfrid Ward, *The Life and Times of Cardinal Wiseman* (London: Longmans, Green, 1900), 1:355, 356.

The question was set at rest for ever by this one great example; a path was opened, pursuing which, works the most beautiful and most touching even to those who are not of the Roman creed, have been produced. Who can listen to them without enthusiasm? Nature herself seems to have acquired voice and utterance; it is as if the elements spoke; and the tones breathing through universal life, poured forth in blended harmony of adoration; now undulating, like the waves of the sea, now rising in songs of triumph to the skies. Amidst the consenting sympathies of creation, the soul is borne upward to the region of religious entrancement.[44]

Mysterium Fidei These words were part of the traditional words of consecration in the old Latin Mass; they mean the *mystery of faith*:

Accipite et bibite ex eo omnes. Hic est enim calix sanguinis mei, novi et aeterni testamenti, mysterium fidei, qui pro vobis et pro multis effundetur in remissionem peccatorum.

Take ye all and drink of it. For this is the chalice of my blood of the new and everlasting covenant, the mystery of faith, which shall be shed for you and for many unto the forgiveness of sins.

They were removed from the formula in the wake of the Second Vatican Council and made an acclamation after the consecration:

Accipite et bibite ex eo omnes. Hic est enim calix sanguinis mei, novi et aeterni testamenti, qui pro vobis et pro multis effundetur in remissionem peccatorum.
    Mysterium fidei.
    Mortem tuam annuntiamus Domine, et resurrectionem tuam confitemur donec venias.

Take ye all and drink of it. For this is the chalice of my blood of the new and everlasting covenant, which shall be shed for you and for many unto the forgiveness of sins.
    The mystery of faith!
    We proclaim Thy death, O Lord, and confess Thy resurrection, until Thou comest.

The words *Mysterium Fidei* were moved because they are not in the New Testament. But then the words of consecration are also not exactly as found in the corresponding biblical texts, which differ among themselves.

---

44. Leopold von Ranke, *The History of the Popes during the Last Four Centuries*, trans. Mrs. Foster and G. R. Dennis (London: G. Bell & Sons, 1912), 1:398–99.

Πίετε ἐξ αὐτοῦ πάντες· τοῦτο γάρ ἐστιν τὸ αἷμά μου τῆς διαθήκης τὸ περὶ πολλῶν ἐκχυννόμενον εἰς ἄφεσιν ἁμαρτιῶν.[45]

Bibite ex eo omnes: Hic est enim sanguis meus novi testamenti, qui pro multis effundetur in remissionem peccatorum.

Drink ye all of it, for this is my blood of the new testament, which is shed for many for the remission of sins. (Authorized Version)

Τοῦτό ἐστιν τὸ αἷμά μου τῆς διαθήκης τὸ ἐκχυννόμενον ὑπὲρ πολλῶν.[46]

Hic est sanguis meus novi testamenti, qui pro multis effundetur.

This is my blood of the new testament, which is shed for many.

Τοῦτο τὸ ποτήριον ἡ καινὴ διαθήκη ἐν τῷ αἵματί μου, τὸ ὑπὲρ ὑμῶν ἐκχυννόμενον.[47]

Hic est calix novum testamentum in sanguine meo, qui pro vobis fundetur.

This cup is the new testament in my blood, which is shed for you.

Τοῦτο τὸ ποτήριον ἡ καινὴ διαθήκη ἐστὶν ἐν τῷ ἐμῷ αἵματι· τοῦτο ποιεῖτε, ὁσάκις ἐὰν πίνητε, εἰς τὴν ἐμὴν ἀνάμνησιν.[48]

Hic calix novum testamentum est in meo sanguine; hoc facite, quotienscumque bibetis, in meam commemorationem.

This cup is the new testament in my blood. This do ye, as oft as ye drink it, in remembrance of me.

The accentuation of the noun *fidei* in the phrase *Mysterium Fi′dei* is a test of whether a celebrant has prepared properly; if he says *Mysterium Fide′i*, then he has a problem.

Mysterium Tremendum et Fascinans This is a Latin expression of Rudolf Otto used in his book *Das Heilige* to describe the effect that the presence of the Deity has on the believer. It means "the indescribable impression that brings on shivering and goose pimples."

Mystery The Greek verb μυέω means *to initiate, to instruct*, and the associated noun μύστης means an *initiate*. Since this was often done with blindfolds, there is a connection with μύω, *to be shut or closed* (of the eyes or mouth). The noun μυστήριον, which was taken over into Latin as *mysterium*, means a *sacred rite*.

45. Matthew 26:28
46. Mark 14:24
47. Luke 22:20
48. 1 Corinthians 11:25

Mythology The Greek noun μῦθος means *anything delivered by word of mouth, speech, conversation,* a *tale.* A myth was understood to be a legendary tale as opposed to an historical account. Μυθολογία, or mythology, is the study (λογία) of myths.

Narthex The Greek noun νάρθηξ, νάρθηκος, *m.*, was the name of a plant, called in Latin *ferula*, which meant in general a *reed*. The word also means a small case or casket for perfumes. The shape of such a casket was evidently considered by the early Christians to be similar to the ante-nave of a church. The narthex of a church is the porch or hall at the west end opening onto the nave; it was the place where penitents, and others not admissible to the interior of the church, would congregate.

Neologism The Greek adjective νέος means *young*, and the noun λόγος means *word* or *reason*. From their concatenation was produced the English word *Neologism*, the name of a philosophical school also denominated *Eclecticism* or *Neo-Platonism*.

The essential mark of Neologism is the denial of the exclusive divine mission and peculiar inspiration of the Scripture Prophets.[1]

Neophyte The Greek adjective νέος means *young*, and the verb φύω means *to bring forth, produce, make to grow, plant*; from their concatenation proceeded the adjective νεόφυτος with the meaning *someone newly planted*, a *recent convert*. A neophyte is a new Christian, one who has only lately been baptized.

Neo-Platonism In the third century there was a revival of the Platonic philosophy under the leadership of Ammonius Saccas, Plotinus, and

---

1. John Henry Cardinal Newman, *The Arians of the Fourth Century*, new ed. (London: Longmans, Green, 1897), 103.

Porphyry. Later generations called these people Neo-Platonists, but they identified themselves merely as Platonists. Their system is described by Duchesne as follows:

It speaks of three constituent elements in the Divine nature, emanating one from the other, and passing down from the abstract to the concrete, from the simple to the composite, and from absolute perfection to varying degrees of imperfection. Behind all, is absolute essential Being, without determinateness or properties, ineffable and inaccessible to thought. It is the first single cause of all being in others; and thus, all other beings are It, and It is the whole being of every being. In the second degree comes Intelligence (νοῦς), which is also the Intelligible, an image of the Supreme Being, capable of being known, but of an absolute unity. This is the prototype of all other beings. Last comes the Soul (ψυχή), which emanates from the Intelligence as the Intelligence emanates from absolute essential Being. The Soul animates the world; it must, therefore, be capable of diversity; it includes individual souls. The visible world proceeds from it; and some only of these souls are attached to individual bodies. But unfortunately harmony does not reign amongst the elements of the world; and the soul does not fully control the body. Hence follows disorder.

Being, having become more and more imperfect by becoming concrete and diversified, must be brought back to perfection. This effort to return begins with virtue; at first social, civic virtue (πολιτική), which adorns the soul but is not sufficient to deliver it; then asceticism, or purifying virtue, which brings it back to goodness. Thus purified, the soul is able to attain to the sphere of the Intelligence (νοῦς) by the exercise of reason. As to absolute essential Being, as reason does not reach it, no one can be in touch with it except through ecstasy. This can be cultivated; and when ecstasy results, the soul sees God. But this is rare. Plotinus, during the six years that Porphyry was with him, only attained four times to this immediate communion with the Supreme Being. And Porphyry himself only reached it once in his whole life.[2]

Neo-Vulgata To indicate that something is new, the correct Latin prefix is *novo-*. Thus, *York* in Latin is *Eboracum*, and *New York* is *Novoëboracum*. However, it has been the long-standing tradition of the Roman Curia to use the Greek prefix *neo-*, from νέος, new, and thus produce *Neoëboracum*. Similarly, the new edition of the Vulgate Bible is, in Latin, the *Nova Vulgata Editio*, but is sometimes denominated the *Neo-Vulgata*.

The Neo-Vulgata, or New Vulgate Edition of the Bible, was declared to be the Church's official edition of the holy scriptures by the apostolic con-

---

2. Louis Duchesne, *Early History of the Christian Church from Its Foundation to the End of the Third Century* (London: John Murray, 1914), 400–401.

stitution *Scripturarum Thesaurus* of Pope John Paul II, issued on April 25, 1979. This document is printed at the beginning of the one-volume edition of this bible published by the Libreria Editrice Vaticana in 1979.

The pope began this constitution by pointing out that the Church has always concerned herself with ensuring that the Community of Saints had the word of God available to it, especially in the liturgy. Of the many versions of the biblical texts, he went on to say, the Church has always held the Vulgate edition of St. Jerome as preeminent, so that as late as 1933, Pius XI had entrusted the Benedictine monks of the Abbey of St. Jerome in Rome with the care of preparing a critical edition of the Vulgate based on modern principles and according to modern standards. On the other hand, the Second Vatican Council, he pointed out, had directed that the Psalter in the Vulgate be revised so that the Psalms might be more easily understood when they were read in the Liturgy of the Hours. Pope Paul VI had therefore established a special pontifical commission on November 29, 1965, to prepare a new edition of the Latin Bible required by the progress of biblical studies, which would be of particular use in the Latin liturgy. Pope John Paul then quoted from an allocution of his predecessor of December 23, 1966, during which Pope Paul had explained the method to be used in producing the new edition: Where Jerome's version accurately rendered the original Hebrew or Greek text, it was to be retained, but where it was in error, it was to be changed; the corrections, however, were to be made in the style of Christian biblical Latin. Pope John Paul, in presenting the finished work to the Catholic world, then asked that all other translations into modern tongues be brought into agreement (*referantur*) with it, and, again quoting Pope Paul, agreed that it would serve as a sound foundation for biblical studies for those to whom the original texts were unintelligible, or more specialized books unavailable. Formerly, Pope John Paul wrote, the Church held that the Vulgate sufficed for teaching the Word of God; even more, he now said, should the Neo-Vulgata suffice in our own time. He concluded by declaring the Neo-Vulgata official (*typica*), notwithstanding any complaints that might be raised by quarrelsome people.

The method by which the Neo-Vulgata was produced had already been explained in an article printed in *L'Osservatore Romano*,[3] three weeks after Pope Paul had received the three top officials of his special commission in private audience. The author of the essay was Tarcisio Stra-

---

3. Tarcisio Stramare, "La Neo-Vulgata," *L'Osservatore Romano*, November 21, 1977, p. 6.

mare, third-in-command at the commission. The purpose for the audience was for the president of the commission, Eduard Schick, bishop of Fulda, to present the last fascicule of their edition to the pope, the one on the Books of Kings, Chronicles, Ezra, and Nehemiah. Stramare pointed out that modern advances in the knowledge of Hebrew and Greek made it obvious that there were errors and obscurities in the Vulgate, and that if these were not corrected, the Vulgate would be left in the dust and the field abandoned to the modern vernacular Bibles. The Neo-Vulgata was not to be a critical edition of Jerome's text, a reconstruction, as far as possible, of what actually left his hand; that work was to be left to the Benedictines of the Pontifical Abbey of St. Jerome, whom Pius XI, as we have seen, had authorized to produce a critical edition. No, the New Vulgate was to be a correction of Jerome's Vulgate where that Father's work was seen to wander from or mistranslate the best Hebrew and Greek texts available to us today. The commission worked as follows. Each book of the Bible was examined by two committees, one of exegetes and the other of Latinists, at first individually, and then assembled in joint session. Their findings were then submitted to the whole commission, and then sent out for criticism to a hundred biblical scholars, amongst whom were laymen, Protestants, and Jews, so that no competent authority was neglected. After their observations came back, the final text was published, the first being that of the Book of Psalms in 1969, the last, that of the historical books in 1977. The readings of this Neo-Vulgata edition were to be official in the sense that they were the ones to be quoted by councils and synods and in encyclicals, and they were to be introduced into the Liturgy of the Hours and the Lectionary of the Mass at the direction of the pope and the Roman Curia. As Padre Stramare had foreseen, the Congregation for Divine Worship issued a second edition of the *Liturgia Horarum* on April 7, 1985; the main difference between this edition and the first edition of 1971 was the introduction of the readings of the Neo-Vulgata throughout the four volumes.

Further information about the work of the commission can be found in the prefaces to the individual fascicules written by the president, Bishop Schick. In the preface to the Neo-Vulgata edition of the New Testament, he explained that he and his colleagues had begun with the latest critical edition of Jerome's Vulgate, that published in Stuttgart by the Deutsche Bibelgesellschaft, and then had accommodated it where necessary to the best Greek text currently available (that of Nestle and Aland). Whenever the Greek reading was uncertain, the benefit of the doubt was given to Jerome's reading.

For the history of Jerome's Vulgate, see the article **Vulgate** below.

It is to be emphasized that the Neo-Vulgata and the critical edition of the Vulgate are two entirely different things. The latter seeks to discover the exact text of the Vulgate as it left the hands of St. Jerome; the former changes the text of the Vulgate whenever necessary to bring it into agreement with the best Hebrew and Greek Bibles. Let us now consider some passages that illustrate how the Neo-Vulgata differs from the Vulgate.

Before doing so, however, it should be noted, lest anyone be left wondering, that the Latin edition of the Psalter produced in 1945 by the Pontifical Biblical Commission under Augustin Bea at the command of Pius XII was not an edition of the Vulgate Psalter; it was a new Latin translation that met with resistance when Pius XII tried to introduce it into the liturgy and has vanished entirely from the scene.

For our first example, let us consider the introit for Pentecost, the text for which in the Vulgate reads:

Spiritus Domini replevit orbem terrarum, et hoc, quod continent omnia, scientiam habet vocis. (Wisdom 1:7)

The Spirit of the Lord has filled the whole world, and that, which contains all, understands speech.

Now what, one may ask, is "that which contains all"? That is, to what does *hoc* refer? It cannot be the Spirit, because *Spiritus* is masculine, whereas *hoc* is neuter. The question will have occurred to any learned fellow who reads his Latin Missal. The answer lies in the original Greek text:

πνεῦμα κυρίου πεπλήρωκεν τὴν οἰκουμένην καὶ τὸ συνέχον τὰ πάντα γνῶσιν ἔχει φωνῆς

The word πνεῦμα, which is the *Spirit* in Greek, is neuter, so τὸ, which is *that which* in Greek, is neuter in agreement with it. When the Latin translator put *Spiritus* for πνεῦμα, he slavishly put the neuter *hoc quod* for τὸ, even though he thereby produced a grammatical monstrosity. "That which contains all" is the Spirit, though the Vulgate text obscures the fact; in the Neo-Vulgata, therefore, the two words *hoc quod* are changed to *ipse qui*, so that everything is now of the masculine gender. The passage thus reads in the Neo-Vulgata:

Spiritus Domini replevit orbem terrarum, et ipse qui continet omnia, scientiam habet vocis.

This is typical of the Neo-Vulgata; it removes obscurities introduced in ancient times by translators who sometimes imitated the text before them more literally than the requirements of clarity allowed.

An example of a somewhat more daring change can be found at John 1:9, the "Last Gospel" of the old Latin Mass. The Vulgate reads:

Erat lux vera, quae illuminat omnem hominem venientem in hunc mundum.

The true light was that which enlightens every man who comes into this world.

It is clear how to translate the Latin text, but the Greek whence it came is ambiguous. The original reads:

τὸ φῶς τὸ ἀληθινὸν ὃ φωτίζει πάντα ἄνθρωπον ἐρχόμενον εἰς τὸν κόσμον.

There are two possibilities for translating ἐρχόμενον. It is either neuter singular, nominative case, modifying φῶς, *light*, or masculine singular, accusative case, modifying ἄνθρωπον, *man*. The Vulgate has understood it in the latter sense, "The true light was that which enlightens every man who comes into the world." Brooke Foss Westcott (1825–1901), Church of England bishop of Durham and one of the greatest New Testament textual critics, argued against this possibility, saying that the proper Greek for "every man who comes" would be πάντα τὸν ἐρχόμενον; he promoted the first alternative, which, in English, would be "It was the true light, coming into this world, which enlightens every man." The authors of the Neo-Vulgata have sided with Westcott and replaced the reading *venientem* of the Vulgate with *veniens*, so that the participle modifies *lux*, light, rather than *hominem*, man. This is an example of how the commission for the Neo-Vulgata made changes in the undisputed text of the Vulgate whenever they felt that Jerome had translated the Hebrew or Greek original incorrectly.

The next example is Psalm 109 (110). This poem, which is about a priest-king whom the Deity helps to crush the armed forces of the nations, will be familiar from Vespers. The Neo-Vulgata makes no change in the first verse:

Dixit Dominus Domino meo: Sede a dextris meis, donec ponam inimicos tuos scabellum pedum tuorum.

Jahweh said unto My Lord, "Sit on my right, while I make your enemies a footstool for your feet."

In the second verse, they have made but one change. The Vulgate reads:

Virgam virtutis tuae emittet Dominus ex Sion. "Dominare in medio inimicorum tuorum."

The Hebrew original here means:

Jahweh will send forth your mighty scepter from Sion. He says, "Be victorious over your enemies."

The authors of the Neo-Vulgata have replaced *virtutis* with *potentiae*. The noun *virtutis* appears twice in the Vulgate version of this psalm, because the Vulgate here is following the Greek Septuagint, which has δυνάμεως twice. The Hebrew text, though, has two different words עֻזְּ and חֵילָךְ; the authors of the Neo-Vulgata have therefore used two different Latin words and reserved *virtutis* for the second Hebrew noun. With respect to the Hebraism *virgam virtutis tuae*, literally, *the rod of your strength*, the authors of the Neo-Vulgata did not go so far as Theodore Beza, who had swept the Hebraism away entirely by putting *sceptrum robustum tuum* for it. (Hebrew is weak in adjectives and uses nouns in the genitive—the *status constructus*—to express them.) The reason for their moderation was that the Hebraisms have become part of Christian biblical Latin, which Pope Paul had told them to preserve.

The third verse of this psalm is one of the most disputed texts in the Bible. It is important for Catholic theology.

The Greek and Latin Fathers, following the rendering of the LXX and Vulgata, build on this verse the eternal generation of the Son and his oneness of nature with the Father.[4]

The Hebrew Masoretic text is corrupt and has some meaning like the following:

Your people will offer themselves willingly on the day you lead your forces on the holy mountains. From the womb of the morning, like dew, your youth will come to you. (New Revised Standard Version)

In such cases of manifest corruption, one looks at the Septuagint, which may preserve a reading from an incorrupt Hebrew manuscript no

---

4. J. J. Stewart Perowne, *The Book of Psalms* (Grand Rapids, Mich.: Zondervan, 1978), 308.

longer in existence. The Septuagint, however, which the Vulgate follows, interprets the text differently, omitting טל לך and pointing ילדתיך differently. The Septuagint reads:

μετὰ σοῦ ἡ ἀρχὴ ἐν ἡμέρᾳ τῆς δυνάμεώς σου ἐν ταῖς λαμπρότησιν τῶν ἁγίων· ἐκ γαστρὸς πρὸ ἑωσφόρου ἐξεγέννησά σε.

The Vulgate accordingly has:

Tecum principium in die virtutis tuae, in splendoribus sanctorum. Ex utero, ante luciferum, genui te.

Yours is the power in the day of your strength, amidst the splendors of the saints. From the womb, before the day-star, have I begotten you.

The authors of the Neo-Vulgata originally (in the 1969 separate edition of the Book of Psalms) had:

Tecum principatus in die virtutis tuae, in splendoribus sanctis. Ex utero matutini velut rorem genui te.

Yours is the government in the day of your strength in the sacred vestments. From the womb of the morning, like dew, have I begotten you.

However, they restored the reading of the Vulgate (*Ex utero, ante luciferum, genui te*) in their final, one-volume edition of the whole Bible in 1979. It is necessary to remember that the original Vulgate reading was from an Old Latin translation that Jerome revised. Later on, when he translated the Psalms directly from Hebrew, a translation that never made it into the Vulgate, his version was similar to the first of the three English translations that I have given above:

Populi tui spontanei erunt in die fortitudinis tuae in montibus sanctis. Quasi de vulva orietur tibi ros adulescentiae tuae.

In verse 4, the Neo-Vulgata is the same as the Vulgate:

Iuravit Dominus et non poenitebit eum: "Tu es sacerdos in aeternum secundum ordinem Melchisedek."

Jahweh has sworn, and will have no regrets, "You are a priest forever after the fashion of Melchisedek."

The final three verses relate how the priest-king shall reduce his enemies to heaps of corpses, after which he shall refresh himself with a drink from a stream of fresh water. The authors of the Neo-Vulgata make one change in verse 5; they replace the verb *confregit* with *conquassabit*. The Vulgate has:

Dominus a dextris tuis confregit in die irae suae reges.

Jahweh, at thy right hand, shall break their kings to pieces in the day of his wrath.

The Neo-Vulgata reads:

Dominus a dextris tuis conquassabit in die irae suae reges.

Jahweh, at thy right hand, shall smash their kings in the day of his wrath.

The reason for this is that the same Hebrew word, מחץ, occurs in the next verse, where the Vulgate has *conquassabit*; the editors therefore thought that the same Latin word should be in both places.

The main problem in the sixth verse is the confusion due to the similarity of the Hebrew words for valleys (גאיות) and corpses (גויות); the Hebrew has *full [of] corpses*, while the Septuagint has πληρώσει πτώματα, *he will fill corpses*, and the Vulgate has *he will fill the valleys*:

Iudicabit in nationibus, implebit ruinas.
    Conquassabit capita in terra multorum.

He will judge among the nations, he will fill the valleys.
    He will smash the heads on the ground of many.

The *apparatus criticus* of Kittel's *Biblia Hebraica* suggests the emendation *He will fill the valleys with corpses*. The critical editions of the Vulgate produced at Rome and Stuttgart have replaced *ruinas* with *cadavera*; in so doing they follow an old manuscript of the eighth century. The authors of the Neo-Vulgata made two further changes here; they replaced *implebit* with *cumulantur* and *multorum* with *spatiosa*. The former change looks to me like a paraphrase; the latter is required to bring the Latin into conformity with the Hebrew רבה על־ארץ, which has a singular adjective, not a plural one. The Neo-Vulgata text therefore is:

Iudicabit in nationibus; cumulantur cadavera,
    Conquassabit capita in terra spatiosa.

He will judge among the nations; corpses pile up.
    He will smash heads over a wide area.

The seventh and final verse of the Psalm is the same in the Vulgata and the Neo-Vulgata:

De torrente in via bibet, propterea exaltabit caput.

He shall drink from the stream along the way, and then he shall lift up his head.

We may finally look at the changes introduced into the Magnificat (Luke 1:46–55), of which there are three. In verse 47, *et exsultavit spiritus meus in Deo salutari meo* has been changed to *et exsultavit spiritus meus in Deo Salvatore meo*, a correction required by the Greek (σωτῆρι = *savior*). In verse 50, *Et misericordia eius a progenie in progenies timentibus eum* has been modified to *Et misericordia eius in progenies et progenies timentibus eum*, again, in order to bring it into conformity with the Greek text (εἰς γενεὰς καὶ γενεὰς) according to the Codex Vaticanus and the Codex Ephraëmi; the traditional reading, which would require an ἀπό in the Greek, is very poorly attested. Finally, in verse 54, *Suscepit Israel puerum suum, recordatus misericordiae suae* was in 1969 changed to *Suscepit Israel puerum suum, memorari misericordiae*, in order to conform to the critical edition of the Vulgate as published by the Stuttgart Deutsche Bibelgesellschaft, which agrees with the Greek μνησθῆναι ἐλέους. However, the 1979 edition adopts the compromise reading *Suscepit Israel puerum suum, recordatus misericordiae*.[5]

Nepotism The Latin word *nepos, nepotis, m.*, means both *grandson* and *nephew*. *Nepos* became *nipote* in Italian. From the fifteenth through the eighteenth centuries, the popes appointed one of their nephews to be a cardinal and their right-hand man. The reason was to have someone they could trust at their side. In the case of Alessandro Farnese, cardinal nephew of Paul III, the cardinal nephew actually was the pope's grandson. This custom led to the coining of the noun *nepotismo* with the meaning, *the favoring of one's relatives*. Weekley says that the noun *nepotism* came into English in a translation from the Italian in 1667.

Nestorian The Greek name Νεστώριος is the diminutive of Νέστωρ (Nestor), the name of the Homeric hero. Nestorius was the patriarch of Constantinople who denied the accuracy of the title Theotokos, or *Mother of God*, given to the Virgin Mary. This was considered dangerously close to denying the divinity of Jesus, so at the Council of Ephesus (431) he

---

5. Those who read Italian may consult the following article: Tarcisio Stramare, "La Neo-Vulgata: impresa scientifica e pastorale insieme," *Lateranum* 45 (1979): 10–35. The allocution of Pope John Paul II to the Pontifical Commission for the New Vulgate on the occasion of the completion of their work may be found in *Notitiae* 154 (May 1979): 236–37.

was accordingly anathematized and deprived of his see. His party was insultingly denominated *Nestorians*. They were the predominant Christian body in Mesopotamia and Persia, whence they spread to India.

For the Bishop of Carthage, Capreolus, he who had sent a deputy to the Council of Ephesus, the Nestorian heresy was identified with the following doctrine: "We must not say that God is born. A simple man was born of the Virgin Mary, and God has later dwelt in him."[6]

Cyril was a clear-headed, constructive theologian. He saw what Thoedoret did not see. He was not content with anathematizing Nestorius; he laid down a positive view of the Incarnation, which the Universal Church accepted and holds to this day as the very truth of revelation. It is this insight into, and grasp of the Adorable Mystery, which constitutes his claim to take his seat among the Doctors of Holy Church. And he traced the evil, which he denounced, higher up, and beyond the person and the age of Nestorius. He fixed the blame upon Theodore of the foregoing generation, "the great commentator," the luminary and pride of the Antiochene school, the master of Theodoret; and he was right, for the exegetical principles of that school, as developed by Theodore, became little less than a system of rationalism.[7]

Milman wrote:

If (according to Nestorius) the Eternal and Coequal Word were *born*, this was a denial of his preëxistence; and to assert that he could be liable to passion or suffering, in the same manner violated the pure spirituality of the Godhead. He proposed, therefore, that the appellation, Christ, should be confined, and, as it were, kept sacred, as signifying the Being, composed of the blended, yet unconfounded, God and man; and that the Virgin should be the mother of Christ, the God-man, not the mother of God, of the unassociated divinity.[8]

Nicene Creed The Greek noun νίκη means *victory*, and from it was derived the adjective νικαῖος with the meaning *belonging to victory*. Related to this adjective is the female proper name Νίκαια. The city in Bithynia was so renamed by Lysimachus, king of Macedon, upon his reconquest of the place in 301 B.C., in memory of his late wife. The French *Nice* is really the same name. It was, in 325, the location of the First Ecumenical Council of the Christian Church.

6. Louis Duchesne, *Early History of the Christian Church from Its Foundation to the End of the Fifth Century*, vol. 3 (London: John Murray, 1924), 212.

7. John Henry Cardinal Newman, "Trials of Theodoret," in *Historical Sketches*, vol. 2 (London: Longmans, Green, 1917), 345.

8. Henry Hart Milman, *History of Latin Christianity, Including That of the Popes, to the Pontificate of Nicholas V* (New York: Sheldon, 1860), 1:204.

The story of the participation of the Roman Church in the Council of Nicaea is told by Duchesne:

The Roman Church had received in the days of Silvester, official intimation of the condemnation of Arius by the Bishop of Alexandria. Being invited to the Council of Nicaea, the Pope had sent there, as in the case of the Council of Arles, two priests to represent him. With regard to doctrinal questions, the Roman Church was at peace. The days of Hippolytus, Callistus, and Tertullian were now far away. In the matter of formulas, when any need was felt for making use of them, there was that of Tertullian and of Novatian, "One Substance, Three Persons," which seemed sufficient for every need. Formerly, when Greek was spoken, the term *homoousios* had been made use of; it was now translated by *consubstantialis*, thus identifying the two words οὐσία and ὑπόστασις. This was the terminology which Silvester's legates recommended to the Council of Nicaea, and of which they secured the adoption.[9]

The Creed produced by the Council was the following:

Πιστεύομεν εἰς ἕνα Θεόν, πατέρα παντοκράτορα, πάντων ὁρατῶν τε καὶ ἀοράτων ποιητήν. Καὶ εἰς ἕνα κύριον Ἰησοῦν Χριστὸν τὸν υἱὸν τοῦ Θεοῦ, γεννηθέντα ἐκ τοῦ πατρὸς μονογενῆ, τοῦτ' ἐστιν ἐκ τῆς οὐσίας τοῦ πατρός, Θεὸν ἐκ Θεοῦ, φῶς ἐκ φωτός, Θεὸν ἀληθινὸν ἐκ Θεοῦ ἀληθινοῦ· γεννηθέντα οὐ ποιηθέντα, ὁμοούσιον τῷ πατρὶ, δι' οὗ τὰ πάντα ἐγένετο, τά τε ἐν τῷ οὐρανῷ, καὶ τὰ ἐπὶ τῆς γῆς, τὸν δι' ἡμᾶς τοὺς ἀνθρώπους καὶ διὰ τὴν ἡμετέραν σωτηρίαν κατελθόντα, καὶ σαρκωθέντα, καὶ ἐνανθρωπήσαντα. Παθόντα καὶ ἀναστάντα τῇ τρίτῃ ἡμέρᾳ, καὶ ἀνελθόντα εἰς τοὺς οὐρανούς. Καὶ ἐρχόμενον πάλιν κρῖναι ζῶντας καὶ νεκρούς. Καὶ εἰς τὸ πνεῦμα τὸ ἅγιον. Τοὺς δὲ λέγοντας· ἦν ποτε ὅτε οὐκ ἦν, καὶ πρὶν γεννηθῆναι οὐκ ἦν, καὶ ἐξ οὐκ ὄντων ἐγένετο, ἢ ἐξ ἑτέρας ὑποστάσεως ἢ οὐσίας φάσκοντας εἶναι, ἢ κτιστὸν, ἢ ἀλλοιωτὸν, ἢ τρεπτὸν τὸν υἱὸν τοῦ Θεοῦ· τούτους ἀναθεματίζει ἡ καθολικὴ καὶ ἀποστολικὴ ἐκκλησία.

We believe in one God, the father almighty, maker of all things visible and invisible, and in one lord Jesus Christ, the son of God, begotten of the father, only-begotten, that is, of the being of the father, God of God, light of light, true God of true God, begotten, not made, of the same being as the father, through whom all things came to be, both those in heaven and those on earth, who, for us men and for our salvation came down and became flesh and became man. He suffered and arose on the third day, and went up into the heavens. And he will come again to judge the living and the dead. And in the holy spirit. And as for those who say, "There was when he was not, and he was not before he was begotten, and he came to be from what are not," and those who claim that the son of God was of another

9. Louis Duchesne, *Early History of the Christian Church from Its Foundation to the End of the Fifth Century*, vol. 2 (London: John Murray, 1931), 357.

substance or being, or that he was created, or variable, or changeable, these the catholic and apostolic church anathematizes.

Niceno-Constantinopolitan Creed The Creed sung at the Mass is called Niceno-Constantinopolitan because it did not come into use until sometime after the first two ecumenical councils. According to Duchesne, it was first called such in 451 at the Council of Chalcedon.[10]

... the creed called Niceno-Constantinopolitan, which is now sung in the Mass. The latter has nothing to do with the Council of 381. Upon this often debated question, see the article of Harnack, in Hauck's Encyclopädie. Vol. xi, pp. 12–28.[11]

Duchesne wrote of Epiphanius of Salamis (late fourth century) as follows:

It was at the request of certain people at Syedra in Pamphylia that he composed first (on the Trinitarian heresies of the day) a treatise called *Ancoratus*, at the end of which appeared, for the first time, the Creed which we now use under the name of the Creed of Nicaea.[12]

Denzinger points out that this Niceno-Constantinopolitan Creed came into use in the East after the Councils of Ephesus (431) and Chalcedon (451) in order to prevent the introduction of any other creed.[13] Its adoption in the West occurred much later. Newman, however, writes:

The Creed of Constantinople is said to be the composition of Gregory Nyssen.[14]

The Greek and Latin texts are as follows:

Πιστεύομεν εἰς ἕνα Θεὸν, πατέρα παντοκράτορα, ποιητὴν οὐρανοῦ καὶ γῆς, ὁρατῶν τε πάντων καὶ ἀοράτων. Καὶ εἰς ἕνα κύριον Ἰησοῦν Χριστὸν τὸν υἱὸν τοῦ Θεοῦ τὸν μονογενῆ, τὸν ἐκ τοῦ πατρὸς γεννηθέντα πρὸ πάντων τῶν αἰώνων, φῶς ἐκ φωτὸς, Θεὸν ἀληθινὸν ἐκ Θεοῦ ἀληθινοῦ, γεννηθέντα οὐ ποιηθέντα, ὁμοούσιον τῷ πατρί, δι' οὗ τὰ πάντα ἐγένετο. Τὸν δι' ἡμᾶς τοὺς ἀνθρώπους καὶ διὰ τὴν ἡμετέραν σωτηρίαν κατελθόντα ἐκ τῶν οὐρανῶν καὶ σαρκωθέντα ἐκ πνεύματος ἁγίου καὶ Μαρίας τῆς παρθένου καὶ ἐνανθρωπήσαντα· σταυρωθέντα τε ὑπὲρ ἡμῶν ἐπὶ Ποντίου Πιλάτου, καὶ παθόντα καὶ ταφέντα, καὶ ἀναστάντα τῇ

10. Louis Duchesne, *Early History of the Christian Church from Its Foundation to the End of the Fifth Century*, vol. 3 (London: John Murray, 1924), 302.

11. Louis Duchesne, *Early History of the Christian Church from Its Foundation to the End of the Fifth Century*, vol. 2 (London: John Murray, 1931), 350n1.

12. Ibid., 467.

13. Denzinger, *Enchiridion Symbolorum et Definitionum*, 7th ed. (Würzburg, V. J. Stahel, 1895), page 14.

14. John Henry Cardinal Newman, *The Arians of the Fourth Century*, new ed. (London: Longmans, Green, 1897), 392. Gregory of Nyssa lived c. 335–95.

τρίτῃ ἡμέρᾳ κατὰ τὰς γραφάς· καὶ ἀνελθόντα εἰς τοὺς οὐρανούς, καὶ καθεζόμενον ἐκ δεξιῶν τοῦ πατρός, καὶ πάλιν ἐρχόμενον μετὰ δόξης κρῖναι ζῶντας καὶ νεκρούς· οὗ τῆς βασιλείας οὐκ ἔσται τέλος. Καὶ εἰς τὸ πνεῦμα τὸ ἅγιον, τὸ κύριον, τὸ ζωοποιόν, τὸ ἐκ τοῦ πατρὸς ἐκπορευόμενον, τὸ σὺν πατρὶ καὶ υἱῷ συμπροσκυνούμενον καὶ συνδοξαζόμενον, τὸ λαλῆσαν διὰ τῶν προφητῶν. Εἰς μίαν ἁγίαν, καὶ ἀποστολικὴν καθολικὴν ἐκκλησίαν. Ὁμολογοῦμεν ἓν βάπτισμα εἰς ἄφεσιν ἁμαρτιῶν. Προσδοκῶμεν ἀνάστασιν νεκρῶν, καὶ ζωὴν τοῦ μέλλοντος αἰῶνος. Ἀμήν.

Credo in unum Deum, Patrem omnipotentem, factorem caeli et terrae, visibilium omnium et invisibilium. Et in unum Dominum Iesum Christum, Filium Dei unigenitum. Et ex Patre natum ante omnia saecula. Deum de Deo, lumen de lumine, Deum verum de Deo vero. Genitum non factum, consubstantialem Patri, per quem omnia facta sunt. Qui propter nos homines et propter nostram salutem descendit de caelis. Et incarnatus est de Spiritu Sancto ex Maria Virgine, et homo factus est. Crucifixus etiam pro nobis sub Pontio Pilato, passus et sepultus est. Et resurrexit tertia die secundum Scripturas. Et ascendit in caelum; sedet ad dexteram Patris. Et iterum venturus est cum gloria iudicare vivos et mortuos, cuius regni non erit finis. Et in Spiritum Sanctum Dominum et vivificantem, qui ex Patre [Filioque] procedit, qui cum Patre et Filio simul adoratur et conglorificatur, qui locutus est per Prophetas. Et unam, sanctam, catholicam, et apostolicam Ecclesiam. Confiteor unum baptisma in remissionem peccatorum, exspecto resurrectionem mortuorum, et vitam venturi saeculi. Amen.

Nicolaitans The Greek nouns λαός and δῆμος both mean *people*, and the verb νικάω means *to conquer*. The names Νικόλαος (Nicholas) and Νικόδημος (Nicodemus) are therefore synonymous; they both mean the *man who is the conqueror of the people*. The insertion of the *h* in English is therefore incorrect. The Nicolaitans or Nicolites are a sect whose originator was some Nicholas and who were singled out for censure in Revelation 2:6, 14–15. Their teaching was that it was necessary to surrender to the urges of the flesh. At a later time, the name was conferred upon the incontinent clergy.

ἀλλὰ τοῦτο ἔχεις, ὅτι μισεῖς τὰ ἔργα τῶν Νικολαϊτῶν, ἃ κἀγὼ μισῶ…. οὕτως ἔχεις καὶ σὺ κρατοῦντας τὴν διδαχὴν τῶν Νικολαϊτῶν ὁμοίως. μετανόησον οὖν· εἰ δὲ μή, ἔρχομαί σοι ταχὺ καὶ πολεμήσω μετ’ αὐτῶν ἐν τῇ ῥομφαίᾳ τοῦ στόματός μου.

Yet this you have, you hate the works of the Nicolaitans, which I also hate…. So you also have some who hold the teaching of the Nicolaitans. Repent then. If not, I will come to you soon and war against them with the sword of my mouth. (Revised Standard Version)

The First Council of the Lateran (1123) under Calixtus II condemned the Nicolaitans of the time, that is, the incontinent clergy, who were held to be heretics in this respect, that they not only broke the ecclesiastical law of celibacy, but taught that this law was impossible to observe and that it was harmful to morality.

Canon 3. Presbyteris, diaconibus vel subdiaconibus concubinarum et uxorum contubernia penitus interdicimus et aliarum mulierum cohabitationem, praeter quas synodus Nicaeana propter solas necessitudinum causas habitare permisit, videlicet matrem, sororem, amitam, vel materteram, aut alias huiusmodi, de quibus nulla valeat iuste suspicio oriri.[15]

We absolutely forbid priests, deacons, and subdeacons to be intimate with mistresses or wives, and prohibit them to live together with other women, except those whom the Council of Nicaea allowed to dwell with them solely for necessary reasons, such as a mother, a sister, a paternal aunt, a maternal aunt, or the like, concerning whom there can arise no just suspicion.

Lea says of this Council summoned by Calixtus II:

Nearly a thousand prelates obeyed his call, and that august assembly promulgated a canon which not only forbade matrimony to those bound by vows and holy orders, but commanded that if such marriages were contracted they should be broken, and the parties to them subjected to due penance.

This was a bold innovation. With the exception of a decretal of Urban II in 1090, to which little attention seems to have been paid, we have seen that, previous to Calixtus, while the sacrament of marriage was held incompatible with the ministry of the altar and with the enjoyment of Church property, it was yet respected and its binding force was admitted, even to the point of rendering those who assumed it unfitted for their sacred functions. At most, and as a concession to a lax and irreligious generation, the option had been allowed of abandoning either the wife or the ministry. At Rheims, Calixtus had deprived them of this choice, and had ordered their separation from their wives. He now went a step further, and by the Lateran canon he declared the sacrament of marriage to be less potent than the religious vow: the engagement with the Church swallowed up and destroyed all other ties. This gave the final seal to the separation between the clergy and the laity, by declaring the priestly character to be indelible. When once admitted to orders, he became a being set apart from his fellows, consecrated to the service of God; and the impassable gulf between him and the laity bound him for ever to the exclusive interests of the Church. It is easy to perceive how important an element

---

15. Denzinger, *Enchiridion Symbolorum et Definitionum*, 7th ed. (Würzburg: V. J. Stahel, 1895), §302, p. 106.

this irrevocable nature of sacerdotalism became in establishing and consolidating the ecclesiastical power.[16]

Lea has the following to say about the Second Council of the Lateran (1139) under Innocent II:

Surrounded by a thousand prelates at the second great Council of the Lateran in 1139, he no longer dreaded to offend the susceptibilities of the clergy, and he proceeded to justify the canon of 1123 by creating a doctrine to suit the practice there enjoined. After repeating the canons of Clermont and Rheims, he unhesitatingly pronounced that a union contracted in opposition to the rule of the Church was not a marriage. He condescends to no argument, while he admits the innovation by alleging as its object the extension of the law of continence and of the purity pleasing to God.[17]

Certain purists, for example, Peter de Bruys and Arnold of Brescia, had presumed to declare that the sacraments dispensed by priests who were married or who kept concubines were invalid. This notion was condemned by the Second Lateran Council:

Canon 23. Eos autem, qui religiositatis speciem simulantes, Domini corporis et sanguinis sacramentum, baptisma puerorum, sacerdotium et caeteros ecclesiasticos ordines et legitimarum damnant foedera nuptiarum, tamquam haereticos ab Ecclesia Dei pellimus et damnamus et per potestates exteras coërceri praecipimus. Defensores quoque ipsorum eiusdem damnationis vincula innodamus.[18]

As for those, however, who, faking the appearance of religion, condemn as invalid the Most Holy Sacrament of the Altar, the baptism of babies, and Holy Orders when those sacraments are celebrated by married priests, we cut them off, heretics as they are, from the Church of God and decree that they be restrained by the secular power, and we punish any who defend them with a similar condemnation.

Nihil Obstat This Latin phrase means, "There is nothing to prevent [sc. publication]." It is a finding issued by a censor that there is no heresy in a manuscript that he was asked to review.

Noble Guard The Greek verb γιγνώσκω means *to know*, and related to it is the Latin verb *nosco, noscere, novi, notus* meaning *to become acquainted*

---

16. Henry Charles Lea, *History of Sacerdotal Celibacy in the Christian Church* (n.p.: University Books, 1966), 264–65.

17. Ibid., 266.

18. Denzinger, *Enchiridion Symbolorum et Definitionum*, 7th ed. (Würzburg: V. J. Stahel, 1895), §309, p. 109.

with, and in the perfect tense, *to know*. From *nosco* was derived the adjective *nobilis* meaning *well-known, renowned, famous, high-born*, hence our *noble*. The word *guard* is a corruption of the Anglo-Saxon word *weard*, which means a *keeper*, whence came the verb *weardian*, to keep. The Noble Guard was a contingent of seventy-seven men, each of whom was of a family that had been noble for at least sixty years; it was founded by Pope Pius VII to be the bodyguard of the sovereign pontiff. They frequently served on horseback. The position of Commander of the Noble Guard was filled alternately by the princes of the House of Barberini and Altieri, but in 1901 Pope Leo XIII appointed the Prince Camillo Rospigliosi to the position. The Noble Guard was abolished by Pope Paul VI in 1970. The last commander was Prince Mario Filippo Benedetto del Drago.

Non-Canonical For the etymology of *canonical*, see the entry **Canon**. Non-canonical books are those books that have not been admitted to the Old or New Testament, for example, the *Third Book of Maccabees* and the *Shepherd of Hermas*.

We may observe in passing, as a point of real distinction between the Canonical and Non-Canonical Books, that the writers of the latter, especially the son of Sirach, display an amount of self-consciousness on the subject of authorship which is wanting in those of the former. The passage first quoted from Ecclesiasticus [24:30–34] is not free from boastfulness—a quality wholly absent from the Canonical Scriptures, and in that respect a speaking witness to their inspiration. The writers of these Scriptures knew that their words were not (in any sense of which they could boast) their own words at all.[19]

With regard to the *Shepherd of Hermas*, we may note that Hermas, the brother of Pope Pius I, wrote this work, which was considered so important that it was included in the Codex Sinaiticus, one of the three or four most important biblical manuscripts, at the end. It contains the heresy that the son of God and the Holy Ghost are one and the same, and that the Savior, a human being, was raised to the Godhead as a result of his merits.

Nones The Latin indeclinable noun *novem* means *nine*, and the related adjective *nonus* means *ninth*. The Nones are the prayers of the Divine Office sung at the ninth hour of the day. By corruption it became our *noon*. In the Roman calendar, the Nones of the month were the ninth day before

---

19. William Sanday, *Inspiration, Eight Lectures on the Early History and Origin of the Doctrine of Biblical Inspiration, Being the Bampton Lectures for 1893* (London: Longmans, Green, 1896), 260.

the Ides. Thus, the Nones of March would be March 7 in our method of calculation.

Novatians The Latin verb *novo, novare, novavi, novatus* means *to make new*, and from it were derived the proper names Novatus and Novatianus. The Novatians (they called themselves καθαροί—the Puritans) were the followers of the Roman priest Novatian. He was the leader of the party in Rome that demanded the retention of the strict, traditional policy toward those who had lapsed during the persecution of Decius (249–251) and had then sought readmittance into the Church; such specimens were disapprovingly denominated *libellatici* after *libellus*, the certificate of sacrifice issued by the authorities to people who had conformed.

Discipline demanded a life-long penance for apostasy. No doubt, as the guilty were so many, a relaxation of the old rules would be necessary.[20]

Novatian was elected antipope after the death of Fabian in opposition to the lenient Pope Cornelius. Novatian is not to be confused with the Carthaginian Novatus of similar views.[21] A disagreement on this matter had arisen in the diocese of Carthage, and the faction that wanted a laxer policy had appealed to Rome.

Novus Ordo This is a pejorative term for the reformed rite of Mass introduced by Pope Paul VI in 1969; it is used by people who deplore what they consider to be its novelties. It means "New Order" in Latin, an expression never applied to the current rite in any official document, where it is simply *Ordo Missae*, the Order of Mass. At one time in the Catholic Church, to say that something was an innovation was not a compliment; indeed, the motto of Alfredo Cardinal Ottaviani was *Semper idem*—Always the same. Nowadays, the negative connotation of *new* has commonly been lost; on the contrary, people boast about the innovations that they have made. I am required on an annual basis by my employer to list all the innovations that I have introduced over the past year, as if all such things must by their very novelty be wonderful; this is not the traditional point of view.

---

20. Louis Duchesne, *Early History of the Christian Church from Its Foundation to the End of the Third Century* (London: John Murray, 1914), 293.

21. *Encyclopaedia Britannica*, 11th ed. (New York: The Encyclopaedia Britannica Company, 1911), s.v. "Novatianus."

Numinous The Greek verb νεύω means *to nod*, and from it was derived the Latin noun *numen* with the meaning *nod*, the divine nod whereby the decisive will of the Deity is announced.

> Ὣς φάτο· τὸν δὲ πατὴρ ὀλοφύρατο δάκρυ χέοντα,
> Νεῦσε δέ οἱ λαὸν σόον ἔμμεναι οὐδ᾽ ἀπολέσθαι.[22]

> Thus pray'd the king, and heav'n's great father heard
> His vows, in bitterness of soul preferr'd;
> The wrath appeas'd, by happy signs declares,
> And gives the people to their monarch's pray'rs.[23]

It was used by Rudolf Otto in *Das Heilige* to describe the impression made on the believer by the divine presence. The people were formerly alerted to the corresponding moments in the liturgy by the ringing of hand-bells.

Nun The Italian words for *grandfather* and *grandmother* are *nonno* and *nonna*, derived from, or giving rise to, the mediaeval Latin *nonnus* and *nonna*, which mean *monk* and *nun*; they are terms of endearment, like *daddy* and *mommy*. *Nun*, therefore, was originally something like *granny* or *nanny*. In this connection, Weekley mentions the English *mammy*.

Nunc Dimittis The *Nunc Dimittis* is the prayer of Simeon, who was present at the presentation of Christ in the Temple, and was thereupon content to die (Luke 2:29–32):

> Nunc dimittis servum tuum Domine,
> Secundum verbum tuum in pace:
> Quia viderunt oculi mei salutare tuum,
> Quod parasti ante faciem omnium populorum.
> Lumen ad revelationem gentium,
> Et gloriam plebis tuae Israel.

The best translation is that in the Book of Common Prayer:

> Lord, now lettest thou thy servant depart in peace
> According to thy word.
> For mine eyes have seen thy salvation,
> Which thou hast prepared before the face of all people;
> To be a light to lighten the Gentiles
> And to the glory of thy people Israel.

22. Homer, *Iliad*, 8.245–46.
23. Homer, *The Iliad of Homer*, trans. Alexander Pope (London, 1716), lines 293–296, vol. 2, p. 604.

Nuncio The Latin noun *nuntius* means a *messenger*, and from it was derived the verb *nuntio, nuntiare, nuntiavi, nuntiatus* meaning *to announce*. A nuncio is the messenger, that is, the ambassador of the pope. The spelling *cius* for *tius* was common in the Middle Ages, as the *t* in such cases was pronounced *ts* rather than *t*, and *ts* was the pronunciation of *c* before *e* and *i*. Formerly a nuncio would be appointed only to a country that recognized that ambassador as the dean of the diplomatic corps. If such a distinction was not allowed, then a lesser emissary was employed. The first nuncios were the papal representatives at the court of the Roman emperor in Constantinople; see the entry **Apocrisiary**.

Oath The word *oath* descends from the Anglo-Saxon noun *āth*. Forty-six Catholic bishops were condemned to hard labor by the Vandal King Huneric in the fifth century for refusing to swear an oath of loyalty to his son; they refused on the pretext that all oaths were forbidden by Christ (Matthew 5:33–37).[1]

ἐγὼ δὲ λέγω ὑμῖν μὴ ὀμόσαι ὅλως.... ἔστω δὲ ὁ λόγος ὑμῶν ναὶ ναί, οὒ οὔ· τὸ δὲ περισσὸν τούτων ἐκ τοῦ πονηροῦ ἐστίν.

Ego autem dico vobis: Non iurare omnino, ... Sit autem sermo vester: "Est, est", "Non, non"; quod autem his abundantius est, a Malo est.

But I say unto you, Do not swear any oath whatsoever.... Let your speech be "Yes, yes," and "No, no," because anything more than that comes from the devil.

Obelus The Greek verb βάλλω means *to throw*, and from it was derived the noun noun τὸ βέλος meaning *anything thrown*, or a *dart*. The addition of an omicron produced the noun ὀβελός with the meaning a *pointed pillar*, an *obelisk*, an *arrow-like projection into the sky*. It was the name of the horizontal-line symbol — or ÷ used by Origen to indicate passages whose right to be in a text he considered doubtful.

Observants The Latin verb *observo, observare, observavi, observatus* means *to watch, regard, attend to*. From this verb is formed the present participle *observantes* with the meaning *those who observe*. Franciscan

---

1. Louis Duchesne, *Early History of the Christian Church from Its Foundation to the End of the Fifth Century*, vol. 3 (London: John Murray, 1924), 441.

friars who held to the rule of their founder and refused to seek or avail themselves of dispensations therefrom were so named. The Observant Franciscans are entrusted with the Custody of the Holy Land, where they staff the Basilica of the Holy Sepulcher and the other shrines.

Octave The Latin word *octo* means *eight*, and the ordinal adjective *octavus* means *eighth*. The octave of a feast is the eight-day-period consisting of the feast and the following seven days. The number of octaves was reduced to two, those of Christmas and Easter, in the reforms following the Second Vatican Council.

Offertory The Latin verb *offero, offerre, obtuli, oblatus* means *to bring* (fero) *before* (ob), *to offer*, and from it is derived the noun *offertorium, a ceremony during which an offering is made*. The Offertory of the Mass is that part in which the bread and wine are offered to the Father.

Operation The Latin verb *opus, operis, n.*, means *work*, and from it is derived the verb *operor, operari, operatus sum* meaning *to toil*. From this verb there proceeded the noun *operatio, operationis, f.*, with the meaning *the act of bringing something about*. It was debated in the seventh century, at the time of the Monothelite controversies, whether the Christ acted with one or two ἐνέργειαι—*operationes*—that is, one or two sources of action, "energies," or "operations."

Opus Dei The Latin phrase *Opus Dei* means the *Work of God* and was in times past understood as referring to the liturgy. In modern times, it is the name of an organization of Catholics, both laymen and priests, founded by St. Josemaría Escrivá de Balaguer and who form the sole personal prelature in the Catholic Church.

Orate Fratres This is the prayer in the Mass that reads "Pray, brethren, that my sacrifice and yours may become acceptable before God the Father Almighty." When judging a translation of the Mass, it is the first sentence to examine in order to discover the philosophy of the translators. So *fratres* is translated *sisters and brothers* by those afraid to seem to discriminate against women. I once attended a Latin Mass in which the pontificating bishop changed the words to *Orate sorores et fratres*.

Oratory The Latin noun *os, oris, n.*, means *mouth*, and the associated verb *oro, orare, oravi, oratus* means *to speak*, and then *to beg, to entreat*, *to pray.* The fellow doing the speaking is the *orator,* and the place where this activity takes place is the *oratorium,* whence proceeds the English *oratory.* This word acquired the connotation of a small chapel or place of prayer, and was adopted by St. Philip Neri for the place of assembly of his community, whence his congregation came to be called the *Congregation of the Oratory.* At these oratories there were regular musical performances of an elevated nature. Since St. Philip Neri thus encouraged musical refreshment with religious content in his oratorios, the musical pieces themselves, compositions like Vivaldi's *Judith* and Handel's *Messiah, Samson,* and *Judas Maccabeus,* became known as *oratorios.*

Ordinary The Latin noun *ordo, ordinis, m.,* means a *series, line, row, arrangement,* and the related adjective *ordinarius* means *in the usual way, regular,* whence we get our word *ordinary.* As a noun, *ordinarius, -i, m.,* means an *overseer who keeps order,* a *centurion of the first cohort,* but in the Catholic Church the word is a synonym for one's diocesan bishop, or, if one is a member of a religious order, of one's major superior. On occasion in the Catholic Church there may arise an entity that is imagined not to fit comfortably into existing administrative structures. Such an entity may then be subtracted from the territorial diocesan system and be called an *ordinariate (ordinariatus, ordinariatūs, m.),* and its head denominated the *Ordinary.* Thus, one finds in the United States the unique *Personal Ordinariate of the Chair of St. Peter* for former Anglicans who want to retain their liturgy upon admission into the Catholic Church.

The *Ordinary of the Mass* is the body of unchangeable parts of the Mass.

To refer to the Sundays *per annum* as *Sundays in Ordinary Time* is liturgical cant. The change from the traditional system of identifying those Sundays by counting from Epiphany and from Pentecost has no mathematical benefit and seems to diminish the importance of those two feasts.

Ordinary Form of the Mass A consul elected in the usual way, that is, on election day, was called a *consul ordinarius,* whereas a consul elected to fill the term of a consul who had died in midterm was called a *consul suffectus,* that is, a consul supplied for the special circumstance (from *sufficio, sufficere, suffeci, suffectus,* which means *to supply* or *provide*). Thus, when William Henry Harrison died one month into his term, his successor, Tyler, the first American vice president to succeed to the presidency on the death of the incumbent, would have been called in Latin *praeses suffectus.* Some people took this too literally and wrote letters to him addressed "to the Acting President"; Tyler, resolved to be called president and not acting president, nipped this development in the bud by ordering the Post Office to return all such mail with the marking: "No such person."

The expression *Ordinary Form of the Mass* is a name for the usual modern way of celebrating Mass, that is, in accordance with the revised Roman Missal; the phrase first appeared as a technical term in the motu proprio *Summorum Pontificum* of Benedict XVI. This motu proprio eased restrictions on the celebration of the old Latin Mass, which it called the *Extraordinary Form of the Mass.*

Ordination The Latin noun *ordo, ordinis, m.*, means a *series, line, row, arrangement*, and from it is derived the noun *ordinatio* with the meaning a *setting in order, arrangement*. The ranks of priest, deacon, and subdeacon are called the *Ordines Maiores* or *Major Orders*, and the ranks of acolyte, exorcist, lector, and porter are called the *Ordines Minores* or *Minor Orders*. In the Catholic Church, these orders have always been reserved for men. After the minor orders were abolished, women were allowed in some places to serve and in all places to read at Mass. It is a very great controversy in modern times whether women should be ordained priests. The word *priestess* has a pejorative connotation and is never used. Certainly if there is no disqualifying reason why women should not be ordained priests, then the Catholic Church has erred for two millennia, and the doctrine of infallibility would have to be revised, for the weight of such a terrific change would have an effect on people capable of consecutive thought. Attention is also focused on a more modest goal, that of female deacons. The use of the word *deaconesses* has less of a pejorative connotation than the word *priestesses*, but it is still not used. In 2016, Pope Francis appointed a commission to study the subject of women deacons. The CBS *Evening News* reported that one of the commission members had said that popes in the Middle Ages had authorized bishops to ordain females deacons. I am unaware of any such authorization. It is probably a matter of misunderstanding or exaggeration.

Oremus Up until 1965, this word, which means *let us pray*, was part of the common vocabulary of Catholicism. In Rome, it has now been replaced by *preghiamo*.

Organ The Greek noun ἔργον means *work*, and related to it is the noun ὄργανον with the meaning *instrument, implement*. This last word was transliterated into Latin as *organum*, and became in English *organ*. The meaning that is of interest to us is that of the musical instrument, which is traditionally installed in all Catholic Churches. It rarely leads to liturgical abuse, since the lower sort of composers and performers cannot get the knack of it. For those who love traditional music, the replacement of the organ by pianos and guitars is the atomic bomb on the liturgy.

Origenism The scholar Origen (c. 185–253) was the greatest of Christian academicians and the father of many heresies. His name Ὠριγένης is composed of two parts, the first part of which—Ὠρι—must be declared to be of uncertain origin. The syllables γένης are a suffix derived from the noun γένος, γένεος, *n.*, meaning *race, descent*. As the name *Diogenes* means the *offspring of Zeus*, so the name *Origenes* means the *offspring of N.*, where the identity of N. is hidden in the syllables Ὠρι. The verse 1 Corinthians 15:28 made a great impression on Origen:

ὅταν δὲ ὑποταγῇ αὐτῷ τὰ πάντα, τότε καὶ αὐτὸς ὁ υἱὸς ὑποταγήσεται τῷ ὑποτάξαντι αὐτῷ τὰ πάντα, ἵνα ᾖ ὁ θεὸς πάντα ἐν πᾶσιν.

And when all things have been subjected unto him, then shall the Son also himself be subjected to him that did subject all things unto him, that God may be all in all. (Revised Version)[2]

It was considered the preeminent heresy of Origen that on the basis of this verse he denied eternal damnation, even of the fallen angels. His interpretation implied various other heresies that were condemned three centuries later by the emperor-theologian Justinian and, at his request, by the Fifth Ecumenical Council. The anathematization of Origen was noteworthy as setting a precedent for anathematizing long after their death people who were accepted as belonging to the Church during their lifetimes. Gibbon wrote on this matter:

It was not three hundred years since the body of Origen had been eaten by the worms: his soul, of which he held the pre-existence, was in the hands of its Creator; but his writings were eagerly perused by the monks of Palestine. In these writings the piercing eye of Justinian descried more than ten metaphysical errors; and the primitive doctor, in the company of Pythagoras and Plato, was devoted by the clergy to the *eternity* of hell-fire, which he had presumed to deny. Under

---

2. I myself will have a massive stroke before I forget the violent reaction of my teacher when he read the Revised Standard Version of this verse, which translates πάντα ἐν πᾶσιν by "everything to everyone."

the cover of this precedent a treacherous blow was aimed at the Council of Chalcedon.[3]

For more on Origen, see the entry **Alexandrian School**.

Original Sin The Latin verb *orior, oriri, ortus sum* means *to rise*, and from it was derived the noun *origo, originis, f.*, meaning *source, beginning*. Thence came the adjective *originalis* with the meaning *pertaining to the source*, whence came our adjective *original*. See the entry **Sin** for the etymology of that word. St. Paul taught the doctrine of original sin, which he based on the story of the fall of Adam and Eve in the Book of Genesis. Paul read the story of Adam and Eve as absolute truth, not as a myth. To Paul, the fall of Adam and Eve was the explanation for the biological fact of death. The Jews believed that death was the result of original sin, as one can see from Genesis 2:17, but they did not attach so much significance to it as Paul did. According to the Pauline doctrine, if Adam and Eve had not sinned, they would not have died or aged, just lived eternally. The doctrine of original sin was St. Paul's solution to the problem of the fact of death, with which he was concerned.

Orphrey The French noun *orfroi* means *frieze* (froi) *of gold* (or), and from it came the English corruption *orphrey*. The orphrey is the elaborately embroidered frieze of the cope or mantum. Pains were often taken to place in the bottom compartment the arms of the bishop or pope by whom the vestment was to be worn. A magnificent specimen of a mantum with orphrey was made for John XXIII, who used it at the Second Vatican Council.

Orthodox The word *orthodox* is the transliteration of the stem of the Greek adjective ὀρθόδοξος, which means *holding the right belief*. Its opposite is ἑτερόδοξος (heterodox), which means *holding the other belief*. In common speech it refers to the members of the Eastern Churches in union with the patriarch of Constantinople.

O Salutaris Hostia Thomas Aquinas composed the Eucharistic hymn *Verbum Supernum Prodiens*, of which the last two stanzas are:

---

3. Edward Gibbon, chapter 47 of *The History of the Decline and Fall of the Roman Empire*, ed. Betty Radice (London: The Folio Society, 1995), 6:56.

O salutaris hostia,
Quae caeli pandis ostium,
Bella premunt hostilia,
Da robur, fer auxilium.

Uni trinoque Domino,
Sit sempiterna gloria,
Qui vitam sine termino
Nobis donet in patria. Amen.

The translation by Edward Caswall (1814–1878) is the best.

O Saving Victim, op'ning wide
The gate of Heav'n to man below!
Sore press our foes from every side;
Thine aid supply; Thy strength bestow.

To Thy great name be endless praise,
Immortal Godhead, One in Three!
Oh, grant us endless length of days
In our true native land, with Thee![4]

Ousia The word *ousia* is the transliteration of the Greek noun οὐσία, which means *being, essence*.

However, Athanasius thought it possible to bring about intercourse between Rome and Basil. A deacon of Milan, evidently unattached, for he was not in the service of Auxentius, landed at Alexandria, bearing a synodal letter in which Damasus, at the head of ninety-two bishops, notified to Athanasius the condemnation of Auxentius and of the Council of Ariminum. Sabinus, as the deacon was called, was sent on to Caesarea with his document. It was not calculated to please Basil; for it said that the Father, the Son, and the Holy Spirit are all of one sole Divinity, one sole virtue, one sole image, one sole *substance*. But the word *substance* in Latin is equivalent to *hypostasis* in Greek. The Bishop of Caesarea could not possibly admit this statement except by a liberal interpretation. But Basil knew that Latin was a comparatively poor language, and in particular that the term *essence* (οὐσία) was lacking in it.[5]

Duchesne quotes from the Creed of the Council of Ariminum (Rimini) of 359:

---

4. Edward Caswall, *Lyra Catholica: Containing All the Breviary and Missal Hymns, with Others from Various Sources* (London: Burns & Oates, 1884), 115–16.

5. Louis Duchesne, *Early History of the Christian Church from Its Foundation to the End of the Fifth Century*, vol. 2 (London: John Murray, 1931), 320.

As to the term Essence (οὐσία) which the Fathers have employed in good faith, but which, being unknown to the faithful, has been the cause of scandal to them, since the Scriptures do not contain it, it has seemed good to suppress it, and to avoid entirely for the future all mention of Essence in reference to God, the Scriptures never speaking of Essence in reference to the Father and the Son. But we say that the Son is like to the Father in all things, as the Scriptures say and teach him to be.[6]

Oxford Movement The name *Oxford* evidently means the *place where the oxen cross*. Once the town in England was established and became famous, it was accorded the Latin name *Oxonia*. The Latin verb *moveo, movere, movi, motus* means *to move*, and from it was formed the late noun *movimentum*, a *movement*. The Oxford Movement was a nineteenth-century movement in the Church of England that promoted the catholic aspect of that entity and deprecated the protestant aspect. Its most famous figure was John Henry Newman, who was priest at the Church of St. Mary the Virgin at Oxford. Many of its figures converted to the Roman Catholic Church; the first such convert was William George "Ideal" Ward, whose son Wilfrid was the foremost historian of the Movement, by means of his biographies of his father, of Cardinal Wiseman, and of Cardinal Newman.

6. Ibid., 237.

Paedo-baptism The Greek noun παῖς, παιδός, ὁ and ἡ, means *child*; see the entry **Baptism** for the etymology of that word. Paedo-baptism is the baptism of infants. This became necessary when the doctrine *Extra ecclesiam nulla salus*, based on John 3:5, was accepted.

ἀπεκρίθη ὁ Ἰησοῦς Ἀμὴν ἀμὴν λέγω σοι, ἐὰν μή τις γεννηθῇ ἐξ ὕδατος καὶ πνεύματος, οὐ δύναται εἰσελθεῖν εἰς τὴν βασιλείαν τοῦ θεοῦ.

Jesus answered, "Amen, amen, I say unto thee, unless one be born of water and spirit, he can not enter into the Kingdom of God."

In the first centuries of Christianity, it was common for people to postpone their baptism to the hour of death, for falling into sin after baptism was a serious matter with tremendous consequences. Thus, the emperor Constantine, though most involved in the affairs of the Church, was not baptized until his end was nigh. Infant baptism was common enough to be discussed for the first time (as far as we know) in the literature of the first half of the third century, by Tertullian (*De Baptismo* 18.1, 200–206 A.D.), Hippolytus (*Apostolic Tradition* 21.16, 215 A.D.), Origen (*Homilies on Leviticus* 8.3, 248 A.D.), and Cyprian (*Letters* 64.2, 64.5, 253 A.D.).

Pagan The Greek verb πήγνυμι means *to stick* or *fix in*, and related to it is the Latin verb *pango, pangere, pepigi, pactus* meaning *to fasten, fix, drive in*. In the perfect forms *pepigi, pactus* it can mean *to settle, fix upon*, such

367

as in the phrase *pepigisse fines* or *terminos*, to fix or agree upon boundaries. Related to *pango* is the noun *pagus, -i, m.*, meaning *village*. The inhabitants of the *pagus* were called *pagani*, or *pagans*. Since, in the early centuries of our era, the practice of Christianity was more common in the cities, the pagans were predominantly non-Christian. The word therefore lost its original meaning of *rustic villager* and came to mean *non-Christian* exclusively. The original meaning is retained in the Neapolitan dialect of Italian, in which *paese*, the corruption of *pagus*, means the *town in which one was born*. The inhabitants of the same town refer to one another as *paesani*, the corruption of *pagani*.

The essence of the traditional polytheism of the pagans was summarized by the great historian of the Romans under the early empire:

If neither the architecture nor religion of the Roman pointed heavenwards, or led to spiritual aspirations, not the less did they combine to impress upon him, in their harmonious development, the great idea of Paganism, the temporal protection with which the Powers of Nature, duly honoured and propitiated, encircle their favourites among men.[1]

Palace According to Lewis and Short, the root *pa-* involves the idea of *protecting* or *nourishing*, whence the Latin verb *pasco* means *to feed* and the Greek noun αἰπόλος means a *goatherd*. The Palatium was one of the seven hills of Rome, the *Mons Palatinus*, and because the family of Augustus took up residence there, it came to indicate a royal residence, and its English corruption is our noun *palace*. The usual residence of the Roman pontiffs was the Lateran Palace, but that edifice burnt down during the Babylonian captivity of the papacy, and when the popes returned to the Holy City, they took up residence at the Vatican Palace, whose location near the Tiber was, however, considered unhealthy. As a result, Gregory XIII started the construction of the Apostolic Palace on the Quirinale, where the popes dwelt during most of the seventeenth, eighteenth, and nineteenth centuries. Pius IX was the last pontiff to live at the Quirinale, for after the occupation of Rome on September 20, 1870, he became the proverbial *Prisoner of the Vatican*, where the popes have lived ever since. The Italian government demanded that he turn over the keys to the Quirinale Palace, which he refused to do; they thereupon blew open the doors, and the Palace became a royal, rather than an apostolic, palace; four kings

1. Charles Merivale, *A History of the Romans under the Empire*, 2nd ed. (London: Longman, Green, Longman, & Roberts, 1862), 4:492–93.

of Italy lived there in the period 1870–1946. These kings received the acclamations of the multitude from the same balcony from which the popes had imparted the apostolic benediction. After 1946 the Quirinale Palace became the residence of the presidents of Italy, and so it remains to this day. The Apostolic Palace of the Lateran was rebuilt by Sixtus V, and in its Sala della Conciliazione was signed the Concordat of 1929. For a while it was a museum. This palace is now inhabited by the offices of the Vicariate of Rome. Sixtus V is also the builder of that portion of the Vatican Palace that contains the private apartment of the pope and the window from which he salutes the faithful gathered in St. Peter's Square.

Palafreniere The Greek preposition παρά means *beside*, and the Latin noun *verēdus* (of Celtic origin, according to Weekley) means a *swift light hunting horse*. From their concatenation was produced the Late Latin noun *parafredus*, which was corrupted into *palafreno* under the influence of the Latin noun *frenum*, a *bridle*. The English word for this horse is *palfrey*. A *palafreniere* is the groom of a palfrey. The papal *palafrenieri* formed an archconfraternity, which employed Caravaggio to paint St. Anne with the Virgin and Child Jesus, a painting now in the Borghese Gallery.

Palatine Guard The Latin adjective *palatinus* means *belonging to the Palatium*, one of the seven hills of Rome. For the etymology of *Palatium*, see the entry **Palace**. For the etymology of *guard* see the entry **Noble Guard**. The Palatine Guard was a corps of militia, the *Guardia Palatina d'Onore*, founded by Pio Nono in 1850; they were foot soldiers, infantry. Its members had to be Romans, but they did not need to be noble, which was required for service in the Noble Guard, who at one time served on horseback. The events of 1870 brought about a modification of their duties.

The Palatine Guard, which is really a sort of Papal Militia, has been recruited from the petty bourgeoisie and tradesmen ever since Pius IX's time.... Like the Noble Guards, the Palatine Guards are for court rather than military duties. They are never used *en masse* except for great ceremonies, but both of them furnish every day a picket for the antechamber of the Pope. No drill is demanded of them: they have only to know how to present and order arms.[2]

The Palatine Guard was abolished by Pope Paul VI in 1970.

Pall This word is an abbreviation of *pallium*.

---

2. Douglas Sladen, *The Secrets of the Vatican* (London: Hurst and Blackett, 1907), 154–55.

Pallium The pallium was the Latin name of an oblong mantle called by the Greeks ἱμάτιον. St. Cyprian considered wearing the pallium an ostentatious form of dress associated with philosophers.[3]

Justin was a philosopher, that is, a citizen of the world, travelling from town to town, with his short cloak and freedom of speech.[4]

The short cloak mentioned is the pallium. The pallium is a vestment of the Roman pontiff granted by him as a favor to metropolitan archbishops. Pope Benedict XVI wore the type of pallium that was common in the first millennium and that can be seen in the sixth-century mosaics in Ravenna and Rome; that worn commonly by present-day prelates is in the form that became common later.

The *pallium* (or pall) consists of a circular band of white lamb's wool from which hang two pendants of the same material, one of which is meant to fall down the middle of the back, and the other over the center of the breast. Six little black crosses are embroidered on the band and its lappets. The pallium is worn over the chasuble at solemn High Mass, on certain days determined by the Ceremonial of Bishops.[5]

Pange Lingua Gloriosi Corporis Mysterium These are the opening words of a composition of Thomas Aquinas written for Vespers for the Feast of Corpus Christi. Lentini, however, says that the attribution to the Angelic Doctor is doubtful ("con qualche dubbio").[6]

> Pange lingua gloriosi
> Corporis mysterium,
> Sanguinisque pretiosi
> Quem in mundi pretium,
> Fructus ventris generosi,
> Rex effudit gentium.
>
> Nobis datus, nobis natus,
> Ex intacta virgine,
> Et in mundo conversatus,

---

3. Edward White Benson, *Cyprian: His Life, His Times, His Work* (London: Macmillan, 1897), 5.

4. Louis Duchesne, *Early History of the Christian Church from Its Foundation to the End of the Third Century* (London: John Murray, 1914), 150. The reference is to Justin Martyr, the author of the *Apology* that was addressed to the emperor Antoninus Pius.

5. John A. Nainfa, *Costume of Prelates of the Catholic Church according to Roman Etiquette* (Baltimore, Md.: John Murphy, 1909), 19–20.

6. Anselmo Lentini, *Te Decet Hymnus, L'Innario della "Liturgia Horarum"* (Vatican City: Typis Polyglottis Vaticanis, 1984), 139.

Sparso verbi semine.
Sui moras incolatus
Miro clausit ordine.

In supremae nocte cenae,
Recumbens cum fratribus,
Observata lege plene
Cibis in legalibus.
Cibum turbae duodenae
Se dat suis manibus.

Verbum caro, panem verum,
Verbo carnem efficit,
Fitque sanguis Christi merum,
Et si sensus deficit,
Ad firmandum cor sincerum
Sola fides sufficit.

Tantum ergo sacramentum,
Veneremur cernui,
Et antiquum documentum
Novo cedat ritui.
Praestet fides supplementum
Sensuum defectui.

Genitori genitoque
Laus et iubilatio,
Salus, honor, virtus quoque
Sit et benedictio.
Procedenti ab Utroque
Compar sit laudatio. Amen.

The best translation is by Edward Caswall (1814–1878).

Sing, my tongue, the Saviour's glory,
Of His Flesh, the mystery sing;
Of the Blood, all price exceeding,
Shed by our immortal King,
Destined, for the world's redemption,
From a noble womb to spring.

Of a pure and spotless Virgin
Born for us on earth below,
He, as Man, with man conversing,
Stay'd, the seeds of truth to sow;

Then He closed in solemn order
Wondrously his life of woe.

On the night of that Last Supper,
Seated with his chosen band,
He the Paschal Victim eating,
First fulfills the Law's command;
Then as Food to his Apostles
Gives Himself with his own hand.

Word made Flesh, the bread of Nature
By his Word to Flesh He turns;
Wine unto his Blood He changes:—
What though sense no change discerns?
Only be the heart in earnest,
Faith her lesson quickly learns.

Down in adoration falling,
Lo! the sacred Host we hail;
Lo! o'er ancient forms departing,
Newer rites of grace prevail;
Faith for all defects supplying,
When the feeble senses fail.

To the Everlasting Father,
And the Son who reigns on High,
With the Holy Ghost proceeding
Forth from Each eternally,
Be salvation, honour, blessing,
Might and endless majesty[7]

Pange Lingua Gloriosi Praelium Certaminis This hymn, by Venantius Fortunatus (530–609), is sung on Good Friday at the ceremony of the creeping to the cross. It is "in the very first class of Latin Hymns."[8] With regard to the first strophe, Neale observes:

The recension of Urban VIII here entirely spoils the original

Pange, lingua, gloriosi
Praelium certaminis

---

7. Edward Caswall, *Lyra Catholica: Containing All the Breviary and Missal Hymns, with Others from Various Sources* (London: Burns & Oates, 1884), 111–12.

8. Rev. J. M. Neale, trans., *Mediaeval Hymns and Sequences*, 2nd ed. (London: Joseph Masters, 1863), 1.

by substituting the word *lauream*. It is not to the glory of the termination of our Lord's conflict with the Devil that the poet would have us look, but to the glory of the struggle itself, as indeed he tells us at the conclusion of the verse.[9]

Pange, lingua, gloriosi
Praelium certaminis,
Et super Crucis trophaeo
dic triumphum nobilem:
Qualiter Redemptor orbis
immolatis vicerit.

De parentis protoplasti
fraude Factor condolens,
Quando pomi noxialis
in necem morsu ruit:
Ipse lignum tunc notavit,
damna ligni ut solveret.

Hoc opus nostrae salutis
ordo depoposcerat:
Multiformis proditoris
ars ut artem falleret,
Et medelam ferret inde,
hostis unde laeserat.

Quando venit ergo sacri
plenitudo temporis,
Missus est ab arce Patris,
natus orbis Conditor,
Atque ventre virginali
carne amictus prodiit.

Vagit infans inter arcta
conditus praesepia,
Membra pannis involuta
Virgo Mater alligat,
Et Dei manus pedesque
stricta cingit fascia.

Lustra sex qui iam peregit,
tempus implens corporis,
Sponte libera Redemptor
passioni deditus,

9. Ibid., 4n1.

Agnus in Crucis levatur
immolandus stipite.

Felle potus ecce languet;
spina, clavi, lancea,
Mite corpus perforarunt,
unda manat, et cruor;
Terra, pontus, astra, mundus,
quo lavantur flumine!

Flecte ramos, arbor alta
tensa laxa viscera,
Et rigor lentescat ille,
quem dedit nativitas,
Et superni membra Regis
tende miti stipite.

Sola digna tu fuisti
ferre mundi victimam,
Atque portum praeparare
arca mundo naufrago,
Quam sacer cruor perunxit,
fusus Agni corpore.

Sempiterna sit beatae
Trinitati gloria;
Aequa Patri Filioque,
par decus Paraclito;
Unius Trinique nomen
laudet universitas. Amen.

The best translation is by the Anglican priest John Mason Neale (1818–1866):

Sing, my tongue, the glorious battle,
With completed victory rife:
And above the Cross's trophy
Tell the triumph of the strife:
How the world's Redeemer conquer'd
By surrendering of His Life.

God His Maker, sorely grieving
That the first-made Adam fell,
When he ate the fruit of sorrow,
Whose reward was death and hell,
Noted then this Wood, the ruin
Of the ancient wood to quell.

For the work of our Salvation
Needs would have his order so,
And the multiform deceiver's
Art by art would overthrow,
And from thence would bring the med'cine
Whence the insult of the foe.

Wherefore, when the sacred fullness
Of th' appointed time was come,
This world's Maker left His Father,
Sent the Heavenly Mansion from,
And proceeded, God Incarnate,
Of the Virgin's Holy Womb.

Weeps the Infant in the manger
That in Bethlehem's stable stands;
And His Limbs the Virgin Mother
Doth compose in swaddling bands,
Meetly thus in linen folding
Of her God the feet and hands.

Thirty years among us dwelling,
His appointed time fulfill'd,
Born for this, He meets His Passion,
For that this He freely will'd:
On the Cross the Lamb is lifted,
Where His life-blood shall be spilled.

He endured the nails, the spitting,
Vinegar, and spear, and reed;
From that Holy Body broken
Blood and water forth proceed:
Earth, and stars, and sky, and ocean,
By that flood from stain are freed.

Faithful Cross! Above all other,
One and only noble tree!
None in foliage, none in blossom,
None in fruit thy peers may be:
Sweetest Wood, and sweetest Iron!
Sweetest Weight is hung on thee.

Bend thy boughs, O Tree of Glory!
Thy relaxing sinews bend;
For awhile the ancient rigour,
That thy birth bestowed, suspend;

And the King of Heavenly Beauty
On thy bosom gently tend!

Thou alone wast counted worthy
This world's ransom to uphold;
For a shipwrecked race preparing
Harbour, like the Ark of old;
With the sacred Blood anointed
From the smitten Lamb that roll'd.

To the Trinity be glory
Everlasting, as is meet:
Equal to the Father, equal
To the Son, and Paraclete:
Trinal Unity, Whose praises
All created things repeat. Amen.[10]

Panis Angelicus See the entry **Sacris Solemniis**.

Pantheon The Greek adjective πάνθειος means *sacred to all the gods*, and the phrase τὸ πάνθειον means the *temple sacred to all the gods*. *Pantheon* is the name of two famous buildings, one in Rome and one in Paris. The Roman Pantheon has been in uninterrupted use for over two thousand years. Though perhaps not originally a temple, for it was next to the Baths of Agrippa and may have been a hall of that complex, it became a place of worship no later than the time of the aforementioned son-in-law of Augustus, who built the vestibule with the famous inscription. In 608, Boniface IV obtained the building from Emperor Phocas and turned it into a Christian church dedicated to the Virgin Mary and the martyrs.

To a Pope of the same century, Boniface IV (608–615) belongs the inscription in the crypt, saved, with several others, out of old St. Peter's. But it is not of his own period, having been placed over him by Gregory IV, and afterwards renewed by Boniface VIII. It is in Leonine verses, and most remarkable because it states that Boniface IV received the Pantheon as a gift of the Emperor Phocas, exorcised all the demons out of it, and consecrated it to all the Saints.[11]

In 1520, the painter Raphael was buried here. The bronze supports of its roof were removed by Urban VIII (Maffeo Barberini) to be melted into cannons and to provide supports for the beautiful baldacchino over the

---

10. Ibid., 1–4.

11. Ferdinand Gregorovius, *The Tombs of the Popes, Landmarks in the History of the Papacy*, trans. Mrs. L. W. Terry (Rome: Victoria Home, 1895), 30.

high altar of St. Peter's Basilica, a crime that called forth the verse called immortal by Gregorovius:

Quod non fecerunt Barbari, fecerunt Barberini.

What the Barbarians did not do, the Barberini did.[12]

In 1878, permission was granted for the body of King Victor Emmanuel II to be laid to rest here, and his son Umberto I and daughter-in-law Margherita, first queen of Italy, were also buried in this church. The honor was denied to the next two royal pairs, who were buried abroad, King Victor Emmanuel III in the Church of St. Catherine in Alexandria, Egypt; Queen Elena, his wife, in the municipal cemetery of Montpellier, France; and King Umberto II and his consort Queen Marie José in the Abbey of Hautecombe, France. In 2017 the Italian state permitted the bodies of Victor Emmanuel III and Queen Elena to be reinterred on Italian soil at the sanctuary of Vicoforte in Piedmont.

During the solemn high Mass of the Feast of Pentecost, the firemen of Rome climb onto the roof and release rose petals into the oculus, which then rain down on the congregation. Similarly, during the Capitular Mass for the Feast of Our Lady of the Snows in the Basilica of St. Mary Major, August 5, white rose petals are released from an opening in the ceiling of the basilica above the high altar in imitation of snowflakes.

Papacy This is the English form, through the mediation of the French *papauté*, of the ecclesiastical Latin noun *papatus, -ūs, m.*, which means the *reign of a pope*, or the *institution of the popedom*.[13]

The biblical passages on which the papacy rests are the following, which are written in six-foot high letters high up on the frieze of the nave and transepts and under the dome of St. Peter's Basilica.

Matthew 16:15–19: λέγει αὐτοῖς· ὑμεῖς δὲ τίνα με λέγετε εἶναι; ἀποκριθεὶς δὲ Σίμων Πέτρος εἶπεν· σὺ εἶ ὁ χριστὸς ὁ υἱὸς τοῦ θεοῦ τοῦ ζῶντος. ἀποκριθεὶς δὲ ὁ Ἰησοῦς εἶπεν αὐτῷ· μακάριος εἶ, Σίμων Βαριωνᾶ, ὅτι σὰρξ καὶ αἷμα οὐκ ἀπεκάλυψέν

12. Ferdinand Gregorovius, *History of the City of Rome in the Middle Ages*, 2nd ed., trans. Mrs. Gustavus W. Hamilton (London: G. Bell & Sons, 1902) 2:107n1.

13. The best authors for the study of the Roman papacy are three: Mandell Creighton, *History of the Papacy from the Great Schism to the Sack of Rome*, 6 vols. (New York: Longmans, Green, 1901); Horace K. Mann, *The Lives of the Popes in the Early Middle Ages* and *The Lives of the Popes in the Middle Ages*, 18 vols. in 19 (St. Louis, Mo.: B. Herder, 1914–1932); Ludwig Freiherr von Pastor, *History of the Popes from the Close of the Middle Ages*, 40 vols. (London: Kegan Paul, Trench, Trübner, 1908–1952).

σοι ἀλλ' ὁ πατήρ μου ὁ ἐν τοῖς οὐρανοῖς. κἀγὼ δέ σοι λέγω ὅτι σὺ εἶ Πέτρος, καὶ ἐπὶ ταύτῃ τῇ πέτρᾳ οἰκοδομήσω μου τὴν ἐκκλησίαν, καὶ πύλαι ᾅδου οὐ κατισχύσουσιν αὐτῆς. δώσω σοι τὰς κλεῖδας τῆς βασιλείας τῶν οὐρανῶν. καὶ ὃ ἐὰν δήσῃς ἐπὶ τῆς γῆς ἔσται δεδεμένον ἐν τοῖς οὐρανοῖς, καὶ ὃ ἐὰν λύσῃς ἐπὶ τῆς γῆς ἔσται λελυμένον ἐν τοῖς οὐρανοῖς.

Dicit illis, "Vos autem quem me esse dicitis?" Respondens Simon Petrus dixit, "Tu es Christus, Filius Dei vivi." Respondens autem Iesus dixit ei, "Beatus es, Simon Bar Iona, quia caro et sanguis non revelavit tibi, sed Pater meus, qui in caelis est. Et ego dico tibi: Tu es Petrus, et super hanc petram aedificabo ecclesiam meam, et portae inferi non praevalebunt adversus eam. Tibi dabo claves regni caelorum. Et quodcumque ligaveris super terram, erit ligatum in caelis, et quodcumque solveris super terram, erit solutum in caelis.

He saith unto them, But whom say ye that I am? And Simon Peter answered and said, Thou art the Christ, the Son of the living God. And Jesus answered and said unto him, Blessed art thou, Simon Bar-jona, for flesh and blood hath not revealed it unto thee, but my Father, which is in heaven. And I say also unto thee, That thou art Peter, and upon this rock I will build my church, and the gates of hell shall not prevail against it. And I will give unto thee the keys of the kingdom of heaven, and whatsoever thou shalt bind on earth shall be bound in heaven, and whatsoever thou shalt loose on earth shall be loosed in heaven. (Authorized Version)

Luke 22:32: ἐγὼ δὲ ἐδεήθην περὶ σοῦ ἵνα μὴ ἐκλίπῃ ἡ πίστις σου· καὶ σύ ποτε ἐπιστρέψας στήρισον τοὺς ἀδελφούς σου.

Ego autem rogavi pro te, ut non deficiat fides tua. Et tu, aliquando conversus, confirma fratres tuos.

But I have prayed for thee, that thy faith fail not, and when thou art converted, strengthen thy brethren.(Authorized Version)

John 21:15–17: Σίμων Ἰωάννου, ἀγαπᾷς με πλέον τούτων; λέγει αὐτῷ ναί, κύριε, σὺ οἶδας ὅτι φιλῶ σε. λέγει αὐτῷ βόσκε τὰ ἀρνία μου. Λέγει αὐτῷ πάλιν δεύτερον· Σίμων Ἰωάννου, ἀγαπᾷς με; λέγει αὐτῷ· ναί, κύριε, σὺ οἶδας ὅτι φιλῶ σε. λέγει αὐτῷ ποίμαινε τὰ πρόβατά μου. Λέγει αὐτῷ τὸ τρίτον· Σίμων Ἰωάννου, φιλεῖς με; ἐλυπήθη ὁ Πέτρος ὅτι εἶπεν αὐτῷ τὸ τρίτον φιλεῖς με; καὶ λέγει αὐτῷ· κύριε, πάντα σὺ οἶδας, σὺ γινώσκεις ὅτι φιλῶ σε. λέγει αὐτῷ· βόσκε τὰ πρόβατά μου.

"Simon Ioannis, diligis me plus his?" Dicit ei, "Etiam, Domine, tu scis quia amo te." Dicit ei, "Pasce agnos meos." Dicit ei iterum secundo, "Simon Ioannis, diligis me?" Ait illi, "Etiam, Domine, tu scis quia amo te." Dicit ei, "Pasce oves meas." Dicit ei tertio, "Simon Ioannis, amas me?" Contristatus est Petrus quia dixit ei tertio, "Amas me?" et dicit ei, "Domine, tu omnia scis, tu cognoscis quia amo te. Dicit ei, "Pasce oves meas."

Simon, son of Jonas, lovest thou me more than these? He saith unto him, Yea, Lord, thou knowest that I love thee. He saith unto him, Feed my lambs. He saith to him the second time, Simon, son of Jonas, lovest thou me? He saith unto him, Yea, Lord, thou knowest that I love thee. He saith unto him, Feed my sheep. He saith unto him the third time, Simon, son of Jonas, lovest thou me? Peter was grieved because he said unto him the third time, Lovest thou me? And he said unto him, Lord, thou knowest all things. Thou knowest that I love thee. Jesus saith unto him, Feed my sheep. (Authorized Version)

The translation of ἐπιστρέψας in the excerpt from Luke (*thou art converted*, in the Authorized Version) has always been a problem. Notice that in the passage from John, the Authorized translators wiped out the distinction between ἀγαπᾷς and φιλεῖς, putting *thou lovest* for both.

Quite worth reading and very famous is Macaulay's essay in review of the English translation of Leopold von Ranke's *History of the Popes*.[14] The following sentences are the most frequently quoted:

There is not, and there never has been on this earth, a work of human policy so well deserving of examination as the Roman Catholic Church.... She was great and respected before the Saxon had set foot on Britain, before the Frank had passed the Rhine, when Grecian eloquence still flourished in Antioch, when idols were still worshipped in the temple of Mecca. And she may still exist in undiminished vigour when some traveller from New Zealand shall, in the midst of a vast solitude, take his stand on a broken arch of London Bridge to sketch the ruins of St. Paul's.[15]

Papist During the Reformation of the sixteenth century, the suffix *-ista* was added to the stem of the noun *papa* to form the first-declension noun *papista* with the meaning, a *follower of the Pope*. The noun is a pejorative term, like the modern construction *Islamist*. It is a mistake to use it as a positive word to denominate Catholics loyal to the Pope. Those aware of the history of a word blameworthily use it in a sense contrary to its original force. Nevertheless words like *Lutheran* and *Calvinist*, which were originally meant to be pejorative, came to be accepted by those so denominated, who turned an insult into a compliment. The Muslims, however, are insulted when called *Mohammedans*.

With regard to making nouns in this manner, the *Oxford English Dictionary* says that they are

14. Thomas Babington Macaulay, *Critical and Historical Essays contributed to the Edinburgh Review*, 6th ed. (London: Longman, Brown, Green, and Longmans, 1849), 3:99–146.

15. Ibid., 100–101.

formed from other abs. (chiefly Latin) without accompanying words in *-ize* or *-ism*, and denoting one whose profession or business it is to have to do with the thing or subject in question.[16]

Paraclete The Greek verb καλέω means *to call*, and the addition of the preposition παρά (*beside*) produces the compound verb παρακαλέω with the meaning *to call to one's side*. The derived noun παράκλητος means an *advocate, lawyer, helper, comforter*. Jesus calls the Holy Ghost the *Paraclete* in John 15:26.

Paradise The Greek noun παράδεισος is probably a transliteration of a Persian word for a great garden. The Romans transliterated it into the Latin *paradisum*. It is a poetic word for the dwelling place of the Deity. The words *paradise* and *heaven* mean the same, but people use the former for the place where one goes after death because it sounds more appealing than *heaven*. *Heaven* is used to refer to the Kingdom of God; *paradise* is used with an eschatological connotation. It cannot be deduced from Revelation 2:7 that there is real eating in heaven; man is able to think of things only in human terms, and life in paradise is something that is beyond human comprehension.

Paralipomena The Greek verb λείπω means *to leave*, and the Greek preposition παρά has the radical sense *beside*. The compounding of the two produces the verb παραλείπω with the meaning *to leave on one side, neglect, omit*. The present participles τὸ παραλειπόμενον (singular) and τὰ παραλειπόμενα (plural) means *something* or *somethings omitted*. What we call the Two Books of Chronicles are called in the Septuagint τὰ παραλειπόμενα; each of them is therefore called in the Vulgate *Paralipomenon*. The Greeks called these books the *books of omitted material*, as if they consisted of material that had been left out of the Books of Samuel and Kings.

Parallelismus Membrorum The Greek preposition παρά means *beside*, and the reciprocal pronoun ἀλλήλων means *of one another* (the word has no nominative), and their conjunction produced the mathematical adjective παράλληλος with the meaning *along one another, parallel*. The associated noun παραλληλισμός means the *state of being parallel*. The Latin noun *membrum* means *limb*. It is the genius of Hebrew poetry that each

16. *Oxford English Dictionary*, number 4 s.v. "–ist."

line of verse consist of two parts, the latter part developing or often re-peating in different words the idea in the first part. This characteristic is called in Latin *parallelismus membrorum*. Thus in Zechariah 9:9 we read:

עָנִי וְרֹכֵב עַל־חֲמוֹר וְעַל־עַיִר בֶּן־אֲתֹנוֹת:

Humble and riding upon a he-ass, and upon a male ass, the son of she-asses.

This does not mean that the rider is seated upon two he-asses; the male ass in the second half of the verse is the same as the he-ass in the first part.

Parce Domine This antiphon is from Joel 2:17.

Parce Domine, parce populo tuo, ne in aeternum irascaris nobis.

Spare, O spare thy people, Lord; be not angry with us forever.

Pascendi The Latin verb *pasco, pascere, pavi, pastus* means *to feed* (sc. ani-mals). This is the first word of the encyclical of Pope Pius X of September 8, 1907, against the heresy of modernism. It refers to the obligation of the pope to lead the flock of the Lord to pasture. The biographer of Wilfrid Ward summed up modernism as follows:

This, it seems to me, was largely the story of Modernism—an emptying out of the supernatural, an increasing reliance on the natural alone in life and in religion.[17]

As for the encyclical *Pascendi*, Ward wrote to a correspondent:

The document seems to me a terrible muddle, and I personally cannot interpret at all the parts I have above referred to so as to square with the disclaimer from Rome.[18]

His daughter commented:

What brought him to sheer agony was the fear that the sequel to the Encyclical might be an explicit condemnation of his hero Newman.[19]

She furthermore wrote:

The Encyclical was "difficult", Wilfrid Ward held, only because, being now done into English and offered to the laity at large, when it stated certain positions, which were in truth false as held by Modernists, it did *not* explain wherein they

17. Maisie Ward, *The Wilfrid Wards and the Transition*, vol. 2, *Insurrection versus Resurrection* (New York: Sheed & Ward, 1937), 181.

18. Ibid., 271.

19. Ibid., 274.

differed from those true doctrines from which they were verbally indistinguishable.[20]

With regard to what was at stake in the controversy about modernism, she concluded:

What was involved was the whole theory of the relation of Rulers to Thinkers in the Church.[21]

Paschal Controversy The Hebrew word פסח means *Passover*, and it was transliterated into Greek as πάσχα, which in turn became the Latin *pascha*. From *pascha* was produced the adjective *paschalis* with the meaning *pertaining to Easter*. The paschal controversy was the dispute in the early Church about the day on which one should celebrate Easter: on the same day as the Jewish Passover, or on the first Sunday thereafter.

Passibility The Latin deponent verb *patior, pati, passus sum* means *to suffer*, and from its third principal part is derived the Late Latin adjective *passibilis* meaning *capable of suffering*. From this adjective proceeded the noun *passibilitas* with the meaning the *capability to feel pain*. During the controversies of the fifth century concerning the Incarnation, it was debated whether or not it was correct to say that God had suffered on the cross. The slogan *Deus passus* was an expression to which the Monophysites would assent, but which the Nestorians would abhor.

Passion This noun is derived from the Latin *passio, passionis, f.*, which means *suffering*, from *patior, pati, passus sum*, to suffer. In the Catholic Church, the noun *passion* usually refers to the suffering and death of Jesus Christ. It was formerly a highlight of Holy Week in Rome to hear the accounts of the passion sung in Latin on Palm Sunday, on the following Monday and Wednesday, and on Good Friday, but these performances are now given in Italian.

The life and death of Jesus Christ is an event of the greatest importance in the history of the human race. The barest facts about the Passion of the Christ are recorded by the historian Tacitus, who, about 100 A.D., explaining the origin of the name *Christian*, wrote:

---

20. Ibid., 277.
21. Ibid., 294. Fr. John Norris had stated in a letter to the *Times*, on the highest authority, that the encyclical did not censure Newman.

Auctor nominis eius, Christus, Tiberio imperitante, per procuratorem Pontium Pilatum supplicio adfectus erat.[22]

The original of this name, Christ, had suffered the death penalty when Tiberius was emperor, under the procurator Pontius Pilate.

For further details we must have recourse to the Holy Gospels according to Matthew, Mark, Luke, and John. There are no Nixon tapes or video cassette recordings of the trial and crucifixion of Christ. Those, therefore, who demand that every assertion as to what happened be demonstrated with mathematical certainty can never be satisfied, and are behaving as impossibly as those who have recourse to absolute skepticism.

The four gospels are great works of literature. They are not written according to modern ideas; they are written in accordance with first century ideas.

A modern writer, making a history with the aid of older records, masters their contents and then makes a wholly new book.[23]

This is not the way of the first three evangelists, nor of most ancient and mediaeval authors. In books on the same subject,

We often find passages occurring almost word for word in each. All use directly or indirectly the same sources and copy these sources verbally as far as is consistent with the scope and scale of their various works.[24]

The ancient writer

was at one time a transcriber, at another time an abridger, at another an original author. With him plagiarism was no crime and no degradation, for what others had done well before him, he felt it unnecessary to recast in another and perhaps less perfect form. He epitomized, or curtailed, or adopted the works of his predecessors in the same path without alteration and without acknowledgment. [His motives and objects] were different from those of the modern historian. He did not consider himself tied to those restrictions to which the latter implicitly submits.[25]

---

22. Tacitus, *Annals* 15.44.

23. William Roberson Smith, *The Old Testament and the Jewish Church* (Edinburgh: Adam & Charles Black, 1881), 325–26.

24. Ibid.

25. Sir Thomas Duffy Hardy, quoted in Walter Farquhar Hook, "Matthew Parker, Chapter 15," in *Lives of the Archbishops of Canterbury*, n.s. vol. 4, *Reformation Period* (London: Richard Bentley & Son, 1872), 497n1.

Matthew and Luke copy over almost everything that is in Mark. For this reason, Matthew, Mark, and Luke are called the *synoptic* gospels, seeing things from the same point of view. The Gospel of John, on the other hand, is *sui generis*, a work of comparative individuality in a class by itself.

The four gospels were written in Greek. Therefore, when one reads the four accounts of the passion in English, one does not actually read the four gospels, but whatever English translation of them one happens to own. It is a pleasant fallacy for one to imagine that one is actually reading the gospels.

There are certain main issues that must be considered. The first is to determine on what day Christ died. In the Orthodox Church, and among Catholics in the East, the Holy Communion is celebrated with leavened bread. This practice they defend on the basis of the Gospel of John, in which, they say, it is clear that Jesus was crucified on a Friday, the day before the Passover, at the time when the paschal lambs were being sacrificed in the Temple, when eating yeast was still legitimate. It was Nisan 14, not quite yet Nisan 15, which would begin at sunset. In the Western Church, however, the Holy Communion is celebrated with unleavened bread. This practice they defend on the basis of the synoptic Gospels of Matthew, Mark, and Luke, in which, it is evident, the "Last Supper" was a Passover Seder, at which leavened bread would have been prohibited. According to this interpretation, the Christ was crucified on Friday, Nisan 15. This disagreement has always been tolerated in the Catholic Church. If the Eastern point of view be accepted, then it may be asserted, on the basis of mathematical formulas to be found, for example, in the eleventh edition of the *Encyclopaedia Britannica*, that Christ died on April 7, 30 A.D.[26] If, on the other hand, one sides with the Western Church, then one may suppose, on the basis of the same learning, that Christ was crucified on April 23, 34 A.D. The situation is summed up by the Abbé Duchesne thus:

In Asia, where they [the Christians] still made a point of keeping to the 14th Nizan, their thoughts seem to have centred round Jesus as being the true Paschal Lamb. So they replaced the ritual feast of the Jews that evening by the Feast of the Eucharist. According to the synoptic Gospels, indeed, the Lord was crucified, not on the 14th but on the 15th; in those days, however, things were not gone into so minutely, and by a slight anticipation, the Sacrifice of calvary was made to agree

---

26. *Encyclopaedia Britannica*, 11th ed. (New York: The Encyclopaedia Britannica Company, 1911), s.v. "Calendar".

with that of His symbolic prototype, the Paschal Lamb. At any rate, the Fourth Gospel soon rectified this discrepancy, by altering the date of the Passion from the 15th back to the 14th.

Apollinaris reproached his adversaries for suggesting a discordance between the Gospels. No doubt he believed he could reconcile the Synoptics with St. John. I also have tried to do so, following many others. It is wiser to acknowledge that, on this point, we are not in a position to reconcile the evangelists.[27]

That Jesus was arrested in a suburban garden, whither he had withdrawn with some of his students ("disciples") to pray, all four gospels agree. The disciples, after some slight resistance, ran away—the first example, as Cardinal Ottaviani used to say, of episcopal collegiality. Who arrested Jesus? According to Matthew, Mark, and Luke, it was a detachment of religious police at the disposal of the Temple authorities. Such ecclesiastical forces are commonplace even today in Saudi Arabia and Iran. John, however, describes the armed men with the word commonly used to indicate a Roman cohort of 480 soldiers, and, on this basis, many have suggested that a large contingent of Roman forces was involved.

What happened next is the subject of the greatest controversy. In the accounts of Matthew and Mark, Jesus is brought to trial during the night, before the Sanhedrin, the supreme council of the Children of Israel, under the presidency of the high priest Caiaphas. Geza Vermes argued that this would have been impossible,[28] because in those gospels, the Passover had already begun, and it would not have been allowed to hold a session of the court on that feast. For example, in 2005, Pope Benedict XVI invited the Jews of Rome to send a delegation to his installation ceremony in St. Peter's Square. The Jews, however, respectfully declined, pointing out that the pope was being installed on the Passover, on which day they were not authorized by the Deity to do business as usual. This is the major objection to the historicity of the synoptic account of the passion, that no meeting of the Sanhedrin could have taken place on the Passover. Others are not convinced by this objection, though they admit that it is very important. The reason that it does not convince them is because it does not take into account that there are people in the world, as we all now know, who justify any crime under the pretext that it is a necessary act to defend

---

27. Louis Duchesne, *Early History of the Christian Church from Its Foundation to the End of the Third Century* (London: John Murray, 1914), 208–9, 209n4. Apollinaris was a second-century bishop of Hierapolis in Phrygia.

28. Geza Vermes, *The Passion* (London: Penguin, 2005).

the interests of the Deity. According to Bury, the last editor of Gibbon and the preeminent modern historian of the Roman Empire, the Jewish authorities of the time were corrupt. In this case, it is not inconceivable that they might have stooped to commit a crime on the Passover.

When reading the synoptic accounts of the trial, one must notice that Jesus makes no reply to the court until the high priest provokes him into admitting that he is the promised Messiah, whereupon the court is disgusted and pronounces him guilty of the capital crime of blasphemy. However, to proclaim oneself the Anointed Messiah is not blasphemy; blasphemy is taking the unutterable name of God in vain. Thus, according to this account, a great miscarriage of justice took place. Also, according to Jewish law, the death sentence could not be pronounced on the same day as the guilty verdict; one had to wait twenty-four hours and hold another session. Here is another miscarriage of justice.

The Gospel of John is the only one to report that the police first brought Jesus to Annas, the high priest emeritus, before delivering him up to Caiaphas. There is nothing incredible about this, since Annas was influential, and his deposition was considered irregular by many Jews. He was probably the oldest of all the chief priests. Why the synoptic evangelists left him out, they are not here to explain.

The trial of the Christ before Pontius Pilate is reported by Tacitus as well as by all four evangelists. Jesus must have been considered a threat to public order for the governor to have become involved. The religious authorities reported to Pilate that Jesus had announced that he was king. The assumption of the royal title was treason. These authorities do not bring the charge of blasphemy, because in that case Pilate might not have condescended to get involved. The trial would have been conducted in Latin, because the majesty of Rome did not allow for any other language to be used in legal proceedings. An interpreter would have been summoned if this was necessary.

There is no trace of the Romans seeking in any quarter to impose their own language on the conquered races, or proscribing the native tongue. The furthest extent to which they allowed themselves to go in obtruding a single, favoured idiom on their subjects, was in conducting public business throughout the empire in Latin, a practice dictated by convenience, though sanctioned no doubt by a feeling of national pride. The majesty of Rome, that moral charm on which her authority was made to rest even more than on her arms, might seem to require that her chief magistrates and generals should use no other language than her own and allow no other to be addressed to them in the provinces.[29]

Geza Vermes objected that the relatively favorable view taken of Pilate in the gospels is not in harmony with what Josephus had to say of him in his history of the Jews. Vermes believed that the compilers of the gospels, writing at a time when Christianity had given up trying to win over the Jews, decided that nothing was to be lost by blaming them for everything and letting the Romans off easy, for the future was in Rome. On the other hand, it is not impossible to allow the possibility that Pontius Pilate was a complex personality, and that he occasionally took seriously his role as the representative of the Roman legal system, which was eventually to produce, under the emperor Justinian, the Code of Civil Law.

That Pilate interrupted his proceedings to offer Herod Antipas the honor of deciding the case of the Galilean Jesus is reported by Luke alone among the evangelists. It is a believable incident, since the Roman government worked through such specimens whenever possible, just as the Americans in Baghdad worked through Alawi, and then al-Jaafary and al-Maliki.

The Passover amnesty offered by Pilate, which led to the release of Bar Abbas, is related by all four evangelists, but it is otherwise unheard of. That it happened has in its favor that it would explain why such a large crowd had gathered at the seat of government so early in the morning. Such a crowd would have contained both supporters and opponents of Jesus. Since Jesus had a large enough following to be viewed as a threat, it has been remarked that one would have expected his partisans to have argued for him as those of Bar Abbas supported their man. If this was the case, it will not be shocking to you to be told that the authors of books select what to tell you, and what not to tell you.

People often imagine that all the words assigned to the various personalities in the gospel accounts of the passion are their exact utterances, as if a tape recorder had taken them down. It would be very daring to think this, although many passages might have been delivered as written. Ancient authors did not consider it important, as we do, to distinguish precisely between the first and third persons; this is a modern concern, not an ancient one. They considered it more important to make the necessary affect.

29. Charles Merivale, *A History of the Romans under the Empire*, 2nd ed. (London: Longman, Green, Longman, & Roberts, 1862), 4:376.

The words of Pilate in the fourth gospel (John 19:5), ἰδοὺ ὁ ἄνθρωπος—
Behold the man!—just meant, "Look at this guy!" Since Jesus must have
been in a sorry state at that point, it was an attempt to solicit pity. The episode of Simon of Cyrene reported in the synoptic gospels sounds realistic.
That a mercilessly beaten man would not have had the strength to carry
the horizontal beam of the cross is something that can be believed. Illustrations portraying Jesus carrying the full cross are a mediaeval invention;
that is not how it was done.

In the Gospel of Mark, one reads that Jesus hung on the cross from the
third until the ninth hour (15:24, 34); John says, though, that he was not
nailed to the cross until the sixth hour (19:14). This is one of a large number of disagreements in the accounts that vigilant readers notice. There
are three ways in which such inconsistencies have been handled through
the ages. One is through the exercising of the harmonizing instinct, which
tries to explain it all away.

But the cleverest defenders of a faith are its greatest enemies; for their subtleties
engender doubt and stimulate the mind.[30]

The second approach is to live with the uncertainty until the increase of
knowledge permits the difficulties to be solved at some future date. For
example, when people were wondering whether Christianity and evolution were compatible, Pius XII was asked to weigh in on the matter. He
said that he did not see how polygenesis could be squared with the doctrine of original sin, and he left it at that. In other words, he left it an open
question. The idea that an infallible pronouncement issues from those
authorities in every morning's newspaper is a mistake. The last approach
is to argue that the gospel accounts contain a large amount of guesswork
and fiction over a skeleton of reality, and the differences in the accounts
are in large measure due to this legendary element. A century ago, this
would have been called modernism.

The occasional miraculous episode presents a great difficulty for many
modern readers. Their presence has led some thinkers to deny that Jesus
Christ ever existed, and to decide that the accounts of the passion are
like episodes from *War and Peace* or *Anna Karenina*. This is not the right
solution, although great men have arrived at it. The people of the time of
Christ were not like the people of Erie or Baltimore. If my thyroid acts
up and requires my physician's attention, I say that Dr. Euler gave me

30. Will Durant, "Spinoza," in *The Story of Philosophy* (New York: Simon & Schuster, 1926), 165.

prednisone and cured me. They would have said that God cured me. Every sentence in Arabic begins with *and* and has the word *God* in it. If a strong wind blows, the Semitic idiom is to say that it is a wind of God. If a feeling of peace and serenity comes over them, they say that an angel was ministering unto them.

Modern archaeology has found that the Church of the Holy Sepulcher satisfies the usual necessary conditions to be considered a candidate for the site of the crucifixion. It used to be objected that the location of this basilica is within the walls, where no one could be buried, but the current walls, built by Suleiman the Magnificent in the sixteenth century, are not those that stood in the time of Christ.

Much has been written on how to interpret the meteorological phenomena reported to have occurred at the death of Christ. It is wrong to go looking for eclipses. I recall that newspaper reports from Rome in 1870 described how the proclamation of the doctrine of papal infallibility took place during the worst lightning and thunder storm ever recorded in Rome. Some exegetes of the time used this example as an admonition to those colleagues who had suggested that the storm in the gospels was a metaphor.

One of the "Seven Last Words (actually, statements) of Christ" recorded in the gospels, Luke 23:34 ("Father, forgive them, for they know not what they do"), is not found in the earliest manuscripts, that is, those of the third and fourth centuries, such as Codex Vaticanus and Codex Sinaiticus. There is therefore considerable doubt as to whether that verse was originally a part of Luke's gospel. This does not imply, of course, that it is not authentic.

It has been said that the gospel accounts of the passion are anti-Semitic. In Europe for centuries, Jews kept out of sight on Good Friday, lest they be attacked in the streets. It is certainly true that the Jews of the time of Christ are represented in a very bad light in the passion narratives. What are we to make of the cry, "Let his blood be upon us and upon our children!" (Matthew 26:25), which presents the greatest problem in this regard? In the tribal society of the Middle East, if my father kills someone's son, then his family is justified in killing me; if they do not retaliate, they are considered cowards and lose face. If these words were actually spoken, what the crowd was telling Pilate was, "If his people have a problem with this, let them come after us, not you." It is an anachronism to read mediaeval or Hitlerite views into the production of a first-century author. At any rate, at least in the Catholic Church, it has become impossible, since the reigns of the recent popes, to be an anti-Semite.

One must keep in mind that the Jewish priests of the first century and their dependents were not the object of veneration from the part of the mass of the Children of Israel of the time. With regard to the Jewish Revolt of the years after 66 A.D., the Abbé Duchesne wrote:

> The high priest Ananias and all the leaders of the sacerdotal aristocracy were massacred by the rioters; fanatics and brigands contended for the Temple and the fortresses.[31]

One should perhaps say a few words about the movie. On Ash Wednesday, 2004, Mel Gibson presented his movie *The Passion of the Christ* to the consideration of the world. Everyone who was qualified to have an opinion, and many more who were not, appeared on television and instructed humanity on the truths that their wide reading and liberal education had enabled them to discover. One might expect much in an age when there is a college on every street corner, and a university in every abandoned garage. The actors speak in Aramaic and in Latin, and since they do not, for the most part, pronounce it like English, it is a stroke of genius rather than a comedy, like an American production of an Italian opera. Gibson makes various interpolations into the biblical narratives from the pretended revelations of mediaeval and modern visionaries; for example, the devil is introduced into the Garden of Gethsemane scene. I do not think that this is an improvement. His method is the traditional one of intertwining the four gospel accounts into one narrative. In the trial before Pilate, the governor converses with the high priest in Aramaic. This is almost certainly wrong, as it was not the way of the Roman authorities to learn the languages of the subject peoples over whom they presided. Even today, do you think that J. Paul Bremer conversed with the members of the Iraqi Governing Council in Arabic? Jesus addresses Pilate in Latin, and converses with him at length in that language. This is unrealistic. He must have spoken in Aramaic, and his remarks would have been translated into Latin.[32]

---

31. Louis Duchesne, *Early History of the Christian Church from Its Foundation to the End of the Third Century* (London: John Murray, 1914), 86.

32. For those who want to read books whose authors deal with this matter as they would treat the assassination of Julius Caesar or the execution of Charles the First, the best modern discussions are by Geza Vermes, *The Passion* (London: Penguin, 2005); and by Haim Cohn, *The Trial and Death of Jesus* (Old Saybrook, Conn.: Konecky & Konecky, n.d.)—Haim Cohn was for many years a justice of the Supreme Court of Israel.

We conclude by noting the etymologies of those names that appear in the narratives of the passion. The Hebrew root יָשַׁע means *to deliver*, and from it was believed to descend the name יְהוֹשׁוּעַ with the meaning *the Lord saves*. This name later shortened to יֵשׁוּעַ. Both the longer and the shorter form were transliterated by the Greek Ἰησοῦς, which became in Latin *Iesus*, whence is derived our *Jesus*. For the longer form of the Hebrew name, one finds the Latin translation *Iosue* used for the name of the eponymous sixth book of the Old Testament. Brown, Driver, and Briggs do not list the name יְהוֹשׁוּעַ under the root יָשַׁע but instead present the entry alphabetically as the name is spelled; they note that whatever the origin, the name was eventually understood to come from יָשַׁע. They point out that the Arabic root وسع means *to be wide, spacious, be* or *live in abundance*, and they offer the additional possibility of *the Lord is opulence* as the original meaning of the name.

The father-in-law of the high priest Caiaphas was Ἅννας—חָנָן—Annas, whose name means *gracious*.

The High Priest who presided at the trial of the Christ was Καϊάφας—קַיָּפָא—Caiaphas. The etymology of this name is uncertain, although Dalman, quoting Lagarde, notices that قايف means a *practitioner of physiognomy*[33] (from the root قيف, which, according to Wehr,[34] means, in the second conjugation, *to follow the tracks of someone, to study, examine, investigate*). Cheyne supports Lagarde.[35]

Herod, in Hebrew הוֹרְדוֹס, is the corruption of the Greek name Ἡρῴδης, the contraction of name Ἡρωΐδης, which means the *son of a hero*, the patronymic suffix -ίδης having been appended to the noun ἥρως, *hero*. The Herod in question was Herod Antipas, Ἀντίπας being the hypocoristic abbreviation of Ἀντίπατρος.

The name of the revolutionary Βαραββᾶς—בַּר־אַבָּא—Barabbas—means *Son of the father* (i.e., student of a rabbinic teacher). *Son of Abba*, says Cheyne,[36] is not possible because at that time *Abba* had not yet become a personal name as it did later (e.g., Abba Eban).

33. Gustaf Dalman, *Grammatik der Jüdisch-Palästinischen Aramäisch, nach den Idiomen des Palästinischen Talmud, des Onkelostargum und Prophetentargum und der Jerusalemischen Targume, zweite Auflage* (Leipzig: J. C. Hinrichs'sche Buchhandlung, 1905), 161n2

34. Hans Wehr, *A Dictionary of Modern Written Arabic (Arabic–English)*, 4th ed., ed. J. Milton Cowan, (Wiesbaden: Otto Harrassowitz, 1979).

35. Rev. T. K. Cheyne and J. Sutherland Black, eds., *Encyclopaedia Biblica, A Critical Dictionary of the Literary, Political, and Religious History, the Archaeology, Geography, and Natural History of the Bible* (London: Adam & Charles Black, 1899), 1:171–72, 172n1.

36. Ibid., 1:476–77.

We do not know the given name of the Governor of Judaea who condemned Christ to the cross; we know only his gentilic name *Pontius* and his cognomen (family name) *Pilatus*. The etymologies of these two names are uncertain. See the entry **Gentiluomini di Sua Santità**.

Pastor The Latin verb *pasco, pascere, pavi, pastus* means *to feed* (of animals), and from its fourth principal part proceeds the noun *pastor*, the shepherd. It figures in the parable of the Good Shepherd in John 10:1–21. It is consequently a common metaphor used to refer to priests, bishops, and popes. It is also the family name of the greatest historian of the popes, Ludwig, Freiherr von Pastor (1854–1928).

Paten The Greek noun πατάνη means a *flat dish*. It came into Latin as *patina*, whence our noun *paten*. It is the plate upon which the sacred host is placed during the Mass.

Pater Noster These are the first words of the Lord's Prayer in Latin and mean *Our Father*.[37] The singing of the Lord's Prayer in Latin is a part of the lost heritage of Catholics.

Πάτερ ἡμῶν, ὁ ἐν τοῖς οὐρανοῖς· ἁγιασθήτω τὸ ὄνομά σου· ἐλθέτω ἡ βασιλεία σου· γενηθήτω τὸ θέλημά σου, ὡς ἐν οὐρανῷ καὶ ἐπὶ γῆς· τὸν ἄρτον ἡμῶν τὸν ἐπιούσιον δὸς ἡμῖν σήμερον· καὶ ἄφες ἡμῖν τὰ ὀφειλήματα ἡμῶν, ὡς καὶ ἡμεῖς ἀφήκαμεν τοῖς ὀφειλέταις ἡμῶν· καὶ μὴ εἰσενέγκῃς ἡμᾶς εἰς τὸ πειρασμόν, ἀλλὰ ῥῦσαι ἡμᾶς ἀπὸ τοῦ πονηροῦ.

Pater noster, qui es in caelis, sanctificetur nomen tuum. Adveniat regnum tuum. Fiat voluntas tua, sicut in caelo et in terra. Panem nostrum quotidianum da nobis hodie, et dimitte nobis debita nostra, sicut et nos dimittimus debitoribus nostris. Et ne nos inducas in tentationem, sed libera nos a malo. Amen.

Patriarch The Greek noun Πατρίαρχος means the *ruler of fathers*. It is a title granted in the early Church to the bishops of Rome, Constantinople, Alexandria, Antioch, and Jerusalem. Later on, the number of authorities who boasted this title was multiplied.

Patrinus and Matrina The Greek nouns πατήρ and μήτηρ mean *father* and *mother* respectively; the corresponding Latin nouns are *pater* and *mater*. The addition of the diminutive and caritative suffix -*inus* (feminine, -*ina*) produces the words *patrinus* and *matrina* which mean *godfather* and *godmother*. According to canon law, each baptized Catholic must have at

37. Matthew 6:9–13.

least one Catholic godparent, who may be male or female, or a Catholic godparent of each sex, but not two of the same sex; having more than two godparents is not allowed. Non-Catholic witnesses may be multiplied as necessary, but they do not count as godparents.

Patripassians The Latin noun *pater* means *father*, and the verb *patior, pati, passus sum* means *to suffer*. *Patripassian* was a derogatory name for *Modalist*, since, if the Father and Jesus were one and the same person, then the Father suffered on the cross. The Patripassians were thus people who denied the distinction of persons in the godhead.

Patron Saint The Latin noun pater means *father*, and from it is derived the noun *patronus* with the meaning, *one who protects or defends like a father*. A patron saint is a saint who is especially recognized as the protector of a specific place or class of people. For example, the saints Cosmas and Damian are the patron saints of twins.

Paulianists The followers of Paul of Samosata, bishop of Antioch (260–269), were denominated *Paulianists*. They denied the doctrine of the Holy Trinity; for them, Jesus of Nazareth was a man whom God adopted. *Paulianus* is an alternative form of *Paulinus*. See the following entry.

Pauline The Greek adjective παῦρος means *small, little*, and related to it is the Latin adjective *paulus* of the same meaning. According to Egger, the word is derived from the primitive word *paue-s-los*, so the earlier form of the adjective and the name was *Paullus*.[38] The Latin adjective *Paulinus* means *that which pertains to Paul*, and its English form is *Pauline*. Thus, the chapel built in the Vatican Palace by Paul III Farnese and adorned by Michelangelo with the frescoes of the martyrdoms of Saints Peter and Paul is called the *Cappella Paolina*, as is that in the Quirinal Palace built by Paul V Borghese. Similarly, the Pauline Epistles are those letters of St. Paul the Apostle that are to be found in the New Testament.

Pavilion The Latin noun *papilio, papilionis, m.*, means a *butterfly*. Tents that looked like the outspread wings of a butterfly were called *pavilions*. In the Catholic Church, the word is used of the large umbrella granted to a basilica as a symbol of its dignity.

---

38. Karl Egger, *Lexicon Nominum Virorum et Mulierum*, 2nd ed. (Rome: Editrice Studium, 1963), 193–94, s. v. "Paolo."

Pax This is the Latin word for *peace*. It is also the name of that part of the Mass after the *Pater Noster* that begins with the words *Pax Domini sit semper vobiscum*, after which the clergy ceremoniously embrace one another. In English, it is called the ceremony of the Kiss of Peace, where *kiss* is supposed to be understood in its archaic sense of *embrace*. The laity nowadays exchange greetings not *per amplexum*, but usually by shaking hands or merely verbally. In the High Middle Ages, when it was considered unseemly and vulgar to touch a stranger, the greeting was extended by means of the paxbred.

Paxbred This word is the combination of the Latin *pax* (peace) with the Anglo-Saxon *bred* or *bord*, (board). It is also spelled *paxbrede*. In Latin, it is the *instrumentum pacis* or *osculatorium pacis*. The paxbred is

A tablet of gold, silver, ivory, glass, or other material, round or quadrangular, with a projecting handle behind, bearing a representation of the Crucifixion or other sacred subject, which was kissed by the celebrating priest at Mass, and passed to the other officiating clergy and then to the congregation to be kissed; an osculatory.

It came into use during the 13th c. as a symbolic substitute for the kiss of peace.... In England its use died out after the Reformation; in the Roman Church it is now used in certain monastic communities on special occasions.[39]

Pax Domini These are the opening words of the sentence in the Mass:

Pax Domini sit semper vobiscum.

May the peace of the Lord be always with you.

In former times, the clergy would at this point embrace one another. In the modern Mass, all in attendance are invited to exchange greetings. It is one of the most noticeable differences between the two rites.

Pelagianism The Greek noun πέλαγος means the *open sea*, and its transliteration *pelagus* had the same meaning in Latin. The adjectives πελάγιος and *pelagius* mean *pertaining to the sea, marine*. This word became a proper name, whose most famous bearer was the heretic Pelagius (died 418), who denied predestination and original sin and taught the doctrine of free will.

For Pelagius, and in this respect he represents to us a considerable body of his contemporaries, things present themselves under quite a different aspect. A man

39. *Oxford English Dictionary* (Oxford: Oxford University Press, 1988), s.v. "Pax."

is virtuous because he wills it strongly and because he gives himself the trouble to be so. God helps him in this, no doubt, but as it were from without, by means of the free will with which He has provided us, by means of His Law, which enlightens and commands us, by means of the example and the exhortations of the saints, and especially of Christ, and by means of the purifying grace of Baptism. In other respects, the good that we do is attributable to us. This good we are under obligation to do, for it would not be commanded us if it were not in our power to attain it. God enjoins the avoidance of all sin: a man can, then, be without sin; and in Pelagius' thought, sin means not only grave and external faults but interior defects which occur in the secret recesses of the soul. This austere and heroic morality fitted in well enough with the conception of virtue held in the ancient schools, with the popular Stoicism on which the life of good people was ordinarily based. Pelagius admitted neither Original Sin nor Original Fall. What talk is this of sin transmitted by heredity? was a question in Pelagian circles. A sin is an act of will; he only who has committed it is responsible for it. It has no consequence which affects his descendants. If we feel within us the assaults of concupiscence, if our body is frail and subject to the law of death, that means that such is the nature of man. Thus, Adam was created by God in the state in which we ourselves come into the world; what we derive from our first father are the original conditions of human nature, not the consequences of an initial fault.[40]

Pellegrina The Latin prepositional phrase *per agros* means *through the fields,* and in a time before the interstate highway system there was derived from it the adverb *peregre* with the meaning *abroad, in a foreign country.* From *peregre* there was derived the adjective *peregrinus, -a, -um* meaning *foreign, strange,* which, as a noun, meant *a foreigner,* someone who has travelled through the countryside to get here. The Italian noun *pellegrino* and the English noun *pilgrim* are corruptions of the Latin *peregrinus.* The *pellegrina* is a shoulder cape open in front that forms part of the prelatial attire known as the simar. It is also part of some cassocks. It was evidently derived from a garment worn by foreigners who came to visit shrines.

Penance The Greek noun ποινή means a *ransom paid for the shedding of blood,* and it was taken over into Latin as *poena* with the meaning *money paid for atonement, a fine,* hence *punishment, penalty.* The associated Latin impersonal verb *paenitet, paeniteri* means *to be the cause of regret,* and from it proceeds the noun *paenitentia,* regret, which came into English as

---

40. Louis Duchesne, *Early History of the Christian Church from Its Foundation to the End of the Fifth Century,* vol. 3 (London: John Murray, 1924), 143–44.

penance. The interchange of the diphthongs *ae* and *oe* does not indicate a different origin.

Penitentiary The *paenitentiarii* are those specially deputized priests in Rome who can absolve in confession those whose sins are so serious that they are required to apply to the Holy See for absolution. Their body is called the *Apostolic Penitentiary*, and their head, who is always a cardinal, is called the *Major Penitentiary*.

Pentateuch The Greek word πέντε means *five*, and the noun τεῦχος means *implement* or, later on, a *book*. The adjective πεντάτευχος, there-fore, means *consisting of five books*. It is the name of the Hebrew Torah, that is, of the Books of Genesis, Exodus, Leviticus, Numbers, and Deuter-onomy taken together.

Perhaps it is as yet rather too soon to speak of the "results" of modern criticism, but if not its "results," at least its strongly pronounced tendency is to spread the composition of the actual Pentateuch as we have it over the period covered by the Monarchy and the Exile. If we ignore minor subdivisions, which are numerous, and look only at the broad distribution of the masses, the component parts of the Pentateuch may be said to be three: (1) a double stream of narrative, the work of prophets, variously dated between 900 and 750 B.C., which forms the greater part of the Book of Genesis, but also runs through Exodus and Numbers: (2) the Book of Deuteronomy, the greater part of which belongs to a date not very long before 621 B.C.; and lastly (3) the Priest's Code, which either falls at the end of the Exile or else had a latent existence somewhat before it.[41]

Pentecost The Greek word πεντήκοντα means *fifty*, and from it was de-rived the adjective πεντηκοστός with the meaning *fiftieth*, whose stem is the English *Pentecost*. The Feast of Pentecost is the fiftieth day—ἡ ἡμέρα ἡ πεντηκοστή—after Easter; it is the birthday of the Church.

Pentecostal The addition of the Latin adjectival suffix *-alis* to the root of the Greek adjective πεντηκοστή produces the modern English word *Pentecostal*, a word commonly used as the name of those people for whom speaking in tongues is a major or common form of religious expression.

Perfidis The old prayer *Oremus et pro perfidis Iudaeis* before the Mass of the Presanctified was a cause of complaint from the part of those who

---

41. William Sanday, *Inspiration, Eight Lectures on the Early History and Origin of the Doctrine of Biblical Inspiration, Being the Bampton Lectures for 1893* (London: Longmans, Green, 1896), 172.

wanted to promote better relations between Catholics and Jews. Since most of the early Jews considered Christianity a heresy, they impeded its progress, with the result that Christians viewed them as enemies. One can see evidence of this in the New Testament. After Christianity triumphed, the failure of the Jews to convert was imputed to blindness and stubbornness.

Oremus et pro perfidis Iudaeis, ut Deus ac Dominus Noster auferat velamen de cordibus eorum, ut et ipsi agnoscant Iesum Christum Dominum nostrum.

Let us also pray for the treacherous Jews, that the Lord Our God might remove the veil from upon their hearts, that they too might acknowledge Our Lord Jesus Christ.

In modern times, there was much learned controversy about whether the correct English translation of *perfidis* is *perfidious* (i.e., treacherous) or *unbelieving*. What is certain is that it is not a complement, but rather a term of opprobrium, and modern people, embarrassed and motivated by shame, certainly wanted it to mean no more than *non-believing*. Retaining the prayer was impossible after the events of 1933–1945. John XXIII acted wisely in cutting the Gordian Knot and removing the word from the prayer, the whole of which was then abolished in the next pontificate and replaced by a new and noncontroversial version. The Latin adjective *perfidus, -a, -um* means *faithless, not to be trusted, promise-breaking, treacherous*.

Persecution The Latin verb *sequor, sequi, secutus sum* means *to follow*. When this verb is compounded with the preposition *per*, the sense is intensified, so that the compound verb *persequor, persequi, persecutus sum* means *to pursue with the intention of doing harm, to persecute*. The corresponding Greek word is καταδιώκω. From the last principal part of the Latin verb comes the associated noun *persecutio*. The first persecution of Christians took place in Rome during the reign of the emperor Nero, who had accused them of arson. Sometime around then the practice of Christianity became illegal, although nobody knows exactly when. The enforcement of the law was intermittent and depended on the attitude of the emperor and of the local governor. Emperors who left the Christians alone included Commodus, Alexander Severus, Philip the Arab, and Gallienus. The persecution under Decius was especially severe, as that monarch required every Christian to appear before a magistrate and receive a certificate (called a *libellus*) attesting that he had sacrificed to the gods or burned incense before one of their images or that of the emperor, a sort of ancient way of saluting the flag; this was a major reversal of the "Don't ask, don't tell" policy of the emperor Trajan hitherto in force.

The majority of recognized Christians had the certificate of sacrifice. The more obstinate would, no doubt, after a taste of prison discipline, end by complying with the regulations. But multitudes were forgotten, who had either concealed their Christianity, or baffled the police. If so many bishops, priests, and deacons succeeded in hiding, and even in continuing their ministries at the most critical moments, it must have been because the authorities either could not or would not see all that was going on. When the persecution ended, there still remained a great many Christians, who, never having been called upon to sacrifice, were neither apostates nor confessors. The success of this edict, which seemed so complete, was in reality but very partial.[42]

Pharisee The Hebrew verb פרש means *to separate*, and the past participle פרוש means a *separatist, one separated*. From this word the Greeks formed the noun Φαρισαῖος, whence comes our noun *Pharisee*. They are first mentioned by Josephus.

At this time there were three sects among the Jews, who had different opinions concerning human actions; the one was called the sect of the Pharisees, another the sect of the Sadducees, and the other the sect of the Essenes.[43]

The Abbé Duchesne describes them as follows.

The Pharisees, so often condemned in the Gospels for their hypocrisy, their false zeal, and their peculiar practices, did not form a special sect; the name was applied generally to all those who were ultra-scrupulous in following the Law, and not the Law only, but the thousand observances with which they had amplified it, attributing as much importance to them as to the fundamental precepts of morality.[44]

Philomena The Greek verb φιλέω means *to love*, and the feminine singular present passive participle φιλουμένη means *beloved lady*. In ancient times it became a personal name; a woman so named is mentioned in Eusebius's *History*.[45]

---

42. Louis Duchesne, *Early History of the Christian Church from Its Foundation to the End of the Third Century* (London: John Murray, 1914), 271.

43. Josephus, *Antiquities of the Jews*, 13.5.9, trans. William Whiston. This book is available at http://www.sacred-texts.com/jud/josephus/index.htm

44. Louis Duchesne, *Early History of the Christian Church from Its Foundation to the End of the Third Century* (London: John Murray, 1914), 10.

45. Eusebius, *The History of the Church from Christ to Constantine*, V 13.

– P –

Philosophy The Greek adjective φίλος means *loved*, and as a noun it means a *friend*. The noun σοφία means *wisdom*, or rather, originally, *cleverness*. (The accurate word corresponding to our *wisdom* would be σωφροσύνη, as Duchesne had pointed out.)[46] The two words were combined by Pythagoras, who referred to himself as a φιλόσοφος, a *lover of knowledge*. The love of knowledge is φιλοσοφία, *philosophy*. In his essay on Plato, Emerson wrote:

Philosophy is the account which the human mind gives to itself of the constitution of the world.

When Pius II founded the University of Basel in 1460, he wrote that man was able to attain knowledge by a gift of God.

Ex dono Dei mortalis homo adipisci valet scientiae margaritam, quae eum in infimo loco natum evehit ad sublimes.

By divine gift the human being can acquire the pearl of knowledge, which elevates him who was born in the humblest state up into the ranks of the leadership.

It is the teaching of the Catholic Church that since the truths revealed in the various sciences are all part of this divine gift, the truths discovered by these branches of knowledge are never in contradiction, but rather complement one another, one explaining what the other cannot. *Praestet fides supplementum sensuum defectui*. This harmony was a central teaching of the encyclical *Providentissimus Deus* of Leo XIII (1893); "truth cannot contradict truth" (II D 5). John Henry Newman gave a famous definition of philosophy in the beginning of the ninth discourse ("Duties of the Church towards Knowledge") of *Idea of a University*. He began by providing a summary of his doctrine on the relationship of the various sciences professed in the university:

I have accordingly laid down first, that all branches of knowledge are, at least implicitly, the subject matter of its [sc, the university's] teaching; that these branches are not isolated and independent of one another, but form together a whole or system; that they run into each other, and complete each other, and that, in proportion to our view of them as a whole, is the exactness and trustworthiness of the knowledge which they separately convey.[47]

46. Louis Duchesne, *Early History of the Christian Church from Its Foundation to the End of the Third Century* (London: John Murray, 1914), 120n2.
47. John Henry Cardinal Newman, *Idea of a University* (Garden City, N.Y.: Image Books, 1959), 221.

399

Each science has its own subject matter and area of competence, from which it is not permitted to wander without causing mischief.

No science whatsoever, however comprehensive it may be, but will fall largely into error if it be constituted the sole exponent of all things in heaven and earth, and that, for the simple reason that it is encroaching on territory not its own, and undertaking problems which it has no instruments to solve.[48]

One type of interference occurs when one science attempts to impose its particular method on another. For example, in his *Age of Reason*, Thomas Paine argued that theology should abandon its deductive method, based on revelation through certain texts, and adopt the inductive method of modern science, based on facts observed in experiment. Similarly, certain professors, colleagues of Galileo, held that the correct "way of arriving at truth in astronomy was by theological reasoning on texts of Scripture."[49] Such a point of view was possible because, as von Ranke pointed out,

The investigation of physics and natural history was at that time almost inseparably connected with philosophical inquiry.[50]

Newman wrote:

I observe, then, that the elementary methods of reasoning and inquiring used in theology and physics are contrary the one to the other; each of them has a method of its own; and in this, I think, has lain the point of controversy between the two schools, viz., that neither of them has been quite content to remain on its own homestead, but that, whereas each has its own method, which is the best for its own science, each has considered it the best for all purposes whatsoever, and has at different times thought to impose it upon the other science, to the disparagement or rejection of that opposite method which legitimately belongs to it.[51]

For example,

The history of the last three centuries is only one long course of attempts, on the part of the partisans of the Baconian philosophy, to get rid of the method proper to theology and to make it an experimental science.[52]

---

48. Ibid., 166. Cf. Lord Bacon, *De Augmentis* 4.2: Let us "rest the sciences each in its proper place."

49. Andrew Dickson White, *A History of the Warfare of Science with Theology in Christendom* (New York: D. Appleton, 1896), 1:131.

50. Leopold von Ranke, *The History of the Popes during the Last Four Centuries*, trans. Mrs. Foster and G. R. Dennis (London: G. Bell & Sons, 1912), 1:393.

51. John Henry Cardinal Newman, *Idea of a University* (Garden City, N.Y.: Image Books, 1959), 400.

52. Ibid., 405.

It is evident, then, that there are great dangers in confusing the boundaries and methods of the various sciences, and Newman assigned the name *philosophy* to that super-science which concerns the mutual relations, boundaries, and methods of the different branches of knowledge:

The comprehension of the bearings of one science on another, and the use of each to each, and the location and limitation and adjustment and due appreciation of them all, one with another, this belongs, I conceive, to a sort of science distinct from all of them, and in some sense a science of sciences, which is my own conception of what is meant by philosophy, in the true sense of the word, and of a philosophical habit of mind, and which in these discourses I shall call by that name.[53]

The student of this science is the truly great intellect, and his alone is real enlargement of mind:

And therefore a truly great intellect, and recognized to be such by the common opinion of mankind, such as the intellect of Aristotle, or of St. Thomas, or of Newton, or of Goethe … is one which takes a connected view of old and new, past and present, far and near, and which has an insight into the influence of all these one on another; without which there is no whole, and no centre. It possesses the knowledge not only of things, but also of their mutual and true relations; knowledge, not merely considered as acquirement, but as philosophy.… That only is true enlargement of mind which is the power of viewing many things at once as one whole, of referring them severally to their true place in the universal system, of understanding their respective values, and determining their mutual dependence. Thus is that form of universal knowledge, of which I have on former occasion spoken, set up in the individual intellect, and constitutes its perfection.[54]

Piazza The Greek adjective πλατύς means *flat, wide, broad*, and thus the phrase ὁδὸς πλατεῖα means a *wide road*. From this feminine form πλατεῖα came the Latin transliteration *platea*, whence proceeded the French *place* and the Italian *piazza*. The combined Latin consonants *pl* often become *pi* in Italian; compare, for example, *placet* and *piace*, *plus* and *più*. A *piazza* is a large broad space or square before a church or palace; St. Peter's Square is the piazza *par excellence*. The Flaminian Gate in Rome became in Italian *Porta del Popolo*, the square within the gate the *Piazza del Popolo*, and the famous church upon the square *Santa Maria del Popolo*, but *popolo* here

---

53. Ibid., 87–88. Again, cf. Bacon, *De Augmentis*, 1.18: "For as no perfect view of a country can be taken from a flat; so it is impossible to discover the remote and deep parts of any science by standing upon the level of the same science, or without ascending to a higher."

54. Ibid., 156–58.

is actually a remnant of the Latin *pōpulus, -i, f.* (poplar tree), not *pŏpulus, -i, m.,* (people).

Pilgrimage In former times, there was no such thing as a tourist. People did not go places where they had no business. It was common, however, for people to go on pilgrimages to various shrines. Since there was no interstate highway system in those days, such travel required them to proceed through the open country, *per agros*, whence developed the noun *peregrinus*, a foreigner who has come through the countryside to some place. From it was derived the Latin noun *peregrinatio* meaning *travelling or studying abroad*. It was then corrupted into the Italian *peregrinaggio* and thence into the English *pilgrimage*.

Pleroma The Greek verb πληρόω means *to fill, to make full*, and related to it is the noun πλήρωμα meaning *fullness*, which appears in the Pauline literature. In the gnostic system, the pleroma was the perfect society of ineffable beings. The Abbé Duchesne gives a list of them.[55] Gibbon calls the pleroma the *world of spirits*.

Pluviale This is a raincoat, the name of which is derived from the Latin noun *pluvia*, rain, and the related adjective *pluvialis*, having to do with rain. It is another name for the cope. The decorative flap on the back is the remnant of a hood.

Polyphony The Greek adjective πολύς, πολλή, πολύ means *much* or *many*, and the noun φωνή means *sound*. Thus, the compound adjective πολύφωνος means *having many tones or sounds*. After Gregorian chant, the polyphonic repertoire is the most suitable music to accompany the sacred liturgy. It requires a trained choir for its performance, an ensemble that ought to be found in all the great churches.

Polytheism The Greek adjective πολύς, πολλή, πολύ means *much* or *many*, and the noun θεός means *god*. From their combination came forth the adjective πολύθεος with the meaning *dedicated to many gods*, and the noun πολυθεῖα (for there is no diphthong) meaning *belief in many gods*. Not satisfied with this latter word, the moderns have made an *ism* out of it. Polytheism is the belief in many gods; it was originally opposed to *monotheism*, the belief in one sole god. Modern scholars have gotten carried

55. Louis Duchesne, *Early History of the Christian Church from Its Foundation to the End of the Third Century* (London: John Murray, 1914), 160.

away and have invented other similar words, such as *henotheism* and *apatheism*, the last being the same sort of word as *labradoodle* and *mathlete*.

Pontiff This word is the corruption of the Latin *pontifex*, literally, a *bridge-maker*, a class of the most eminent priests in Rome, who formed a *collegium* whose chief was the Pontifex Maximus, the highest official of the Roman religion. This office was soon assumed into the imperial dignity. The emperor Valentinian I was the last emperor to take the title Pontifex Maximus; at his death in 375, his son and successor Gratian refused the title.[56] In the Catholic Church, the title is reserved for the bishop of Rome. Pope Leo the Great was the first pope to be called Pontifex Maximus.[57]

Pontificale For the etymology and formation of this Latin word, see the entries **Pontiff** and **Missal**. The *Pontificale Romanum* is the book containing the text of ceremonies that are performed by bishops, such as confirmations, ordinations, consecrations, and coronations.

Pontificate This English word is both a noun and a verb. As a noun, it is a synonym for *papacy*. The denominative verb *pontifico, pontificare* is derived from the noun *pontifex* and is used of a bishop, *to celebrate Mass in style*, that is, with pomp; it is a technical term that is defined by the rubrics in the rituals specified for pontifical celebrations.

Pope The Latin noun *papa, -ae, m.,* means *father; pope* is the English corruption of *papa*. The Greeks have the corresponding word πάππας, the childish pronunciation of πατήρ. In the Catholic Church, this name is reserved for the bishop of Rome. In Egypt, however, it is used of the patriarch of Alexandria of the Copts. In Latin, the plural of *papa* is *papae*; in Italian it is *papi*. The title of *pope* was given to many prominent bishops in the first centuries of the Church; for example, the Roman clergy once sent a letter to the clergy of Carthage about the behavior of their bishop St. Cyprian that began, "We have heard that the holy Pope Cyprian has left the city."[58] Archbishop Benson lists some of the sees whose incumbents were honored with this appellation.[59] In 1073, Gregory VII restricted the use

56. Louis Duchesne, *Early History of the Christian Church from Its Foundation to the End of the Fifth Century*, vol. 2 (London: John Murray, 1931), 498.

57. Ferdinand Gregorovius, *History of the City of Rome in the Middle Ages*, 2nd ed., trans. Mrs. Gustavus W. Hamilton (London: G. Bell & Sons, 1902) 2:96n1.

58. Louis Duchesne, *Early History of the Christian Church from Its Foundation to the End of the Third Century* (London, John Murray, 1914), 291.

59. Edward White Benson, *Cyprian: His Life, His Times, His Work* (London: Macmillan, 1897),

of the title to the Roman pontiff. Since his sway did not extend to Egypt, the Coptic patriarch of Alexandria is to this day called *pope*. Duchesne has observed:

This term was at that time [sc. about 335], and long remained, employed to denote bishops, whoever they might be. Later on, it was reserved for the Bishop of Rome in the West, and the Bishop of Alexandria in the East. He still takes the title of Pope in his official style.[60]

Popery From the English noun *pope* there was formed in the sixteenth century the pejorative term *popery* to denominate the recognition of the bishop of Rome as the visible head of the Catholic Church.

Popish The addition of the adjectival suffix *-ish* to the stem of the English noun *pope* produced the derogatory adjective *popish*, applied to post-Reformation, sixteenth-century Englishmen who acknowledged the authority of the bishop of Rome. The iconic use of the adjective *Popish* is with regard to the Gunpowder Plot of November 5, 1605, the day of the state opening of parliament, whereon it was proposed to blow up the sovereign together with both lords and commons; since the conspirators were Catholics, the generality of people referred to the crime as the *Popish Plot*.

Portantina The Latin and Italian verb *porto* means *to carry*, and from it was derived the noun *portantina* with the meaning of an *enclosed sedan-chair* or *litter*. It was frequently used by popes to get about without the extravagance of the *sedia gestatoria*. The last pope to use one was Leo XIII.

Portiera The *portiera* is the tapestry that contains the arms of the pope and is hung from the balcony of St. Peter's (and elsewhere) when he appears to give his blessing. The original meaning is *door-curtain*.

PP. This is an abbreviation for *papa*; it is to be found in inscriptions, and in the form *Pp.* in the formal signature of the pope: *Franciscus Pp., Benedictus Pp. XVI.*

Praecordia The Latin neuter plural noun *praecordia* means the *midriff, diaphragm*, and then the *heart and certain organs that are in its vicinity*. The praecordia (i.e., the heart and contents of the abdominal cavity) of all

---

29–31. Archbishop Benson was the father of Msgr. Robert Hugh Benson (1871–1914), a famous convert of the early twentieth century and the author of *Lord of the World*.

60. Louis Duchesne, *Early History of the Christian Church from Its Foundation to the End of the Fifth Century*, vol. 2 (London: John Murray, 1931), 142n2.

the popes who died during the period from 1590 to 1903 were removed during the process of embalmment and placed in jars that were, either at once or eventually, preserved in the Church of Saints Vincent and Anastasius, which was the parish church of the Apostolic Palace of the Quirinale, where the popes lived during the period from Sixtus V to the Roman Republic of 1849. The last such translation of the praecordia was that of the viscera of Leo XIII, and the details were recorded by Hartwell de la Garde Grissell:

At 11:30 the same night, the Pope's 'Praecordia' were carried in a terracotta jar by two of the Noble Guard, accompanied by others of the same corps, and by Mgr. Maestro di Camera and the Dean of the Scopatori Segreti, and others carrying lighted torches, through the different ante-chambers and down the great staircase to the Cortile of San Damaso. Here the jar was placed in one of the Palace carriages and taken by Mgr. Angeli, the late Pope's private secretary, and Mgr. Mazzolini, his private chaplain, to the Church of SS. Vincenzo ed Anastasio a Trevi, where for the night it was deposited in a small Chapel in the Convent. On the following morning it was placed within the wall of the Church on the Epistle side of the Altar, under the jars containing the 'Praecordia' of Pius VIII, Leo XII, and Gregory XVI. The 'Praecordia' of Pius IX had in 1878 been placed in the Crypt of St. Peter's, but will eventually be removed to this Church, a space having been left for his name over that of Leo XIII. The 'Praecordia' preserved in this Church include those of all the Popes from Sixtus V, in 1590, and were removed to this spot (it being the parish Church of the Palazzo Quirinale) by Benedict XIV.[61]

Praegustatio This Latin word means the *tasting* (gustatio) *beforehand* (prae). It is the name of the ceremony wherein a minister first tastes the bread and wine to be consecrated, as a proof against the poisoning of the celebrant. It was performed in papal Masses, and is described by Hartwell de la Garde Grissell as it was done at the Coronation Mass of Pius X, August 9, 1903.

Mgr. Pifferi, the Sacristan, having left the Pope's Throne, went to his credence, where the humeral veil was put over his shoulders: with it he carried the chalice, paten, golden spoon, and two purificators, and accompanied by a '*Votante di Segnatura*' acting as an acolyte, who carried a cup and two empty cruets, he went to the Pope's credence on the Gospel side of the Altar. They placed on the credence what they carried, and one of the Pope's servants (Mgr. Sagrista having purified

---

61. Hartwell de la Garde Grissell, *Sede Vacante, Being a Diary Written during the Conclave of 1903, with Additional Notes on the Accession and Coronation of Pius X* (Oxford: James Parker, 1903), 3–4.

the paten, chalice, and cruets) then tasted the wine and water. The Sacristan then washed with the wine the chalice, paten, spoon, cruets and cups, and filled the cruets with wine and water, pouring a little of each into a small cup that the servant might taste them. He then carried them to the Altar. The Cardinal Deacon then placed three wafers on the Paten. He took one of them, touched it with the other two, and gave it to the Sacristan, who ate the two wafers. The third was kept for consecration. The Cardinal Deacon then took the cruets, and poured from them some wine and water into the cup held by the Sacristan, who drank from it. This ceremony is called the 'Praegustatio' or 'Proba'.[62]

Pragmatic Sanction The Greek verb πράττω means *to pass through, to complete a journey,* hence *to achieve, to do,* and the related noun πρᾶγμα means a *deed, something done.* From this noun was derived the noun πραγματικός, an *attorney* or *agent,* which, as an adjective, meant *related to law-business.* The Latin adjective *sacer* means *sacred, holy, consecrated,* and to it is related the verb *sancio, sancire, sanxi, sanctus* meaning *to consecrate, make holy,* and of laws *to confirm, ratify, decree.*

It was a decision of the state dealing with some interest greater than a question of dispute between private persons, and was given for some community (*universitas hominum*) and for a public cause. In more recent times it was adopted by those countries which followed the Roman law, and in particular by despotically governed countries where the rulers had a natural tendency to approve of the maxims and to adopt the language of the imperial Roman lawyers. A pragmatic sanction as the term was used by them was an expression of the will of the sovereign or "the prince", defining the limits of his own power, or regulating the succession. Justinian regulated the government of Italy after it had been reconquered from the Ostrogoths by pragmatic sanctions. In after ages the king of France, Charles VII, imposed limits on the claims of the popes to exercise jurisdiction in his dominions by the pragmatic sanction of Bourges in 1438.[63]

Prayer The Latin noun *prex, precis, f.,* means *request,* and from it was derived the first conjugation deponent verb *precor* with the meaning *to beg, entreat.* This word became *prier* in French, whence we get *pray* in English. The efficacy of petitional prayer, viewed as the gift of attention to God, rests on a natural human impulse. An unchristian attitude is reported in a famous verse quoted by Plato:

62. Ibid., 67–68.

63. *Encyclopaedia Britannica, 11th ed.* (New York: The Encyclopaedia Britannica Company, 1911), s.v. "Pragmatic Sanction."

Δῶρα θεοὺς πείθει, δῶρ᾽ αἰδοίους βασιλῆας.[64]

Gifts persuade the gods, and turn aside the wrath of kings.

Preachers The Latin verb *praedĭco* of the first conjugation means *to make publicly known, proclaim*. This verb was corrupted into the French *prêcher*, whence we get the English word *preach*. The official name of the Dominican Order is the *Ordo Praedicatorum*, the Order of Preachers. In England, they were called the *Black Friars* because of the black cape they wore over their white habit. See the entry **Dominicans**.

Predella (Footpace) The *Oxford English Dictionary* gives the following etymology of this word, which it calls *probable*: The Old High German noun *pret* means a *board*, and the addition of the diminutive suffix *-ella* produced the noun *predella*, which is the *suppedaneum*, or *footpace*, before the altar. See the entry **Suppedaneum**.

Predestination The Greek noun ὅρος means *boundary, limit*, and from it was derived the verb ὁρίζω with the meaning *to divide* or *separate, to mark out with boundaries*. In combination with the preposition πρό there was produced the compound verb προορίζω with the meaning *to mark out beforehand*. The Latin preposition *prae* gives the force of *before*, and the verb *destino, destinare*—which is related to *sto, stare*, meaning *to stand*—means *to make fast, to resolve to do*. From their combination is formed the verb *praedestino, praedestinare*, which is used in the Vulgate to translate the Greek προορίζω. Predestination is the act whereby the Deity foreordains everything that is to happen, in particular, whether a particular creature will be damned or achieve salvation. Its origin is to be found in Romans 8:28–30:

οἴδαμεν δὲ ὅτι τοῖς ἀγαπῶσιν τὸν θεὸν πάντα συνεργεῖ εἰς ἀγαθόν, τοῖς κατὰ πρόθεσιν κλητοῖς οὖσιν. ὅτι οὓς προέγνω, καὶ προώρισεν συμμόρφους τῆς εἰκόνος τοῦ υἱοῦ αὐτοῦ, εἰς τὸ εἶναι αὐτὸν πρωτότοκον ἐν πολλοῖς ἀδελφοῖς· οὓς δὲ προώρισεν, τούτους καὶ ἐκάλεσεν· καὶ οὓς ἐκάλεσεν, τούτους καὶ ἐδικαίωσεν· οὓς δὲ ἐδικαίωσεν, τούτους καὶ ἐδόξασεν.

Scimus autem quoniam diligentibus Deum omnia cooperantur in bonum, iis, qui secundum propositum vocati sunt sancti. Nam quos praescivit, et praedestinavit conformes fieri imaginis Filii sui, ut sit ipse primogenitus in multis fratribus. Quos autem praedestinavit, hos et vocavit: et quos vocavit, hos et iustificavit: quos autem iustificavit, illos et glorificavit.

---

64. Quoted by Plato in the third book of the *Republic* (390e).

And we know that all things work together for good to them that love God, to them that are the called according to his purpose. For whom he did foreknow, he also did predestinate to be conformed to the image of his Son, that he might be the firstborn among many brethren. Moreover whom he did predestinate, them he also called, and whom he called, them he also justified, and whom he justified, them he also glorified. (Authorized Version)

In the writings of St. Paul, predestination is always something positive: predestination to salvation. Negative predestination, to hell, came later in Christian theology. Gottschalk (c. 808–867?) was the first to teach predestination to damnation as well as to salvation.[65] If one inquires too persistently into this, one may get the reply of Exodus 33:19:

וחנתי את אשר אחן
ורחמתי את אשר ארחם

> I will be gracious unto whom I will be gracious,
> And I will have mercy upon whom I will have mercy.

In other words, "Mind your own business."

Prefect The Latin verb *praeficio, praeficere, praefeci, praefectus* is compounded of the preposition *prae* (before) and the verb *facio* (to make) and means *to put in front of*. A prefect was a civil or military officer of lower status than someone of senatorial rank, like a proconsul or propraetor. Thus some low-born fellow like Sejanus, the head of the Praetorian Guards under Tiberius, had the rank of prefect. The Roman governor of Egypt was also a prefect, because the emperor Augustus considered it dangerous to exalt the superintendent of faraway Egypt, such an important part of the Roman Empire, lest such a fellow become a potential rival.

Prefigure The Latin verb *fingo, fingere, finxi, fictus* means *to shape, fashion, mold*. Related to this verb is the noun *figura* with the meaning *form, shape*. From this noun there proceeded the denominative verb *figuro, figurare* with the meaning *to form, mold, shape*. The addition of the preposition *prae* produced, in the third century, the compound verb *praefiguro* with the meaning *to represent beforehand*; according to the *Oxford English Dictionary*, the word was used by Cyprian in the year 250. To look for prefigurings is the method of the allegorical interpretation of scripture.

---

65. John Henry Cardinal Newman, "The Benedictine Schools," in *Historical Sketches*, vol. 2 (London: Longmans, Green, 1917), 480.

Deus, qui Abrahae filios per mare Rubrum sicco vestigio transire fecisti, ut plebs, a Pharaonis servitude liberata, populum baptizatorum praefiguraret.[66]

O God, who caused the children of Abraham to cross the Red Sea without wetting their feet, so that those people, freed from slavery to Pharaoh, might prefigure the baptized.

Prelate The Latin verb *praefero, praeferre, praetuli, praelatus* means *to carry* (fero) *before* (prae), and from its fourth principal part is derived the noun *praelatus, -i,* whence the English *prelate,* with the meaning of a *clergyman of high rank, one who has been lifted up and made conspicuous.* One formerly would have said a *member of the clerical nobility.* From this noun was derived the ecclesiastical term *praelatura* with the meaning *prelacy* or *prelature.* Nowadays *praelatura* is a technical term that may designate a sort of diocese without territorial bounds; it is the category assigned to the organization Opus Dei by Pope John Paul II in 1982.

Prelates "di Fiocchetto" The Latin noun *floccus* means a *lock of wool, something trifling;* our noun *flake* is related to it. Derived from *floccus* is the Italian noun *fiocco* meaning a *tassel;* the diminutive *fiocchetto* means a *small tassel.*

The name of these prelates is derived from the tassel ... formerly decorating the heads of their horses in the grand cavalcades on special occasions or in ceremonial processions. In the earliest period of knightly heraldry, the horse was decorated heraldically as well as its rider: it is, therefore, not surprising that the horses bore a decoration on their gala harness symbolic of the prelate's position of honour. There were only four of these high ranking prelates of the Papal Curia: the Vice-Camerlengo of the Holy Roman Church, the Auditor General and the Treasurer General of the Apostolic Chamber, and the Majordomo to His Holiness.
 These last three titles are no more granted. Only the office of the Vice-Chamberlain has remained and is at present held by an archbishop.[67]

However, in 2013 Benedict XVI appointed Bishop Giuseppe Sciacca Auditor General of the Apostolic Camera.

Presbiterio The Latin noun *presbiterium* is the transliteration of the Greek τὸ πρεσβυτέριον, which is the *place where the elders congregate.* In

66. *Ordo Baptismi Parvulorum,* edition typica altera (Vatican City: Libreria Editrice Vaticana, 1986), 29.
 67. Bruno Bernard Heim, *Heraldry in the Catholic Church: Its Origin, Customs and Laws* (Gerrards Cross, England: Van Duren Publishers, 1981), 117–18.

the Catholic Church, it is a synonym for *sanctuary*; that is, it is the place where the priests function. There is, moreover, another meaning:

The Pope, having given the Blessing and said the last Gospel, left his maniple on the Altar, and took his seat on the Sedia Gestatoria. Still wearing the vestments of the Mass, he now assumed the miter, gloves and ring, and received from Cardinal Rampolla, the Arch-priest of the Basilica, accompanied by two Canons, a white silk purse embroidered in gold, containing 25 Giulii in ancient coin, called the 'Presbiterio', the Cardinal offering it with these words:

"Beatissime Pater, Capitulum et canonici huius Sacrosanctae Basilicae, Sanctitati Vestrae consuetum offerunt presbyterium pro Missa bene cantata."

The Pope's hand was then kissed by the Cardinal Arch-priest, and his foot by the two Canons, and he delivered the purse to the Cardinal Deacon Segna, who had sung the Gospel, who in his turn gave it to his train-bearer who after the ceremony obtained from the chief Sacristan of St. Peter's in exchange for it the sum of 25 lire.[68]

Presbytera This was the Latin name for the wife or concubine of a priest.[69] Similarly, the wife or concubine of a bishop was in the Middle Ages called an *episcopissa*.[70]

Presbyterian The Greek adjective πρεσβύτερος means *elder*; it is the comparative degree of πρέσβυς, *old*. The Vulgate transliterates, always putting *presbyter* for πρεσβύτερος. In the seventeenth century, the English adjective *Presbyterian* was coined to describe the followers of Calvin and Knox, whose church was ruled by elders. This was the form of Protestantism that prevailed in Switzerland, Scotland, France, and Hungary.

President The Latin verb *praesideo, praesidere* means *to sit* (sedeo) *before* (prae) or *in front of*. Its present participle is *praesidens, praesidentis*, whence comes our word *president* or presiding officer. The president is someone who sits in front.

Priest This word is the corruption of the Latin *presbyter*, the transliteration of the stem of the Greek πρεσβύτερος, *elder*. The Vulgate always puts *presbyter* for πρεσβύτερος. The Geneva translators, who did not believe

68. Hartwell de la Garde Grissell, *Sede Vacante, Being a Diary Written during the Conclave of 1903, with Additional Notes on the Accession and Coronation of Pius X* (Oxford: James Parker, 1903), 72–73.

69. Henry Charles Lea, *History of Sacerdotal Celibacy in the Christian Church* (n.p.: University Books, 1966), 201.

70. Ibid., 122.

in a sacramental clergy, put *elder* instead of *priest* for this word, and this is the sense in which they were referred to as *Presbyterians*, that is, *people governed by elders*. In reaction, the Rhemes translators retained the traditional *priest*. Bishops (ἐπίσκοποι), the Presbyterians believed to be a general designation for pastors and elders, as opposed to deacons, who handled the money and the care of widows. The Abbé Duchesne writes of the Christians of Jerusalem in the decade after the death of Jesus:

In those first days the desire for a common life was so intense that they even practised community of goods. This led to administrative developments; the apostles chose out seven helpers who were the fore-runners of the Deacons. A little later there appeared an intermediate dignity, a council of elders (*presbyteri*, priests), who assisted the apostles in general management and took counsel with them.[71]

The Latin word for a Jewish or pagan priest, *sacerdos*, is not used of Christian priests in the New Testament. Conversely, the New Testament word for Christian priest, *presbyter*, is scarcely used for Catholic priests in modern times. The word lingers, however, in the title *cardinal priests*, who are called in Latin *presbyteri cardinales*, not *sacerdotes cardinales*. The Greek noun πρεσβύτεροι was used not for the Jewish priests, who were the ἱερεῖς, *sacerdotes*, but for the Jewish elders, the זקנים, who were men distinguished both by age and by learning and whose opinion was therefore considered in the discussion of matters of importance. The name ἱερεῖς was in common use for Catholic priests at least by the beginning of the fourth century, for Eusebius used it when addressing the priests in his sermon at the dedication of the cathedral of Tyre.[72]

Prime The Latin numerical adjective *primus* means *first*. It was the name of the first canonical hour during daylight.

Prince Assistant at the Throne See the entry **Assistant**.

Priscillianists The Latin adjective *priscus* means *ancient*, and the forms *Priscus* and *Prisca* and their diminutives *Priscillus*, *Priscilla* and *Priscillianus* became proper names. The notorious Priscillian was a Spanish bishop of Avila who gave his name to a heresy. The Priscillianists were a

71. Louis Duchesne, *Early History of the Christian Church from Its Foundation to the End of the Third Century* (London: John Murray, 1914), 13.

72. Eusebius, *The History of the Church from Christ to Constantine*, trans. G. A. Williamson (London: The Folio Society, 2011), X 4, p. 277.

Christian ascetic body that arose in fourth-century Spain. The practices of the Priscillianists were described by Duchesne.

> Asceticism was not unknown in Spain. The Council of Elvira speaks much of celibates (*confessores*) and consecrated virgins, meaning by those terms persons who practised continence and abstinence according to the already time-honoured customs of the Church, and within the bounds of its organization. The disciples of Priscillian went further in marking themselves out as distinct from these. In the first place they were disciples of a particular man, and of a man who had no mission to teach from the Church, who claimed to some extent an inspiration of his own and took his stand in his teaching, not only upon the received Scriptures, but also upon the apocryphal writings, and notably upon those lives of the Apostles Peter, John, Andrew, and Thomas, which were so strongly imbued with the Encratite spirit opposed to marriage, to wine, and to any kind of substantial food. Moreover, there prevailed among them a tendency to despise other Christians. They separated themselves at certain times of the year, during Lent and in the days before the Epiphany; at such times they disappeared from sight; no one saw them; they kept themselves shut up in their own houses or in the mountains. It was known that they held secret meetings in lonely villas, and it was remarked that they generally walked barefooted. They fasted on Sundays. If they came to Church they allowed the Eucharist to be given to them; but no one saw them communicate. Finally, and this was a more serious matter still, women who are always delighted with any novelty, even and especially of a religious character, fluttered continually round the celebrated teacher. He held meetings for women only, over which he presided, either in person or by means of assistants.[73]

The study of the history of the Priscillian heresy is of interest because it was the first instance in which some authorities of the Catholic Church called in the secular power to arrest and even execute heretics. St. Ambrose, however, opposed this behavior.

> He did not wish to have any relations with bishops "who had demanded the death of the heretics."[74]

> "No shedding of blood!" he said, "Ecclesiastical penalties, such as deposition, are quite enough."[75]

In this attitude he was joined by St. Martin of Tours.

---

73. Louis Duchesne, *Early History of the Christian Church from Its Foundation to the End of the Fifth Century*, vol. 2 (London: John Murray, 1931), 419–20.
74. Ibid., 426.
75. Ibid., 424.

On his arrival at the imperial Court, Martin refused to hold communion with the bishops, amongst whom he saw the blood-stained Ithacius.[76]

Prisoner of the Vatican The Greek verb χανδάνω means *to hold*. The combination of its root and the prefixed preposition *prae* (in front of) produced the Latin verb *prehendo, prehendere, prehendi, prehensus* with the meaning *to lay hold of*. This Latin verb has the abbreviated ("syncopated") form *prendo, prendere, prendi, prensus*, from whose fourth principal part proceeded the noun *prensio, prensionis, f.*, which means the *act of seizing*. Our English word *prison* is derived from this noun. When the Italian army captured Rome on September 20, 1870, by breaking through the Aurelian Walls at Porta Pia, Pio Nono considered himself despoiled and shut himself up within the Vatican, which he never left again. His successors Leo XIII, Pius X, and Benedict XV similarly remained within the walls of the Vatican. For this reason, these popes were referred to as the "Prisoners of the Vatican." After the conclusion of the Lateran Treaty of 1929, Pius XI resumed moving about Rome and travelling to Castel Gandolfo, and his successor Pius XII did no more than this. John XXIII ventured as far away as Loreto and Assisi, all in one day. The era of papal world travel began with Pope Paul VI and was taken to the next level by his successors. Duchesne explained the reason why popes typically stayed at home.

The Council of Arles, in 314, was of special importance. It was a kind of Oecumenical Council, as was speedily said, in which the bishops assembled from all parts of Constantine's empire. The Pope was not present; he sent in his stead two Roman priests. This was the inauguration of a practice which was long observed. Very few were the Popes who quitted Rome, especially for ecclesiastical affairs: *maior a longinquo reverentia.*[77]

Privilege The Latin adjective *privus* means *single, particular, special*. The noun *lex* means *law*. From their combination proceeds the noun *privilegium*, a special law relating to one person or class only. Privilege in the Catholic Church often has to do with attire, with who is allowed to wear what. Nainfa makes a wise comment about those who refuse to avail themselves of a privilege:

---

76. Ibid., 425. Ithacius was bishop of Ossonova and the accuser of Priscillian.
77. Ibid., 355–56.

When a privilege is granted to a class of dignitaries, each one of them is considered as bound to make use of the privilege; otherwise, he wrongs the body of which he is a member. Moreover, he has no right to refuse a privilege, the concession of which has been made rather to the body than to him individually.[78]

Privy Chamberlain See the entry **Camerieri Segreti Partecipanti.**

Proba The Latin verb *probo, probare* means *to test, to try*, and from it was derived the noun *proba*, with the meaning a *test*, a *trial*. *Proba* is another name for the ceremony of the *Praegustatio*.

Pro-cathedral The Latin preposition *pro* means *for*. See the entry **Cathedra Petri.** When the actual cathedral of a diocese is for some reason unavailable, or if there is no suitable edifice at all, the church that is designated as the temporary headquarters of the bishop is called the pro-cathedral. This is the case for the Archdiocese of Dublin. The two churches that served as cathedrals before the Reformation, Christ Church and St. Patrick's, were not available to the Roman Catholics in the nineteenth century, since they were in the possession of the Church of Ireland. The Catholics therefore built St. Mary's Pro-cathedral, which has served as the center of the archdiocese ever since.

Procession The Latin verb *cedo, cedere, cessi, cessus* means *to go*, and when compounded with the preposition *pro*, which gives the meaning *forward*, produces the verb *procedo, procedere, processi, processus* with the meaning *to go forward, proceed*. From the fourth principal part of this latter verb came the noun *processio, processionis, f.*, whence we get our word *procession*. A procession, whether academic or religious, is supposed to be a dignified progress. Clergy who behave in a casual or familiar manner during processions display no very lofty conception of the dignity of their profession. In most towns in Italy, on the feast day of the town's patron saint, the saint's statue is carried out of the church on procession; at the *uscita*, or coming out of the church, the local band plays suitable music, such as Rossini's march *Mosè*.

Procession of the Holy Ghost The Greek verb πορεύω means *to convey*, and in the middle voice, *to convey oneself, to go*. The addition of the preposition ἐκ (*from*) produces the compound verb ἐκπορεύω meaning

---

78. John A. Nainfa, *Costume of Prelates of the Catholic Church according to Roman Etiquette* (Baltimore, Md.: John Murphy, 1909), 88.

to make go out, whose middle voice ἐκπορεύομαι has the meaning *to go forth*. The Greek verb ἐκπορεύομαι was translated into Latin by *procedo*. It is the word used in the Nicene Creed:

τὸ ἐκ τοῦ πατρὸς ἐκπορευόμενον

qui ex patre procedit

which proceeds from the Father.

The doctrine of the procession of the Holy Ghost has for centuries been a cause of dispute between the Latin and Greek Churches. The relevant scriptural passage is John 15:26:

Ὅταν ἔλθῃ ὁ παράκλητος ὃν ἐγὼ πέμψω ὑμῖν παρὰ τοῦ πατρός, τὸ πνεῦμα τῆς ἀληθείας ὃ παρὰ τοῦ πατρὸς ἐκπορεύεται, ἐκεῖνος μαρτυρήσει περὶ ἐμοῦ·

Cum autem venerit Paraclitus, quem ego mittam vobis a Patre, Spiritum veritatis, qui a Patre procedit, ille testimonium perhibebit de me.

When however the Helper will have come, whom I shall send to you from the Father, the Spirit of truth who proceeds from the Father, he will bear witness about me.

For the addition of the phrase *filioque* in the Western Church, which changed the relevant clause in the Creed to *qui ex patre filioque procedit* ("who proceeds from the Father and the Son"), see the entry **Filioque**.

Procurator The Latin noun *cura* means *concern*, and the associated first conjugation verb *curo, curare, curavi, curatus* means *to take care*. When this verb is compounded with the preposition *pro*, there is produced the verb *procūro, procūrare, procūravi, procūratus* with the meaning *to take care of, look after*. From the fourth principal part of this verb is derived the noun *procurator*, the name of a rank in the Roman government. According to Tacitus, it was the position held by Pontius Pilate in Judaea and Samaria; see the passage in question in the entry **Martyr**. The gospels refer to Pilate as ἡγεμών, a generic term for a leader; even the emperor could be indicated thereby. In one place (Luke 3:1) the Codex Bezae substitutes ἐπιτροπεύοντος Ποντίου Πιλάτου for ἡγεμονεύοντος Ποντίου Πιλάτου, ἐπίτροπος being the usual Greek translation of *procurator*; the Vulgate has *procurante Pontio Pilato* at this passage, though at Matthew 27:2 the phrase Πιλάτῳ τῷ ἡγεμόνι is rendered by *Pilato praesidi*; *praeses* is another general name for a high "presiding" official. The procurator was an imperial appointee who managed the financial affairs—that is, the collection of taxes and the payment of the troops—of an area. In 1961, a monument dating from the first half of the first century was uncovered at Caesarea (it is now in the Israel Museum) in which Pontius Pilate was denominated a *praefectus* or *prefect*, a different title from *procurator*. See the entry **Prefect**.

Profane The Latin noun *fanum, -i, m.*, means a *place solemnly consecrated to a god*, a *temple*. The associated adjective *profanus* means *that which is before and therefore outside the temple, not sacred, common, ordinary*.

> Procul, O procul este, profani.[79]

> Far hence be, souls prophane![80]

Pro Multis The words of consecration of the wine contain the phrase *pro multis*, for many, a literal translation of the Greek ὑπὲρ πολλῶν of the gospel. The International Commission on English in the Liturgy (ICEL), the entity that produced the English Mass, translated this by "for all," and a great controversy ensued. For decades, the priest said *for many* if he celebrated in Latin and *for all* if he celebrated in English, an absurd situation. *For all* is an example of a *theologoumenon*, a correction of the original text, which, it was feared, would be perceived by the commonality of people as an example of divine discrimination. Eventually *for all* was taken out and replaced by the literal translation. ICEL tried to reconcile theology and philology, a difficult if not impossible task.

Pro-nuncio For the etymology, see the entry **Nuncio**. When a consul or a praetor finished his term of office, he was sent off to be governor of a province and was given the title *proconsul* or *propraetor* respectively. It was by an analogy with these titles that the Apostolic See established the dignity of pro-nuncio. This was the name given by the Holy See to the papal ambassador to a country that did not accord that ambassador the status of dean of the diplomatic corps. The title was discontinued in 1991. The force of *pro* here is that of *like* or *as good as*. Compare the German *Ich bekenne mich für unschuldig*—I plead not guilty.

Pro Opportunitate This is one of the most common phrases in the *Institutio Generalis Missalis Romani* (General Instruction of the Roman Mis-

---

79. Vergil, *Aeneid* 6.258.
80. Virgil, *The Works of Virgil, containing his Pastorals, Georgics, and Aeneis*, trans. John Dryden (London, 1697), p. 373, line 368.

sal); it means, "It is optional." In this regard, see also the entry **His Vel Similibus Verbis**.

Prophet From the Greek verb προφημί, *to say ahead of time*, proceeds the noun προφήτης, *he who foretells, a prophet*. The Hebrew word for such a seer is נביא.

The three so-called Major Prophets and twelve Minor are the central representatives of Israel's religion, the culmination of all religion before the coming of Christ.[81]

The distinguishing characteristics of the prophets, first of their speech and action and afterwards of their writings, was the firm and unwavering belief that they were instruments or organs of the Most High, and that the thoughts which arose in their minds about Him and His Will, and the commands and exhortations which they issued in His name, really came at His prompting, and were really invested with His authority. There is no alternative between accepting this belief as true and regarding it as a product of mental disease or delusion....

A world-wide religion which for more than thirty centuries has been taking increasing hold on the most highly developed races could not have its origin in mere mental disease.[82]

Protestant The Latin noun *testis* means *witness*, and the associated deponent verb *testor, testari, testatus sum* means *to bear witness*. When this verb is combined with the preposition *pro*, the force is strengthened in the resulting compound verb *protestor*, which means *to bear witness openly and solemnly*. From the present participle *protestans, protestantis* of this verb comes the name *Protestant* for the followers of Martin Luther, a designation that arose in the following manner. The reformed representatives issued a solemn declaration, called the *Protestatio*, in which they dissented from the *recess* of the Diet of Speyer (1529), according to which the practice of the Catholic religion was to be allowed everywhere in the Empire, but the toleration of the Reformed Faith was to be admitted only in those places where it had already taken root.

Protocol The Greek noun κόλλα means *glue*, and the adjective πρῶτος means *first*. When combined they produce the compound πρωτόκολλον— the *sheet first glued*—which, when used in the phrase τὸ κόλλημα τὸ πρωτόκολλον, means the first leaf, the fly-leaf glued inside a volume or first on a papyrus roll, containing an account of the manuscript.

---

81. William Sanday, *Inspiration, Eight Lectures on the Early History and Origin of the Doctrine of Biblical Inspiration, Being the Bampton Lectures for 1893* (London: Longmans, Green, 1896), 143.
82. Ibid., 394.

In the Middle Ages, the word *protocol* acquired the meaning of the official list of details or minutes of a transaction, and then of the list of rules of etiquette to be observed in audiences with a high dignitary. Cardinal Nasalli Rocca di Corneliano reports that Pius XI said, in reply to a lackey who had commented that there was too much protocol at the Vatican, that protocol kept in their place people who did not know their place.[83]

Proverbs The book of the Old Testament called מִשְׁלֵי שְׁלֹמֹה was called in the Septuagint Παροιμίαι and in the Vulgate *Proverbia*. The Hebrew verb מָשַׁל means *to represent, to be like*, and the מְשָׁלִם were sentences constructed in parallelism in accordance with the Hebrew practice of writing poetry that uses *parallelismus membrorum*. The Greek adjective πάροιμος means *by the wayside*, and it is the compound of the preposition παρά (along) and the noun οἶμος (road). From it is derived the noun παροιμία with the meaning *adage*. The Latin noun *proverbium*, compounded of *pro* (for) and *verbum* (word), already in the time before Christ had the same meaning as its English derivative *proverb*. According to Sanday, Proverbs 7:7–20 was the main reason that the acceptance of that book into the canon was delayed.[84]

Psalm The Greek verb ψάλλω means *to touch, to pluck, to play the harp, to sing to a harp*, and from it is derived the noun ψαλμός with the meaning a *song sung to a stringed instrument*. It is the Greek translation of the Late Hebrew noun, תְּהִלִּים, the name for the Book of Psalms, from the verb הָלַל, which, in the Piel conjugation, means *to praise*. The psalms were evidently songs of praise sung with musical accompaniment. The noun ψαλμός became in Latin *psalmus*, whence we get our noun *psalm*. The collection of psalms was called the *psalterium*, whence we get our noun *psalter*. In speaking of children brought to the Benedictine schools to be educated, Newman mentioned that at the age of seven they became *pueri* and began the study of the Psalter.[85]

Pseudepigrapha The Greek verb γράφω means *to write*, and the addition of the preposition ἐπί produces the compound verb ἐπιγράφω meaning *to*

---

83. Mario Nasalli Rocca di Corneliano, *Accanto ai Papi* (Vatican City: Libreria Editrice Vaticana, 1976), 17: "Il protocollo serve a tenere al loro posto le persone che non ci sanno stare."

84. William Sanday, *Inspiration, Eight Lectures on the Early History and Origin of the Doctrine of Biblical Inspiration, Being the Bampton Lectures for 1893* (London: Longmans, Green, 1896), 108n1.

85. John Henry Cardinal Newman, "The Mission of St. Benedict," in *Historical Sketches*, vol. 2 (London: Longmans, Green, 1917), 459.

write on, to inscribe; thus the associated noun ἐπιγραφή means an *inscription*, whence comes the English word *epigraphy*, the science of inscriptions. The verb ψεύδω means *to cheat*, and from it comes the adjective ψευδής with the meaning *lying, false*. From these words was formed the adjective ψευδεπίγραφος with the meaning *having a false inscription*. The neuter plural of this adjective produced the English word *pseudepigrapha* with the meaning *writings falsely ascribed to biblical personalities*. One of the main propositions of modern higher criticism was that certain books of the Old and New Testaments are pseudepigraphal in the sense of not having been written by the fellow whose name is given in the inscription, for example, the *Wisdom of Solomon* and the *Second Epistle of St. Peter*. To accept such a view creates a problem with regard to divine inspiration. Of this issue, Sanday has written:

> We must then, I think, distinctly contemplate the possibility, if not the probability, that we have in the New Testament a book which is not by the writer whose name it bears. What this would mean is that the New Testament is not upon a different footing to the Old; that there would be a real parallel to a case like that of *Ecclesiastes*, in which a book has found its way into the Canon under an assumed name....
>
> To many modern readers the critical doubtfulness of the Epistle [2 Peter], combined with its claim to speak with the authority of St. Peter, is a more serious stumbling block....
>
> But in this, as in other things, the Providence of God does not absolutely exclude the infirmities of men.[86]

There is also a second meaning of the word; the *Pseudepigrapha* are those books present in the Septuagint but not included in the canon of scripture by the Catholic Church, that is, 1 Esdras, 3 and 4 Maccabees, Psalm 151, and the Epistle of Jeremiah. There is an express quotation from the Pseudepigrapha, namely, from the Book of Enoch (1:9), in Jude 14–15.

Purgatory The Latin verb *purgo, purgare* means *to clean*, and from it was derived the noun *purgatio*, a cleaning, whence there developed in Ecclesiastical Latin the noun *purgatorium*, a location where the cleaning of the soul takes place. In the Western Church, it was conceived of as the place where the souls are cleaned up before admission to the divine presence. Its biblical basis is 2 Maccabees 12: 43–45:

---

86. William Sanday, *Inspiration, Eight Lectures on the Early History and Origin of the Doctrine of Biblical Inspiration, Being the Bampton Lectures for 1893* (London: Longmans, Green, 1896), 348, 349.

ποιησάμενός τε κατ᾽ ἀνδρολογίαν εἰς ἀργυρίου δραχμὰς δισχιλίας ἀπέστειλεν
εἰς Ἱεροσόλυμα προσαγαγεῖν περὶ ἁμαρτίας θυσίαν πάνυ καλῶς καὶ ἀστείως
πράττων ὑπὲρ ἀναστάσεως διαλογιζόμενος· εἰ μὴ γὰρ τοὺς προπεπτωκότας
ἀναστῆναι προσεδόκα, περισσὸν καὶ ληρῶδες ὑπὲρ νεκρῶν εὔχεσθαι· εἴτε
ἐμβλέπων τοῖς μετ᾽ εὐσεβείας κοιμωμένοις κάλλιστον ἀποκείμενον χαριστήριον,
ὁσία καὶ εὐσεβὴς ἡ ἐπίνοια· ὅθεν περὶ τῶν τεθνηκότων τὸν ἐξιλασμὸν ἐποιήσατο
τῆς ἁμαρτίας ἀπολυθῆναι.

He also took up a collection, man by man, to the amount of two thousand drach-
mas of silver, and sent it to Jerusalem to provide for a sin offering. In doing this
he acted very well and honorably, taking account of the resurrection. For if he
were not expecting that those who had fallen would rise again, it would have been
superfluous and foolish to pray for the dead. But if he was looking to the splendid
reward that is laid up for those who fall asleep in godliness, it was a holy and
pious thought. Therefore he made atonement for the dead, so that they might be
delivered from their sin. (New Revised Standard Version)

The Vulgate reading is as follows. Notice the last sentence.

Et facta conlatione duodecim milia dragmas argenti misit Hierosolymam offerri
pro peccato sacrificium bene et religiose de resurrectione cogitans. Nisi enim eos
qui ceciderant resurrecturos speraret, superfluum videretur et vanum orare pro
mortuis, et quia considerabat quod hii qui cum pietate dormitionem acceperant
optimam haberent repositam gratiam. Sancta ergo et salubris cogitatio pro de-
functis exorare ut a peccato solverentur.

It is the Vulgate text of the last sentence that is translated by the Doway
fathers:

It is therfore a holie, and healthful cogitation to pray for the dead, that they may
be loosed from sinnes.

By the time of the Second Council of Lyons, in 1274, its existence had
become a doctrine of the Catholic Church, a dogma confirmed by the
Councils of Florence and Trent:

Quod si vere poenitentes in caritate decesserint, antequam dignis poenitentiae
fructibus de commissis satisfecerint et omissis: eorum animas poenis purgatoriis,
seu catharteriis, sicut nobis frater Joannes explanavit, post mortem purgari: et ad
poenas huiusmodi relevandos prodesse eis fidelium vivorum suffragia, Missarum
scilicet sacrificia, orationes, eleemosynas, et alia pietatis officia, quae a fidelibus
pro aliis fidelibus fieri consueverunt secundum ecclesiae instituta.[87]

87. From the Confession of Faith of the Roman emperor Michael Palaeologus, proposed to him
in 1267 by Pope Clement IV and offered by him to Pope Gregory X in 1274 at the Second Ecumenical

If they should die truly penitent in a state of grace, but before they should have made satisfaction for their sins of commission and omission by such acts as are the proper consequences of penance, their souls are cleaned after death by the purgatorial, that is, the cleansing, pains, as Brother John has explained to us. And the intercession of the living faithful help them obtain relief from these pains, that is, the holy sacrifice of the Mass, prayers, alms, and other acts of piety, which are accustomed to be offered by the faithful for other faithful in accordance with the customs of the Church.

Pyx The Greek noun πυξίς, πυξίδος, *f.* (also ἡ πύξος) means *box*, and the word was transliterated into Latin by *puxis*. It is a small covered container in which the consecrated species is kept when it is carried to the sick. In such a case, in former times, the priest would ideally be accompanied by two acolytes, one holding an ombrellino over him, and the other ringing a hand-bell, which alerted the passers-by to kneel.

Council of Lyons. Denzinger, *Enchiridion Symbolorum et Definitionum*, 7th ed. (Würzburg, V. J. Stahel, 1895), §387.

Quadragesima This is the Latin adjective for *fortieth*, nominative case, feminine singular; it became the Latin word for *Lent*. The Italian corruption is *Quaresima*.

Quarant' Ore The Italian phrase *Quarant' Ore* means *Forty Hours*. It is the name of the devotion that consists of the public exposition of the reserved sacrament for that period of time.

Quartodeciman The Latin indeclinable numerical adjective *quattuordecim* means *fourteen*, and the associated ordinal number *quartus decimus* means *fourteenth*. The quartodecimans were those Eastern Christians who ended the Lenten fast on Nisan 14, the day the Jews sacrificed the paschal lamb in the Temple of Jerusalem. Whether they celebrated the resurrection of Christ two days later or on the next following Sunday is unknown.

Quicumque Vult These are the opening words of the Athanasian Creed and mean "Whoever wants." The Athanasian Creed is of the fifth century and was formerly to be found in the Roman Breviary for the Hour of Prime for Sundays after Pentecost, after Psalm 118. It was removed after the Second Vatican Council in the transition to the Liturgy of the Hours. Its first sentence is famous.

Quicumque vult salvus esse, ante omnia opus est, ut teneat catholicam fidem. Quam nisi quisque integram inviolatamque servaverit, absque dubio in aeternum peribit.

422

Whoever will be saved, before all things it is necessary that he hold the Catholic Faith. Which Faith, except everyone do keep whole and undefiled, without doubt he shall perish everlastingly.[1]

This warning is repeated in the last verse:

Haec est fides catholica, quam nisi quisque fideliter firmiterque crediderit, salvus esse non poterit.

This is the Catholic Faith, which except a man believe faithfully and firmly, he cannot be saved.

Quinisext in Trullo The Greek numerals πέντε and ἕξ mean *five* and *six* respectively, and from their combination was formed the bizarre feminine adjective πενθέκτη, fifth-sixth, to modify the noun σύνοδος in the phrase πενθέκτη σύνοδος, Fifth-Sixth Council, used to denominate the assembly summoned by the emperor Justinian II at the end of the seventh century. This council was intended to be ecumenical, and was called in Latin by the equivalent name *Quinisexta*. The story is nicely told by Gregorovius:

A few years after the succession of Sergius, the Trullan Council was held in Constantinople. The Byzantine theologians had announced that neither the Fifth nor the Sixth Synod had propounded a Canon of Discipline, and a Council was therefore summoned to frame one.[2] A hundred and two laws were promulgated, approved, and signed by the papal nuncios. These articles had been sent for ratification to Sergius, whose sharp eye, however, discovered among them some suspicious doctrines, such as the condemnation of celibacy among presbyters and deacons, the prohibition of Saturday fasts, and other rules, esteemed at that time of gravest import. The Pope refused his signature, and forbade the publication of the articles.[3]

The decrees of this council with regard to celibacy codified the discipline in that regard for the Eastern Churches, a discipline that was less severe than that adopted by the Church in the West. The Trullan Council allowed the ordination of married men and prohibited the separation of married clergy from their wives. Priests and deacons who married after ordina-

---

1. Marquess of Bute's translation of the Athanasian Creed in *The Catholic Encyclopedia* (New York: The Encyclopedia Press, 1913), 2:33b, s.v. "Athanasian Creed."

2. [Note of Gregorovius]: "The date of this Council has disappeared together with the Acts. Pagi and Muratori assume that it was held in 691. Its name was derived from the cupola (*trullus*) of the palace. It was also called *Quini-Sextum* from the circumstance that it was summoned to supplement the Fifth and Sixth Oecumenical Councils."

3. Ferdinand Gregorovius, *History of the City of Rome in the Middle Ages*, 2nd ed., trans. Mrs. Gustavus W. Hamilton (London: G. Bell & Sons, 1902), 2:182.

tion, however, were ordered to separate from their spouses. See the entry **Trullan**.

Quinquagesima This is the Latin adjective for *fiftieth*; it modifies the noun *dominica* (Sunday) understood. It is the Sunday falling fifty days before Easter.

Quirinale When Romulus became a god, he was accorded the name *Quirinus*, a denomination derived either from the name of a Sabine town or from the noun *curia*. The associated adjective *Quirinalis* means *having to do with Quirinus*, that is, *with Romulus*. The Quirinal is the highest of the seven hills of Rome; the popes dwelt there during most of the seventeenth, eighteenth, and nineteenth centuries. The palace that they built was called the Apostolic Palace of the Quirinale. Other palaces, like the Consulta and the Datary, were built nearby for the sake of convenience. In 1870, the palace was seized by Victor Emmanuel II, first king of united Italy, and the Quirinale became the Royal Palace of the Italian State. The Republic was established in 1946, and in due course the palace became the residence of the Italian president, which it remains to this day.

Quod Semper, Quod Ubique, Quod ab Omnibus This is a Latin adage from the year 434, found in the *Commonitorium* of St. Vincent of Lérins; it means, "What has always [been believed], and [believed] everywhere, and by everyone." It describes a characteristic of what Christians should believe.

Quo Primum These are the first two words of the papal bull *Quo Primum Tempore* of Pius V, dated July 14, 1570, promulgating the edition of the Roman Missal revised in accordance with the decrees of the Council of Trent. It used to be printed at the front of all missals until the reforms of the Second Vatican Council. The document begins, "From that time when We were first raised to the Apostolic throne ..."

Rabbi The Aramaic and Late Hebrew word רבּי means *My Lord*; it was a polite way of addressing one's superior. It became the title of a teacher. Quite unrelated to this is the use of the word as a name for an article of clerical attire.

That which today is known as the "rabbi" is the true Roman collar, called in Italian *collaro*.... The "rabbi" is probably a corruption of the French word rabat (rabattu). The rabbi is a loose breastpiece of silk or woolen material.[1]

The French verb *rabattre* means *to turn down*.

Radio The Latin noun *radius, -i, m.*, means a *staff, rod, stake*, or *ray of light*. From it was concocted in the nineteenth century the name *radium* for the chemical element discovered by the Curies. Bacci says that the modern appliance is *radiophonicum instrumentum*. Vatican Radio was established by Guglielmo Marconi in 1931 and inaugurated with a visit to its premises on February 12 of that year by Pope Pius XI, who made the inaugural speech, which was in Latin. It began:

Qui arcano Dei consilio succedimus in loco Principis Apostolorum, eorum nempe quorum doctrina et praedicatio iussu divino ad omnes gentes et ad omnem creaturam destinata est, et qui primi in loco ipso mira sane ope Marconiana uti frui possumus, ad omnia et ad omnes primo Nos convertimus atque, hic et infra Sacro Textu iuvante, dicimus, "Audite caeli quae loquor; audiat terra verba oris mei. Audite haec omnes gentes, auribus percipite omnes qui habitatis orbem,

1. Henry J. McCloud, *Clerical Dress and Insignia of the Roman Catholic Church* (Milwaukee, Wis.: Bruce Publishing, 1948), 73, 74.

simul in unum dives et pauper. Audite insulae et attendite populi de longe." Sitque primum verbum Nostrum, "Gloria in altissimis Deo, et in terra pax hominibus bonae voluntatis."[2]

We who, by the mysterious plan of God, have succeeded in the room of the Prince of the Apostles, namely, of those whose teaching and instruction are intended by divine dispensation for all peoples and every living thing, We who are able to enjoy the use of the marvelous invention of Marconi, now first address Ourselves to all things and to all peoples in the words of the Sacred Scripture and say, "Give ear, O ye heavens, and I will speak, and hear, O earth, the words of my mouth. Hear this, all ye people, give ear, all ye inhabitants of the world, both low and high, rich and poor together. Listen, O isles, unto me, and hearken, ye people, from far!" Let Our first words be, "Glory to God in the highest, and on earth peace to men of good will."

The late Cardinal Foley, while still archbishop, regularly performed the duties of English language commentator for those papal Masses and other ceremonies transmitted by Vatican Radio. In this capacity he was outstanding, as was Fulton Sheen, when that prelate provided commentary to religious events. They have no successor.

Rationalism The Latin verb *reor, reri, ratus sum* means *to think*, and from the last principal part proceeded the noun *ratio, rationis, f.*, with the meaning a *reckoning, account, calculation*, and eventually, the *faculty of mind that calculates, the reason*. From *ratio* came the adjective *rationalis* with the meaning, *that which is in conformity with the reason*. According to the *Oxford English Dictionary*, the earliest known use in English of the noun *rationalism* is from 1800; it is the program of explaining by natural causes what heretofore was ascribed to supernatural causes. For example, the star in the sky that brought the Magi to Bethlehem was imagined by rationalists to be a comet. This is not the same thing as the method of David Strauss (1808–1874), who went all the way and held that there was neither star nor comet, that the whole story was fiction.

Rebaptism The Latin prefix *re-* gives the sense of *again* when added to the verb *baptizo, baptizare*, thereby producing the Late Latin compound *rebaptizo, rebaptizare* with the meaning *to baptize again*. See the entry **Baptism**. St. Cyprian believed in the rebaptism of repentant apostates. Lea says that according to the Penitential ascribed to Theodore, Archbishop of Canterbury (688–690),

2. Deuteronomy 32:1, Psalm 49:1, Isaiah 49:1, Luke 2:14.

the bishop, priest, or deacon who was guilty of fornication was degraded, and all who had been baptized by him were required to be re-baptized—an expression of reprobation which it would be hard to parallel elsewhere in the history of the Church.[3]

Recess The Latin verb *cedo, cedere, cessi, cessus* means *to go*, especially in the sense of *to go away*. This special sense was emphasized by the addition of the prefix *re-* to form the verb *recedo* with the meaning *to withdraw*. From this compound verb there arose the fourth declension noun *recessus* with the meaning *withdrawal*. The decrees of the diets of the Holy Roman Empire were denominated *recessūs* because they were written out before the assembled delegates left for home.

Codex deliberationum in dietis seu conventibus habitarum, ideo sic dictus, quod scribi soleat antequam a conventibus recedant procures congregati.[4]

The minutes of the debates that take place in the diets and congresses, so called because they are accustomed to be written before the assembled authorities adjourn.

Most famous was the recess of the Diet of Speyer (1529), which provoked the protest of the reformers and gave birth to the name *Protestant*.

Redemption The Latin verb *emo, emere, emi, emptus* means *to buy*, and the addition of the prefix *re-* produces the compound verb *redimo, redimere, redemi, redemptus* with the meaning to *buy back, ransom*. The noun *redemptio* formed from the fourth principal part means a *buying back*, a *ransoming*.

Et ipse redimet Israel ab omnibus peccatis eius.[5]

The Greek word for *redemption* is ἀπολύτρωσις. The Hebrew word is פְּדוּת, from the root פדה.

Reformation The Latin noun *forma* means *figure, shape*, and from it was formed the verb *formo, formare, formavi, formatus* with the meaning *to fashion, arrange*. The addition of the prefix *re-* produces the compound verb *reformo* with the meaning *to form again, to mould anew*. From the fourth principal part of this verb is formed the noun *reformatio* which

---

3. Henry Charles Lea, *History of Sacerdotal Celibacy in the Christian Church* (n.p.: University Books, 1966), 129.
4. Charles du Fresne Du Cange, *Glossarium Mediae et Infimae Latinitatis* (Paris, 1845), 5:616a, s.v. "Recessus."
5. Psalm 129 (130):8.

came into English as *reformation*. The Protestant Reformation of the sixteenth century was the reformation *par excellence*. The reformers did not consider that they were founding new churches; rather they believed that they were straightening out the existing Church.

Regina Caeli The famous antiphon *Regina Caeli* is at least as old as 1200. The translation is by Caswall (1814–1878).

> Regina caeli, laetare, alleluia.
> Quia quem meruisti portare, alleluia.
> Resurrexit, sicut dixit, alleluia.
> Ora pro nobis Deum, alleluia.
>
> Joy to thee, O Queen of Heaven! Alleluia.
> He whom thou wast meet to bear, alleluia,
> As He promis'd hath arisen, alleluia.
> Pour for us to Him thy prayer. Alleluia.[6]

Regular The Latin verb *rego* means *to rule*, and from it was derived the noun *regula* with the meaning a *straight length, rule, ruler, pattern, model*. The regular clergy were those who lived by a rule, such as the Benedictines, Dominicans, Franciscans, and Jesuits. Those clergy who do not live by a rule are denominated *secular clergy*.

Religion The Latin noun *religio, religionis, f.*, is related to the verb *religo, religare* which means *to tie* (ligo), *to fasten* (ligo) *behind* (re-). The noun means *scrupulousness, conscientious exactness, respect for what is sacred*. The related adjective *religens* means *careful* and is the opposite of *negligens*, careless. Alfred North Whitehead defined religion as follows:

Religion is what the individual does with his own solitariness.[7]

Sanday offers a definition of religion, a thing not attempted any more by most modern scholars.

Religion consists not only in the knowledge of God and of His Will, but in the realization of that knowledge in the heart and conscience, in its effect upon conduct, and in its recognition by acts of worship and praise.[8]

---

6. Edward Caswall, *Lyra Catholica: Containing All the Breviary and Missal Hymns, with Others from Various Sources* (London: Burns & Oates, 1884), 39.

7. From a lecture "Religion in History" given at King's Chapel, Boston, in February, 1926 and available at http://alfrednorthwhitehead.wwwhubs.com/ritm1.htm.

8. William Sanday, *Inspiration, Eight Lectures on the Early History and Origin of the Doctrine of Biblical Inspiration, Being the Bampton Lectures for 1893* (London: Longmans, Green, 1896), 396.

The religious impulse is natural to man, in accordance with the yearning of Augustine, *Cor nostrum inquietum est, donec requiescat in te.* The function of religion is specified by William James in *The Varieties of Religious Experience*:

Religion makes easy and felicitous what in any case is necessary; and if it be the only agency that can accomplish this result, its vital importance as a human faculty stands vindicated beyond dispute.[9]

Requiem Mass The Mass for the Dead begins with the following words of the *Introit*:

Requiem aeternam dona ei, Domine, et lux perpetua luceat ei. Te decet hymnus, Deus, in Sion, et tibi reddetur votum in Jerusalem. Domine, exaudi orationem meam. Ad te omnis caro veniet.

Eternal rest grant unto him O Lord, and let perpetual light shine upon him. It is fitting to sing hymns unto Thee, O God, in Sion, and to fulfill our vows unto Thee in Jerusalem. Lord, hear my prayer. Unto Thee all flesh must come.

As a result, the ceremony has from time immemorial been called the *Requiem Mass*. As the Latin noun *quies, quietis, f.* (rest, repose) is derived from the verb *quiesco, quiescere, quievi, quietus* (to rest), so is the noun *requies, requietis, f.* (the rest of the dead) derived from the compound verb *requiesco*, to rest (used especially of the dead). *Requiem* is one of those words that entered all languages from the Latin Mass.

Resurrection The Latin verb *rego, regere, rexi, rectus* means *to make straight*, and the addition of the preposition *sub* (up from under) produces the compound verb *surgo, surgere, surrexi, surrectus* meaning *to get up, to rise*. The addition of the prefix *re-* (again) produces the compound verb *resurgo, resurgere, resurrexi, resurrectus* meaning *to rise again*. From its fourth principal part is formed the noun *resurrectio* with the meaning a *rising again*. In the Catholic religion, it means the *coming back from the dead*.

Et resurrexit tertia die.

Among the Jews, it was and is an optional doctrine. *Resurrectio* is the translation of the Greek ἀνάστασις.

---

9. William James, "Circumscription of the Topic," in *The Varieties of Religious Experience: A Study in Human Nature* (London:Folio Society, 2008), 43.

Revelation The Latin noun *velum, -i, n.*, means a *covering*, a *veil*, and the associated verb *velo, velare* means *to veil, to cover*. The verb *revelo* is compounded of *velo* and the prefix *re-*, back, and means *to unveil, to disclose*. The noun *revelatio, -onis, f.*, derived from it means an *uncovering*, a *pulling back of the veil that covers something*. It is the translation of the Greek ἀποκάλυψις.

There is a principle, the importance of which has long been recognized by theologians, the progressiveness of revelation, its adaptation, at different periods, to the moral and spiritual capacities of those to whom it was primarily addressed.[10]

A true historical view of the growth of the Old Testament, and of the progress of revelation, besides being important for its own sake, is valuable also in another way; it removes, viz., many of the difficulties, sometimes historical, sometimes moral, which the Old Testament presents, and which frequently form serious stumbling-blocks. The older apologists, by the harmonistic and other methods at their disposal, were quite unable to deal with these; historical criticism shows that they belong to the human element in the Bible, and that they are to be explained by reference either to the historical position of the writer, or to the imperfections incident to a relatively immature stage in the spiritual education of mankind.[11]

That revelation is progressive was the opinion of Sanday:

In this as in other things Revelation proceeds by way of growth, by development, by a gradual opening of the eyes to higher ranges of truth. To reach the highest summits of all we must go not to the Former Prophets but to the Latter, not to Genesis or Exodus or to the Books of Samuel and Kings, or even to those of Ezra and Nehemiah, but to Jeremiah and Second Isaiah, to the prophecy of the New Covenant and to the doctrine of the Suffering Servant.[12]

Revert The Latin verb *reverto, revertere* means *to turn back, to return*. The noun *revert* is a modern invention with the meaning *a former Catholic who returns to the faith*. Its use is not recommendable.

Revision The Latin verb *instauro, instaurare, instauravi, instauratus* means *to set up, establish, renew, restore*. What we call a *revision* of the Roman Missal the Latin title page calls a *restoration* or *renewal*. The revision of liturgies was a subject discussed by Rudolf Otto:

10. S. R. Driver and A. F. Kirkpatrick, *The Higher Criticism* (New York: Hodder & Stoughton, 1912), 59.

11. Ibid., 59–60.

12. William Sanday, *Inspiration, Eight Lectures on the Early History and Origin of the Doctrine of Biblical Inspiration, Being the Bampton Lectures for 1893* (London: Longmans, Green, 1896), 164.

Because their [sc. portions of the Latin Mass] design shows but little of regularity or conceptual arrangement, they preserve in themselves far more of the spirit of worship than the proposed recastings of the service put forward by the most practical reformers. In these we find carefully arranged schemes worked out with the balance and coherence of an essay, but nothing unaccountable, and for that very reason suggestive; nothing accidental, and for that very reason pregnant in meaning; nothing that rises from the deeps below consciousness to break the rounded unity of the wonted disposition and thereby point to a unity of a higher order—in a word, little that is really spiritual.[13]

Rhemes Rheims or Reims, the name of the French coronation city, is a corruption of *Remi*, the Celtic tribe that inhabited this part of Gaul in the time of Caesar. Rhemes is the way the sixteenth century English spelled and pronounced Rheims. The Rhemes New Testament is the name of the first English translation of the New Testament made in Rheims for the use of English speaking Catholics. It appeared in 1582. Since most copies were seized at the ports and destroyed, it is a great rarity. For the *Rhemes-Doway Bible*, see the entry **Doway.**

Rite The Latin noun *ritus, ritūs, m.*, means a *religious custom* or *ceremony*. Weekley thinks that it may be related to the Greek noun ἀριθμός, *number.*

Rituale For the etymology and formation of this word, see the entries **Rite** and **Missal**. The *Rituale Romanum*, or *Roman Ritual* in English, is the name of the liturgical book containing the texts of certain ceremonies celebrated by priests, such as baptisms, marriages, and blessings.

Rochet The Anglo-Saxon word *rocc* is the name of an upper garment, a coat. It became the German *Rock*, the French *rochet*, the Italian *rocchetto* and the Latin *rochetum*. The word should be pronounced as in French.

Although it [rochet] is also pronounced as rock′-et or ro-shet′, as is the custom in the Anglican Church, the proper pronunciation remains ro-shay′.[14]

The rochet is a linen or silk vestment that prelates wear in place of the surplice. It differs from the latter by having narrow, tight sleeves. The rochet should be crimped like the alb and the surplice. The main relic of the Cathedral of Trier is *der heilige Rock*, the holy rochet, the coat of Christ.

---

13. Rudolf Otto, "Means of Expression of the Numinous," in *The Idea of the Holy*, trans. J. W. Harvey (Oxford: Oxford University Press, 1923), 67, 68.

14. James-Charles Noonan Jr., *The Church Visible* (New York: Viking, 1996), 319.

Rogation Days The Latin verb *rogo, rogare, rogavi, rogatus* means *to ask*, and the associated noun *rogatio, -onis, f.*, means *something asked, a prayer, a petition*. It is the English name for special prayers of petition, which were offered on certain days by way of litany in procession. These days were April 25 (in the old Roman Missal, *in Litaniis Majoribus*), on which the *Missa de Rogationibus* was sung after a procession, and the Monday, Tuesday, and Wednesday before Ascension Day (in the Roman Missal, *in Litaniis Minoribus*), on which the same Mass was sung. The Rogation Days were removed from the Roman Missal as part of the reform after the Second Vatican Council.

Roma Locuta, Causa Finita This sentence means *Rome has spoken, and the case is closed*. It was used at the time of the Roman Empire to allude to the fact that there was no appeal from a decision of the bishop of Rome. Its use continued in the Church as a reference to the finality of a verdict reached by the supreme pontiff. Nevertheless, people did appeal occasionally from the pope ill informed to the pope better informed, but such appeals were never allowed. The sentence is a traditional summary of words found in a sermon of St. Augustine.

Iam enim de hac causa duo concilia missa sunt ad Sedem Apostolicam; inde etiam rescripta venerunt. Causa finita est; utinam aliquando finiatur error![15]

Concerning this matter the decrees of two councils have already been submitted to the Apostolic See, whose confirmations have since arrived. The case is closed. If only we are now finished with this heresy!

Rome The etymology of the Latin noun *Roma* is unknown. The Greeks called the city Ῥώμη. The city of Rome has for two thousand years been *Caput Mundi*, the capital of the world and the headquarters of the Catholic Church. The text of the following hymn was found by Niebuhr in his researches in the Vatican Library; he dated the hymn to the fifth century.[16] It was the pilgrim's song, sung when Holy Rome first came into sight.

> O Roma nobilis orbis et domina,
> Cunctarum urbium excellentissima,
> Roseo martyrum sanguine rubea,

15. *The Oxford Dictionary of Quotations*, 4th ed., ed. Angela Partington (Oxford, Oxford University Press, 1992), 37. They cite Sermon Number 131, section 10, of the Antwerp edition of the sermons (1702). The sermon can be read online at www.augustinus.it/latino/discorsi/index2.htm.

16. Ferdinand Gregorovius, *History of the City of Rome in the Middle Ages*, trans. Mrs. Gustavus W. Hamilton (London: G. Bell & Sons, 1909), 1:397.

Albis et liliis virginum candida.
Salutem dicimus tibi per omnia,
Te benedicimus, Salve per saecula!

Petre tu praepotens caelorum claviger,
vota praecantium exaudi iugiter.
Cum bissex tribuum sederis arbiter,
factus placabilis iudica leniter.
Tu poenitentibus nunc temporaliter,
ferto suffragia misericorditer.

O Paule suscipe nostra precamina,
cuius philosophos vicit industria.
Factus economus in domo regia,
divini muneris appone fercula.
Ut quae repleverit te sapientia,
Ipsa nos repleat tua per dogmata.

O Noble Rome, of all the world the head,
No place on earth thine equal can we tread,
With martyrs' blood adorned a rosey red,
With virgins' lilies white thy gardens spread.
All hail thee now, the living and the dead,
And bless thee more than ever can be said.

O Peter, thine's the power of the keys,
Hear all our prayers, our vows, our litanies.
The tribes of Israel are thy diocese.
Give judgment soft, be easy to appease,
Them that repent release from penalties.
To intercede for us may it thee please.

O Paul who didst philosophers refute,
Who dared with thee foolishly to dispute,
Steward of the king, not meat, not bread, not fruit,
But truth divine provide, the absolute.
Accept our prayer, in us thy wisdom root,
Thy teaching for our errors substitute.

Gregorovius, at the end of his masterpiece, spoke of the history of the papacy and the city of Rome as "the history most full of passion, the most glorious and sublime in the annals of mankind".[17] Dr. Arnold of Rugby used to say, "The History of Rome must in some sort be The History of the

17. Ferdinand Gregorovius, *History of the City of Rome in the Middle Ages*, trans. Mrs. Gustavus W. Hamilton (London: G. Bell & Sons, 1902), vol. 8, pt. 2, p. 702.

World."[18] To see how Rome looked before the transformation brought on by the unification of Italy in 1870, consult the collection of photographs published by the Thorvaldsen Museum.[19]

Rose The English word *rose* is derived from the Latin *rosa*, which is related to the Greek ῥόδον. The Golden Rose was an award that in former times the popes used to present to worthy female royalty. The last time that the Golden Rose was awarded with the fullest possible ceremony was when it was given to Queen Elena of Italy in 1937. The royal coaches of the House of Savoy were sent to the apostolic nunciature on Via Nomentana to bring the nuncio, Monsignor Borgongini Duca, and the Bearer of the Golden Rose, Prince Sacchetti, to the Quirinale, where there was a solemn high Mass in the Pauline Chapel at which the Sistine Choir under the direction of Monsignor Perosi provided the music. The whole royal court and the diplomatic corps were present.

Rota The Latin noun *rota, -ae, f.,* means *wheel.* The *Tribunal Apostolicum Rotae Romanae* is the supreme court of appeals of the Holy See. It is called the *Rota* because it used to meet in a circular room.

Rubric The Latin adjective *ruber, rubra, rubrum* means *red.* From it was derived the first-declension noun *rubrīca* meaning *red earth, red ochre,* or the *pigment derived therefrom.* Copyists used red ink for the titles of laws in legal manuscripts; other additional matter to which one wanted to attract attention would similarly be written in red. In the composition of missals and other liturgical books, copyists and, later on, type-setters used red ink for whatever directions and other material were included on a page as information for the celebrant, in this way drawing attention so as to ensure that such matter would not be misinterpreted as part of the sacred text, which would itself be in black ink. The expression *red ink* in reference to critical annotations by teachers made in red ink to a text composed by students in black ink derives from this usage.

18. Arthur Penrhyn Stanley, *The Life and Correspondence of Thomas Arnold, D. D.*, two volumes, fifth edition, London, B. Fellowes, 1845, volume 1, page 211.

19. *Rome in Early Photographs, The Age of Pius IX, Photographs 1846–1878 from Roman and Danish Collections*, trans. Ann Thornton (Copenhagen: The Thorvaldsen Museum, 1977).

Sabellianism The *Sabines* or *Sabini* were an ancient people of Italy; *Sabelli* was a poetic name for *Sabini*. *Sabellus* means a *Sabine*, and *Sabellius* is a proper name originally formed from it by the addition of the adjectival suffix *-ius*.[1] The Sabellian heresy arose in the middle of the third century and takes its name from Sabellius, a priest of Cyrenaica, who was a sort of Unitarian. The Sabellians formed a distinct church by the year 381, when the Council of Constantinople declared that their baptism was invalid.

Its peculiar tenet is the denial of the distinction of Persons in the Divine Nature.[2]

Sack of Rome The Hebrew noun שַׂק means a *bag, sackcloth*; it appears to be derived from a root שקק, which is, however, according to Brown, Driver, and Briggs, nowhere found. The Greek noun σάκκος means a *coarse cloth of goat's or camel's hair, a bag*; it is transliterated into Latin by *saccus*. Since plunderers steal items that they then put into a bag, the verb *to sack* acquired the meaning *to pillage*. The sacks of Rome by Alaric in August 410 and by Genseric in 455 astonished the world and were the subject of investigation by Gregorovius in the first volume of his history. *The Sack of Rome*, which occurred in the week of May 6–13, 1527, marked the end of the Renaissance. Unpaid mutinous German, Spanish, and Italian troops nominally loyal to the emperor-elect Charles V captured the Holy City and subjected it to criminal vandalism for more than a week. Six thousand

---

1. See *Allen and Greenough's New Latin Grammar for Schools and Colleges*, ed. J. B. Greenough, A. A. Howard, G. L. Kittredge, Benj. L. D'Ooge (Boston: Ginn, 1916), §247.
2. John Henry Cardinal Newman, *The Arians of the Fourth Century*, new ed. (London: Longmans, Green, 1897), 117.

people died, half the buildings were burnt, and St. Peter's Basilica and other churches were used as stables for horses. One hundred forty-seven soldiers of the Swiss Guard perished, an event that they remember with an annual memorial, during which new recruits take their oath. The damage to works of art, manuscripts, and archives was tremendous. Pope Clement VII, together with the cardinals and the Curia, fled into the Castel Sant'Angelo where he remained until it was safe for him to come out, after which he moved to Orvieto and Viterbo, not daring to return to Rome until October 1528.[3] During this period of retirement, he grew a beard, a practice that was copied throughout Europe, even by Henry VIII. After Clement VII, the popes invariably were bearded for two centuries. The last bearded pontiff was Innocent XII.

Sacrament The Latin adjective *sacer, sacra, sacrum* means *holy, consecrated*, and from it was derived the verb *sacro, sacrare* with the meaning *to dedicate to a deity*. From this verb is derived the noun *sacramentum*, which means *something that obliges a person, a civil suit, a military oath, any oath or solemn promise*. According to Weekley, it is the Latin translation of the Greek μυστήριον, which is otherwise merely transliterated by *mysterium*. In the Catholic religion, the definition of *sacramentum* is given by Cardinal Gasparri:

Nomine *Sacramenti novae legis* intelligitur signum sensibile, a Iesu Christo institutum, ad gratiam significandam eamque Sacramentum digne suscipientibus conferendam.[4]

By the name "Sacrament of the New Law" there is understood a visible sign instituted by Jesus Christ, which signifies a grace and which confers that grace on those who receive the sacrament worthily.

Sacramental The addition of the adjectival suffix *-alis* to the stem of the noun *sacramentum* produces the adjective *sacramentalis* with the meaning *pertaining to a sacrament*. The noun *sacramentale, sacramentalis, n.*, formed from the adjective is either a pious action, like making the sign of the cross, or a religious object, like holy water.

---

3. Bernhard Schimmelpfennig, *Das Krönungszeremoniale Kaiser Karls V* (Stuttgart: Belser Verlag, 1989), 22. This is a companion volume to the facsimile edition of Codex Borgianus Latinus 420 in the Vatican Apostolic Library.

4. *Catechismus catholicus, cura et studio Petri Cardinalis Gasparri concinnatus*, 15th ed. (Rome: Typis Polyglottis Vaticanis, 1933), 188–89.

Sacrarium The *sacrarium* was in ancient times the sacristy of a temple, a place where holy objects were kept. In the Catholic Church, it is the name of the drain that leads into the basin or *piscina*, into which one pours the water that was used in washing the sacred vessels of the Mass.

Sacrilege The Latin adjective *sacer, sacra, sacrum* means *holy*, and the verb *lego, legere* means to gather. From their concatenation is formed the noun *sacrilegium* with the meaning the *theft of consecrated things*. It has acquired the meaning of an unspeakable offense against religious etiquette.

Sacris Solemniis Thomas Aquinas composed this hymn for Matins of the Feast of Corpus Christi. The last two stanzas are the famous *Panis Angelicus*. It was wonderfully set to music by Michael Haller (1840–1915).

> Sacris solemniis iuncta sint gaudia,
> Et ex praecordiis sonent praeconia:
> Recedant vetera, nova sint omnia,
> Corda, voces, et opera.
>
> Noctis recolitur cena novissima,
> Qua Christus creditur agnum et azyma
> Dedisse fratribus, iuxta legitima
> Priscis indulta patribus.
>
> Post agnum typicum, expletis epulis,
> Corpus Dominicum datum discipulis,
> Sic totum omnibus, quod totum singulis,
> Eius fatemur manibus.
>
> Dedit fragilibus corporis ferculum,
> Dedit et tristibus sanguinis poculum,
> Dicens: Accipite quod trado vasculum,
> Omnes ex eo bibite.
>
> Sic sacrificium istud instituit,
> Cuius officium committi voluit
> Solis presbyteris, quibus sic congruit,
> Ut sumant, et dent ceteris.
>
> Panis angelicus fit panis hominum;
> Dat panis caelicus figuris terminum:
> O res mirabilis! Manducat Dominum
> Pauper, servus, et humilis.

Te trina Deitas unaque poscimus,
Sic nos tu visita, sicut te colimus:
Per tuas semitas duc nos quo tendimus,
Ad lucem quam inhabitas. Amen.

The best translation is by Edward Caswall (1814–1878):

Let old things pass away;
Let all be fresh and bright;
And welcome we with hearts renew'd
This feast of new delight.

Upon this hallow'd eve
Christ with his brethren ate,
Obedient to the olden law,
The Pasch before Him set.
Which done,—Himself entire,
The true Incarnate God,
Alike on each, alike on all,
His sacred hands bestow'd.

He gave His Flesh; He gave
His precious Blood; and said,
"Receive, and drink ye all of this,
For your salvation shed."

Thus did the Lord appoint
This Sacrifice sublime,
And made his Priests its ministers
Through all the bounds of time.

Farewell to types! Henceforth
We feed on Angels' food:
The slave—oh, wonder!—eats the Flesh
Of his Incarnate God!

O Blessed Three in One!
Visit our hearts we pray;
And lead us on through thine own paths
To thy eternal Day.[5]

Sacristy In mediaeval times, the noun *sacristia*, derived from *sacrum* (see the entry **Sacrament**, above), came to mean the place where the priest vested for Mass and where the sacred paraphernalia were kept. The corre-

---

5. Edward Caswall, *Lyra Catholica: Containing All the Breviary and Missal Hymns, with Others from Various Sources* (London: Burns & Oates, 1884), 113–14.

sponding place in Roman temples was called the *sacrarium*. Bacci, quoting Jacopo Pontano, condemns the word:

Sacristiam qui nominat, nulla necessitate loquitur barbare.[6]

Whoever uses the word *sacristia* unnecessarily adopts a barbarism.

The fellow in charge of the sacristy was called the *sacrista* or, in English, the *sacristan*. This last word was later corrupted to *sexton*.

Sadducee The Hebrew noun צדק means *righteousness*, and from it was derived the proper name צדוק from whom later priests claimed descent.

Unxerunt Salomonem Sadoc sacerdos et Nathan propheta regem in Gihon, et ascendentes laeti dixerunt, "Vivat Rex in aeternum."

This Latin antiphon was sung at the coronation of Catholic kings, at the anointing. The free English translation was set to music by Handel for the coronation of George II in 1727 and sung as recently as 1953 for the coronation of Elizabeth II.

Zadok the Priest and Nathan the Prophet anointed Solomon King. And all the people rejoiced and said, "God save the King! Long live the King! May the King live forever! Amen. Amen. Alleluia. Alleluia. Amen.[7]

From the noun צדוק was later formed the word צדוקי transliterated into Greek as Σαδδουκαῖος, whence proceeded our *Sadducee*. The Sadduccees were one of the three parties of the Jews mentioned by Josephus; see the entry **Pharisee**. They were prominent among the temple establishment.

Saint The Latin adjective *sacer* means *holy, consecrated*, and related to it is the verb *sancio, sancire, sanxi, sanctus* with the meaning *to consecrate, hallow*. From the fourth principal part is derived the French and English *saint*, the *c* being lost. Among certain speakers of English, the *t* may also be lost, as in the British pronunciation of *St. John*.

Two reasons may be hinted especially, though there are many others which we have not space to enlarge on, for the strong preference which, we are convinced, is due to the guidance of living individuals over that of printed documents. The one, that the very principal difficulties through which earnest and practical men are anxious to see their way will always be peculiar to their own time: and to resort for

6. Antonio Bacci, *Vocabolario Italiano-Latino delle Parole Difficili a Tradurre* (Rome: Editrice Studium, 1963), 664.
7. Coronation anthem of the kings of England.

their solution to writers living in the period of Charles the First is like consulting St. Chrysostom on a subject of political economy. The other is that, partly for this very reason, partly for others, the credentials of living and breathing men are far more open to our inspection; we have far better means of attaining a deep and intimate conviction that we may safely to so great an extent trust the awful affair of our eternal salvation to their hands.[8]

Salve Regina These are the opening two words of the famous Latin prayer of the Middle Ages; they mean *Hail, O Queen!*

Salve, Regina, mater misericordia, vita, dulcedo, et spes nostra, salve! Ad te clamamus, exsules filii Hevae. Ad te suspiramus, gementes et flentes in hac lacrimarum valle. Eia ergo, advocata nostra, illos tuos misericordes oculos ad nos converte, et Iesum, benedictum fructum ventris tui, nobis post hoc exilium ostende. O clemens, O pia, O dulcis virgo Maria.

The following translation is by Caswall (1814–1878).[9]

> Mother of mercy, hail, O gracious Queen!
> Our life, our sweetness, and our hope, all hail!
> Children of Eve,
> To thee we cry from our sad banishment;
> To thee we send our sighs,
> Weeping and mourning in this veil of tears.
> Come, then, our Advocate;
> Oh, turn on us those pitying eyes of thine:
> And our long exile past,
> Show us at last
> Jesus, of thy pure womb the fruit divine.
> O Virgin Mary, mother blest!
> O sweetest, gentlest, holiest!

Samaritan The Hebrew place name שֹׁמְרוֹן refers to an ancient city in central Palestine, the inhabitants of whom were called הַשֹּׁמְרֹנִים. The Septuagint transliterates the name of the city by Σαμαρεία and calls the inhabitants οἱ Σαμαρῖται. From the last word we get the Latin *Samaritani*, the *Samaritans*. The Jews who returned from the Babylonian Exile found them in the land and disapproved of them, and they were considered heretics. They, on the other hand, considered themselves descendants of the

---

8. Wilfrid Ward, *William George Ward and the Oxford Movement* (London: Macmillan, 1889), 237.

9. Edward Caswall, *Lyra Catholica: Containing All the Breviary and Missal Hymns, with Others from Various Sources* (London: Burns & Oates, 1884), 40.

ancient Israelite tribes who had dwelt in their area. They would have nothing to do with the rebuilt temple in Jerusalem.

Sanctuary From the fourth principal part of the verb *sancio, sancire, sanxi, sanctus* (to consecrate, to hallow, to make sacred or inviolable by a religious act) was derived the noun *sanctuarium* with the meaning a *place for keeping holy things*; it is the Late Latin equivalent for the classical *sacrarium*. The sanctuary was formerly reserved for the clergy and was separated from that part of the church where the people congregated by an altar screen or at least by an altar rail. Lay folk would have trembled to cross into it.

A story very characteristic of Pugin's intense feeling on this subject is told. Pugin was showing to an Anglican friend the rood screen which he had erected at St. Barnabas's, Nottingham. "Within," he said, "is the Holy of Holies. The people remain outside. Never is the sanctuary entered by any save those in sacred orders." At this moment a priest appeared within the sanctuary in company with two ladies. Pugin in acute excitement said to the sacristan, "Turn those people out at once. How dare they enter?" "Sir," said the sacristan, "it is Bishop Wiseman." Pugin, powerless to do anything, sank down on a neighboring bench, and burst into tears.[10]

Sanctus *Sanctus* is the Latin adjective meaning *holy*. It is therefore also used as the name of the prayer in the Mass after the Preface and before the Canon: *Sanctus, Sanctus, Sanctus, Dominus Deus Sabaoth*. See the entry **Seraphim**.

Sanhedrin The word *Sanhedrin* is the corruption of the Greek noun συνέδριον, the deliberative body of the Jews of Jerusalem at the time of Christ. It means a *sitting* (ἕδρα, a *seat*) *together* (σύν).

Santo Bambino The Greek verb βαμβαίνω means *to stammer*; it is formed from the sound, like *babble*. From it was formed the onomatopoetic Italian noun *bambino* applied, like *baby*, to an infant, because of the manner of its speech. The Italian phrase, which means *Holy Baby*, is the name of a small statue of the Infant Christ preserved in a chapel in the Basilica of Santa Maria in Araceli on the Capitoline Hill in Rome. The Roman banker Prince Alessandro Torlonia (1800–1886), after having had to dispatch his own carriage to bring the image to the bed of his sick daughter, provided, after her recovery, a suitable carriage of its own for the

10. Wilfrid Ward, *The Life and Times of Cardinal Wiseman* (London: Longmans, Green, 1900), 1:359.

sacred image, in which it was transported about town in its visits to the dying. The statue was stolen from the church in 1994 and has never been recovered; it has been replaced by a replica in the meantime.

Satan The Hebrew noun שׂטן means *adversary* and then the *superhuman adversary* whom Christ referred to as *the Evil One*, ὁ πονηρός, in the Lord's Prayer; its English transliteration is *Satan*.

Saturno Saturnus was the Roman god considered equivalent to the Greek Κρόνος, the father of Zeus. It is the name given to the ringed planet. The *saturno* is a black hat with a wide circular brim and a hemispherical crown, so called because of an alleged similarity to the planet Saturn, with the rings providing the brim. It used to be common in Rome, wherefore the Italians call it *il cappello Romano*, the Roman hat.

Scala Santa The Latin verb *scando, scandere, scandi, scansus* means *to climb*, and related to it is the noun *scalae, -arum, f.*, meaning a *flight of stairs. Scala Santa* means *holy staircase* in Italian and is the name of the staircase of the palace of the Roman procurator in Jerusalem, believed to have been removed by St. Helena and brought to Rome as a relic of the passion, since Christ must have walked up and down it. It is kept in a small edifice near the Lateran basilica, and the faithful are allowed to ascend it only on their knees. A visit to the Scala Santa on September 19, 1870, the day before the fall of Rome, was the last time Pius IX left the Vatican. William Barry, the author of the lives of Ernest Renan and Cardinal Newman, remarks in the former biography that he was present on this occasion.[11]

Scandal The Greek noun σκάνδαλον means a *trap laid for an enemy*, a *stumbling-block*. From it is derived the verb σκανδαλίζω with the meaning *to cause to stumble, to give offense*. In the theological sense, a scandal is something that by its enormity causes one to be distracted or interrupted in the practice of the faith, like the details of clerical sexual abuse.

Schism The Greek verb σχίζω means *to rend asunder, to split*, and from it was derived the noun σχίσμα, σχίσματος with the meaning *division*. This Greek noun, most serviceable in view of the quarrelsomeness of Christians, was taken over in the Latin West as *schisma, schismatis, n.*, with the meaning *a split in the Church*. The most famous schism is that of the Greeks, which resulted in the division of Christianity into Catholic and

---

11. William Barry, *Ernest Renan* (New York: Charles Scribner's Sons, 1905), 66.

Orthodox branches. The most scandalous schism was the Great Schism of the fourteenth and fifteenth centuries, in which there were two and later three claimants contending for the papal throne.

Scholastic The Greek noun σχολή means *leisure, spare time*, and the derived verb σχολάζω means *to be at leisure, to have spare time to devote to something*. From this verb proceeded the adjective σχολαστικός with the meaning *having spare time* and later, *devoting one's spare time to learning*. From this connection with learning, the noun σχολή acquired the meaning *school*, which word is anyway its corruption. In the Catholic Church, the adjective *scholastic* is reserved for the philosophy of Thomas Aquinas and others like him, who made philosophy the handmaiden of the Church. In his *Dictionary*, Blackburn defines *scholasticism* as follows:

The philosophy taught in the Church schools and theological training-grounds in the medieval period. Scholasticism was the dominant philosophical approach in Europe from perhaps the 11th until the 16th century, or the time of Abelard to that of Suárez. It combined religious doctrine, study of the Church fathers, and philosophical and logical work based particularly on Aristotle and his commentators, and to some extent on themes from Plato. Prominent scholastics included Aquinas, Buridan, Duns Scotus, and Ockham.[12]

Scrutiny The Greek noun γρύτη means *frippery, rags*, and related to it is the Latin noun *scruta, scrutorum, n.*, with the meaning *frippery, trash*. From this noun is derived the verb *scrutor, scrutari* meaning *to examine carefully, to hunt out* (perhaps by going through the trash). From this verb is derived the Late Latin noun *scrutinium* with the meaning *investigation*. In the language of the Conclave, the scrutiny is a round of voting and the counting of how many votes each candidate has received. Each cardinal takes the following oath before he places his ballot onto the paten and drops it into the chalice:

Testor Christum Dominum, qui me iudicaturus est, me eligere, quem secundum Deum iudico eligi debere, et quod idem in accessu praestabo.[13]

I call to witness Christ Our Lord, who is to sit in judgment over me, that I am voting for that man whom I judge before God ought to be elected, and that I shall remain steadfast in this if we should we proceed to accession.

12. Simon Blackburn, *The Oxford Dictionary of Philosophy* (Oxford: Oxford University Press, 1994), 342a.

13. Hartwell de la Garde Grissell, *Sede Vacante, Being a Diary Written during the Conclave of 1903, with Additional Notes on the Accession and Coronation of Pius X* (Oxford: James Parker, 1903), 80.

The last six words of the Latin oath were dropped after the option of proceeding to election by accession was abolished by Pius X.

Secretarium The Latin noun *secretarium* is formed from the fourth principal part of the verb *secerno, secernere, secrevi, secretus*, which means *to separate*. The *secretarium* is a side chapel set up for the vesting of a bishop during Terce before pontifical high Mass.

Secretary The Latin verb *secerno, secernere, secrevi, secretus* means *to separate*, and the neuter plural perfect passive participle became a noun with the meaning *things set apart for privacy's sake*, particularly papers. The fellow in charge of these private documents was in Late Latin denominated *secretarius*. Such a person signs his name *N. a secretis*, that is, *so-and-so in charge of private affairs*.

Secular Clergy The Latin noun *saeculum* means a *generation*, and then a *long period of time*, either a century or a whole age, in particular the current age. From its use to translate the Hebrew עוֹלָם it came in later times to mean the *world*.

Dum veneris iudicare saeculum per ignem.[14]

When thou shalt come to judge the world with fire.

The secular clergy are those who are not regular clergy, that is, those who do not live by the special rule of a founder.

Securus Iudicat Orbis Terrarium This Latin sentence means *the verdict of the whole world must be right*. One of the arguments of St. Augustine against the Donatists was that the whole world was against them.[15] John Henry Newman decided that the Church of England similarly stood in opposition to the whole world. A similar idea is expressed by the saying *Vox populi, vox Dei*. It has been taken to the next level by political scientists, pollsters, and the organizers of focus groups.

Sedia Gestatoria *Sedia* is the Italian corruption of the Latin *sedes, -is, f.*, which means *seat*; it is derived from the verb *sedeo, sedere, sedi, sessus*, to sit. The verb *gero, gerere, gessi, gestus* means *to carry*, and from it was derived the frequentative verb *gesto, gestare, gestavi, gestatus* meaning *to carry about*.

---

14. From the prayer *Libera me, Domine*, of the Requiem Mass, familiar to all lovers of Verdi.
15. Wilfrid Ward, *William George Ward and the Oxford Movement* (London: Macmillan, 1889), 144.

From the fourth principal part of this latter verb came the Italian adjective *gestatoria*, portable. The phrase *sedia gestatoria* means *portable throne* and refers to the sedan chair on which the pope was carried in his public appearances. This contrivance allowed him to be easily seen. It was always carried by twelve porters called in Italian *sediari*, six on each side. The last pope to avail himself of this method of locomotion was John Paul I in 1978. It was conducive to the maintenance of dignity. When Pope John Paul II became infirm, he was wheeled around in a modern metamorphosis of the *portantina*, which was a less elevated portable throne carried by bearers, though not on their shoulders. The Latin name for the *sedia gestatoria* is *sella gestatoria*, as we learn from Suetonius:

Interdiu quoque clam gestatoria sella delatus in theatrum, seditionibus pantomimorum e parte proscaeni superiore signifer simul ac spectator aderat.[16]

He would even secretly visit the theater by day, in a sedan chair, and watch the quarrels among the pantomime actors, cheering them on from the top of the proscenium.[17]

The following account of the institution of the *sedia gestatoria*, if not true, is a good story:

30. The clergy and people, gathered together in the church of St. Mary Major, elected by acclamation a new Pope, under the name of Stephen III (March 26, A.D. 752). So lively was the joy awakened by his election, that the enthusiastic multitude bore him upon their shoulders to the basilica of St. John Lateran. The usage has since been renewed, at the installation of each new pontiff, and was the origin of the *sedia gestatoria*—the pontifical chair, borne by twelve of the noble guards. This imposing ceremony gives to the Roman pomps a splendor never equaled by any other sovereign court.[18]

Sediarii The *sediarii* were the gentlemen who carried the *sedia gestatoria* or the *portantina*, on which the pope was transported from place to place in accordance with his dignity.

Sedilia Greek verb ἕζομαι means *to sit*, and related to it is the Latin verb *sedeo, sedere, sedi, sessus* with the same meaning. From this Latin verb

---

16. Suetonius, *Life of Nero*, §26.

17. Suetonius, *The Twelve Caesars*, rev. ed., trans. Robert Graves (London: the Folio Society, 1964), 224.

18. Joseph-Epiphane Darras, *General History of the Catholic Church from the Commencement of the Christian Era to the Twentieth Century*, 13th ed. (New York: P. J. Kennedy, n.d.), 2:339.

is derived the noun *sedīle, sedīlis, n.*, with the meaning a *seat*. The plural *sedilia* are used of those chairs in which the priest, deacon, and subdeacon sit during Mass. If the altar is at the east end of the church, the sedilia should be placed at the south of the sanctuary, so that the seated clergy are facing north.

See This is an English corruption of the Latin *sedes* (chair). It is found in such expressions as the *Holy See*, and *the See of Constantinople*. Similar expressions are to be found in the other languages (der Heilige Stuhl, le Saint Siège, la Santa Sede, etc.). Observe that *sedes* changed gender when it migrated from Latin into French. A similar fate befell *arbor*, tree. It may be useful to consider here the difference between the three terms the *Holy See*, the *Vatican City*, and the *Vatican*. The *Holy See* is the bishopric of Rome, at whose head is the sovereign pontiff, the bishop of Rome; the term *Holy See* is used of the Diocese or Church of Rome especially in its capacity as the governing body of the Catholic Church. The *Vatican City* is the sovereign state established on February 11, 1929, by agreement of the Holy See and the Kingdom of Italy. It established an independent state upon whose territory the offices of the Holy See could function. *The Vatican* is used by metonymy for the collective of decision-making bodies whose headquarters are in the Vatican Palace and in the surrounding buildings. However, for many centuries the popes and their closest advisers lived not at the Vatican but in the Lateran Palace or in the Quirinal Palace or even at Avignon; in those times one could not have referred to the papal government as *the Vatican* without confusion; it is an anachronism to use the expression "the Vatican" to refer to a decision of the papal regime at a time when the pope resided at Avignon or operated from the Lateran or the Quirinal in Rome.

Semi-Arian The Greek prefix ἡμι- means *half*, and related to it is the Latin prefix *semi-* with the same meaning. The Semi-Arians were a party of prominent fourth-century heretics who approximated to the Catholic doctrine more closely than did the Arians. Their doctrine was that the Christ was ὁμοιούσιος, of like being as the Father, rather than ὁμοούσιος, of the same being as the Father. Their chief was Basil, bishop of Ancyra.

Septuagesima This is the Latin adjective for *seventieth*; it modifies the noun *dominica* (Sunday) understood. It is the Sunday falling roughly seventy days before Easter. It begins a preparatory period before Lent.

Septuagint The Latin word for *seventy* is *Septuaginta*, and that name is given to the Greek translation of the Old Testament, because it was believed to have been made by seventy authorities.

Before the Romans established their empire, while the Macedonians still held Asia, Ptolemy son of Lagus was anxious to equip the library he had established in Alexandria with worthwhile books from every quarter, so he asked the people of Jerusalem to provide him with a copy of their Scriptures translated into Greek. Being at that time still subject to the Macedonians, they sent him seventy men of mature age, the most skilled they had in the Scriptures and in both languages. Thus was God's purpose fulfilled. Ptolemy wished to test them in his own way, fearing that they might put their heads together and manipulate their translation to conceal the true meaning of the Scriptures. So he separated them from each other, and told them they must all produce the same translation: he laid down this rule for every one of the books. When they reassembled before Ptolemy and compared their respective versions, God was glorified and the Scriptures were recognized as truly divine; they all said the same things in the same phrases and the same words from beginning to end, so that even the heathen who were present knew that the Scriptures had been translated by the inspiration of God.[19]

Sè non è vero, è ben trovato. The critical edition of the Septuagint is that edited by Rahlfs.[20] The serious study of the Old Testament is impossible without the Septuagint, since it often preserves readings from better Hebrew manuscripts than those that have survived to this day. The Septuagint is frequently indicated in the Roman manner by LXX.

Sepulcher (Holy) The Latin verb *sepelio, sepelire, sepelivi, sepultus* means *to bury*, and from it is derived the noun *sepulcrum*, which means *a place of burial*. The tomb of Christ in Jerusalem, around which was built the Basilica of the Holy Sepulcher, has been the destination of pilgrims for two millennia. The present structure dates from the Crusader period. The ownership of the basilica is in accordance with a decree of the Ottoman Sultan in 1852, referred to as the *Status Quo*, which confirmed the existing compromise between the six Christian Churches with rights in the holy places: the Catholic Church, the Greek Orthodox Church, the Armenian Church, the Syrian Church, the Coptic Church, and the Ethi-

---

19. Eusebius, *The History of the Church from Christ to Constantine*, trans. G. A. Williamson (London: The Folio Society, 2011), V 8, p. 141. He is quoting Irenaeus. The reign of Ptolemy I began in 305 and ended in 283 or 282 B.C.

20. Alfred Rahlfs, ed., *Septuaginta, Id est Vetus Testamentum graece iuxta LXX*, 8th ed. (Stuttgart: Württembergische Bibelanstalt, 1985).

opian Church; the last three named have very minor privileges. Since, by the *Status Quo* of 1852, the placement of altars, the times for ceremonies, and other such details cannot be changed, this was the one church in the world where the liturgical reforms that followed the Second Vatican Council could not be fully implemented.

Sequence The Latin verb *sequor, sequi, secutus sum* means *to follow*. The participle (nominative case, neuter plural) *sequentia* means *things that follow*. In Late Latin, it became the first declension noun *sequentia, -ae, f.*, with the meaning *continuation*. Thus in the old days the deacon sang *Sequentia Sancti Evangeli secundum N*, "the continuation of the Holy Gospel according to N." *Sequentia* has in the new missal been changed to *lectio*, a reading, a noun formerly used to introduce the reading or chanting of the epistle.

The word *sequence* is used also for the name of the five famous poems that are sung following the Gradual verses on certain days: *Dies Irae* (Requiem Masses), *Lauda, Sion, Salvatorem* (Corpus Christi), *Stabat Mater* (Sorrows of the Blessed Virgin Mary), *Veni, Sancte Spiritus* (Pentecost), and *Victimae Paschali Laudes* (Easter).

Seraphim The Hebrew verb שָׂרַף means *to burn*, and from this root is derived the plural noun שְׂרָפִים, the name of the six-winged angelic beings, in the vision of Isaiah 6, who stood above the throne of the Lord and chanted:

קָדוֹשׁ קָדוֹשׁ קָדוֹשׁ יהוה צְבָאוֹת
מְלֹא כָל־הָאָרֶץ כְּבוֹדוֹ:

From this verse is derived the Sanctus of the Mass:

Sanctus, Sanctus, Sanctus, Dominus Deus Sabaoth. Pleni sunt
caeli et terra gloria tua.

The seraphim are conspicuous in the *Te Deum*:

Tibi omnes angeli, tibi caeli et universae potestates,
Tibi Cherubim et Seraphim incessabili voce proclamant.

They also appear in a famous aria of Handel:

Let the bright Seraphim, in tuneful row,
Their loud uplifted angel trumpets blow.

Sermon The Greek verb εἴρω means *to join* or *fasten together, to connect,* and related to it is the Latin verb *sero, serere, serui, sertus* with the same meaning. The noun *sermo, sermonis, m.,* is derived from this verb. The word means *discourse* or *language,* but nowadays it is usually understood to mean the homily of a clergyman.

Servus Servorum Dei This Latin phrase means *Servant of the Servants of God* and is a title of the pope. Thus papal bulls would begin with the words *N. Episcopus Servus Servorum Dei, ad perpetuam rei memoriam.* The title was taken by Gregory the Great in response to the megalomania of the patriarch of Constantinople, who had assumed the title Πατρίαρχος Οἰκουμενικός, Worldwide Patriarch. The ecumenical patriarch now has direct rule over four thousand Greeks who have remained in Turkey.

Sexagesima This is the Latin adjective for *sixtieth;* it modifies the noun *dominica* (Sunday) understood. It is the Sunday falling roughly sixty days before Easter.

Sext The Greek word ἕξ means *six,* and related to it is the Latin word *sex* with the same meaning. The related adjective *sextus* means *sixth. Sext* is the name of the prayers of the Divine Office sung at the sixth hour of daylight, about noon.

Sfumata The Greek verb θύω means *to sacrifice,* and the related noun θυμός means *soul, life, breath.* Since the major sacrifices were accomplished by burning, the related Latin noun *fumus, -i, m.,* came to mean smoke. The *sfumata* is the Italian name for the smoke signal whereby the result of a scrutiny in the papal conclave is announced to the outside world. The smoke (*fumo*) is either *bianca* (white) or *nera* (black) depending on whether a pope is elected or not. The initial *s* of the Italian word is a remnant of the preposition *ex* as in *ex fumo.*

Shema The Hebrew verb שמע means *to hear.* It is the first word of the main prayer of the Jews:

שמע ישראל יהוה אלוהינו יהוה אחד

Hear, O Israel, Yahweh is our God, Yahweh is one.

Shrine The Latin verb *scribo, scribere, scripsi, scriptus* means *to write,* and from it was derived the noun *scrinium* with the meaning a *case* or *box for books or papers,* a *casket* in general. The word *scrinium* became in German *der Schrein*, whence it entered English as *shrine*. Such a container might also contain bones, and these bones might be those of a saint, whence the modern meaning of the word arose.

Signatura Apostolica The noun *signum* means *mark, sign, token*, and from it were formed the diminutive noun *sigillum*, or *seal*, and the denominative verb *signo, signare, signavi, signatus*, which means *to sign or seal*. *Signatura* therefore meant *a signing or sealing*, such as by a witness to a legal document, and, by extension, the office where such signings and sealings of legal documents took place. The officials of the papal court who received petitions and appeals from Christendom and to whom the preparation of the necessary responses was referred were called *referendarii* and collectively denominated the *signatura iustitiae*, which dealt with legal disputes, and the *signatura gratiae*, which dealt with requests for exemptions and favors. They formerly met in the room, decorated by Raphael, in the Apostolic Palace of the Vatican called the *Stanza della Segnatura*, the Hall of the Signatura. Among the frescoes to be found there are paintings illustrating the publication of the Code of Civil Law under Emperor Justinian and of the Decretals under Pope Gregory IX. (The most famous of the works in the Hall, though, are the *Disputa* and the *School of Athens*.) In the reorganization of the Roman Curia by Pius X, every former entity called a *signatura* was abolished, and there was created the Signatura Apostolica under Vincenzo Cardinal Vannutelli as a sort of Supreme Court of the Catholic Church, with its headquarters in the Palace of the Cancelleria, where it remains to this day.

Sign of the Cross These four English words are the translation of the two Latin words *Signum Crucis*. It is the name of the well-known blessing made with the right hand over the front of the body, all the while saying *In nomine Patris, et Filii, et Spiritus Sancti*. The Protestants avoid the sign as a product of superstition. The Eastern Christians make the sign from right to left, the Western from left to right. As the ISIS terrorists, when rounding up arbitrary crowds of people, spare those who can recite verses from the Quran, some Yugoslav war criminals, during the Second World War, spared those who made the sign of the cross in the Western way. The clergy give their blessing in the sign of the cross. In former times, the priest was instructed in the preliminary matter to the old Roman Missal to give his blessing at Mass with his fingers joined.[21]

21. *Ritus Servandus* XII 1: "iunctisque digitis."

Simar Weekley says that this word is of unknown origin. In English, it is also spelled *cymar*. It is the outer dress of prelates outside of choir, always covered with a pellegrina, over which one wears the pectoral cross. The appearance of the simar was simplified by Pope Paul VI, who, alas, ordered the removal of the false buttoned half sleeves. It is also not an improvement to omit hooking the pectoral cross on a button and instead to wear it hanging free. Formerly the ferraiolo was invariably worn with it, but this now seems to happen only at graduations and St. Patrick's Day parades. The custom of wearing the simar became established in the nineteenth century, when it was promoted by Pius IX, whence prelates so attired were said to be dressed in the *Pian habit*.

Sin The Greek verb ἁμαρτάνω means *to miss the mark, to fail*, and from it was derived the noun ἁμαρτία, *failure, error, mistake, sin*. The word ἁμαρτάνω was used to translate the Hebrew verb חטא, which means *to miss a goal or way, to go wrong, to sin*. The Romans translated ἁμαρτάνω by the Latin verb *pecco, peccare, peccavi, peccatus*, which means *to make a mistake, to go wrong*. From it is derived the noun *peccatum*, which means an *error* or *fault*. It was translated by the Anglo-Saxon *synn*, which means *evil, wickedness*.

Sirmium The site of this ancient capital of the Roman province of Pannonia Secunda is now occupied by the city of Mitrovica, Serbia. In 357, the bishops in the entourage of Emperor Constantius, who was then at Sirmium, issued a statement that attempted a compromise solution to the Arian controversy by avoiding new technical terms. Their communiqué summarized the Arian doctrine at that time.

The document in question was not a confession of faith, but a simple theological declaration. "Some dissension having arisen in regard to the Faith, all the questions have been carefully considered and discussed, at Sirmium, in the presence of the holy bishops, our brethren, Valens, Ursacius, and Germinius. We believe that there is but One God, etc." The idea of the existence of two gods is set aside, and the terms "substance" and "essence" are repudiated; there must no longer be a question either of *homoousios* or *homoïousios*, expressions which are not in Scripture, and which, besides, presume to express in words relations which are inexpressible. The Father is greater than the Son; His attributes are described as those of the One Only God, while the Son is always placed below Him.[22]

---

22. Louis Duchesne, *Early History of the Christian Church from Its Foundation to the End of the Fifth Century*, vol. 2 (London: John Murray, 1931), 228.

These views were based upon John 14:28:

ὁ πατὴρ μείζων μού ἐστιν.

The Father is greater than I.

Cardinal Newman explained the Catholic interpretation of verses such as this as follows.

The very name of Son, and the very idea of derivation, imply a certain subordination of the Son to the Father, so far forth as we view Him as distinct from the Father, or in His personality: and frequent testimony is borne to the correctness of this inference in Scripture, as in the descriptions of the Divine Angel in the Old Testament, revived in the closing revelations of the New (Revelation VIII 3; and in such passages as that above cited from St. John's Gospel.)[23]

Sistine This English adjective comes from the Italian *sistino, -a*, which means *having to do with Sixtus*. See the following entry.

Sixtus The Greek verb ξύω means *to scrape, to smooth, to polish*, and from it was derived the adjective ξυστός with the meaning *polished*. The adjective became a proper name and is transliterated into Latin as *Xystus*; the transliteration *Sixtus* is incorrect, though sanctioned by custom. The derived Italian adjective *sistino* means *pertaining to Sixtus*; thus, the chapel built by Sixtus IV (1471–1484) in the Vatican was called the *Cappella Sistina*, the straight road built by Sixtus V (1585–1590) from the Spanish Steps to Santa Maria Maggiore was called the Via Sistina, and the Sistine Hall is the main hall of the Vatican Library built by the same pontiff. The name *Sixtus* is unrelated to the Roman proper name *Sextus*. *Sextus* became a personal name on the analogy of *Quintus*, one of the most common ancient Roman *praenomina*. The name *Sextus* would have been given originally to the sixth child, or to a child born in the sixth month (August), and then, later on, merely because it was a popular name in the family.

Snuffer The noun *snuff*, with the meaning the *wick of a candle*, is of uncertain origin. The same English word with the meaning *powdered tobacco* is of Dutch origin. *Snuffers* are instruments whereby candles are extinguished. In former times, the candles on the high altars of great churches might be several feet high, and snuffers of significant length were needed to reach the flames at the top.

23. John Henry Cardinal Newman, *The Arians of the Fourth Century*, new ed. (London: Longmans, Green, 1897), 163.

Solā Scripturā This is a Latin phrase in the ablative case that means *by scripture alone*. It refers to the dogma of the Reformers that the Bible is the sole source of doctrine, and that tradition is mostly an accumulation of corruptions and superstitions. In the Catholic Church, it is a heresy condemned by the Council of Trent, which in its fourth session put tradition on an equal footing.

Omnes libros tam Veteris quam Novi Testamenti, cum utriusque unus Deus sit auctor, nec non traditiones ipsas, tum ad fidem, tum ad mores pertinentes, tanquam vel oretenus a Christo, vel a Spiritu Sancto dictatas, et continua successione in Ecclesia catholica conservatas, pari pietatis affectu ac reverentia suscipit et veneratur.[24]

[The Most Holy and Worldwide General Council of Trent] accepts and honors all the books both of the Old and the New Testaments, since the One God is the author of each, and at the same time, with equal sentiments of religious awe and reverence, she accepts and honors the traditions themselves, whether they have to do with faith or with morals, since they come either orally from Christ or have been dictated by the Holy Ghost and preserved in the Catholic Church continuously from the beginning.

Thus, the Catholic Church hesitates to touch long-standing tradition. The higher critics undermined the doctrine *sola scriptura* among the Protestants; indeed, one of the most illustrious higher critics, Charles Augustus Briggs, was declared a heretic by the Presbyterians in a notorious trial and thereupon joined the Episcopalians.

Solemnity The Latin adjective *sollemnis* is the combination of two words, *sollus*, an Oscan form of *totus* meaning *whole*, and *annus*, which means *year*. *Sollemnis* means *that which recurs annually*. Such recurring occasions were considered especially holy. From this adjective there was formed the noun *sollemnitas* for the name of such a festivity. To spell the word with only one *l* is an early mistake on the part of the inadequately educated, who confused *sollus* with *solus*. Since the introduction of the new Roman Missal, the word is used for the highest-ranking days in the ecclesiastical calendar.

Soprana The Greek preposition ὑπέρ means *above*, and related to it is the Latin adverb and preposition *super* with the same meaning. There is also the Latin adjective *superus* meaning *situated above*, from which

24. Denzinger, *Enchiridion Symbolorum et Definitionum*, 7th ed. (Würzburg: V. J. Stahel, 1895), §666, p. 179.

is derived the adverb and preposition *supra* meaning *above, over*. From this last word comes the Italian adverb and preposition *sopra* with the same meaning, from which proceeds the noun *soprana*, an outer garment worn over one's other clothes. As a technical term, it was the name of the outer garment or cassock of seminarians being educated in Rome, each seminary having a different color soprana for its students. It is similar to the *mantellone*, but without its silk bands; it is full cut and made of wool.[25]

Soprintendente Generale delle Poste The Greek verb τείνω means *to stretch*, and the related Latin verb *tendo, tendere, tetendi, tentus* (also *tensus*) has the same meaning. The addition of the preposition *in* produced the compound verb *intendo, intendere, intendi, intentus* with the meaning *to stretch, to direct one's course toward, to apply the mind, to direct the thoughts to*. The further addition of the preposition *super* produced the Ecclesiastical Latin verb *superintendo, superintendere* meaning *to have the oversight of*. From the present participle *superintendens, superintendentis* of this verb proceeded the Italian noun *soprintendente* and the English *superintendent*. The Greek noun γένος, γένεος, *n.*, means *kind, type*, and related to it is the Latin noun *genus, generis, n.*, of the same meaning. From it was derived the adjective *generalis* with the meaning *belonging to all the members of a certain ensemble, universal*. The Latin verb *pono, ponere, posui, positus* means *to place*. Fresh horses and riders were placed at stations along the main routes for the forwarding of official messages by relay, and these places were called in Late Latin *postae*, shortened from *positae*. The position of Superintendent General of the Mail in the Papal States was hereditary in the family of the Principe Massimo, one of the oldest families of Rome. He was one of the five *camerieri segreti di spada e cappa partecipanti*.

Soul It may be assumed that everyone knows what is meant by the *body*. The soul, on the other hand, is difficult to define. Our word *soul* is the descendant of the Anglo-Saxon *sāwol, sāwl*. In each of the three biblical languages, there are two words for *soul*, and all have a connection with *breath* or *wind*.[26] The Hebrew word נֶפֶשׁ means *that which breathes*; recall that in

---

25. James-Charles Noonan Jr., *The Church Visible* (New York: Viking, 1996), 326.

26. In cases like this, the books by Girdlestone and Archbishop Trench are invaluable aids. Robert B. Girdlestone, *Synonyms of the Old Testament: Their Bearing on Christian Doctrine*, 2nd ed. (1897; repr. Grand Rapids, Mich.: Wm. B. Eerdmans, 1981); and Richard Chenevix Trench, *Synonyms of the New Testament*, 9th ed. (1880; repr. Grand Rapids, Mich.: Wm. B. Eerdmans, 1976).

Genesis 2:7, God breathes into the body to bring it to life. This word נפש is translated by ψυχή in Greek, a noun derived from the verb ψύχω, which means *to breathe*. Both נפש and ψυχή are translated by the Latin *anima*, which is connected with the Greek ἄημι, *to breathe*. The Hebrew word רוח means *breath* or *wind*; it is usually translated into Greek by πνεῦμα, which is derived from πνέω, *to blow* or *breathe*. Both רוח and πνεῦμα are usually translated by the Latin *spiritus*, from *spiro, spirare*, which means *to blow* or *breathe*.

Soutane The Latin adverb *subtus* means *below* or *under*, and the Italian preposition and adverb *sotto* is derived from it. *Soutane* is a corruption of *sotto*. *Soutane* is a synonym of *cassock*.

Spirit The Latin verb *spiro, spirare, spiravi, spiratus* means *to breathe*, and from it was derived the noun *spiritus* meaning *breath*. Thus, etymologically the soul is related to breath, though philosophers as late as Descartes identified it with the mind.

Squadrone Volante The Greek numeral τέτταρες means *four*, and related to it is the Latin numeral *quattuor* with the same meaning. Cognate with *quattuor* is the Latin noun *quadrum*, which means a *square*. From *quadrum* there were produced the Italian noun *squadra*, with the meaning a *company of soldiers in square formation*, and then the noun *squadrone*, meaning a *large company of soldiers in square formation*, whence came our *squadron*. The Latin and Italian verb *volo, volare* means *to fly*. The term *squadrone volante* or *flying squadron* was a term applied by the Spanish ambassador in the conclave of 1655 to those cardinals who declined to follow the leadership of any cardinal nephew and instead acted as free agents. This was possible because the leading adviser of Pope Innocent X (1644–1655) had been a woman, his sister-in-law Donna Olimpia Maidalchini, and not, as was usual, a nephew who had been made a cardinal.

S.R.E. This is the abbreviation for *Sanctae Romanae Ecclesiae*, "of the Holy Roman Church." It is particularly to be noticed in inscriptions and in the formal signatures of cardinals. The following inscription is taken from the façade of St. Hedwig's Cathedral on Unter den Linden in Berlin, built in the period 1747–1773 during the reign of Frederick the Great (1740–1786) for the Catholics of the capital of Prussia.

Federici Regis Clementia
Monumentum Sanctae Hedwigi
A. M. Quirinus, S. R. E. Card.
Suo Aere Perfecit.

Angelo Maria Cardinal Quirini,
Cardinal of the Holy Roman Church,
Paid with His Own Money
For This Monument to Saint Hedwig
Made Possible by the Clemency of King Frederick.

It is curious that in this case the words *S. R. E. Card.* were not placed in between *Maria* and *Quirini* in the expected idiomatic manner. If a school student had done this, it would have been marked wrong by a vigilant teacher. The reference is to Angelo Maria Cardinal Quirini (1680–1755), Benedictine scholar and bishop of Brescia.

Stabat Mater Dolorosa The rhyming sequence *Stabat Mater Dolorosa* was composed in the thirteenth century and is of unknown authorship. It is sung on September 15 in the Mass of the Seven Dolors of the Blessed Virgin Mary. The most famous musical settings are the Gregorian chant setting and those by Palestrina and Rossini.

Stabat Mater dolorosa
Iuxta Crucem lacrimosa,
Dum pendebat Filius.

Cuius animam gementem,
Contristatam et dolentem,
Pertransivit gladius.

O quam tristis et afflicta
Fuit illa benedicta
Mater Unigeniti!

Quae maerebat, et dolebat,
Pia Mater, dum videbat
Nati poenas incliti.

Quis est homo, qui non fleret,
Matrem Christi si videret
In tanto supplicio?

Quis non posset contristari,
Christi Matrem contemplari
Dolentem cum Filio?

Pro peccatis suae gentis
Vidit Iesum in tormentis,
Et flagellis subditum.

Vidit suum dulcem natum
Moriendo desolatum,
Dum emisit spiritum.

Eia Mater, fons amoris,
Me sentire vim doloris
Fac, ut tecum lugeam.

Fac, ut ardeat cor meum
In amando Christum Deum,
Ut sibi complaceam.

Sancta Mater, istud agas,
Crucifixi fige plagas
Cordi meo valide.

Tui nati vulnerati,
Tam dignati pro me pati,
Poenas mecum divide.

Fac me tecum pie flere,
Crucifixo condolere,
Donec ego vixero.

Iuxta Crucem tecum stare,
Et me tibi sociare
In planctu desiděro.

Virgo virginum praeclara,
Mihi iam non sis amara:
Fac me tecum plangere.

Fac, ut portem Christi mortem,
Passionis fac consortem,
Et plagas recolere.

Fac me plagis vulnerari,
Fac me Cruce inebriari,
Et cruore Filii.

Flammis ne urar succensus,
Per te, Virgo, sim defensus
In die iudicii.

Christe, cum sit hinc exire,
Da per Matrem me venire
Ad palmam victoriae.

Quando corpus morietur,
Fac, ut animae donetur
Paradisi gloria. Amen. Alleluia.

Most famous is the English translation of this sequence by Denis Florence MacCarthy (1817–1882):[27]

By the cross, on which suspended,
With his bleeding hands extended
Hung that Son she so adored,
Stood the mournful Mother weeping,
She whose heart, its silence keeping,
Grief had cleft as with a sword.

O, that Mother's sad affliction—
Mother of all benediction—
Of the sole-begotten One;
O, the grieving, sense-bereaving,
Of her heaving breast perceiving
The dread sufferings of her Son.

What man is there so unfeeling,
Who, his heart to pity steeling,
Could behold that sight unmoved?
Could Christ's Mother see there weeping,
See the pious Mother keeping
Vigil by the Son she loved?

For his people's sins atoning,
She saw Jesus writhing, groaning,
'Neath the scourge wherewith he bled,
Saw her loved one, her consoler,
Dying in his dreadful dolour,
Till at length his spirit fled.

O, thou Mother of election,
Fountain of all pure affection,
Make thy grief, thy pain, my own;

27. *Annus Sanctus, Hymns of the Church for the Ecclesiastical Year*, selected and arranged by Orby Shipley, M. A. (London: Burns & Oates, 1884), 1:89–90. This book is available at https://archive .org/details/AnnusSanctusV1/page/n151.

Make my heart to God returning,
In the love of Jesus burning,
Feel the fire that thou hast known.

Blessed Mother of prediction
Stamp the marks of crucifixion
Deeply on my stony heart,
Ever leading where thy bleeding
Son is pleading for my needing.
Let me in his wounds take part.

Make me truly, each day newly
While life lasts, O Mother, duly
Weep with him, the Crucified;
Let me, 'tis my sole demanding,
Near the cross, where thou art standing,
Stand in sorrow at thy side.

Queen of virgins, best and dearest,
Grant, oh, grant the prayer thou hearest.
Let me ever mourn with thee;
Let compassion me so fashion
That Christ's wounds, his death and passion,
Be each day renewed in me.

Oh, those wounds do not deny me;
On that cross, oh, crucify me;
Let me drink his blood, I pray;
Then on fire, enkindled, daring,
I may stand without despairing
On that dreadful judgment day.

May the cross be my salvation;
Make Christ's death my preservation;
May his grace my heart make wise;
And when death my body taketh,
May my soul when it awaketh
Ope in heaven its raptured eyes.

Equally noteworthy is the version by Caswall (1814–1878):[28]

At the Cross her station keeping,
Stood the mournful Mother weeping,

---

28. Edward Caswall, *Lyra Catholica: Containing All the Breviary and Missal Hymns, with Others from Various Sources* (London: Burns & Oates, 1884), 138–42.

Close to Jesus to the last.
Through her heart, his sorrow sharing,
All his bitter anguish bearing,
Now at length the sword had passed.

Oh, how sad and sore distress'd
Was that Mother highly blest
Of the sole-begotten One!
Christ above in torments hangs;
She beneath beholds the pangs
Of her dying glorious Son.

Is there one who would not weep
Whelm'd in miseries so deep
Christ's dear Mother to behold?
Can the human heart refrain
From partaking in her pain,
In that Mother's pain untold?

Bruised, derided, cursed, defiled,
She beheld her tender Child
All with bloody scourges rent;
For the sins of his own nation,
Saw him hang in desolation,
Till His Spirit forth He sent.

O thou Mother! fount of love!
Touch my spirit from above,
Make my heart with thine accord:
Make me feel as thou hast felt;
Make my soul to glow and melt
With the love of Christ my Lord.

Holy Mother! pierce me through;
In my heart each wound renew
Of my Saviour crucified:
Let me share with thee His pain,
Who for all my sins was slain,
Who for me in torments died.

Let me mingle tears with thee,
Mourning Him who mourn'd for me,
All the days that I may live:
By the Cross with thee to stay;
There with thee to weep and pray;
Is all I ask of thee to give.

Virgin of all virgins best!
Listen to my fond request:
Let me share thy grief divine;
Let me, to my latest breath,
In my body bear the death
Of that dying Son of thine.

Wounded with his every wound,
Steep my soul till it hath swoon'd
In His very blood away;
Be to me, O Virgin, nigh,
Lest in flames I burn and die,
In His awful Judgment day.

Christ, when Thou shalt call me hence,
Be thy Mother my defence,
Be Thy Cross my victory;
While my body here decays,
May my soul Thy goodness praise,
Safe in Paradise with Thee.

Station The Latin verb *sto, stare, steti, status* means *to stand*, and from it was derived the noun *statio* with the meaning *stopping place*. The word is found in the "Stations of the Cross" and in the "Stational Churches" of Rome.

Stigmata The Greek verb στίζω means *to prick, puncture,* or *brand,* and from it was derived the noun τὸ στίγμα, τοῦ στίγματος, with the meaning *a brand mark, a mark in general.* The nominative plural τὰ στίγματα is transliterated into Latin by *stigmata;* since the middle alpha in Greek is short, the word is in Latin an antepenultimate, and when taken over into English it should be pronounced *STIG-ma-ta* not *stig-MA-ta,* but the incorrect pronunciation is so common that usage prohibits it from being marked wrong anymore. The *stigmata* are the five wounds of Christ made by the four nails and the lance. The Portuguese boast that these wounds are remembered in the five white bezants inside each of the five small blue shields in the coat-of-arms on their flag.

Stoic The Greek verb ἵστημι means *to stand,* and from it was derived the noun στοά with the meaning a *place enclosed by standing pillars, a cloister.* From this noun was derived the adjective στωικός with the meaning *colonnade-like, having to do with a cloister.* Since the philosopher Zeno taught in the ποικίλη στοά or Painted Piazza, his followers were called Στωικοί or Στοϊκοί, *Stoics*. They are mentioned along with the Epicureans in Acts 17:18, where they are reported to have engaged St. Paul in conversation. The motto of the Stoic Epictetus was ἀνέχου καὶ ἀπέχου, or in Latin, *Sustine et abstine*—Endure and do without.

Stole The Greek noun στολή means a *kerchief* or *shawl*. It was merely transliterated into Latin to produce the noun *stola*, whence our English *stole*. The stole is worn by all clergy of the rank of deacon and above. Deacons wear the stole over the left shoulder, with the ends fastened on the right hip. Priests and bishops wear it around the neck.

Strepitus The Latin verb *strepo, strepere, strepui, strepitus* means *to make a loud noise*, and from the fourth principal part was derived the noun *strepitus, strepitūs, m.*, with the meaning a *loud noise*. At the end of the Tenebrae service, noise was made to simulate the convulsion of the world at the death of Christ.

Stylite The Greek noun στῦλος means a *pillar*, and the associated noun στυλίτης means *someone who lives on a pillar*. The first and most famous of such celebrities was Simeon the Stylite (died 459), of whom Butler had the following to say:

St. Simeon, to remove these causes of distraction, projected for himself a new and unprecedented manner of life. In 423 he erected a pillar six cubits high, and on it he dwelt four years; on a second, twelve cubits high, he lived three years; on a third, twenty-two cubits high, ten years; and on a fourth, forty cubits high, built for him by the people, he spent the last twenty years of his life. Thus he lived thirty-seven years on pillars, and was called Stylites, from the Greek word stylos, which signifies a pillar. This singularity was at first censured by all as a piece of extravagance. To make trial of his humility an order was sent him in the name of the neighboring bishops and abbots to quit his pillar and give up his new manner of life. The saint at once made ready to come down; but the messenger said that, as he had shown a willingness to obey, it was their desire that he should follow his vocation in God.

His pillar did not exceed six feet in diameter at the top, which made it difficult for him to lie extended on it; neither would he allow a seat. He only stooped, or leaned to take a little rest, and often in the day bowed his body in prayer.[29]

---

29. *Butler's Lives of the Saints, Complete Edition*, ed. Herbert J. Thurston, SJ, and Donald Attwater (Norwalk, Conn.: Easton Press, 1995), 1:36 (January 5). A note of Attwater to this passage reads, "A cubit was a measure of from 18 to 22 inches."

The phenomenon of the stylites persisted for over five hundred years. The details of St. Simeon's life, as well as those of St. Daniel the Stylite, next only to him in fame, may be read in the pages of Butler, the latter under December 11.

Subcinctorium The Latin verb *cingo, cingere, cinxi, cinctus* means *to surround, encircle, to gird oneself.* From it was derived the noun *cinctorium* with the meaning a *sword-belt*, a *girdle*; the addition of the preposition *sub* to this noun resulted in *subcinctorium*, the name of a vestment so called because it was fastened on the cincture as the maniple is fastened on the arm. The subcinctorium is also denominated *subcingulum*, and the corresponding Italian word is *succintorio*. It was a papal vestment, formerly used by the pope when he celebrated solemn pontifical high Mass.

Subdeacon The Greek verb διακονέω means *to serve*, and the corresponding noun διάκονος means *servant, minister*; Latin just transliterates it into *diaconus*, of which *deacon* is the corruption. The force of the preposition *sub* is to give the meaning *almost a deacon*. The dignity of subdeacon was the lowest of the major orders in the Latin Church, until it was abolished by Pope Paul VI. The Eastern Church still has subdeacons, called in Greek ὑποδιάκονοι. Since the subdeacon was required to chant the epistle at a solemn high Mass, significant education in Latin and music was required to do the job right. Innocent III decided that marriage was incompatible with the subdiaconate.[30]

Substance The Latin noun *substantia* is the literal translation of the Greek ὑπόστασις, *foundation, something standing underneath*, from the verb ὑφίστημι, *to place under. Substance* is a philosophical term used to indicate that which is the underlying determinative factor of something, everything else being accidental or secondary. With regard to the Deity, the question argued was, "What is the correct description of how the one God can be in three persons?"

The acknowledgment of Jesus as divine required the elucidation of his relation with the Father; a similar requirement followed from the acknowledgment of the Holy Ghost as divine. The Greek language used the technical terms οὐσία, πρόσωπον, and ὑπόστασις to explain the situation with precision. The first of these nouns has been taken over into English

---

30. Henry Charles Lea, *History of Sacerdotal Celibacy in the Christian Church* (n.p.: University Books, 1966), 273.

as *ousia*, and the last as *hypostasis*; the middle has escaped such adoption. The Latin language employed the nouns *essentia*, *persona*, and *substantia*, from which we derive the English words *essence*, *person*, and *substance*. The Greek ὑπόστασις is etymologically the same as the Latin *substantia*. In addition, there developed the compounds ὁμοούσιος and *consubstantialis* to meet certain needs, as will be seen below.

The Catholic doctrine of the Holy Trinity is, if expressed in the theological vocabulary of the Greek language, that there are three *hypostases* (ὑποστάσεις) in one *ousia* (οὐσία). In Latin, one says that there are three *personae* in one *essentia*.

Ut in confessione verae sempiternaeque Deitatis, et in personis proprietas, et in essentia unitas, et in maiestate adoretur aequalitas.

One can also say in Latin that there is a Trinity of one substance:

in unius Trinitate substantiae,

which, however, must be taken in the sense "in a Trinity of one being," not "in a Trinity of one hypostasis." Thus the Latins sometimes used *substantia* where the Greeks would not use ὑπόστασις, its etymological equivalent. This can lead to confusion, and I shall have more to say about the matter below.

To say that there were three persons (τρία πρόσωπα) in the godhead was not sufficient, since this might easily be misinterpreted to mean three individuals, that there were three gods. Furthermore, an actor in a Greek drama would play several parts, changing his mask in the transition from one character to another. The word for *mask* was the same as the word for *person*, πρόσωπον; thus, one might get the impression from the sole expression τρία πρόσωπα that the persons of the godhead were like three different characters played by the same actor in a play, that the godhead was unitarian. Something more was felt to be needed.

The Greeks eventually decided to describe what was shared by the three persons as οὐσία, being, and to describe what was not shared as ὑπόστασις, *hypostasis*; there were thus three hypostases but one being. However, before the time when this decision as to the choice of words was made official, the words οὐσία and ὑπόστασις had been commonly used as synonyms, and they had both been translated by the same Latin word *substantia*. This fact is clear from the New Testament itself, where *substantia* translates οὐσία in Luke 15:12 and ὑπόστασις in Hebrews 1:3:

Πάτερ, δός μοι τὸ ἐπιβάλλον μέρος τῆς οὐσίας. ὁ δὲ διεῖλεν αὐτοῖς τὸν βίον.

Pater, da mihi portionem substantiae, quae me contingit. Et divisit illis substantiam.[31]

Father, give me the part of the property that belongs to me. And he divided the property between them. (Luke 15:12)

ὃς ὢν ἀπαύγασμα τῆς δόξης καὶ χαρακτὴρ τῆς ὑποστάσεως αὐτοῦ, …

Qui cum sit splendor gloriae, et figura substantiae eius, …

Who, being the reflection of his glory and the imprint of his nature, … (Hebrews 1:3)

In the fourth century, the Latin world was established in the habit of using *substantia* where the Greek world used οὐσία. The most famous case is the Nicene Creed, where *consubstantialem Patri* was put for ὁμοούσιον τῷ Πατρὶ. The same sort of thing happened in the hymn *Summae Parens clementiae* to be found in the Roman Breviary and appointed to be sung on Trinity Sunday. The hymn speaks of God as "of one substance," which must mean "of one being"; to say "of one hypostasis" (and recall that etymologically *substantia* and ὑπόστασις are the same) would be heresy.

> Summae Parens clementiae,
> Mundi regis qui machinam,
> Unius et substantiae
> Trinusque personis Deus.
>
> O Thou eternal Source of love!
> Ruler of Nature's scheme!
> In Substance One, in Persons Three!
> Omniscient and Supreme![32]

Readers who are confused by this situation will rejoice that even the highest authorities have fumbled in their attempt to use the right word. When the Mass became English in the decade following the Second Vatican Council, the official translation of the phrase *consubstantialem Patri* in the Creed was *one in being with the Father*. This translation was true to the Greek text ὁμοούσιον τῷ Πατρὶ, but it surprised Catholics accustomed to the translation *consubstantial with the Father* formerly found in the old missals and the catechism. The official translation was revoked in 2011 and changed back to *consubstantial with the Father*.

---

31. Note that *substantia* translates both οὐσία and βίος in this verse.

32. Edward Caswall, *Lyra Catholica: Containing All the Breviary and Missal Hymns, with Others from Various Sources* (London: Burns & Oates, 1884), 109.

Suffragan The Latin verb *suffragor, suffragari*, means *to vote in favor*, and the related Latin noun *suffragium* means a *voting tablet*, a *vote*, usually a favorable one. From it was formed the Late Latin adjective *suffraganeus* with the meaning *qualified to cast a vote*, said of those bishops who were heads of dioceses in the province of the metropolitan and who therefore had the right to vote at the provincial synods.

Superstition The noun *superstitio* means a *system of unreasonable ideas*; it was used both by Pliny and by Suetonius of the Christians. For the passages, see the entries **Martyr** and **Christian**. It is derived from the Latin compound verb *supersto*, to stand (*sto*) over or upon (*super*), to be left standing, to survive. How the sense developed from being a survivor to being a sectary of a cult is unknown.

Suppedaneum The Greek noun πούς, ποδός, *m.*, means *foot*, and related to it is the Latin noun *pes, pedis, m.*, with the same meaning. The addition of the preposition *sub* (under) and the nominal suffix *-aneum* produces the compound noun *suppedaneum* meaning *that which is under the feet*.

The top step before the altar forms a platform on which the celebrant stands while he says Mass. This is the FOOTPACE (*suppedaneum, predella*).[33]

Surplice The Latin noun *pellis, pellis, f.*, means *skin, hide*, and from it is formed the adjective *pellicius*, made of skin or hide. The addition of the preposition *super* results in the adjective *superpellicius*, worn over the skin or hide, whence comes the phrase *superpellicium vestamentum*, an article of clothing worn over one's winter outfit of fur. *Superpellicium* became in French *surplice*, and in English we use the same word. The surplice is a knee-length garment of linen or silk worn over the cassock in choir. Prelates wear the rochet in its stead. Its bottom portion should be crimped, as one learns from the following episode from the life of Ronald Knox.

Those who knew him only in later life, when his clothes were barely respectable, will learn with surprise that there was a touch of the dandy about him in those days. "Slig, dear," he wrote from Manchester to F. F. Urquhart, "do you happen to know or can you find out for me, whether there is a Catholic laundry in Oxford that would iron surplices properly, i. e. in accordion pleats? If so, I hope to trade with them. My sister thinks ordinary wash people won't do it."[34]

33. Adrian Fortescue and J. B. O'Connell, *The Ceremonies of the Roman Rite Described* (Westminster, Md.: Newman Press, 1962), 27.
34. Evelyn Waugh, *Monsignor Ronald Knox, Fellow of Trinity College, Oxford and Protonotary Apostolic to His Holiness Pope Pius XII* (Boston: Little, Brown, 1959), 110.

Swiss Guard *Schwyz* is the name of a town and canton from which the name of the country Switzerland is derived. Its etymology is unknown. The Swiss, like the Hessians of the time of the American Revolution, frequently served as paid troops for foreign powers, and Pope Julius II began their uninterrupted employment in the papal service in 1505; in 1527 most of the Swiss perished as they held back the Imperial troops long enough to allow Clement VII to escape through the Passetto into the Castel Sant'Angelo. The march commonly used for the entrance of the Swiss Guard is the *Marcia Cracovia* by S. Marcellini; it will be familiar to anyone who has been present at a benediction *Urbi et Orbi*.

Syllabus This is a ghost-word that has come into existence by error, like *Sarum* or *mumpsimus*. The story is well told in the entry in the *Oxford English Dictionary*:

Syllabus Pl. **syllabi** or **syllabuses** [mod. L. *syllabus*, usually referred to an alleged Gr. σύλλαβος, *Syllabus*, appears to be founded on a corrupt reading *syllabos* in some early printed editions—the Medicean MS. has *sillabos*—of Cicero Epp. ad Atticum IV. iv, where the reading indicated as correct by comparison with the MS. readings in IV. v. and viii. is sittybas or Gr. σιττύβας. acc. pl. of sittuba, σιττύβα parchment label or title-slip on a book. (Cf. Tyrrell and Purser *Correspondence of Cicero* nos. 107, 108, 112, Comm. and Adnot.Crit.) *Syllabos* was graecized by later editors as συλλάβους, from which a spurious σύλλαβος was deduced and treated as a derivative of συλλαμβάνειν, to put together, collect (cf. Syllable).

In the passage from St. Augustine's *Confessions* XIII. XV ("ibi legunt [sc. angeli] sine syllabis temporum quid velit aeterna voluntas tua") commonly adduced as further evidence of L. syllabus, the word is clearly *syllaba*, syllable.]

Thus the use of the word *syllabus*, whether in Latin or in English, is the result of a comedy of errors, and its use in the title of the appendix to the encyclical *Quanta Cura* shows the limits of infallibility. The use of *syllabus* as an English word was already well established in the seventeenth century. It is a popular word on American college campuses.

Synod The Greek noun ἡ ὁδός means *the way*, *path*, *road*, and the addition of the preposition σύν produced the compound noun σύνοδος with the meaning a *coming together*, a *meeting*. In the Church, it is used of an assembly of clergy, especially a council of bishops.

Syriac The word Ἀσσυρία, or its shortened form Συρία, is the Greek transliteration of the Hebrew אשּׁור, a city in Mesopotamia that gave its name to a great empire. From Συρία is derived the adjective συριακός with the meaning *pertaining to Syria*, which came into Latin via transliteration as *syriacus*. In particular, the adjective refers to the branch of the Aramaic language spoken in Mesopotamia before the triumph of Arabic. No sane person undertakes the study of Syriac who has not first mastered Latin, Greek, and Hebrew.[35]

35. The best textbook for beginners is L. Palacios, *Grammatica Syriaca* (Rome: Desclée, 1954). (It is written in Latin.) Also excellent and very thorough, with an emphasis on Eastern Syriac, is Thomas Arayathinal, *Aramaic Grammar*, 2 vols. (Mannanam, India: St. Joseph's Press, 1957), which was dedicated to Cardinal Tisserant.

Tabarro The *tabarro* is the outdoor winter cloak of a clergyman; it has a cape reaching to the elbows. The etymology of the word is uncertain; it cannot be traced further back than the Middle Ages, where one finds the Latin noun *tabardum*. Cardinals used to wear red ones; the archbishops of New York, for example, would wear the red tabarro as they watched the St. Patrick's Day Parade from the steps of St. Patrick's Cathedral. Pope Paul VI outlawed this red tabarro in 1969;[1] they must now make do with black ones, which do not look right when worn over red choir dress.

Tabernacle The Latin noun *taberna* means a *booth* or *hut,* and the addition of the suffix *-culum* produces the diminutive noun *tabernaculum* meaning a *small hut* or *tent.* In the Catholic Church, it is the repository of the reserved Sacred Species.

Tanak *Tanak* is an acronym formed from the first three letters of the Hebrew words תורה, נביאים, and כתובים, which mean *Law, Prophets,* and *Writings,* that is, the three divisions of the Hebrew Bible. The books of each part of the Hebrew Bible were admitted by the Jews to canonicity at roughly the same time.

The canon of the Law was practically complete at the time of the promulgation of the Pentateuch by Ezra and Nehemiah in the year 444 B.C., and that of the Prophets in the course of the third century B.C.... A common view is that the

---

1. *Ut Sive Sollicite* (instruction of the Secretariat of State, March 31, 1969), *Acta Apostolicae Sedis* 61, no. 5 (1969), 334–40, §8. The text is also available at www.shetlersites.com/clericaldress/utsivesollicite.html.

distinct recognition of these books [the Writings] as Scripture would be not later than 100 B.C.[2]

Tantum Ergo Sacramentum These are the opening words of the last two stanzas of the hymn "Pange Lingua Gloriosi Corporis Mysterium" of St. Thomas Aquinas.

> Tantum ergo sacramentum,
> Veneremur cernui,
> Et antiquum documentum
> Novo cedat ritui.
> Praestet fides supplementum
> Sensuum defectui.
>
> Genitori genitoque
> Laus et iubilatio,
> Salus, honor, virtus quoque
> Sit et benedictio.
> Procedenti ab Utroque
> Compar sit laudatio. Amen.

The English translation by Edward Caswall (1814–1878) is the best.

> Down in adoration falling,
> Lo! The sacred Host we hail.
> Lo! O'er ancient forms departing
> Newer rites of grace prevail.
> Faith for all defects supplying
> Where the feeble senses fail.
>
> To the everlasting Father
> And the Son Who reigns on high
> With the Holy Sp'rit proceeding
> Forth from each eternally,
> Be salvation, honor, blessing
> Might and endless majesty.[3]

Te Deum Laudamus These words mean *We praise thee as God*. They are the opening words of the hymn attributed to St. Ambrose. However, speaking of Nicetas of Remesiana (c. 335–414), Duchesne wrote:

2. William Sanday, *Inspiration, Eight Lectures on the Early History and Origin of the Doctrine of Biblical Inspiration, Being the Bampton Lectures for 1893* (London: Longmans, Green, 1896), 101–2.

3. Edward Caswall, *Lyra Catholica: Containing All the Breviary and Missal Hymns, with Others from Various Sources* (London: Burns & Oates, 1884), 112.

It seems likely that there is ground for attributing to him the composition of the *Te Deum*. If so, this famous hymn which the whole of Latin Christendom chants in hours of deep emotion must have first resounded in a forgotten corner of Moesia. It is the fairest relic of the churches which flourished there in ancient times.[4]

This hymn has been set to music by many of the greatest composers.

Te Deum laudamus, Te Dominum confitemur.
Te aeternum Patrem omnis terra veneratur.
Tibi omnes angeli, tibi caeli et universae potestates,
Tibi Cherubim et Seraphim, incessabili voce proclamant:
Sanctus, Sanctus, Sanctus Dominus Deus sabaoth.
Pleni sunt caeli et terra maiestatis gloriae tuae.
Te gloriosus Apostolorum chorus, Te prophetarum laudabilis numerus,
Te martyrum candidatus laudat exercitus.
Te per orbem terrarium sancta confitetur Ecclesia.
Patrem immensae maiestatis, Venerandum tuum verum et unicum Filium,
Sanctum quoque Paraclitum Spiritum.
Tu rex gloriae, Christe. Tu Patris sempiternus es Filius.
Tu ad liberandum suscepturus hominem non horruisti Virginis uterum.
Tu, devicto mortis aculeo, aperuisti credentibus regna caelorum.
Tu ad dexteram Dei sedes, in gloria Patris.
Iudex crederis esse venturus. Te ergo quaesumus, tuis famulis subveni,
Quos pretioso sanguine redemisti.
Aeterna fac cum sanctis tuis in gloria numerari.
Salvum fac populum tuum, Domine, et benedic hereditati tuae.
Et rege eos, et extolle illos usque in aeternum.
Per singulos dies benedicimus te.
Et laudamus nomen tuum in saeculum, et in saeculum saeculi.
Dignare Domine die isto sine peccato nos custodire.
Miserere nostri, Domine, miserere nostri.
Fiat misericordia tua, Domine super nos,
Quemadmodum speravimus in te.
In te, Domine, speravi; non confundar in aeternum.

In former times, it was sung on New Year's Eve (St. Sylvester's Day) in thanksgiving for the blessings of the year then drawing to a close; the pope would attend this thanksgiving at the Church of the Gesù in Rome; this ceremony has been transferred to St. Peter's Basilica. The best translation is that of John Dryden (1631–1700), published for the first time by

---

4. Louis Duchesne, *Early History of the Christian Church from Its Foundation to the End of the Fifth Century*, vol. 3 (London: John Murray, 1924), 127.

Sir Walter Scott in 1808 in the first volume of his eighteen-volume edition
of the collected works:

> Thee, Sovereign God, our grateful accents praise;
> We own thee Lord, and bless thy wondrous ways;
> To thee, Eternal Father, earth's whole frame,
> With loudest trumpets, sounds immortal fame.
> Lord God of Hosts! For thee the heavenly powers,
> With sounding anthems, fill the vaulted towers.
> Thy Cherubims thrice Holy, Holy, Holy, cry;
> Thrice Holy, all the Seraphims reply,
> They owe their beauty to thy glorious ray.
> Thy praises fill the loud apostles' choir:
> The train of prophets in the song conspire.
> Legions of martyrs in the chorus shine,
> And vocal blood with vocal music join.
> By these thy church, inspired by heavenly art,
> Around the world maintains a second part;
> And tunes her sweetest notes, O God, to thee;
> The Father of unbounded majesty;
> The Son, adored co-partner of thy seat,
> And equal everlasting paraclete.
> Thou King of Glory, Christ, of the most high,
> Thou co-eternal filial Deity,
> Thou who, to save the world's impending doom,
> Vouchsaf'st to dwell within a virgin's womb;
> Old tyrant Death, disarmed, before thee flew
> The bolts of heaven, and back the foldings drew,
> To give access, and make thy faithful way;
> From God's right hand thy filial beams display.
> Thou art to judge the living and the dead;
> Then spare those souls for whom thy veins have bled.
> O take us up amongst thy bless'd above,
> To share with them thy everlasting love.
> Preserve, O Lord! Thy people, and enhance
> Thy blessing on thine own inheritance.
> For ever raise their hearts, and rule their ways,
> Each day we bless thee, and proclaim thy praise;
> No age shall fail to celebrate thy name,
> No hour neglect thy everlasting fame.
> Preserve our souls, O Lord, this day from ill;
> Have mercy on us, Lord, have mercy still:

As we have hoped, do thou reward our pain;
We've hoped in thee—let not our hope be vain.[5]

Temple The Greek verb τέμνω means *to cut* and is related to the noun
τέμενος, a piece of land cut off and allotted for some purpose, a piece of
land sacred to a god. The related Latin noun *templum, -i, n.*, means *a section, a part cut off, a consecrated piece of land*. Weekley says that it is "the
section of earth and sky marked out by the augur for observing the flight
of birds (cf. *contemplate*)." A Reform rabbi once told me that the best thing
that ever happened to the Jews was when the Romans destroyed their
Temple, for this cut out the cancer of animal sacrifices from their religion
forever. The Temple, he said, was a slaughterhouse, and not all the frankincense of the East could cover up the stench of the gory carcasses, nor
all the Psalms of David drown out the screams of the terrified beasts. He
would quote for support Rabbi Eliezer in the Talmud, who said, "On the
day when the Temple was destroyed, there fell an iron curtain, which had
raised itself up between Israel and their Father in Heaven."[6] However, I am
not sure that it was the welfare of the animals that concerned Rabbi Eliezer.

Temporal Power The Greek verb τέμνω means *to cut*, and related to it is
the Latin noun *tempus*, with the meaning a *portion of something*, a *portion
of time*. From this noun proceeds the adjective *temporalis* with the meaning *temporary, lasting only for a certain amount of time*; it is from this
adjective that we get our English word *temporal*. As all things of this world
are temporary, the German equivalent of *temporalis*, *weltlich*, has much
to recommend itself. The temporal power of the papacy is the sovereign
authority of the pope over territory, formerly the Pontifical States of the
Church, nowadays the Vatican City.

The religious obligations of the popes were sometimes in direct opposition to their political interests. The temporal power also enabled the
popes to gratify the inclination to nepotism. Leopold von Ranke had the
following to say when commenting on the policies of Pope Paul III vis-à-

---

5. John Dryden, *The Works of John Dryden*, ed. Walter Scott (London: William Millar, 1808),
1:343–44.

6. The Babylonian Talmud, Berakoth 32b, quoted by Leo Baeck in *The Essence of Judaism*, trans.
Victor Grubwieser and Leonard Pearl (London: Macmillan, 1936), 170. This book can be read at
https://archive.org/details/in.ernet.dli.2015.215950/page/n5. The passage in the Talmud can be found
at https://www.sefaria.org/Berakhot.32b.7?lang=b&with=al&lang2=en. It reads:

ואמר רבי אלעזר מיום שחרב בית המקדש נפסקה חומת ברזל בין ישׂראל לאביהם שבשמים:

vis the emperor Charles V at the time of the transference of the Council of Trent to Bologna:

The ecclesiastical duties of the papacy were again in direct collision with its political interests.[7]

He similarly cited the policy of Pope Urban VIII, who, at the point of the Thirty Years War when the forces of Emperor Ferdinand had triumphed on all fronts and were restoring the practice of the Catholic religion in places that had been under Protestant domination, transferred his support to the alliance of which Gustavus Adolphus of Sweden was the military genius, in order to prevent in imbalance of power in the Italian peninsula unfavorable to the independence of the Pontifical State.

Von Ranke dated the establishment of the temporal power of the popes to an event of the eighth century:

When Pepin the Younger, not content with the reality of kingly power, desired also to possess himself of the name, he felt that a higher sanction was needful. This the pope afforded him. In return, the new monarch undertook to defend "the Holy Church and the Republic of God" against the Lombards. Nor did he content himself with merely defending them. On the contrary, he compelled the Lombards to evacuate that portion of territory called the Exarchate, which they had wrenched from the Roman empire. In strict justice this should have been restored to the emperor from whom it had been taken, but when the proposal for such restoration was made to Pepin, his reply was, "That for no favour of man had he entered the strife, but from veneration to St. Peter alone, and in the hope of obtaining forgiveness for his sins." He caused the keys of the conquered towns to be placed on the altar of St. Peter, and in this act he laid the foundation of the whole temporal power of the popes.[8]

Julius II (1503–1513) enjoyed the incalculable advantage of finding opportunity for promoting the interests of his family by peaceable means; he obtained for his kindred the inheritance of Urbino. This done, he could devote himself, undisturbed by the importunities of his kindred, to the gratification of that innate love for war and conquest which was indeed the ruling passion of his life. To this he was invited by the circumstances of the times, and the consciousness of his eminent position; but his efforts were all for the Church—for the benefit of the papal see. Other popes had labored to procure principalities for their sons or their nephews:

---

7. Leopold von Ranke, *The History of the Popes during the Last Four Centuries*, trans. Mrs. Foster and G. R. Dennis (London: G. Bell & Sons, 1912), 1:201.

8. Ibid., 15.

it was the ambition of Julius to extend the dominions of the Church. He must, therefore, be regarded as the founder of the papal states.[9]

Tenebrae The plural Latin noun *tenebrae, -arum, f.*, means *darkness*. It is the name of the celebration of Matins and Lauds without intervening interruption during Holy Thursday, Good Friday, and Holy Saturday, during which the fifteen candles of a candelabrum are successively extinguished.

Terce The Latin adjective *tertius*, sometimes spelled *tercius* by the mediaeval authors, means *third*. It is the name of that hour of the Divine Office that is celebrated at the third hour of daylight, about 9 A.M.

Testament The Latin noun *testis, testis, m.*, means *witness*, and from it was derived the verb *testor, testari, testatus sum* meaning *to give evidence*. From this verb, there proceeded the noun *testamentum* with the meaning a *last will*. The corresponding Greek noun is διαθήκη, which has the additional meaning a *covenant*, and so in due course, by the time of Jerome, *testamentum* acquired this sense also. The use of the name Old Testament for the books of the Hebrew Bible was originally a term of disparagement, since it supposes the existence of a superseding New Testament.

The Books of the Law were collected first; the Prophets and Histories second, and the reason why the Book of Daniel was not included among the one and the Books of Chronicles among the other was simply that at the date when the second collection was made they had not been composed, or at least were not currently accepted in the same sense as the other books.... There is now a large amount of consent among scholars that the Canon of the Law was practically complete at the time of the promulgation of the Pentateuch by Ezra and Nehemiah in the year 444 B.C., and that of the Prophets in the course of the third century B.C. As to the closing of the Canon of the third group, the *Kethubim*, there is perhaps more room for difference of opinion. A common view is that the distinct recognition of these books as Scripture would be not later than 100 B.C. Many data seem to make this at least a *terminus ad quem*.[10]

Tetragrammaton The Greek numeral τέτταρες means *four*, and the verb γράφω means *to write*. From this verb proceeded the noun γράμμα, γράμματος, *n.*, with the meaning *anything drawn or written*, a *letter*. The adjective τετραγράμματος means *having four letters*, and in the nomina-

---

9. Ibid., 42.

10. William Sanday, *Inspiration, Eight Lectures on the Early History and Origin of the Doctrine of Biblical Inspiration, Being the Bampton Lectures for 1893* (London: Longmans, Green, 1896), 101–2.

tive case, neuter singular, it is used as a noun, τὸ τετραγράμματον, meaning *the four-letter word*, namely יהוה, the ineffable, that is, not to be spoken, personal name of God Almighty. See the entry **Jehovah**.

Tetrarch The Greek numeral τέτταρες means *four*, and the verb ἄρχω means *to rule*, and from them arose the noun τετράρχης, *tetrarch*. A *tetrarch* was originally a fellow who ruled one-fourth of a domain, or ruled in conjunction with three other authorities. The domain of a tetrarch was a τετραρχία, or *tetrarchy*. The connection with four eventually weakened, and the noun *tetrarch* eventually came to be applied to minor potentates like Herod Antipas, tetrarch of Galilee, who was actually one of three heirs of Herod the Great. A real government by tetrarchy was introduced into the Roman Empire in the late third century by the emperor Diocletian, who decided that the Empire was too big for one man to control, and that it would be more easily governed by two emperors (*Augusti*) and two subordinates (*Caesares*), one of each in the East and one of each in the West. Procopius, a reader at Scythopolis, thought it wrong that there should be four emperors, and quoted to the audience a verse from Homer, in which *monarchy* was commended.[11] In the system of Diocletian, the eastern emperor lived at Nicomedia and his deputy, the eastern Caesar, at Sirmium; the western emperor was stationed at Milan, and his deputy Caesar at Trier.

Theatine The Italian city Chieti in the Abruzzi was called in ancient times *Teate*, and its inhabitants, *teatini*. The Greeks called the place Θεάτη, whence we have the letter *h*. Giovanni Pietro Caraffa (later Pope Paul IV), at that time archbishop of Chieti, together with Gaetano da Teano, founded in 1524 the order of the Theatines.

Thus, these two men agreed in their desire for seclusion; the one from an instinct of his nature; the other impelled by yearnings after an ideal perfection; both were disposed to religious activity and, convinced that reform was needed, they combined to found an institution (since called the Order of Theatines), having for its objects at once the reformation of the clergy and a life of contemplation.[12]

---

11. Louis Duchesne, *Early History of the Christian Church from Its Foundation to the End of the Fifth Century*, vol. 2 (London: John Murray, 1931), 33–34. The allusion is to Homer, *The Iliad*, 2.204–5. See the entry **Bishop**.

12. Leopold von Ranke, *The History of the Popes during the Last Four Centuries*, trans. Mrs. Foster and G. R. Dennis (London: G. Bell & Sons, 1912), 1:137.

Theism The Greek noun θεός means *god*, and the suffix *-ism* is the transliteration of the stem of the Greek suffix -ισμός, which forms nouns of action from verbs ending in -ίζειν. *Theism* is a word first found in the sixteenth century and used to denote belief in a god; therefore both Catholics and deists are theists. Learned after-dinner discussion of the main issues involving Theism was the purpose of two famous London clubs in the Victorian era. In 1869, William George Ward joined Dean Church, James Anthony Froude, William E. Gladstone, R. H. Hutton, Thomas Henry Huxley, Archbishop Manning, James Martineau, John Morley, John Ruskin, Henry Sidgwick, Dean Stanley, Lord Tennyson, and many other eminent British thinkers of the time to found the Metaphysical Society, whose purpose was "to bring together in friendly and free debate on the fundamental problems of man's life and destiny representatives of all the various schools of opinion which made up the world of thought at the time of its foundation."[13] In the next generation (1896), Wilfrid Ward, son and biographer of William George Ward, joined Arthur Balfour, J. A. Bryce, G. K. Chesterton, Baron Friedrich von Hügel, R. H. Hutton, Sir Richard Jebb, James Martineau, Dean Armitage Robinson, Henry Sidgwick, Father Tyrrell, George Wyndham, and others to found the Synthetic Society, the successor to the Metaphysical Society; its purpose was to discuss whether there was a unifying principle in the world. Wilfrid Ward taught "the necessity of some form of Theism to explain the facts of man's ethical nature."[14] John Stuart Mill (1806–1873) wrote a famous essay "Theism," in which he concluded that the probabilities favored the existence of God, but that God was not sufficiently powerful to remove all evil from the world. He had been invited to join the Metaphysical Society by his friend William George Ward but declined because he felt too old to engage in verbal discussion.

Theodicy The Greek noun θεός means *god*, and the noun δίκη means *custom, usage, right,* for in primitive, unsophisticated times that which was customary was right. By compounding these words Leibniz produced in 1710 the noun *Théodicée* (whence our *theodicy*) with the meaning, the *justification of the ways of God to men.*

---

13. Wilfrid Ward, *William George Ward and the Catholic Revival* (London: Macmillan, 1893), 297. Chapter 12 gives an account of the Metaphysical Society.

14. Maisie Ward, *The Wilfrid Wards and the Transition,* vol. 1, *The Nineteenth Century* (New York: Sheed & Ward, 1934), 375.

Taking the Book of Job as a whole, it might be urged that it struggles with a problem to which it does not furnish a completely satisfactory or final solution. The prosperity of the wicked and unmerited suffering of the righteous was a stone of stumbling to the Hebrew mind. It is repeatedly coming up, as in the didactic Psalms to which reference has been made, but nowhere is there such a sustained attempt to grapple with it as here in the Book of Job. And even here only once, and that obscurely and almost doubtfully, does the argument pierce through to that belief in a future life which gives the best answer to Job's perplexities.[15]

Theodotians The Greek proper name Θεόδοτος means *God-given*. Theodotus of Byzantium was a heretic of the second century whose follows were denominated *Theodotians*.

According to him, Jesus, except for his miraculous birth, was a man like other men. He grew up under ordinary conditions, manifesting a very high degree of sanctity. At His baptism, on the banks of the Jordan, the Christ, otherwise called the Holy Ghost, descended upon Him in the form of a dove: He thus received the power to work miracles. But He did not thus become God, and according to the Theodotians, this prerogative only became His after His resurrection, and only a section of them conceded even so much.[16]

Theology The Greek noun θεολογία is the compound of the noun θεός and the suffix -λογία; it means *talk about God*. The suffix is derived from the verb λέγω, to speak.

Theopaschite The Greek noun θεός means *God*, and the verb πάσχω means *to suffer*. From the concatenation of these two words was produced the adjective *theopaschite*, which means *believing that God suffered*. It was a doctrine rejected by the Nestorians, favored by the Monophysites, and confirmed by Pope John II (533–535). It was suggested by the emperor Justinian to Catholics and Monophysites in an attempt to make a formula of conciliation acceptable to both sides.[17]

Theotokos The Greek noun θέος means *God*, and the verb τίκτω means *to bear*, and their concatenation produced the adjective θεοτόκος with the meaning *God-bearing*. Its application to the Virgin Mary in the early fourth century aroused the indignation of Nestorius, patriarch of Con-

---

15. William Sanday, *Inspiration, Eight Lectures on the Early History and Origin of the Doctrine of Biblical Inspiration, Being the Bampton Lectures for 1893* (London: Longmans, Green, 1896), 204–5.

16. Louis Duchesne, *Early History of the Christian Church from Its Foundation to the End of the Third Century* (London: John Murray, 1914), 217.

17. See J. B. Bury, *History of the Later Roman Empire* (New York: Dover, 1958), 2:376.

stantinople, who opposed it as an anthropomorphic term not to be found in scripture. The result was an international controversy resulting in the Third Ecumenical Council at Ephesus in 431, where Nestorius was condemned and the appellation in question was approved. The corresponding Latin term is *Deipăra* from the compounding of *Deus* (God) and *pario, parere* (to bear).

The Three Chapters The Greek nouns κεφαλή and κεφάλαιον both mean *head*, and the latter noun acquired the meaning of *chapter*, because such a section of a book was begun with a title at its head. See the entry **Chapter**. *The Three Chapters* (τὰ τρία κεφάλαια) were a list of quotations from three authors compiled circa 543 by the emperor Justinian for the purpose of having those passages and their authors condemned. The first chapter contained statements from the writings of Theodore of Mopsuestia (c. 350–428), the second chapter from the writings of Theodoret, bishop of Cyrrhus (c. 393–458), and the third chapter from a letter of Ibas, bishop of Edessa (died 457). Since all three of these authorities had been acknowledged as Catholics by Leo the Great and the Council of Chalcedon (in fact, Theodoret had even attended that council), Pope Vigilius (537–555) and the Latin West hesitated to anathematize them. In fact, the papal legates at the Council of Chalcedon had read the aforementioned letter of Ibas and declared:

Ἀναγνωσθείσης γὰρ τῆς ἐπιστολῆς αὐτοῦ ἐπέγνωμεν αὐτὸν ὑπάρχειν ὀρθόδοξον.

Having read his letter, we came to the conclusion that he is Orthodox.[18]

It would be a problem for one ecumenical council to condemn someone whom a previous ecumenical council and the Roman pontiff had declared orthodox. There was the additional problem that they had all been dead for over a century, and they had died in the bosom of the Church. Nevertheless, the Imperial Majesty wanted them condemned, perhaps at the instigation of his wife, the empress Theodora, who wanted to appease, it seems, the irritation of the Monophysites, who had a low opinion of the Council of Chalcedon. Vigilius was carried off to Constantinople and forced to reverse his former teaching on the matter and accept the anathematization of the three bishops in question. Gibbon wrote of the dispute about the Three Chapters, that it "has filled more volumes than it deserves lines."

18. Louis Duchesne, *Early History of the Christian Church from Its Foundation to the End of the Fifth Century*, vol. 3 (London: John Murray, 1924), 309n2.

Under the cover of this precedent a treacherous blow was aimed at the Council of Chalcedon. The fathers had listened without impatience to the praise of Theodore of Mopsuestia; and their justice or indulgence had restored both Theodoret of Cyrrhus and Ibas of Edessa to the communion of the church. But the characters of these Oriental bishops were tainted with the reproach of heresy; the first had been the master, the two others were the friends, of Nestorius: their most suspicious passages were accused under the title of the *three chapters*; and the condemnation of their memory must involve the honour of a synod whose name was pronounced with sincere or affected reverence by the Catholic world. If these bishops, whether innocent or guilty, were annihilated in the sleep of death, they would not probably be awakened by the clamour which, after a hundred years, was raised over their grave. If they were already in the fangs of the demon, their torments could neither be aggravated nor assuaged by human industry. If in the company of saints and angels they enjoyed the rewards of piety, they must have smiled at the idle fury of the theological insects who still crawled on the surface of the earth. The foremost of these insects, the emperor of the Romans, darted his sting, and distilled his venom, perhaps without discerning the true motives of Theodora and her ecclesiastical faction. The victims were no longer subject to his power, and the vehement style of his edicts could only proclaim their damnation, and invite the clergy of the East to join in a full chorus of curses and anathemas. The East, with some hesitation, consented to the voice of her sovereign: the fifth general council, of three patriarchs and one hundred and sixty-five bishops, was held at Constantinople; and the authors, as well as the defenders of the three chapters, were separated from the communion of the saints, and solemnly delivered to the prince of darkness. But the Latin churches were more jealous of the honour of Leo and the synod of Chalcedon; and if they had fought as they usually did under the standard of Rome, they might have prevailed in the cause of reason and humanity. But their chief was a prisoner in the hands of the enemy; the throne of St. Peter, which had been disgraced by the simony, was betrayed by the cowardice, of Vigilius, who yielded, after a long and inconsistent struggle, to the despotism of Justinian and the sophistry of the Greeks.[19]

Throne The Greek noun θρόνος means a *seat* or *chair*. It acquired the sense of the *chair of a judge or teacher*, and then of a sovereign, whether secular or religious. In this latter sense it was transliterated into the Latin *thronus*, whence we get our English word *throne*. Nowadays, in speaking of the bishop's *cathedra*, we are admonished to avoid the word *throne*, as it smacks of ostentation.

19. Edward Gibbon, chapter 47 of *The History of the Decline and Fall of the Roman Empire*, ed. Betty Radice (London: The Folio Society, 1995), 6:56–57.

Thurible The Greek verb θύω means *to sacrifice*, and from it is derived the noun τὸ θύος, τοῦ θύεος, *n.*, meaning a *burnt sacrifice*, and later *incense, fragrant stuffs*. The proper Greek noun for *incense* is θυμίαμα, and the proper word for fragrant stuffs is its plural, θυμιάματα. The noun θύος was taken over into Latin as *tus, turis, n.*, with the meaning *incense, frankincense*, and from it was derived the noun *turibulum* meaning a *vessel in which one burned incense*, from which word descends our noun *thurible*. The thurible contains hot coals on which the celebrant sprinkles incense from a boat, the *navicula*, with a spoon. English retains the Greek theta by inserting an *h* after the *t*; this is a possibility also in Latin. The biggest thurible in current use is the enormous *botafumeiro* of the cathedral of Santiago da Compostela in Spain, well known to those who undertake the pilgrimage to St. James.

Thurifer The Latin noun *tus, turis, n.*, means *incense*, and the verb *fero, ferre, tuli, latus* means *to bear*. From their concatenation is produced the adjective *turifer, turifera, turiferum* meaning *incense-bearing*. The masculine form is also a noun, the *thurifer*, who is the acolyte who carries with his right hand the thurible on a chain and with his left hand the *navicula* filled with incense.

Tiara This word is the Latin transliteration of the Greek noun τιάρα, τιάρας, which was originally a Persian word for the name of a headdress worn by the Persian king. The tiara is the triple crown used by the popes from the fourteenth century until it was set aside by Paul VI, who used it for only a few years. Of its origin, Gregorovius had the following to say:

For this haughty Pope [Boniface VIII] was the first to adopt the double crown, all his predecessors had used only the simple miter. Later, Urban V added a third crown to these.[20]

It remains the symbol of papal power and is traditionally flanked by the crossed keys of St. Peter. The last coronation with the tiara was that of Paul VI in 1963, when Cardinal Ottaviani pronounced the formula:

Accipe tiaram tribus coronis ornatam, et scias te esse patrem principum et regum, rectorem Orbis, in terra vicarium Salvatoris nostri, cui est honor et gloria in saecula saeculorum.

---

20. Ferdinand Gregorovius, *The Tombs of the Popes, Landmarks in the History of the Papacy*, trans. Mrs. L. W. Terry (Rome: Victoria Home, 1895), 90.

Receive the tiara adorned with three crowns, and know that thou art the father of princes and of kings, the ruler of the world, the vicar on earth of our savior, to whom are honor and glory forever and ever.

Tintinnabulum The Latin verb *tinnio, tinnire* means *to ring* or *tinkle*, and the duplication of the stem produced the verb *tintinno, tintinnare* with the meaning *to ring* or *jingle*. From this latter verb there proceeded the noun *tintinnabulum* meaning a *little bell*. The tintinnabulum is a bell formerly used to alert the populace to the approach of the Roman pontiff. It became a necessary implement at basilicas. A similar bell should be rung to alert the people to the approach of the Most Holy in processions, whether indoor or outdoor. Indeed, if there is no umbrella or canopy over the monstrance, it is difficult to see where the priest carrying the host is.

Titular The Latin noun *titulus* means *inscription* or *label*. Thus, the sign put on the cross of Christ by order of Pilate, which read *Iesus Nazarenus Rex Iudaeorum*, was called in Latin a *titulus*. The Late Latin adjective *titularis* means *holding a title*, even one purely honorary.

Toleration The Latin verb *tollo, tollere, sustuli, sublatus* means *to take up*, and from it is derived the verb *tolero, tolerare, toleravi, toleratus* with the meaning *to carry, to support*. From the fourth principal part of this latter verb comes the noun *toleratio, tolerationis, f.*, with the meaning an *enduring*, from which we derive our noun *toleration*. Toleration is the policy whereby contradictory opinions are allowed to be maintained without penalty.

We can form some idea of the extent of this toleration, when we consider that it was permissible to side either with Philo, or with Akiba, to believe either in the resurrection of the dead, or in absolute annihilation, to look forward to the Messianic hope or to scoff at it, to philosophize like Ecclesiastes, or like the Wisdom of Solomon, etc.[21]

Tolle Lege St. Augustine, at the moment of his conversion, heard a voice commanding him, *Tolle, lege*—"Pick up and read!"[22] He thereupon took up the open Bible that he had put down where his friend Alypius was sitting and read the first verses that came to his attention, Romans 13:13–14:

---

21. Louis Duchesne, *Early History of the Christian Church from Its Foundation to the End of the Third Century* (London: John Murray, 1914), 89n2.

22. *Confessions*, 8.26–30.

Non in comessationibus, et ebrietatibus, non in cubilibus, et impudicitiis, non in contentione, et aemulatione: sed induimini Dominum Iesum Christum, et carnis curam ne feceritis in desideriis.

Not in rioting and drunkenness, not in chambering and impurities, not in contention and envy, but put ye on the Lord Jesus Christ, and make not provision for the flesh in its concupiscences.

Tome of Pope Leo The Greek verb τέμνω means *to cut,* and from it was derived the noun τόμος with the meaning a *slice,* a *piece cut off,* a *part of a book rolled up by itself,* a *section,* a *roll of papyrus,* a *volume.* If the thing being cut was a tree, the stump that was left was called the τομή and the piece cut off the τόμος. The Latin language transliterated τόμος into *tomus,* from which we get our English word *tome;* in the Catholic vocabulary *tome* is used of an authoritative pontifical communication. The *Tome of Pope Leo* was a letter from Pope Leo the Great to Patriarch Flavian of Constantinople, which was accepted by the Council of Chalcedon as the teaching of the Catholic Church with regard to the Second Person of the Trinity.

The doctrine of the Incarnation is there expressed in terms simple and precise: Two Natures, in the unity of a single Person; two true Natures, capable of action and each acting on its own account, in agreement of course, and in co-operation.[23]

Tone (of a Lesson, of Prayers) The Greek verb τείνω means *to stretch* or *strain,* and derived from it is the noun τόνος with the meaning *that which strains and tightens a thing,* a *tone* or *note.* The same word exists in Latin, *tonus, -i, m.,* with the same meaning. In Gregorian chant, the word is used of any one of the various melodies to which the verses of a psalm or canticle or other passage from scripture are sung.

Tonsure The Latin verb *tondeo, tondere, totondi, tonsus* means to *shave,* whence came the noun *tonsura,* a *shaving.* The tonsure was the shaving of the crown of the head; it indicated one's admittance to the clerical state. The practice of tonsuring was abolished by Pope Paul VI in the motu proprio *Ministeria Quaedam* of August 15, 1972.[24]

---

23. Louis Duchesne, *Early History of the Christian Church from Its Foundation to the End of the Fifth Century,* vol. 3 (London: John Murray, 1924), 286. Duchesne offers in a note (286n5) the original Latin of a passage from the letter: "*In integra veri hominis perfectaque natura verus natus est Deus, totus in suis, totus in nostris.... Agit utraque forma (forma Dei, forma servi) cum alterius communione quod proprium est.*"

24. *Ministeria Quaedam* (motu proprio of Pope Paul VI, August 15, 1972), *Acta Apostolicae Sedis* 64

Tourist The Greek noun τόρνος means a *lathe*, and it was transliterated into the Latin language as *tornus*. From *tornus* came the verb *torno*, *tornare* meaning *to turn on the lathe*, whence proceeded the French verb *tourner* with the meaning *to turn* and the French masculine noun *tour*, a *turn*. The English noun *tourist* made its appearance, according to Weekley, around 1800 and was applied to a gentleman who completed his education by seeing the sites of Italy, France, Germany, and Switzerland.

Tradition The Latin verb *do, dare, dedi, datus* means *to give*, and the preposition *trans* means *across* or *over*. The resulting compound verb *trado*, *tradere, tradidi, traditus* means *to hand over, to betray*. The related noun *traditio, -onis, f.*, means *surrender*. Bacci says that the full Latin equivalent of the English *tradition* is *memoriae a maioribus traditae*. Tradition is one of the two fountains of Catholic doctrine, the other being the holy scriptures. Of those two sources the Council of Trent wrote that the Church "*pari pietatis affectu suscipit et veneratur*," accepts and respects them with equal sentiments of reverence. (See the entry **Solā Scripturā**.)

Traditional The Late Latin adjective *traditionalis* was formed from the noun *traditio, traditionis, f.*, by the addition of the adjectival suffix *-alis*. From it is derived the English *tradition*. In the times after the Second Vatican Council, this adjective has been commonly applied to Catholics displeased by the liturgical changes.

Traditores The Latin verb *trado, tradere, tradidi, traditus* means *to hand over*, and the related noun of action *traditor* means *traitor*. The Circumcellions called *traditores*, traitors, all Christians who lapsed during a persecution.

Train The Latin verb *traho, trahere, traxi, tractus* means *to draw*, and Weekley writes that Vulgar Latin derived from this verb the word *tragino*, *traginare* with the meaning *to trail* or *drag along the ground*. A corruption of this verb, *traino, trainare*, entered the Italian language with the meaning *to drag* or *haul*; the English noun *train* is related to this verb, probably through the medium of Old French. It is the name of the skirts of a vestment, such as the *cappa magna*. The train of the *cappa magna* of a cardinal was five meters long; Pius XII shortened this to three meters in 1946.

(1972): 529–34, section 1. The text is also available at http://w2.vatican.va/content/paul-vi/la/motu_proprio/documents/hf_p-vi_motu-proprio_19720815_ministeria-quaedam.html.

Train-Bearer This is the English translation of the Latin *caudatarius*. The train bearer holds up the skirts of vestments like the *falda* and *cappa magna*, which would otherwise render the dignitary wearing them immobile. See the entry **Caudatarius**.

Transfiguration *Transfiguratio* is the Latin translation of the Greek μεταμόρφωσις, whose transliteration is *metamorphosis*. It means a *change* (for such is the force of the prefixed preposition μετά) *of appearance* (μορφή). In the Catholic Church it is used of the event related in Matthew 17:1–13, Mark 9:2–13, and Luke 9:28–36.

Translation The Latin verb *fero, ferre, tuli, latus* means *to carry*, and the preposition *trans* means *across*. Their combination produced the compound verb *transfero, transferre, transtuli, translatus* meaning *to carry across, to translate from one language to another*. From the fourth principal part of this verb comes the noun *translatio* with the meaning *a removal from one place to another, a translation*. When it was determined to revise the King James Version of the Bible, Theodore Dwight Woolsey (1801–1889), chairman of the American New Testament Committee and ex-president of Yale University, had the following to say:

We would here guard against a wrong inference which might be drawn from our remarks, as if in a translation for the nineteenth century the words most in use in the century, and most familiar to the ears of the people, ought always to take the place of others less in use, which, however, retain their place in the language. This is far from being a safe rule. One of the most important impressions which the Word of God makes is made by its venerableness. The dignity and sanctity of the truth are supported by the elevation of the style, and woe to the translator who should seek to vulgarize the Bible, on the plea of rendering it more intelligible. Understood it must be, and this must be provided for by removing the ambiguities and obscurities to which changes in society and changes in the expression of thought give rise. But as long as the English is a living tongue, the style of the scriptures must be majestic, and removed from all vulgarity. Indeed, it must be such as it is now, with those exceptions, few in number, which time brings with it, and most of which will hardly be noticed by the cursory reader.[25]

Another one of the revisers, A. B. Davidson (1831–1902), professor of Hebrew, New College, Edinburgh commented on the same topic:

25. Theodore Dwight Woolsey, "Reasons for a New Revision of the Scriptures in English," in *Anglo-American Bible Revision*, by members of the American Revision Committee (New York: American Sunday School Union, 1879), 45.

The antique cast of style must be retained. Nothing that is not absolutely wrong, or not absolutely out of use, should be removed. The modern vocabulary, and the modern order of words, and the modern cast of sentence must be avoided. Any change of familiar passages will grate on the ear, and even on the heart, of the devout reader.[26]

The result of their work was the Revised Version of the Bible, which appeared in 1881 (Old Testament) and 1885 (New Testament). Another point of view was that to be discovered in the literary principle of the Roman Consilium, which in a different but not altogether unrelated enterprise, the translation of the Roman Missal, set the following guideline:

The language chosen should be that in "common" usage, that is, suited to the greater number of the faithful who speak it in everyday use, even "children and persons of small education".[27]

Transubstantiation Transubstantiation is the preeminent doctrine of the Catholic Church, whereby it is distinguished from all other Christian denominations. It is

The conversion of the substance of bread and wine into the substance of the body of Christ, whilst its appearance remains unaltered. The distinction between substance and accident that this entails formed one of the main stimuli to scholastic metaphysical thought.[28]

Transubstantio was an original Mediaeval Latin technical term, not a mere Latin translation of a Greek word. It was formed by the compounding of the preposition *trans*, meaning *across*, and the noun *substantia*; see the entry **Substance**.

Tridentine The Latin numerical adjective *tres* means *three*, and the noun *dens, dentis, m.*, means *tooth*; from these words was formed the adjective *tridens, tridentis* meaning *having three teeth*. This adjective was also used as a noun with the meaning *trident*, the symbol of the god Neptune. Our *Trent* is the corruption of the Latin *Tridentum*, the name of the city in

---

26. Andrew Bruce Davidson, "The Bible and Its Revision" in *Biblical and Literary Essays*, 2nd ed., ed. J. A. Paterson (London: Hodder & Stoughton, 1903), 210.

27. *Comme le prévoit* (instruction of the *Consilium ad Exsequendam Constitutionem de Sacra Liturgia*, January 25, 1969), *Notitiae* 5 (1969), 3–12. The official English translation can be read at http://www.natcath.org/NCR_Online/documents/comme.htm. The quotation is from the allocution of Pope Paul VI of November 11, 1965.

28. Simon Blackburn, *The Oxford Dictionary of Philosophy* (Oxford: Oxford University Press, 1994), 381a.

the south Tyrol. The city was so named, in honor of the god Neptune, because of its location in the vicinity of three peaks. The adjective *Tridentinus, -a, -um* means *belonging to Tridentum*. The adjective *Tridentine* is correctly accented in English either on the first or on the second syllable.[29] Words must be accented on the syllable that allows them to be understood when spoken. Disputes about correct accentuation, like all points of usage, should be settled by the practice of the best authors and speakers. Should, however, a pronunciation that is wrong be universally adopted, then the matter is thereby settled according to the principle *vox populi, vox Dei*. Thus the word *senator* is properly accented in English on the first syllable, though in Latin it is accented on the second syllable; if it were to be pronounced nowadays as it always should have been, it would not be understood.

Trent was the location of the ecumenical council that convened on December 13, 1545, at the command of Pope Paul III. This council called for a revision of the Roman Missal, an enterprise that was accomplished by Pius V in 1570, who issued an edition of the *Missale Romanum* to which the preface was the bull *Quo Primum*. For this reason, the word *Tridentine* is also a commonly used adjective for the old Latin Mass celebrated in the Catholic Church before the reform of the liturgy that followed the Second Vatican Council. In this sense, it was not originally a phrase used by the learned.

There are three great works on the Council of Trent. The modern four-volume history of Hubert Jedin, SJ, is definitive; the first two volumes were translated into English with the title *History of the Council of Trent*. The author worked in the Vatican during the Hitler time because he had a Jewish mother. A great classic is the history of Fr. Paolo Sarpi, *Istoria del Concilio Tridentino* (published anonymously in 1619); the 1620 translation by Nathaniel Brent made a sensation in England. Sarpi's history called forth the rebuttal *Istoria del Concilio di Trento* of Pietro Sforza Pallavicino in two magnificent and immense quarto volumes in 1656.

Triduum This neuter Latin noun of the second declension means *a period of three days*. It is used in the Church for the ceremonies of Holy Thursday, Good Friday, and the Easter vigil.

---

29. The *Oxford English Dictionary* allows both; it lists the former possibility first.

Trinity The Latin adjective *trini, -ae, -a* means *three at a time* or *three to-gether*, and from it is derived the Christian noun *trinitas, -atis, f.*, the name for the triune God. The Trinity is mentioned by Christ in Matthew 28:19:

πορευθέντες οὖν μαθητεύσατε πάντα τὰ ἔθνη, βαπτίζοντες αὐτοὺς εἰς τὸ ὄνομα τοῦ πατρὸς καὶ τοῦ υἱοῦ καὶ τοῦ ἁγίου πνεύματος.

Euntes ergo docete omnes gentes, baptizantes eos in nomine Patris et Filii et Spiritus Sancti.

Go ye therefore, and teach all nations, baptizing them in the name of the Father, and of the Son, and of the Holy Ghost. (Authorized Version)

In his discussion of the Council of Sardica (343), Duchesne wrote:

Besides these questions of individuals, the Council also wished, after the example of the Council of Nicaea, and as the Eastern prelates had just done [at Antioch], to draw up a profession of faith. With this intention, a composition of considerable length was prepared, which, for the most part, either justified or disguised certain ideas for which Marcellus had been blamed, and which affirmed the unity of hypostasis, this word being taken, be it understood, in the sense of its Latin equivalent *substantia*.[30] Hosius and Protogenes, who approved of this rather tenuous creed, had even prepared a letter to Pope Julius, to induce him to give it his approval. However, the proposal miscarried. The council was made to understand, and Athanasius seems to have exerted himself strongly to this end, that there was already quite sufficient difficulty in maintaining the Creed of Nicaea, without complicating it with appendices, which would only increase the centers of opposition to it; and that therefore it was much better to keep to the text unanimously adopted by that venerable assembly, and not to imitate the opposing party, who every year brought out a new creed.

Athanasius was quite right, as the sequel showed. The Nicene Council, inspired solely by the desire to save the absolute Divinity of Christ, had accepted the Western *homoousios*, which really safeguarded the point assailed, but gave no explanation of the personality of the preexisting Christ. Such a formula was incomplete in itself; it was necessary to supplement it by that of the Three Persons. This latter dogma the Western Bishops at Nicaea may have held in the spirit: Tertullian and Novatian speak unhesitatingly of the *tres personae*. But it had not been introduced into the Creed of Nicaea; and, besides, the word persona, πρόσωπον in Greek, was not sufficiently explicit. *Persona* has undoubtedly the sense of ratio-

30. [Note of Duchesne]: For people who translated ὁμοούσιος by *consubstantialis*, the terms οὐσία and ὑπόστασις were equivalent. We must note carefully that the word *essentia*, by which we translate οὐσία, was not at that time in use; that, for the two Greek words οὐσία and ὑπόστασις, there was but one Latin term, *substantia*. We can therefore understand the Council of Sardica being tempted to pass from the "consubstantial" to the unity of hypostasis.

nal individuality, but it equally well signifies a character, a mask, a personage. The most orthodox among the Easterns clung to a greater precision of language. This they expressed by the term *hypostasis*, which was itself inadequate, for its proper meaning is substance, and, when one speaks of the three divine hypostases, one has the appearance at first of speaking of three divine substances, of three gods. However, without really comprehending what they were trying to explain—and how can anyone comprehend such relations in the Infinite Being?—they ended by acknowledging the one essence and the three hypostases of the Easterns. It was finally agreed that that which, in the Trinity, was common to the Father, to the Son, and to the Holy Spirit, should be called "essence" (οὐσία), and that which was proper to each of them should be designated by the terms "hypostasis" or "Person". But, at the time of which we are now writing, that solution was still far off. It would certainly have been compromised, if the Council of Sardica had prejudiced it by proscribing the three hypostases. It was a wise inspiration on the part of Athanasius to oppose such a declaration.[31]

On the subject of the Holy Trinity, Cardinal Newman wrote:

Language then requires to be refashioned even for sciences which are based on the senses and the reason; but much more will this be the case, when we are concerned with subject-matters of which, in our present state, we cannot possibly form any complete or consistent conception, such as the Catholic doctrines of the Trinity and Incarnation. Since they are from the nature of the case above our intellectual reach, and were unknown until the preaching of Christianity, they required on their first promulgation new words, or words used in new senses, for their due enunciation; and, since these were not definitely supplied by Scripture or by tradition, nor, for centuries, by ecclesiastical authority, variety in the use, and confusion in the apprehension of them, were unavoidable in the interval....

Moreover, there is a presumption equally strong, that the variety and confusion that I have anticipated, would in matter of fact issue here or there in actual heterodoxy, as often as the language of theologians was misunderstood by hearers or readers, and deductions were made from it which the teacher did not intend. Thus, for instance, the word *Person*, used in the doctrine of the Holy Trinity, would on first hearing suggest Tritheism to one who made the word synonymous with *individual*; and Unitarianism to another, who accepted it in the classical sense of a *mask* or *character*.[32]

Trisagion The Greek adverb τρίς means *three times*; it is the adverb of the numeral τρεῖς. The verb ἅζομαι means *to stand in awe of*. From it

---

31. Louis Duchesne, *Early History of the Christian Church from Its Foundation to the End of the Fifth Century*, vol. 2 (London: John Murray, 1931), 176–77.

32. John Henry Cardinal Newman, *The Arians of the Fourth Century*, new ed. (London: Longmans, Green, 1897), 433.

are derived the noun τὸ ἄγος, which denoted any matter of religious law, and the adjective ἄγιος, *devoted to the gods*. According to Duchesne, the acclamation known as the *Trisagion*—τὸ τρισάγιον—was first to be heard at the Council of Chalcedon in 451.[33] It is part of the Improperia of the Good Friday service:

> Hágios o Theós.
> Sanctus Deus.
> Hágios Ischyrós.
> Sanctus Fortis.
> Hágios Athánatos, eléison hýmas.
> Sanctus Immortalis, miserere nobis.
>
> Holy God.
> Holy Mighty One.
> Holy Immortal One, have mercy on us.

It became the cause of controversy at the end of the fifth century when Peter the Fuller, patriarch of Antioch, enforced the addition to the Trisagion of the relative clause ὁ σταυρωθεὶς δι᾽ ἡμῶν—who was crucified for us. Such a statement could not be admitted by Nestorians, but since Peter was a Monophysite, even the Catholics were at first suspicious of it. The result was the first religious war in history, which humbled the Byzantine emperor Anastasius.

And such was the event of the first of the religious wars which have been waged in the name and by the disciples of the God of Peace.[34]

The title *Trisagion* is also given to the cry of the Seraphim before the throne of the Almighty (Isaiah 6:3):

Ἅγιος ἅγιος ἅγιος κύριος σαβαωθ

Holy, Holy, Holy is the Lord of Hosts.

Trullan The Greek noun τροῦλλος means a *vessel* or *basin*; the word came into Latin as *trullus*, and was eventually used to denote a cupola, which was deemed an upside-down basin. Because the Quinisext Council, held at Constantinople sometime in the period 690–692, met in a hall

---

33. Louis Duchesne, *Early History of the Christian Church from Its Foundation to the End of the Fifth Century*, vol. 3 (London: John Murray, 1924), 301n1.

34. Edward Gibbon, *The History of the Decline and Fall of the Roman Empire*, ed. Betty Radice (London: The Folio Society, 1995), 6:52.

of the Imperial palace that was surmounted by a cupola, that Council was known as the Council *in Trullo*. See the entry **Quinisext in Trullo**. The adjective associated with *trullus* is *trullanus*, and its stem is the English adjective *Trullan*.

Truth The Anglo-Saxon noun *trēow* means *faith*, and the adjective *true* originally meant *faithful, truthworthy*—what the Latins called *fidus*. The later and current meaning of *truth* as *veracity* is related to the Latin *verus* and the German *wahr*.

Tu Es Petrus These are the first three words of the verse Matthew 16:18, which is sung upon the entrance of the pope into a church. The three preeminent musical settings are those of Gregorian chant, Palestrina, and Perosi. The words mean *Thou art Peter*.

Tunicle The Roman *tunica* was a *tunic*, a *garment with sleeves*, and the diminutive *tunicula* indicated a small tunic. This was the outer garment of the subdeacon at Mass, similar to a dalmatic but less ornate, and since the subdeaconate has been suppressed, the tunicle has also disappeared except at celebrations of the traditional Latin Mass. Whereas a dalmatic with stripes should have two horizontal stripes, a tunicle with stripes should have but one.

Type The Greek verb τύπτω means *to strike*, and from it was formed the noun τύπος with the meaning a *blow*, the *mark of a blow*, an *outline*, a *system*. In his *Typos*, or outline of the faith, of 648, the emperor Constans II ordered that it was forbidden to cause trouble by openly debating whether there were one or two wills in the Christ, and whether Christ had one or two energies. People who ignored this decree were to be severely punished. The emperor needed domestic harmony in view of the Muslim advance, and he was upset about the wrangling amongst the Christians over the Monothelite issue.

U

Ultramontanism The Latin prepositional phrase *ultra montes* means *beyond the mountains*. It was used of those individuals who exaggerated the authority of the Holy See, which was beyond the Alps.

Umbella (Umbrella) The Latin word *umbra* means *shadow*. From it was derived the noun *umbella*, a sun-shade. *Umbra* became in Italian *ombra*, and *umbella* became *ombrella*. In modern times, *ombrella* became masculine, *ombrello*, with the diminutive *ombrellino*. The ombrellino was used to protect the Host in its progress to or from the tabernacle and the baldacchino. In some ceremonies, its use is omitted, an omission that makes it difficult to see where the monstrance is during a progress.

Unction The Latin verb *unguo, unguere, unxi, unctus* means *to anoint, besmear,* and from its fourth principal part is derived the noun *unctio* which means a *smearing*, an *anointing*. *Extreme Unction* is the English transliteration of the Latin *extrema unctio* ("the Last Rites"); it is a learned term for the anointing of people *in periculo mortis*.

Uniate The Latin adjective *unus* means *one*, and from it was formed the verb *unio, unire, univi, unitus* with the meaning *to unite*. The perfect passive participle *unitus* means *one who has been united*. The English noun *uniate* is an illiterate and pejorative corruption of this word, as if *unio* were of the first conjugation. It is used disparagingly and even insultingly of the members of the Eastern Catholic Churches.

Union See the entry **Uniate** above. The Latin noun *unio, unionis, f.,* means *oneness*; in later times it acquired the meaning *union*.

Urbi et Orbi This is the name of the traditional papal blessing, given *to the city and to the world* on Christmas and Easter and on other rare occasions when the pope appears on the central balcony of the Vatican Basilica, such as on the day of his election to the papacy. It used to be given from St. John Lateran on Ascension Day, and from the balcony of Santa Maria Maggiore on Assumption Day.

Sancti Apostoli Petrus et Paulus, de quorum potestate et auctoritate confidimus, ipsi intercedant pro nobis ad Dominum. Amen.

Precibus et meritis beatae Mariae semper Virginis, beati Michaëlis Archangeli, beati Ioannis Baptistae et sanctorum Apostolorum Petri et Pauli et omnium Sanctorum, misereatur vestri omnipotens Deus, et dimissis omnibus peccatis vestris, perducat vos Iesus Christus ad vitam æternam. Amen.

Indulgentiam, absolutionem, et remissionem omnium peccatorum vestrorum, spatium verae et fructuosae paenitentiae, cor semper paenitens, et emendationem vitae, gratiam et consolationem Sancti Spiritus, et finalem perseverantiam in bonis operibus tribuat vobis omnipotens et misericors Dominus. Amen.

Et benedictio Dei omnipotentis, Patris, et Filii, et Spiritus Sancti, descendat super vos et maneat semper. Amen.

May the Holy Apostles Peter and Paul, in whose power and authority we trust, intercede for us before the Lord. Amen.

Through the prayers and merits of the blessed Ever-Virgin Mary, of blessed Michael the Archangel, of blessed John the Baptist and the holy Apostles Peter and Paul and all the Saints, may Almighty God have mercy on you, and, after all your sins have been forgiven, may Jesus Christ bring you to eternal life. Amen.

May the almighty and merciful Lord grant you mercy, absolution, and the remission of all your sins, time for true and fruitful penance, a contrite heart, the correction of your life, the grace and consolation of the Holy Ghost, and final perseverance in good works. Amen.

And may the blessing of God almighty, the Father, the Son, and the Holy Ghost, descend over you and remain forever. Amen.

Like all solemn prayers, it is supposed to be sung, the singing imparting a necessary dignity to the occasion. Since there are no musical notes in the great volume from which the pontiff reads, there is much variation in their performances. The standard of excellence in all matters ceremonial was set by Pius XI. Pope Paul VI, when he appeared on the loggia of St. Peter's Basilica for the first time, did not impart the apostolic benediction *Urbi et Orbi*; instead he merely gave the pontifical blessing "*Sit nomen Domini benedictum....*" I supposed at the time that they could not find the book with the proper prayer. Wisely did Pope Francis discontinue the custom begun by Paul VI, whereby the pope wished "Merry Christmas" or "Happy Easter" in many vernacular languages; with John Paul II, this had gotten out of hand. After the pope imparts the *Urbi et Orbi* blessing, the senior cardinal deacon reads out the proclamation of the plenary indulgence. At the coronation of Pope John XXIII, and for centuries before, this proclamation was always, or at least first, in Latin; it is now, alas, only in Italian. One can hear the proclamation made in Latin by Cardinal Canali at the 1958 coronation, which was videotaped by Italian television. Alas, the recording has a commentator who, in the offensive modern manner, gets in the way by talking over all the sounds.

Sanctissimus in Christo Pater et Dominus Noster, Dominus Ioannes, Divina Providentia Papa Vicesimus Tertius, dat et concedit Christi fidelibus cunctis qui hic adsunt et eam pie receperint indulgentiam plenariam in forma Ecclesiae consueta. Rogate igitur Deum pro felici statu Sanctitatis Suae et Sanctae Matris Ecclesiae.

Il Santo Padre Francesco, concede a tutti fedeli presenti la sua benedizione con l'indulgenza plenaria nella forma stabilita dalla Chiesa. Preghiamo Iddio Onnipotente, perchè conservi a lungo il Papa a guida della Chiesa e perchè conceda alla Chiesa pace in tutto il mondo.

The following episode is from the coronation of Pius X in 1903:

The two Cardinal Deacons, having read aloud the Plenary Indulgence in Latin and Italian, threw the formulas (or should have done so) towards the people, who commenced shouting "Viva Pio X," and waving their handkerchiefs.[1]

Utraquist The Latin adjective *uterque, utraque, utrumque* means *each of two, both,* and from it was devised the modern Latin noun *utraquista, -ae, m.*, with the meaning *one who demands to receive the Eucharist in both kinds,* that is, *sub utraque specie*. (Recall that in those days the faithful received only the Host at the Mass; the chalice was reserved to the celebrant.) The *utraquists* formed the predominant party of the Bohemian followers of Jan Hus (burned at the stake in Constance on July 6, 1415), who, in order to put an end to a terrible religious war, reached an agreement

---

1. Hartwell de la Garde Grissell, *Sede Vacante, Being a Diary Written during the Conclave of 1903, with Additional Notes on the Accession and Coronation of Pius X* (Oxford: James Parker, 1903), 75.

called the *Compact of Prague* with the legates of the Council of Basel on November 26, 1433, on the basis of the following four articles:

I. Free preaching of the Word of God; II. Communion in both elements for the laity; III. The clergy to be deprived of all dominion over temporal possessions, and to be reduced to the evangelical life of Christ and the apostles; IV. All offences against divine law to be punished without exception of person or condition.[2]

The Compact was never confirmed by the Holy See, which was on a collision course with the Council of Basel at that time. The Compact was eventually condemned by Pius II (1458–1464), but the use of the chalice in the Czech territories was not eliminated until the time of the Counter-Reformation, when the victory of the emperor Ferdinand II at the battle of the White Mountain (November 8, 1620) terminated the Protestant cause in Bohemia.

2. Henry Charles Lea, *A History of the Inquisition in the Middle Ages* (New York: Harper & Brothers, 1887), 2:519–20.

V

Vatican The Latin noun *vates* means a *seer* or *prophet,* the related deponent verb *vaticinor, vaticinari* means *to foretell,* and the related adjective *vatĭcĭnus* means *prophetical.* The word *Vatican* is commonly derived from these words, but the derivation is uncertain. The greatest of all guide books to Rome has the following to say about the Vatican:

The hollow of the Janiculum between S. Onofrio and the Monte Mario is believed to have been the site of Etruscan divination.

> "Fauni vatesque canebant."
> —Ennius

Hence the name, which is now only used in regard to the papal palace and the basilica of S. Peter, but which was once applied to the whole district between the foot of the hill and the Tiber near S. Angelo.

> "... ut paterni
> Fluminis ripae, simul et jocosa
> Redderet laudes tibi vaticani
> Montis imago."
> —Horace, *Od.* I 20.

Tacitus speaks of the unwholesome air of this quarter. In this district was the Circus of Caligula, adjoining the gardens of his mother Agrippina, decorated by the obelisk which now stands in front of S. Peter's. Here Seneca describes that while Caligula was walking by torchlight he amused himself by the slaughter of a number of distinguished persons—senators and Roman ladies. Afterward it became the Circus of Nero, who from his adjoining gardens used to watch the martyrdom of the Christians—mentioned by Suetonius as "a race given up to a new and evil

496

superstition"—and who used their living bodies, covered with pitch and set on fire, as torches for his nocturnal promenades.

The first residence of the popes at the Vatican was erected by St. Symmachus [A.D. 498–514] near the forecourt of the old S. Peter's, and here Charlemagne is believed to have resided on the occasion of his several visits to Rome during the reigns of Adrian I (772–795) and Leo III (795–816). During the twelfth century, this ancient palace having fallen into decay, it was rebuilt in the thirteenth by Innocent III. It was greatly enlarged by Nicholas III (1277–1281), but the Lateran continued to be the papal residence, and the Vatican palace was only used on state occasions, and for the reception of any foreign sovereigns visiting Rome. After the return of the popes from Avignon, the Lateran palace had fallen into decay, and for the sake of the greater security afforded by the vicinity of S. Angelo, it was determined to make the pontifical residence at the Vatican, and the first conclave was held there in 1378.[1]

The evidence for the visit of the apostles Peter and Paul to Rome and their subsequent deaths there is the subject of the excursus "Peter in Rome" by the great Bishop Lightfoot; this study, which was incomplete at the time of his death in 1889, assembles all the literary authorities from the first three centuries that prove the sojourn of the two apostles in the capital of the world.[2] A briefer presentation of the evidence is given by Fr. Herbert J. Thurston, SJ, in his edition of Butler's *Lives of the Saints*, under January 18.[3] I note some of the most important passages here. First there is the mention of Peter and Paul together in the Epistle of S. Clement to the Corinthians, 5:

Λάβωμεν πρὸ ὀφθαλμῶν ἡμῶν τοὺς ἀγαθοὺς ἀποστόλους· Πέτρον, ὃς διὰ ζῆλον ἄδικον οὐχ ἕνα οὐδὲ δύο, ἀλλὰ πλείονας ὑπήνεγκεν πόνους καὶ οὕτω μαρτυρήσας ἐπορεύθη εἰς τὸν ὀφειλόμενον τόπον τῆς δόξης. διὰ ζῆλον καὶ ἔριν Παῦλος ...[4]

Let us put before our eyes the good apostles, Peter, who, because of wicked fanaticism bore not one nor two but many sufferings, and having thus borne witness journeyed to the promised place of glory, and Paul, who, on account of fanaticism and anger ...

1. Augustus J. C. Hare, *Walks in Rome*, 17th ed. (New York: George Routledge & Sons, n.d.), 603–4.

2. This excursus is an appendix to J. B. Lightfoot's *The Apostolic Fathers: Clement, Ignatius, Polycarp*, 2nd ed. (London: Macmillan, 1889), part 1, vol. 2, pp. 481–502.

3. *Butler's Lives of the Saints*, ed. Herbert J. Thurston, SJ, and Donald Attwater (Norwalk, Conn.: Easton Press, 1995), 1:113–15.

4. J. B. Lightfoot, *The Apostolic Fathers, Clement, Ignatius, and Polycarp*, rev. ed. (Peabody, Mass: Hendrickson, 1989), part 1, vol. 2, pp. 25–28.

Ignatius and Clement of Alexandria, both of the second century, are the authors of the earliest documents expressly reporting that the apostle Peter taught and died in Rome. There is the passage in the Epistle of Ignatius to the Romans, 4:

Οὐχ ὡς Πέτρος καὶ Παῦλος διατάσσομαι ὑμῖν· ἐκεῖνοι ἀπόστολοι, ἐγὼ κατάκριτος·[5]

Not like Peter and Paul do I give you commandments; they were apostles, but I am a convict.

Clement of Alexandria is quoted by Eusebius as saying:

When, at Rome, Peter had openly preached the word and by the spirit had proclaimed the gospel, the large audience urged Mark, who had followed him for a long time and remembered what had been said, to write it all down. This he did, making his Gospel available to all who wanted it.[6]

St Irenaeus of Lyon, in his *Refutation of Heresies* III 2 wrote:

τοῦ Πέτρου καὶ τοῦ Παύλου ἐν Ῥώμῃ εὐαγγελιζομένων καὶ θεμελιούντων τὴν ἐκκλησίαν ...

Cum Petrus et Paulus Romae evangelizarent et fundarent Ecclesiam ...

When Peter and Paul were preaching the Gospel in Rome and founding the Church ...

Of the Emperor Nero, Eusebius writes:

So it came about that this man, the first to be heralded as a conspicuous fighter against God, was led on to murder the apostles. It is recorded that in his reign Paul was beheaded in Rome itself, and that Peter likewise was crucified, and the record is confirmed by the fact that the cemeteries there are still called by the names of Peter and Paul, and equally so by a churchman named Gaius, who was living while Zephyrinus was Bishop of Rome. In his published *Dialogue* with Proclus, the leader of the Phrygian heretics, Gaius has this to say about the places where the mortal remains of the two apostles have been reverently laid: "I can point out the monuments of the victorious apostles. If you will go as far as the Vatican or the Ostian Way, you will find the monuments of those who founded this church."

That they were both martyred at the same time Bishop Dionysius of Corinth informs us in a letter written to the Romans:

5. J. B. Lightfoot, *The Apostolic Fathers, Clement, Ignatius, and Polycarp*, rev. ed (Peabody, Mass: Hendrickson, 1989), part 2, vol. 2, p. 209.

6. Eusebius, *The History of the Church from Christ to Constantine*, trans. G. A. Williamson (London: The Folio Society, 2011), VI 14, pp. 173–74.

In this way by your impressive admonition you have bound together all that has grown from the seed which Peter and Paul sowed in Romans and Corinthians alike. For both of them sowed in our Corinth and taught us jointly: in Italy too they taught jointly in the same city, and were martyred at the same time.[7]

The Vatican City is the sovereign state enclosed by the Vatican walls and the Bernini colonnade; it was established in 1929 as the successor to the Pontifical State, the rump of which was occupied by Italian troops in 1870. See the entry **Lateran Pacts**. The Vatican City is to be distinguished from the Holy See, which is the bishopric of Rome. When Pope Francis came to address the United States Congress, he was awkwardly introduced by the sergeant-at-arms as the "Pope of the Holy See." The Vatican City has its own stamps, coins, and radio station. Viktorin Hallmayer (1831–1872) was the composer of the *Marcia Trionfale*, which was the national anthem of the Papal States during the last decade of their existence. After the Lateran Pacts of 1929, it was used as the anthem of the Vatican City State until Pius XII replaced it with Gounod's *Marche Pontificale* on October 16, 1949.

Two great artists visited Rome in these years, Liszt in 1862 and Gounod in 1869. Gounod was enjoying a pension from the French Academy at Villa Medici, having won the Grand Prix de Composition Musicale in 1839. A religious sentimentalism urged him to enter holy orders, but a short sojourn in the Roman Seminary sufficed to change his views. Returning to Paris, he married and revisited Rome in 1869, as the guest at Villa Medici, of M. Hébert, Director of the Imperial French Academy, on which occasion he occupied the room Galileo inhabited on his second visit. He lived a retired life, but desired to assist at the Holy Week ceremonies. For Pius IX he composed a march performed by military bands on the steps of St. Peter's, in honour of the fiftieth anniversary of the first Mass said by the Pope.[8]

Vatican II "Vatican Two" is a careless way of referring to the Second Vatican Council.

Veneration The Latin deponent verb *veneror, venerari* means *to ask reverently, to beseech with awe, to revere*. From this came the noun *veneratio* with the meaning *respect, veneration*. Veneration is a technical term for the reverence shown to saints. The Greek word for this idea is δουλία. It is to be distinguished from λατρεία, in Latin *adoratio*, the technical term for the worship of God.

---

7. Eusebius, *The History of the Church*, II 25, p. 58.

8. Raffaele de Cesare, *The Last Days of Papal Rome, 1850–1870*, trans. Helen Zimmern (London: Archibald Constable, 1909), 148–49.

Veni Creator Spiritus This hymn is attributed to Rabanus Maurus (d. 856), abbot of Fulda, archbishop of Mainz.

> Veni Creator Spiritus,
> Mentes tuorum visita:
> Imple superna gratia
> Quae tu creasti pectora.
>
> Qui Paraclitus diceris,
> Donum Dei altissimi,
> Fons vivus, ignis, caritas,
> Et spiritalis unctio.
>
> Tu septiformis munere,
> Dextrae Dei tu digitus,
> Tu rite promissum Patris,
> Sermone ditans guttura.
>
> Accende lumen sensibus,
> Infunde amorem cordibus,
> Infirma nostri corporis
> Virtute firmans perpeti.
>
> Hostem repellas longius,
> Pacemque dones protinus:
> Ductore sic te praevio
> Vitemus omne noxium.
>
> Per te sciamus da Patrem,
> Noscamus atque Filium,
> Te utriusque Spiritum
> Credamus omni tempore.
>
> Sit laus Patri cum Filio,
> Sancto simul Paraclito,
> Nobisque mittat Filius
> Charisma Sancti Spiritus. Amen.

The best translation is by John Dryden (1631–1700).

> Creator Spirit, by whose aid
> The world's foundations first were laid,
> Come visit every pious mind;
> Come pour thy joys on human kind;

― V ―

From sin and sorrow set us free,
And make thy temples worthy thee.

O source of uncreated light,
The Father's promised Paraclete!
Thrice holy fount, thrice holy fire,
Our hearts with heavenly love inspire;
Come, and thy sacred unction bring
To sanctify us, while we sing.

Plenteous of grace, descend from high,
Rich in thy sevenfold energy!
Thou strength of his Almighty hand,
Whose power does heaven and earth command.
Proceeding Spirit, our defence,
Who dost thy gifts of tongues dispense,
And crown'st thy gift with eloquence.

Refine and purge our earthly parts;
But, O, inflame and fire our hearts!
Our frailties help, our vice controul,
Submit the senses to the soul;
And when rebellious they are grown,
Then lay thy hand, and hold them down.

Chase from our minds the infernal foe,
And peace, the fruit of love, bestow;
And lest our feet should step astray,
Protect and guide us in the way.

Make us eternal truths receive,
And practise all that we believe:
Give us thyself, that we may see
The Father, and the Son, by thee.

Immortal honour, endless fame,
Attend the Almighty Father's name:
The Saviour Son be glorified,
Who for lost man's redemption died;
And equal adoration be,
Eternal Paraclete, to thee.[9]

9. John Dryden, *The Works of John Dryden*, ed. Walter Scott (London: William Millar, 1808), 11:190–91.

Veni Sancte Spiritus *Veni Sancte Spiritus* is the sequence for Pentecost; of unknown authorship, it was probably composed in the twelfth century.

Veni, Sancte Spiritus,
Et emitte caelitus
Lucis tuae radium.

Veni, pater pauperum,
Veni, dator munerum,
Veni, lumen cordium.

Consolator optime,
Dulcis hospes animae,
Dulce refrigerium.

In labore requies,
In aestu temperies,
In fletu solacium.

O lux beatissima,
Reple cordis intima
Tuorum fidelium.

Sine tuo numine
Nihil est in homine,
Nihil est innoxium.

Lava quod est sordidum,
Riga quod est aridum,
Sana quod est saucium.

Flecte quod est rigidum,
Fove quod est frigidum,
Rege quod est devium.

Da tuis fidelibus,
In te confidentibus,
Sacrum septenarium.

Da virtutis meritum
Da salutis exitum,
Da perenne gaudium.
Amen. Alleluia.

The traditional translation is by John Austin (1613–69):[10]

10. There is more than one version of this translation. See, for example, http://www.preces-latinae
.org/thesaurus/Hymni/VSS-2.html and https://archive.org/details/SongsOfTheSpirit1871/page/n211
(which has the doxology at the end).

Come Holy Ghost,
Send down those beams,
Which sweetly flow in silent streams
From thy bright throne above.
O come, Thou Father of the poor,
O come, Thou source of all our store,
Come, fill our hearts with love.

O Thou, of comforters the best,
O Thou, the soul's delightful guest,
The pilgrim's sweet relief.
Rest art Thou in our toil, most sweet
Refreshment in the noonday heat;
And solace in our grief.

O blessed Light of life Thou art;
Fill with Thy light the inmost heart
Of those who hope in Thee.
Without Thy Godhead nothing can
Have any price and worth in man,
Nothing can harmless be.

Lord, wash our sinful stains away,
Refresh from heaven our barren clay,
Our wounds and bruises heal.
To Thy sweet yoke our stiff necks bow;
Warm with Thy fire our hearts of snow;
Our wandering feet recall.

Grant to Thy faithful, dearest Lord,
Whose only hope is Thy sure word,
The sevenfold gifts of grace.
Grant us in life Thy grace that we
In peace may die and ever be,
In joy before Thy face.

All glory to the sacred Three,
One ever living Deity,
All power ascribe, and bliss, and praise;
As at the first when time begun,
May the same homage still be done,
While time does last, when time decays.
Amen. Alleluia.

The following version is that of Edward Caswall (1814–1878):[11]

Holy Spirit! Lord of light!
From thy clear celestial height
Thy pure beaming radiance give:
Come, Thou Father of the poor!
Come, with treasures which endure!
Come, Thou Light of all that live!

Thou, of all consolers best,
Thou the soul's delightsome guest,
Dost refreshing peace bestow;
Thou in toil art comfort sweet;
Pleasant coolness in the heat;
Solace in the midst of woe.

Light immortal! light divine!
Visit Thou these hearts of thine.
And our inmost being fill:
If Thou take thy grace away,
Nothing pure in man will stay;
All his good is turned to ill.

Heal our wounds; our strength renew;
On our dryness pour thy dew;
Wash the stains of guilt away:
Bend the stubborn heart and will;
Melt the frozen, warm the chill;
Guide the steps that go astray.

Thou, on those who evermore
Thee confess and Thee adore,
In thy sevenfold gifts, descend:
Give them comfort when they die;
Give them life with Thee on high;
Give them joys that never end.

Verbum Supernum Prodiens It is commonly believed that St. Thomas Aquinas composed this hymn for the Hour of Lauds for the feast of Corpus Christi; however, Lentini puts a question mark in parentheses after the attribution.[12] The last two stanzas are the famous hymn, *O Salutaris Hostia.*

11. Edward Caswall, *Lyra Catholica: Containing All the Breviary and Missal Hymns, with Others from Various Sources* (London: Burns & Oates, 1884), 234–36.

12. Anselmo Lentini, *Te Decet Hymnus, L'Innario della "Liturgia Horarum"* (Rome: Typis Polyglottis Vaticanis, 1984), 141.

Verbum supernum prodiens,
Nec Patris linquens dexteram,
Ad opus suum exiens,
Venit ad vitae vesperam.

In mortem a discipulo
Suis tradendus aemulis,
Prius in vitae ferculo
Se tradidit discipulis.

Quibus sub bina specie
Carnem dedit et sanguinem:
Ut duplicis substantiae
Totum cibaret hominem.

Se nascens dedit socium
Convescens in edulium,
Se moriens in pretium,
Se regnans dat in praemium.

O salutaris hostia,
Quae caelis pandis ostium,
Bella premunt hostilia,
Da robur, fer auxilium.

Uni trinoque Domino,
Sit sempiterna gloria,
Qui vitam sine termino
Nobis donet in patria. Amen.

The following translation is by Edward Caswall (1814 –1878).[13]

The Word, descending from above,
Though with the Father still on high,
Went forth upon his work of love,
And soon to life's last eve drew nigh.

He shortly to a death accursed
By a disciple shall be given;
But, to his twelve disciples, first
He gives Himself, the Bread from Heaven.

Himself in either kind He gave:
He gave his Flesh, He gave his Blood;

---

13. Edward Caswall, *Lyra Catholica: Containing All the Breviary and Missal Hymns, with Others from Various Sources* (London: Burns & Oates, 1884), 114–16.

Of flesh and blood all men are made;
And He of man would be the Food.

At birth our brother He became;
At meat Himself as food He gives;
To ransom us He died in shame;
As our reward, in bliss He lives.

O Saving Victim! opening wide
The gate of Heav'n to man below!
Sore press our foes from every side;
Thine aid supply, thy strength bestow.

To thy great Name be endless praise,
Immortal Godhead, One in Three!
Oh, grant us endless length of days,
In our true native land, with Thee!

Vernacular The Latin noun *verna, -ae, c.*, means a *slave born in the master's house*. The associated adjective *vernaculus, -a, -um* means *pertaining to such a slave*. Someone who did not realize that *vernaculus* was already an adjective superimposed the adjectival suffix *-aris* upon it and produced the English superadjective *vernacular*. It nowadays refers to the common everyday language, especially as distinct from the learned language, Latin. In the decade 1962–1972, the Catholic Church switched from an entirely Latin liturgy to (almost everywhere) a vernacular liturgy. This came as a shock to some who remembered a certain canon of the Council of Trent:

Si quis dixerit, ecclesiae Romanae ritum, quo submissa voce pars canonis et verba consecrationis proferuntur, damnandum esse; aut lingua tantum vulgari Missam celebrari debere, … anathema sit.[14]

If anyone should say that the rite of the Roman Church, wherein a part of the canon and the words of consecration are spoken in a low voice, is to be condemned, or that the Mass should only be celebrated in the vernacular language, … let him be anathema.

An entirely vernacular liturgy is not what was prescribed by the Second Vatican Council, which called for a less drastic policy.

Linguae latinae usus, salvo particulari iure, in Ritibus latinis servetur.

Cum tamen, sive in Missa, sive in Sacramentorum administratione, sive in aliis Liturgiae partibus, haud raro linguae vernaculae usurpatio valde utilis apud

---

14. Council of Trent, Sessio 22.

populum existere possit, amplior locus ipsi tribui valeat, imprimis autem in lectionibus et admonitionibus, in nonnullis orationibus et cantibus, iuxta normas quae de hac re in sequentibus capitibus singillatim statuuntur.[15]

The use of the Latin language in the Latin rites is to be kept, save for particular law.

Since, however, whether in the Mass, or in the administration of the Sacraments, or in other parts of the Liturgy, the adoption of the vernacular language for the people might not rarely be of benefit, a greater role may usefully be allowed to it, especially in readings and warnings, and in some prayers and songs, in accordance with the regulations that are established in this regard in the following sections.

Some compromise combination of Latin and the vernacular language seems to have been envisaged, the sort of thing Dr. Johnson condemned when he observed the epitaph of James Craggs in Westminster Abbey, which was half English and half Latin.

It may be proper here to remark the absurdity of joining, in the same inscription, Latin and English, or verse and prose. If either language be preferable to the other, let that only be used; for no reason can be given why part of the information should be given in one tongue, and part in another on a tomb, more than in any other place, or any other occasion; and to tell all that can be conveniently told in verse, and then to call in the help of prose, has always the appearance of a very artless expedient, or of an attempt unaccomplished. Such an epitaph resembles the conversation of a foreigner, who tells part of his meaning by words, and conveys part by signs.[16]

Today it can no longer be said, as Maisie Ward wrote in 1937:

This union of localization and universality finds expression in the miracle of tongues on Whit Sunday and to-day in the language and liturgy which unites at one altar men severed by national languages and national interests.[17]

The following lines are an excerpt from the poem *De Valera at Ninety-Two* by Brendan Kennelly. The poet "only met De Valera six weeks before he died.... The poem is in the form of answers by De Valera to a series of questions which Kennelly put to him, based on the attitudes of his childhood."[18]

15. Sacrosanctum Concilium, *Constitutio de Sacra Liturgia*, 36 §1, §2.

16. Samuel Johnson, *Lives of the Most Eminent English Poets; with Critical Observations on Their Works* (London, 1781), 4:224–25.

17. Maisie Ward, *The Wilfrid Wards and the Transition*, vol. 2, *Insurrection versus Resurrection* (New York: Sheed & Ward, 1937), 7.

18. Tim Pat Coogan, *Eamon De Valera: The Man Who Was Ireland* (New York: HarperCollins, 1993), 691.

When my grandfather scattered things on the kitchen floor
He used strange words from the Gaelic.
I wonder still about the roots of words.
They don't teach Latin in the schools now.
That's bad, that's very bad.
It is as important to know
Where the words in your mouth come from
As where you come from yourself.
Not to know such origins
Is not to know who you are
Or what you think you're saying. I had a small red book at school,
'Twas full of roots,
I still remember it.

Finally, the religious value of the Latin language was the subject of comment by Rudolf Otto:

There are other manifestations of this tendency of the feeling of the "mysterious" to be attached to objects and aspects of experience analogous to it in being "uncomprehended". It finds its most unqualified expression in the spell exercised by the only half intelligible or wholly unintelligible language of devotion and in the unquestionably real enhancement of the awe of the worshipper which this produces.... [An instance of this is] the Latin of the service of the Mass, felt by the Catholic to be not a necessary evil, but something especially holy.[19]

Versus Populum This Latin phrase means *toward the people*, and is used to describe the modern orientation of the priest when celebrating Mass, facing the congregation, as opposed to the old way, when the priest and people faced in the same direction. The new orientation has caused considerable damage in the rearrangement of churches that was required to make it possible. This orientation has the disadvantage that the priest is perpetually gazing at the assembly, so that his mistakes and the idiosyncrasies of his personal appearance are a constant distraction. It is not edifying to watch him chew the Sacred Host. The following was the practice of the monks of St. Pachomius, the inventor of the cenobitic life.

While eating, they covered their heads with their hoods; in this way they disguised an operation which apparently seemed to them unbecoming, or, at any rate, kept to themselves the secret of the privations which they voluntarily endured.[20]

19. Rudolf Otto, "Means of Expression of the Numinous," in *The Idea of the Holy*, trans. J. W. Harvey (Oxford: Oxford University Press, 1923), 67, 68.

20. Louis Duchesne, *Early History of the Christian Church from Its Foundation to the End of the Fifth Century*, vol. 2 (London: John Murray, 1931), 396.

In churches where the high altar was not destroyed, there are now two altars, one a free standing table, a very strange arrangement offensive to the genius of the building. It is true that even in former times the mass was sometimes celebrated *versus populum*. One reads in the memoirs of a Pontifical Zouave under the date January 23, 1869 (he is speaking of the Basilica of Santa Cecilia in Rome):

> The high altar immediately over the shrine of the Saint is placed at the intersection of the nave and the choir, so that when the priest celebrates Mass he faces the people in the nave.[21]

Vespers The Greek noun ὁ ἕσπερος means *the evening*, and from it was derived the Latin noun *vesper, vesperis* or *vesperi, m.*, with the same meaning. There was also the associated Greek adjective ἕσπερος, ἑσπέρα, ἕσπερον with the meaning *pertaining to the evening*, whence came the phrase ἑσπέρα ὥρα, or *evening hour*. Latin too had the adjective *vesperus, -a, -um*, and the phrase *vespera hora*, the *evening hour*. Our noun *Vespers* is derived from the French feminine plural *vêpres* meaning *evening prayer*, probably an abbreviation of some Latin phrase like *vesperae orationes* or *preces*. Weekley says that it came into English in the seventeenth century in books of travel. *Vespers* is the late afternoon or evening prayer of the Church, and as a result the psalms commonly sung for that ceremony have been frequently put to music by the great composers, in particular, Psalm 109 (110), *Dixit Dominus*.

Vestments The Greek verb ἕννυμι means *to clothe*, and from its perfect passive infinitive ἕσθαι there proceeded the noun ἐσθής, ἐσθῆτος, *f.*, meaning a *garment*. Related to this noun is the Latin noun *vestis, -is, f.*, meaning *clothing*, and the verb *vestio, vestire* meaning *to clothe*. From *vestio* there developed the noun *vestimentum* meaning *an article of clothing*. The reformers greately reduced the use of vestments, some of them not admitting them at all. Billy Graham, for example, never appeared in vestments.

Veterum Sapientia This phrase, which means the *wisdom of the ancients*, is the name of an apostolic constitution of Pope John XXIII, dated February 22, 1962, which called for the promotion of Latin in the Catholic Church, particularly in the seminaries.

---

21. Joseph Powell, *Two Years in the Pontifical Zouaves, A Narrative of Travel, Residence, and Experience in the Roman States* (London: R. Washbourne, 1871), 83.

Veto The Latin verb *veto, vetare, vetui, vetitus* means *to forbid*. In the papal conclaves, the sovereigns of the major Catholic powers, Austria, France, and Spain had the privilege of vetoing the candidacy of a cardinal whose election to the papacy they wished to prevent, one candidate per conclave. The last candidate to be vetoed was Mariano Rampolla del Tindaro, who was vetoed by Emperor Francis Joseph in 1903. This privilege was cancelled thereafter by Pius X in the apostolic constitution *Commissum Nobis* of January 20, 1904.

Vexilla Regis Prodeunt "This world-famous hymn, one of the grandest in the treasury of the Latin Church,"[22] was composed by Venantius Fortunatus (530–609). It is sung at Vespers in Holy Week and on September 14, the Feast of the Finding of the True Cross. The first verse of the penultimate stanza is known to all stamp collectors, since it appears on a series of four stamps issued for the Holy Year of 1933. The second and seventh stanzas were not included in the *Breviarium Romanum*, and the fourth stanza, which was there, has in modern times been omitted from the *Liturgia Horarum* for reasons given by Lentini in his work.[23] The last line of the stanza, *regnavit a ligno Deus*—God hath reigned from the wood—contains what is now known to be an interpolation (*a ligno*) in the text of Psalm 95:5; this condemned the stanza to death. The words in question were added to the psalm by Christians, but in a less ecumenical age the Jews were blamed for their absence in the Hebrew Bible; the Doway Old Testament has the following note on the passage:

Diuers ancient Doctors read more in this place: Our Lord hath reigned from the wood, to witte, Christ by his death on the crosse conquered the diuel, sinne, and death, and thence begane to reigne. S Iustinus Martyr, dialogo aduers. Triphonem. Tertullian li. aduers. Iudaeos. c. 9. & 13. & aduers. Marcionem. li. 3 c. 19. & 21. S Augustin in this place, according to the old Roman Psalter. Before him Arnobius, and after him Cassiadorus and others, wherby it is probable, that it was sometimes in the Hebrew text, and blotted out by the Iewes.

Notice that the second strophe of this anthem contains a grammatical anomaly, an accusative absolute.

22. Rev. J. M. Neale, trans., *Mediaeval Hymns and Sequences*, 2nd ed. (London: Joseph Masters, 1863), 6.

23. Anselmo Lentini, *Te Decet Hymnus, L'Innario della "Liturgia Horarum"* (Rome: Typis Polyglottis Vaticanis, 1984), 103–4.

Vexilla Regis prodeunt;
fulget crucis mysterium,
quo carne carnis conditor
suspensus est patibulo.

Confixa clavis viscera
tendens manus, vestigia,
redemptionis gratia
hic immolata est hostia.

Quo vulneratus insuper
mucrone diro lanceae,
ut nos lavaret crimine,
manavit unda et sanguine.

Impleta sunt quae concinit
David fideli carmine,
dicendo nationibus:
regnavit a ligno Deus.

Arbor decora et fulgida,
ornata Regis purpura,
electa digno stipite
tam sancta membra tangere.

Beata cuius bracchiis
pretium pependit saeculi:
statera facta corporis,
praedam tulitque tartari.

Fundis aroma cortice,
vincis sapore nectare,
iucunda fructu fertili
plaudis triumpho nobili.

Salve, ara, salve, victima,
de passionis gloria,
qua Vita mortem pertulit
et morte vitam reddidit.

O Crux, ave, spes unica,
hoc passionis tempore!
Piis adauge gratiam,
reisque dele crimina.

Te, fons salutis, Trinitas,
collaudet omnis spiritus:
quos per crucis mysterium
salvas, fove per saecula. Amen.

The translation by John Mason Neale (1818–1866) is famous:[24]

> The Royal Banners forward go;
> The Cross shines forth in mystic glow;
> Where He in flesh, our flesh Who made,
> Our sentence bore, our ransom paid.
>
> Where deep for us the spear was dy'd,
> Life's torrent rushing from His side,
> To wash us in that precious flood,
> Where mingled Water flow'd, and Blood.
>
> Fulfill'd is all that David told
> In true Prophetic song of old;
> Amidst the nations God, saith he,
> Hath reign'd and triumph'd from the Tree.
>
> O Tree of Beauty! Tree of Light!
> O Tree with royal purple dight!
> Elect on whose triumphal breast
> Those holy limbs should find their rest.
>
> On whose dear arms, so widely flung,
> The weight of this world's ransom hung,
> The price of human kind to pay,
> And spoil the Spoiler of his prey.
>
> O Cross, our one reliance, hail!
> This holy Passiontide, avail
> To give fresh merit to the Saint,
> And pardon to the penitent.
>
> To Thee, Eternal Three in one.
> Let homage meet by all be done;
> Whom by the Cross Thou dost restore,
> Preserve and govern evermore.

Viaticum This word is the corruption of the Latin phrase *Via Tecum*, which means *on the way with you*. It originally referred to the *traveling money* that the traveler took with him as a provision for the journey. In the Catholic Church, it is another name for the Eucharist administered to the dying as part of the Last Rites; this latter denomination is now out of favor as it emphasizes the imminence of death.

24. Rev. J. M. Neale, trans., *Mediaeval Hymns and Sequences*, 2nd ed. (London: Joseph Masters, 1863), 6–7.

Vicar The Latin defective noun *vicis* (genitive), *vicem* (accusative), *vice* (ablative) means *change, interchange, alternation*, and in the plural, the *duties of one person performed by a substitute*. As we read in Ode 4 of Book 1 of the *Odes* of Horace:

Solvitur acris hiems, grata vice veris et Favoni.
Hard winter breaks, O happy turn to Zephyr and to Spring![25]

The associated noun *vicarius* means a *substitute*. Thus, the pope's substitute for the administration of the diocese of Rome is called the *cardinal vicar*.

From the defective noun *vicis, vicem, vice* we derive our adjective *vice* as in *vice president* and *vice admiral*. Our noun *vice*, the opposite of *virtue*, is derived from a different Latin word, *vitium*, which means *fault*.

Vicar Apostolic In those countries without an established hierarchy, bishops *in partibus infidelium* are appointed to exercise episcopal functions, whether liturgical or administrative. Such prelates are denominated *vicars apostolic*. For the etymologies, see the entries **Vicar** and **Apostle**.

Vicar Capitular Upon the death or incapacity of a bishop, the cathedral chapter elects a temporary official, the *vicar capitular*, to administer the diocese during the interregnum or incapacity. For the etymologies, see the entries **Vicar** and **Chapter**.

Vicar Foraneus For the etymology of the first of these two words, see the entry **Vicar**. The Greek noun θύρα means *door*, and the enclitic suffix -δε gives the meaning *toward*, so that the compound θύραδε or θύραζε has the meaning *toward the door, outward*. The related Latin adverb is *foras*, outside, and from it was formed the adjective *foraneus*, outdoors, whence comes our adjective *foreign*. A *vicar foraneus* is a priest granted some supervisory powers over the other priests in his rural area.

Vicar General The Greek noun γένος, γένεος, *n.*, means *race, kind*, and related to it is the Latin noun *genus, generis, n.*, with the same meaning. From the latter noun was formed the adjective *generalis* with the meaning *belonging to a kind, universal*. The familiar military meaning of *general* arose from the fact that a lieutenant, captain, major, or colonel whose

25. *The William Morris Manuscript of the Odes of Horace, Commentary and Translation* (London: The Folio Society, 2014), 18.

authority was to be emphasized was denominated a *lieutenant general*, *captain general*, *major general*, or *colonel general*. The adjective eventually became a noun, *general*. For the etymology of the word *vicar*, see the entry **Vicar**. A *vicar general* is the chief administrative assistant of a bishop. Henry VIII also appointed a vicar general, Thomas Cromwell, to assist him in his supervision of the Church of England.

Vicegerente The Latin verb *gero, gerere, gessi, gessus* means *to carry, bear, conduct*. Its present participle is *gerens, gerentis* meaning *conducting* [affairs]. The Italian word *vicegerente* comes from the Latin phrase *vice gerens*, which indicates the fellow who comes next after the cardinal vicar for Rome in the administration of that diocese. The full expression would be something like [*Sacras in Urbe*] *vices gerens*. For the etymology of *vice*, see the entry **Vicar**.

Vice-Regent *Vice* is the ablative singular of the defective Latin noun *vicis*; see the entry **Vicar**. The Latin verb *rego, regere, rexi, rectus* means *to guide, direct*, and its present participle is *regens, regentis*, from whence comes our noun *regent*. A *vice-regent* is a fellow who acts in the place of a ruler.

Victimae Paschali Laudes The sequence for Easter Sunday is usually attributed to Wipo of Burgundy (eleventh century). The bracketed mean-spirited lines of this sequence, for what are in modern times obvious reasons, were wisely omitted in the reform of the liturgy undertaken after the Council of Trent.

> Victimae paschali laudes
> immolent Christiani.
>
> Agnus redemit oves:
> Christus innocens Patri
> Reconciliavit peccatores.
>
> Mors et vita duello
> conflixere mirando:
> dux vitae mortuus, regnat vivus.
>
> Dic nobis, Maria,
> quid vidisti in via?
>
> Sepulchrum Christi viventis:
> et gloriam vidi resurgentis.
> Angelicos testes,
> sudarium, et vestes.

Surrexit Christus spes mea:
praecedet vos in Galilaeam.

[Credendum est magis soli
Mariae veraci
Quam Iudaeorum
Turbae fallaci.]

Scimus Christum surrexisse a mortuis vere:
Tu nobis, victor Rex, miserere.
Amen. Alleluia.

The translation of this sequence by Charles Stuart Calverley (1831–1884) is typical of the magnificence attained by that poet.[26]

Our salvation to obtain
Christ our Passover is slain:
Unto Christ we Christians raise
This our sacrifice of praise.

By the Lamb the sheep were bought,
By the Pure the guilty sought:
With their God were made at one
Sinners by the sinless Son.

In a dark mysterious strife
Closed the powers of Death and Life,
And the Lord of Life was slain:
Yet he liveth and doth reign.

"Say what saw'st thou, Mary, say,
As thou wentest on thy way."
"Christ's, the Living's, tomb; the throes
Earth was torn with as He rose:

And the angels twain who bare
Witness that He was not there;
And the grave-clothes of the Dead,
And the cloth that bound His head:

Christ our hope is risen, and He
Goes before to Galilee."
[Trust we Mary: she is true;
Heed we not the faithless Jew.]

26. *The Literary Remains of Charles Stuart Calverley*, with a memoir by Walter J. Sendall (London: George Bell, 1885), 237. The book is available at https://babel.hathitrust.org/cgi/pt?id=coo1.ark:/13960/t7br9bv7j;view=1up;seq=257.

Conqueror, King, to Thee we raise
This our sacrifice of praise:
We believe Thee risen indeed;
Hear us, help us in our need.

Vidi Aquam These Latin words mean "I saw water" and are the first two words of the verse which begins the ceremony of the sprinkling of the congregation with holy water before the main Sunday Mass during the Easter season. Their origin is in the story of the vision of the temple seen by the prophet Ezekiel, chapter 47. It is one of the most beautiful Gregorian chants, rarely sung now because of the overthrow of Latin. The correct way to do the Asperges ceremony is for the priest go up and down the main aisle, all the while blessing one side at a time, the side on his right. It is sloppy to bless both sides alternately. As he returns to the altar, the people on his right should turn to face him, to avoid being sprinkled from the rear, which is unseemly.

Vigil The Latin adjective *vigil, vigilis* means *wide awake*, and as a noun it means a *watchman*. The associated noun *vigilia* means a *watch*, one of the four equal parts of the night. In Ecclesiastical Latin, the *vigilia* was the day before a feast. The word came into English as *vigil*.

Vigilius *Vigilius* is a proper name formed by adding the suffix *-ius* to the adjective *vigil*, which means *wide awake, keeping vigil*. It is the name of one of the three popes whose cases are always brought up by people who dispute the doctrine of papal infallibility: Liberius (352–356), Vigilius (537–555), and Honorius (625–638). When the emperor Justinian presented to Vigilius a list of excerpts ("The Three Chapters") from the writings of three long-dead bishops, Theodore of Mopsuestia, Theodoret of Cyrrhus, and Ibas of Edessa, with the demand that the pope condemn the doctrines therein contained together with their authors, Vigilius hesitated, since the three bishops had been accepted as Catholics by the Council of Chalcedon, and to condemn them a century after their deaths would appear unseemly as well as insulting to that revered council. There was the additional problem that Vigilius was not competent in Greek, a serious disqualification for meddling in theology. Justinian thereupon brought Vigilius to Constantinople, where he was censured by the Fifth Ecumenical Council (553) for refusing to participate in their deliberations and to condone their condemnation of the Three Chapters; his name was stricken from the diptychs, that is, it was no longer to be commemorated in the

Mass. After suffering house arrest and other indignities, Virgilius finally yielded under pressure and did as the emperor asked. Gregorovius had the following to say about Vigilius:

Vigilius meanwhile had remained in Constantinople, engaged in a dogmatic contest with the Emperor concerning the dispute of the Three Chapters. After many difficulties, and after enduring some hard usage, Vigilius, by the shameful recantation of his earlier opinions, acceded to the desire of the Emperor, and accepted the decisions of the Fifth Council (the second held at Constantinople). Justinian now yielded to the entreaties of the Roman clergy, who through Narses had implored the release of their bishop, and allowed Vigilius, and the presbyters or cardinals who accompanied him, to return to Rome. The Pope, however, was taken ill on the way, and died at Syracuse, June 555. The pontificate of a Roman, who had reached the sacred chair by means of intrigue and crime, is memorable in history as being contemporary with the disruption of ancient Rome. The city preserves no memorial of his reign, beyond a metrical inscription lamenting the sack of the churches and cemeteries by the Goths.[27]

The preeminent historian of the Later Roman Empire made the following comment about Vigilius:

Vigilius himself was not much of a theologian, and he seems never to have been quite sure as to the merits of the controversy. He was pressed on one side by the Emperor and the patriarch, on the other by western opinion. His vacillations, due both to intellectual and to moral weakness, presented a pitiable spectacle. In view of his past record, he cannot excite much compassion, but it is not uninteresting to read the story of a Pope trailing in the dust the dignity of the Roman see.[28]

Vimpa The mediaeval Latin noun *vimpa, vimpae, f.*, is related to the archaic English noun *wimple*, which is the concatenation of *wind* and *pallium*; that is, it is a *winding cloak*. The *vimpa* is an unadorned long shawl worn over his shoulders by the acolyte who holds therewith the bishop's miter when that prelate is not wearing it. Another acolyte uses a vimpa to hold the episcopal crosier when the prelate is not himself wielding it.

Vision The Latin verb *video, videre, vidi, visus* mean *to see*, and from its fourth principal part proceeds the noun *visio* with the meaning *something seen*. The iconic account of a vision is that in the sixth chapter of the prophecy of Isaiah:

---

27. Ferdinand Gregorovius, *History of the City of Rome in the Middle Ages*, trans. Mrs. Gustavus W. Hamilton (London: G. Bell & Sons, 1909), 1:491–492.

28. J. B. Bury, *History of the Later Roman Empire* (New York: Dover, 1958), 2:386.

In the year that King Uzziah died, I saw also the Lord sitting upon a throne, high and lifted up, and his train filled the temple. Above it stood the seraphims: each one had six wings; with twain he covered his face, and with twain he covered his feet, and with twain he did fly. And one cried unto another, and said, Holy, holy, holy, is the Lord of hosts: the whole earth is full of his glory. And the posts of the door moved at the voice of him that cried, and the house was filled with smoke. Then said I, Woe is me! for I am undone; because I am a man of unclean lips, and I dwell in the midst of a people of unclean lips: for mine eyes have seen the King, the Lord of hosts. Then flew one of the seraphims unto me, having a live coal in his hand, which he had taken with the tongs from off the altar: And he laid it upon my mouth, and said, Lo, this hath touched thy lips; and thine iniquity is taken away, and thy sin purged. Also I heard the voice of the Lord saying, Whom shall I send, and who will go for us? Then said I, Here am I; send me. (Isaiah 6:1–8, Authorized Version)

Since the Hebrew noun *Seraphim*, like *Cherubim*, is already plural, it was a mistake of the translators to add a final *s*.

Vocation The Latin noun *vox, vocis, f.*, means a *voice*, and from it was derived the verb *voco, vocare, vocavi, vocatus* meaning *to call*. From its fourth principal part there was derived the noun *vocatio, vocationis, f.*, with the meaning, a *calling*. A *vocation* is a calling to practice a certain profession, in particular the religious life.

Votanti di Segnatura The Italian verb *voto, votare* means *to vote*, and its present participle active plural is *votanti*, which means *voting*. The *votanti di segnatura* are the voting members of the Apostolic Segnatura.

Votive The Latin verb *voveo, vovere, vovi, votus* means *to vow*, and from its fourth principal part was formed the adjective *votivus* with the meaning *related to a vow*. A *votive mass* is a mass not corresponding to the divine office for the day but instead celebrated for a special intention.

Vulgate The Latin noun *vulgus, -i, n.*, means *the common folk*. From this noun proceeds the denominative verb of the first conjugation *vulgo, vulgare, vulgavi, vulgatus*, meaning *to make common, to make generally accessible, to publish, to circulate*. Since the Latin translation of the Bible by St. Jerome made that text readily accessible to the Latin West, it was called the *vulgata editio*, the edition for the multitude, and in the English language this edition is known as the *Vulgate*. Jerome made his Latin version of the Bible at the behest of Pope Damasus.

When the Pope had Jerome in Rome entirely at his beck and call, he began to overwhelm him with questions upon the difficult points of the Bible; he encouraged him, with an eagerness that was almost indiscreet, to translate the Greek interpreters; he urged him to revise or rewrite—on the basis of the Hebrew or Greek originals—the Latin version of the Holy Scripture. Jerome greatly protested, but he did it; and in doing it, he enjoyed the purest pleasure possible to persons of his character—that of seeing his learning of some use.[29]

The Vulgate is of mixed origin. In the Old Testament, Jerome translated most books directly from Hebrew, which he learned for that purpose. In the case of the Psalms that we find in the Vulgate, Jerome revised a preexisting Latin translation that had been made from a Greek translation of the Psalter. Some books, like *Wisdom* and *Tobias*, which did not exist in Hebrew at all, but only in Greek, and which some call *apocryphal*, Jerome did not bother to translate into Latin, because he did not consider them canonical; the Latin text of these that we find in the Vulgate are from a preexisting Latin translation earlier than Jerome, the *Vetus Latina* ("Old Latin"). In the New Testament, rather than starting from scratch, he amended the preexisting Old Latin; the same is probably the case with the Old Testament books as well. It took about three hundred years for this hybrid to drive the competition from the field and become the common, or vulgate, edition of the sacred scriptures for the Western Church, and at the fourth session of the Council of Trent (1546), it was declared official, *pro authentica*,[30] a phrase that embarrassed those who interpreted it to mean that a translation could have the same weight as the original text; Pius XII (*Divino Afflante Spiritu*, §16) settled the debate among the believers when he declared:

the original text, having been written by the inspired author himself, has more authority and greater weight than even the very best translation, whether ancient or modern.

Having declared the Vulgate official, the Church now sensed the need to publish an accurate edition, for no manuscript had survived from the time of St. Jerome, and, during a millennium when there were no Xerox machines, the text had been corrupted in many places on account of the

---

29. Louis Duchesne, *Early History of the Christian Church from Its Foundation to the End of the Fifth Century*, vol. 2 (London: John Murray, 1931), 381.

30. Denzinger, *Enchiridion Symbolorum et Definitionum*, 7th ed. (Würzburg: V. J. Stahel, 1895), §667, p. 179.

errors of copyists. This work of compiling an accurate edition began in the pontificate of Sixtus V (1585–1590), who, however, interfered disastrously with the work of his commission, so that the edition he issued commanded no authority and was withdrawn after his death. Ludwig von Pastor, in his history of the pontificate of Sixtus, even felt the need to discuss the question whether the episode was a counterexample to the doctrine of infallibility. (He concluded that it was not.)[31] One matter that was settled at this time, though, was the recognition of the Codex Amiatinus, or manuscript from the Abbey of Mt. Amiata (c. 700 A.D.), as the best of all available manuscripts of the Vulgate. The edition of the Vulgate published by Pope Clement VIII in 1592 was also not altogether satisfactory, because, as Pastor pointed out:

Care was taken not to depart too widely from the wording hitherto in use. Certain things, which from the purely scientific point of view called for change, were for this reason left exactly as they were, in order to avoid scandal or surprise.[32]

The next attempt at producing an accurate edition was that of John Wordsworth, Oxford professor and then Church of England bishop of Salisbury, whose work on the New Testament part of the Vulgate satisfied the highest critical standards.

a copy was also presented to Pope Leo XIII, and was acknowledged by him in a letter so gracious that it aroused the alarm of the more Protestant Church newspapers.[33]

Pius X, four years before Wordsworth's death, ordered the Benedictine monks of St. Anselm's Abbey in Rome, under the leadership of Cardinal Gasquet, to produce a critical edition of the whole Vulgate, both Old and New Testaments (1907).

No chapter on the Vulgate can close without some reference to the enterprise now undertaken by the Benedictine Order, in the preparation of a critical edition of the whole Bible; though the new Catholic Encyclopaedia prints a full account of that enterprise without a word of reference to the work of the Bishop of Salisbury.[34]

The commission set up by Pope Pius X was suppressed by Pius XI in 1933; he organized a separate abbey for the monks who were working on the

31. Ludwig Freiherr von Pastor, *History of the Popes* (St. Louis, Mo.: B. Herder, 1932), 21:208–23.
32. Ludwig Freiherr von Pastor, *History of the Popes* (St. Louis, Mo.: B. Herder, 1952), 24:223.
33. E. W. Watson, *Life of Bishop John Wordsworth* (London: Longmans, Green, 1915), 151.
34. Ibid., 155.

– V –

Vulgate, called it "St. Jerome," and encouraged the monks to continue with their work, which they are carrying on even to this day. The monks have joined forces with the successors of Wordsworth and the Deutsche Bibelgesellschaft of Stuttgart to produce the best critical edition available, which is sold in the United States by the American Bible Society of New York.

W

Whitsunday *Whitsunday* is derived from *White Sunday*, an Old English name for Pentecost, because of the white garments worn at baptisms evidently celebrated with some frequency on that day.

Worship Weekley says that the Anglo-Saxon noun *weorthscope* means *glory* or *dignity*; he points out that the word is equivalent to the combination *worth-ship*. It is a title of respect, as is clear form the form of address "Your Worship" used in England for mayors and some other magistrates, and from the pledge in the old marriage ritual, "With my body I thee worship, and with all my worldly goods I thee endow," but now it is reserved for the appropriate attitude before the Almighty. In that regard it is equivalent to the Latin *adoratio* and the Greek λατρεία.

Wreckovation This is an example of blending of two words, *wreck* and *renovation*, to produce one bad word, *wreckovation*. The practice is common and has produced such indispensable additions to the English vocabulary as *mathlete*. The concoction *wreckovation* refers to the changes made in Catholic churches, such as the taking down of high altars and the removal of communion rails, to render them appropriate, as it was thought, for the celebration of the new rite of Mass. There is a certain type of person who is upset at the taking away of what has become familiar, and another type that cannot have enough of it. Speaking of the damage done to Durham Cathedral by the renovating deans at the time of the Reformation, Archdeacon Stranks wrote:

The worst destruction took place after Whitehead's death. His successor, Robert Horne, was a convinced reformer, but he only held the office two years before Queen Mary's accession forced him to flee to the continent, but he was recalled by Queen Elizabeth and was Dean for two more years before becoming Bishop of Winchester. He smashed up a good deal, but it was his successor William Whittingham, who was Dean for sixteen years, who completed the devastation. To us it all seems wanton vandalism, but only those who have lived through a similar upheaval can understand the passions which inspire men to the strange things they do at such times. No doubt to many the destruction seemed to be necessary.[1]

According to traditional ideas, the church building is the house of God and gate of heaven.[2] William Morris wrote:

If I were asked to say what is at once the most important production of Art and the thing to be most longed for, I should answer, A beautiful House; and if I were further asked to name the production next in importance and the thing next to be longed for, I should answer, A beautiful Book.[3]

The beautiful decoration of the church, which is the house of God, is the most magnificent production of art. The remodeling of church interiors in accordance with the demands of modern people presents a great problem, because the quality of the art in the replacement is rarely equal to the quality of art in what has been destroyed. There will always be certain people for whom what they consider the idiocy of modern life, with its boom boxes and cell phones, provokes the most complete aversion. For them, what has happened to the interior of churches is the product of a general culture that they reject.

Apart from the desire to produce beautiful things, the leading passion of my life has been and is hatred of modern civilisation.[4]

1. C. J. Stranks, *Durham Cathedral* (London: Pitkin Pride of Britain Books, 1970), 16.
2. Genesis 28:17: Non est hic aliud nisi domus Dei et porta caeli.
3. *The William Morris Manuscript of the Odes of Horace, Commentary and Translation* (London: The Folio Society, 2014), 7.
4. Ibid., 11.

Xerophagy The Greek verb ἐσθίω means *to eat*, but its second aorist is supplied by the defective verb φαγεῖν, ἔφαγον. The adjective ξηρός means *dry*. From ξηρός and φαγεῖν is formed the noun ξηροφαγία with the meaning a *diet of dry food*, that is, of food without oil. From this Greek noun proceeds the English word *xerophagy*, which denotes the absolute abstention from oils, such as is practiced by the Eastern Christians in penitential seasons.

Xystus See the entry **Sixtus**.

Y

YHWH These four letters are the transliteration of the name of the Deity, in Hebrew יהוה. See the entries **Tetragrammaton** and **Jehovah**.

Z

Zelanti The Greek verb ζέω means *to boil*, and related to it is the second verb ζηλόω with the meaning *to love ardently, to be jealous of* or *for*.

ἀνθ᾽ ὧν ἐζήλωσε τῷ Θεῷ αὐτοῦ.

Quia zelatus est pro Deo suo.

Because he was enthusiastic on behalf of his God.[1]

From ζηλόω is derived the noun ζῆλος with the meaning *eager rivalry, emulation, zeal*. The verb ζηλόω was transliterated into Latin by *zelo, zelare*, whose participle *zelantes* came into Italian as *zelanti* with the meaning *intransigent people*. The word was used as a pejorative term at various times during the history of the Church to denominate people who would not compromise when it was considered time to do so. Thus, the Spiritual Franciscans of the thirteenth century, who insisted on absolute poverty as indispensable to perfection, were called by the Italians *zelanti*; they taught that Christ and the apostles held no property (a doctrine eventually condemned by John XXII), and they were easily identifiable because they adopted shorter and narrower gowns than those worn by the common Franciscans. When their views did not find favor in the eyes of the authorities, they began to comment on the venality and corruption of the Church, an activity that brought them to the attention of the Holy Office. Their story is told in minute detail by Lea in the first three chapters

---

1. Numbers 25:13

of the third volume of his *History of the Inquisition in the Middle Ages*.[2]
See the entry **Fraticelli**.

The word *zelanti* was also used to describe a party in the papal conclaves of the *settecento*. Speaking of the conclave of 1700, von Ranke wrote:

> The Zelanti, who were first so called on this occasion, would have willingly elected Colloredo, but the rest considered him too austere.[3]

With regard to the same conclave, Pastor wrote:

> The grouping of the parties was accordingly quite simple; one group consisted of the French and the Imperialists, who were implacable opponents, and the other of the "Zelanti", who were inspired by strict ecclesiastical sentiments.
>
> The "Zelanti" had agreed to set aside all worldly considerations of nationality, friendship, enmity, kinship, gratitude or interest, and to keep exclusively before their eyes the welfare of the Church.[4]

Bacci, in his entry "Zelo," says that the proper Latin word for *zeal* is *studium* and that *zelum* is not used by the best authors.

Zona The Greek verb ζώννυμι means *to gird*, and the associated noun ζώνη means a *belt* or *girdle*. The Latin transliteration of this noun is the ecclesiastical sash. Formerly prelates wore the sash with fringes (*cum laciniis*) at home or when not performing ecclesiastical activities, and that with tassles (*cum flocculis*) otherwise. The sash with tassels, however, was abolished by Paul VI, so now the sash with fringes is the only option.[5]

Zouave In times gone by, every empire sooner or later availed itself of colonial troops. So, in the nineteenth century, the French, in their wars against the North African Arabs, made use of troops enrolled from the Berber population of modern-day Algeria, and from the French corruption of the Arabic name of one such people, زواوة, these troops were called *Zouaves*. Their dress indicated their exotic origin. In due course, volunteer or mercenary troops from European sources were also denominated

2. Henry Charles Lea, chapters 1–3 in *A History of the Inquisition in the Middle Ages*, vol. 3 (New York: Harper & Brothers, 1887).

3. Leopold von Ranke, *History of the Popes, Their Church and State*, trans. E. Fowler, rev ed. (New York: The Colonial Press, 1901), 3:433.

4. Ludwig Freiherr von Pastor, *History of the Popes*, vol. 33, trans. Ernest Graf (St. Louis, Mo.: B. Herder, 1941), 3.

5. *Ut Sive Sollicite* (instruction of the Secretariat of State, March 31, 1969), *Acta Apostolicae Sedis* 61, no. 5 (1969), 334–40, §3: "Zona autem cum flocculis aboletur." The text is also available at www.shetlersites.com/clericaldress/utsivesollicite.html.

Zouaves. In 1860, with the encouragement and approval of the papal pro-minister of war, Msgr. Merode, General Lamoricière, a veteran command-er of Zouaves in the Algerian campaigns, became commander-in-chief of the armed forces of the Pontifical State and organized a contingent of volunteers to fight on behalf of the Roman pontiff against the troops both of Victor Emmanuel and of Garibaldi. This force was denominated the *tirailleurs* or sharpshooters. Two hundred and fifty strong, they were part of the *papalini*, or papal army, defeated at the Battle of Castel Fidardo on September 18, 1860. In the following year, the *tirailleurs* were reor-ganized, dressed in their henceforth distinctive grey uniform with red trim, cincture, and kepi, and given the name *Pontifical Zouaves*. All orders were given in French. At the death of Lamoricière in 1865, the position of commander-in-chief of the pontifical army, as well as the position of pro-minister of war, devolved upon General Hermann Kanzler, a native of the Grand Duchy of Baden, and the command of the Pontifical Zouaves passed to a Swiss, Colonel Eugène Allet, and to his assistant, Lieutenant Colonel Athanase de Charette. The exploits of the Zouaves were the sub-ject of a book by one of their veterans, the Englishman Joseph Powell, who served from March 1868 to April 1870.[6] Powell commented as follows on the number of Pontifical Zouaves and their national origin.

On New Year's Day, 1870, the Papal Zouaves formed a regiment of four battal-ions, of six companies each, and of a Depôt battalion of four companies, together with a company called *La compagnie hors range*, composed of officers' servants, of the tailors, shoemakers, and armourers, and of the bandsmen and *Sapeurs* of the regiment.

The numerical strength of the different companies varied much, and as new recruits arrived, and old soldiers left, the same company could vary much in its strength at different periods. About one hundred men was the supposed comple-ment of men to each company, but often it was but sixty or even less, while occa-sionally the numbers increased immensely. At the time of the taking of Rome by Victor Emmanuel's troops, the 5th company, 3rd battalion, numbered nearly 150 men. I should, therefore, think, about the beginning of 1870, the corps numbered about 3500 men in all. Of these the most numerous were the Dutch, then the French, and after these the Belgians, Canadians, English and Irish, Swiss, Ger-mans, and Italians. Spain, Portugal, and many other nations sent their representa-tives, including three or four blacks, and one Chinese.[7]

6. Joseph Powell, *Two Years in the Pontifical Zouaves, A Narrative of Travel, Residence, and Ex-perience in the Roman States* (London: R. Washbourne, 1871).

7. Ibid., 287.

Garibaldi made his last invasion of the Papal State in the fall of 1867 and was defeated by the pope's forces at Mentana (November 3) in a battle in which the Zouaves played the principal part. This victory was the occasion of the last triumph of the pontifical army. The victorious soldiers of the State of the Church marched into Rome through the Porta Pia and were saluted by their Commander-in-Chief Kanzler at a reviewing stand in front of the Church of Santa Maria della Vittoria. He then proceeded to the Vatican to be congratulated by Pio Nono, an occasion for a remarkable display of liberal learning by the pontiff. When Kanzler entered the pontifical presence, Pio Nono greeted him in the words of Tasso:

> Canto l'armi pietose e il capitano
> Che 'l gran sepolcro liberò di Cristo.
> Molto egli oprò co'l senno e con la mano.
> Molto soffrì nel glorioso acquisto.
> E in van l'Inferno a lui s'oppose. E in vano
> S'armò d'Asia e di Libia il popol misto.
> Che il ciel gli diè favore, e sotto ai santi
> Segni ridusse i suoi compagni erranti.

The following is the translation by John Hoole, 1727–1803:

> Arms and the chief I sing, whose righteous hands
> Redeem'd the tomb of Christ from impious bands:
> Who, much in council, much in field sustain'd,
> Till just success his glorious labours gain'd:
> In vain the powers of hell oppos'd his course,
> And Asia's arms, and Lybia's mingled force;
> Heaven bless'd his standards, and beneath his care
> Reduc'd his wandering partners of the war.[8]

The incident was recorded by De Cesare:

Pius IX received him with all honours, but tinctured with that characteristic humour which never deserted him even in the most solemn moments. He was in the throne-room, surrounded by his Court and many cardinals, when Kanzler appeared. Rising, the Pope declaimed in a loud voice the first octave of "Gerusalemme Liberata", to the great amusement of all present.[9]

---

8. Torquato Tasso, *Jerusalem Delivered*, trans. John Hoole, 8th ed. (London: Cuthell, 1803), 1:3.
9. Raffaele De Cesare, *The Last Days of Papal Rome, 1850–1870*, trans. Helen Zimmern (London: Archibald Constable, 1909), 399.

David Maitland Armstrong, the American emissary to the Papal States with the rank of consul, had the following to say about the Zouaves in a report to Secretary of State Hamilton Fish three days after the fall of Rome:

It was an easy victory for the Italians, and the loss, in killed and wounded, on both sides, was not great, they were in over-whelming force, with very heavy artillery and they knew that the mass of Romans were their friends; the Zouaves, on the other hand, although they never could have imagined how much they were detested, must have, at heart, feared the people, and could not fight their best; they were a fine looking body of men, many of them, even the common soldiers, of superior education and refinement, some of them undoubtedly served the Pope from religious feeling, many for the sake of the romance and adventure of the thing, very few for pay, as it was ridiculously small.[10]

Zucchetto The Italian noun *zucca* means a *pumpkin*; it is a slang word for the *head*. The diminutive *zucchetta* is a *small pumpkin*. An incorrect masculine metamorphosis of this noun, *zucchetto*, is now established as the word for the ecclesiastical *skullcap*. The color depends on the dignity of the fellow it decorates. People still come to papal audiences with a zucchetto for the pope. He accepts the gift in exchange for the one already on his head.

10. David I. Kertzer, *Prisoner of the Vatican* (Boston: Houghton Mifflin, 2004), 56.

BIBLIOGRAPHY

Aland, Kurt, Matthew Black, Carlo M. Martini, Bruce M. Metzger, and Allen Wikgren, eds. *The Greek New Testament*. 3rd ed. In cooperation with the Institute for New Testament Textual Research. Münster/Westphalia: United Bible Societies, 1975.

Alighieri, Dante. *Inferno*. Translated by Henry Francis Cary, introduced by Robin Hamlyn, with illustrations by William Blake. London: the Folio Society, 1998.

Allen and Greenough's New Latin Grammar for Schools and Colleges, Founded on Comparative Grammar. Edited by J. B. Greenough, A. A. Howard, G. L. Kittredge, and Benj. L. D'Ooge. Boston: Ginn, 1916.

Allen, Willoughby C. *A Critical and Exegetical Commentary on the Gospel according to S. Matthew*. 3rd ed. The International Critical Commentary. Edinburgh: T&T Clark, 1977.

Arayathinal, Thomas. *Aramaic Grammar*. 2 vols. Mannanam, India: St. Joseph's Press, 1957.

Attwater, Donald. *The Catholic Eastern Churches*. Milwaukee, Wis.: Bruce Publishing, 1935.

————. *The Dissident Eastern Churches*. Milwaukee, Wis.: Bruce Publishing, 1937.

Bacci, Antonio. *Vocabolario Italiano-Latino delle Parole Moderne e Difficili a Tradurre*. Rome: Editrice Studium, 1963.

Baeck, Leo. *The Essence of Judaism*. Rev. ed. New York: Schocken Books, 1948.

Baskerville, Alfred. *The Poetry of Germany, Consisting of Selections from the Most Celebrated Poets, Translated into English Verse with the Original Text on the Opposite Page*. 6th ed. New York: Leypoldt & Holt, 1867.

Benson, Edward White. *Cyprian: His Life, His Times, His Work*. London: Macmillan, 1897.

Biblia Hebraica, adiuvantibus W. Barmgartner, G. Beer, J. Begrich, J. A. Bewer, F. Buhl, J. Hempel, F. Horst, M. Noth, O. Procksch, G. Quell, Th. H. Robinson, W. Rudolph, H. H. Schraeder, edidit Rud. Kittel, Textum Masoreticum curavit P. Kahle, Editionem tertiam denuo elaboratam ad finem perduxerunt editionem septimam auxerunt et emendaverunt A. Alt et O. Eissfeldt, editio quarta decima emendata typis editionis septimae expressa. Stuttgart: Württembergische Bibelanstalt 1966.

Biblia Sacra Iuxta Vulgatam Versionem. Adiuvantibus Bonifatio Fischer OSB, Ioanne Gribomont OSB, H. F. D. Sparks, W. Thiele, recensuit et brevi apparatu instruxit Robertus Weber OSB, editio tertia emendata quam paravit Bonifatius Fischer OSB cum sociis H. I. Frede, Ioanne Gribomont OSB, H. F. D. Sparks, W. Thiele. 2 vols. Stuttgart: Deutsche Bibelgesellschaft, 1985.

Blackburn, Simon. *The Oxford Dictionary of Philosophy.* Oxford: Oxford University Press, 1994.

Boswell, James. *The Journal of a Tour to the Hebrides with Samuel Johnson, LL. D.* London: printed by Henry Baldwin for Charles Dilly, 1785.

Boudens, Robrecht, ed. *Alfred Plummer: Conversations with Dr. Döllinger, 1870–1890.* With the collaboration of Leo Kenis. Leuven: Leuven University Press, 1985.

Brewer, John Sherren. *The Reign of Henry VIII, from His Accession to the Death of Wolsey.* Edited by James Gairdner. 2 vols. London: John Murray, 1884.

Brewer's Dictionary of Phrase and Fable. 18th ed. Edited by Camilla Rockwood. Edinburgh: Brewer's, 2009.

Briggs, Charles Augustus. *A Critical and Exegetical Commentary on the Book of Psalms.* 2 vols. Edinburgh: T&T Clark, 1906.

Brown, Francis, S. R. Driver, and Charles A. Briggs. *A Hebrew and English Lexicon of the Old Testament.* Oxford: Clarendon Press, 1968.

Bury, J. B. *History of the Later Roman Empire.* 2 vols. New York: Dover Publications, 1958.

Butler's Lives of the Saints, Complete Edition. Edited by Herbert J. Thurston, SJ, and Donald Attwater. 4 vols. Norwalk, Conn.: Easton Press, 1995.

Calverley, Charles Stuart. *The Literary Remains of Charles Stuart Calverley,* with a memoir by Walter J. Sendall, with portrait and illustrations. London, George Bell, 1885.

Cassell's New Latin Dictionary. Revised by D. P. Simpson, M. A. New York: Funk & Wagnalls, 1959.

Caswall, Edward. *Lyra Catholica: Containing All the Breviary and Missal Hymns, with Others from Various Sources.* London: Burns & Oates, 1884.

The Catholic Encyclopedia: An International Work of Reference on the Constitution, Doctrine, and History of the Catholic Church. 16 vols. New York: The Encyclopedia Press, 1913.

Cavendish, George. *Thomas Wolsey, Late Cardinal, His Life and Death.* Edited by Roger Lockyer. London: The Folio Society, 1962.

Chadwick, Owen. *Britain and the Vatican during the Second World War.* Cambridge: Cambridge University Press, 1986.

Chambers Biographical Dictionary. Edited by Magnus Magnusson. Edinburgh: W. & R. Chambers, 1993.

Charles, R. H. *The Apocrypha and Pseudepigrapha of the Old Testament in English.* 2 vols. Oxford: Clarendon Press, 1913.

Charles, R. H. *A Critical History of the Doctrine of a Future Life.* London: Adam & Charles Black, 1913. Republished in 1963 under the title *Eschatology: The Doctrine of a Future Life in Israel, Judaism, and Christianity, A Critical History,* New York: Schocken Books.

Chesterfield, Lord. *Letters Written by the Late Right Honourable Philip Dormer Stanhope, Earl of Chesterfield, to His Son, Philip Stanhope, Esq., Late Envoy Extraordinary at the Court of Dresden, together with Several other Pieces on Various Subjects, Published by Mrs. Eugenia Stanhope, from the Originals Now in Her Possession.* 2 vols. London: J. Dodsley, 1774.

Cheyne, T. K., and J. Sutherland Black, ed. *Encyclopaedia Biblica, A Critical Dictionary of the Literary, Political, and Religious History, the Archaeology, Geography, and Natural History of the Bible.* 4 vols. London: Adam & Charles Black, 1899–1907.

Cohn, Haim. *The Trial and Death of Jesus.* Old Saybrook, Conn.: Konecky & Konecky, n.d.

Colwell, Ernest Cadman. *The Study of the Bible.* Chicago: Phoenix Books, The University of Chicago Press, 1964.

Comme le prévoit, instruction of the *Consilium ad Exsequendam Constitutionem de Sacra Liturgia* of January 25, 1969. *Notitiae* 5 (1969), 3–12. Available online at http://www.natcath.org/NCR_Online/documents/comme.htm.

Confalonieri, Carlo. *Pius XI: A Close-Up.* Translated by Regis N. Barwig. Altadena, Calif.: The Benziger Sisters, 1975.

Coogan, Tim Pat. *Eamon De Valera: The Man Who Was Ireland.* New York: HarperCollins, 1993.

Creighton, Mandell. *History of the Papacy from the Great Schism to the Sack of Rome.* 6 vols. New York: Longmans, Green, 1901.

Dalman, Gustaf. *Grammatik der Jüdisch-Palästinischen Aramäisch, nach den Idiomen des Palästinischen Talmud, des Onkelostargum und Prophetentargum und der Jerusalemischen Targume,* zweite Auflage. Leipzig: J. C. Hinrichs'sche Buchhandlung, 1905.

Darras, Joseph-Epiphane. *General History of the Catholic Church from the Commencement of the Christian Era to the Twentieth Century.* 13th ed. New York: P. J. Kennedy, n.d.

Davidson, Andrew Bruce. *Biblical and Literary Essays.* Edited by J. A. Paterson. 2nd ed. London: Hodder & Stoughton, 1903.

De Cesare, Raffaele. *The Last Days of Papal Rome, 1850–1870.* Abridged, with the assistance of the author, and translated by Helen Zimmern. London: Archibald Constable, 1909.

[Franz ספרי הברית החדשה נעתקים מלשון יון ללשון עברית על ידי החכם פראפעסאר פראנץ דעליטש Delitzsch's Hebrew New Testament]. London: Lowe & Brydone, 1960.

Denzinger, Heinrich. *Enchiridion Symbolorum et Definitionum.* 7th ed. Würzburg, Germany: V. J. Stahel, 1895.

Döllinger, John J. Ignaz von. *Fables respecting the Popes of the Middle Ages, A Contribution to Ecclesiastical History.* Translated by Alfred Plummer. London: Rivingtons, 1871.

Driver, S. R., and A. F. Kirkpatrick. *The Higher Criticism.* New York: Hodder & Stoughton, 1912.

Dryden, John. *The Works of John Dryden.* Edited by Walter Scott. 18 vols. London: William Millar, 1808.

Du Cange, Charles du Fresne. *Glossarium Mediae et Infimae Latinitatis.* Paris, 1845.

Duchesne, Louis. *Early History of the Christian Church from Its Foundation to the End of the Third Century.* London: John Murray, 1914.

———. *Early History of the Christian Church from Its Foundation to the End of the Fifth Century,* vol. 2. London: John Murray, 1931.

———. *Early History of the Christian Church from Its Foundation to the End of the Fifth Century,* vol. 3. London: John Murray, 1924.

Durant, Will. *The Story of Philosophy.* New York: Simon & Schuster, 1926.

Egger, Karl. *Lexicon Nominum Virorum et Mulierum.* 2nd ed. Rome: Editrice Studium, 1963.

———. *Lexicon Nominum Locorum.* Rome: Libreria Editrice Vaticana, 1977.

Encyclopaedia Britannica, A Dictionary of Arts, Sciences, Literature and General Information. 11th ed. 32 vols. New York: The Encyclopaedia Britannica Company, 1911.

Encyclopaedia Judaica. 20 vols. Jerusalem: Keter Publishing House, n.d.

Eusebius. *The History of the Church from Christ to Constantine.* Translated by G. A. Williamson. London: The Folio Society, 2011.

Forester, C. S. *Victor Emmanuel II and the Union of Italy.* London: Methuen, 1927.

Fortescue, Adrian, and J. B. O'Connell. *The Ceremonies of the Roman Rite Described.* Westminster, Md.: Newman Press, 1962.

Freytag, Georg Wilhelm. *Lexicon Arabico–Latinum praesertim ex Djeuharii Firuzabadiique et Aliorum Arabum Operibus, Adhibitis Golii Quoque et Aliorum Libris Confectum, Accedit Index Vocum Latinarum Locupletissimus.* 4 vols. Halle: C. A. Schwetschke, 1830–1837.

Frezza di San Felice, Filippo. *Dei Camerieri Segreti e d'Onore del Sommo Pontefice.* Rome, 1884.

Friedländer, Saul. *Pius XII and the Third Reich: A Documentation.* New York: Alfred A. Knopf, 1966.

Gairdner, James. "The Draft Dispensation for Henry VIII's Marriage with Anne Boleyn." *English Historical Review* 5, no. 19 (July, 1890): 544–50.

———. "New Lights on the Divorce of Henry VIII." *English Historical Review* 11, no. 44 (October, 1896): 673–702.

————. "New Lights on the Divorce of Henry VIII (Continued)." *English Historical Review* 12, no. 45 (January, 1897): 1–16.

————. "New Lights on the Divorce of Henry VIII (Continued)." *English Historical Review* 12, no. 46 (April, 1897): 237–53.

Gasparri, Pietro Cardinal. *Catechismus catholicus, cura et studio Petri Cardinalis Gasparri concinnatus.* 15th ed. Rome: Typis Polyglottis Vaticanis, 1933.

Gibbon, Edward. *History of the Decline and Fall of the Roman Empire.* 6 vols. London: Strahan & Cahall, 1776–1788.

————. *The History of the Decline and Fall of the Roman Empire.* Edited by Betty Radice. 8 vols. London: The Folio Society, 1995.

Girdlestone, Robert B. *Synonyms of the Old Testament: Their Bearing on Christian Doctrine.* 2nd ed. 1897. Reproduction, Grand Rapids, Mich.: Wm. B. Eerdmans, 1981.

Goodwin, William W. *A Greek Grammar.* New York: Macmillan / St. Martin's Press, 1968.

Gray, G. Buchanan. *Studies in Hebrew Proper Names.* London: Adam & Charles Black, 1896.

Gregorovius, Ferdinand. *The Tombs of the Popes, Landmarks in the History of the Papacy.* Translated by L. W. Terry. Rome: The Victoria Home, 1895.

————. *History of the City of Rome in the Middle Ages.* 2nd. ed. Translated from the fourth German edition by Mrs. Gustavus W. Hamilton. 8 vols. in 13. London: G. Bell & Sons, 1902–1909.

————. *The Roman Journals of Ferdinand Gregorovius 1852–1874.* Edited by Friedrich Althaus and translated from the second German edition by Mrs. Gustavus W. Hamilton. London: G. Bell & Sons, 1911.

Grissell, Hartwell de la Garde. *Sede Vacante, Being a Diary Written during the Conclave of 1903, with Additional Notes on the Accession and Coronation of Pius X.* Oxford: James Parker, 1903.

Haldane, Elizabeth S. *Descartes: His Life and Times.* London: John Murray, 1905.

Hale, William Gardner, and Carl Darling Buck. *A Latin Grammar.* Boston: Ginn / Athenaeum, 1903.

Hare, Augustus J. C. *Walks in Rome.* 17th ed. New York: George Routledge & Sons, n.d.

Hastings, James, ed. *A Dictionary of the Bible, Dealing with Its Language, Literature, and Contents, including the Biblical Theology.* With the assistance of John A. Selbie. 4 vols. New York: Charles Scribner's Sons, 1900–1902.

Hatch, Carl E. *The Charles A. Briggs Heresy Trial.* New York: Exposition Press, 1969.

Hefele, Carl Joseph von. *Conciliengeschichte, Nach den Quellen bearbeitet.* 9 vols. Freiburg im Breisgau: Herder, 1855–1890.

Heim, Bruno Bernard. *Heraldry in the Catholic Church: Its Origin, Customs and Laws.* Gerrards Cross, England: Van Duren Publishers, 1981.

Hibbert, Christopher. *Il Duce: The Life of Benito Mussolini.* Boston: Little, Brown, 1962.

Hook, Walter Farquhar. *Lives of the Archbishops of Canterbury.* Multiple editions. 11 vols. plus index. London: Richard Bentley & Son, 1865–1875.

Hymns for the Year: A Complete Collection for Schools, Missions, and General Use. New ed. London: Burns, Lambert, & Oates, 1866.

ICEL. *Psalms for All Seasons: From the ICEL Liturgical Psalter Project.* Silver Spring, Md.: National Association of Pastoral Musicians, 1987.

James, William. *The Varieties of Religious Experience: A Study in Human Nature.* London: Folio Society, 2008.

Johns, Alger F. *A Short Grammar of Biblical Aramaic.* Andrews University Monographs 1. Berrien Springs, Mich.: Andrews University Press, 1966.

Johnson, Samuel. *A Dictionary of the English Language: In Which the Words Are Deduced From Their Originals, and Illustrated in Their Different Significations by Examples from the Best Writers, to Which Are Prefixed, a History of the Language, and an English Grammar.* 2 vols. London: W. Strahan, for J. & P. Knapton et al., 1755.

———. *Lives of the Most Eminent English Poets; with Critical Observations on Their Works.* 4 vols. London: 1781.

Faber, Geoffrey. *Jowett, a Portrait with Background.* Cambridge, Mass.: Harvard University Press, 1958.

Katz, Robert. *Death in Rome.* New York: Macmillan, 1967.

———. *Black Sabbath.* London: Arthur Barker, 1969.

———. *The Battle for Rome.* New York: Simon & Schuster, 2003.

Kertzer, David I. *The Kidnapping of Edgardo Mortara.* New York: Knopf, 1997.

———. *Prisoner of the Vatican.* Boston: Houghton Mifflin, 2004.

———. *The Pope and Mussolini.* Oxford: Oxford University Press, 2014.

Kidd, B. J., ed. *Documents Illustrative of the Continental Reformation.* Oxford: Clarendon Press, 1911.

Lane, Edward William. *An Arabic-English Lexicon.* 8 parts. Beirut: Librairie du Liban, 1980.

Lea, Henry Charles. *A History of the Inquisition in the Middle Ages.* 3 vols. New York: Harper & Brothers, 1887.

———. *History of Sacerdotal Celibacy in the Christian Church.* N.p.:University Books, 1966.

Lehnert, Sister M. Pascalina. *His Humble Servant: Sister M. Pascalina Lehnert's Memoirs of Her Years of Service to Eugenio Pacelli, Pope Pius XII.* Translated by Susan Johnson. South Bend, Ind.: St. Augustine's Press, 2014.

Lentini, Anselmo. *Te Decet Hymnus, L'Innario della "Liturgia Horarum."* Rome: Typis Polyglottis Vaticanis, 1984.

Leo XIII. *Carme Secolare del Sommo Pontefice Leone XIII Tradotto in Varie Lingue.* Rome: Federico Pustet, 1901.

Lewis, Charlton T., and Charles Short. *A Latin Dictionary*. Oxford: Clarendon Press, 1969.

Lewy, Guenter. *The Catholic Church and Nazi Germany*. New York: McGraw-Hill, 1964.

Lexicon Recentis Latinitatis. Volumen I, A–L, editum cura Operis Fundati Cui Nomen "Latinitas." Rome: Libraria Editoria Vaticana, 1992.

Liddell, Henry George, and Robert Scott. *A Lexicon Abridged from Liddell and Scott's Greek-English Lexicon*. Oxford: Clarendon Press, 1963.

Liddell, Henry George, and Robert Scott. *A Greek-English Lexicon*. Revised and augmented throughout by Sir Henry Stuart Jones with the assistance of Roderick McKenzie, with a supplement edited by E. A. Barber with the assistance of P. Mass, M. Scheller, and M. L. West. Oxford: Clarendon Press, 1968.

Lightfoot, J. B., ed. and trans. *The Apostolic Fathers, Clement, Ignatius, and Polycarp*. Revised Texts with Introductions, Notes, Dissertations, and Translations. 5 vols. London: Macmillan, 1889. Reprint, Peabody, Mass: Hendrickson Publishers, 1989.

———. *The Apostolic Fathers, comprising the Epistles (Genuine and Spurious) of Clement of Rome, The Epistles of S. Ignatius, The Epistle of S. Polycarp, The Martyrdom of S. Polycarp, The Teaching of the Apostles, The Epistle of Barnabas, The Shepherd of Hermas, The Epistle to Diognetus, The Fragments of Papias, The Reliques of the Elders Preserved in Irenaeus, revised texts with short introductions and English translations*. Edited and completed by J. R. Harmer. New York: Macmillan, 1891.

Lo Bello, Anthony. *Origins of Mathematical Words: A Comprehensive Dictionary of Latin, Greek, and Arabic Roots*. Baltimore, Md.: The Johns Hopkins University Press, 2013.

Macaulay, Thomas Babington. *Critical and Historical Essays contributed to the Edinburgh Review*. 6th ed. 3 vols. London: Longman, Brown, Green, & Longmans, 1849.

———. *The Miscellaneous Writings*. 2 vols. London: Longman, Green, Longman, Roberts, 1860.

MacNutt, Francis Augustus. *A Papal Chamberlain: The Personal Chronicle of Francis Augustus MacNutt*. London: Longmans, Green, 1936.

Mann, Horace K. *The Lives of the Popes in the Early Middle Ages* and *The Lives of the Popes in the Middle Ages*. 18 vols. in 19. St. Louis, Mo.: B. Herder, 1914–1932.

McCloud, Henry J. *Clerical Dress and Insignia of the Roman Catholic Church*. Milwaukee, Wis.: Bruce Publishing, 1948.

Merivale, Charles, B. D. *A History of the Romans Under the Empire*. 7 vols. London: Longman, Brown, Green, and Longmans, 1850–1862.

Mill, John Stuart. *Three Essays on Religion*. New York: Henry Holt, n.d.

———. *On Liberty & Considerations of Representative Government*. With an introductory essay by Isaiah Berlin. London: The Folio Society, 2008.

Milman, Henry Hart. *History of Latin Christianity, Including That of the Popes, to the Pontificate of Nicholas V*. 8 vols. New York: Sheldon, 1860–61.

Ministeria Quaedam, motu proprio of Pope Paul VI, August 15, 1972. *Acta Apostolicae Sedis* 64 (1972), 529–534. Available online at http://w2.vatican.va/content/paul-vi/la/motu_proprio/documents/hf_p-vi_motu-proprio_19720815_ministeria-quaedam.html.

More, Thomas. *Utopia*. Translated by H. V. S. Ogden. Northbrook, Ill.: AHM, 1949.

Morley, John F. *Vatican Diplomacy and the Jews during the Holocaust 1939–1943*. New York: KTAV Publishing House, 1980.

Nainfa, John A. *Costume of Prelates of the Catholic Church according to Roman Etiquette*. Baltimore, Md.: John Murphy, 1909.

Nasalli Rocca di Corneliano, Mario. *Accanto ai Papi*. Rome, Libreria Editrice Vaticana, 1976.

Neale, J. M., trans. *Mediaeval Hymns and Sequences*. 2nd ed. London: Joseph Masters, 1863.

New Catholic Encyclopedia. 17 vols. Washington, D.C.: The Catholic University of America, 1967.

Newman, John Henry Cardinal. "On the Inspiration of Scripture." *The Nineteenth Century* 15, no. 84 (February, 1884): 184–89.

———. *The Arians of the Fourth Century*. New ed. London: Longmans, Green, 1897.

———. *Historical Sketches*. Vol. 2. Longmans, Green, London, 1917.

———. *Idea of a University*. Garden City, N.Y.: Image Books, 1959.

Noonan, James-Charles, Jr. *The Church Visible*. New York: Viking, 1996.

Nova Vulgata Bibliorum Sacrorum Editio, Sacros. Oecum. Concilii Vaticani II Ratione Habita, Iussu Pauli Pp. VI Recognita, Auctoritate Ioannis Pauli Pp. II Promulgata. Rome: Libreria Editrice Vaticana, 1979.

Novum Testamentum Graece et Latine, Textum Graecum post Eberhard et Erwin Nestle communiter ediderunt Barbara et Kurt Aland, Johannes Karavidopoulos, Carlo M. Martini, Bruce M. Metzger. Textus Latinus Novae Vulgatae Bibliorum Editioni debetur. Utriusque textus apparatum criticum recensuerunt et editionem novis curis elaboraverunt Barbara et Kurt Aland una cum Instituto Studiorum Textus Novi Testamenti Monasterii Westphalii. Stuttgart: Deutsche Bibelgesellschaft, 1994.

Novum Testamentum Graece et Latine, Utrumque textum, cum apparatu critico imprimendum curavit Eberhard Nestle, novis curis elaboraverunt Erwin Nestle et Kurt Aland. 22nd ed. Stuttgart: Württembergische Bibelanstalt, 1963.

Ordo Baptismi Parvulorum, editio typica altera. Rome: Libreria Editrice Vaticana, 1986.

Otto, Rudolf. *The Idea of the Holy*. Translated by J. W. Harvey. Oxford: Oxford University Press, 1923.

The Oxford Dictionary of Quotations. 4th ed. Edited by Angela Partington. Oxford: Oxford University Press, 1992.

The Oxford English Dictionary. Compact ed. Complete text reproduced micro-graphically. 2 vols. Oxford: Oxford University Press, 1988.

Paine, Thomas. *The Age of Reason.* New York: The World's Popular Classics Books, n.d.

Palacios, L. *Grammatica Syriaca.* Rome: Desclée, 1954.

Pastor, Ludwig Freiherr von. *History of the Popes from the Close of the Middle Ages, Drawn from the Secret Archives of the Vatican and from Other Original Sources.* 40 vols. London: Kegan Paul, Trench, Trübner, 1908–1952.

Perowne, J. J. Stewart. *The Book of Psalms.* Grand Rapids, Mich.: Zondervan, 1978.

Pius II. *The Commentaries of Pius II.* Translated by Florence Alden Gragg, with historical introduction and notes by Leona C. Gabel. Northampton, Mass.: Smith College Studies in History, 1936–1957.

Plummer, Alfred. *A Critical and Exegetical Commentary on the Gospel according to St. Luke.* 10th ed. The International Critical Commentary. New York: Charles Scribner's Sons, 1914.

Poeschke, Joachim. *Italian Mosaics 300–1300.* Translated by Russell Stockman. New York: Abbeville Press, 2010.

Pontificales Ritus, instruction of the Sacred Congregation of Rites, July 29, 1968. *Acta Apostolicae Sedis* 60, no. 7 (1968), 406–12. Available online at www.vatican.va/archive/aas/documents/AAS-60-1968-ocr.pdf.

Pontificalis Domus, motu proprio of Pope Paul VI, March 28, 1968. The text is available at http://w2.vatican.va/content/paul-vi/la/motu_proprio/documents/ hf_p-vi_motu-proprio_19680328_pontificalis-domus.html.

Pope, Alexander. *The Iliad of Homer.* Translated by Mr. Pope. 6 vols. London: printed by W. Bowyer for Bernard Lintott, 1715–1720.

Powell, Joseph, Z. P. *Two Years in the Pontifical Zouaves: A Narrative of Travel, Residence, and Experience in the Roman States.* London: R. Washbourne, 1871.

Rahner, Karl, and Herbert Vorgrimler. *Theological Dictionary.* Edited by Cornelius Ernst, OP, translated by Richard Strachan. New York: Herder & Herder, 1965.

Ranke, Leopold von. *History of the Popes, Their Church and State.* Translated by E. Fowler, with a special introduction by William Clark. Rev. ed. Vol. 3. New York: The Colonial Press, 1901.

Rhodes, Anthony. *The Vatican in the Age of the Dictators (1922–1945).* New York: Holt, Rinehart, & Winston, 1973.

Rome in Early Photographs, The Age of Pius IX, Photographs 1846–1878 from Roman and Danish Collections. Translated by Ann Thornton. Copenhagen: The Thorvaldsen Museum, 1977.

Runciman, Steven. *A History of the Crusades.* 3 vols. London: The Folio Society, 1994.

Russell, Bertrand. *Why I Am Not a Christian and Other Essays on Religion and Related Subjects.* Edited by Paul Edwards. New York: Simon & Schuster, n.d.

Sanday, William. *Inspiration, Eight Lectures on the Early History and Origin of the*

Doctrine of Biblical Inspiration, Being the Bampton Lectures for 1893. London: Longmans, Green, 1896.

Schechter, Solomon. *Seminary Address and Other Papers*. Cincinnati, Ohio: Ark Publishing, 1915.

Schimmelpfennig, Bernhard. *Das Krönungszeremoniale Kaiser Karls V*. Stuttgart: Belser Verlag, 1989.

Septuaginta, Id Est Vetus Testamentum graece iuxta LXX interpretes edidit Alfred Rahlfs. 8th ed. Stuttgart: Württembergische Bibelanstalt, 1985.

Smyth, Herbert Weir. *A Greek Grammar for Colleges*. New York: American Book Company, 1920.

Sladen, Douglas. *The Secrets of the Vatican*. London. Hurst & Blackett, 1907.

Smith, Denis Mack. *Garibaldi*. The Stratford Library. London: Hutchinson, 1957.

———. *Mussolini: A Biography*. New York: Alfred A. Knopf, 1982.

———. *Cavour: A Biography*. New York: Alfred A. Knopf, 1985.

———. *Italy and Its Monarchy*. New Haven, Conn.: Yale University Press, 1989.

———. *Mazzini*. New Haven, Conn.: Yale University Press, 1994.

Smith, William Roberson. *The Old Testament and the Jewish Church*. Edinburgh: Adam & Charles Black, 1881.

Stanley, Arthur Penrhyn. *The Life and Correspondence of Thomas Arnold, D. D.* 2 vols., 5th ed. London: B. Fellowes, 1845.

Stehlin, Stewart A. *Weimar and the Vatican 1919–1933*. Princeton, N.J.: Princeton University Press, 1983.

Storti, Nicola. *La Storia e il Diritto della Dataria Apostolica dalle Origini ai Nostri Giorni*. Naples: Athena Mediterranea Editrice, 1969.

Stramare, Tarcisio. "La Neo-Vulgata: impresa scientifica e pastorale insieme." *Lateranum* 45 (1979): 10–35.

Stranks, C. J. *Durham Cathedral*. London: Pitkin Pride of Britain Books, 1970.

Swete, Henry Barclay. *An Introduction to the Old Testament in Greek*. Cambridge: Cambridge University Press, 1900.

Tasso, Torquato. *Jerusalem Delivered*. Translated by John Hoole. 2 vols., 8th ed. London: Cuthell et al., 1803.

Thurston, Herbert. "The Canon Law of the Divorce." *English Historical Review* 19, no. 76 (October 1904): 632–45.

Trench, Richard Chenevix. *Synonyms of the New Testament*. 9th ed. 1880. Reproduction, Grand Rapids, Mich.: Wm. B. Eerdmans, 1976.

Tres Abhinc Annos, instruction of the Sacred Congregation of Rites, May 4, 1967. *Acta Apostolicae Sedis* 59 (1967), 442–48. Available online at http://www.vatican.va/archive/aas/documents/AAS-59-1967-ocr.pdf.

Trevelyan, George Otto. *The Life and Letters of Lord Macaulay*. London: Longmans, Green, 1876.

Ut Sive Sollicite, instruction of the Secretariat of State, March 31, 1969.

Acta Apostolicae Sedis 61, no. 5 (1969), 334–40. Available online at www.shetlersites.com/clericaldress/utsivesollicite.html.

Vermes, Geza. *The Passion*. London: Penguin, 2005.

Virgil. *The Works of Virgil, containing his Pastorals, Georgics, and Aeneis*. Translated by John Dryden. London: printed for Jacob Tonson, 1697.

Ward, Maisie. *The Wilfrid Wards and the Transition*. Vol. 1, *The Nineteenth Century*. New York: Sheed & Ward, 1934.

———. *The Wilfrid Wards and the Transition*. Vol. 2, *Insurrection versus Resurrection*. New York: Sheed & Ward, 1937.

Ward, Wilfrid. *William George Ward and the Oxford Movement*. London: Macmillan, 1889.

———. *William George Ward and the Catholic Revival*. London: Macmillan, 1893.

———. *The Life and Times of Cardinal Wiseman*. 2 vols. London: Longmans, Green, 1900.

Watson, E. W. *Life of Bishop John Wordsworth*. London: Longmans, Green, 1915.

Waugh, Evelyn. *Monsignor Ronald Knox, Fellow of Trinity College, Oxford and Protonotary Apostolic to His Holiness Pope Pius XII*. Boston: Little, Brown, 1959.

Webster's New Twentieth Century Dictionary of the English Language. Unabridged 2nd ed. The New York: World Publishing Company, 1962.

Weekley, Ernest. *An Etymological Dictionary of the English Language*. 2 vols. New York: Dover, 1967.

Wehr, Hans. *A Dictionary of Modern Written Arabic (Arabic–English)*. 4th ed. Edited by Milton J. Cowan. Wiesbaden, Germany: Otto Harrassowitz, 1979.

The William Morris Manuscript of the Odes of Horace, Commentary and Translation. London: The Folio Society, 2014.

Woolsey, Theodore Dwight. "Reasons for a New Revision of the Scriptures in English." In *Anglo-American Bible Revision*, edited by members of the American Revision Committee, 43–47. New York: American Sunday School Union, 1879.

Würthwein, Ernst. *The Text of the Old Testament: An Introduction to Kittel-Kahle's Biblia Hebraica*. Translated by Peter R. Ackroyd. Oxford: Basil Blackwell, 1957.

Zahn, Gordon C. *German Catholics and Hitler's Wars*. New York: Sheed & Ward, 1962.

Zuccotti, Susan. *The Italians and the Holocaust: Persecution, Rescue, Survival*. New York: Basic Books, 1987.

———. *Under His Very Windows: The Vatican and the Holocaust in Italy*. New Haven, Conn.: Yale University Press, 2000.

INDEX

Origins of Catholic Words: A Discursive Dictionary was designed in Minion with
Mr Eaves display type and composed by Kachergis Book Design of Pittsboro, North Carolina.
It was printed on 60-pound House Natural Smooth and bound by
Sheridan Books of Chelsea, Michigan.